# THE RUSSIAN RESEARCH CENTER

The Russian Research Center of Harvard University is supported by a grant from the Carnegie Corporation. The Center carries out interdisciplinary study of Russian institutions and behavior and related subjects.

# SOVIET TRANSPORTATION POLICY

# SOVIET

# TRANSPORTATION

# POLICY

## HOLLAND HUNTER

Harvard University Press, Cambridge, 1957

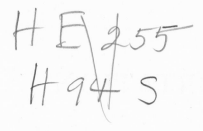

To

*Hester Walrath Hunter*

# PREFACE

In reviewing this study at its completion, I am conscious of many respects in which it represents a preliminary statement rather than a final word. Yet the process of enlarging our understanding is a reciprocal one, and publication of this analysis now may contribute to the work of others, who in turn will widen the basis for further work in the area covered here. Future studies will also be able to make use of new statistical material that has appeared while this book was at the press. I have been able to incorporate data from the April, 1956, statistical handbook issued by the USSR Central Statistical Administration, but not from subsequent volumes, and in particular, not from the handbook on transportation that is being released in the USSR as these words are written. Its figures should provide a check on my appendix series; I hope that the inaccuracies disclosed will be minor ones.

A research grant enabled me to spend the month of June, 1957, in the USSR, traveling in European Russia and talking with several Soviet transportation economists. Galley proofs of the text were available as a basis for the discussions, and I learned of at least two respects in which the study drew criticism. Chapter 7 compares Soviet railroad operations with railroad performance in the United States over the period 1925–1955; Soviet writers look more at the present and future, and see a far more favorable comparison than I present. Chapter 8 presents a critical analysis of the coordination among carriers that has been achieved in the USSR, and a skeptical view of the prospects for water transportation. Soviet transportation economists acknowledge the technical difficulties involved, but believe strongly in the organizational advantages of Soviet administrative arrangements, and in the outlook for greatly increased water transportation. It should also be noted that developments since 1955, such observation of transportation activity as I found time for, and the positions that emerged from the interviews I was granted, all tend to suggest some retreat from the strong conclusion of Chapter 15 that the share of total investment going into transportation need not increase. As a history of the 1928–1955 period, most of the present study may perhaps stand up. As a guide to the future, my provisional forecasts may well require revision.

I am grateful for the generous support of the Russian Research Center, Harvard University, and the encouragement of its executive director, Marshall D. Shulman. Alexander Eckstein gave me valuable advice for revising an intermediate version of the study, and Alexander Gerschenkron stood as a wise mentor throughout its preparation. Help in posing initial questions came from Dean Edward S. Mason, Wassily W. Leontief, and Edward Ames; the study benefited also from my early joint research with M. Gardner Clark. The Library of Congress, and especially Nicholas R. Rodionoff and John T. Dorosh, were most helpful in making source material available. Similar aid came also from Leon M. Herman, Graham E. Getty, Eugene J. Rapoport, and

Victor Fediai. I owe a special debt to James H. Blackman, who gave me the benefit of his own research in this field, and to George Y. Novak, who has checked the accuracy of many of my data. My wife, Helen Manning Hunter, has reviewed the analysis at all stages and provided valuable advice on statistical methodology, especially for chapter 12. The editors of *Railway Age* and of the *National Defense Transportation Journal* have generously given me permission to draw on 1954 and 1955 articles underlying, respectively, chapters 7 and 5. Finally, for critical advice or other assistance, I am grateful to Francis Armbruster, Abram Bergson, Aldo Caselli, Paul E. Garbutt, Milton Giffler, David Granick, Gregory Grossman, Donald R. Hodgman, Edgar M. Hoover, Naum Jasny, Max F. Millikan, John A. Morrison, George M. Saharov, Howard M. Teaf, Jr., Gilbert F. White, and Ernest W. Williams, Jr. Help with the computations came from Herbert W. Hickman, Edward J. Stevens, and Robert W. Kilpatrick. Precise manuscript preparation was supplied by Rose DiBenedetto, Helen Olsen, and Tesse Yacopino. The manuscript was substantially improved through the editorial scrutiny of Ann Staffeld Mendez. All remaining shortcomings reflect my inability to take full advantage of this help.

Three minor details of presentation deserve notice. The map on pages 134-35 shows only the place names and rail lines mentioned in the text, without attempting to give a full picture of Soviet transportation facilities. In tables containing percentage distributions of absolute data, the components will be found to total exactly 100 per cent in spite of rounding off. This departure from accepted practice arises because the absolute data sometimes were obtained through assembly or manipulation of Soviet percentage data, and because rounding errors in one percentage distribution would have projected additional uncertainty into other tables derived from them. Necessary adjustments were made through altering the final digit of the largest components, or of those nearest a dividing line. Throughout the study, time-series charts are presented with a logarithmic vertical scale, so that a 10 per cent annual increase, say, will have the same steepness in the 1950's, when the absolute change is large, as it had in the 1920's, when the sums involved were very much smaller. The procedure permits accurate visual comparisons of growth rates in two different series, or between different periods of time.

HOLLAND HUNTER

Haverford College
July 26, 1957

# CONTENTS

## MAP

## TABLES

## CHARTS

CHARTS                                                                      xvii

# SOVIET TRANSPORTATION POLICY

"What's true is true!"—L. M. Kaganovich

# INTRODUCTION

This is an essay in economic history, dealing with transportation in the USSR, mainly during the period 1928–1955. Rapid economic change has dominated the Soviet scene since 1928, and this central feature of the record has suggested certain inherent issues that have given shape to the study. For this sector of the Soviet economy, we examine a series of economic policies. Now economic policies can be passive, in the sense that decisions seek no more than adjustment to the existing environment, or they can be purposive, in the sense that programs are put in motion to challenge the impact of the environment and reorganize the inherited economic process. Obviously the Soviet regime has pursued highly purposive economic policies. As a consequence, an economic analysis of the USSR is almost automatically given the elements of dramatic unity. Here on one side are the forcefully stated objectives of the regime, harshly demanding structural reorganization of the whole economy, and there on the other are a variety of stubborn, recalcitrant factors underlying the existing situation and resisting change. As Lenin once put the question in a pamphlet, "Who Will Win?"

In such a setting, an analytic review will have several elements. The protagonists in the struggle, both personal and impersonal, are identified, and the major events in the contest over the years are chronicled. On this basis a review of the record can seek to account for observed successes and failures. At the same time the policy objectives themselves can be evaluated and the forces resisting change can be assessed as to strength and permanence. The work as a whole can be at once a dramatic historical narrative and a case study in national economic policy.

The present book has grown out of a belief that Soviet policies toward transportation during a period of rapid industrialization provide significant lessons for many other countries now on the eve of rapid industrial growth. The lessons are both positive and negative — suggesting both policies likely to succeed elsewhere, and courses of action to be avoided. It is admitted, of course, that each country reflects a unique combination of geographic, climatic, and inherited factors bearing on its transportation problems, so that the experience of one cannot be transferred directly to another. Nevertheless, the timing issues that arise in a growing economy are substantially universal, and Soviet experience therefore has general relevance. In other respects too, problems assume a common form even where the variables rank differently from one country to another.

Relations between the transportation sector and the rest of the Soviet economy are significant also in connection with the economic growth potential of the USSR. It has sometimes been argued that future Soviet growth will be slowed down by the need for much larger additions to transportation capacity than have proved necessary to date. The evidence assembled in Part III of this study, while by no means conclusive, suggests on the contrary that the inhibiting influences of the transportation sector on Soviet growth in the near future will be negligible.

For some twenty years, direct and detailed information on the Soviet economy has been very largely suppressed by the Soviet government, and this has given rise in the West to a popular view of "mystery wrapped in enigma." Actually, much of the mystery has reflected insufficient scholarly attention to the Soviet record, and in recent years topic after topic has been clarified through careful winnowing of primary source material available in Western libraries. Such material is especially rewarding in the field of transportation (mainly railroad transportation), for several reasons, which may be briefly listed as follows: (a) Transportation activity generates abundant numerical records all over the world, and this tradition, well established in tsarist Russia, has continued to the present day in the USSR. (b) Records of transportation activity and facilities form an intricate network of relationships, affording multiple opportunities for cross-checking the consistency of the record as it is assembled. (c) Though the last volume of the NKPS (People's Commissariat — renamed Ministry — of Transportation) statistical series to reach the United States covers the year 1933, the material available for later years has been plentiful, including a railroad newspaper (1938–1940 and 1943–1956), two railroad technical journals (1934–1948 and 1956), and innumerable textbooks, manuals, pamphlets, and so on, for transportation workers. This material, identified more precisely in the bibliography, has been the basis for the present study.

But how reliable is all this Soviet information? While the degree of precision varies from field to field, extensive discussion among Western scholars has led to a consensus that Soviet data are not freely invented.[1] They may be misused by Soviet writers, sometimes very seriously, but they provide the fragments with which an accurate reconstruction of the record can be attempted. Appearance of the 1956 Soviet statistical handbook has served to place all such work on a sounder footing. Incidentally, it has confirmed many transportation figures previously arrived at indirectly, and has permitted a notable reduction in the text of this study's appendices. An endemic uncertainty remains, however, in connection with changes of coverage and definition, which have been quite inadequately dealt with in Soviet statistical material, even long before the policy of suppression began. A few such changes have been noted in the present study, and others may remain undetected, but the implications of the record have not been altered by the changes encountered, and the possibility that they could be through the discovery of further statistical manipulation appears a very remote one.

The text of the study is based analytically, though not for reading purposes, on the records compiled in Appendices A–F. These make tedious reading indeed, but, as Professor Gerschenkron has pointed out elsewhere, "while the reader may resent being burdened with masses of statistical detail, he should consider that without such documentation he would neither be able to form an independent judgment of the validity of the conclusions nor even be in a position to appreciate the methods used." [2] Detailed evidence underlying the conclusions reached is thus available, but is separated from the analytic narrative, with the hope that the majority of readers, who need to absorb results with maximum economy of their own attention, will find the text more attractive. Where doubts arise in the reader's mind, he should trace the matter back to the appropriate portions of the appendices.

Part I of this study is chiefly occupied with reviewing the historical and geographic factors that have provided the setting for Soviet transportation, and with a sketch of the governmental objectives that have acted upon this framework to produce the observed record. Part II presents a selective analysis of 1928–1955 transportation developments, designed to bring out the lessons referred to above. In Part III, certain aspects of the railroad sector's relations with the rest of the economy are analyzed to shed light on the prospective role of the railroads in future Soviet economic growth. The final chapter offers a summary.

PART I

THE LOCATIONAL FRAMEWORK

# THE SOVIET
## 1 GEOGRAPHIC SETTING
## IN HISTORICAL PERSPECTIVE

It seems natural that an analysis of Soviet transportation policy should begin with a brief review of the forces that generate a need for transportation in Russia. That will be the task of the present chapter. In the next we can consider the objectives of the Soviet regime as they relate to transportation, and thus set the stage for an analysis of Soviet policy as it has evolved over the years. The underlying issue throughout the discussion will be the extent to which Soviet transportation needs can be modified through governmental policy. Clearly the need for transportation depends in part on certain fixed features of the geographic environment, not subject to alteration by a government. Yet equally clearly, an enormous variety of locational patterns for economic activity is at least theoretically possible, and this suggests a wide range of possibilities for the territorial organization of a growing economy, each with different transportation requirements.

If all the elements of economic activity were locally available wherever men settled, it is evident that the need for transportation would be relatively insignificant. Under conditions of simple agricultural life, self-sufficient communities need only devote resources to local movement of persons, tools, and agricultural products. Transportation on a significant interregional scale develops out of the fact that economic activity can be enormously more productive if resources and products are exchanged among localities. Primarily this is so because individual localities do not, typically, have at hand all the elements desirable for highly productive activity, in sufficient variety and in optimum amounts. Some, at least, can be more effectively obtained from another place, and Adam Smith's familiar observations concerning the benefits of specialization and exchange apply geographically as well as industrially. The underlying geographic basis for transportation, then, is that the elements of economic activity are not uniformly distributed over the surface of the earth. Regions differ very widely in their natural endowments, and transportation facilities which enable heterogeneous regions to co-operate will contribute in a major way to productive economic life.

Seen in this light, the Soviet land mass offers great scope for the contributions transportation can make. It contains a wide variety of resources, in large absolute amounts, but they are very unevenly distributed over the territory of the USSR. This is, of course, a world-wide phenomenon, and most economies suffer from similar disabilities. But the fact remains that the scattered pattern of resources in the USSR creates a need for transportation facilities if these resources are to be drawn into modern productive activity. Going further, one may argue that the need for transportation is directly related to the extent of locational discrepancy that exists among these resources, or putting it the other way, that the need for transportation is inversely related to the degree of correspondence in the regional pattern of resource endowment. Where good land, coal, and iron ore lie close together, for example, a large industrial community can exist with far less transportation than will be required to support a similar community located near good land, but dependent on coal and iron ore from other regions.

Resource endowment is thus a fundamental factor affecting the need for transportation in the USSR. But economic activity also involves the presence of a population making use of the resources, and this immediately introduces an important new variable. In the short run, a country's pattern of population settlement is an inherited fact, reflecting generations of adaptation to the search for a livelihood and reflected in costly development of all the social capital that enables a community to be productive. In the short run, the location of social capital, a labor force, and markets consuming the economy's output will be as decisive in determining the need for transportation as will the pattern of resource endowment. In the long run, however, a population can move to new locations, creating new centers of social capital, relocating the labor force, and presenting a new regional pattern of consuming markets. Such changes have been a regular feature of the industrialization process throughout the world, since industrialization changes man's relation to resources, both in technological and in locational respects. The geographic pattern of combination of resources, labor, social capital, and consumers has typically evolved over time in response to advancing technology. Our review of the Soviet inheritance should therefore have a historical dimension, describing Russian transportation needs as they had evolved up to the time when Soviet forced industrialization began in earnest.

The economy inherited by the Soviet regime had taken shape over many centuries of preindustrial life, but it reflected also the impact of an industrialization process which had gotten under way in the middle of the nineteenth century. Let us therefore give brief attention first to the locational forces and transportation patterns of the preindustrial era, and then to the changes induced by early Russian industrialization. In general, it will be obvious that the location of arable land was the dominant factor in the former era, and that the location of coal, iron ore, and other minerals became a leading factor in the later period.

Soil resources in the USSR, considered (as they must be) in conjunction with rainfall zones, are strongly differentiated, with the most favorable territory being contained within a well-known "wedge" that begins as a wide north-south band at the western frontier and extends eastward across European Russia, growing narrower until it comes to an end around the Yenisei River.[1] It is circumscribed on the north by a line above which it is not feasible to grow cereal grains, and on the south by a line marking the minimum annual rainfall required for irrigationless agriculture. Determined Soviet policy has already made considerable progress in spreading at least a minimum volume of agricultural activity beyond these limits to the north, the east, and the south, and will presumably continue to do so. It remains true, nonetheless, that natural conditions raise the real costs of carrying on agricultural activity outside the "wedge" territory, so that attempts to spread agricultural operations uniformly over the Soviet land mass face increasingly prohibitive barriers in real terms.

From a transportation point of view, therefore, the location of arable land imposes an initial handicap on the growth of a uniformly distributed economy making use of relatively little transportation. It would be entirely possible, of course, to distribute the population and all other economic activity in accordance with the distribution of arable land, so that crudely self-sufficient regions could be established within the wedge, and little use would be made of the remaining territory. History demonstrates that such a pattern actually developed over the centuries preceding the present era. It has left as a legacy a very pronounced concentration of population density within the triangular wedge referred to above, clearly visible in population maps as recent as those derived from the census of 1939.[2] If the Russian economy had remained agrarian, the need for transportation would have been limited to the volume involved in the traditional trade with merchants from Europe and Asia, since the population had come to be distributed in accordance with food supplies. While this is true in a very broad sense, it must be qualified in its application to the eighteenth and nineteenth centuries, and has now become a point of speculative interest only, since the impact of modern technology and the process of industrialization have brought overriding new pressures to bear on the pattern of population distribution.

While the location of arable land went far to determine the pattern of population distribution in preindustrial Russia, one must note also the influence of the river systems in establishing major population concentrations. Here, as elsewhere throughout the world, the largest towns tended to grow at river junctions or at transshipment points. In the early history of the east European plain, it was especially true that river routes formed the basis for political control of the region and for trade among its parts, as well as transit trade through it to other parts of the world. Consequently the major markets and concentrations of skilled artisans, at the beginning of the industrialization period, were located in the ancient cities of central European Russia, and not in the regions where rich supplies of coal, iron ore, petroleum, and other resources later came to be found.

The early locational pattern of the Russian economy also reflected a contest extending over several centuries between the settled agricultural peoples of central European Russia and the nomadic peoples of the east. The forests of central European Russia afforded some protection against the marauding tribes of the eastern steppes, and it was only after several centuries of what might now be called "containment" that the Russian economy spread gradually southward to the Black Sea and eastward to the Volga, the Urals, Central Asia, and finally the Pacific. This fact tended to delay the growth of markets and population centers in the southeast and east, and to reinforce the factors causing industrialization to take root in the center and northwest.

An adequate account of the origins of industrial activity in Russia, even if confined to its locational aspects, would run far beyond the limits of what is appropriate for the present study. With considerable oversimplification, therefore, let us summarize the trends that led to the situation inherited by the Soviet regime, noting only the major forces at work. Obviously nonagricultural activity is founded on the use of fuel and mineral resources, whose geographic distribution will be a powerful influence on the location of growing industries. Hence we should note the location of major resource deposits in the USSR, turning then to other influences at work.

The first coal field to be extensively worked in nineteenth-century Russia was located in the eastern Ukraine, near the Donets River, and it is still a major producer. In recent years it has lost much of its dominant position, but the Donbas (Donets Basin) even now accounts for about 40 per cent of Soviet coal production. On the eve of the 1917 revolutions, several other fields were being opened up, and prospecting for additional supplies has continued during the Soviet period. But the locational influence of coal deposits on prerevolutionary Russian industrialization centered on the Donbas as a domestic source, to which was added a considerable volume of coal imported from Poland and England to supply factories around St. Petersburg (now Leningrad) and in the Baltic region.

The densely populated regions of European Russia contain another coal field in the district south of Moscow, known as the sub-Moscow field, but it yields only a low-grade lignite, and cannot supply coking coal. This is also true of small-scale deposits in the western Ukraine, which are only beginning to be worked. During the last twenty years a new field has been opened at Vorkuta in the Pechora River Basin of north European Russia, designed to supply industry around Leningrad as well as shipping in northern waters. However, it lies above the Arctic Circle, several hundred miles from existing concentrations of population, and has clearly involved high real costs of production. No large high-quality fields have been found in the Caucasus region, and the numerous small fields being worked in the Ural Mountain region yield coal that is generally unsatisfactory for various technical reasons.

The really large deposits of coal available to the Soviet economy lie in Asiatic Russia, at the eastern limit of the soils-population triangle. This is illustrated by the data of Table 1, which shows two percentage distributions of the geographic location of coal reserves, based on Soviet estimates for

Table 1. Estimated coal reserves, USSR, by field, 1937 (percentages of the USSR total)

| Field | "Proven" reserves | Estimated total reserves |
|---|---|---|
| Donets basin | 27.1 | 5.4 |
| Sub-Moscow | 4.5 | 0.7 |
| Vorkuta | 0.4 | 2.2 |
| West Ukraine | 1.2 | — |
| Caucasus | 0.6 | 0.3 |
| Urals | 3.0 | 0.5 |
| Karaganda | 4.3 | 3.8 |
| Central Asia | 0.5 | 1.0 |
| Kuznets basin | 8.0 | 27.3 |
| Minusinsk | 37.7 | } 1.2 |
| Other East Siberian fields | 7.8 | 55.4 |
| Soviet Far East | 4.9 | 2.2 |

Source: Adapted from absolute data in Gosplan, 1939b, pp. 171–72. The term "proven" reserves is used, somewhat loosely, for the Soviet "A + B" reserves. On the meaning of Soviet reserve categories, see Clark, 1956, p. 103.

1937. The figures in the first column reflect the extent of geological exploration carried out in earlier decades, while the estimates of the second column (especially the huge figure for "other East Siberian fields") reflect optimistic government hopes. To the extent that these provisional estimates are well founded, it appears that the widely scattered coal deposits of the USSR are heavily concentrated in the relatively unsettled regions of Asiatic Russia. There has thus been a pronounced locational discrepancy between the pattern of population and industrial concentration inherited by the Soviet regime, and the pattern of coal deposits.

Soviet iron ore resources are distributed in much closer conformity to arable land and population concentrations than is true of coal fields. Table 2 presents percentage figures showing the estimated reserves available in

Table 2. Estimated iron ore reserves, USSR, by region, 1938 (percentages of the USSR total)

| Region | "Proven" reserves | Estimated total reserves |
|---|---|---|
| Krivoi Rog | 14.6 | 12.8 |
| Kerch | 35.8 | 23.9 |
| Other southern deposits | 4.0 | 2.4 |
| Central European Russia | 9.4 | 11.5 |
| Northwest European Russia | 2.9 | 14.0 |
| Caucasus | 3.8 | 1.7 |
| Urals | 25.0 | 20.8 |
| Kazakhstan | 0.2 | 1.5 |
| West Siberia | 1.4 | 1.3 |
| East Siberia | 2.6 | 8.5 |
| Soviet Far East | 0.3 | 1.6 |

Source: Adapted from absolute data for January 1, 1938, presented in Clark, 1956, p. 156.

1938 in each major region. It will be noted that European Russia contains about 70 per cent of the national total. The Krivoi Rog deposits in the eastern Ukraine have been by far the most productive to date, accounting in 1937 for 59 per cent of the annual output. A misleading impression is given, on the other hand, by the figures for Kerch ores in the Crimean Peninsula. While the ore is abundant, it is also very poor, so that the effective contribution of this deposit to Soviet steel-making is very unlikely to be proportional to its relative size.[3]

The coming of railroads made possible the growth of an iron and steel industry in the eastern Ukraine, based on Donets Basin coking coal and Krivoi Rog iron ore. It began in the 1870's, and was already well established by 1917. Transportationwise, it rested on two east-west trunk lines, of which the northern became the more important, connecting the two deposits.

They are about 350 miles apart.[4] A heavy industrial complex grew up around the steel industry, so that the eastern Ukraine became an early major focus of Russian heavy industry. It is well located with respect to food supplies and other necessary inputs, such as water, limestone, and manganese ore. The transportation problems of the eastern Ukraine have been caused, not by serious disproportions among the basic needs of the region, but by its separation from the old established centers to the north and northwest.

Russia at the turn of the century was for a brief period the world's leading producer of crude petroleum, and the location of her oil deposits had some influence on the pattern of industrial growth. The major oil field was situated near the city of Baku, in the Trans-Caucasus region on the western shores of the Caspian Sea. Together with other small fields on the northern slopes of the Caucasian range and at the northeastern edge of the Caspian Sea, these deposits formed the basis for an extractive and refining industry whose output was divided between domestic consumption and exports to Europe. Domestic shipments traveled up the Volga River to ancient cities where heavy fuel oil could be used for power generation in factories, flour mills, and so forth. Export shipments traveled by pipeline or rail to Batumi on the Black Sea, whence they were carried to Europe. From a locational point of view, it was unfortunate that the oil deposits were situated on the very edge of the Russian economy, far from existing centers, though the presence of cheap water transportation routes partially compensated for the long distances, at least during the open navigating season.

But the location of coal, iron ore, petroleum, and other resources not here examined was by no means a decisive influence in determining the geographic pattern of prerevolutionary industrial growth in Russia. Transformation of the old Russian economy proceeded under a strong pull exerted by the West. Even as early as Peter the Great's deliberate transfer of his capital from Moscow to St. Petersburg, there were commercial and cultural ties linking the old cities of central Russia with Western Europe rather than the Russian east. When factories came to be established, they generally employed machinery and equipment imported from Western Europe, and, in the case of the textile industry (a major early focus of industrialization), raw cotton was imported as well. In considerable part the products of the new factories tended to return to Europe as Russian exports; this was especially true at the extractive level. There was thus a noticeable geographic pull from the western border. Frequently the location of enterprises would reflect also the availability of workers or the presence of a concentrated market for the firm's output. Both existed mainly in the established urban centers, to which it then became necessary to bring the requisite fuel and raw material supplies.

The development of the Russian railroad network gave striking evidence of these influences. The earliest lines joined together the ancient river cities and connected the capital with the frontier on the west. Soon a series of lines was extended from the Baltic Sea southeastward into regions that began to export grain to Europe; later similar lines reached up from the Black Sea coast into the same area. The railroad line and pipeline built between Baku on the Caspian Sea and Batumi on the Black Sea were designed to export oil to European markets. It would be an oversimplification, however, to emphasize only these factors underlying the development of Russia's railroad system. Some of the construction in south Russia was directly connected with exploitation of coal and ore resources, and the growth of a domestic steel industry to supply the home market. In the Urals, where a primitive iron industry based on charcoal had flourished in the eighteenth century, a rail network was laid down in the 1870's and 1880's to facilitate exploitation of the region's mineral resources. It was not connected with European Russia until 1896, and therefore cannot be explained as a network designed to export raw materials to Europe.

While the railroad lines built in the nineteenth century reinforced the contemporary locational pattern, they proved at the same time a powerful means for initiating a *new* geographic structure for the Russian economy. Pioneering lines reached out toward the south and east, opening up territory that had previously been relatively little used. In some cases the principal objective was the settlement of fertile grain-growing areas, and in others military conquest of outlying peoples. The Trans-Siberian Railroad was a state venture motivated by a desire to strengthen the position of the Russian Empire on the Pacific, as well as by desires to facilitate settlement of Western Siberian farm lands, and extraction of gold and other minerals in Siberia. By the time the Soviet regime was ready to launch its First Five Year Plan, the fundamentals of a railroad network in the east had been laid down.

Nevertheless, if one examines the location of industrial activity in 1913, it is clear that the markets, labor force, and social investment (such as housing, local transportation, and water supply) of the established cities in European Russia had attracted well over half the total plant and equipment of the economy. This industry depended on raw materials imported from abroad, or brought over long distances from the south and east. It developed where it did because the combined weight of cost advantages, given the existing pattern of population and already established facilities, together perhaps with a certain momentum received from the past, made the importation of raw material seem more attractive than wholesale migration toward the sites of the new resources. From a sufficiently long-run point of view, especially from the standpoint of transportation, this geographic aspect of Russia's prerevolutionary industrialization was unfortunate. It would not have come about to anything like the same extent if the country had been settled for the first time at this moment in history.

The new regime, however, far from starting with unsettled territory, inherited an ancient, well-established economy, deeply embedded at traditional sites and already launched on an industrialization process with strong locational tendencies. During its first decade, the previous locational tendencies were even to some extent reinforced. It will be recalled that for various reasons economic conditions deteriorated catastrophically in Russia during 1917–1920, and that strenuous efforts at recovery occupied the next seven years. The pressing need to restore production focused attention on industrial capacity already built in the old centers. In several primary products recovery here was faster than in outlying areas, with the result that the locational disadvantages of the old pattern were preserved and even exacerbated. Hence the basic problem of locational discrepancies between the resource deposits required for industrialization and the population centers of the inherited economy was brought right down to 1928.

In the railroad sector, on the other hand, developments during the decade and a half up to 1928 were considerably more promising for economic development. First, it appears that railroad-building in Russia was given a tremendous stimulus by the First World War. The annual increments in 1911, 1912, and 1913 were substantial, but they were dwarfed by the additions which came in 1914, 1915, and 1916. This can be seen from the following tabulation of roadway added for permanent operation between 1911 and 1917:[5]

| 1911 | 1309 kilometers | 813 miles |
|------|-----------------|-----------|
| 1912 | 998 | 620 |
| 1913 | 1165 | 724 |
| 1914 | 2920 | 1814 |
| 1915 | 2979 | 1851 |
| 1916 | 4272 | 2654 |
| 1917 | 995 | 618 |

A large part of this new construction was clearly developmental in purpose, reaching out farther to the east, the south, and the European north, for new mineral resources as well as new arable land. As it happened, the additions to the network during 1914–1917 were more than offset by the loss of rail line in the territory ceded under the Treaty of Brest-Litovsk. The new regime therefore inherited a total length of roadway (first main track, excluding second tracks, yard tracks, and so on) within the boundaries of the USSR totaling 70,951 kilometers in early 1918 (44,087 miles), not far different from the total available in the boundaries of the tsarist empire at the end of 1913.

Second, the Soviet heritage included an additional group of projects that had been initiated before but not completed by the end of 1917, and these were gradually added to the network during the next decade. As the head of the NKPS reported to the Central Executive Committee of the USSR in February 1927, "For the most part, we have completed lines begun before the war. We ourselves have begun and finished only a very small number of new lines." [6] Similar observations have been made by other Soviet writers, and analysis of individual projects in this period discloses several that would not have been worth initiating under existing conditions, substantially different from those of 1912–1915. Thus additions to railroad carrying capacity continued to be made during an interval when industry was with difficulty struggling back to the 1913 level. In effect, a reservoir of transportation capacity was created, to be drawn on when fresh industrial growth was resumed. A few of the new lines were only of marginal value, as indicated, but many others proved to be very useful indeed.

Before passing to a consideration of Soviet locational objectives, we should notice a general climatic factor influencing many aspects of Soviet life, and review briefly various environmental factors influencing the ability of the major carriers to serve the transportation needs of the economy. The general climatic factor is of course the northerly location of large portions of the USSR, and the consequences of this position. Perhaps as serious as any other is permafrost, or permanently frozen subsoil, which affects 47 per cent of the USSR.[7] It renders agricultural activity difficult indeed, and creates many cost-raising problems in the construction of buildings, roads, railroads, water-supply facilities, and industrial installations. Only in recent decades have technological advances permitted much headway against these problems, but in the USSR, as in northern Canada, progress is evident. Agricultural exploitation of these regions appears to face prohibitively high costs, but mining, generation of hydroelectric power, and certain other industrial operations seem to have become feasible. One of the large, open questions concerning Soviet economic prospects relates precisely to this matter of overcoming permafrost and the disadvantages of cold, inhospitable northern regions. The answer hinges in part on the state's ability to attract productive labor to such areas. For some twenty-five years the Soviet government has relied heavily on corrective labor camps, containing criminals, political prisoners, and prisoners of war, to develop the northern and eastern regions. By all accounts, productivity has been low, and currently emphasis seems to be shifting to free labor, attracted by high wages and appeals to patriotism. But it is too soon to assess the results. Perhaps the only observation warranted by present knowledge is that real costs of production in taking advantage of the resources of this territory (almost half the USSR) are likely to be substantially higher than costs in settled regions.

Turning now to environmental factors bearing on the abilities of the various transportation media to serve the Soviet economy, we should note climatic influences and topographic features of the Soviet land mass. The continentality of the Soviet climate leads to extremes of heat and cold; while hot weather does not bring any major carrier to a halt, cold weather does. The point is strikingly illustrated by the data in Table 3, showing the extent to which internal waterway and coastal maritime carriers are penalized at various points because the rivers and seas are frozen.

Table 3. *Average annual length of shipping season, USSR, at major rivers and ports*

| Location | Length of season (days) | Percentage of time navigable |
|---|---|---|
| *River* | | |
| Dnepr at Kiev | 267 | 73.2 |
| Lower Volga | 264 | 72.3 |
| Upper Volga | 224 | 61.4 |
| Western Dvina | 236 | 64.7 |
| Northern Dvina | 177 | 48.5 |
| Ob at Salekhard | 152 | 41.6 |
| Irtysh at Tobolsk | 189 | 51.8 |
| Yenisei at Krasnoyarsk | 197 | 54.0 |
| Southern (upper) Lena | 145 | 39.7 |
| Northern (lower) Lena | 88 | 24.1 |
| *Seaport* | | |
| Odessa | 328 | 89.9 |
| Mariupol | 288 | 78.9 |
| Taganrog | 252 | 69.0 |
| Astrakhan | 238 | 65.2 |
| Tallin | 283 | 77.5 |
| Leningrad | 200 | 54.8 |
| Murmansk | 365[a] | 100.0 |
| Archangel | 175 | 47.9 |
| Nizhne-Kolymsk | 110 | 30.1 |
| Vladivostok | 255 | 69.9 |

[a] Kept open by icebreaker for 50 days.
Sources: The river data are from Obraztsov, 1948c, p. 61, except that the Ob and Irtysh river figures come from Suslov, 1947, p. 22. The port data are from Suiazov, 1949, p. 35.

The intermittent character of water transportation in the USSR is a very serious drawback in an industrial economy. In the preindustrial era, when the seasonal rhythm of economic activity, primarily agricultural, was pronounced, there was simultaneous and co-ordinated variation among all major activities. Now, however, manufacturing and mining can be carried on at an almost uniform rate throughout the year, and this creates a need for equally uniform transportation of raw materials and finished products. Here the water carriers break down, unless large stockpiles are accumulated at the beginning and end of each shipping season. When the prospective roles of the several carriers are discussed in a later chapter, Soviet experience on this point will be examined. Here it is sufficient to note that the Soviet climate imposes substantial handicaps on river and sea transportation.

The climate is responsible for another peculiar difficulty for those rivers which flow north, as do all the important rivers in Siberia. At the time of the annual spring thaw, the upper course of these rivers melts, while the lower (northern) portions are still icebound. Consequently great masses of water flow toward the mouths of the rivers, spread out over the frozen lower reaches, and produce large floods. Such floods increase the difficulty of maintaining and operating port facilities along the upper part of the rivers, while bridges across the middle portion of these rivers are periodically endangered. The rivers of Siberia originate in high mountains and are characterized by a rapid descent in their upper course, rendering them unnavigable until they reach the Siberian lowlands. For both these reasons, combined with the short shipping season, it appears that the contribution that her river systems can make to the economic development of Siberia will be limited, and that major reliance will have to be put on rail, road, and air carriers.

A less pervasive but still significant climatic influence on Soviet transportation is the scanty rainfall that characterizes large regions in southeast European Russia and in Central Asia. Use of many rivers in these regions is hampered in certain months by inadequate water flow, lowering the channel below the depth required even for shallow-draft vessels. Railroad operations in these regions face serious difficulties in obtaining the rather large quantities of water required for steam locomotive boilers. A water-condensing tender for use with steam locomotives in these regions was developed in the 1930's specifically to meet this problem, and diesel-electric locomotives are increasingly coming into use here for the same reason.

Seasonal variation in railroad freight operations is far less severe than that imposed on Soviet water carriers by frozen water periods. At no time do railroad operations cease, though winter snowstorms, floods, earthquakes, and so on may interrupt service on particular lines for a few days or weeks. Under strong governmental pressure for maximum performance, Soviet

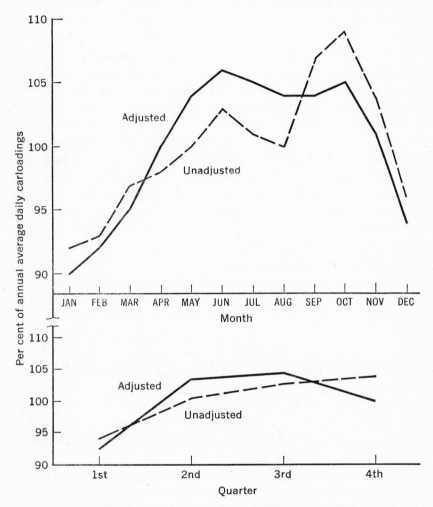

*Chart 1. Seasonal index of average daily carloadings, 1921–1938, USSR railroads. Source: Table 29.*

railroads have developed a seasonal pattern for freight traffic (using monthly figures for average daily carloadings), in which the June peak is no more than roughly 18 per cent above the January low. To put it another way, the January level is about 90 per cent, and the June level about 106 per cent of the year-round monthly average. The pattern is indicated in Chart 1, which shows an unadjusted seasonal index calculated strictly on the basis of continuous monthly data for the 18 years from 1921 through 1938, and an adjusted index reflecting the pattern which became typical in the 1930's.

When rail operations were recovering from a very low level in the 1920's, month-to-month changes were large and erratic. When the system was being pressed to capacity under the forced industrialization program, month-to-month changes became more regular. The whole shape of the annual pattern was altered. Before the mid-1930's the fall harvest brought an annual peak in October. With agricultural freight being displaced, relatively, by industrial traffic, this effect diminished. In the early years there was a tendency for traffic to fall off in April and May, reflecting the spring rains. This tendency too disappeared in the 1930's. The pattern that took shape as a result consisted of a fairly level rate of operations between May and October, followed by a continuous drop to the annual low in January, after which monthly traffic rose again. In effect, the rate of operations was pushed up to take advantage of unutilized potential in the first part of the warm season. Yet the cold-weather fall in the rate of operations has persisted, though on a diminished scale.

Soviet internal waterways suffer from a second disability by comparison with the railroads. The major rivers of the Soviet Union flow, with few exceptions, out to the edges of the land mass, and in so doing fail to join together the major concentrations of natural resources and economic activity. No river links are available between the iron ore and coal deposits of the eastern Ukraine, or between the coal and iron ore deposits of the Urals, Kazakhstan, and Western Siberia. In both territories short stretches of various rivers pass through the intervening areas, but do not by themselves furnish through communications. As will be seen later on, transshipment to and from river carriers in connection with rail-water shipments is a strong deterrent to their use.

Neither of these basic industrial complexes is directly connected by river with Moscow or Leningrad. The Volga River has been a great interregional connection in the past, and the new Volga-Don Canal will extend its sphere of activity farther to the west, but even the Volga has not taken much part in traffic between the old industrial center and the eastern Ukraine. In conjunction with the Kama River, a tributary that comes to the upper Volga from the northern Urals, the Volga can be used to bring timber southward for the mines of the Donbas, and of course it has been the main channel of petroleum traffic northward from the Caucasus to central European Russia. The growth of heavy industry in the cities along the middle Volga is enhancing the interregional transportation significance of the great river of Russian history, but nevertheless the railroad network that is gradually filling the territory all around it is responsible for more and more of the traffic.

The huge river systems of Western and Eastern Siberia unfortunately flow northward rather than in an east-west direction, and hence do not provide direct connection with European Russia. Their connection by way of the Northern Sea Route, from their mouths west to Archangel or Murmansk, is severely limited by the short shipping season and the high cost of navigating the northern seas. The Amur River in the Soviet Far East has proved of negligible value in developing the territory that surrounds it. In Soviet Central Asia, the rivers have not been important aids to regional transportation, and they can make little contribution as connecting routes between Central Asia and the regions to the north or west. In earlier days the Dnepr and the rivers of northwestern European Russia were the main traffic arteries of the territories through which they ran, but with the coming of railroads their role has steadily declined, and even the building of several canals during the interwar period has failed to re-establish their relative position.

All in all, the evidence indicates conclusively that the rivers of the USSR are not well located to serve the transportation needs of an industrial economy, and this factor, combined with their enforced idleness during the winter, goes far to explain their small and probably declining role.

Geographic shortcomings also account to a large extent for the failure of maritime carriers to contribute on a major scale to domestic transportation in the USSR. Except for the Aral Sea, which is located in a sparsely settled, semidesert region, the seas available to the Soviet Union are all peripheral and isolated from one another. The Caspian Sea was wholly landlocked until joined with the Black Sea by the Volga-Don Canal in 1952. The canal now makes possible, for a few months each year, water connections on Soviet territory between the Black Sea and the Baltic Sea, at least for shallow-draft vessels. But year-round connections between the south and north of European Russia by sea still require a trip around the whole circumference of Western Europe. Sea passage from the Black Sea to the Soviet Far East calls for a voyage almost halfway around the world, by way of the Suez Canal, skirting India and China to reach Vladivostok. The

Northern Sea Route, connecting the White Sea with the Pacific Ocean, has gradually been opened for traffic, but does not seem likely to become a major artery for bulk freight in the foreseeable future.[8]

The total length of the borders of the USSR is approximately 60,000 kilometers (37,000 miles), of which 70 per cent represents a water boundary; yet only a small fraction of these surrounding waters is geographically suited to the carriage of freight between points in the USSR. If the seas across the north of the USSR could somehow be transformed into open water, making available a passage like that below Australia, or if some sort of Panama Canal could magically cut through the continents separating Russia's western and eastern coasts, her maritime transportation system would be revolutionized. Simply to suggest the notion is to illustrate, by contrast with reality, the limitations laid on Russia's maritime transportation. The USSR is a land power, and it must depend on land transportation to meet its domestic needs. In respect to water transportation, it is less well endowed than any other major power of the world.

The topography of the USSR, on the other hand, is unusually favorable for the construction and low-cost operation of railroads. European Russia consists primarily of a flat plain, with elevations varying from 18 meters (60 feet) below to 350 meters (1100 feet) above sea level.[9] As a result, the gradients to be surmounted in laying out railroads seldom exceed 1 per cent, and can for the most part be kept below 0.5 per cent. Apart from the Caucasus and Ural Mountains, the central continental land mass contains no barriers equivalent to the mountain chains in the eastern and western United States, and a fortiori is free of the kind of massive barrier that has impeded railroad communications in South America. Along the southern edge of Central Asia and Western Siberia, and throughout the territory lying to the east, topographical conditions grow increasingly unfavorable for railroad construction, but in general it can safely be said that the USSR is fortunate in the topographical conditions it offers for railroads. This can be seen clearly from the data of Chart 2, which presents a frequency distribution of the total length of operated railroad roadway by class of ruling gradient, in 1933. Only 4 per cent of the total first main track operated had ruling gradients in excess of 1 per cent, while at the other end of the scale, more than a quarter of the line was horizontal, and over 60 per cent had gradients below 0.5 per cent.

Our discussion of the need for transportation in Russia has stressed interaction between the location of the population and the location of the resources they use, as a basic determinant of that need. The interaction

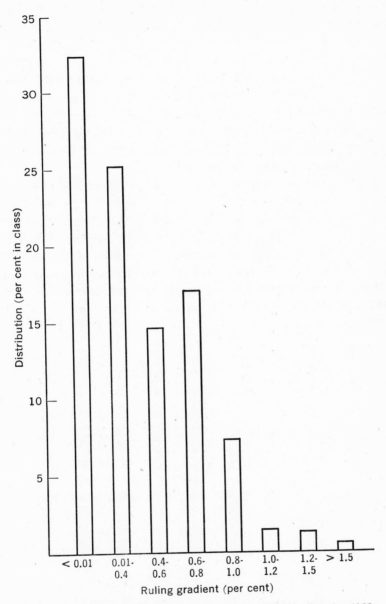

*Chart 2. Distribution of total road operated, USSR railroads, 1933.
Source: Table 30, which also gives data for 1913 and 1940.*

depends on the kind of economic activity pursued and on the level of technology employed; as these change, previous patterns of locational adjustment become in greater or lesser degree untenable, but the process of adjustment is slow. The need for transportation also depends on the extent of locational discrepancy among the resources themselves, and it has been suggested that Russia's rich resources are scattered very unevenly over her territory, thus generating an inherent need for transportation if they are to be effectively united in production. Attention has been called, finally, to the disadvantages imposed on almost half the Soviet land mass by its northern climate, especially by permafrost.

Turning to the factors affecting the ability of various transportation agencies to serve the economy (and leaving highways, pipelines, and air carriers for later consideration), we have seen that river and sea carriers labor under several handicaps in the USSR. The freezing of their routes forces both to cease operations for substantial fractions of the year. Neither form of transportation is well located to serve conveniently among the main traffic-originating centers. By contrast, the railroads can provide relatively continuous service, over favorable terrain, throughout most of the Soviet realm.

# 2    SOVIET LOCATIONAL OBJECTIVES AND PROBLEMS

The all-inclusive Soviet goal of "building socialism" meant, in the economic sphere at least, a determined drive to renew and speed up the industrialization of Russia. We have now to consider the spatial aspects of this drive. In building heavy industry, one must decide where to put the new plants, and such decisions will obviously play a large part in determining the transportation needs associated with the new economic activity. Let us therefore examine briefly the locational principles expressed by the new regime, and note the policy problems encountered in applying these principles to the environment described in the preceding chapter. Reflection will soon persuade the reader that locational matters are very complex — instead of attempting to trace their intricacies here, it seems best to present only a broad review of policies and forces at work. We can then turn to an analysis of transportation developments, which will follow the impact of these forces and policies as reflected in actual transportation performance. In Part III of the study, after the record has been reviewed, we can return to the issues and consider some theoretical observations suggested by an evaluation of Soviet experience.

Among the Marxian notions that Lenin subjected to further development was the idea that under capitalism different parts of the world, and even different parts of the same country, grow "unevenly," that is, at different rates. The "center" waxes fat, while the colonies, or the provinces, are held back and exploited.[1] If it were true that capitalism unfairly promoted the interests of certain "home" areas at the expense of other outlying areas, then it would be a natural deduction that one task when the capitalists were expropriated would be to redress this unfairness, to remove the unevenness of economic location. Hence one of the slogans, or lines of thought influencing Soviet location theory and policy in the postrevolutionary period, centered on this concept of locating economic activity more "evenly."

In the tsarist empire the ethnic situation was complicated, with Great Russians making up about half the population, Ukrainians and White

Russians about a fourth, and a large number of smaller minorities the remaining fourth.[2] As revolutionists wishing to appeal to all disaffected elements in the population, the Bolsheviks understandably had a plank in their platform calling for special attention to the peoples trampled on by the Great Russians of the tsarist regime. This whole sphere of nationality relations had been the special province of I. V. Stalin since 1912, and consequently came to assume more prominence as he gradually consolidated his position in the party. It was generally true of the minority groups that they lived "out in the provinces" and that their culture was (from a European point of view) "backward." A regularly repeated slogan affecting locational policy was, therefore, that it should help to raise the level of these backward groups and regions.

The international environment surrounding the new government added still a third strand to the thinking of Bolsheviks on locational matters. Intervention during 1918–1920, and hostility thereafter, made the concept of "capitalist encirclement" a vivid one in the minds of the leaders. Even admitting that Soviet attitudes played a part in engendering hostile responses from the West, it must be recognized that a lively fear of pressure from abroad, including actual invasion, influenced Soviet domestic planning. In a fundamental way it led to a policy of autarky, bringing almost to a complete halt the previous path of the Russian economy toward industrial growth through participation in the world economy, and leading the Bolsheviks instead to give national self-sufficiency a very high place on their agenda.[3] Not wishing to be dependent on outside sources of supply for any important element of national power, the Bolsheviks spurned the advantages that might have accrued to them through taking part in international specialization and exchange. Under conditions of capitalist encirclement, it was only to be expected, too, that distance from the frontier would be taken into account when location alternatives were being considered.

These three general injunctions — to remove capitalist unevenness, to advance the backward regions, and to beware of capitalist encirclement — have been persistent themes in Soviet discussion of location and transportation problems to this day. They coincide with the concept of moving production closer to sources of raw material and fuel, since the latter typically lie in relatively undeveloped, interior areas of the USSR. The geographic thrust of all these notions is outward and eastward, in historical perspective a continuation of Great Russian expansion from Muscovy during the last few centuries. In crude summary, therefore, the regime's locational objectives can be identified with raising the proportion of the USSR's output which comes from the eastern and underdeveloped parts of the country.

One finds, however, in examining the record of Soviet development, that the eastward movement has proceeded rather slowly, and that the old centers of European Russia have usually received more attention than outlying regions. Part of the explanation no doubt lies in the climatic and geographic disadvantages of the Soviet east and north described in the last chapter. But in addition there appear to have been two counterforces at work among the regime's economic objectives, and it is instructive to note their impact on what would otherwise seem a straightforward program for development.

The first of these counterforces was Soviet determination to obtain the benefits of economies of scale in production. Both where the capacity of existing industries was to be increased and where entirely new industries were to be established, the technicians who drew up the First Five Year Plan, spurred on by their political overseers, called for absolutely large production units. Their output would be cheaper, in real terms, than the output of small or medium-sized plants. They could utilize the latest German, British, and American technology. And they would unquestionably be dramatic symbols of the giant strides being taken by the regime, potent instruments for persuading domestic and foreign persons of the virtues of the system.

Now when individual production units are large, the necessary locational consequence is that the territory over which their output will be distributed must be larger than the market area surrounding a smaller production unit. The giant plant can supply the needs of a large region, or even of a whole country. Unit production costs will be low, but they will be at least partly offset by the transportation costs incurred in distributing the plant's output. If the large plant is established in thickly settled territory with large consumption needs, the plant's radius of distribution may be small, and many such plants can be spread evenly over the countryside.

But giant plants in the Soviet setting have not been consistent with spreading economic activity more "evenly," except in a very gross sense. By contrast with a set of small plants more uniformly located throughout a territory, the Soviet giants of the 1930's carried with them a considerable degree of geographic centralization. At the same time this tendency reflected the fact that Soviet mineral resources, especially those then known, occur in clusters widely separated from each other. Thus what developed under the five-year plans was a pattern in which new plants dotted the map very widely, yet in which the major ones formed definite clusters in about five districts.

Each of these districts was unbalanced in the sense that it required imports of certain supplies or produced an exportable surplus of certain outputs. The transportation requirements that arose from the pursuit of economies of scale in production were therefore not uniformly spread throughout the USSR, but instead were focused on routes connecting the major producing regions. Large plants in major districts, that is to say, led to a large volume of interregional exchange concentrated on inter-regional trunk lines. There was thus a direct technological relationship be-tween the policy of "gigantomania" and the policy of "super-trunklining" major arteries, which will be described in Chapter 3. These concentrated flows of freight traffic did not appear in cases where supply sources were scattered widely over large areas, as was true for many agricultural outputs like grain, or in cases where consumers were widely spread over large regions, as was true of kerosene for Machine Tractor Stations. But in gen-eral, because of the geography of resource deposits, supplies tended to originate at a few points; and, because of the large-plant policy, industrial consumers tended to be locationally concentrated too.

The second counterforce influencing Soviet location and transportation policy in the 1928–1940 period was the tremendous emphasis on speed of development. It was clear that if substantial increments of industrial output were to be obtained rapidly, the place to obtain them was in the old estab-lished centers of European Russia. The inherited "unevenness" of industrial location would not thereby be lessened, nor would the backward regions be raised. As for safety from invasion, both Leningrad and the eastern Ukraine were uncomfortably close to the western frontier. Nevertheless it appears to have been recognized that, in the absence of massive capital imports from abroad, the fastest way to spread heavy industry into the less developed regions was to enlarge heavy industrial capacity first in the old centers of European Russia, so that they could act as springboards from which new bases could be launched.

Questions of timing are usually just as important as issues of direction in formulating national policy, and they loom large in any analysis of Soviet affairs. The reader will recognize an unyielding insistence on "keeping up the tempo" of heavy industrial advance as perhaps the central feature of what may be called "Stalinist industrialization." This is, however, not the place to explore the causes and consequences of the emphasis on speed,[4] except in relation to the sphere of location and transportation. Here it seems to have retarded the eastward movement.

The emphasis on rapid expansion of heavy industry and the emphasis on large production units both tended to deflect energy away from the even spread of industry into backward, interior regions of the USSR that was called for by the leading slogans of the party. In Soviet presentations of the evidence, however, judicious arrangement of regional data could make it appear that the party slogans were meeting with great success, and of course there were undeniable revolutionary changes in economic life throughout the USSR. But as will shortly be shown in connection with economic developments during World War II, the 1928–1940 period represented only an initial step toward attaining the regime's locational objectives.

Moreover, the objectives themselves underwent changes in balance and emphasis during the period, and on the eve of the war were restated in an emphatic form which will repay brief examination. To understand the changes, one must note four developments of the intervening years. The first was the gradual completion of major industrial projects launched during the First Five Year Plan. During the period between 1934, when the Second Five Year Plan was officially promulgated, and 1939, when the Third Five Year Plan received official confirmation, efforts were devoted to finishing construction of uncompleted installations and to bringing them into full operation. The leading slogan of "mastering technique" meant in effect that the new Soviet managers and industrial labor force were engaged in raising the efficiency and productivity with which they could operate the large production units installed.

Consolidation of these major centers had the effect of removing one degree of freedom from the situation confronting planners in the late 1930's. The principal foci toward which fuel and raw materials would flow, and from which industrial output would be distributed, were fixed and given to a much greater extent than was true a decade earlier. The change was not a black-and-white reversal, of course, but the balance of forces at work certainly shifted substantially. Given the location of these major centers, how could increments of industrial capacity best be locationally distributed?

Another marked shift in the forces at work related to the international situation, or in Soviet terms, the threat of capitalist encirclement. At both the Seventeenth Party Congress in January 1934 and the Eighteenth Party Congress in March 1939, Stalin laid great stress on the menace of Japan and Germany. One has presumably to discount these pronouncements somewhat in the light of their domestic function as instruments promoting unity and enthusiasm in the population, but it was a readily observable fact that Japan and Germany were rearming and explicitly discussing their hostility toward the USSR. Japan and Russia had had conflicting interests around China for many decades, and in 1931 Japan had occupied Manchuria. How could this help but influence location policy in the Soviet Far East?

By March 1939, most major powers recognized that large-scale rearmament appeared necessary and that Nazi aggression seemed imminent. In the USSR, recognition of this ominous danger seems to have come earlier, as indeed was understandable in view of Hitler's explicit remarks about the Slavs and the Ukraine. Considerations of national defense and strategic security, therefore, were given steadily increasing attention in Soviet location policy as the 1930's wore on. Again, the change was one of emphasis, since even in 1928 these factors played an appreciable part in Soviet thinking; by 1939 the sense of urgency and danger seemed to dominate the situation.

Still a third set of altered pressures on location policy arose from developments in the sphere of transportation itself. In the late 1920's the Soviet transportation system contained a good deal of slack, and the planners made use of it in their calculated-risk policy of intensifying the utilization of existing transportation facilities. It became necessary to channel a large volume of resources and attention to transportation after a few years in order to overcome the crisis that had developed. But it gradually became clear that only a temporary solution had been found, that large additional increments of freight traffic were in prospect, and that existing location policy, far from reducing the relative need for transportation by bringing production closer to sources of raw materials, was somehow systematically generating huge traffic demands.

Transport writers in the middles thirties began to introduce a new argument into the discussion. For instance, in 1935 the head of the Transport Section of Gosplan spoke of "the accomplishment of a rational distribution of productive forces in the country, with the aim of facilitating the work of transport. . . ."[5] A major 1937 article on "Problems of Railroad Transportation in the Third Five Year Plan" went further, discussing "irrational shipments" and "regional self-sufficiency."[6] It may be surmised that the traffic demands implied by the draft Third Five Year Plan output targets (assuming recent relationships between production and freight traffic continued) were alarmingly high. The foreseeable volume of freight traffic, that is, would probably have called for a volume of investment in enlarged freight-carrying capacity that was unacceptable to the Bolshevik leadership because it diverted too much investment away from rearmament. Under these circumstances it was perfectly logical to investigate seriously the possibilities of reducing the volume of transportation associated with a given amount of industrial production.

When the plan era began, there were optimistic hopes that through locating new facilities nearer to raw material and fuel supplies, the distances over which freight had to move would be shortened. The First Five Year Plan put the average length of haul for railroad freight in 1932–33 at 579 kilometers, slightly below the preliminary figure of 584 kilometers for the 1927–28 base period used as a reference. The actual 1932 average length of haul was about 9 per cent longer than anticipated, or 632 kilometers. When the Second Five Year Plan was announced in 1934, the planners assumed that the 1937 average length of freight shipments on the railroads would remain at 632 kilometers. But again there was an unintended rise, and the actual 1937 figure was 686 kilometers. In 1938 it increased to 718 kilometers.

This persistent lengthening in average railroad freight hauls meant that the railroads were forced to carry each ton for longer and longer distances, absorbing some of the capacity otherwise available for carrying a larger number of tons. If the average length of haul in 1938 had been what it was in 1932, the railroads might have originated approximately 585 million metric tons of freight instead of the 516 million tons actually loaded. It appeared to railroad officials that the roads were being made to perform unnecessary work, that the specialization of regions and plants had gone too far, and that not enough attention was being paid to minimizing the need for transportation. Diversion of some short-haul traffic from railroads to trucks, and of long-haul traffic from rivers to railroads, was also raising the average railroad haul, but the railroads were encouraging the former and unable to prevent the latter. And average hauls had risen secularly for United States railroads, but this was not, evidently, a relevant consideration among Soviet officials.

These appear to have been the major changes among the factors influencing Soviet location policy since the early formulations of the late 1920's. Major centers had taken shape, the Second World War loomed near, transportation capacity faced prospective heavy demands, and the average railroad haul had risen alarmingly. After trial balloons like the Obraztsov-Zemblinov article in 1937, a sweeping new policy was organized and promulgated at the Eighteenth Congress of the Communist Party, in March 1939. The major address introducing the Third Five Year Plan was made by V. M. Molotov, who devoted several sections of his speech to location matters.[7] At the same congress, L. M. Kaganovich, who had been in charge of transportation for several years, in his speech regaled the audience with many examples of what he called "outrageous instances of irrational consignment of goods," driving home the central point of the new policy.[8] The final resolution of the congress embodied the main slogans of the new policy, which were as follows:[9]

1. Build new plants closer to sources of raw materials *and* to centers of consumption.
2. Develop each of the main economic regions "comprehensively."
3. Combat the mania for building giant factories.
4. Eliminate irrational shipments, crosshauls, and excessively long hauls.

In the months following the congress, many articles and books were written to explain the implications of these slogans in detail.[10] The principles were admirably fitted to the war period of 1941–1945, and have been adhered to ever since, in the Fourth, Fifth and Sixth Five Year Plans. It is worthwhile, therefore, to indicate a little more fully what each one meant.

The first precept, that plants should be built closer to sources of raw materials *and* to centers of consumption, clearly shows bland unconcern for the central problem of location theory — that except in rare instances plants cannot possibly do both. It is not the only example of a platform plank drawn to enhance its dramatic quality at the expense of its precision, either in Soviet affairs or in the West, but it is mildly exasperating to anyone seeking workable criteria for plant location. The notion of building plants near raw material sites had been put forward long before, as we have seen, in connection with the goal of reducing unevenness in the location of economic activity. In the actual developments of the 1930's, however, many plants had been located to take advantage of other important factors, such as a labor supply or existing social capital, and they therefore required long-haul imports of raw materials and fuel.

At the Eighteenth Congress, planning officials were being exhorted once again to put new facilities out near new mineral deposits, so that weight-losing products could be fabricated there and then be shipped to market. In furtherance of this objective, the Central Committee of the Party and the Council of People's Commissars jointly issued a decree prohibiting the building of new factories and mills in Moscow and Leningrad, and the Eighteenth Congress Resolution on the Third Five Year Plan suggested that the prohibition be extended to Kiev, Kharkov, Rostov-on-Don, Gorky, and Sverdlovsk.

The additional injunction that production should be located closer to centers of consumption, when spelled out in detail, seemed to relate primarily to consumer-oriented production, especially to such food-supply activities as truck gardening and potato-growing. It was suggested that each major city should have nearby sources of supply for all such products. The first slogan in practice, therefore, was not quite so meaningless as it appears standing by itself.

The second of the new locational principles called for developing each major region "comprehensively," and the meaning of this term can perhaps best be brought out negatively, through a passage criticizing "noncomprehensive development":

In the positive geographical shift of the economy toward new regions, especially in the east, the full, well-rounded development of the new regions was not provided for. Rapid promotion of individual industries in new regions was not always accompanied by simultaneous transfer of related industries. Therefore the development of new industries in the formerly economically backward regions did not provide for a full range of the necessary raw materials, fuel, and so on, and led to bringing them from far away.[11]

While the term was not used directly in this connection, the objective of this proposal for "comprehensive" development was clearly regional self-sufficiency. A comprehensively developed region would have the necessary minerals, fuels, and secondary activities at hand, and therefore would not need to import large quantities from other parts of the country. It is easy to see the advantages of such a situation in the event of war, when parts of the country might be occupied by the enemy.

The third slogan called for an end to "gigantomania," or the practice of building huge works rather than medium- or small-sized plants. It will be recalled that in pursuit of economies of scale and the latest technology, many giant installations had been launched during the First Five Year Plan. Quite apart from the shipping problems created thereby, it was belatedly recognized that an interrelated group of complex installations could not function effectively until every last one of the components had been completed, and this turned out to be a very lengthy process. The Magnitogorsk iron and steel works was a case in point.[12] Speed of completion had always been important to the Bolshevik leadership, but with the international outlook steadily deteriorating, prompt completion of smaller plants seemed absolutely imperative.[13] Getting increments of output from new, smaller installations dispersed throughout the country, instead of adding to capacity at the old centers, would have the special advantage of providing stand-by or duplicate capacity in the event that other plants were knocked out. And with local distribution supplanting previously imported supplies from distant plants, there would be savings in the volume of freight traffic associated with the additional output.

The fourth major slogan, condemning irrational shipments, crosshauls, and excessively long hauls, placed the full weight of party and government authority behind a long-standing complaint of transportation officials and many others. Even before the five-year plans began, the then Commissar of Transportation, IAn Ernestovich Rudzutak, reporting to the Central Executive Committee of the Congress of Soviets in 1927, said: "Therefore, I repeat, if there are transport difficulties they can be laid at the door primarily of uneconomic freight consignments, and only thereafter at the door of our weak transport facilities." [14] In January 1932, G. K. (Sergo) Ordzhonikidze, the then Commissar of Heavy Industry, inveighed against the existing practice of supplying railroads around Vladivostok with coal from Cheremkhovo, 2650 miles away, while there were, as he pointed out, perfectly adequate supplies of locomotive coal near Vladivostok.[15] Similar pleas for traffic-economizing shipping practices were regularly voiced, but they had never before been given such prominence at the top policy level.

As spelled out in hundreds of examples discussed since 1939, "irrational shipments" are those which use "unnecessary" amounts of transportation. For example, transportation writers frequently point out that sawmills should be located at or near timber stands, or at least at transshipments points from water to rail movement, since 25 to 30 per cent of a log's weight is lost in the process of obtaining sawn boards, and in addition some 25 to 30 per cent of a freight car's capacity is wasted when logs rather than boards are carried.[16] From the same point of view, flour mills should be located near harvest areas so that grain is not shipped away for conversion and flour shipped back for consumption, and also to spread traffic more evenly throughout the year.

Since 1939, transportation, especially railroad, writers have emphasized the "rationality" of fostering new industries for the purpose of lightening the load on transportation facilities. Natural gas, carried in pipelines, is recommended in place of long-haul coal or firewood for heating purposes in several metropolitan areas.[17] Expansion of hydroelectric generating capacity can reduce the need for steam-generated electricity making use of long-haul coal carried by the railroads. Development of synthetic petroleum fuels produced from coal would lessen the demand for rail distribution of petroleum products over extremely long distances.

The indignation over crosshauls led to a June 1939 order giving railroad officials the right to review the short-run shipping plans of their clients, in regard to both points of origination and points of termination. The railroads were intent on inducing their clients to draw supplies from the nearest available source and to ship output to the nearest available customer. A 1941 textbook for railroad employees stated in the section on making up shipment plans that "transport offices must not permit crosshauls . . . ," [18] and when Khachaturov described Soviet transportation for a London audience in 1945, he stated that "the interconnection between areas of origin and destination for each commodity is made with a view to the shortest possible total haul of all goods." [19]

The phenomenon of crosshauling, if narrowly defined to cover the simultaneous movement in opposite directions between two points of precisely identical products, can only arise through ignorance, scheduling difficulties, or special surrounding circumstances. This kind of crosshauling came under attack, but in addition a much looser form of crosshauling was criticized, one which arose directly out of the economies-of-scale policies applied in the previous period. If one selects a whole category of products for examination, iron and steel products, for example, it is easy to show that large quantities were being shipped from the eastern Ukraine to the Urals just at the moment that similarly large quantities of the same category were moving from the Urals to the eastern Ukraine. The answer, of course, was that plants were specialized, and that certain specific products could be obtained from one region but not, on short notice, from the other.

For a wide variety of manufactured products, low production costs are obtained through volume operations, employing long, uninterrupted production runs that will keep specialized equipment in relatively continuous use. What transportation writers called for, on the other hand, was a diversified product mix in each major region. If each large works turned out a broad range of products tailored to the needs of its territory, there would be little need for obtaining special product types from similar plants in other regions. This again was an argument for regional self-sufficiency. In 1939 it was directed especially at iron and steel rolling mills, who were ordered in a directive of the Eighteenth Congress to "see to it that all the principal iron and steel producing centers of the country have locally produced rolled steel of all generally used specifications." Even at the expense of certain advantages from specialization, the 1939 policy called for a substantial modification of existing patterns of distribution.

In the chapter thus far, the account of Soviet locational objectives and problems has perhaps brought home to the reader the intricate manner in which various forces combined to shape the Soviet industrial landscape before the war. The regime's over-all objective called for development of the relatively unsettled portions of the USSR, in spite of geographic difficulties, but the inherited regional pattern proved resistant to change, and short-run urgencies gave strong weight to expansion at established centers. While no single measure can express adequately an economy's locational "evenness" or "unevenness," one can form a crude impression of Soviet progress toward its over-all locational objective through examining the eastward movement in the USSR.

When forced industrialization began, the western part of the USSR contained almost exactly three quarters of the population, though it accounts for only one quarter of total Soviet territory. (The dividing line between "east" and "west" in the USSR is discussed below.) By 1939, before the incorporation of new territory in the west, the east's share of total population had risen from 24.3 per cent to 26.6 per cent of the national total — a noticeable but scarcely revolutionary change. In mining activities, on which government interest centered, changes were more marked; the east's share of coal output rose from 20 per cent to 36 per cent, and in crude oil production the rise was from 3 per cent to 12 per cent. The railroad freight tonnage originating in the eastern regions increased from 16 per cent to 28 per cent of the country's total between 1928 and 1940, while the east's share of total minerals production showed approximately the same change. In terms of industrial output, as aggregated in the official Soviet production index, the percentage ascribable to the eastern regions in 1928 was around 10–12 per cent; by 1940 these territories had come to account for over 16 per cent of total industrial production.

It seems clear from these figures that the growth of mining and manufacturing in many parts of the eastern regions must have been most impressive, beginning from essentially nothing in 1928. Nevertheless, in the case of coal for example, some 59 per cent of the increase in coal production, subtracting 1928 output from 1940 output, came from European Russia, primarily the Donbas. The industrial output of all eastern territory in 1940 amounted to just about half the output of Moscow and Leningrad together, two of the inherited centers whose capacity had been greatly expanded.[20] These and other similar comparisons show the need for some such conception as the springboard policy adduced above to account for the observed record.

When we come to the 1941–1945 period, further surprises are in store.

In a general sense, it is obvious that Soviet victory over the Nazis in World War II must have been based on the territory lying to the east of that huge portion of European Russia occupied by the Nazi invaders during 1941 and 1942. Not only had industry been expanded in the east during the 1930's, but additional facilities were evacuated during the retreat of the Russians in the summer and fall of 1941, to be re-established for war production "in the eastern regions." It would seem to follow that Soviet survival is to be explained primarily in terms of the party's foresight in preparing an eastern base before the war and using it in enlarged form during the war.

This is the impression given by Nikolai A. Voznesenskii, whose *Economy of the USSR During World War II* (1947), is the most detailed official chronicle of the period so far available. For example, he says:

There was a period in the history of the USSR's war economy when a large part of the armament industry was on wheels, traveling eastward. . . . This was a unique period of industrial relocation in the east. . . . A powerful industrial base for the Great Patriotic War was established in the Urals, along the Volga, and in Siberia. [pp. 9–10]

The first half year of the war (second half of 1941) saw a great transfer of Soviet industry to the east. . . . During some three months of 1941, more than 1360 large plants, mainly for armaments, were evacuated to the eastern regions of the USSR, including 455 to the Urals, 210 to Western Siberia, 250 to Central Asia and Kazakhstan. . . . [p. 41] and about 200 to the Volga Valley. [p. 49]

Yet if the regional details supplied by Voznesenskii are combined with otherwise available fragments, it appears that the role of the Russian east has been considerably exaggerated. Two devices have been employed — a shift of the dividing line between east and west that transfers certain districts from west to east, and a simple failure to discuss developments in the territory lying between Nazi-occupied areas in the west and the true eastern regions. Both presumably helped to strengthen an impression during the war that Soviet power had been transferred decisively out of danger from the Nazis, moved far off to the east. One thinks of the phrase "Behind the Urals," which is the title of John Scott's widely read 1942 book describing the growth of Magnitogorsk. In fact, while the Russian east did contribute decisively to Soviet victory, half the output of war years continued to come from Russian western territory. Let us examine each of these devices briefly.

Identification of the Russian "east" is probably just as nebulous in Russian minds as is the "west" in the United States. To the Boston dowager, everything beyond Newton in the Boston suburbs is "west." For the Atlantic Seaboard, the west begins on the other side of the Appalachians. Seen from

Chicago, these regions are all eastern, while from Denver even the Mississippi Valley appears eastern, in geography if not in ideology.

In the context of Russian history, the "east" might almost be said to begin at the eastern approaches to Moscow. Certainly in earlier centuries, towns like Nizhnii Novgorod (now Gorky) and Kazan on the Volga were out in "the east." Around 1740, however, the Ural Mountains were taken to be a kind of "continental divide" between Europe and Asia, and to this day the convention is marked by the railroad station of Evropeiskaya near where the Serebranka River rises to flow west, the station of Aziatskaya thirty kilometers away, near where the Baranch River rises to flow east, and the "Summit of the Urals" station halfway between them.[21] When, for administrative reasons in the nineteenth century, the distinction between European and Asiatic Russia came to have statistical expression in the compilation of data for "fifty provinces of European Russia," the effect was to cross the Urals and extend the boundary of Europe even farther to the east. Perm guberniia included all the eastern slope of the Urals and almost reached Tiumen, while Orenburg guberniia, extending almost to Kurgan, covered part of the West Siberian lowland.

Since 1917, however, the boundary has moved westward. As administrative divisions within the USSR became stabilized, there was considerable experimentation in Gosplan and elsewhere with delineation of so-called economic regions, which would have some rationale in terms of homogeneity, coherence, or self-sufficiency. It became usual to consider the Ural economic region as lying in the "east," and this had the effect of moving the west-east boundary substantially westward from where it had been in prerevolutionary days.[22] Farther south, the west extended up to Kazakhstan and Central Asia. In Voznesenskii's presentation of 1940 and in wartime regional data, the concept of "eastern regions" reverts still more toward that of early days. He specifically discusses the Volga Valley as a component of the "east," and his totals for the "eastern regions" involve a large unexplained component that must be ascribed to parts of eastern European Russia.

The second device for concentrating public attention on the "eastern regions" can be illustrated through the figures presented in Chart 3. Rough estimates for the value of industrial production during 1940–1944 are presented for three parts of the USSR: the occupied west, the eastern regions, and an intervening territory here christened the "middle band." The underlying absolute figures and their year-to-year trends are not to be taken very seriously, since they reflect undisclosed Soviet value weights subject to serious

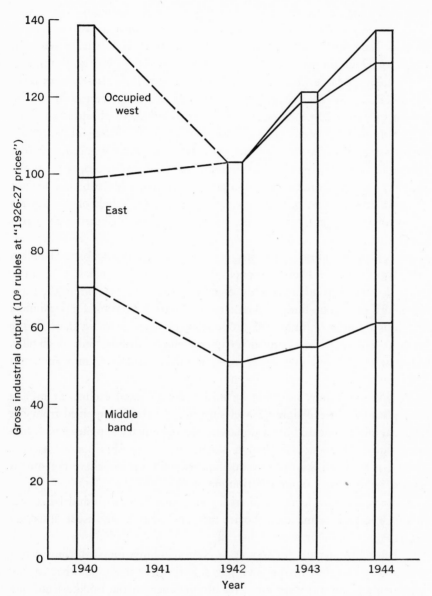

*Chart 3. Gross industrial output, USSR, 1940–1944. Source: Table 31.*

interpretative reservations. But the *relative* contributions of the three territorial divisions emerge even from faulty data, and the point here is that the "middle band" was almost as important as the Russian east.

The Nazi invasion produced a sharp drop in industrial production during 1942 in middle band territory, even with higher valued military output taking a larger role in the 1942 product mix. But this drop was more than made up for by a remarkable growth of output in the east. The 1942 eastern total was 2.3 times as large as its 1940 output. In physical terms the growth must have been more modest, and of course it was accompanied by a drastic fall in living standards, yet beyond cavil this was a noteworthy achievement. An increment of 30 billion rubles in eastern output offset the 20 billion drop in middle band output and contributed 10 billion toward the 46 billion lost on occupied territory. Almost exactly half of the USSR's output in 1942 came from the east, which had only contributed a sixth two years before.

In 1943, total industrial production rose some 18 billion rubles; 11 billion came from the east. There was another rise of 16 billion rubles in 1944, but this time the east contributed only about 4 billion. Still, combining the three years, 1942–1944, one finds eastern territory to be responsible for 183 out of 361 billion rubles of industrial production, or a shade more than 50 per cent. At a time when occupied territory could contribute only negligibly, it can safely be said that eastern output made a decisive contribution to Soviet victory.

At the same time, it would be misleading to focus exclusively on the eastern regions in explaining Soviet survival. The USSR received from her Western allies some 12 billion dollars worth of military supplies and equipment during the war, and though Voznesenskii[23] brushes it aside as only about 4 per cent of domestic production, it is difficult to believe that this is an accurate measure of its contribution.

Moreover the evidence of Chart 3 shows that half the industrial output of the war years came from Soviet territory west of the usual boundary of the eastern regions. Even when the middle band regions were immediately behind the front, and subject to Nazi bombing, they contributed half the country's output. In the later stages of the war it appears that further increments of output were more readily obtained in the middle band and from temporarily occupied regions than from the east. As the need for both military and reconstruction supplies shifted steadily westward, the disadvantage of eastern industrial locations from a freight-traffic point of view must have begun to weigh more heavily. Thus if it can be granted without qualification that the eastern part of Soviet territory provided an indispensable margin toward Soviet victory, it must be admitted that the various regions of European Russia, and in particular the middle band territory, played an equally fundamental role. It is this role which is lost sight of in Voznesenskii's discussion.

The evidence so far reviewed suggests that up to 1941 no very fundamental shift of the Soviet economy's center of gravity toward the east had taken place. Outlying regions had grown remarkably, but so had old centers like Moscow and Leningrad. During World War II, however, the industrial relocation forced on the USSR by the Nazi invasion did produce a basic transfer of activity toward the eastern edge of European Russia and beyond. As the Red Army moved west, bringing under Soviet authority the rich, settled areas that had been reduced largely to wasteland, there began a process of rehabilitation and restoration almost as impressive, in its way, as the previous rapid expansion of output in the east. This restoration of occupied territory since 1944 has clearly tended to counteract the wartime eastward movement; by 1949 it appears that the regions that had accounted for one third of national industrial output before the Nazi invasion had rebuilt their production to a point accounting for roughly 22 per cent of the country's total. Yet in spite of this impressive restoration of industrial activity in the areas that had been badly damaged during the war, western European Russia has suffered a permanent setback in its relative position among Soviet regions.

In passing to a summary review of the "east"'s current position, one meets again the annoying problem of dealing with the westward shift of its boundary. The Volga Valley economic region, which Voznesenskii included with the "east" in his chronicle of World War II, appears to have remained there for record-keeping purposes since the war. Thus if, say, 1950 figures for the proportion of economic activity carried on in the "east" are compared with data for 1940, or 1928, or 1913, and the latter are not adjusted to cover comparable territory, a purely spurious boost is given to the genuine eastward movement under way. It does not appear, however, that the "eastern regions" as presently defined are as vague and inclusive as those alluded to by Voznesenskii in his book.

The following passage, from G. M. Malenkov's report to the Nineteenth Congress in October 1952, is representative of recent Soviet statements:

An important result of our industrial development in this period has been the rapid growth of industry in the eastern regions of the USSR, and this has considerably altered the geographical distribution of our industries. A powerful industrial base has been built up in the eastern regions — in the Volga Valley, in the Urals, in Siberia, in the Far East, in the Kazakh SSR and in the Central Asian SSR's. By 1952, the total volume of industrial output in these areas had increased threefold compared with 1940. In 1951, the eastern regions accounted for nearly a third of the Soviet Union's aggregate industrial output, for over half of its output of steel and rolled metals, for nearly half of the coal and oil output, and for over 40 per cent of the electricity output.[24]

There is evidence, however, of a profound locational dilemma confronting the Soviet regime, and before we turn to a review of transportation developments it may be well to fix the problem in our minds. Between 1950 and 1955, while the east's share of mining and electric power production has no doubt continued to rise, its over-all share of industrial production has *fallen* slightly, from 27 per cent to 26 per cent (presumably excluding the Volga Valley region).[25] Evidently the forces attracting additional industrial capacity to the old established centers are continuing to operate. Moreover, recent Soviet thinking appears to acknowledge the permanence of these forces in comments like the following (by the geographer V. F. Vasiutin): "While in the European part of the USSR some three quarters of industrial production is concentrated, in 1954 only somewhat more than 50 per cent of total USSR coal production was mined here. This . . . led to imports of coal from Kuznetsk and Karaganda, 11 million tons of it in 1954 . . . which, coming 2000–3000 kilometers, wastes 20 to 30 billion ton-kilometers of freight traffic, costing the country more than half a billion rubles a year." [26] This frequently voiced complaint is now accompanied by a demand that more coal be found and mined in European Russia — obviously a retreat from the earlier doctrine of moving industry out to the sources of fuel and raw materials.

# PART II

## RAILROADS AND OTHER CARRIERS IN ACTION

# 3  INDUSTRIALIZATION AND TRANSPORTATION

The stage is now set for a critical analysis of Soviet experience with the transportation sector during a period of rapid forced industrialization. Freight transportation being an ancillary service required to facilitate the central activities of production, within the specific framework of an economy's inherited geographic setting, we have had to gain some impression of the locational pattern on which the Soviet industrialization drive was imposed. It has been suggested that the Soviet economy's need for transportation depends on complex interaction among a variety of governmental objectives and historico-geographic factors, and their main features have been quickly sketched. The interaction itself, and the problems of the major carriers in meeting the demands placed on them, will occupy us in this and the next few chapters.

In the fall of 1928 the Soviet government launched its First Five Year Plan, designed to set in motion once again the process of industrialization that had been under way before the revolution, and to force the process at a higher rate than had ever been attempted before. Transportation, especially railroad freight transportation, had a minor but essential role to play in this process, and in the present chapter we will examine the first years of interaction between the industrialization drive and the functioning of the transportation system. But before addressing ourselves to a detailed scrutiny of transportation under the first two five-year plans, we should note certain features of the doctrinal environment and policy objectives that were uppermost in the minds of the Soviet leaders at this time.

First of all, it may be suggested that, in this respect at least, the Bolshevik leaders were agents of historical continuity rather than doers of the Marxian Word: resumption of rapid industrial growth in Russia was not the result of doctrinal innovation.[1] The problems and policies of the plan era are quite understandable without recourse to the tenets of Marx-Engels-Lenin-Stalinism. The new regime may have forced the pace, and devised sterner institutional vehicles for the process, but it was resuming a task already begun under the late tsarist regime.[2] It is fortunate that this is so, for it means that we may explore the causes and consequences of such developments as, for example, Stalin's drive against wage-leveling,[3] without having to rely solely on the categories of dialectical and historical material-ism. There remains a need, of course, to be sufficiently conversant with the sacred works to understand the slogans and peculiar terminology of party literature. But this is a problem in translation, and once the phrases have been understood, they are seen to relate to objective phenomena of modern industrial economic life. And the essential point is that one then sees the struggles of the five-year plan period not as political events in a Marxist framework, but as economic, social, and political elements in the process of industrialization.

Although doctrine was not the decisive factor in shaping the policies of the five-year plan period, it was possible to reach back into the rich store of party literature and find doctrinal support for whatever current policy recommended itself. As a result, Soviet discussions of economic policy give a surface impression of being concerned in large part with interpreta-tion of received doctrine. One has only to study the statistical record of the contemporary period, however, to see clearly on returning to the policy literature that behind the ritualistic slogans lay objective, difficult issues to be met and solved. And the solutions appear to have been forced by events, not deciphered from Marxian tablets.

In retrospect the outstanding characteristic of over-all policy since 1928 has been its Draconian emphasis on speed. When the First Five Year Plan was being evolved, one group of economists took the approach of projecting forward into the future the rates of growth that had characterized the recent past, or had proved feasible in other countries. This quite understandable method of estimating what might be possible in the immediate future was dubbed the "genetic" approach. It proved unacceptable to the party leader-ship, and went down to defeat at the hands of the so-called "teleological" approach. The latter was not so much a difference in technique as a differ-ence in attitude. Its flavor can best be conveyed by a famous statement of Stalin's, in February 1931, to the effect that "there are no fortresses which Bolsheviks cannot capture." [4] It is perhaps surprising to discover a body of men who subscribed to a highly materialist and determinist view of human affairs laying such emphasis on Bolshevik "will," on their ability to mold events in the face of "objective" (a highly disparaging term) difficulties. Thus it was, however, that the more optimistic of the two drafts was adopted as the first plan. And thus it was, also, that when the first year's results proved better than expected, the targets of the plan were immediately raised still higher.

The emphasis on speed was accompanied by two corollaries: a determination to eliminate dependence on imports of foreign engineering equipment as soon as possible, and a single-minded concentration on heavy industry. In the early 1930's Soviet imports of capital equipment from Germany, England, the United States, and elsewhere showed a temporary spurt, but thereafter they fell rapidly to a very low level. Attention on the iron and steel industry, machine tool industry, and a few others was so concentrated that shortages were in almost every case deflected off to light industry, especially to the consumer goods industry. This tendency, as will be shown in Chapter 10, took the form on the railroads of constricted passenger transportation during the worst of the crisis in freight transportation.

Just as the First Five Year Plan was being launched, the government became involved in what the official party history itself calls "a profound revolution . . . equivalent in its consequences to the revolution of October 1917." This was the mass collectivization of agriculture, "not," to quote the party history again, "just a peaceful process. . . ."[5] In the early 1930's the contest between the Kremlin and the peasants must have absorbed a major share of the government's attention. The outcome was not clear for several years, and in fact the underlying issues have not yet been resolved. Be that as it may, the argument here is that during the period of the First Five Year Plan transportation problems had to compete for the government's attention with collectivization problems, and that this is probably an important factor explaining why the transportation situation was permitted to deteriorate so seriously.

If a set of general directives can be imagined as passing from the Politburo to those directly charged with formulating transportation and location policy, Chapter 2 has shown that it would have run somewhat as follows: "The formerly backward regions of the USSR, especially the regions inhabited primarily by non-Russian ethnic groups, are to be brought up to a closer parity with the regions of central European Russia. Economic activity is to be distributed more evenly over the whole territory of the USSR. Industry is to be expanded at sites closer to the supplies of raw materials and fuel. At the same time, industrial output is to be increased as rapidly as possible, and allocations for capital formation in the transportation sector will be strictly limited." As a theme running somewhat counter to this more or less explicit set of directives, there appears to have been a body of thought derived from existing trends in Russian economic development. Reduced to a simple formulation, it stressed the fact that regional specialization and geographic division of labor held the most promise for rapid industrial growth. In connection with railroad-building, ambitious developmental projects were proposed, in the Russian tradition of recent decades. Going even further, several of the proposals for new lines implied a renewal of Russia's prewar *international* division of labor, with grain exports from the east as the basis for manufactured imports from the outside world.

The final text of the First Five Year Plan reflected both views.[6] The uneven economic development of Russia under the tsars was criticized in strong Bolshevik language, and concern was expressed for the prompt raising of formerly oppressed peoples to relative equality with the "center." On the other hand, the major regions of the USSR were described as having individual advantages, some being especially well endowed for agricultural production, and others peculiarly fitted for industrial activity.

The largest single piece of railroad construction completed during the First Five Year Plan period, and one that obtained widespread publicity throughout the world, was the Turkestan-Siberia Railroad. It was explicitly intended to further regional specialization. The line connected Soviet Central Asia, where the output of cotton to supply the domestic textile industry was being sharply increased, with Western Siberia, where recently opened wheat regions were expected to produce a substantial excess of grain for consignment outside Siberia. Grain was to be shipped south from Western Siberia through Kazakhstan to Central Asia, where it would feed those who would be concentrating on cotton-growing. This project clearly stems from the second of the two themes outlined above. Central Asia would specialize in cotton-growing, and at least part of western Siberia would specialize in producing wheat. The line came into permanent operation in 1931.

The most important development for transportation during the First Five Year Plan period was not, however, the Turk-Sib Railroad, which was relatively lightly loaded until the end of the 1930's, but the grandiose project known as the "Ural-Kuznetsk Kombinat," or "second iron and steel base" of the USSR. As it took shape, it proved to involve a far heavier load on the transportation system than was ever envisaged for the Turk-Sib. In fact, its transportation implications are dealt with at some length in the following section. We can note immediately that the project conforms closely to the directive imputed above to the Politburo. Iron and steel plants were to be established near rich supplies of coal and iron ore, in districts that had previously been little developed. Their output would be converted into capital plant and equipment throughout the Soviet eastern territory. As a result the previous differentiation between primary-product regions in the east and established industrial centers in the west would be reduced.

In considering specifically the relation between increased production of raw materials and finished products on the one hand, and increments of freight transportation on the other, the drafters of the First Five Year Plan were quite optimistic. For example, S. A. Bessonov is quoted as writing, in May 1930:

It cannot be doubted that with a growth in production, the total volume of freight to be carried will always increase also. Nevertheless, industrialization need not be fully accompanied by a proportionate increase in transport facilities. Newly built enterprises can be located near sources of raw materials and fuel, so that the total volume of shipments, in spite of a considerable growth of production, either does not grow at all, or grows to a considerably smaller extent.[7]

It was apparently argued further that if location nearer sources of raw material and fuel would serve to check transport demands proportional to output growth, then the existing railroad system would be able to handle the traffic without substantial requirements for capital improvements. According to a 1931 critic, "right opportunists" among the party officials concluded that 93 per cent of the network would need no reconstruction, and that the main routes of the Donets Basin and in Western Siberia already had sufficient carrying capacity to handle prospective traffic. Within the People's Commissariat of Transportation itself, where one would expect to find claimants for the railroad sector, the bureau of the party cell (presumably at Moscow headquarters) in 1930 supported Bessonov's position that "internal resources" rather than "reconstruction" was the answer. The "internal resources" slogan meant that more efficient operating methods, together with repair and development programs financed out of savings from operating efficiency, could be expected to see the railroads through. "Reconstruction," on the other hand, implied that in order to handle prospective traffic the railroads would have to be allocated the materials and labor necessary for a large-scale capital construction program.

Those who took the position that "reconstruction" of railroads should not be the policy in 1930 (and this seemed pretty clearly to be the way the wind was blowing at that moment) argued that it would take too much iron and steel. A writer in the railroad newspaper is quoted as advising against extensive "reconstruction" on the following grounds: "This would disrupt the whole industrialization program, would drastically slow down the expansion of heavy industry. This line has nothing in common with the line of the party. The party is holding to the course of maximum expansion of heavy industry in the immediate future. Only on this basis will it be possible to set about the radical reconstruction of transportation." [8]

Another general view characterizing the First Five Year Plan period was that economies of scale could be obtained in freight transportation just as they could in large production units. There was evidence that an attitude of "the bigger, the better" influenced the planners of the USSR, somewhat as a similar attitude held sway in the United States during the 1920's. This position was disowned at the end of the 1930's, but for about a decade it colored the regionalization policies of the USSR, and left an enduring mark. In the field of freight transportation, the argument was that if volume shipments of basic materials were concentrated on a few trunk lines, the ton-mile costs of carrying them could be brought down to a very low level. Since a large part of the cost of railroad operations represents fixed costs, invariant with respect to the volume of traffic (though this is less true in the USSR than elsewhere, as explained in Chapter 11), a substantial rise in the density of traffic could be expected to bring with it a proportionate fall in unit costs. That this was the planners' expectation is indicated by the following statement of Gleb Maximilianovich Krzhizhanovskii, head of the State Planning Commission, in 1929:

In the five-year plan as promulgated . . . there are two especially crucial points: . . . agriculture . . . and the proper linking together of the energies of each major economic region. In the latter, we are taking the line of concentrating freight traffic on the basic routes, trunklining them technically, and lowering the cost of shipping the mass freights. In this way we hope to change the whole face of our industrial geography, regardless of the difficulties of distance. In our hands, transport is a more powerful means than with the bourgeoisie, but it is a means, not an end in itself.[9]

The concept of lower unit costs through higher traffic densities and the concept of less-than-proportionate traffic increases due to a shift toward raw materials, together with the two locational themes sketched earlier, appear to have been the major elements in the thinking of transportation specialists at this time. We are in the fortunate position now of being able to follow actual developments thereafter, and thus to see how well these concepts bore the test of application to reality. Before doing so, however, we must examine a little more closely the locational and transportation implications of the Ural-Kuznetsk Kombinat.

Writing after World War II, one cannot help seeing the Soviet decision of 1928 to launch the Ural-Kuznetsk Kombinat as one of a handful of key decisions in Soviet history. It was argued in Chapter 2 that Soviet publicity has exaggerated the extent to which the regions "behind the Urals" were responsible for winning the war. Nevertheless, their coal and steel, together with the heavy industry founded on them, probably provided the margin of victory when the Germans overran all of the eastern Ukraine and brought Leningrad industry virtually to a halt.

The problem of combining the rich iron ore of Magnitnaya, known since 1747, on the eastern slopes of the southern Urals, with the high-grade bituminous coking coal deposits in the Kuznets Basin of Western Siberia, was almost entirely a transportation problem. In the first place it was necessary to assemble these two basic inputs, which lay some 1500 miles apart. Once this was done, it would be necessary to ship finished iron and steel products to the market, and while industrial construction in the region itself would absorb much of the output, it would be still true at that time that the major markets remained in European Russia. The rail distance from Magnitogorsk north to Chelyabinsk in the Urals was 258 miles; to Sverdlovsk it was 414 miles. For steel works at Stalinsk in the Kuznets Basin, the distance to Novosibirsk was 262 miles; the distance to Chelyabinsk was 1210 miles, and the distance to Sverdlovsk was 1274 miles.

These were the "local" distances to the main centers of the regional market. If shipments from the new bases back to the old established centers of European Russia were made, the distances to be faced were initially as follows:[10]

| | |
|---|---|
| Magnitogorsk–Moscow (via Kuibyshev) | 1507 miles |
| Magnitogorsk–Leningrad (via Kuibyshev) | 1912 miles |
| Stalinsk–Moscow | 2492 miles |
| Stalinsk–Leningrad | 2896 miles |

The mere fact of long distances does not by itself demonstrate that the Ural-Kuznetsk Kombinat was uneconomical. Supplying the anticipated demand arising in the Urals and Western Siberia, to say nothing of potential needs farther east and in Central Asia, from the eastern Ukraine would require equally long shipments to the east. These distances do emphasize, however, the immense importance of ton-mile shipping costs in planning the development of eastern steel production. How was it proposed to overcome the disadvantages they entailed?

Here the slogan was "super-trunklining," a term adapted from the German and employed in the 1920 Goelro plan. To convert a weak, low-capacity railroad line into a trunk line meant to raise its carrying capacity through reducing ruling gradients, reducing curvature, laying heavier rail, introducing stone or gravel ballast, strengthening bridges, adding passing tracks, improving signaling facilities, and making other such engineering improvements. It might involve improving the motive power employed, once the track would support heavier locomotives, and improving the rolling stock used, especially through introducing automatic couplings and automatic brakes. It might require double-tracking the road, or even electrifying it. In all these ways, with no apparent change in the length of road operated, a railroad line could be made into a trunk line or a "super–trunk line," and could thereby be made to carry large amounts of traffic at low costs per ton-mile. This was the sort of development in which the party placed its hope, as suggested by Krzhizhanovskii's remark above.

One of the factors that lay behind the government's decision to build steel works at Magnitogorsk and Stalinsk in spite of the high costs involved was apparently a decision that national defense required an interior base. The First Five Year Plan suggested, for example, that "as a region far from the frontiers, with a completely favorable composition of production (ferrous metals, high-grade steel, nonferrous metals, chemicals, and fuel), the Urals are the natural base for the defense of the USSR." [11] A transport writer, discussing the new project in 1931, stated that it "also has great significance for defense interests," and quoted Comrade Krzhizhanovskii at the Sixteenth Party Congress in 1930 as saying that the Urals were the backbone (*stanovoi khrebet*), which guaranteed the defense of the proletarian world.[12] Another writer, in a 1930 pamphlet about the "great Siberian super–trunk line" argued that shipment of iron and steel from the Ukraine and center to the east "is unquestionably disadvantageous from a defense point of view. For this it is very important to have large steel production precisely in the Urals and Siberia, in the depths of the country, and not near the western frontier, which is vulnerable to air bombardment by an enemy." [13]

It is difficult, when two or more considerations press in the same direction, to weigh the relative importance of each. The decision to organize the Ural-Kuznetsk Kombinat reflected several objectives of the regime, as suggested earlier, and national defense appears fairly far down the list in contemporary discussion of the project. It might well have been launched in the complete absence of a strong sense of "capitalist encirclement." In any case, there can be little doubt that national defense was not the ruling consideration when the First Five Year Plan was drawn up, since approximately two thirds of the total investment was allocated to the established centers of

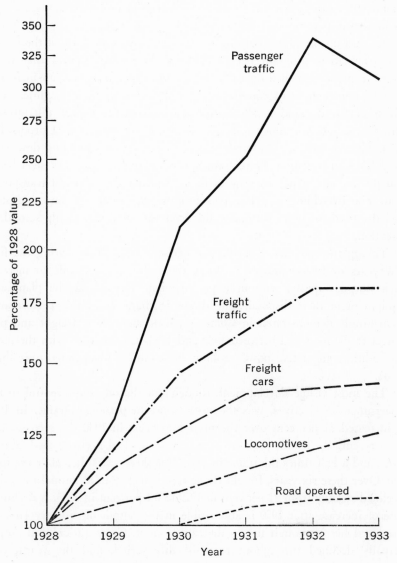

*Chart 4. Railroad traffic and railroad facilities, 1928–1933. Source: Table 32.*

European Russia. We can assume, however, that in the state's scale of preferences, the defensive significance of the project added some positive quantity to its marginal social net product, perhaps just enough to outweigh its high transportation costs.

To sum up the discussion thus far, it has been suggested that the forced industrialization program began with objectives and policies that more or less consciously called on the transportation system to bear an increased load without benefit of commensurate improvements in its facilities. The extent of the demand it would face was, as matters turned out, grossly underestimated. Too much reliance was placed on relocation of production in the direction of raw materials and fuel as a means of holding down the need for transportation. Development of the "second iron and steel base" was put on the agenda in spite of its huge demand for freight transportation. The overriding objective was prompt expansion of heavy industry, and the needs of other sectors of the economy were given only secondary attention.

Taking the calendar year 1928 as a base, we find that during the first few years of forced industrialization, the railroads were able to increase their output rapidly, without a proportionate increase in the plant and equipment at their disposal. The dramatic character of this performance is strikingly demonstrated in Chart 4, which shows how freight and passenger traffic increased between 1928 and 1933, as contrasted with the modest additions to motive power, rolling stock, and road operated over these years.

The most visible development, though not the one most central to the government's objectives, was the great spurt in passenger traffic. In 1929 it increased 31 per cent over the preceding year; in 1930 the increase was 62 per cent. By 1932 a peak in passenger traffic had been reached, almost three and a half times the traffic in 1928. For three years thereafter the total fell. Over these six years, freight traffic rose 82 per cent, at annual rates that declined steadily from 21 per cent in 1929 to 0.1 per cent in 1933. A declining rate of increase after 1930 is also visible in the output of industry (not reproduced here), though not to the same extent. Gross agricultural output actually declined throughout most of this period, and the year-to-year changes were quite erratic.

These gains in the railroads' output were accomplished principally through raising the productivity of existing roadway and equipment, as is clear from inspection of the chart. The number of freight cars actually in service rose 44 per cent, the number of freight locomotives rose 26 per cent, and the length of road operated rose 7 per cent between 1928 and 1933, yet freight traffic rose 82 per cent. The freight-car records reflect substantial increments in the early years, partly due to repair of existing unserviceable cars. Road operated, on the other hand, rose only toward the end of the period.

The trouble with this performance was that it was not good enough. The demand for freight transportation was increasing even more rapidly than actual traffic carried. There is no question here of hostile foreign criticism magnifying a minor maladjustment in the system; Soviet writers at the time and since have been perfectly frank in describing the situation which arose. It is usually referred to as the "bottleneck" (*uzkoe mesto*) period.

In discussing the transportation crisis, it is important to distinguish between attacks on the railroads from consignees who blamed the carrier for delays that were actually caused by the shipper, and criticism justly leveled at the railroads. Harassed officials of enterprises whose production schedules were threatened by shortages of raw materials and supplies could easily assume that their most direct contact with the chain of supply was the source of the trouble. If it were only in this sense that outcries arose against the railroads, the carriers could be absolved of blame. For purposes of the present analysis, a transportation bottleneck will be defined as a situation in which, simultaneously with the unsatisfied demands of consignees, there exist substantial unshipped stocks of freight at shippers' sidings. Under such conditions the shipper has performed all prerequisite operations, and any subsequent delay can be clearly ascribed to the carrier. It is the existence or nonexistence of appreciable backlogs of unshipped freight, then, that measures the presence of a transportation "bottleneck."

A certain backlog of unshipped freight is a normal part of railroad operations, especially at certain times of year when shippers reach seasonal peaks of production. In March 1926, the maximum volume of unshipped freight was 46,300 carloads; in March 1927, the volume dropped to 29,900 carloads; and by March 1928, the spring preceding inauguration of the First Five Year Plan, the March balance of unshipped freight had been brought down to 7,500 carloads.[14] However, the burst of activity that began in earnest in the spring of 1929 quickly reacted on the transport situation, and by September 1929 there were 26,072 carloads of freight awaiting shipment.

In the fall of 1929, petroleum refineries began to complain that fuel oil (*mazut*) was accumulating in their storage tanks, and that operations would have to be shut down soon if the railroads didn't take the oil away. At the same time that this fuel oil was lying in the Tuapse and Grosny storage depots, southern iron and steel works were reduced (in October) to a 2–5 days' supply of fuel oil, instead of the standard 20 days' supply. Other supplies were endangered too: at the Yugostal' iron and steel works ore supplies in October 1929 fell to 18 days' worth, with a standard of 45 days; coal and coke fell to 6 days in lieu of 20; and the stockpile of scrap dropped to 5 days' supply, while 15 days was the norm.[15]

The 1929 difficulties were apparently not widespread, for a transportation history of this period published in 1941 states that "transport began to lag in the fall-winter of 1930–31." [16] The fourth quarter of 1930 was the so-called "special quarter," statistically distinct as a result of the changeover to calendar-year accounting for 1931, and was made the occasion for special production campaigns throughout the economy. The quantity of ore mined, for example, was 18.5 per cent larger than the quantity mined in the fourth quarter of 1929, but average daily carloadings of ore on the railroads were 24.6 per cent *lower*. Grain collections (*zagatovka*) in the special quarter were 42 per cent above the corresponding quarter a year earlier, but average daily carloadings of grain rose only 18.9 per cent. According to the government's grain-collecting agency, Soiuzkhleb, as much as 2,000,000 tons of grain lay under the open sky, awaiting loading at railroad stations, during the special quarter of 1930. The timber organization, Soiuzlesprom, stated that, at the end of the special quarter, timber enough to load 142,000 freight cars lay unshipped for lack of rolling stock.[17]

The government's immediate reaction was to issue a decree that was intended to improve the railroads' operating efficiency. It was considered that the system of "depersonalized driving," in which locomotive engineers were assigned to whatever locomotive came out of the pool, was causing inadequate operation and repair of locomotives. The decree instituted "paired driving," a system in which two locomotive crews were regularly assigned to each locomotive, and also revised wage scales in locomotive repair shops to stimulate better work.[18]

The evidence indicates, however, that the situation was not relieved by this decree. The 1941 history of transport development states that "at the end of 1932 a huge backlog of unshipped freight had accumulated. [There were] about 12 million tons of unshipped timber, about 2 million tons of unshipped ore, more than 1 million tons of unshipped coal; in all, about 20 million tons." [19] One must note here that 60 per cent of the backlog was in timber; this implies that the breakdown strongly affected the northern timber-carrying lines, such as the Archangel-Vologda line, which were not part of the industrial trunk-line network of routes. It is probably also related to a much greater consumption of timber in the construction program than was anticipated by the original five-year plan, which assumed that existing timber lines could carry the load.

In 1933 the situation deteriorated still further. "The backlog of unshipped freight grew sharply. Mines, steel works, light-industry plants, and food enterprises became choked up with unshipped output. . . . The railroads could not even deal with shipments of rails, fastenings, and pipe, the needs of transport itself." [20] In July, the government issued four important decrees dealing with the crisis. The first contained a general statement of the seriousness of the situation and listed the measures proposed to solve it; the second outlined a thorough administrative reorganization of the People's Commissariat of Transportation and the individual railroad administrations; the third set forth a new scale of differentiated wage rates for railroad workers; and the fourth, issued by the party alone, established "political sections" at all levels of railroad administration. [21]

The emphasis continued to rest primarily on more efficient operation of existing facilities, rather than extensive additional allotments of materials and labor for improved roadway and equipment. Inspection of monthly figures for average daily carloadings shows that operations did not improve appreciably in the latter half of the year, and 1933 closed with a total of freight traffic moved only 0.1 per cent larger than the 1932 total. Passenger traffic actually showed a contraction of 10.3 per cent. The backlog of unshipped freight on Jan. 1, 1934, was estimated at 1,338,000 cars, or about 20,000,000 tons. [22]

Nineteen thirty-three was a year of crisis at many points in the economy, with output showing absolute decreases or only modest increases as compared to the preceding rapid growth. In 1934, however, the economy moved forward again at a renewed high rate of advance. Railroad freight traffic increased by 21.4 per cent over the preceding year. Nevertheless, the problem of unshipped backlogs still remained. At the end of 1934, there were almost 1,000,000 tons of unshipped ore, more than 2,000,000 tons of unshipped coal, and more than 3,000,000 tons of unshipped timber to be dealt with. The total still amounted to 15,000,000 tons. The backlog of needs for heavy industry, the chief claimant, was estimated at 650,000 cars, equivalent to about 10,000,000 tons.

The transportation bottleneck was a major topic of discussion at the Seventeenth Party Congress (January 26 — February 10, 1934), and A. A. Andreev, who had been Commissar of Transportation for two years, was heavily criticized. After the congress the railroads did begin to receive more attention from the government, but it was not until 1935 that a vigorous drive to eliminate the difficulties got into high gear. Before examining the measures taken, it may be worthwhile to pause and review the circumstances under which the crisis arose. Why did it develop? Could it have been forestalled?

There was no lack of warning, certainly. As far back as February 1927, before the First Five Year Plan had even been launched, Rudzutak, the newly elected Politburo member who was then head of the People's Commissariat of Transportation (see note 6, Chapter 1), told the government's Central Executive Committee that "transport in the near future can become a brake on the development of the economy." He explained that "maximum attention must be put on planned and correct rational use of transportation, or we will with our own hands turn transport into a brake on the further development of the economy." Rudzutak pointed out that before the revolution the railroads used to get as much investment per year as industry — sometimes more than industry — while in recent years investment (in millions of rubles) in industry and railroads had been as follows:[23]

| Year | Industry | Railroads |
|------|----------|-----------|
| 1923–24 | 245 | 141 |
| 1924–25 | 339.5 | 181 |
| 1925–26 | 779 | 216 |
| 1926–27 (proposed) | 1000 | 315 |

A reply to this warning came six months later in the August ninth resolution of a joint plenum of the Party's Central Committee and Central Control Commission. The plenum

noted that delay in the development of transport might be a threat to the carrying out of the industrialization of the country, and that to prevent this it was necessary to increase outlays on railroad fixed capital, for strengthening the existing network, building new lines, etc. The plenum pointed out also that the means for doing this must be sought first of all within railroad transport itself, through improved organization of the whole railroad system, lowering of operating expenses, and higher labor productivity. Along with utilization of the railroads' internal accumulation, the plenum considered it necessary to provide supplementary means from the budget.[24]

The party's position was clear. Improvement of the transportation system would have to depend primarily on savings plowed back by the railroads themselves, supplemented perhaps by a little help from the central budget. We will shortly see how much capital investment the railroads actually obtained during these years.

In the middle of 1930, at the height of the collectivization crisis, Stalin referred to transportation toward the end of his long report to the Sixteenth Party Congress, with the following admonition:

There is no necessity for enlarging upon the tremendous significance of transportation for the whole economy. And not only for the economy. As is known, transportation also has serious significance for the country's national defense. And yet, in spite of the tremendous significance of transportation, transport operations and reconstruction of the transportation system are still lagging behind the general rate of development. Is it still necessary to prove that in such a situation we run the risk of having transport become a "bottleneck" in the economy, forcefully holding back our forward advance? Is it not time to put an end to such a situation? [25]

Again we see that the government was aware of potential dangers in the current situation. At this moment, however, no decisive action was taken. A year later Tverskoi, the fiery young author cited above, entitled a chapter of his pamphlet, "Transport is still a bottleneck in our economy," and said: "For three years now, the development of industry and agriculture has met with serious difficulties in shipment of industrial raw materials, agricultural, and industrial products." [26] His vigorous polemics apparently furthered his own career, but in 1932 and 1933 the transportation system was not similarly aided.

By 1934, the tone of party discussion had grown more serious, and real attention began to be given to the railroads. Stalin's speech at the Seventeenth Party Congress referred to transportation rather misleadingly in connection with retail trade. He said: "Transportation is a bottleneck that can check, and is already beginning to check, our whole economic policy, and first of all our distribution of commodities." He went on to diagnose the difficulty as "the well-known disease called bureaucratic-routine methods of management," and concluded: "Hence, in addition to helping the transportation system by providing workers and equipment, our task is to root out the bureaucratic-routine attitude prevalent in transport administration and make it more efficient." [27]

Stalin's lead was followed by the many other speakers who discussed the transportation crisis — it was recognized that more plant and equipment was needed, but primary emphasis was laid on shaking up and streamlining the existing organization. K. E. Voroshilov, Commissar of War, spoke of the railroads' importance for national defense, referring to transport as the "twin brother of the Red Army," and calling for stricter discipline among transportation workers. A. A. Andreev as Transportation Commissar, Ian E. Rudzutak as former Transportation Commissar and present head of the

Party's Control Commission, L. M. Kaganovich as a Politburo member already devoting time to transportation supervision, V. M. Molotov and V. V. Kuibyshev as introducers of the Second Five Year Plan, IU. L. Piatakov as Commissar of Heavy Industry, and several others — all demanded more energetic, "Bolshevik" performance from transportation people. Moreover a significant and ominous note was struck by Voroshilov, who said: "Now that Comrade Stalin is really turning his attention to transportation, comrades, you may be sure that all joking is going to be laid aside." The passage is italicized in the transcript of the congress and its implications must have been clear to the 1934 audience, reflecting on what had happened when Comrade Stalin turned his attention to agriculture.[28]

Thus it can be seen that throughout the whole period from 1927 to 1934, the government's position was essentially that the transportation system, and this meant mainly the railroads, could cope with the requirements it faced if only the people in this sector of the economy, from top officials down to rank-and-file workers, would bestir themselves sufficiently. For such reconstruction of transportation facilities as proved necessary even with greater operating efficiency, the transportation sector was urged to rely primarily on internally financed capital development. Since the question of capital development was obviously of central importance here, let us examine in some detail both the money and real flow of capital resources to the railroads.

Rudzutak's data on investment, cited above, showed that even in the restoration period of the middle 1920's the railroads were getting a much smaller share of the country's investment capital than they had obtained before the First World War. In spite of his plea for more investment in transportation, there was no immediate change. Contemporary records indicate that, in the four years before the beginning of the First Five Year Plan, the fixed assets of the railroad system increased by 4.6 per cent, while the economy's aggregate fixed assets increased 17.3 per cent and industry's fixed plant and equipment increased in value by 32.7 per cent (see Table 77 in Appendix F). The source for Table 77 contains no details explaining the price basis for the data, which should therefore be treated with some caution, though between 1925 and 1929 the price level was quite stable relative to subsequent periods. Nevertheless, the contrast between the capital growth of railroads and of industry is so striking that it would certainly be maintained under any plausible adjustment of the data for price changes.

It will be noted that, according to contemporary data, the value of fixed capital in railroads was some 44 per cent larger than the value of fixed capital in industry, at the beginning of this period, and that the railroads still had 13 per cent more plant and equipment than industry at the beginning of the First Five Year Plan. On October 1, 1924, railroad plant and equipment accounted for 17.3 per cent of the economy's total; the railroads' share fell during the next five years, but on October 1, 1928, it was still 15.4 per cent of the total.

If we turn to the record for annual investment in the railroads, and compare it with total investments in all sectors of the economy, it becomes

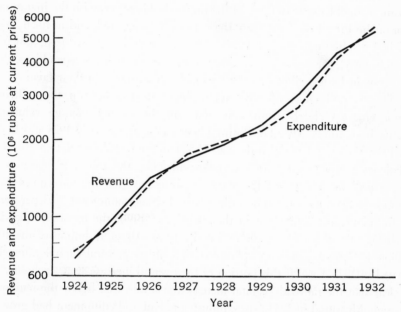

Chart 5. *Government budget revenue and expenditure in railroad sector, 1924–1932. Source: Table 33.*

vividly clear that the era of "railroadization" had drawn to a close. Government policy quickly brought the railroads' share of annual ruble investments down from the 19 per cent that characterized the middle 1920's to an average of 13 per cent for the First Five Year Plan period. The data, in millions of rubles at current prices, are set forth in Table 71 of Appendix D.

These investment data are from centrally compiled studies that presumably segregated capital expenditures from current expenditures. For this period, we have another way of examining financial relations between the railroads and the government, namely, the unified government budget. Until 1932, railroad operations were included in the budget on both the revenue and expenditures sides. The bulk of the sums involved of course related to current finances, but some capital financing appears to have been included too.[29] In Chart 5, the annual ruble sums collected by the government from the railroad sector are compared with annual sums spent on this sector to see what net balance existed in each year.

Inspection of the chart discloses that perhaps Rudzutak's plea had a certain short-lived effect. After having exacted a net toll from the railroads in fiscal 1925 and 1926, the government relented in fiscal 1927 and 1928 to permit a small balance in favor of the railroads. However, with the inauguration of the First Five Year Plan, the net drain reappeared, and in fiscal 1930 reached a substantial magnitude. Thereafter the drain was reduced, and for calendar 1932, the last year before the railroads' financial independence, the government budget showed a not inconsiderable balance in their favor.

The over-all effect of government investment policy on the railroad sector emerges clearly from some data on the annual average value of "active basic funds" (fixed operating plant and equipment) in 1928 and 1933. In 1928, the sum for railroads was 11,529 million rubles and that for the whole economy, 49,394 million rubles; in 1933, the railroads' share was 15,513 million rubles and the whole econmy's, 99,188 million rubles (all figures at 1933 prices).[30] The railroads in 1928 accounted for 23.3 per cent of the plant and equipment in the socialist sector of the economy, that is, excluding the value of privately owned capital. About 10 billion of the 100 billion 1933 total represents collectivization of agricultural capital privately owned in 1928. Even if this portion of the over-all increase were excluded, it is clear that the railroads' capital increased at a rate well below the national average. Measured in 1933 prices, industry's plant and equipment had grown threefold, and Group A (that is, heavy) industry showed a fourfold increase. The over-all rise in national fixed capital was to 201 per cent of the 1928 level. But railroad capital rose only 35 per cent. As a result, 15.6 per cent of the socialist plant and equipment was to be found in the railroad sector in 1933, as opposed to 23.3 per cent five years earlier.

These asset data make it clear that by comparison with earlier periods, the railroads were put on short rations by the government. In a gross sense, therefore, it could be concluded that this shortsighted policy produced the transportation crisis. Such a view, however, would neglect at least two important considerations. The first is the demonstrated capacity of the railroad system to increase its output greatly, using existing facilities. We must ask: "How close did the railroads come to meeting the demands placed on them?" Perhaps a relatively small increment of investment would have prevented the growth of backlogs in freight tonnage. In this case the government's policy would have to be considered on the whole correct, with its error reduced to a failure to supply the small additional capital required.

The second consideration relates to the supply, not of rubles but of the critical materials and other resources necessary for capital formation in real terms. And in this connection one must also consider the question of timing. Perhaps the volume of steel, say, which would have been necessary in 1931 to forestall the shipping backlogs of 1933, could not have been diverted from other uses without undercutting the very increments of output that give rise to freight backlogs in 1933. The data at present available do not permit a thorough analysis of the intricate set of alternatives suggested by these considerations, but the following preliminary attempts are at least suggestive.

We may begin by comparing the backlogs of unshipped freight at various times throughout this period with the then-existing level of traffic actually carried, to form an impression of the relative scale of the deficiency. The figures in Table 4 can be variously interpreted. It will be seen, for example, that in December 1933 the railroads took up for carriage only about half of the tonnage requiring shipment. Such a situation appears rather desperate. Yet if one calculates roughly what increase in the current rate of operations would have been necessary to work off the backlog completely over the next six months, a different impression emerges. Column 4 in Table 4 shows the data. Assuming equality between seasonal variation in

Table 4. *Rail freight originated and unshipped during selected months, 1928–1934*

| Month | Freight originated (10⁶ m t) | Freight unshipped (10⁶ m t) | Ratio of unshipped to originated freight | Percentage increase required for 6-month elimination |
|---|---|---|---|---|
| March 1928 | 13.8 | 3.1 | 0.22 | 4 |
| September 1929 | 16.7 | 10.3 | .62 | 10 |
| December 1932 | 22.0 | 20.0 | .91 | 15 |
| December 1933 | 21.9 | 20.0 | .91 | 15 |
| December 1934 | 26.3 | 15.0 | .57 | 10 |

Sources: Monthly data for tons originated appear in TsUNKhU, 1936b, p. 341. Estimated unshipped backlogs at the end of the specified months are taken from SNK, 1929, p. 367, for 1928; from p. 322 of the following year's volume in this series for the 1929 figure; from Vol'fson, 1941, p. 202, for 1932 and 1934; and from Vol'fson, 1934, p. 100, for 1933. This last source compares monthly average daily carloadings from May 1933 through October 1933 with estimated requirements, and shows a deteriorating ratio from 85 per cent coverage in May to 51 per cent in October, the seasonal peak month. V. V. Kuibyshev at the Seventeenth Congress (Kommunisticheskaia partiia, 1934, p. 383) stated that current production then called for average daily carloadings of 61 thousand cars while the railroads were handling 52–54 thousand, and pointed out that at this rate the backlog would continue to accumulate. His estimate suggests that a 15 per cent increase in carloadings would have covered current demands.

carrying capacity and seasonal traffic demand in the six months following each date, and assuming parallel movement of the annual upward trend in carrying capacity and traffic demand, the calculation shows what *additional* effort would have been necessary to wipe out in half a year the existing backlog of unshipped freight. The dimensions of the crisis take on a new perspective. Apparently when the situation was at its worst, a 15 per cent increase in originated tonnage, sustained for six months, would have eliminated the backlog. In addition, of course, the railroads would have to raise current output enough to cover current shipping demands.

The rough data in Table 4 show that something like a quarter of the task was accomplished during 1934. To anticipate our story slightly, it appears that by the end of 1935 the excess backlog had been entirely eliminated. Such prompt success in mastering the crisis argues in favor of accepting our second interpretation of its relative dimensions. If the railroads were thought of as doing only half the job expected of them in December 1933, it would indeed be difficult to explain how their difficulties were solved in two short years.

In order to examine the implications for the railroads' resource needs during these years, let us carry away from this crude calculation upper and lower figures of 10 per cent and 20 per cent as suggesting the scale of additional capacity the railroads needed to overcome the crisis and keep up with the demands placed on them. Clearly the figures are heroic oversimplifications. Even as measures of demand, they neglect the many specific details of commodity composition in freight traffic, regional location of demand, and time pattern of demand that lie behind the aggregative summary. The planning and operating tasks confronting officials on the spot at that time required consideration of all sorts of transfer and substitution alternatives that are here ignored.

An equally serious difficulty arises in passing from a measure of incremental demand to its equivalent in input requirements. The railroad production function was anything but stable during these years, and in fact the very heart of the government's campaign was the drive to *change* the function. As will be shown in a later section, considerable success was achieved between 1928 and 1933, though not so much as had been counted on. Moreover, in the next three years really substantial improvements in the coefficients of the railroad production function contributed decisively to solution of the transportation crisis.

Despite both these sets of complications, it will nevertheless be instructive to proceed with an examination of the flow of resources and labor to the railroad sector during these years. In each case we can apply the 10 per cent and 20 per cent figures derived above to see what the impact on supplies for the rest of the economy would have been if the railroads had been accorded more generous allocations.

Leaving aside such small critical items as copper for communications wire, on which little information is available, it seems likely that the most critical input for the railroads during these years was steel. Here we have information from 1923 through 1936 covering the tonnage of rails supplied to the railroads, figures for the period 1931–1938 covering the railroads' consumption of rolled steel products, and 1932–1938 data covering the railroads' share of total steel consumption in the USSR. The rail data are presented in Table 78 of Appendix F.

A railroad system requires very substantial amounts of rail every year, even if no new construction is under way. The Russian railroad system in 1913 is said to have consumed 660 thousand tons of rail.[31] In the 1920's the railroads obtained steadily increasing amounts of rail until 1928, but did not reach even half the 1913 volume. When the First Five Year Plan started, the railroads were cut back 5 or 10 per cent from the 1928 level, certainly an inauspicious beginning when the demands on the system were rapidly rising. In 1930 and 1931 supplies increased appreciably, though the railroads obtained only 79 per cent and 58 per cent of their planned allocation respectively.

The planned supply of rails in 1932 and 1933 was reduced somewhat from the 1931 target, in spite of the railroads' difficulties. In April 1932 one of the participants in a conference on industrial location, discussing Ural-Kuznetsk Kombinat transportation problems, said: "The shortage of rails is the basic limitation on transport construction. This circumstance has forced the holding up of several lines already being built, and prevents the building of several important routes." [32] Not only was the allocation cut back, but the tonnage actually received by the railroads dropped, according to railroad records, by 18 per cent in 1932; the plan was only 52 per cent fulfilled.

It appears, incidentally, that the iron and steel industry was producing appreciably more railroad rails than the railroads were receiving, to judge by the discrepancies between the records kept in the two sectors. The steel industry data specifically exclude tramway and mine rails, and cover only "railroad rails." It is not clear how the discrepancy should be explained. The trackage not operated by the NKPS, consisting mainly of sidings and intraplant spurs and narrow-gauge timber spurs, could hardly have absorbed the differences involved. Perhaps rejects or defective rails were included in the industry's records. In any case, the year-to-year trends are similar.

In 1934 the railroads received 67 per cent more rails than in 1933, and the annual allocation was 96 per cent fulfilled. This sharp increase perhaps

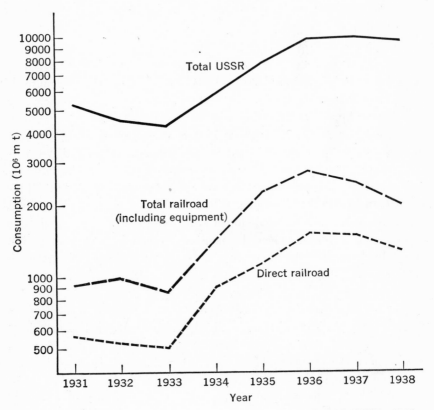

*Chart 6. Rolled steel consumption, USSR railroads and total USSR, 1931–1938. Source: Table 34.*

reflects the attention that Stalin reportedly gave to the transportation situation. In 1935 and 1936, the more generous allocations continued, with annual rises of 19 per cent and 33 per cent, though rates of plan fulfillment dropped back to 89 per cent and 74 per cent respectively. The tonnage of rails received in 1936 was three times the quantity delivered in 1928, and undoubtedly this had a good deal to do with the railroads' success in overcoming their shortcomings.

Although rails make up a large part of the railroads' steel consumption, many other forms of iron and steel are required in their operations, and a more comprehensive view of their situation can be gained through reviewing trends in the supply of all rolled steel products to the railroad sector. In Chart 6, annual data for 1931–1938 are recorded, showing the amounts consumed both directly by the railroads and indirectly through the acquisition of rolling stock and motive power. The graph also shows total USSR consumption of rolled steel products, so that the railroads' share may be examined. The last two columns of Table 34, Appendix A, illustrate the impact on supplies of rolled steel products for the rest of the economy in each year if the railroads had been assigned 10 per cent more, or 20 per cent more, tonnage than in fact they received.

The general trends apparent in the record for rail supplies alone are visible in these more comprehensive data, but many revealing details come to light also. Total USSR consumption of rolled steel products in 1932 and 1933 was appreciably smaller than in 1931. The explanation appears to lie in a failure of the domestic industry to maintain the pace set in 1930, plus a decision not to maintain the 1931 level of imports, as indicated in Table 5.

Table 5. Production, imports, and consumption of rolled steel, USSR, by year, 1930–1934
(thousands of metric tons)

| Year | Domestically produced rolled steel | Imports of semifinished steel | Total steel available | Consumption |
|------|------|------|------|------|
| 1930 | 4259[a] | 764 | 5023 | — |
| 1931 | 3927 | 1703 | 5630 | 5217 |
| 1932 | 4060 | 1040 | 5100 | 4500 |
| 1933 | 4486 | 633 | 5119 | 4289 |
| 1934 | 6189 | 401 | 6590 | 5719 |

[a] For 12 months including 3 months of the preceding calendar year.
Sources: Production — TsUNKhU, 1936a, p. 135; imports — Bakulin, 1939, pp. 78–80; consumption — Shul'kin, 1940, pp. 20–28. The imports may include ingots with rolled steel. For lower figures, see TsUNKhU, 1936a, p. 692.

The years 1932 and 1933 are thus seen to have been years of over-all shortage for all steel consumers, and this puts the railroads' experience in quite a different perspective from what might be imagined otherwise. For example, reference to Table 34 shows that with a 14 per cent cutback in over-all consumption during 1932, the railroads' consumption actually increased 8 per cent, due to a 32 per cent rise in steel used for locomotive and car manufacture. The shrinkage in railroad consumption during 1933 reduced them to a level only 4 per cent below 1931, whereas over-all consumption had dropped 18 per cent. Evidently the contraction forced on the railroads was less stringent that the contraction imposed on the rest of the economy.

Moreover, when domestic production of rolled steel began to increase rapidly, the railroads shared more than proportionately in the enlarged consumption this made possible. Total consumption in 1934 increased by 33 per cent over 1933, but the railroads' consumption rose 60 per cent. The rise was especially great in the railroads' direct consumption, though it was substantial for transport equipment also. In 1935 an additional 60 per cent increase in consumption was accorded the railroads, while total USSR consumption grew by 34 per cent. The 1935 increment was directed more heavily into the building of freight cars and locomotives; consumption for this end use more than doubled in one year. After these two years of favored treatment, the railroads in 1936 shared somewhat less munificently in continued gains; their consumption increased 21 per cent while over-all consumption rose 28 per cent. Most of the railroad increment in 1936 was used directly by the railroads for maintenance and construction.

Total rolled steel consumption leveled off in 1937 with no appreciable gain over 1936, and the railroad sector registered an absolute decrease of 11 per cent. It applied almost entirely to equipment consumption, indicating perhaps that the backlog of needs here had been met. In 1938 the over-all situation deteriorated somewhat; total consumption declined by 3 per cent. The railroads suffered a contraction of 19 per cent, affecting both equipment building and roadway programs. The railroads' falling share after 1935 apparently reflects diversion of steel to munitions facilities as well as mastery of the transportation crisis.[33]

Examination of the railroads' share of total USSR consumption of rolled steel products shows clearly how seriously this one sector of the economy imposed on the total available. Between 20 and 30 per cent of all rolled steel had to be allocated to railroad transportation, even when several other sectors stood higher in the government's scale of priorities. The precise fraction devoted to the railroads differs according to the comprehensiveness of the data used; the percentage series above may be slightly high. It was obtained through compiling numerator and denominator in each year from Shul'kin's tables. In his introduction, however, he presents a different series, based on a somewhat larger national total. Two other writers, analyzing the situation in a 1937 article, reach still different magnitudes.[34] It is encouraging, nonetheless, to note that year-to-year trends within the four series are strikingly close, as can be seen in the accompanying tabulation of railroad consumption as a percentage of total USSR consumption of rolled steel.

| Year | Computed from Shul'kin | Given by Shul'kin | Guttsait and Spivak (p. 72) | Guttsait and Spivak (p. 69) |
|---|---|---|---|---|
| Average during First FYP | — | — | 19.1 | — |
| 1931 | 17.7 | 17.7 | — | — |
| 1932 | 22.1 | 19.9 | — | — |
| 1933 | 20.6 | 17.4 | 19.1 | 17.2 |
| 1934 | 24.7 | 20.6 | 22.5 | 20.6 |
| 1935 | 29.6 | 24.6 | 27.3 | 22.0 |
| 1936 | 28.0 | 23.0 | 24.9 | 23.3 |
| 1937 (plan) | — | — | — | 22.6 |
| 1937 (actual) | 25.0 | 20.3 | — | — |
| 1938 | 20.9 | 16.4 | — | — |

The marked increase going to the railroads during 1935 and 1936 emerges clearly from all four series, as does the subsequent fall in their share during 1937 and 1938. Evidence for 1939 is available from a statement that "in 1939, rails . . . [and other named products for transportation] made up 21.2 per cent of all rolled steel in our country." [35] The coverage of this statistic is not clear, but it perhaps indicates that no further cuts were made in the railroads' share of total consumption.

The last two columns of Table 34 demonstrate that a 10 per cent increase in rolled steel for railroad consumption during 1931–1933 would have meant about a 3 per cent reduction in supplies available for the other sectors of the economy; a 20 per cent increase would have required a 4 to 6 per cent cut. If we take account only of direct effects, the failure to make such a diversion appears to have been a mistake. In 1934, when "joking was laid aside," it proved possible to increase railroad consumption of rolled steel by 60 per cent in one year. True, the increment came from added production, and the balance available for nonrailroad consumption rose simultaneously. Nevertheless, the step could have been taken a year earlier with beneficial results in transportation (reflected back in other sectors), which probably would have outweighed the disadvantages of a 5 per cent cut distributed over other sectors of the economy.

Shul'kin's consumption data make it possible to calculate, as a final measure of the railroads' share of Soviet iron and steel supplies, their consumption of pig iron, cast iron pipe, steel pipe, and alloy steel products. Adding all these to the figures for ordinary rolled products, we obtain total iron and steel consumption by the railroads, and compare it with over-all consumption in Chart 7.

Again, the pattern of stringency followed by greatly increased allocation through 1936 emerges, with a few interesting differences. Total Soviet consumption in 1933 was not absolutely smaller than in 1932, nor did it level off in 1937, as was true for rolled products alone. Railroad consumption was

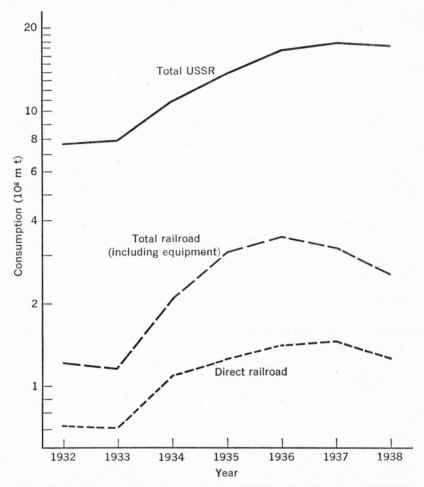

*Chart 7. Total iron and steel consumption, USSR railroads and total USSR, 1932–1938. Source: Table 35.*

a smaller part of total iron and steel consumption than was true for rolled products alone. Even here, however, the railroads in 1935 took 22.5 per cent of the country's steel, which was clearly a substantial drain on the total. When all forms of iron and steel are included, it appears that the cutback in 1937 and especially in 1938 reduced the railroads' share to a level appreciably below that of 1933; the absolute quantity, of course, was almost twice as large as in 1933.

Although in a relatively undeveloped economy traversing the early stages of industrialization, labor is by definition more abundant than capital, in the USSR of the early 1930's the supply of nonfarm labor was extremely tight. The scarcity was most acute in the upper categories of skilled labor.

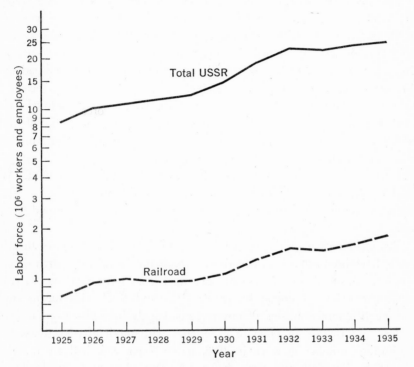

*Chart 8. Labor force, USSR railroads and total USSR, 1925–1935. Source: Table 36.*

Hence it will throw additional light on the relation between railroad transportation and the rest of the economy if we examine the trend of labor force developments under forced industrialization. Chart 8 shows annual trends in the railroad labor force and total nonfarm[36] labor force from 1925 through 1935.

The broad conclusion evident from inspection of the labor data is that in respect to this crucial input, just as was the case for steel, the program of forced industrialization led to a shrinkage in the railroads' relative position in the economy. In the late 1920's some 9 per cent of the labor force was employed in the railroad sector. By the middle 1930's, this percentage had fallen to around 7 per cent. It is also clear that in the difficult days of 1933 the over-all labor force declined by almost 3 per cent, after having almost doubled since 1928. In 1934 and 1935 the railroad sector gained workers and employees at rates above the national average, indicating that here too, more attention was being devoted to transportation.

The railroads' need for additional labor to cope with growing traffic requirements, and to carry out the reconstruction program plus some new building, led to a substantial influx of new labor. Presumably most of the new workers were untrained. By 1932 roughly one third of the railroad labor force consisted of workers with less than five years of railroad experience, a factor that must have weighed adversely on operating efficiency. Railroad operations require closely co-ordinated and well-disciplined performances from the various services involved. Deficiencies here are reflected in reduced output from the given rolling stock and equipment, maladjustments in meeting localized demand or peak demands, a high rate of collisions and accidents, and accelerated depreciation of equipment. All of these symptoms plagued railroad operations during the early 1930's, and were ascribed in part to inadequate performance by the railroad labor force.

But examination of the record for the total labor force shows that it would have been difficult at this time to assist the railroads through diversion to them of additional workers. The total labor force came within two percentage points of doubling between 1928 and 1932. This means that half the 1932 total consisted of raw recruits, largely fresh from agricultural villages and lacking in previous experience with mechanized activity. Of the average number at work in 1932, some 37 per cent had entered the labor force less than two years before. Among them were, at the least, a million or so "kulaks," forcibly ejected from their villages.

The final two columns of Table 36, Appendix A, show that substantial increments to the railroad labor force, amounting to 10 or 20 per cent, would not have reacted seriously on the supply remaining for the rest of the economy. In 1933 a 20 per cent additional allotment of labor to the railroads would have deducted only 1.4 per cent from the balance of labor available for other sectors. Just as was the case for rolled steel, it appears that such a reallocation should have been made. It may be that with respect to certain categories of skilled workers, such as locomotive repair shop machinists, a transfer to the railroads from the small number on hand would have worked serious hardship on heavy industry. Moreover, it can be seen that the increments of labor during 1934 and 1935, when the rail-roads mastered their difficulties, were not large, which implies that labor may not have been the decisive factor. We touch here on the consideration that while a ton of steel has an output potential that varies within rela-tively narrow limits, a worker's productivity can vary enormously. The government hoped throughout this period for greater productivity from the existing labor force, and in the next section we shall examine the role it played in finally eliminating the bottleneck.

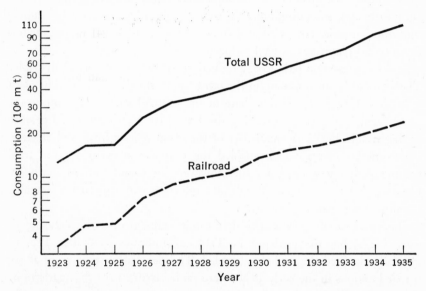

*Chart 9. Coal consumption, USSR railroads and total USSR, 1923–1935. Source: Table 37.*

Examination of trends in the average wage paid to railroad workers, as compared to wages paid in industry, shows that between 1925 and 1935 the two moved closely together.[37] Railroad wages were usually slightly below average wages in industry, but in 1932 and 1934 the average railroad wage rose to levels slightly above those in industry. While this probably reflects wage revisions designed to raise incentives in transportation, the difference does not appear large enough to have constituted a powerful inducement for skilled industrial labor to transfer to the railroad sector. Actually, the rise in average wage rates between 1928 and 1935 in both industry and railroad transportation was well below the over-all average rise. The largest percentage gains were made by agricultural workers not members of collective farms, timber workers, bureaucrats, doctors, and teachers. It seems clear that in this period wage inducements were not employed to attract labor to the railroads.

Besides steel and labor, the other input that makes up an important part of railroad costs is fuel, primarily coal. This review of trends in railroad supplies will therefore conclude with a brief examination of annual coal data to see how the railroads fared in this aspect of their needs. Chart 9 presents the record for total USSR coal production and railroad coal consumption by year from 1923 through 1935. The production series covers anthracite and sub-bituminous as well as bituminous coal; the railroad consumption series covers all coal consumed by railroads, including general heating and plant uses as well as locomotive firing.

Taking 1928 as a base, coal production by 1935 had more than tripled. The railroads' consumption, on the other hand, stood at 241 per cent of the 1928 level. Hence the relative share of the railroad sector fell from around 28 per cent in the years preceding the First Five Year Plan to 22 per cent in the middle 1930's. A small part of this drop reflects improved efficiency in locomotive firing, which enabled the railroads to carry a given traffic volume with fewer tons of coal. However, the major portion of the explanation lies in the rapid growth of production and associated channeling of output increments to industry.

The coal supply was a critical factor in railroad operations during the early 1920's, but the evidence in Table 37 indicates that after 1926 the railroads obtained the coal they needed. The deficiencies that arose at particular locations in the early 1930's were probably due to traffic snarls rather than an inability of the railroad sector to acquire an adequate allocation from total supplies available. Hence there is no reason to examine carefully the results of increased railroad coal allocations in 1932 or 1933, as was done above for steel and labor. Because the railroads absorbed a larger fraction of total supplies in this field, the impact of a 20 per cent increase in their 1933 consumption would have been more serious for the rest of the economy than was true for labor. There would have been some 6 or 7 per cent less coal for other users, though the absolute growth of coal production in 1933 was so ample that no consumer would have been required to accept an absolute decrease. This 1933 increase in the output of coal was a bright spot in the otherwise unfavorable developments we have noted for that year.

In 1934, when the railroads were receiving more generous allocations of steel and labor, their coal consumption increased substantially, at a rate almost twice the percentage increase of 1933. However, they were accorded only 15.4 per cent of the added output, though they consumed 24 per cent of the previous year's output, and hence their share dropped again. It would appear that if the railroad sector had depended on still further coal allocations in order to overcome their difficulties, the extra amounts would have been made available. Thus the tentative conclusion for this particular input is that a more generous policy on the part of the government would not have contributed decisively to prevention or solution of the transportation crisis.

To sum up this record of policy in action, it is revealing to survey ruble figures for annual investments made in the railroad sector and for the whole economy, to trace the railroads' share and the year-to-year changes in investment allocations. Data for 1928–1934 (taken from Table 71), in millions of rubles at current prices, are given in the accompanying tabulation.

| | Invested in railroads | | Invested in the whole economy | | |
| Year | Amount | Annual percentage increase | Amount | Annual percentage increase | Railroads' percentage share |
| --- | --- | --- | --- | --- | --- |
| 1928 | 731 | 2.2 | 4,088 | 11.5 | 17.9 |
| 1929 | 873 | 19.5 | 5,885 | 44.0 | 14.8 |
| 1930 | 1,112 | 27.4 | 9,786 | 66.3 | 11.4 |
| 1931 | 1,910 | 71.9 | 15,681 | 60.3 | 12.2 |
| 1932 | 2,569 | 34.5 | 20,086 | 28.1 | 12.8 |
| 1933 | 2,107 | −18.0 | 19,707 | −1.9 | 10.7 |
| 1934 | 2,928 | 39.0 | 25,528 | 29.5 | 11.5 |

The rapid growth of these ruble figures reflects marked price inflation as well as real expansion in capital formation, but the data can still be taken as indicators of year-to-year trends, and of allocations to the railroad sector. It is clear that though the railroads received substantial increments in annual investment, especially for 1931, their share of total allocations was quickly reduced to about two thirds of what it had been before the plan era began. It is clear also that the rapid gains of 1929–1932 had petered out by 1933, a crisis year in which total investment fell off 2 per cent from the preceding year and railroad investment suffered an 18 per cent absolute decrease. This 18 per cent cut in investment during 1933 appears to have been a central element in the circumstances giving rise to the transportation crisis. The railroads' share of total investment fell to 10.7 per cent, lower than in any subsequent prewar year, and 43 per cent lower than the average percentage share obtained by the railroads in 1925–1928.

The impact on the rest of the economy, if the railroads had been given 20 per cent more investment funds in 1933 than they actually were, would have been slight. Investment in all other sectors would have been 2.4 per cent lower. Under these conditions the railroads would have borne a 1.6 per cent cut in their 1932 allocations, and the rest of the economy a 1.9 per cent cut; the railroads' share of the total would have remained at 12.8 per cent. In view of the backlogs that had developed by the end of 1932, it appears to have been a serious mistake to impair the railroads' carrying capacity still further. Note that the decisions which produced these 1933 results went beyond a failure to improve the railroads' relative position. A more than proportionate share of the year's cut was assigned to the railroad sector. Perhaps if enough were known of the problems confronting other sectors of the economy (especially, I suspect, the steel industry), the government's policy could be justified. As it stands, however, and seen only from a transportation point of view, the 1933 investment cut was sheer folly.

On balance it seems clear that a more farsighted government policy could have prevented the transportation difficulties of 1931–1934. If less reliance had been placed on driving existing equipment and personnel harder, and more steel, labor, and so on had been allocated for capital development, the backlogs in freight would not have arisen. Moreover, the dimensions of the deficiency in railroad performance were not so large but what such a diversion of resources could prove feasible. Even in the crisis year of 1933, reductions amounting to from 2 to 7 per cent in supplies for the rest of the economy would have provided the railroads with 20 per cent increases in their needs. After unnecessary delay, resources *were* diverted to the railroad sector, and the transportation bottleneck was quickly overcome.

# 4  SURMOUNTING THE TRANSPORTATION CRISIS

We have seen, in the narrative up to this point, how the transportation crisis arose, and something of how government policy was changed in 1934 to initiate a recovery. But it remains to trace further the details of investment and allocation policies after 1934, and to see what was done with the rubles, tons, and man-hours made available in order to build a more effective railroad system. The record for steel has already been presented. A more comprehensive indicator of resources flows is provided by the record for annual investments, in millions of rubles, continued in the accompanying tabulation for the years 1934–1940 (data from Table 71).

| | Invested in railroads | | Invested in the whole economy | | |
| Year | Amount | Annual percentage increase | Amount | Annual percentage increase | Railroads' percentage share |
|---|---|---|---|---|---|
| 1934 | 2,928 | 39.0 | 25,528 | 29.5 | 11.5 |
| 1935 | 4,038 | 37.9 | 27,693 | 8.5 | 14.6 |
| 1936 | 4,428 | 9.7 | 31,750 | 14.6 | 14.0 |
| 1937 | 3,576 | −19.2 | 32,813 | 3.3 | 10.9 |
| 1938 | 4,650 | 30.0 | 35,700 | 8.8 | 13.0 |
| 1939 | 4,950 | 6.5 | 34,300 | −4.0 | 14.4 |
| 1940 | 5,000 | 1.0 | 38,000 | 10.8 | 13.2 |

For the economy as a whole, 1934 marked a considerable improvement over 1933 — the harvest was good, steel output rose substantially, and total investment increased by 30 per cent. Having by now decided that the railroads required special attention, the government accorded a 39 per cent increase to them, bringing their share of the year's total up to 11.5 per cent. This was of considerable assistance, as we have seen, but still kept the railroads below their previous relative position. In 1935 the generous policy was amplified; this year the national total rose by 9 per cent, while investment in railroads increased 38 per cent.

The year 1935 marks the high point of government concern for railroads during the period of forced industrialization before World War II. Annual investment in the railroad sector was planned at 16.8 per cent of the national total (as compared with 13.1 per cent in the Second Five Year Plan, issued early in 1934), and the railroads' share of realized investment reached 14.6 per cent. In the following year the increment for railroad investment was 10 per cent, while the national total rose 15 per cent, so that the railroads slipped back to 14 per cent of the whole. By 1937, the government's concern had clearly turned to other sectors of the economy. The railroads suffered a 19 per cent cut in their investment funds, though the total invested for the whole economy increased by 3.3 per cent. The annual plan for 1937 apparently allocated 17 per cent of total investment funds to the railroads, which may indicate that the shrinkage in realized investment was due to lagging capital development work on railroads. A large program of new railroad construction was getting under way, and as the tabulation above shows, investment allocations to the railroads in 1938 and 1939 were generous, both absolutely and in relation to the rest of the economy.

On December 14, 1935, V. M. Molotov stated in the course of a major address that "transportation is not now a bottleneck. Now our transportation, overfulfilling traffic plans, is not only not an obstacle, but is a tremendous help in the improvement and cheapening of construction." [1] Thus it appears that less than two years from the time the transportation crisis was at its height, the official view was that it had been eliminated. In the present chapter, developments from 1934 through 1940 will be reviewed with the aim of discovering the factors responsible for rapid solution of the crisis and satisfactory performance of the railroads thereafter.

A framework for the discussion can be provided through a summary tabulation of annual data for railroad traffic and railroad facilities, as was previously done for the 1928–1933 period. In Chart 10, major features of the 1932–1940 record are displayed. Again, the most notable development is the trend of railroad passenger traffic, dropping for three consecutive years and then gradually making its way back to a level somewhat above the early 1932 peak. Freight traffic grew extremely rapidly in 1934–1936, while the railroads caught up with the economy's demands. Thereafter the rate of growth fell off substantially.

Inspection of the series for railroad equipment will show that the expanded flow of inputs to the railroads clearly had an important bearing on their capacity to carry traffic. It is worthwhile to analyze these developments briefly. Then we can pass to a consideration of the qualitative changes that properly fall under the heading of "human engineering." The two sets of factors in combination led to considerable improvements in productivity.

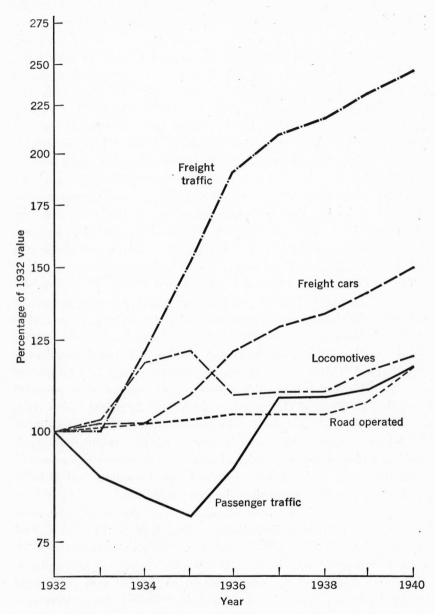

275 —
250 —
225 —
200 —
175 —

Percentage of 1932 value

150 —
125 —
100 —
75 —

Freight
traffic

Freight cars

Locomotives

Road operated

Passenger traffic

1932     1934     1936     1938     1940

Year

*Chart 10. Railroad traffic and railroad facilities, 1932–1940. Source: Table 32.*

The latter, in turn, when reviewed for trends, are instructive about the limits beyond which it seems difficult to advance under Soviet conditions.

Beginning with the record for the average length of roadway operated, one finds that additions to the system had very little to do with traffic growth between 1933 and 1940. New line added for permanent operation declined to an annual total of 278 kilometers (173 miles) in 1937. The emphasis during these years lay rather in improving the carrying capacity of existing roadway. In 1939 and 1940, the substantial additions to operated roadway reflect mainly acquisition of almost 17,000 kilometers (10,500 miles) of rail line in territory added to the USSR along its western frontier, though during these two years a revival of new building brought over 4,000 kilometers (2,500 miles) of new line into permanent operation. (For details, see Table 59.) Over the whole period from 1932 to 1940, if the acquired line and its traffic are excluded, the railroad system raised its index of freight traffic from 100 to about 240, while the average length of operated roadway increased only 10 per cent.

The railroads' freight locomotive stock in service increased substantially during 1934, and again in 1935. It appears probable that a large part of the explanation for these increases involves a reduced percentage of unserviceable locomotives, and a pressing into service of every available old locomotive. In 1936, it will be noted, the average number of freight locomotives at work declined. This does not, however, indicate a decline in total tractive power available. Rather it probably reflects exchange of new, more powerful locomotives for the small old types that were very likely retired from service. It would be desirable to have a series for annual tractive power available in freight service, but it has not been attempted in the present study. Such a series would show no early peak and subsequent decline, or at least would reduce the extent of the change, since each new locomotive had 25 to 30 per cent more tractive power than the average old one.[2]

The locomotive series has been compiled through the use of performance data rather than by assembling absolute figures from Soviet records. And the approach involved very likely understates the actual number at work by about 15 per cent. But the error, if it is one, is systematic and uniform, so that considerable reliance can be placed on the index of year-to-year changes. Excluding the additions to stock in 1939–1940 due to incorporations, the 140 per cent increase in freight carried was associated with approximately a 15 per cent increase in the number of locomotives in road freight service.

Along with new locomotives, a substantial number of new freight cars was built for the railroads between 1932 and 1940. The increments of steel received in 1934 and 1935 made it possible to increase the average number of two-axle units on line by 35,000 in 1935 and 60,000 in 1936. Increments thereafter were smaller, but the total stock continued to grow, and, including the cars acquired in 1939–1940, the 1940 total reached a level 50 per cent above 1932. Comparing the index of freight traffic in 1940 with the number of freight cars at work, excluding acquisitions, we find the 140 per cent growth in traffic associated with roughly a 42 per cent growth in the freight car stock.

Clearly these additions to railroad facilities improved their capacity to carry traffic. But equally clearly, the rise in output was more than proportional to the expansion in facilities, in fact strikingly so. Hence other factors must have been at work. One such factor was the strenuous campaign to reform transportation that was led by Lazar Moiseevich Kaganovich. It is interesting to attempt an evaluation of this campaign. Could similar results be obtained by other railroad systems? Why did it go no further than it did?

The government had asked for greater energy and effectiveness from railroadmen from the beginning of the plan period. In mid-1933, as was mentioned earlier, "political sections" were attached to all railroad organizations specifically to stimulate productivity. But apparently the results left something to be desired, for on February 28, 1935, Kaganovich was relieved of his duties as Commissar of Heavy Industry and made the head of the People's Commissariat of Transportation.[3] He had already demonstrated great capacity as an administrator and galvanizing agent, and the transfer meant that the government was assigning its crack trouble shooter to straighten out the railroad situation. Even before relieving A. A. Andreev, he had apparently devoted part of his time to transportation.[4]

Kaganovich set to work vigorously. His first important decree was issued March 19, 1935, and was entitled "On the Fight Against Accidents and Wrecks." It called for stricter observance of operating rules and elimination of careless, slipshod performance of duties. At the beginning of April he called a large meeting of railroad officials to discuss the carrying out of this order, methods for speeding up freight car movement, and the 1935 capital development program. On April 15 came a decree "On Speeding Up Freight Car Turnaround Time," which outlined steps for a strong campaign along this line. The decree "On Improving the Utilization of Locomotives and the Organization of Train Movement" was issued after another large meeting held between July 25 and July 29.[5]

This second meeting closed with a full-dress session in the Kremlin, at which both Kaganovich and Stalin addressed the railroadmen in ringing speeches.[6] The theme of the occasion was that the railroad system was very important to the USSR, and that every railroad worker, right down to the lowliest trackwalker, was therefore important to the USSR. The Soviet railroadman was worthy of respect, held a post of dignity and responsibility, fulfilled a vital function. Consequently it was his duty to serve punctiliously, to play his part in enabling the system to operate like the smoothly adjusted mechanism of a fine watch. To commemorate this July 30, 1935 meeting in the Kremlin, a nearby Sunday has been set aside every year thereafter as Railroadmen's Day. Stalin's phrases: "The USSR would be inconceivable without a first-class railroad system," and "a conveyer, run like clockwork" have appeared with numbing frequency, probably millions of times, in the railroad newspaper and other railroad literature, until recently.[7]

The railroads also developed a version of Stakhanovism appropriate to their field. In July 1935, Petr Fedorovich Krivonos ran his freight locomotive between Slavyansk and Lozovaya (near Kharkov in the eastern Ukraine) at a speed of 31.9 kilometers per hour, when the "limiting norm" was 23 kilometers per hour. Later he raised his average speed for the run to 48 kilometers per hour (30 mph), and increased the steam pressure of his boiler by 50 per cent.[8] Krivonos thereupon became a national hero, and a sweeping campaign to spread the "Krivonos movement" throughout railroad transportation got under way. Railroadmen who showed initiative in devising improved operating methods were rewarded not only with prizes and publicity, but with rapid promotion to top administrative positions.[9]

After scanning the flamboyant publicity associated with Kaganovich's 1935 and 1936 campaigns, especially the remarks of party workers in the political sections, one might think that the verbal clamor would find no counterpart in operating performances. This was emphatically not the case. Somehow the previously accepted standards for what could be expected in the speed of freight train movement, the time necessary to load and unload freight cars, or the number of miles per day a locomotive could run, were broken through. Performance measures that had remained within 10 per cent or 20 per cent of their 1928 level, and had fallen off appreciably in 1933, now rose as much as 30 per cent in one year. There was evidently a real sense in which the previous level of operations had concealed unutilized reserves of productivity in the railroad system.

Chart 11 provides some illustrations of these changes in operating efficiency. For example, a series is shown for "Gross freight ton–kilometers per freight train–hour," a measure that rose 30.6 per cent in 1936. In American railroad practice, this index is considered the most revealing single measure of train operating efficiency, since it combines the weight and the speed of freight trains in a single indicator.

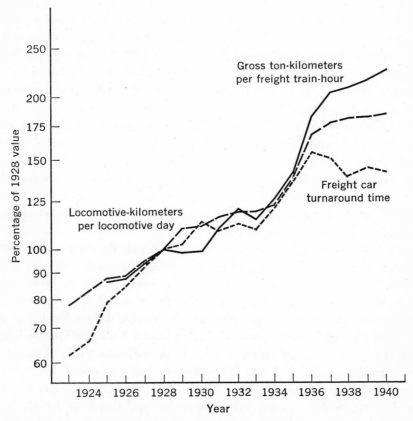

*Chart 11. Indexes of railroad operating averages, USSR, 1923–1940. Source: Table 38.*

Gross freight ton–kilometers equals the average gross weight per freight train times the total distance trains travel annually. The total distance trains travel annually, divided by the total number of hours trains use for movement, equals the average speed of freight trains. When gross ton–kilometers are divided by total train-hours, the total distance traveled by trains cancels out, and in effect average train weight is multiplied by average train speed. Soviet railroad records do not contain this particular operating average, but do contain train weights and train speeds, so the measure may easily be computed.

Changes in the level of this and the other operating averages provide a comprehensive measure of annual developments in operating efficiency. During the years of the First Five Year Plan, the weight-times-speed indicator lagged for two years and then rose to a level 20 per cent above the 1928 value, principally as a result of heavier average freight trains. The average daily mileage of freight locomotives rose immediately by 10 per cent and then gradually advanced to 120 per cent of 1928. The average number of days per freight car trip was shortened appreciably in 1930, but did not improve thereafter. In 1933 all three measures deteriorated, giving one more indication of the precarious state of the railroads at that time.

Improvements in 1934 were noticeable, and Kaganovich's campaign led to substantial further improvements in 1935. The really impressive gains were registered in 1936, the year that stood as a high-water mark in Soviet railroad advance during the 1930's. The average turnaround time for freight cars was brought down to less than seven days; freight locomotives averaged 232 kilometers per day, and, as just pointed out, gross ton–kilometers per freight train–hour rose 30.6 per cent.

In 1937 matters appeared to be proceeding well during the first half year, and on August 27 Kaganovich was transferred from the railroads to a supervisory post as Commissar of Heavy Industry. Railroads operations promptly slumped. The momentum of his reforms carried the weight-times-speed index up another 10 per cent, and locomotive daily mileage rose 6 per cent, but freight car turnaround time suffered a 3 per cent setback. The winter of 1937–38 saw a serious faltering in the railroads' work, as average daily carloadings dropped well below the previous year's level. In a post-mortem the next summer, A. V. Bakulin, who succeeded Kaganovich as head of the NKPS, was accused of "loosening up," that is, of letting discipline deteriorate, and of smugness, conceit, and resting on his laurels.[10] On April 5, 1938, Kaganovich was ordered back to the railroads, though this time the Presidium of the USSR Supreme Soviet directed him to serve simultaneously as Commissar of Transportation and Commissar of Heavy Industry.

Again Kaganovich called meetings to discuss the situation with railroad officials. From April 22 to April 28 they analyzed the lessons to be learned from the previous winter's difficulties, and in addition took up the problem of introducing *khozraschet* into the operations of individual railroads.[11] The latter was roughly equivalent to a reorganization of cost-accounting procedures to isolate each operating unit financially, in order to stimulate profitable operation by each road. Even Kaganovich's drive could not produce a repetition of his previous success. Average turnaround time deteriorated in 1938 by more than 7 per cent, and the other two measures showed negligible improvement. He apparently stayed on as head of the NKPS in 1939 and 1940, but, as the records make clear, no further notable gains in operating efficiency were achieved.

It is interesting to speculate on the reasons for this failure to maintain the pace of improvement attained in the middle 1930's. Our present knowledge of the domestic scene in these years will not support anything more than tentative hypotheses, since many forces were at work. But a few general notions may be advanced as apparently consistent with the available evidence, in hopes that additional research will prove or disprove them. It could be asserted, for example, that the sharp gains resulted from two forces, neither of which lasted for long. The first was the expanded flow of steel and other resources to the railroads, which, as we have seen, was severely cut back after 1936. Improved facilities were certainly a necessary, even if not a sufficient, basis for higher operating averages. The second was the rise in living standards that came in 1935 and 1936 with the abolition of rationing and a general easing of living conditions. It would be difficult to demonstrate a direct connection between the general climate of affairs and the performance of operating railroadmen, but this factor must have at least reinforced the appeals made by Kaganovich for better work. And the remainder of the argument, perhaps equally tenuous, calls attention to the radically different climate imposed by the widespread purges of 1937–1938. According to two observant and analytically minded *émigrés* who saw the purges from prison cells, "the proportion of arrests among the intelligentsia, railway workers, and Red Army officers was substantially above the average," and "those who fell under the ax were . . . high officials in the People's Commissariats, particularly the transport organization. . . ." [12]

The railroad system apparently approached some sort of limit to its effectiveness. It was partly a technological limit, given the ill-assorted mixture of advanced and obsolete equipment in use, although average train speeds and some other measures were appreciably below contemporary American levels. The state of roadbed and superstructure on most of the network, plus the low proportion of freight cars with automatic brakes and couplings,[13] probably prevented any further increases in train speeds.

The daily mileage accomplished by freight locomotives was substantially higher than is usual on Western railroads, and here too, a technological limit may have been approached.

The concept of a psychological or administrative limit may also be relevant in this context. Railroad workers, and for that matter shippers and receivers too, had been subjected to great strain by the government's efforts to minimize turnaround time. Prompt loading and unloading of freight cars became almost an obsession with the NKPS. The system-wide average in 1936 and 1937 was about sixteen hours for each operation, which means that a freight car spent well under a day at each end of its trip being emptied and filled again.[14] Such speed is absolutely unknown in American railroad practice, and the contrast will be further discussed in Chapter 7. The point here is that it did not prove possible to make any additional reductions in the time required for loading and unloading, perhaps because the administrative strain of operations keyed up to this level was more than could be sustained. The average time spent at classification yards and in trains also rose after 1937, indicating a similar situation.

The unanswered question, of course, is whether this leveling-off of performance shows that technological and administrative limits had been reached, or merely that the purges disorganized railroad operations. If the latter explanation could be established, it would imply that further gains were internally possible, given a favorable environment — a point of some interest for other industrializing economies speculating on potentialities within their own transportation systems. If the failure of operating averages to show much improvement in 1939 and 1940, after the purges were over, is taken to mean that the purges were not a decisive influence in 1937 and 1938, then the case for the existence of limits is thereby strengthened.[15]

The discussion so far has reviewed the transportation crisis and its elimination only in over-all terms. An essential feature of the Soviet solution is thereby neglected, and we need to note its importance. The geography of transportation demand and transportation supply, that is, the regional distribution of traffic requirements and traffic capacities, suggested one of the keys to solution of the bottleneck problem.

In earlier chapters the major centers of economic activity have been listed and the locational program of the First Five Year Plan was summarized. The chief focuses from a transportation point of view were (1) the eastern Ukraine, (2) the Moscow industrial region, (3) the Leningrad industrial region, and (4) the Ural-Kuznetsk Kombinat. Almost every district in the USSR felt the impact of the industrialization program, but these four were the ones which gave rise to most of the additional railroad traffic.

In July and August of 1930, a group of American railroad officials visited the USSR as consultants to the government, retained to inspect the Soviet railroad system and write an evaluatory report with suggestions for improvement. Their report listed sixteen specific suggestions and included additional comment on a wide variety of technical matters.[16] No doubt many of the changes recommended were obvious and had already been proposed previously by Soviet engineers. It would therefore be unjustified to ascribe all the reforms introduced during the 1930's to this one advisory report. But there is observable a correspondence between the American recommendations and subsequent technical developments in Soviet railroading. One notes, however, that in respect to railroad electrification, the report's conclusions were ignored (See Chapter 6).

The clear implication of the specific suggestions in the Americans' report was that the existing railroad network would require a whole series of technical improvements in order to carry heavier traffic densities. But, as just indicated above, the major increments of traffic were generated to a marked extent in four regional centers. It was therefore obvious on pragmatic grounds that the improvement program should not be uniformly applied to the whole railroad network, but should be concentrated on the bottleneck routes. Within the eastern Ukrainian industrial complex, for instance, and in the Ural-Kuznetsk Kombinat territory, substantial programs of betterment were launched in the First Five Year Plan period. And improved connections between the eastern Ukraine and Moscow, the eastern Ukraine and Leningrad, the eastern Ukraine and the Urals, were required to carry the sharply growing interregional traffic among these centers. Thus began the policy of "differentiating" certain railroad lines from the general network and "concentrating" development work on them, as proposed in the 1920 Goelro plan.

It will be observed that a transportation policy of building up high-capacity interregional arteries is the necessary corollary of a locational policy stressing large-scale facilities concentrated around raw material sites. That is to say, there was a close causal connection between "gigantomania" and "super-trunklining." The output of a giant plant, especially if it was located in the east, had to be shipped, at least in part, to other regions perhaps thousands of miles away. It was this upsurge of interregional traffic that made the improvement of main interregional routes an urgent matter. Moreover, it will also be recognized that the restoration and further development of industry around Leningrad and Moscow prolonged and even aggravated the heavily transport-using locational pattern inherited from the old regime. Since these regions lacked the fuel and raw materials to match their labor force and fixed capital, expansion of their output required greatly increased capacity on the interregional trunk lines coming to them. Thus both the building of large-scale facilities and the growth of established centers acted selectively on the railroad system, bearing down heavily on parts of the network and having little influence on the remainder.

The essential feature of the transportation crisis geographically, then, was simply that it was spatially focused on certain parts of the railroad system. The appropriate government policy was therefore to notice where "bottlenecks" (the term is nicely adjusted to the meaning in this case) had developed or were impending, and then apply the measures outlined in the report of the American railroad officials. This simple and straightforward conception will go far toward explaining, one by one, the scores of betterment projects carried out between 1928 and 1940. A lengthy review of individual projects could be made to build a case for the thesis, but would be of doubtful value for most readers of this study. Perhaps the argument can be sufficiently established through enumeration of a handful of outstanding examples.

The oldest bottleneck situation was already causing difficulty on the eve of the First World War. Traffic originating in the eastern Ukraine, consisting especially of coal, was blocking up the lines running north to the Moscow region as early as 1910–1914.[17] Of these there were two, the route north from Kharkov through Kursk and Orel to Moscow, and the route north from Rostov-on-Don through Voronezh and Ryazan to Moscow. Both had been double-tracked by 1917, yet a new line, built directly into the coal fields, seemed necessary. Location surveys for a new route had been made almost annually from 1913 on,[18] but no action was taken until 1927.

The location problem for a line in this territory was basically whether to combine a number of existing sections of old line into a new through route or to lay out an entirely new line lying slightly more to the east. The old lines crossed several watersheds, and a patchwork route using them would therefore have higher operating costs than a new line laid out to minimize ruling gradients. Apparently not foreseeing the full extent of the impending traffic growth, the government decided in 1927 to build a 44-kilometer connecting link that would complete the patchwork route for a third Moscow-Donbas line. It came into permanent operation in 1928.[19] By 1931, it became clear that this patchwork route, lying between the Kursk route on the west and the Voronezh route on the east, was going to require a great deal of improvement. The building crews who constructed the Turk-Sib Railroad, when they had completed that task in 1931, were transferred en masse to rebuild the "Moscow-Donbas Trunk Line." [20] By the end of 1934, the project was being called the "Magnitostroi of Railroad Transport," implying that it was as large and important a project for the railroads as the Magnitogorsk works were for the steel industry.[21] In December 1934, a separate railroad administration was created to operate the road,[22] though its renovation continued throughout the 1930's. On August 20, 1939, the rebuilt trunk line was accepted by a government commission for permanent operation.[23]

In order to concentrate northbound coal traffic more heavily on the Moscow-Donbas trunk line, two extensions were built in the eastern Ukraine. The first connected Kupyansk with Svyatogorskaya, a point on the line coming north from Debaltsevo; this 73-kilometer stretch came into permanent operation in 1940. The second ran south from Valuiki into the eastern (and newer) districts of the coal fields; a single-track section 229 kilometers south to Kondrashevskaya came into temporary operation in 1936. By 1939 it had been double-tracked, and in 1940 it came into permanent operation. By 1942 it had been extended another 89 kilometers south to Dolzhanskaya.

This brief history of the Moscow-Donbas trunk line provides a clear illustration of Soviet policy, described by Khachaturov* in his 1945 talk as being based on the following principles:

---

* Tigran Sergeevich Khachaturov is perhaps the most thoughtful writer on transportation economics in the USSR, and it is worthwhile to describe his background in some detail. He was born in Moscow on October 6, 1906, and graduated from Moscow University in 1926 (aged 19), having worked under the "faculty of social science." He promptly began to publish articles in transportation journals; a good example is his article on freight rates in *Transport i Khoziaistvo,* 1929, no. 2, pp. 54–66. During the 1930's he apparently spent several years on a massive study comparing transportation in other countries and in prerevolutionary Russia with Soviet transportation. It was submitted as a dissertation in competition for the degree of Candidate in Economic Science (a rank somewhat below Ph.D.).

In an unusual development, one to excite the envy of graduate students all over the world, this dissertation was discussed at a session of the Economics Institute of the USSR Academy of Sciences, and "it was recognized that in breadth of coverage of material, in thoroughness, and in seriousness of study of the question, the work was not inferior to a doctor's dissertation. At this same meeting it was decided to confer a doctor's degree on T. S. Khachaturov, bypassing his candidacy" (story with photograph in *Gudok,* 24 Nov. 1940, p. 4). Hence Khachaturov became a Doctor of Economic Science in 1939, at the age of 33, and the book was published by the State

  a) concentration of traffic on trunk lines;
  b) radical technical reconstruction of railway transport, in the first place on these trunk lines;
  c) rationalization of the work of railway transport as a whole;
  d) construction of new railways to connect up new areas, and improvement of the configuration of the whole railway network.[24]

A series of old, low-capacity grain feeder lines was combined with three short new lines and thoroughly renovated to become a double-tracked trunk line with the roadbed improved sufficiently to support the new, heavier locomotives. It was intended especially for freight traffic, with the Kursk route being somewhat freed for its relatively heavy passenger traffic.[25]

The development of through connections between the eastern Ukraine and Leningrad, where coal was needed to replace imports from England and Poland, is another example of selective improvement, confined to a minimum number of lines in the relatively well-developed grid of western European Russia. In the middle and late 1930's, it proved necessary to raise traffic capacity on a route running northeast from the eastern Ukraine to the middle Volga Valley and the Urals. Consequently the prerevolutionary line from Valuiki northeast through Liski, east through Balashov, and northeast to Penza was double-tracked. The double-tracking continued east through Syzran and Kuibyshev to Ufa and Chelyabinsk in the Urals. In addition, a second track was laid between Rtishchevo on this line and Saratov on the middle Volga.[26] In 1939 and 1940, the whole route was being equipped with automatic block signaling.[27]

The selective improvement of lines in response to the concentration of traffic demands on those lines led to a marked differentiation of trunk lines from the remainder of the network. Present-day maps that show all railroads in the USSR as equally prominent lines give a very misleading impression of their capacity and importance. Nevertheless, if frequency

---

Social-Economic Publishing House, a more august press than the railroad publishing house.

In 1943 Khachaturov was elected a corresponding member of the Academy of Sciences, at the age of 37, thus joining a handful of elderly engineers who were the only other transportation representatives in this select body. For several years after the war he was Director of the All-Union Scientific-Research Institute of Railroad Transportation in Moscow, and since 1954 he has been Director of the USSR Academy of Sciences Institute of Complex Transportation Problems.

A partial list of his works appears in the bibliography of the present study. In connection with the discussion of "concentration and differentiation," reference should be made to an excellent talk given by Khachaturov in London on January 4, 1945 and reprinted as "The Organization and Development of Transport in the USSR," *International Affairs* (London), April 1945, pp. 220–35.

distributions of total freight traffic classified according to the intensity of use of the roadway are examined, it appears that traffic was heavily concentrated on a relatively small portion of the network even at the beginning of the forced industrialization period. As a result the extent of *further* concentration during the 1930's was not so great as might be supposed. Lorenz curves drawn for freight traffic in 1932, 1937, and 1940 show appreciable changes in the lower range, but do not disclose significant shifts in the upper range.[28] In all three years it was roughly true that 90 per cent of the roadway operated carried only two thirds of the freight traffic, but in 1932 the limiting traffic density for this part of the whole was five million ton-kilometers per kilometer of line per year, while in 1940 it had risen to eleven million. Perhaps if 1928 data were compared with those for 1940, the contrast would be more marked, not only in change of average traffic densities, but in the extent of differentiation among parts of the network.

What seems to have taken place is a widespread increase in freight traffic densities, affecting most of the road operated. Where lines had previously been very lightly loaded, the added traffic did not require substantial improvements in their capacity. On the other hand, where the industrialization program called for traffic loads well above the capacity of a line, it became necessary to improve the route. As a result, the critical interregional trunk lines, and the main lines within each industrial center, emerged from the relatively primitive web of railroads to become modernized, high-capacity routes. Clearly this selective approach facilitated prompt mastery of the transportation crisis. If it had been necessary to raise traffic capacity more uniformly throughout the whole railroad system, the development program obviously would have required both more time and more investment.

In retrospect it seems clear that the transportation crisis was overcome through a combination of capital improvements and pronounced gains in operating efficiency. Measuring separate contributions does not appear possible, however, especially since efficiency gains were, in part at least, direct consequences of the introduction of modern equipment. It is significant, at the same time, that the productivity gains did not continue to the end of the decade. There appear to have been both engineering and psychological limits to further gains. Alternatively, the failure to improve performance may be explained as a consequence of the purges, which affected the railroads severely.

In its territorial aspect, the transportation bottleneck was eliminated through selective improvement of the railroad network, responding to the selective impact of traffic demands. Modernization of the principal inter-regional trunk lines led to a sharp differentiation of these lines from the bulk of the railroad system, which remained a network of low-capacity lines. This concentration of traffic and capital development work on trunk lines reflected the over-all location policy of the industrialization program in its "gigantomania" period, and might be less appropriate under a different location policy.

# 5 SOVIET RAILROADS IN WORLD WAR II

Looking back on the early years of the Second World War, one might find it difficult now to recall fully the low estimate placed on Russia's defensive capacities by observers all over the world. Soviet military power was questioned on a number of grounds, and, conversely, it appeared after the spring of 1940 that the *Wehrmacht* was almost invincible. In the event of a German-Russian war, all the evidence seemed to point toward a rapid and decisive German victory. And one of the elements in the usual analysis was the weakness of Soviet transportation.

There was historical precedent for such a view. Inadequate transportation had proved to be a difficulty during the Crimean War in 1854, and played a part in the 1904–1905 fiasco of the Russo-Japanese War.[1] In the war of 1914–1918, the overburdened railroad system of tsarist Russia proved incapable of maintaining adequate communications between the front and rear, or between the food and raw material–exporting regions on the one hand, and the industrial, food-deficit regions on the other. Military operations at the front were hampered by an almost complete absence of lateral lines across the radial network leading back to the interior, in contrast with which the Central Powers had available a fairly elaborate web of lines for transferring troops and supplies from one sector to another. In the Russian rear, freight traffic bottlenecks on the exits from the Donets Basin in the eastern Ukraine leading toward Moscow and Leningrad gave rise to backlogs of unshipped freight. Connections with the eastern parts of the Russian Empire were strained by the growing volume of traffic, especially at the crossing of the Volga River near Samara (now known as Kuibyshev).[2] One of the final irritants that cumulated in the collapse of the tsarist government was a failure of food supplies for Petrograd and Moscow, to which railroad difficulties contributed. On the basis of all these precedents, it was easy for observers to conclude that the railroad system would again prove a weak spot if the USSR were involved in war.

This was the view, for example, of A. Piotrowski, an expert from the

Eastern European Institute at Vilna, Poland. In an article published in October 1939, he reviewed the Soviet railroad system and concluded that in a war it would collapse.[3] It appeared to him that "the level of carloadings reached in the third quarter of 1937 (97,700 cars per day) seems to show the maximum that Soviet transport in its present state can attain with all its efforts." [4] The state of track, superstructure, and rolling stock was precarious, even for the existing level of operations. Therefore, he argued, "in case of war in the near future, leading to expanded pressure on transport, attrition of the whole railroad system can be foreseen, since they have almost no reserves of material for making good existing deficiencies that could cause the complete disorganization of railroad traffic."

Carrying the argument further, Piotrowski cited the words of K. E. Voroshilov, head of the People's Commissariat of Defense: "The most modest foresight allows us to predict that in case of war, transport will be burdened with additional work two or three times the peacetime normal, and in the regions immediately around the front, even eight or nine times as great," and concluded: "It is clearly evident that the lines of the USSR are not in a position to bear such pressure. In particular, the lines of the frontier zone are not in a position to bear it. The proof is that while freight traffic on all lines has grown fourfold since 1913, it has increased almost fivefold in the Belorussian SSR. Stations in the Ukrainian SSR have loaded more cars than all the stations of Russia in 1913. And now if we compare the problems that must eventually confront transport in wartime with the condition of track and equipment, it will be clear to us that Soviet transport would not be able to surmount the difficulties it would have to face."

Soviet officials were aware of doubts in the outside world. D. G. Pavlov, a military commander discussing railroads and the Red Army on July 30, 1938, the annual Railroadmen's Day, prophesied that "those who try to build an estimate of the work of Soviet railroads on the basis of facts about the work of transport in tsarist Russia will err severely." [5] They were also aware of impending danger. An article by Colonel V. Vorob'ev in the fall of 1938 begins: "In the war that the Fascist barbarians are getting ready against the country of the Soviets, transport, especially railroads, will play an extremely important part," and goes on to indicate that considerable thought was being given to placing Soviet railroads on a mobilized basis.[6] Two years later, a *Pravda* editorial on Railroadmen's Day said: "the complex international situation requires standing mobilized readiness of railroad workers. No complacency!" [7]

Although details were not available to the outside world, the railroads were receiving some preliminary training in military operations at this time. According to official Soviet history, "In 1938, Japan fell on our country in the region of Lake Khasan near Vladivostok, and in the next year Japan repeated her invasion in the region of the Mongolian People's Republic, around Khalkin-Gol, with the aim of getting onto Soviet territory, cutting our Siberian trunk line, and isolating the Far East from Russia." [8] At the other end of the country, during 1939 and 1940, several new territories were incorporated into the USSR along the western frontier. Another 1940 editorial on Railroadmen's Day asserted that "military shipments at the time of the Lake Khasan incident, at Khalkin-Gol, in the days of suppression of the Polish gentry, and in the battles against the White Finnish warmongers, have shown that USSR railroads are prepared to carry out the task of defending the country." [9] Reviewing the record toward the end of the war, a senior engineering spokesman for the railroads, Vladimir Nikolaevich Obraztsov, stated: "Soviet transport was prepared for the war. Experience with transport work at the time of the liberation of western Ukraine and western Belorussia, and in the war against the White Finns in 1939, permitted the introduction of several corrections and improvements in railroad operations." [10]

The outcome of the Nazi-Soviet conflict makes it appear, pragmatically, that the confident Soviet editorials of 1940 offered more accurate forecasts than did Piotrowski's analysis. Yet this is simply to refer to the eventual outcome, and sheds no light on the factors that could explain the railroads' performance. Surely the mere fact of readiness, plus the small-scale experience gained in 1938–1940, cannot provide an adequate answer.

Some years ago an article of mine began by noting the expectation that the Soviet transportation system would collapse under the pressure of the Nazi invasion, and adding, "Yet somehow it did not." When L. M. Kaganovich was concluding a major address to Soviet railroadmen in May 1954, he took occasion to cite this undiplomatic comment, and to add, no doubt with great vigor: "The Soviet transportation system held up, not 'somehow,' but because it is an integral part of a unified, all-conquering system of Socialist economy, and because Soviet railroadmen are part of a heroic free people, led by the great Communist Party." [11] The record does suggest, as Kaganovich implies, that centralized controls and popular patriotism were part of the explanation, but in the following pages it will be shown that several other factors played an essential role.

We have seen that, under the stringencies of the middle 1930's, emphasis was put on raising the traffic capacity of major interregional trunk lines.

As a result, although an ambitious list of new railroad lines had been put on the agenda in the Second Five Year Plan (issued in 1934), the actual volume of completed construction soon dwindled to insignificance. In 1937 and 1938 together, 409 miles of new roadway were added for permanent operation in all of the USSR, spread out over a handful of minor projects. But in 1938, attention shifted back toward the new building program, and construction of a large number of projects became active again. The fruits of this activity began to appear in 1939, when 850 miles of new line came into permanent operation. Hand in hand with the development of the war, construction of new railroad line attained the dimensions of a major boom, just as it had in Russia during the First World War. Evidently many projects adjudged postponable in the middle 1930's, and crowded off the docket by heavy industrial investment, were now considered, with the outbreak of hostilities, to be critically necessary. Since an interval of anywhere from a year to five years is necessarily involved between the decision to build a new line and completion of the project, we can safely conclude that the lines built during this boom had genuine importance in the eyes of the government. Moreover, the selectivity observed in carrying through construction projects is itself revealing. Many new lines listed in the Third Five Year Plan (issued in the spring of 1939) had not yet been begun at the time of the Nazi invasion, and were put over to the postwar five-year plan. In at least one case, construction was stopped on a line already partly completed, and it does not seem to have been revived in the same form since the war. Conversely, several other lines were hurriedly built to serve war needs, though they had not previously been on the agenda.

The assumption appears reasonable that the new line put into permanent operation between 1938 and July 1941 was considered by the government as contributing appreciably to the strength of the Soviet economy and the ability of the railroad system to serve that economy. It can also be assumed that the line brought into permanent operation between July 1941 and the end of 1944 was considered essential to the war effort. Since, in the aggregate, the almost 7600 miles of new roadway added for permanent operation between the end of 1938 and the end of 1944 represented a 14.4 per cent addition to total road operated at the end of 1938, it seems incontrovertible that the new line was an important factor in enabling the railroads to emerge from the war successfully.

The reader's patience would be taxed unduly by an exhaustive listing of the lines making up the 7600-mile total, and it would not reveal the over-all pattern very clearly. For purposes of classification, the individual projects can be divided into three groups according to the major function they were intended to fulfill, though of course some lines served two or more purposes. One group of new railroad lines clearly seems to have been built primarily for military purposes. Another group can be classed as developmental lines, in the sense that they were built to initiate or improve access to new regions or new deposits of natural resources. Still a third group of lines appears to have primarily interregional significance, that is, to provide new or shorter connections between points on the existing network.[12]

For the USSR, the war against Germany lasted forty-seven months, or almost four years, and during three quarters of this period the fighting was on Soviet territory. We can observe immediately, therefore, that this wartime record provides very little direct evidence for predicting the performance of the Soviet railroad system in a military conflict *outside* the borders of the USSR. Success in dealing with the domestic transportation problems of 1941–1945 does not *ipso facto* demonstrate a capacity for success in supporting military operations beyond Soviet frontiers. But the argument can be carried further. During about half the war, Soviet railroad operations were territorially compressed within only part of the network previously operated. Obviously this gave rise to serious problems. On the other hand, it brought certain favorable consequences too, and these should not be overlooked in explaining the record.

The crux of the matter, somewhat simplified, is that railroads make use of three types of equipment in performing their services: line, motive power, and rolling stock. The Nazi invasion resulted in the loss of about 40 per cent of the roadway operated, but since locomotives, freight cars, and passenger cars could be evacuated, Soviet railroads still had available at the beginning of 1943, the turning point of the war, 85 per cent of their locomotives and 80 per cent of their freight cars.[13] Some of this evacuated equipment, however, could not be used. The FD locomotives, for example, were too heavy for use in unoccupied territory, and various lines in the east lacked the sidings to accommodate available cars. Still, performance data for equipment in use shows that this drastic change in relative availabilities was of fundamental importance.

Its significance can be illustrated by crude calculations of the amount of work actually performed, on the average, by freight locomotives and freight cars during 1942–1944, as shown in Table 6. In 1940, the average freight locomotive accounted for about 65 million ton-kilometers of freight carried per year. But the shrinkage in the size of the network, and in the volume of freight traffic, meant that during 1942, 1943, and 1944 the average freight locomotive accounted for something like 42, 45, and 50 million freight ton-kilometers respectively. The underlying data are not firm, but there can be little doubt that the volume of freight traffic per freight locomotive, on the average, declined appreciably. Put this way, the phenomenon

Table 6. *Freight ton-kilometers per freight locomotive and freight car, USSR railroads, 1940, 1942, 1943, 1944*

| Year | Total ton-kilometers $(10^9)$ | Average no. locomotives in road service | Average no. cars on line | Ton-kilometers per locomotive $(10^6)$ | Ton-kilometers per car $(10^3)$ |
|---|---|---|---|---|---|
| 1940 | 415 | 6,430 | 721,000 | 64.5 | 576 |
| 1942 | 228 | 5,500 | 589,000 | 41.5 | 387 |
| 1943 | 256 | 5,750 | 574,000 | 44.5 | 446 |
| 1944 | 297 | 6,000 | 632,000 | 49.5 | 470 |

Sources: The ton-kilometer estimates are from Table 46. The locomotives estimates are derived from a 1940 average in column 6, Table 61, plus the statements that the locomotive stock at the beginning of 1943 was 15 per cent smaller than at the beginning of 1941 (Voznesenskii, 1947, p. 100) and that during 1943 it rose by 2000 units (*ibid.*, p. 102). These remarks probably refer to the total stock, of which freight locomotives in road service comprise about 40 per cent. If on January 1, 1943, 85 per cent of the January 1, 1941 stock in this category was on hand, the number would have been 5525, assuming 6500 for the end of 1940. The estimate in Table 61 for 1945, independently computed, is 6070, and the 1943 and 1944 estimates above are interpolated accordingly. The freight car estimates are derived as products of carloadings figures from Table 46 and turnaround times from Table 75.

sounds like deterioration, and in a real sense, it was. Operating efficiency, under the stress of wartime conditions, evidently declined substantially. But the observed relationship resulted from a sharper drop in traffic than in the number of locomotives in use. Consequently it shows that motive power was relatively abundant, compared to the amount of work to be performed.

A similar situation developed with respect to the freight car fleet. The volume of freight traffic in 1942 was about 46 per cent below the 1940 level, while the number of freight cars in use during the year was only 18 per cent smaller. Here too, in a relative sense, rolling stock was more available than it had been before the invasion.

That this is a plausible reconstruction of events is indicated by a number of contemporary remarks in Soviet sources. An editorial in the railroad newspaper in September 1942 said: "Some railroadmen try to excuse the congestion they have permitted in train movement by saying that there is nowhere to spread out, that it is difficult to maneuver, that the number of freight cars is large. Yes, the railroads' load has increased, and the freight car stock of several trunk lines has considerably increased, precisely on account of growth in the volume of traffic and also on account of rolling stock evacuated from regions temporarily occupied by the Germans." [14]

Evidently there was no shortage of cars at important points in unoccupied territory. The altered ratio of rolling stock to line capacity gave rise, however, to problems of overcrowding, as the following comments show: "Our railroad network has contracted considerably, and hence we need maximum activity and initiative in using the carrying capacity of each line and section. Without waiting for winter, we must immediately free junctions and stations from excess cars, especially on the railroads in the Urals and Siberia, and carry out exactly the assignments for unloading and transfer of cars." [15] In the fall of 1942 the problem was apparently not where to find the rolling stock to carry wartime freight, but how to keep the ample stock from impairing operations through congestion at classification and marshaling yards, or on overcrowded line sections.

Wartime manpower shortages, plus other dislocations, evidently led to a reversal of the conditions typical of the early 1930's, when lagging railroad operations permitted backlogs of unshipped freight to accumulate on clients' sidings. An August 1943 editorial in *Pravda* indicates that two years after the beginning of the war freight cars were still available in ample numbers: "However . . . the task is not carried out for all commodities . . . because on the other hand some branches of the economy are not fully using the rolling stock presented for loading. Coal and metallurgy workers were justly disgruntled with railroadmen when the latter held up shipments of raw material and fuel. Now cases are observed where transport sends cars and the client does not use them." [16]

Before the war, great pressure was put on clients to load and unload cars promptly, and the railroads themselves strained to minimize the time spent by cars in classification yards, at division points, and en route. The average time between one loading and the next, for a freight car, was held down to about seven days, whereas in the United States it was about fifteen days. (See Chapter 7.) Under wartime conditions, however, average freight car turnaround time increased alarmingly, as the following figures show:

| | | | |
|------|------------|------|-----------|
| 1940 | 7.37 days  | 1943 | 12.6 days |
| 1941 (first half) | 6.92 | 1944 | 11.4 |
| 1942 | 13.8 | 1945 | 10.92 |

In his review of wartime transportation, Voznesenskii draws attention to this change, ascribing it partly to a longer average length of haul and partly to a worsening of car utilization averages. The average haul for freight traffic did rise to about 17 per cent above its 1940 level, but this cannot have accounted for more than three percentage points of increase in turnaround time, other things being equal, since cars at that time were only spending about 18 per cent of their time in motion from origin to destination. His second explanation is a tautology. It appears from a comparison of turnaround time components in 1940 and 1945 that the major cause for delayed freight car movement was longer time spent in classification and marshaling yards. This again tends to confirm the analysis set forth above.

If we turn from examining the relations between wartime freight traffic and rolling stock to consider the relation between traffic and line facilities, a somewhat similar pattern emerges. Chart 12 presents 1938–1946 trends for freight traffic, total road operated, and freight traffic density. It will be seen that, in 1942, the estimated annual average road operated was only 72 per cent of the 1940 average. Traffic, however, had dropped to 54 per cent, and the result was a fall in the over-all density of freight traffic per mile of road operated to three quarters of its prewar level. In 1945 and 1946, when all the prewar network was recaptured and most of it put back into at least temporary operation, and when additional roadway was operated in acquired territory, the average density of freight traffic dropped to two thirds of its 1940 level.

It must be emphasized that the war greatly intensified the density of freight traffic on many lines that had suddenly become trunk lines in unoccupied territory, after having previously been secondary lines "out in the provinces." Moreover, the figures for line operated in 1943–1946 cover many thousands of kilometers of line with only a fraction of its former capacity. The resulting problems were serious, and will be taken up shortly. Nevertheless, the record indicates that on an over-all basis the density of freight traffic for the system as a whole was lower during the war than in the late 1930's. It was still, of course, extremely high by Western standards, and the comparison with 1938–1940 points up the taut operating level of "normal" peacetime Soviet railroad operations. But the fact of diminished wartime traffic densities remains.

This chapter began with quotations from a Polish analyst who argued that the Soviet railroad system would prove incapable of handling the greatly increased traffic densities that would logically be associated with a war. We can now see that the actual course of events did not, for the railroad system as a whole, subject this proposition to a test. Over-all freight traffic densities did *not* increase, and this must be counted as one of the factors explaining Soviet railroad performance during World War II.

A cursory review of the main characteristics of wartime freight traffic, on which the extent of released information is extremely limited, will never-theless disclose a few points that can be fitted into our explanation of the railroads' performance. We note, first of all, that the Nazi invasion excised

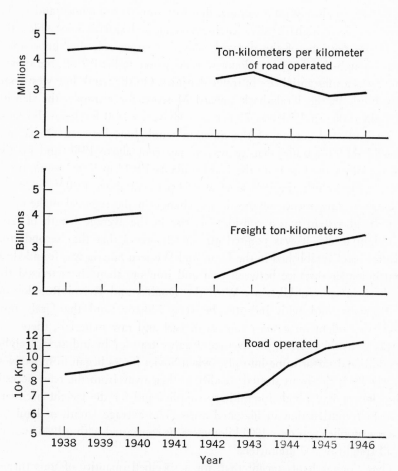

Chart 12. Freight traffic density, USSR railroads, 1938–1940 and 1942–1946. Source: Tables 46 and 59.

a large block of normal freight traffic from the demands placed on the railroad system. In fact one can gain a crude impression of what was in-volved through imagining that all the traffic carried in the United States "eastern district" was severed from the national total, along with the road-way and track. It was the most developed part of the Soviet railroad system that was occupied, and it included much of the densest traffic. The unoccupied two thirds of the system resembled western and southern districts in the United States in having, for the most part, lower traffic densities and longer hauls. The drop in traffic densities can therefore be interpreted as a change in the over-all average, due to removal of territory and traffic characterized by high density, leaving a truncated situation in which the low-density portions of the network played a larger role. On unoccupied lines, although there were no doubt sections where traffic fell off, the typical change was a substantial *rise* in traffic densities. On the trunk line west from Chelyabinsk in the Urals back toward Moscow, for example, the density of freight traffic in 1944 was 75 per cent above its 1940 level; on the most heavily burdened section of the Siberian trunk line, between Omsk and Novosibirsk, 1944 traffic density was 47 per cent above 1940; and on the head section of the line from the Karaganda coal field in Kazakhstan, north as far as Akmolinsk, the 1944 level was 58 per cent above 1940.[17]

Another consequence of the drastic change in the regional make-up of the railroad system was a considerable rise in the average length of haul for freight traffic. It was pointed out in Chapter 3 that the "second iron and steel base" established in the Urals and Western Siberia was founded on a much longer distance between coal and iron ore than characterized the first base in eastern Ukraine. With the Donbas and Krivoi Rog lost to the Russians, and with industry between Moscow and the Urals now wholly dependent on eastern sources of fuel and raw materials, there was no way to avoid a rise in the average distance traveled by industrial freight. An additional factor came into play when Soviet forces began to move west in early 1943; the front shifted steadily farther away from the rear, necessitating longer hauls both for military supplies and for the freight necessary to begin reconstruction in liberated areas. The average length of haul for military supplies was over 1000 kilometers, as contrasted with a 1940 average for all freight of 700 kilometers.[18]

These longer hauls meant that, for a specified quantity of tons turned over to the railroads for shipment, a larger quantity of ton-kilometers of movement had to be produced than before the war, and this increased the railroads' burden. From another point of view, however, it may be pointed out that for any given quantity of ton-kilometers to be produced, the burden placed on the railroads by long-haul traffic is smaller than the burden associated with short-haul traffic. If the average length of haul in 1943 had been 700 kilometers (the 1940 level), instead of the 817 kilometers it actually was, then the 256 billion ton-kilometers of freight traffic carried in that year would have been associated with 366 million tons of originating traffic, instead of the actual 313 million tons. There would have been 17 per cent more tonnage to deal with at loading and unloading points, and these terminal operations are the most costly portions of a railroad's work, in real terms. Thus there is a sense in which the longer hauls permitted the railroads to turn out their wartime levels of ton-kilometers more easily than would have been possible under peacetime conditions. Yet while we can recognize the ameliorating effect of this change in the ratio of line to terminal services, the fact remains that the longer hauls of World War II demanded an absolute increase in the physical volume of transportation contributed by the railroads to each ton of output delivered to its destination.

The composition of wartime freight traffic, commodity-wise, presumably mirrored the drastic changes in the output of the wartime economy, but the details available for analysis in the present study will suffice for only a few general observations. In the opening stages of the invasion, for example, the railroads bore the brunt of a large-scale evacuation operation that removed plant and equipment, and people, from the path of the advancing enemy. The railroads carried something like twelve to fourteen billion short ton–miles of evacuation freight during the second half of 1941, and this represented about 10 per cent of total freight traffic at that time.[19] The volume of military railroad traffic in the narrow sense during these early months was apparently of a comparable magnitude. Consequently it appears that over three quarters of the railroads' work in the second half of 1941 continued to involve nonwar traffic.

During 1942–1944, the category of "military traffic," a vague and broad term in modern warfare, accounted for roughly 30 per cent of railroad carloadings, and since the average length of haul for such traffic was above the national average, for possibly one third of the total ton-kilometers of freight traffic. Wartime trends in military and nonmilitary traffic are shown in Chart 13. This chart illustrates in a slightly different way the important difference between wartime developments and prewar predictions, which was pointed out in the preceding section. Wartime traffic did not have to be added on to peacetime traffic, as Piotrowski had assumed, logically enough, that it would. In 1942, the volume of nonmilitary railroad freight traffic was only about one third its 1940 level. How could two thirds of the normal traffic disappear so promptly? Ruthless suppression of nonessential traffic presumably accounted for some of the cut, though to the extent that the 1940 economy was already stripped to a semimobilized basis, the possibilities here must have been limited. The balance of the cut must evidently be ascribed to the elimination of all the normal, industrial, nonmilitary traffic that had previously taken place on the 40 per cent of the network occupied by the Nazis.

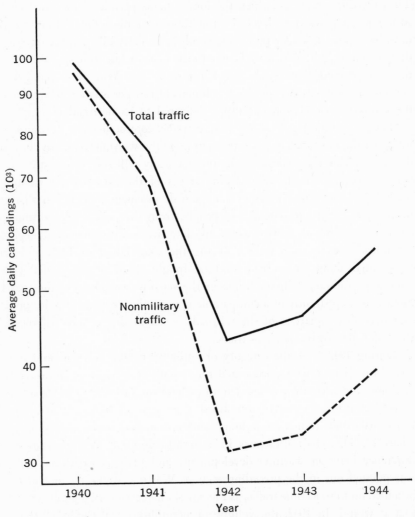

*Chart 13. Military traffic, USSR railroads, 1940–1945. Source: Table 39.*

The Soviet railroad system was able to expand its carriage of military freight in 1942–1943 to about five times the 1940 level, partly because the volume of nonmilitary freight in 1942–1943 was only one third of the 1940

level. It is quite clear that, in any military conflict that required maintenance of nonmilitary traffic at a level close to its peacetime volume, this
facilitating feature of the World War II experience could not again come
into play. The reasoning here must be kept within bounds; it is scarcely
rational to describe the Nazi invasion as a "facilitating feature" of the war
from a Russian point of view. *Within* the nonoccupied part of the USSR,
military freight traffic did have to displace, forcibly, an appreciable part of
the previously carried peacetime traffic, and in addition means had to be
found to move larger amounts of freight than before on many lines. But
the special circumstances of this period mean that we must guard against
ill-considered transfer of the World War II record to hypothetical problems.
It could not be deduced, for example, that two thirds of normal peacetime
railroad freight traffic could be removed from the railroads for two years
without having the total economy collapse. In 1942 and 1943 only about
60 per cent of the USSR, effectively, was available for Soviet use, and while
this meant that the other 40 per cent could not produce for Russia, it also
meant that two fifths of normal consumption was removed from consideration.

Chart 13 permits another kind of comparison, which also has interesting implications for evaluation of Soviet transportation. The prewar level of
average daily carloadings in the USSR was around 100,000. Evidently it
was possible to transport supplies for the large-scale military operations of
1942–1944 through loading about 15,000 cars per day with military freight.
This was about 30 per cent of total average daily carloadings at the time,
since the total was much reduced. But it represents only a 15 per cent increase over the 1940 level, and with average daily carloadings at their 1955
level of roughly 175,000, the increment would amount to under 9 per cent.
Evidently the order of magnitude of military traffic on the railroads during
World War II was utterly different from the "two or three times the peacetime normal" anticipated by Voroshilov, as cited in the opening pages of
this chapter. Piotrowski was probably quite right in supposing that the Soviet
system could not carry two or three times its normal traffic, but the point
is that this did not prove necessary. A prudent calculation for current conditions would suggest that the Soviet railroad system could transport supplies for an all-out military operation with perhaps a 10 per cent addition to
(or substitution within) its current rate of average daily carloadings.

The shift toward the east in economic activity, and therefore in railroad
traffic, that followed the Nazi invasion created serious bottleneck problems
at many points on the remaining Soviet railroad system. They were promptly

and vigorously dealt with. The capacity of classification and marshaling yards, terminal facilities, and certain line sections was increased through laying additional track and adding the other necessary facilities.[20] As a result, the railroads were able to cope with the intense strains of the early stages of the war, from the middle of 1941 to the end of 1943. Among the factors explaining Soviet railroads' wartime success, these prompt expansion projects clearly deserve a place.

But the really impressive performance of Soviet railroad maintenance and construction crews came with the great drive westward. Recognizing that the Soviet advance would depend heavily on transportation, the Nazis made determined efforts to demolish all railroad lines as thoroughly as possible before retreating. There must have been situations in which line could be recaptured intact, but most of the line seems to have been badly damaged. Yet it was imperative that through communications be re-established immediately after each military advance, in order that further advances could be made. In this sphere, the evidence indicates that Soviet railroadmen were extremely competent.

The railroad engineering journal toward the end of 1943 began to publish technical articles concerning methods for reconstructing roadway and superstructure. Some included photographs of wrecked line, and it appears that the Naxis used three different techniques for making railroad line impassable. One was to chop out sections of rail, or explode rail joints, at frequent intervals (three to a rail in one photograph). Another was to pull the rails away from their crossties. The third is described as follows: "At the beginning of January 1944, the Germans used for the first time a new kind of obstruction — a trackwrecker of the *kriuk* [hook] type — which wrecks ties. It consists of a specially strengthened two-axle flatcar on which is mounted a rolled-iron hook. . . . It is pulled by two locomotives."[21] An accompanying diagram gives its dimensions — the device was about seventeen feet long — and a photograph shows the manner in which the hook plowed a furrow between the rails, snapping every tie. The articles describe a number of makeshift methods for welding short lengths of rail together, using short ties, and in one way or another reconstructing line so that trains could again pass over it. Clearly the difficulties involved were formidable.

The amount of roadway destroyed and reconstructed can be determined within fairly narrow limits through splicing together a series of figures drawn from Soviet sources. Their reliability hinges on the definition of "destruction" and "reconstruction," but it seems prudent not to underestimate either one. Published Soviet totals for German damage, compiled in connection with reparation demands, are vague and somewhat larger than the figures appearing in railroad literature, which are the ones used here. The figures for the amount of reconstruction accomplished, when subtracted from the alleged amount of destruction, precipitate residuals that tally quite closely with the data published in 1946 on the amount of reconstruction that remained to be done under the Fourth Five Year Plan.

Tabulating the length of roadway (first main track) involved, we find the following:

| | |
|---|---|
| Total destroyed in the USSR during World War II | 52,400 kilometers |
| Total restored to operation by May 1945 | 48,800 |
| | |
| Balance still out of operation in May 1945 | 3,600 |

The time schedule for reconstruction, that is, number of kilometers returned to operation, is as follows:

| | During period | Cumulative |
|---|---|---|
| First half 1943 | 6,600 | — |
| Second half 1943 | 12,400 | 19,000 |
| First half 1944 | 16,000 | 35,000 |
| Second half 1944 | 8,000 | 43,000 |
| January–April 1945 | 5,800 | 48,800 |

In addition, Soviet railroadmen are said to have reconstructed and put back in operation, outside the USSR, 19,100 or 28,800 or over 30,000 kilometers of roadway, depending on the compiler.

The figures for second tracks, excluding yard tracks, are as follows:

| | |
|---|---|
| Total destroyed | 17,513 kilometers |
| Repaired by May 1945 | 7,846 |
| Repaired by end of 1945 | 10,725 |
| Balance out of operation | 6,788 |

It is clear that restoration of the second track on a double-track trunk line lagged well behind the reopening of first main track. This was foreseen by T. S. Khachaturov, who wrote in 1943: "In the prewar period, the through capacity on several of our railroads was limited, usually not by line sections, but by stations. Destruction on the liberated railroads is less severe for line sections than for stations. Therefore, reconstruction of only one track of individual double-track lines, in the first stage, can be assumed." [22]

As to yard tracks, approximate data indicate that some 30,000 kilometers (over half the national total) were destroyed. Of this, 20,070 kilometers were repaired during the war, leaving another 10,000 to be restored to operation in the following period. A total of 2,323 large- and medium-sized bridges was recorded as having been destroyed, with 550 being restored to at least temporary operation during 1943, 1,307 more coming into operation during 1944–1945, and 466 left unrepaired at the war's end. The damage to passenger terminals in occupied territory was drastic: 2,455 stations were destroyed out of a national total of 3,013, and, as will be seen in the review of postwar developments, restoration on a permanent basis did not come on a large scale for about five years.[23]

As a result of the vigorous emergency repair programs reflected in these figures, combined with the completion of newly built lines noted earlier, the total length of road operated had been brought back to the prewar level by the end of 1944. Consequently, in the late stages of the war, the favorable ratio of rolling stock and motive power to road operated diminished or vanished. An acute British analyst had noted in the early fall of 1943 that the improved ratio of locomotives and cars to line facilities was a factor aiding the Russians during 1941 and 1942, but he went on to point out that: "The real Russian problem will be when a rapid advance begins and large areas of territory are recovered. . . . the advances of August and September 1943 may provide an even greater test and strain for the Russian railways than the retreats of 1941 and 1942." [24] The compression of the Soviet railroad system, which led to a relative abundance of cars and locomotives in unoccupied territory, could no longer assist railroad officials in their work. Locomotives and freight cars had to be returned to the liberated lines. Moreover, since sizable quantities of rolling stock and motive power had been damaged or captured during the invasion and later battles, the initial stock was no longer available for redistribution. Under these conditions it seemed obvious that serious shortages would make their appearance.

Hindsight and the availability of crude numerical records for the wartime period reveal to us that, while the re-expanded network tended to dilute the relation of rolling stock to road operated even below the prewar level, this was *not* true for the volume of freight traffic. The railroads recaptured from the Germans were relatively lifeless, and were not burdened with anything like their prewar density of freight traffic until the end of the recovery period. In 1941, the Nazi invasion had extinguished a huge block of freight traffic; the Soviet advances of 1943 and 1944 meant that the railroad lines that had formerly carried this traffic came back under Soviet control, but without their previous traffic. It was crucially important, of course, that liberated lines at the front carry military supplies for attacks, and that interregional connections be maintained across the widening band of liberated territory separating the front from the unoccupied rear. There was also a prompt beginning of restoration activities in the Donbas and elsewhere, which placed demands on recaptured rail lines. But without having detailed records of the traffic volumes involved, we can nevertheless be sure that these traffic demands combined did not amount to even a third of the dense peacetime industrial traffic on these roads in 1940.

The Soviet railroad system was thus able to supply the transportation requirements of the latter stages of World War II in part through making use of the motive power and rolling stock that before the war had been carrying peacetime traffic in occupied territory. The shortages foreseen in 1943 were to this extent much smaller than might have been anticipated.

The actual number of freight cars available was evidently a closely guarded military secret during the war, and Soviet sources since the war have not disclosed any significant data for these years. In the summer of 1945 an imposing list of Nazi damage was drawn up to support reparations claims, however, and it stated that 428,000 freight cars had been "destroyed, damaged, or taken away to Germany."[25] The obvious deduction was that there must have been a severe shortage of freight cars, and since 400,000 was about half the estimated prewar stock, that this shortage would hinder postwar reconstruction. Here, it seems, the West was seriously misled.

The average number of freight cars in use at any time can be calculated indirectly as the product of average daily carloadings times average turn-around time. For example, if 50,000 cars are loaded each day, and it takes twelve days for a complete freight car trip, the total stock of cars in use will have to be 600,000. Continuous series for both carloadings and turnaround time can be compiled, fortunately, and we therefore have in Table 7 reasonably accurate estimates for the years 1940–1947.

Instead of a reduction of 428,000 in the freight car stock, the performance data show a fall of about 166,000. How is this to be explained? The gross figure for reparations purposes evidently covered not only those freight cars permanently destroyed by the Nazis, but also those which were damaged but quickly repaired and those which were recaptured as the Soviet Army moved westward. Two thirds of the loss in cars was made good during 1944 and 1945, while the Russians were sweeping over the western boundaries of the USSR and into Eastern Europe. It may be conjectured that along with the Soviet cars recaptured from the Nazis, the Russians took over freight cars previously owned by eastern European or German railroads.[26]

A similar discrepancy between asserted losses and wartime availabilities appears in connection with locomotives: 15,800 were said to have been destroyed, damaged, or removed, yet the number of freight locomotives in road service fell by something like 1,000. Lend-lease shipments of almost 2,000 locomotives evidently made a substantial contribution at this point.

Table 7. *Average number of freight cars (2-axle units) in use, USSR railroads, by year, 1940–1947*

| Year | Number of cars | Change from preceding year | Index (first half of 1941 = 100) |
|------|---------------|---------------------------|----------------------------------|
| 1940 | 721,000 | — | — |
| 1941 (first half) | 740,200 | +19,000 | 100.0 |
| 1942 | 589,000 | −151,000 | 79.6 |
| 1943 | 574,000 | −15,000 | 77.5 |
| 1944 | 632,000 | +58,000 | 85.4 |
| 1945 | 676,500 | +44,500 | 91.4 |
| 1946 | 700,700 | +24,200 | 94.7 |
| 1947 | 732,900 | +32,200 | 99.0 |

Sources: Compiled as products of carloadings data in Table 46 and turnaround time data in Table 75. These estimates are broadly consistent with Voznesenskii's statement (1947, p. 100) that the freight car stock at the end of 1942 was 80 per cent as large as the stock at the end of 1940. If the end-of-year figure for 1940 is taken to be 730,000, then 80 per cent of it would be 584,000 for the end of 1942. He states (*ibid.*, p. 102) that during 1943 the total stock of freight cars rose by 56,000 units, whereas the annual average indicated above is 15,000 units smaller than the 1942 average. He may have included bad-order cars in his increment, or they may have entered the "working fleet" late in the year.

The discussion thus far has drawn attention to four major factors that appear to account for the successful record of Soviet railroads during World War II. Before concluding the chapter, we may note briefly three other factors, probably less important in their effects, which nevertheless contributed to the railroads' performance.

The first was the substantial shipments of transportation equipment under Lend-Lease and Mutual Aid agreements between the USSR and her allies. These included almost 2,000 locomotives, 475,000 trucks, 14,500 aircraft, and 11,000,000 pairs of boots and shoes, along with many thousands of tons of rails, signaling equipment, and other transportation supplies.[27] The transport demands of a modern army have evidently shifted appreciably from rail to road carriers (trucks, tanks, and other wheeled equipment), and to this extent these supplies eased the burden on the Soviet railroad system. There was some loss in transit, due mainly to ship sinkings, especially in the early years of the war, but it was roughly 10 to 12 per cent of the tonnages dispatched.[28] Soviet writers even during the war acknowledged such aid only very rarely, so that it is not at present possible to evaluate its contribution except by conjecture. A detailed analysis of United States Lend-Lease records would probably support the view that, in addition to the end products noted above, Russia received many other items which contributed to transport operations. In particular, the prompt restoration of movement on recaptured rail lines probably owed a good deal to supplies received from abroad.

A second, less tangible factor that supported wartime railroad operations was the tightening of discipline among railroad workers. For several years before the war, railroad and enterprise officials were subject to fines and jail sentences for excessive delays in loading or unloading freight cars, or similar offenses. After the Nazi invasion, such cases were dealt with more severely, and certain other infractions were dealt with very harshly indeed. In July 1942, three railroad workers were caught stealing sacks of millet from railroad cars at night; the leader was sentenced to be shot, and the others were sentenced to ten years' imprisonment. A few days later, a switch operator who reported for duty drunk was sentenced to seven years' loss of freedom. The head of a mailcar on the Moscow-Murmansk run, who opened eighteen parcels addressed to soldiers and officers at the front and took the contents, was sentenced to be shot. An editorial in the railroad newspaper in September 1942 cited two cases of train wrecks due to carelessness, and urged stricter discipline regarding observance of regulations governing train movements.[29]

On April 15, 1943, the Presidium of the USSR Supreme Soviet issued a decree establishing martial law on the railroads, with the following provisions: (1) all railroad workers are considered mobilized and fixed at their jobs; (2) railroad workers are responsible for their crimes just as soldiers are; (3) railroad military tribunals are to try cases using wartime law; (4) guilty workers are to be fired and sent to penal companies at the front, unless given sterner treatment; and (5) regular operating rules are to be enforced more sternly, with up to twenty days of administrative arrest for infractions.[30] In September 1943 the government extended to the railroads the ranks and insignia that had been restored to the armed forces in the fall of 1942. The change was intended "to have great significance for strengthening military discipline and for raising the authority of commanders."[31] It will be recalled that strong government pressure for strict discipline had been applied to railroad workers ever since 1935, so that there was presumably not a great deal of slack to be taken up through these added measures. However, they probably acted to check a decline in efficiency due to wartime dislocations.

A final factor that contributed to the railroads' success was the resourceful use of new and untrained workers, especially women. Details are fragmentary, but there was evidently a substantial cut in the regular railroad labor force, with the gap being filled, to the extent that it was filled, by young, inexperienced workers. The use of women in heavy work had been growing throughout the Soviet economy under the five-year plans, and was not peculiar to railroads. A 1932 regulation that excluded women from the jobs of locomotive engineer, assistant engineer, and fireman was abandoned in November 1938, at which time there were already fifteen women locomotive engineers, running freight trains on their own. Considerable publicity was given to Zinaida Petrova Troitskaia, a girl from a railroading family, who in 1930 began working in a locomotive depot and by 1936 was running a passenger locomotive so well she received the Order of Lenin. Relatively few women reached the glamorous post of locomotive engineer, but many became assistant engineers; in September 1939 there were forty-four of the former and forty-five hundred of the latter.[32]

Wartime exigencies led to further use of women in railroad operations. A 1943 pamphlet proudly recounts the story of a freight train run from Omsk to Moscow with an all-woman train crew of fourteen persons: "One need not think that the trip passed without difficulties. But the crew always came through them with honor. On the South Urals Railroad, the sanders broke down on the steepest grade. Then four women ran ahead of the train for six kilometers and spread sand. Another time a locomotive axle box heated up. Razumova went out onto the runway, with the train going full steam ahead, and for two sections, in frost and wind, kept the hot box quenched."[33] The train, carrying 1650 tons of coal, reached its destination.

Inventively used manpower evidently replaced destroyed or unobtainable equipment in wartime railroad operations. For example, a November 1942 article described a "living block signaling" system for use on lines near the front. Off-duty railroad workers or soldiers from nearby military units were to be placed alongside the track at intervals from 1000 to 2600 feet, to signal the presence or absence of trains. A yellow flag and a red flag during the day, or white and red lantern lights at night, would permit the chain of signalers, standing just within sight of each other, to transmit information forward and back.[34] Prewar evaluations of Soviet railroad capacities probably made quite inadequate allowance for makeshift solutions such as this, with the result that wartime potentials were underestimated.

Soviet railroadmen have good reason to be proud of their World War II record. They weathered a smashing blow against the most developed part of their network, mastered the strains of heavier traffic in unoccupied territory, and successfully restored movement on recaptured line as the Soviet

Army moved westward to Berlin. The contrast with earlier Russian wars is striking.

It should be noted, however, that the gloomy forecasts of outside observers in the late 1930's were not proved wrong — they simply were not put to a test. The Nazi invasion eliminated from the demands placed on the railroads more than it eliminated from their ability to meet those demands, and this provided a margin of capacity for dealing with military traffic. Evacuation of locomotives and freight cars to unoccupied territory made them relatively abundant during most of the war.

A combination of strict discipline, inventiveness, and patriotic fervor led Soviet railroad repair crews to perform remarkable feats of restoration in the westward drive. They were assisted in this to an undetermined extent through provision of supplies from Russia's wartime allies. Moreover, the need for restoration was exaggerated in some respects by the Soviet government in connection with reparations claims.

Rough calculations indicate that railroad military traffic made up a much smaller fraction of total traffic during World War II than had been anticipated, and suggest that at present a 10 per cent addition to (or substitution within) current traffic would support a large-scale military effort. It should be noted also that emergency restoration of damaged railroad facilities has become a highly developed art, as demonstrated in the record we have reviewed and more recently in the Korean War. On both counts it must be concluded that Soviet railroad transportation has become a capable and reliable element of Soviet military strength.

In his 1954 speech, Kaganovich reported my conclusion that the railroads would not be a Soviet Achilles' heel in a future war, and added: "What's true is true! Our heel is tougher than that of the ancient Greek, Achilles. On this heel we reached Berlin, and if some imitator of Hitler comes along, then on this heel we, basing ourselves on the power of our great Soviet Army, will get even farther." While one readily recognizes the morale-building function of such remarks, the reference to truth, implying as it does a respect for evidence, may seem more hopeful. If the present study contributes to understanding, both within and outside the USSR, derived from objective evidence, it will have achieved its purpose.

# 6  POSTWAR RECOVERY AND EXPANSION

During the last decade and a half the USSR has recovered from its wartime setback and advanced substantially beyond prewar levels. While the transportation sector cannot, of course, claim major responsibility for the rapid economic growth that has been achieved, the record indicates that this time the carriers have at least not hampered industrial expansion. Confining ourselves to the railroads, which have continued to dominate Soviet transportation, we will trace in this chapter the main developments of the recovery period and the subsequent expansion.

After we have noted the over-all trend of the recovery period, it will prove interesting to compare the railroads' performance with their record during the previous Soviet postwar recovery in the 1920's. The growth of freight traffic and railroad facilities between 1948 and 1955 can be similarly contrasted with parallel developments during the 1928–1940 period. The recent impressive gains in Soviet railroad utilization deserve review, and there is topical interest, finally, in Soviet responses to the great current debate over railroad motive power.

Recovery from wartime lows, at least in industrial activity, had already begun before the end of World War II, but officially the Fourth Five Year Plan period begins with 1946. Its targets for 1950 appeared rather ambitious when they were announced in March 1946, yet, after a slow start in 1946 and 1947, the important industrial goals were in most cases met or slightly exceeded. Heavy industry by 1950 had reached a level considerably above its previous peak of 1940; the agricultural sector, on the other hand, appears scarcely to have regained its 1940 level by 1950. The result of these divergent recovery rates was to carry forward still further the displacement of agriculture by industry that had marked the 1928–1940 period. For consumers, the harsh deprivations of the war years gradually gave way, after 1947, to steadily improving living conditions, though again it is not clear that the 1940 level had been regained by 1950.

The Fourth Five Year Plan anticipated that the output growth it envisaged would give rise to a 1950 volume of freight traffic, for all carriers, some 81 per cent above their 1945 traffic. Moreover, it stipulated that railroad freight ton-kilometers should only grow by 69 per cent, while the other carriers were to carry almost 2.5 times their 1945 traffic. Previous Soviet experience was repeated, however, and neither basic intention for the transportation sector was fulfilled. Aggregate traffic rose by 93 per cent, some 6 per cent more than had been hoped, and the minor carriers fell 20 per cent short of their target. As a consequence, railroad freight traffic increased, not 69 per cent, but 91 per cent from 1945 to 1950. In an over-all sense, therefore, it seems evident that the railroads' ability to do considerably more than had been expected of them must have contributed to postwar Soviet recovery.

The dominant contribution of the railroads can be illustrated in another way, through examining the absolute growth in over-all freight traffic each year and noting the railroads' contribution. This has been done in the accompanying tabulation (derived from Table 52), in billions of ton-kilometers.

| Year | Absolute increment in over-all freight traffic | Contributed by railroads | Contributed by the four other carriers |
|---|---|---|---|
| 1946 | 27.0 | 21.1 | 5.9 |
| 1947 | 29.5 | 15.8 | 13.7 |
| 1948 | 107.8 | 95.4 | 12.4 |
| 1949 | 90.3 | 77.2 | 13.1 |

Freight traffic recovered slowly during 1946 and 1947, while the economy was undergoing reconversion and suffering from the effects of a severe crop failure, and in 1947 the other carriers contributed almost as much to the year's increase as the railroads did. But as will shortly be made clear, 1948 was the decisive year in the postwar recovery, and for the attainment of that year's successes, about 88 per cent of the credit must go to the railroads. The absolute increment in 1949 fell back slightly after this great spurt, but the railroads continued to account for more than four fifths of the additional freight traffic.

Historical perspective on the impressive growth of Soviet railroad freight traffic since 1942 is provided by comparing the recovery from World War II with the Soviet Union's previous recovery experience, following World War I. In each case a trend of steady growth was sharply reversed by war, and several years were required to regain the prewar trend line. In each case the recovery years saw remarkably high annual percentage increases of railroad freight traffic. But in what respects did the two recoveries differ? Chart 14 suggests an answer.

The two curves of Chart 14 trace, against a logarithmic vertical scale, the annual level of railroad freight ton-kilometers from 1913 through 1928, and from 1937 through 1952. The years 1916 and 1940 are juxtaposed as the prewar peaks; 1918 and 1942 appear as the wartime troughs. Several significant differences between the two periods are immediately apparent. The recovery of Soviet railroad freight traffic from 1922 to 1926 was extraordinarily rapid; the growth rates of the 1940's came nowhere near matching

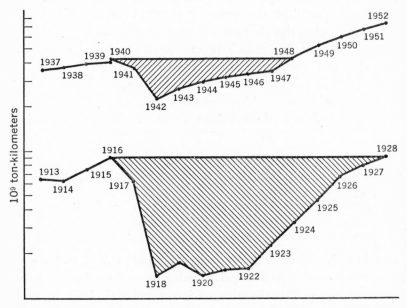

Chart 14. Railroad freight, USSR, by year, 1913–1928 and 1937–1952. Source: Table 46.

the earlier experience. At the same time, it is obvious that, relatively speaking, the fall in railroad freight traffic during the First World War was very much more drastic than during the Second. Reflection will suggest a number of essential dissimilarities between the underlying factors in the two periods, and a causal analysis would be extremely intricate. But we may note in summary fashion that the recent record shows both less fall and less rise than the 1916–1928 record. In a sense, there was less need for extraordinary growth in the 1940's than existed in the 1920's, since the prior contraction had been less severe. Or, to put it another way, there was more opportunity for rapid expansion in the 1920's than in the 1940's, since there was so much more ground to be regained.

After the First World War, it required ten years to reach the 1916 level of railroad freight traffic in the USSR. Regaining the 1940 level after the Second World War required only six years. The areas enclosed by the two level lines suggest the relative differences in ground lost as a result of the

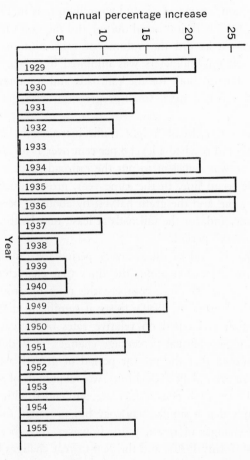

*Chart 15. Annual percentage increases, railroad freight traffic, USSR, 1928–1940 and 1949–1955. Source: Table 46.*

two conflicts. It is clear that, through checking the initial drop in railroad freight traffic and maintaining steady growth after 1942, the Soviet government was able to avert a recurrence of the calamitous deficiencies that had to be made up during the 1920's.

Further examination of the upper curve shows that between 1944 and

1947 only modest increases in railroad freight traffic were obtained. These were the years of reconversion and adjustment, and other sectors of the economy were experiencing great difficulties. The gross output of all industry fell from a wartime peak in 1944 by about 12 per cent in 1945, and declined again by about 17 per cent in 1946.[1] A disastrous drought reduced the subnormal grain harvest of around 66 million tons in 1945 to 61 million in 1946. During 1947, both industrial output and the grain harvest registered substantial increases, as did the volume of railroad tons originated, but growth in railroad ton-kilometers was inhibited by a marked drop in the average length of haul. Both for the railroads and for total transportation, the gains of 1946 and 1947 made small progress toward regaining the prewar level.

In 1948, however, railroad freight traffic increased by 27 per cent over the previous year, and reached a level 8 per cent over 1940. As can be seen on Chart 14, this rise was sufficient to put the railroads back on a crude 1942–1952 logarithmic trend line. In the same year, gross industrial output rose by about 27 per cent, and the grain harvest by about 19 per cent. All in all, it was a good year, and, for the railroads at least, may be thought of as completing the "recovery" period.[2]

If 1948 marks the end of the recovery period for railroads, subsequent growth represents expansion along the lines that characterized the 1928–1940 period. We may therefore compare the rates of growth observed in recent years with those of the 1930's, to see if significant differences emerge. Since our attention is focused on relative rates of increase, it should be interesting to compare annual percentage changes, as is done in Chart 15.

It will be recalled that the prewar period of growth was divided by a temporary plateau around 1932–1933 into two subperiods of rapid expansion. Each began with very high rates of increase, and ended with quite low rates. Chart 15 indicates that a similar tendency has prevailed during 1949–1954. The percentage changes of recent years, however, have been more modest than those of the stormy 1930's, and the year-to-year changes have been more regular. Inauguration of the First Five Year Plan led to a burst of railroad freight traffic growth, which petered out to a 0.1 per cent rise in 1933. The strenuous campaign to overcome freight backlogs then led to annual rises of 20 to 25 per cent for three years, but toward the close of the 1930's the yearly increases sank to below 5 per cent. In 1949 railroad freight traffic increased by some 17 per cent over 1948, while thereafter the annual growth subsided gently to around 7.5 per cent in 1953 and 1954. The 1955 rise of 13 per cent marks a renewed spurt of rail freight traffic, though a far less violent one.

If there were theoretical and historical justification for assuming a regular five- or six-year pattern of freight traffic growth in the USSR, these three periods would certainly lend empirical weight to a cyclical theory.

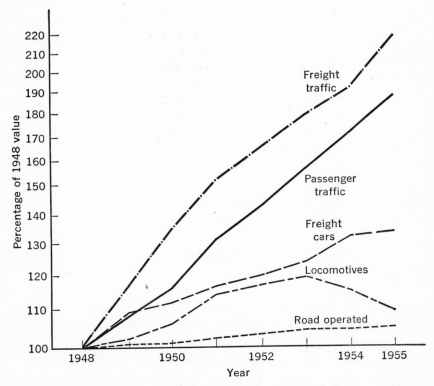

*Chart 16. Railroad traffic and railroad facilities, 1948–1955. Source: Table 32.*

However, the rationale for such a theory would have to rest on recurrence of underlying causal factors; and, since so many of the relevant factors (such as structure of governmental economic policy, composition of party leadership, and relation of freight traffic to physical output) have clearly been different during 1949–1954 from what they were in 1928–1933 or 1934–1940, there does not seem to be any basis here for positing a stable five- or six-year pattern. In any case, a weighing of the factors determining rail freight traffic trends will be deferred to the final chapter of this study.

Turning now to trends in Soviet railroad traffic and railroad facilities during the 1948–1955 period, and comparing them with developments during the prewar industrialization years, we find another set of significant differences and similarities. Chart 16 presents the record visually in the form employed for Chapters 3 and 4. Annual figures for freight and passenger traffic are plotted on a logarithmic vertical scale, together with data for the number of freight cars, freight locomotives, and kilometers of road utilized to produce this traffic. It is clear that once again output growth has substantially exceeded the expansion of railroad facilities — that more intensive utilization of equipment has been a major factor in railroad performance during the postwar expansion period. Railroad freight traffic in 1955 was about 118 per cent more than it had been in 1948, and passenger traffic was about 88 per cent larger, yet road operated had increased by less than 5 per cent, locomotives in road freight service by some 9 per cent, and freight cars by 34 per cent. The locomotive series shows a decline of roughly 700 locomotives after 1953 — a development that may reflect retirement of old locomotives and replacement with a smaller number of more powerful engines, or which may merely reflect estimating error.

While postwar expansion for the railroads shows a family resemblance to both the prewar subperiods, pronounced differences in absolute dimensions must also be emphasized. The absolute growth in rail freight traffic from 1949 through 1955 was 525 billion metric ton-kilometers, or about 75 billion per year. By contrast, the increment of 1940 over 1928 was about 322 billion ton-kilometers, or approximately 27 billion per year. Annual additions in the postwar period, that is, were almost 3 times the prewar standard. Passenger traffic, however, showed no such expansion, rising in 1949–1955 by about 66 billion passenger-kilometers, and in 1929–1940 by 73 billion. On an annual basis the recent passenger increments have been about as large as those of 1930–1932, though the level of passenger traffic is approaching twice that of the early peak. The freight traffic growth in 1929–1940 was 4.4 times the passenger traffic growth; in 1949–1955 the freight traffic increment has been almost 8 times the passenger growth. Clearly the railroads in recent years have reflected the economy's emphasis on industrial activity.

These increments of railroad output have been obtained with smaller additions to railroad facilities than were associated with the 1928–1940 growth. In the prewar period the railroad system added 12,259 kilometers of first main track (excluding acquisitions), 2,070 freight locomotives in road service, and 380,000 freight cars (in two-axle units) to its plant between 1928 and 1940. By contrast, the 1948–1955 additions amounted to some 5,000 kilometers of new roadway, 720 freight locomotives in road service, and 265,000 freight cars. That the Soviet railroad system, which in 1948 could plausibly be described as straining its capacity to the utmost, should have proved capable of drawing on still further "internal reserves" to obtain these increments of output is unquestionably a remarkable achievement. The evidence appears to cast doubt on any easy assumption that additions to traffic output require proportional additions to railroad plant and equipment. In the period since the railroads regained the prewar level, the governmental policy of demanding increased output in the absence of correspondingly enlarged facilities seems to have borne fruit, just as it did in the 1928–1940 period. It is understandable that modernization of the fairly primitive 1928 railroad system should have permitted greatly improved performance — the postwar record of continued intensification in the use made of a more up-to-date system seems still more impressive.

In this frame of reference it may be instructive to inquire briefly into the nature of the additional facilities that have assisted the railroads, along with more effective utilization of existing facilities, in achieving this record. Clearly there must have been qualitative improvement in, as well as quantitative growth of, operated roadway, freight locomotives, and freight cars to handle additional traffic, along with generally improved integration of men and equipment. How has it been done? The technical character of Soviet railroad operating practice will be dealt with briefly in the next chapter; here only some quantitative indicators will be examined.

Not the least surprising aspect of this record is the fact that, in a formal sense at least, it has been completely unplanned. Developments between 1945 and 1955 have taken quite a different course from what was laid down in the Fourth and Fifth Five Year Plans. This can be seen in the accompanying tabulation of plans and performance, showing absolute increments for each quinquennium.[3] (See p. 118.) The data are rough, but the railroads clearly have handled much larger increments of freight traffic in these two five-year periods than was intended, while receiving only from a third to three quarters of the new facilities assigned to them. In 1950, the freight traffic increment was 32 per cent larger than planned, and in 1955 the excess was 57 per cent, comparing performance with the terminal year targets of the Fourth and Fifth Five Year Plans. Yet only about half the new trackage, signaling facilities, and freight cars scheduled for delivery to the railroads were actually received. Obviously this required the railroads to load their facilities even more heavily than they were supposed to.

| Increments | 1946–1950 Plan | 1946–1950 Actual | 1951–1955 Plan | 1951–1955 Actual | 1956–1960 Plan |
|---|---|---|---|---|---|
| First main track (kilometers) | 10,300 | 5,000 | 8,500 | 3,800 | 6,500 |
| Second track (kilometers) | 12,500 | 4,000 | 6,500 | 4,700 | 6,600 |
| Other tracks (kilometers) | 8,400 | 4,400 | 6,200 | 3,800 | 3,600 |
| Auto. signaling (kilometers) | 10,400 | 4,800 | 9,500 | 4,200 | 15,000 |
| Freight cars (thousands) | 472.5 | 210.0 | — | 169.3 | 255.0 |
| Freight traffic (billion ton-km.) | 218 | 288 | 235 | 369 | 403 |
| Passenger traffic (billion pass.-km.) | 32 | 21 | — | 54 | — |

Comparison of the three postwar plans shows also that the government expects to continue benefiting from intensified utilization during the current plan period. The freight traffic increment in 1960 is set down as some 174 per cent of the planned increment for 1950–1955, in spite of the fact that planned additions to trackage are smaller. Of course with less ambitious facilities targets, the proportion of fulfillment can presumably be higher, though there is no railroad precedent for overfulfillment. It should be noted, in comparing 1951–1955 with 1946–1950, that the early postwar years involved considerable restoration of damaged plant, as opposed to new construction, and that the latter was probably larger during the Fifth Five Year Plan than during the fourth. In connection with freight cars, the figure for actual increments is a net increase in the number at work, while the plan targets are for new units built, so the comparison understates the degree of accomplishment. Nevertheless, the crude data make it clear that there is no marked upward trend in plans for railroad expansion — if anything, there is evidence of a modest decline.

These comparisons between over-all plans and performance suggest an observation that is borne out by detailed review of individual projects. Soviet discussions of building plans, and some of the foreign observations derived from them, have a certain breathless quality that is quite misleading. Projects generally have a long history, and almost always take longer to complete than was anticipated. Seen in their true time perspective, the grandiose construction feats of the plan era appear both less awesome and more credible. The South Siberian trunk line, which has been the biggest new line of the postwar period, is a case in point. When the Minister of Transportation discussed railroads in the Fourth Five Year Plan (in a public lecture on October 30, 1946, of which 110,000 copies were printed), he said "the South Siberian trunk line from Abakan to near Kuibyshev will extend for almost 4000 kilometers." [4] What he did not point out was that 31 per cent of the total length of the new route was already built, and that construction of another 17 per cent would not even begin until after 1950. Thus the actual amount scheduled for near-term construction was 2003 kilometers,[5] or half the total. Moreover, it developed that none of this construction was finished during the fourth plan period, with just under 1000 kilometers coming into operation during the fifth plan period and the balance still under construction during the Sixth Five Year Plan. Now that five Soviet five-year plans can be compared with their subsequent operating periods, we may note an important plan characteristic: project lists are exhaustive, and the emerging situation has determined which projects among the total should be carried out at any given time. In this case, for example, other demands were evidently given priority over the South Siberian trunk line. To point this out is not to disparage Soviet construction planning, but merely to suggest that future five-year plan project lists should be considered agenda rather than firm commitments.

Not only are projects listed in a five-year plan frequently deferred to subsequent periods, but occasionally a project not on the docket at all will, because of a changed situation, be rapidly brought to completion. A good example is provided by the Chardzhou-Kungrad line, built along the Amu Darya River (the Oxus of ancient times), toward the Aral Sea. There has long been a dream of connecting the middle Volga Valley with Central Asia by a line south of the Aral Sea, and it was mentioned from time to time during the 1928–1940 period, but no action was taken.[6] It was not among the lines slated for construction in the Fourth Five Year Plan. Yet in the summer of 1947 the government decided to build a line northwest from the Bukhara region to the cotton-growing oases on the lower Amu Darya. The work was put in charge of an energetic official, who made rapid progress until (as he complained in *Gudok*) a shortage of secondhand rail from neighboring railroads developed in the summer of 1948.[7] Construction languished somewhat in 1949 and 1950, but the decision late in 1950 to divert the lower Amu Darya back into its prehistoric stream bed west to the Caspian Sea, and to erect a hydroelectric power station at Takhia Tash south of the Aral Sea, revived the project. The first train reached Takhia Tash in February 1952. Under the Fifth Five Year Plan the line as far as Kungrad has been completed, and surveying has started on an extension northwestward to Makat, near Guryev at the head of the Caspian Sea.

The South Siberian trunk line has rapidly taken on the function of off-loading the most heavily taxed portion of the main Siberian trunk line, and it exemplifies a number of smaller projects of this type. The Chardzhou-Kungrad line is typical of several other postwar lines built to initiate or improve access to specific resource sites. In each case the construction can be defined as intensive rather than extensive, in the concrete sense that it facilitates higher-density use of an established system rather than spreading lightly traveled line into pioneer country. Thus part of the answer to the question of how Soviet railroads managed their traffic and line increments lies in their having confined new construction to projects with a high capacity to release traffic pressures.

While the preceding comparison of plans with performance accurately portrays the shortfalls in new facilities, it fails to emphasize the usefulness of the additional facilities that were obtained. The length of second main track operated did not regain its 1940 level until around 1954, but the 8700 kilometers brought into use between 1945 and 1955 probably includes a good deal of new second track in heavily burdened stretches of the system, while old second tracks in the Baltic Republics and western European Russia may still not have been restored to operation. The 5000 or 6000 kilometers of yard tracks added to the network since 1948 similarly can be assumed to have contributed substantially to traffic-handling capacity at bottleneck points throughout the country. Even in the sphere of signaling facilities, where Soviet railroads are quite backward by Western standards, several thousand kilometers of modern signaling have been installed since 1948, raising very greatly the train-occupancy abilities of many parts of the network.

These forms of intensive development have contributed to a steady rise in the over-all density of traffic on the Soviet railroad system. Comparative data for prewar and postwar periods are set forth in Table 8, showing the ratio of freight traffic to the length of the railroad network.

Columns one and two in Table 8 use route mileage or the length of first main track as a denominator, while columns three and four show the ratio of freight traffic to the sum of first, second, and yard tracks. Results are not significantly different. The 1940 density was 3.2 times the 1928 density according to the first measure, and 3.0 according to the second. Density in 1945 was about 26 per cent below the 1940 level, and by 1948 the prewar peak had been regained or slightly exceeded. In 1950, Soviet railroads were being crowded with about one third more freight traffic per mile than in 1940, and by 1955 the density of freight traffic was slightly more than twice the prewar level. Anticipations for 1960 under the Sixth Five Year Plan run

Table 8. *Average freight traffic densities, USSR railroads, selected years, 1928–1960 plan* (thousands of metric tariff ton–kilometers per year)

| Year | Per kilometer of road operated | | Per kilometer of total trackage | |
|---|---|---|---|---|
| | Density | Index (1940 = 100) | Density | Index (1940 = 100) |
| 1928 | 1,215 | — | 759 | — |
| 1940 | 4,344 | 100 | 2,259 | 100 |
| 1945 | 2,781 | 64 | 1,733 | 77 |
| 1948 | 3,876 | 89 | 2,349 | 104 |
| 1950 | 5,169 | 119 | 3,111 | 138 |
| 1955 | 8,057 | 185 | 4,715 | 209 |
| 1960 (plan) | 10,862 | 250 | 6,173 | 273 |

Source: Computed as ratios of freight traffic data in Table 46 over road operated data (annual averages) in Table 59 and total trackage data (year-end figures) in Table 60.

in terms of increasing freight traffic density by still another 32 to 35 per cent, and if the past is any guide, the rise will be even more marked. Comparing the prewar growth period of 1928–1940 with a postwar period, 1948–1960 (plan), of equal length, we find a 2.8-fold rise anticipated currently, as contrasted with the earlier 3.2-fold rise. Again it is clear that government policy continues to rest on squeezing substantially greater output from only moderately increased facilities.

Turning to the freight car stock as another essential component of railroad freight operations, we find a similar situation. Table 9 presents rough

Table 9. *Estimated freight cars on line, USSR railroads, selected years, 1928–1955* (thousands of cars)

| Year | Two-axle cars | Four-axle cars | Total |
|---|---|---|---|
| 1928 | 305.8 | 17.8 | 323.6 |
| 1940 | 410.1 | 155.5 | 565.6 |
| 1945 | 380.5 | 148.0 | 528.5 |
| 1950 | 413.1 | 236.5 | 649.6 |
| 1955 | 289.0 | 383.2 | 672.2 |
| Increments | | | |
| 1928–1940 | 104.3 | 137.7 | 242.0 |
| 1945–1950 | 32.6 | 88.5 | 121.1 |
| 1950–1955 | −124.1 | 146.7 | 22.6 |

Source: These are synthetic figures, estimated through applying percentage with four axles data from Table 65 to computed figures for that fraction of the total freight car fleet actually at work, from column 3 of Table 63.

estimates for the number of freight cars in active use, divided between the small, two-axle, European type and the large, four-axle, American type, at various times from 1928 through 1955. The railroads in 1940 were using about 100,000 more small cars and 140,000 more large cars than in 1928 — clearly a substantial investment and one that enabled them to handle much more freight traffic. The 1945 supply in use was some 5 to 7 per cent lower than in 1940, but it increased steadily, first largely as a result of reconditioning damaged and bad-order cars. From about 1948 on, a large-scale program of freight car construction has provided carrying capacity for the increments of freight traffic pressed on the railroads.

It might appear that the 1950–1955 increment in active freight cars was less than a fifth of the 1945–1950 increment, and thus that the building program of recent years has not matched earlier feats. Closer examination shows, on the contrary, that during the Fifth Five Year Plan somewhat more four-axle cars were added to the active fleet than during the whole 1928–1940 period, and that the modest net addition reflects retirement of almost 125,000 old-fashioned two-axle cars. This qualitative change in the composition of the freight car fleet, since the new cars all have automatic couplings, automatic brakes, and lower relative tare weights, must have contributed appreciably to the recent performance of the railroad system.

It has become clear in the last decade that railroads all over the world face a technological revolution in their motive power. In a few countries, such as the United States, the old steam locomotive has practically disappeared, while in others the change is just beginning. The diesel-electric locomotive has emerged in the United States as the new dominant form, but electric locomotives still have a place, and other engines, such as the gas turbine locomotive, may gain in importance. It is to be expected that each country will react to these technological changes in its own individual way, depending on its stage of development and on the age composition of its existing equipment, among other things. However, a brief review of the Soviet record in this sphere will at least provide perspective on the factors that make one form of power more attractive than another.

In the 1920's Soviet railroads used only steam locomotives. There was, however, a special party attitude on power sources that influenced the railroad system as well as the rest of the economy. Lenin and others had evidently noticed that electric power was a glamorous and rapidly expanding feature of advanced industrial economies in the 1890–1920 era, and they consequently made it a dramatic element in their early blueprints. With the advent of five-year plans, the electric power industry received special attention, and the output of electric power has increased more rapidly than any of the other major indicators of Soviet industrialization.

In the railroad sector, the introduction of electric traction on lines previously operated with steam locomotives was somewhat vaguely proposed in 1920 for almost all major trunk lines, and continued to be regularly proposed thereafter for a considerable list of key routes. By 1940, starting from no electrified line at all prior to 1929, electric traction had actually been introduced on 1870 kilometers (almost 1200 miles) of operated roadway. About three quarters of this total consisted of line electrified to carry long-haul freight, with the remainder electrified to handle suburban passenger traffic around major cities. The total represented only a small fraction of the early grandiose plans, and was less than half the mileage currently operated in the United States, but it nevertheless constituted a substantial beginning.

The Fourth Five Year Plan called for electrification of 5325 kilometers of railroad line, including several hundred kilometers of restoration on previously electrified line in occupied territory. By the end of 1950, only 1047 kilometers of new electrification had been put into operation, representing 20 per cent of the ambitious 1946 construction target.

During the Fifth Five Year Plan period, railroad electrification speeded up considerably, with an additional 2,267 kilometers of electrified line coming into operation, or 58 per cent of the amount called for in the plan. The increment represented a 74 per cent increase over the length of electrified line on hand in 1950. The Sixth Five Year Plan calls for another 8,100 kilometers of electrification, and if the target is, say, 75 per cent fulfilled, the Soviet railroad system will have about 11,400 kilometers of electrified line, including the major route from Moscow as far east as Lake Baikal.

The question of the economic feasibility of large-scale railroad electrification in the USSR would make a fascinating topic for combined technical and economic research. One of the central elements in such an analysis would have to be the treatment of capital charges. When a group of American railroad experts toured the Soviet railroad system in the summer of 1930 as consultants to the Soviet government, their final report stated:

We do not think electrification of USSR railroads is justified to any considerable extent. Possibly some electric passenger train service should be provided for a short distance out of Leningrad and perhaps also the electric passenger service out of Moscow should be expanded somewhat. No freight traffic conditions exist or are in prospect for the near future which cannot, in our opinion, be met more economically by modern steam railway operation than by electric operation, considering the high cost of electrification.

Electric motors are in many ways more satisfactory for handling railway trains than steam locomotives. They are cleaner; they require no water or fuel service; they are capable of more nearly continuous operation between stoppings; they will handle trains at more nearly uniform speed and perform as efficiently in winter as in summer.

The only reason electric motors do not replace steam locomotives is that it costs more to use them than it does to use steam, including, of course, the interest and depreciation on the cost of installation.[8]

During the 1930's Soviet engineers persisted in electrifying suburban passenger lines around Moscow, and several long-haul freight lines where special conditions favored the change, though the grandiose schemes of the Politburo remained unimplemented. Traffic densities soon doubled or tripled over the levels reviewed by the American technicians, thus bringing down the cost of electrification per ton-mile of traffic carried, and some projects could perhaps be supported as yielding valuable experimental evidence.

But the crucial question here, as suggested in the report cited above, concerns the treatment of capital charges. It has been shown by Gregory Grossman that doctrinal phobias in the USSR have weakened the normal market barrier against overly capital-intensive construction projects.[9] That is, in cases where adequate recognition of capital costs would have brought a clear decision against, for example, electrification of a railroad line, the scheme might nevertheless be carried through. Have there been such cases on Soviet railroads? It would be a feasible research project to assemble the data for a case-by-case analysis of 1928–1940 railroad electrification projects, designed to evaluate their contemporary economic validity.

At present a new range of technical-economic issues presents itself for evaluation. We have seen that freight traffic densities have already reached twice the 1940 level and will increase still further. Since 1945 several engineering developments have made railroad electrification cheaper and more feasible, and many European rail systems have increased their electrified mileage substantially. Moreover there is now the alternative of the diesel-electric locomotive to be considered. In recent years there has been a quickening stream of discussion among Soviet railroad technicians as to the optimum balance of motive power on Soviet railroads, the trend of which is most revealing.

Around 1948 a relative shortage of petroleum seemed to be a decisive consideration. When V. N. Obraztsov, the railroads' senior engineering spokesman, gave a public lecture in 1948 on railroad electrification prospects in the USSR, he reviewed the many advantages of diesels, but then added:

However, the diesel-electric locomotive has one very great disadvantage: it requires liquid fuel. Comrade Stalin noted the desirability of having 60 million tons of oil per year in place of the 35.4 million planned for 1950. But we need oil for aviation, warships, automobiles, and tractors. It would hardly be expedient to exchange all our steam locomotives for diesel-electrics. Besides, electric power from hydroelectric stations is much cheaper. From this, the desirable direction for our future power policy is perfectly clear.[10]

Since then, however, Soviet petroleum production has increased very rapidly, and by March 1955 the official in charge of the Diesel-Electric Locomotive Administration of the Railroad Ministry could say, "Our fuel balance now permits wider use of diesel-electric locomotives. Rapidly growing petroleum production has led to some use of fuel oil instead of coal for steam locomotives, and diesel-electrics are more economical of fuel oil than this." [11] The implication is, clearly, that petroleum had become available even for relatively low-priority uses.

Scattered data indicate that by 1955 electric locomotives were handling 8.4 per cent of Soviet freight ton-kilometers, diesel-electric locomotives were handling 5.7 per cent, and the balance of 85.9 per cent was still being handled by steam locomotives. Diesel-electric motive power was employed on about 7,000 out of 121,000 kilometers of roadway; diesel-electric locomotives made up 2.2 per cent of the total locomotive stock. This form of motive power, with its small water requirements as compared to steam traction, was especially concentrated in regions where the water supply was deficient in quantity or quality. Electrified sections, on the other hand, were principally concentrated in regions with steep gradients or around major cities.

At a major railroadmen's conference in May 1954, L. M. Kaganovich said: "I am for the steam locomotive and against those who imagine that we will not have any steam locomotives in the future. This machine is sturdy, stubborn, and won't give up, but it must not be idealized. We must say frankly that in the future the steam locomotive will remain, but that the leading locomotives will be diesel-electric and electric." [12] This proved to be a transition statement. By the summer of 1955 the Party Central Committee had issued a decree calling once more for a huge program of railroad electrification, and at the Twentieth Congress in February 1956 Kaganovich said: "The Central Committee of the Party correctly and decisively raised the question of a rapid transfer of the railroads to electric traction, which is the main link in their technological reorganization. . . . Railroad electrification, and also the introduction of diesel-electric locomotives, will be the main factor in raising the railroads' carrying capacity." [13] Under the Sixth Five Year Plan, these two forms of motive power are to handle 40 to 45 per cent of the freight traffic by 1960. The locomotive-building program calls for 2000 electric locomotives and 2250 diesel-electrics over the five years, with production of steam locomotives to cease after 1957.[14] The change will evidently be concentrated at the end of the five-year period, since anticipated annual production of locomotives appears to be scheduled somewhat as follows:[15]

| Year | Electric | Diesel-electric |
|------|----------|-----------------|
| 1955 (actual) | 194 | 134 |
| 1956 | 200 | 150 |
| 1957 | 300 | 150 |
| 1958 | 400 | 160 |
| 1959 | 550 | 170 |
| 1960 | 550 | 1630 |

With eight or nine thousand locomotives currently in active freight service, such a production program will clearly only initiate the motive power revolution. It is perhaps roughly comparable to developments on American railroads in the late 1940's, some ten years earlier.

But as the USSR moves away from steam locomotives, should the trend be to electric traction, or to diesel-electrics? The factors involved are largely objective, technical elements of railroad activity, quite independent of political forms, and faced by railroads all over the world. This appears to be a field in which Soviet technicians could usefully exchange views with European and American railroad officials for the mutual benefit of all concerned, including the railroad officials of countries like India. Traffic densities, relative costs of electricity and fuel oil, capital availability, and other relevant considerations will of course vary from one economy to another, but each could learn from the experience of the others.

It may be worth while to make one final observation concerning the investment and resource impact of the coming Soviet motive power revolution. Obviously the construction of thousands of electric and diesel-electric locomotives, to say nothing of power transmission facilities and servicing installations, will require a huge outlay of resources. But current maintenance and replacement of the steam locomotive fleet also involves a substantial drain on steel and other supplies — one of the chief attractions of the diesel-electric locomotive is its economy in this respect. Consequently the net impact of a changeover will be substantially reduced, and is perhaps fully compatible with continuation of strict government rationing of investment in the railroad sector.

# 7 SOVIET RAILROAD OPERATIONS

A Western observer of the Soviet transportation system is frequently puzzled by technical aspects of Soviet railroad operations. As we have seen, certain measures indicate higher efficiency and more intensive utilization than we are used to, while other performance indexes suggest that Soviet railroads are technologically backward. Gaps in the statistical record raise doubts concerning the meaning and reliability of such fragments as come to light. Under these conditions, speculation on Soviet railroad capabilities can range from the extreme of applying engineering coefficients derived from experience with the most backward and undeveloped railroad systems, to the other extreme of applying intensified versions of the factors appropriate to advanced United States railroad practice. Clearly it would be desirable to narrow the range of such speculations.

Although, broadly speaking, railroad technology is standardized all over the world, it permits significant variation in the way its elements are combined. General economic principles would lead us to expect that differences from one country to another in the relative scarcity of inputs and the relative demand for types of transportation output could plausibly be used to explain observed differences in railroad operations. If the unusual features of Soviet railroad operating practice can be associated with specific characteristics of the supply and demand situation facing Russian railroads, the Soviet record should become both more understandable and more believable.

The present chapter, therefore, has two purposes: first, to sketch the main characteristics of Soviet railroad operating practice in such a way as to indicate precisely its strong and weak points; second, to suggest economic reasons for the observed developments, thereby enhancing the credibility of an unfamiliar set of relationships. The discussion makes use of fairly extensive figures from the appendices, converted to American units of measurement (miles and short tons) so that Soviet practice may be more readily compared with our own. The analysis here is confined to freight transportation, leaving comparative review of passenger operations to Chapter 10.

Probably the most important difference between Soviet and American railroad practice lies in their relations with the senders and receivers of freight. In the United States, the kind of railroad domination that gave rise to the Granger movement in the Middle West after the Civil War has passed, and the typical railroad attitude toward clients stresses a willingness to serve and an almost humble eagerness to retain or obtain business. Not so in the USSR. Since the middle 1930's, although the railroads' duty to provide prompt, reliable freight service for enterprises sending and receiving freight is noted, the balance of power has been on the railroads' side. They are not anxious to obtain more business. Government policy instead emphasizes the enterprise's duty to keep its demand for freight transportation to a minimum, and if possible to use other carriers than the railroads.

Many of the implications of this aspect of Soviet transportation theory and practice have already been analyzed; it is here only necessary to recall them to the reader's mind, and point out their relevance for operating procedures. The managers of any economic unit attempting to maximize internal efficiency, that is, to minimize costs, are likely to find that in their relations with other economic units, clashes of interest arise. Practices that reduce costs for an enterprise may raise costs for the units it deals with. This ungainly feature of modern industrial organization is not exorcised by "government ownership of the means of production." The steel industry and the railroads, for example, may both be owned by the state, yet their respective interests in matters of freight transportation may diverge significantly. It becomes necessary, then, to adjudicate the problems that arise, and Soviet policy for the last twenty years has tended to favor the railroads in resolving issues between them and their clients.

The matter of trainload consignments will provide a clear-cut example of what is involved. Railroad operating costs can be substantially reduced if an entire train can be loaded at the point of origination, with all the cars consigned to a single destination. The original assembly of cars need not be co-ordinated with loadings at neighboring enterprises to form a trainload consigned to a given general area. While the train is under way, no cars need be detached for delivery to particular consignees. And at the point of termination, the railroad's task in sorting the cars for delivery to clients' sidings is reduced to a minimum. This kind of train movement maximizes efficiency from the carrier's point of view.

But consider the effect on the shipper and receiver. For them, the smooth flow of relatively small receipts and shipments, which would in general minimize their costs, is supplanted by intermittent mass arrivals and departures. Clearly much more storage space will be required. The plant's shipping department will have a serious peak-load problem. If cheapness and convenience for the carrier come at the expense of higher costs and inconvenience for the client, then in the USSR the railroads' interests tend to prevail.[1]

These trainload consignments are most easily arranged for commodities like coal and iron ore, and the practice is by no means unknown in the United States. But in the USSR, determined efforts are made to extend the same principle to movements of other commodities too, involving clients for whom the practice is, to say the least, highly inconvenient. American shippers and receivers, within limits, can expect the railroads to call for and deliver even single cars in a kind of custom service. While such service exists also in the USSR, it appears that the railroads are far more reluctant to provide it, and that Soviet clients are under pressure to arrange their transportation demands so as not to complicate the railroads' work.

The most striking measurable symbol of this difference in relationship is provided by figures for the average number of hours spent in loading and unloading freight cars. Over the past 25 years, loading and unloading operations at each end of a freight car trip have required from as much as 60 hours to as little as 32 hours in the USSR (reviewing yearly averages for all freight traffic). United States records do not provide a breakdown of freight car time, since evidently it is not of so much concern, and hence year-to-year variation cannot be studied. But a 1933 analysis showed that in 1932, 47 per cent of a freight car's time was spent being loaded or unloaded, and it was estimated in 1955 that some 125–135 hours per trip were used in United States loading and unloading operations.[2]

Why are loading and unloading operations in the USSR so much faster than in the United States? Again, the explanation appears to be a difference in the balance of forces. American railroads have not found it expedient to press their clients for prompt loading and unloading. The level of demurrage charges has evidently not been a strong deterrent when cars provide a kind of auxiliary warehouse for crowded plants, or when the costs of rapid loading and unloading would be high. In the USSR, on the other hand, relatively high demurrage charges have been traditional, and for the last twenty years or more they have been reinforced through the application of criminal proceedings against plant officials who systematically delay freight cars. Soviet railroads can afford to insist on prompt loading and unloading, being backed up by the government.

Behind this difference in bargaining power lies a more fundamental explanation for the operating practice of the two systems. The stock of freight cars in the United States, while not adequate to meet seasonal peak demands in particular territories, has been relatively ample in terms of over-all traffic demands during the last 20 or 30 years. This is demonstrated by the fact that in 1943, the peak year for wartime railroad freight traffic, revenue ton-miles were more than three times as large as in 1932 at the trough of the depression, while the 1943 stock of freight cars was 18 per cent smaller than the 1932 stock. Evidently the United States stock of freight cars was not being taxed in the 1930's. After 1943 a similar situation developed. The 1950 stock of freight cars was 2 per cent smaller than the 1943 stock, but revenue ton-miles of freight traffic in 1950 were 19 per cent below the 1943 peak.

Soviet experience has been quite different. During the prewar period of forced industrialization, from 1928 through 1940, the number of freight cars in use (measured in two-axle units) more than doubled, but the volume of freight traffic increased almost 4.5 times. Clearly the pressure on freight cars grew more intense. The Nazi invasion gave rise to a somewhat different situation, as pointed out in Chapter 5; the number of freight cars in use fell by 18 per cent from 1940 to 1942, but the volume of freight traffic dropped 45 per cent, so that in a relative sense the pressure on freight cars was eased. Growth since that time, however, has brought a return of car stringency. The 1950 volume of freight traffic was 2.6 times the 1942 level, while the number of freight cars in use increased by a little more than 50 per cent. Under these conditions it is not hard to understand why Soviet freight cars must be kept in motion as much as possible.

Not only are the clients of Sovet railroads urged to load and unload freight cars quickly, but they feel considerable pressure to perform the operations straight around the clock. With the objective of approaching continuous operation, Soviet railroads have carried on a postwar campaign to raise nighttime loading and unloading to half the daily total. For shippers and receivers working on a three-shift basis, this drive may not be seriously inconvenient, but for many enterprises it must present appreciable difficulties. Again the attempt is to induce clients to conform to practices increasing railroad efficiency. There is no Soviet counterpart for the American practice of allowing loading and unloading to cease on Saturdays, Sundays, and holidays.

A second set of factors that throw light on the operating characteristics of Soviet railroads relates to the mixed technical background of the system. In its present state it represents an unusual mixture of European and American steam railroad practice, combined with certain unique features of its own. The Soviet transportation economist T. S. Khachaturov has expressed the matter this way:

It is possible to recognize two main technical types of railway transport in economically developed countries: the American and European types. The American railways use heavy trains with a low density of movement. European railways use light trains with a high density of movement. Accordingly American railways employ heavy types of engines and four-axle freight cars of great capacity, but the number of double-track lines is low. The railways of most European countries use locomotives of considerably less power and almost exclusively double-axle freight cars, but the European railways have a high percentage of double-track lines. . . .

Before the revolution, Russia used the European type of railways, light engines and small double-axle wagons, and in addition the percentage of double-track lines was low.

[However] . . . the USSR with its extremely great distances and heavy bulk transport had to have that type of transport which could ensure the lowest freight costs. . . .

The railways of old Russia used light trains similar to those employed in Europe, but with a low density of traffic as in America. The railways of the USSR use heavyweight trains that approximate American weights. At the same time, they have a high density of traffic, as do European railways. Indeed, a new type of railway transport has been created, combining the best features of the American and European types of transport and ensuring a high level of efficiency in operation.[3]

As will become clearer in subsequent discussion, certain features of this argument are inaccurate, but it contains a large kernel of truth. The present Soviet railroad system does utilize heavier equipment than most European railways, and does attain much higher (over-all) traffic densities than American railroads. But waiving the issue of "better" or "worse," the point to be emphasized is that Soviet railroad practice corresponds to neither familiar type.

The process referred to by Khachaturov of transforming the old Russian railroad system into a heavier and more modern system has not yet been completed, and has not been applied uniformly over the whole network. On important trunk lines, for example, improved roadway has made possible the introduction of American-type freight locomotives and freight cars, while secondary branch lines are still operated (as in other countries) with light, old-fashioned equipment. Even on the modernized trunk lines, the roadway and equipment in general correspond to American practice of about twenty-five years ago, with a few recent improvements added.

In a broader sense, the contrast between Soviet and United States rail-

road operations reflects a simple difference in historical timing, for which
political blame or praise cannot be claimed. The American railroad system
was built before the appearance of the automobile, and was largely built
ahead of traffic. In Russia, although extensive railroad-building characterized
the final decades of the tsarist regime, the Soviet government inherited an
economy at a relatively early stage of economic development, with a thin
railroad network. The traffic capacity of American railroads in the twentieth
century has been ample, even more than ample, in relation to the demands
confronting it. In the USSR since 1928, on the other hand, traffic demands
have expanded much more rapidly than railroad facilities, and the government, far from building ahead of traffic, has held new construction to a low
level. The United States is thus fortunate in having inherited an ample
railroad network that is not hard pressed by current traffic demands. The
Soviet Union has not been so fortunate in its inheritance, and under its
leaders' policy of forced industrialization, the country has seen traffic demands outrun capacity. To a certain extent, therefore, American railroad
operating characteristics reflect pronounced underutilization while Soviet
indexes reflect intense overutilization. The explanation, in each case, is not
so much engineering desirability as historical necessity.

"The basic type of locomotive on the railroads of the USSR is the steam
locomotive, serving 97.8 per cent of the whole length of the network. Out
of the total number of locomotives on our railroads, 98.8 per cent are steam
locomotives." [4] While this 1948 statement relates to an era approaching its
end, as shown in the preceding chapter, it remains an accurate characteriza-
tion of the system we are reviewing. The small fraction of the locomotive
stock that is not steam-powered consists of both electric and diesel-electric
units, with the former outnumbering the latter. Not since 1930 has the
United States railroad system been so dominated by steam power.[5] Since
both diesel-electric and electric locomotives outperform the steam locomotive
in most respects, Soviet reliance on steam traction places the system at a
disadvantage in comparisons with current United States practice.

When we consider Soviet freight cars, the combination of European
and American practice that Khachaturov referred to is strikingly clear.
The 1928 freight car fleet consisted almost entirely of two-axle cars, with
hand brakes and hand couplings, carrying about 18 short tons of freight.
Soviet efforts in the 1930's and since have been directed toward replacing
these cars with large four-axle freight cars, of 44 to 65 ton capacity, equipped
with automatic brakes and couplings. However, contrary to the impression
left by Khachaturov in 1945, the transformation is only now being completed;

in 1955 less than 60 per cent of the freight cars had four axles, about 77 per cent had automatic couplings, and about 87 per cent had automatic brakes.[6] Consequently train speeds, train weights, and labor efficiency on the Soviet railroad system have until recently suffered seriously from the continued presence of old-fashioned rolling stock.

Another instance of mixed practice is provided by signaling facilities, which reflect a blend of modern automatic control systems with the primitive train-staff system still found in Europe. Major trunk lines have been equipped with automatic block signaling, and in recent years a few thousand miles of road have been operated with centralized traffic control, automatic train control, or automatic cab signaling. But the dominant method still appears to be an electrified version of the old Webb-Thompson-Smith train-staff system, which in 1940 accounted for about 70 per cent of the road operated. Track capacity and train speeds will clearly be limited by this kind of equipment, as compared with the devices familiar in United States practice.

The general condition of operated roadway varies widely from major trunk line to little-used outlying feeder, as is also true in the United States. In 1930, when the American railroad officials visited the USSR as advisory consultants, they stressed the need for improved ballast, more and larger ties, improved and heavier rails, more accurate track alignment, and reduction of gradients, as important elements of a modernization program.[7] Gradually these improvements have been applied to key routes. Nevertheless, such data as are available suggest that train speeds and operating safety in Russia are still limited by deficiencies on all these points. The average weight of rail, for example, which was 104 pounds per yard in the United States at the end of 1954, was then about 85 pounds per yard in the USSR.[8]

These differences between the railroad systems of the USSR and the United States, in respect to locomotives, freight cars, signaling equipment, roadway, and track, act in every case to place Soviet railroads at an operating disadvantage in comparison with American railroads. Train weights, train speeds, and operating safety are all adversely affected. In fact, the net impression they leave with an observer is considerable surprise that Soviet performance figures are as high as they are. For a review of the most important measures, we turn now to a comparison of operating averages.[9] A general measure of the intensity with which a railroad system is utilized is provided by the ratio of freight traffic moved to the length of the network. Table 10 shows the trend of this measure over the last thirty years in the USSR and the United States.

BOUNDARY
BETWEEN
"WEST" AND "EAST"

LIMIT OF NAZI
OCCUPATION

Murmansk
KOLA
PENINSULA
Vorkuta
COAL
FIELD
Salekhar

WHITE
SEA

Archangel

URAL
REGION

Baltic-
White Sea
Waterway

Lake
Ladoga

Kotlas

MIDDLE

Tallin
Leningrad

Vologda

Kirov

Europeiskaya Tavda
Aziatskaya
Tiumer
Molotov
Sverdlovsk

Riga

BAND

Sinarskaya
Kurga
Chelyabins

Warsaw
Minsk

OCCUPIED
Moscow
Gorky
Cheboksary
Kazan
Kanash
KAMA
Ufa
Magnitogorsk

SUB-MOSCOW
COALFIELD
Ryazan
Venev
Uzlovaya

TERRITORY

Orel
Penza
Syzran
Ekaterinovka
Kuibyshev

TERRITORY
Kursk
Voronezh

Kiev

Orsk

Liski
Balashov
Saratov

UKRAINE
Kharkov
Valuiki

Kandagach

Krivoi Rog
DONBAS
DON

Stalingrad
KAZA A

Odessa
Zaporozhy
Stalino
Lake Baskunchak
Makat

Mariupol
Kerch
Rostov-
on-Don
VOLGA-DON
CANAL
Astrakhan
Guryev

CRIMEA

ARA
SEA

See enlarged railroad plan right page
Tuapse

BLACK SEA
Sochi
CAUCASUS
Grozny
Makhach
Kala
CASPIAN
Kungrad
Takhia Tash

Batumi
Tbilisi
MTS
SOVIE

Baku
Krasnovodsk

SEA
Ashkhab

0    50    100         200 MILES

100  0  100         500 KILOMETERS

Railroads

Sam'l H Bryant '57

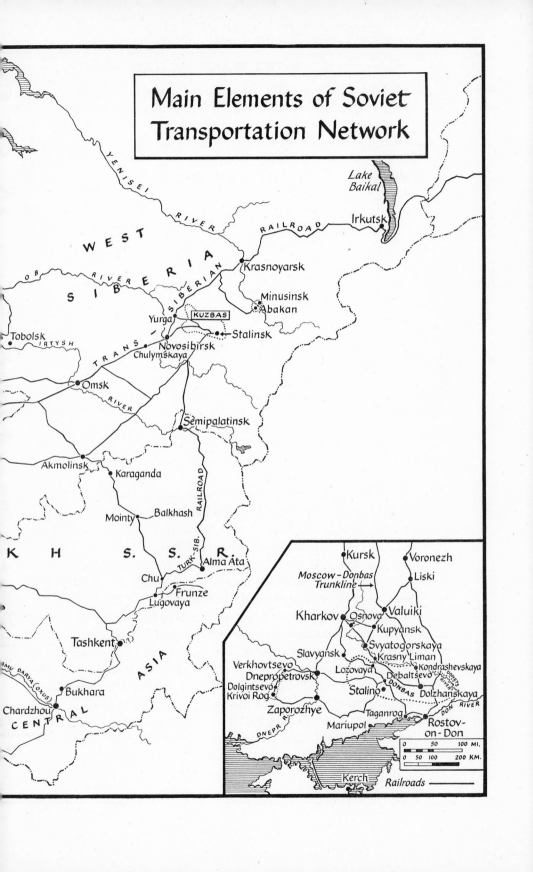

# Main Elements of Soviet Transportation Network

*Lake Baikal*

Irkutsk

YENISEI RIVER

RAILROAD

WEST

OB RIVER

S I B E R I A

Krasnoyarsk

Minusinsk
Abakan

TRANS - SIBERIAN

KUZBAS

Yurga

Stalinsk

Tobolsk

IRTYSH

Novosibirsk
Chulymskaya

Omsk

RIVER

Semipalatinsk

Akmolinsk

Karaganda

RAILROAD

Mointy

Balkhash

K H

S.

S. R.

Alma Ata

TURK-SIB.

Chu

Frunze
Lugovaya

Tashkent

A S I A

AMU DARYA (OXUS)

Bukhara

C E N T R A L

Chardzhou

### Inset map

Kursk

Voronezh

Liski

Moscow – Donbas
Trunkline →

Kharkov

Osnova

Valuiki

Kupyansk

Svyatogorskaya

Slavyansk

Krasny Liman

Verkhovtsevo

Lozovaya

Kondrashevskaya

Dnepropetrovsk

Debaltsevo

Dolgintsevo

DONBAS

Krivoi Rog

Stalino

Dolzhanskaya

Zaporozhye

Taganrog

DON RIVER

Mariupol

Rostov-
on-Don

DNEPR R.

| 0 | 50 | 100 MI. |
| 0 | 50 | 100 | 200 KM. |

Kerch

*Railroads* ————

In the second half of the 1920's, when United States railroads were busy and Soviet forced industrialization was just beginning, freight traffic density in the USSR was 89 per cent of the United States figure. With the advent of depression in America and five-year plans in the Soviet Union, density on USSR railroads moved quickly to over twice the United States level in the early 1930's. Furthermore, the second half of the decade saw a density

Table 10. *Freight traffic densities, USSR and United States railroads, five-year averages, 1926–1955* (*thousands of short ton–miles of revenue and nonrevenue freight per mile of road operated per year*)

| Period | USSR | United States | USSR as percentage of United States |
|--------|------|---------------|-------------------------------------|
| 1926–1930 | 1784 | 1994 | 89 |
| 1931–1935 | 2693 | 1228 | 219 |
| 1936–1940 | 4841 | 1583 | 306 |
| 1941–1945 | 3771[a] | 3029 | 124 |
| 1946–1950 | 4489 | 2808 | 160 |
| 1951–1955 | 7883 | 2830 | 279 |

[a] Average for 1942–1945 (1941 not available).

Sources: The USSR figures are ratios of total "operating ton-kilometers" (column 1 in Table 46 plus column 1 in Table 58) over the annual average of total road operated (column 1 of Table 59), computed as quotients of five-year sums. The factor for conversion to short ton–miles is 1.1023. The United States figures are from ICC, 1934, p. S-52; 1940, p. 56; 1950, p. 60; and AAR, 1956, p. 24. Exclusion of Class II and III railroads tends to raise average density slightly, but inclusion of trackage rights in road operated tends to lower it. Use of annual averages instead of year-end road operated figures would not alter the results appreciably. The traffic coverages for each country are roughly comparable, since the United States series includes nonrevenue freight and the Soviet series reflects actual distances moved rather than tariff distances.

on the Soviet system more than three times the current United States level, which had risen from depression lows but had not regained the levels of a decade earlier. It is in this kind of comparison that the contrast between overutilization and underutilization becomes striking.

During the 1941–1945 period, the density of freight traffic on United States railroads almost doubled the level of the preceding five years, reaching a point about 50 per cent above the density of the late 1920's. American railroads were brought into something approaching full use. In the USSR, on the other hand, invasion and destruction combined to lower freight traffic density by about one quarter. These divergent trends reduced the Soviet margin in density levels to only one-fourth over the American. The second half of the decade, however, saw a slight reduction in average United States freight density, and a rise in the Soviet average to 60 per cent above the United States level. During 1951–1955 the American average showed no gain, while Soviet freight traffic density increased some 75 per cent.

Hence once again the Soviet figure is about three times the network average for the United States.

These system-wide comparisons properly reflect the more intensive use of roadway in the USSR than in the United States. What they do not show is the extent to which the contrast is due to a very large mileage of lightly traveled feeder line in the United States. If all the mileage on which freight traffic amounted to less than 500,000 tons a year were excluded from the calculations for each country, the disparity in over-all densities would be substantially reduced. The results, in other words, do not mean that Soviet rail traffic densities are higher than American densities on every part of the network.

To illustrate the point, we may compare maximum densities on the two systems for a particular stretch of trunk line. In the USSR, the most heavily traveled freight sections are the Krasnyi Liman-Osnova line southeast of Kharkov in the Ukraine, and the Novosibirsk-Chulymskaya portion of the Trans-Siberian, in Western Siberia just west of Novosibirsk. Density on the former in 1940 was 27 million short ton–miles per mile of operated road, and by 1950 this level was probably at least regained. Density on the latter was 23 million in 1947 and by 1950 was probably over 27 million.[10] Detailed information covering short stretches of line in the United States is not readily available, but these levels are clearly exceeded. The most heavily traveled section of the Pennsylvania Railroad system, just west of Philadelphia, which is probably the most densely loaded stretch on the United States network, had a density of over 62 million short ton–miles per road mile in 1947, and in 1944 this figure was at least 74 million.[11] Over-all Soviet freight traffic density has roughly doubled since 1948, so by 1955 there were probably individual sections of line with densities of over 50 million short ton–miles per mile.[12]

It would be interesting to compare briefly the intensity with which freight locomotives and cars are used on the two systems, to see whether the high ratio of freight traffic to road operated is matched with respect to these other major categories of equipment. Unfortunately, the Soviet locomotive and car data collected in the present study are too fragmentary to establish securely their coverage and meaning. Hence the significance of comparative computations would at present be doubtful. However, a partial indication of relative performance is provided by comparing available Soviet statistics for the daily mileage of freight locomotives and cars with United States figures, as is done in Table 11.

Table 11. *Daily mileage of freight locomotives and cars, USSR and United States railroads, 1926–1955*

| Period | Locomotives | | Freight cars | |
|--------|-------|-------|-------|-------|
| | USSR | United States | USSR | United States |
| 1926–1930 | 86.4 | 87.9 | 51.5 | 32.6 |
| 1931–1935 | 105.1 | 90.4 | 66.1 | 26.4 |
| 1936–1940 | 153.3 | 104.1 | 87.4 | 35.9 |
| 1945 | 137.3 | 118.4 | 74.9 | 49.3 |
| 1950 | 156.0 | 119.3 | 90.9 | 46.5 |
| 1955 | 179.0 | 147.2 | 118.2 | 48.2 |

Sources: The USSR figures are derived from yearly data in Tables 74 and 75. Their coverage is not entirely clear, but it seems to correspond to the series for "locomotives in road freight service, serviceable, not stored," and "serviceable freight-carrying cars on line," in Interstate Commerce Commission records.

The United States figures for locomotives are computed from annual data in AAR, 1956, p. 24, and cover freight locomotive–miles per locomotive-day for active, i.e., serviceable (not stored), locomotives of Class I railroads. The freight-car figures are derived from annual data for serviceable cars in the same source.

It will be seen that over the last twenty years Soviet freight locomotives and cars have been put to considerably harder use than American freight locomotives and cars. In 1955, the daily mileage of an average Soviet freight locomotive was about 22 per cent above the mileage of its American counterpart, and for freight cars, 145 per cent higher. These comparisons overstate the relative productivity of Soviet freight locomotives and cars in terms of freight ton–miles moved, since tons per locomotive and per car are considerably lower in the USSR than in the United States. Nevertheless, the performance of Soviet motive power and rolling stock is impressive.

Another measure of operating efficiency is provided by average train speeds, for which comparative Soviet and American data are set forth in Table 12. It is clear that the terminal-to-terminal speeds of Soviet freight

Table 12. *Average freight train speeds, USSR and United States railroads, five-year averages, 1926–1955*

| Period | USSR (mi/hr) | United States (mi/hr) | USSR as percentage of United States |
|--------|--------------|------------------------|-------------------------------------|
| 1926–1930 | 8.2 | 12.8 | 64 |
| 1931–1935 | 8.9 | 15.6 | 57 |
| 1936–1940 | 12.0 | 16.4 | 73 |
| 1941–1945 | — | 15.8 | — |
| 1946–1950 | 11.0 | 16.4 | 67 |
| 1951–1955 | 14.4 | 18.0 | 80 |

Sources: The USSR figures are five-year averages of annual data in Table 73. They are computed in Soviet records as the quotient of principal locomotive-miles divided by principal locomotive-hours, including locomotive-hours at intermediate stations. See Kochetov, 1948, p. 139.

The United States figures are five-year averages of annual data in ICC, *Statistics*, Table 165 (formerly Statement No. 56), plus AAR, 1956, p. 24. They are computed as the quotient of total freight train–miles divided by total freight train–hours, including train-switching hours at way stations, for Class I railways.

trains have regularly been far below United States levels. Running speeds, that is, average miles per hour when trains are under way, have of course been much higher than the above terminal-to-terminal speeds, in both countries. The average Soviet running speed has been 65 to 70 per cent faster than terminal-to-terminal speed. Although data for the United States are not readily available, this ratio is probably somewhat higher, since train-handling at way stations probably takes up a larger share of total freight train–hours in the United States than in the USSR.

Slower train movement in the USSR than in the United States is partly a reflection of differences in the state of roadbed and track, and the quality of signaling equipment. It must also be related to the number of trains per day, since (as every motorist has observed) when moving objects are running close together their speed tends to be lowered. The Soviet pattern of train operation, reverting to Khachaturov's earlier comparison, is still more European than American in this respect; frequent trains at slow speeds rather than occasional trains at high speeds.

The pronounced improvement in Soviet freight train speeds during the latter half of the 1930's illustrates one facet of the railroad Stakhanovite drive launched by L. M. Kaganovich in 1935. Wide publicity was given to Petr Krivonos and other "daredevil" locomotive engineers who raised their running speeds sharply. The somewhat lower postwar figure evidently shows the effects of deteriorated track and roadbed after World War II, together with more delays at stops en route. During 1951–1955, the average speed of Soviet freight trains rose to 14.4 miles per hour, which was 80 per cent of the United States average of 18.0 miles per hour.

Along with speed, the weight of freight trains is an important index of operating effectiveness, and one that has been greatly emphasized in Soviet railroad improvement programs. Comparative figures for train weights on the two systems are presented in Table 13. When Soviet forced industrialization began, the level of gross freight train weights on Soviet railroads was only half the American level. (Gross weight combines the weight of the cars themselves with the weight of their contents.) Evidently because of a heavier commodity composition of freight traffic in the USSR, the average net weight (lading only) of Soviet freight trains was 62 per cent of the contemporary American level. United States train weights dropped somewhat in the early 1930's, while Soviet weights rose, thereby reducing their lag appreciably. Improvement of USSR railroads in the latter half of the 1930's outran United States recovery in this respect, and the net weight of Soviet freight trains reached 96 per cent of the American level. Thus Khachaturov's assertion is borne out.

Table 13. *Average gross and net freight train weights, USSR and United States railroads, five-year averages, 1926–1955*

| Period | USSR short ton–miles per freight train–mile | | United States short ton–miles per freight train–mile | | USSR as percentage of United States | |
|---|---|---|---|---|---|---|
| | Gross | Net | Gross | Net | Gross | Net |
| 1926–1930 | 924 | 483 | 1817 | 781 | 51 | 62 |
| 1931–1935 | 1085 | 611 | 1763 | 704 | 62 | 87 |
| 1936–1940 | 1370 | 767 | 1939 | 797 | 71 | 96 |
| 1941–1945 | — | — | 2313 | 1066 | — | — |
| 1946–1950 | 1458 | 824 | 2497 | 1154 | 58 | 71 |
| 1951–1955 | 1760 | 1093 | 2879 | 1311 | 61 | 83 |

Sources: The USSR figures are derived from annual data in Table 73. They are computed in Soviet records as the ratio of gross ton–miles (excluding locomotives and tenders) to principal locomotive-miles (for gross weight), and the ratio of "operating" ton–miles of revenue and nonrevenue freight to principal locomotive-miles (for net weight). See Kochetov, 1948, p. 138. The United States figures are five-year averages of annual data in Table 58 (formerly Statement No. 26), in annual volumes of ICC, *Statistics*, plus AAR, 1956, p. 24.

However, in recent years marked advances have been made in United States practice, while Soviet train weights have suffered from war and postwar difficulties. As a result, the Soviet position relative to the United States has been set back. During 1951–1955, average gross and net freight train weights in the USSR were 61 per cent and 83 per cent, respectively, of their United States counterparts. This is a particular instance of a common phenomenon in Soviet-American industrial rivalry; as the Soviet government strives to reach and surpass American levels, the United States target proves to be a moving one, and some Soviet objectives are thereby made more difficult of attainment.

These comparisons of the weight and speed of freight trains on the two systems may be combined in a single criterion of operating efficiency, widely employed in United States performance analysis, though not in the USSR. Multiplying the two together shows how many ton-miles of movement are produced in an hour's run of the average freight train. Table 14 records this index for the USSR and the United States. Gross ton–miles per freight train–hour on Soviet railroads in the late 1920's were only one third the American level, and the net figure was somewhat less than half its current American counterpart. Gains were made in both countries during the 1930's, but Soviet railroads showed the greater improvement, and in the latter part of the decade they were producing 52 per cent and 71 per cent of the gross and net train output being registered on the United

States system. Since that time, however, as noted earlier, United States progress has exceeded that in the USSR. During 1951–1955 the Soviet average for gross train output was 49 per cent of the American figure, and in net output the Soviet average was still at only two thirds the advancing United States level.

Table 14. Gross and net ton–miles per freight train–hour, USSR and United States railroads, five-year averages, 1926–1955

| Period | USSR short ton–miles per freight train–hour | | United States short ton–miles per freight train–hour | | USSR as percentage of United States | |
|---|---|---|---|---|---|---|
| | Gross | Net | Gross | Net | Gross | Net |
| 1926–1930 | 7,574 | 3,970 | 23,322 | 10,077 | 33 | 39 |
| 1931–1935 | 9,677 | 5,441 | 27,384 | 10,992 | 35 | 50 |
| 1936–1940 | 16,448 | 9,195 | 31,461 | 12,958 | 52 | 71 |
| 1941–1945 | — | — | 36,081 | 16,632 | — | — |
| 1946–1950 | 16,069 | 9,033 | 40,427 | 18,689 | 40 | 48 |
| 1951–1955 | 25,344 | 15,739 | 51,366 | 23,383 | 49 | 67 |

Sources: This measure may be computed either as the ratio of total ton-miles (gross or net) to total freight train-hours, or as the product of average freight train weight and speed. In the absence of firm annual data for total Soviet freight train-hours, the latter method has been used for the USSR figures above, which are derived from the five-year averages of Tables 12 and 13. The United States figures are five-year averages of annual data for Class I railroads in Table 60 of ICC, Statistics, plus AAR, 1956, p. 24.

It is clear that the average Soviet freight train is neither so heavy nor so fast as American trains. But a comparison which stopped at this point would be seriously incomplete. As Khachaturov pointed out in the passage cited earlier, Soviet railroads utilize relatively more freight trains to carry out their work than do American roads. With a certain exaggeration to dramatize the contrast, one may visualize a thick population of lighter, slower trains constantly spread over the Soviet railroad network, while in the United States a much more elaborate network is sparsely populated with fast, heavy freight trains that only occasionally appear. In accomplishing any given volume of freight transportation work, a considerably larger number of freight train-hours will be used in the USSR than in the United States. The contrast emerges clearly from the figures for total ton-miles and total train-hours in Table 15.

Over the last twenty-five years, the Soviet railroad system has annually expended about the same aggregate of freight train-hours as was being recorded for United States railroads. Recently, in fact, Soviet totals have been a third above the reduced American level. Yet the remaining "European" component of Soviet railroad practice has meant that these train-hours have produced net traffic volumes far below American standards.

When a freight train is light and slow, it is relatively unproductive. For example, in 1936–1940, when annual average freight train–hours were identical for the two systems, actual ton-miles of freight moved on Soviet railroads were only 71 per cent of the United States figure, and in 1946–1950, when Soviet train-hours were slightly above United States levels, Soviet traffic stood at 51 per cent of the American average.

Table 15. *Total annual net ton–miles and freight train–hours, USSR and United States railroads, five-year averages, 1926–1955 (millions of short ton–miles and hours)*

| Period | USSR | | United States | | USSR as percentage of United States | |
|---|---|---|---|---|---|---|
| | Ton-miles | Freight train–hours | Ton-miles | Freight train–hours | Ton-miles | Freight train–hours |
| 1926–1930 | 70,540 | 17.8 | 468,350 | 47.0 | 15 | 38 |
| 1931–1935 | 137,560 | 25.3 | 295,020 | 27.0 | 47 | 94 |
| 1936–1940 | 263,740 | 28.7 | 371,510 | 28.7 | 71 | 100 |
| 1941–1945 | 161,180[a] | — | 695,950 | 41.6 | 23 | — |
| 1946–1950 | 322,740 | 35.7 | 638,430 | 34.3 | 51 | 104 |
| 1951–1955 | 584,700 | 37.1 | 636,400 | 27.3 | 92 | 136 |

[a] Excluding calendar 1941.

Sources: "Net" ton–miles combines revenue and nonrevenue freight movement. The USSR figures are five-year averages of annual data in column 1 of Table 46 plus column 1 of Table 58, converted from metric ton–kilometers using the factor of 0.68494. The United States figures are five-year averages of annual data in ICC, *Statistics*, Statement 55 (Table 165), plus AAR, 1956, p. 20. The USSR train-hour figures are approximate only, being computed as the quotient of the above ton-mile data divided by the net figures in column 2 of Table 14.

American railroads have receded from their wartime traffic peaks in recent years, while greater train productivity has permitted additional reduction in freight train–hours. Hence while the USSR has not yet reached the 1941–1945 American average for total annual freight train–hours, its recent average has been 36 per cent above the 1951–1955 United States level. In net ton–miles of traffic moved, the USSR actually surpassed contemporary American railroad output by about 10 per cent in 1954 and 1955, though the Soviet record of 711 billion net ton–miles in 1955 still fell 9 per cent short of the 785 billion ton-miles produced by American railroads in 1944.

What may appear to be inconsistency between these relatively low train performance levels and the very high traffic densities noted earlier can easily be resolved through examination of the average number of trains per day at an average point on the network, as set forth in Table 16. American railroad practice is such that, taking the system as a whole, only about 6 freight trains a day pass over the average stretch of line. In the early 1930's the figure fell below 5, and during World War II it reached 8. But the

Soviet system, even before the industrialization drive reached its height, showed a frequency of freight trains of about 8 per day, and in the latter part of the 1930's this figure was raised to about 17 trains a day. Reconstruction difficulties reduced the 1946–1950 average to about 15 freight trains per mile of road per day, but in 1951–1955 the network average was almost 20, as compared with 6 for the United States. Thus the freight train popula-

Table 16. *Average freight train frequencies, USSR and United States railroads, five-year averages, 1926–1955 (total freight train–miles per mile of road operated in freight service per day)*

| Period | USSR | United States | USSR as percentage of United States |
|--------|------|---------------|-------------------------------------|
| 1926–1930 | 7.9 | 6.5 | 122 |
| 1931–1935 | 11.8 | 4.8 | 248 |
| 1936–1940 | 17.2 | 5.5 | 313 |
| 1941–1945 | — | 7.8 | — |
| 1946–1950 | 14.6 | 6.7 | 218 |
| 1951–1955 | 19.7 | 6.0 | 328 |

Sources: The USSR figures are derived from approximate annual data in column 1 of Table 73, divided by average annual road operated in Table 59. To obtain the United States figures, annual data were compiled for total ordinary freight train–miles and average annual road operated in freight service. Five-year totals were taken and their ratio divided by 365 to put it on a daily basis. The train-mile data cover Class I railways, and were taken from ICC, *Statistics*, Table 53 (formerly Statement No. 30), plus AAR, 1956, p. 20. The 1926–1930 average does not reflect allocation of mixed train-miles (initiated in 1936), but the 1931–1935 average does. The road operated data are from ICC, *Statistics*, Table 158 (formerly Statement No. 55) and AAR, 1956, p. 5.

tion on the railroad system of the USSR, reduced to a per-mile basis, has come to be over three times the usual US figure.

The picture is now relatively complete. Starting with a much smaller total of line, motive power, and rolling stock to work with, Soviet railroads have attained outstanding over-all traffic densities through crowding the line with a large number of lighter, slower trains. This has meant that locomotives and freight cars, especially freight cars, are kept on line more continuously than in the United States. At the same time, the ton-mile productivity of trains, locomotives, and cars is substantially below American levels. The juxtaposition of performance indexes well above and well below familiar standards has turned out to be understandable.

Moreover, it can be argued that under the circumstances this type of operating practice is economically justified. The use of relatively fast, heavy freight trains in the United States is a means of economizing on the labor costs of train crews, while the use of advanced, mechanized roadway (necessary to support such movement) is a means of economizing on the labor costs of maintaining that roadway. American practice is thus relatively labor-saving and capital-using. In the USSR, on the other hand, while skilled labor has been in short supply for twenty-five years, the supply of capital equipment is even scarcer. This has been especially true on the railroads, where a much larger investment program than the leaders would countenance would have been necessary to keep pace with traffic demands. Consequently the hard-pressed officials of Soviet railroads have logically been driven to make intensive use of roadway, motive power, and rolling stock, while at the same time employing "excessively" large quantities of labor, from an American standpoint. The observed characteristics of Soviet railroad operations are therefore consistent with what could be expected on the grounds of rational resource management.

It may be well to close this discussion with a mild suggestion to United States readers who have gained an impression of great superiority for the American railroad system in this comparison. The thirty year trend has deliberately been presented, in lieu of a 1955 comparison alone, so that a "catching-up process" could be observed. It must be expected that Soviet railroad practice will continue to improve, as it has in the past, approaching more closely that "new type of railway transport" described by Khachaturov. Certainly this is the intention of Soviet railroad men. Furthermore, the present system, with all its differences from accepted American practice, is already a remarkably effective one. Hence the indicated conclusion should be one of respect rather than complacency.

# 8 INTERCARRIER RELATIONS IN FREIGHT TRANSPORTATION

One of the attractive features of a planned economy, in theory at least, has been its prospect of facilitating the co-ordinated operation of several freight-carrying agencies in a rational and unified way. It is argued that organizational barriers, at least, can be reduced or eliminated. In the present chapter, we shall examine the way in which the Soviet transportation system in fact co-ordinates the activities of the various carriers. It will appear that there are a number of serious, technologically based problems, problems not exorcised by political slogans, to be surmounted in achieving an effectively unified transportation system. The chapter will also present, in more detail than has previously been offered, information about the role of the minor carriers, and observations on their future prospects. If this book has appeared so far to place excessive emphasis on the railroads, it is in the present chapter that the rationale for this approach will be set forth.

It may be as well to begin by indicating the dimensions of the roles played by the various carriers in Soviet freight transportation. Chart 17 presents five-year averages for most of the period from 1928 through 1955, showing the percentage share each carrier contributed to the total volume of freight ton-kilometers produced by the Soviet transportation system. One is struck immediately by the dominant position of the railroads. Even during the First Five Year Plan period, they handled more than three quarters of total freight traffic. Thereafter, in spite of the government's intentions, the railroads' share steadily increased, so that recently they have accounted for more than 84 per cent of total freight traffic. This rise of the railroads has been at the expense of the water carriers. Accounting for more than 20 per cent of total freight traffic in the late 1920's, internal waterway and maritime carriers in the postwar period have carried about 12 per cent of the total. The tiny remainder not accounted for by these three mass carriers is handled by trucks, whose share has risen from practically nothing to over 3 per cent recently, and petroleum pipelines, which have handled about 1 per cent of total traffic throughout the whole period.

The first of the minor carriers to deserve our attention is the fleet of barges and ships operating on Soviet internal waterways. For many centuries, the rivers were the principal arteries of interregional communication across

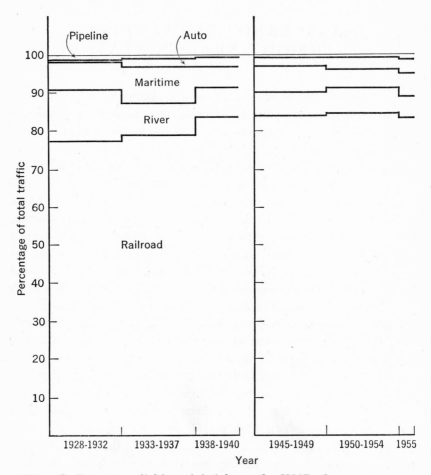

*Chart 17. Percentage division of freight traffic, USSR, five-year averages, 1928–1954, plus 1955. Source: absolute annual data in Table 52.*

the great land mass of Russia. The "river road" connecting Scandinavia and the Byzantine Empire via the Dnepr River, the Volga as a link between Central Asia and northwestern Europe, and lesser examples, too, are well known to students of Russian history. But with the coming of railroads to Russia, the relative contribution of her rivers has steadily diminished. In

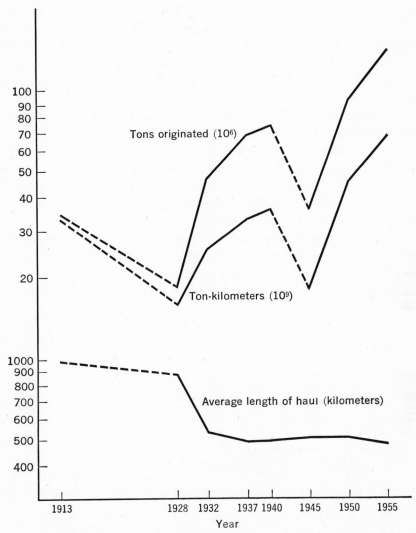

Chart 18. River freight traffic, USSR, selected years, 1913–1955. Source: Table 47, plus a 1913 estimate excluding timber floated loose or in rafts (and not drawn by power).

1913, the rivers handled some 33 billion ton-kilometers of freight traffic compared to the 66 billion handled by railroads. Subsequent trends in the volume of river freight traffic are indicated in Chart 18, which shows that river freight traffic has not significantly exceeded the prerevolutionary level until very recently. By contrast, the railroads during the 1930's expanded their volume of freight traffic to some six times the prerevolutionary level, and by 1954 were producing 13 times as much freight transportation as in 1913.

As can be seen in Chart 18, river carriers found it possible to reach the prerevolutionary level of originated tonnage during the First Five Year Plan period. However, a drastic decline in the average distance for which freight was carried on the rivers held back recovery in river freight ton-kilometers. This decline in average hauls has been a serious deficiency of river transportation in the eyes of the government, but it has continued to plague the rivers even in recent years.

While it is true that the total length of rivers on Soviet territory, even of so-called "navigable waterways," is perfectly enormous, it is equally true that the great bulk of river freight traffic moves only on a single river together with its tributaries. Table 17 indicates the regional pattern of river

*Table 17. River freight traffic, USSR, by river system or region, selected years, 1913–1950 plan (per cent of total ton-kilometers carried on rivers)*

| Year | Volga-Kama | N. European Russia[a] | S. European Russia[b] | Eastern rivers[c] |
|------|-----------|-----------------------|-----------------------|-------------------|
| 1913 | 65.6 | 17.9 | 10.1 | 6.4 |
| 1935 | 70.2 | 17.5 | 5.2 | 7.1 |
| 1940 | 68.6 | 14.3 | 5.9 | 11.2 |
| 1945 | 72.7 | 8.5 | 3.7 | 15.1 |
| 1950 (plan) | 71.5 | 11.8 | 6.1 | 10.6 |

[a] Includes northwestern European Russia.
[b] The Dnepr and several smaller rivers.
[c] Ob'-Irtysh, Amur, Yenesei, and Central Asian rivers.
Sources: Summarized from more detailed data for 1913 in MPS, 1916, Part II, p. 39 and p. 71; for 1935 in TsUNKhU, 1936a, p. 448; and for 1940, 1945, plan 1950 in Shashkov, 1947, p. 19.

freight traffic. The Volga River, rising in central European Russia and threading its way down to the Caspian Sea, has accounted for about two thirds of total Soviet river traffic throughout the period. Moreover, the Volga and the other rivers of European Russia account for nine tenths of total Soviet river traffic: the huge rivers of Siberia, and to some extent of Central Asia, have not yet come to play a very large role.

As will be shown in the next chapter, railroad freight traffic is dominated by coal, followed by a considerable range of other mass freight and fabricated commodities. By contrast, river freight traffic is taken up very largely with two commodities: timber and petroleum. Table 18 presents summary

Table 18. River freight traffic, USSR, by major commodity group, selected years, 1913–1950 plan
(per cent of total river ton-kilometers)

| Year | Timber[a] | Petroleum | Other |
|------|-----------|-----------|-------|
| 1913 | 35.4 | 27.6 | 37.0 |
| 1928 | 29.1 | 49.8 | 21.1 |
| 1932 | 35.6 | 45.6 | 18.8 |
| 1937 | 49.4 | 27.2 | 23.4 |
| 1940 | 40.5 | 33.7 | 25.8 |
| 1945 | 34.8 | 34.6 | 30.6 |
| 1950 (plan) | 44.9 | 27.0 | 28.1 |

[a] Including timber rafted under power.
Sources: Derived from absolute data in the sources noted under Table 17, plus (for 1937) tons originated data from Vodnyi Transport, 1940, no. 9, p. 5, and various length-of-haul references.

data indicating the structure of river freight traffic. Measured in ton-kilometers, timber traffic has regularly been a third or more of total traffic. Similarly, petroleum traffic has usually made up another third of total traffic. One might have thought that forced Soviet industrialization would produce substantial changes in the composition of river freight traffic, leading away from primary products and toward industrial output, but no such trend is evident in the record to date. In fact, the target for 1950 established in 1946 called for a higher concentration on timber traffic than existed in 1913.

For a somewhat more detailed review of the composition of internal waterways freight traffic, Table 19 presents both ton-kilometers and tons-

Table 19. River freight traffic, USSR, by commodity, 1940

| Commodity | Ton-kilometers (10⁹) | Average length of haul (Km) | Tons originated (10⁶) |
|-----------|----------------------|------------------------------|------------------------|
| Timber in boats | 2.82 | 378 | 7.46 |
| Timber in rafts | 11.65 | 356 | 32.72 |
| Total timber | 14.47 | 360 | 40.18 |
| Petroleum | 12.07 | 1259 | 9.59 |
| Grain | 2.19 | 424 | 5.17 |
| Salt | 1.76 | 1224 | 1.44 |
| Mineral building materials | 1.44 | 193 | 7.46 |
| Coal | 1.15 | 540 | 2.13 |
| Other | 2.72 | 392 | 6.94 |
| Total | 35.80 | 491 | 72.91 |

Sources: Derived from absolute 1950 targets and percentage increases over 1940 (ton-kilometers), plus stated average hauls in Shashkov, 1947, p. 18.

originated data for 1940, covering eight subgroups within the total. In terms of tons originated, timber floated in rafts drawn by tugboats accounts for 45 per cent of all traffic. Together with timber carried in boats, it makes up well over half the total. However, the distance it is carried on the average is below that for other freight, and its position therefore in total river ton-kilometers is relatively smaller.

Petroleum's share of originated tonnage is much smaller, but its average haul is so long that the proportion of river ton-kilometers accounted for by petroleum (and petroleum products) is substantial. Grain in 1940 still made up about 6 per cent of river ton-kilometers, and salt made up an additional 5 per cent. The latter is to be explained by distribution of salt from the large deposits at and near Lake Baskunchak in the lower Volga Valley. Mineral building materials, including cement, made up some 4 per cent, and coal added some 3 per cent of total traffic. The remaining 8 per cent was distributed among iron and steel, ores, other products of agriculture, and so on, in very small amounts.

The Soviet government has devoted considerable attention to improving its system of river transportation. Much publicity was given to construction of the Baltic–White Sea Waterway in the 1930's, and to construction of the Volga-Don Canal, completed in 1952. Moscow is sometimes referred to as the "port on five seas," a reference to its water connections with the White Sea, the Baltic Sea, the Black Sea, the Sea of Azov, and the Caspian Sea. Substantial investment has gone into deepening river channels, lighting them, and otherwise improving their navigabilty.

In canals and waterways, however, the volume of freight traffic carried, while large in absolute terms, has so far remained infinitesimal as a share of total freight transportation. For example, the Baltic–White Sea Waterway, in its first five years of operation, from August 2, 1933 to August 2, 1938, carried about 1.4 billion ton-kilometers of freight; in 1940 its traffic amounted to about 0.5 billion ton-kilometers of freight, at a time when internal waterways as a whole produced 36 billion, and all carriers produced 488 billion.[1] In its first three years of operation, the Volga-Don Canal appears to have carried considerably less traffic than was hoped for.

Soviet internal waterways are important not only for freight transportation, but, as in other countries, for several other purposes as well. The Soviet government has devoted extensive resources to hydroelectric power development, in such grandiose projects as the dam at Zaporozhye on the Dnepr, and the current hydroelectric dams at Stalingrad and near Kuibyshev on the Volga River. Without entering into an evaluation of Soviet water-use pro-

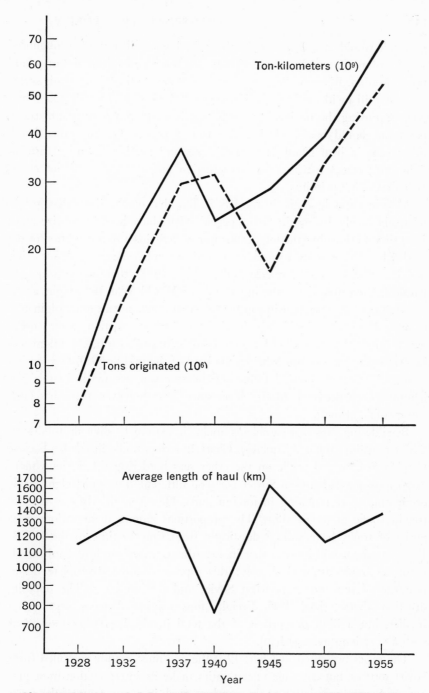

*Chart 19. Maritime freight traffic, USSR, selected years, 1928–1955. Source: Table 48.*

grams, it would appear that the basic limitation on all uses is a pronounced scarcity of water supplies in relation to needs for agriculture, industry, and transportation. River basin development to extend utilization of this scarce resource will incidentally have the effect of deepening channels and otherwise improving the navigability of Soviet rivers. Hence river freight transportation should benefit during the ice-free season. On the other hand, investment in boat channels around dams and similar expensive installations must compete with other construction projects, and need not necessarily have high priority.

Maritime freight traffic in the USSR, like that on the rivers, has grown relatively slowly during the Soviet period. There have been impressive gains from time to time, but the total traffic moved remains a minor portion of the total. Chart 19 presents a summary record of ton-kilometers and tons originated on Soviet seas. From 1928 to the middle 1930's, there was marked expansion; thereafter the gathering clouds of World War II brought about an appreciable contraction in ton-kilometers, though not in tons originated. Conversely, the war itself brought about a sharp contraction in tons originated, compensated for by a longer average trip, so that total ton-kilometers in 1945 were not very much below the level of the middle 1930's. Expansion during the recovery period following the war was not marked, since the length of trip declined. In the years since 1950, however, there has been considerable growth.

Bewildering coverage problems make it extremely difficult to discuss Soviet maritime traffic adequately. Chart 19 covers traffic in the landlocked Caspian Sea, coastal traffic on the other seas bordering the Soviet Union, cargo movements between Soviet ports on different seas, and freight traffic originating or terminating in foreign ports. However, the data cover only freight traffic in Soviet ships. The proportions among these various categories of traffic have shifted drastically from time to time in the USSR. For example, it will be seen that in 1940 the average length of haul for all maritime traffic dropped sharply; this represents almost complete disappearance of movements between Soviet and foreign ports. The opposite situation characterized 1945. Freight tons originated were very much smaller, but a high proportion of the total involved overseas movement with a very long average haul.

The series presented in Chart 19 is the one most readily compiled from Soviet sources, but coverage uncertainties make its interpretation most precarious. Some appreciation of the trends at work in components of the series can be obtained from Table 49, Appendix B, though it should be emphasized that the estimates therein are no more than crude calculations.[2] Examining first the trend for freight traffic within particular seas, it appears that there was unbroken expansion and a high rate of growth straight through the period from 1928 to 1940. On the other hand, the volume of freight traffic between Soviet seas rose sharply to 1933, fell back seriously through 1937, spurted temporarily in 1938 and 1939, and declined in 1940 to the 1929 level. Similarly, the volume of freight traffic between Soviet and foreign ports rose dramatically to a peak in 1936, and then fell just as drastically to almost nothing in 1940. These conflicting movements would be still further altered if the freight carried in non-Soviet ships in foreign and intersea domestic movement could be added to this record of traffic carried in Soviet bottoms.

In 1913, almost half the tons originated in maritime freight traffic, including those moved by foreign ships, took place in the Black and Azov seas. The Caspian at that time accounted for only about 20 per cent of the total. Soviet isolation in the 1920's led to a drastic shrinkage in overseas freight traffic, while Caspian Sea traffic had again reached its prerevolutionary level. In the middle 1930's, foreign trade associated with the First and Second Five Year Plans restored the absolute volume of Black Sea traffic, though not that of the Baltic. Meanwhile Caspian Sea traffic more than doubled its 1928 volume. By 1940, tons originated on the Caspian Sea accounted for 51 per cent of total maritime tons originated, and the share of Black and Azov sea traffic was 33.5 per cent. It was intended in 1946 to reduce the Caspian Sea's share to 40 per cent in 1950, with 34 per cent to be originated in the Black and Azov seas, and considerable expansion in the Baltic Sea and Far Eastern waters.[3] Recently there appears to have been another marked shift in proportion among the Soviet seas, since Kaganovich reported in 1954 that some 26 per cent of all maritime freight shipments took place in the Far Eastern Basin.[4] Maritime freight traffic appears to be dominated by petroleum. In 1940, the percentage shares of various commodities in total intrasea tons originated were as follows:[5]

| | |
|---|---|
| Petroleum | 65.0 |
| Timber | 5.6 |
| Coal | 4.9 |
| Ores | 4.7 |
| Mineral building material | 2.3 |
| Iron and steel | 0.9 |
| Other | 16.6 |

In the USSR, intercity truck transportation as defined in the United States is just coming into existence. The kind of truck traffic that has been estimated and recorded in Soviet freight traffic statistics would be excluded entirely from American records.[6] It relates to freight pickups and deliveries within major cities, together with rural communication between collective farms and neighboring railroad stations. The average length of haul for Soviet truck traffic is ten to twelve kilometers, or around seven miles.

Nevertheless, as shown in Table 50, this kind of truck traffic has grown very rapidly in the USSR since 1928. It reached 1 billion ton-kilometers in 1932, 9 billion in 1940, and some 20 billion in 1950. It has now come to account for 4 per cent of total Soviet freight traffic, and can be expected to continue its rapid absolute and relative growth.

In countries where truck transportation has made substantial inroads on the position of the other major carriers, it will seem natural to ask why intercity truck transportation has not so far developed in the USSR. A plausible answer would probably emphasize the enormous investment in highways required to permit such transportation. In the United States, citizens have been willing since World War I to devote a substantial part of state taxes to highway construction, involving a huge aggregate investment in this form of social capital. The purpose, of course, has been free movement of passenger vehicles, and the rise of intercity common-carrier truck transportation has been merely a by-product. No similar pull from the consumer side has existed in the USSR, and the government has not seen fit to devote a large volume of resources to highway construction when it was cheaper to expand the carrying capacity of the railroad network.

Since the late 1940's, intercity automobile transportation, at least for bus carriage of passengers, has begun to develop. (See the concluding portion of Chapter 10 for details.) In September 1953, administration of truck freight operations was transferred from the individual Soviet republics, where it had previously resided, to a new Union-Republic Ministry charged with developing what we would call common-carrier truck transportation. The new ministry has since been endeavoring to take over blocks of traffic previously carried in the truck fleets operated by various other ministries.[7] On the whole, it is clear that local truck traffic has been expanding very rapidly, and it seems likely that intercity truck traffic will begin to develop in the coming years.

Extraction of petroleum had begun in Russia well before World War I, around Baku on the shores of the Caspian Sea, at two points on the northern slopes of the Caucasus Mountains, and at the mouth of the Emba River on the northeastern shores of the Caspian Sea. A pipeline came into operation in 1906 from Baku westward below the Caucasian range to Batumi, a port on the Black Sea whence kerosene was exported. Two short lines were brought into operation from oil fields to refineries in the North Caucasus shortly before World War I. Since that time, a number of additional pipelines have been built, but the Soviet pipeline network, by American standards, is still very small.

Table 20. Petroleum pipelines, USSR, as of 1940, by region, year, and capacity

| Termini | Year started | Length (Km) | Diameter (inches) | Annual capacity ($10^3$ tons) |
|---|---|---|---|---|
| *Trans-Caucasus* | | | | |
| Baku-Batumi | 1906 | 883 | 8 | 900 |
| Baku-Batumi | 1930 | 822 | 10 | 1650 |
| *North Caucasus* | | | | |
| Maikop-Krasnodar | 1910 | 108 | 8 | 900 |
| Grosny-M. Kala | 1914 | 162 | 8 | 790 |
| Grosny-Tuapse | 1928 | 618 | 10 | 1650 |
| Armavir-Trudovaya | 1932 | 488 | 12 | 1660 |
| Malgobek-Vrezka | 1934 | 25 | 10 | — |
| Grosny-M. Kala | 1940 | — | — | — |
| *Ural-Emba* | | | | |
| Dossor-Rakusha | 1930 | 84 | 6 | — |
| Gur'ev-Orsk | 1936 | 758 | 12 | 2500 |
| Koschagil-Makat | 1935 | 130 | 8 | — |
| Koschagil-Kulsary | 1939 | 20 | 8 | — |
| Baichunam-Iskine | 1939 | 22 | 8 | — |
| *Second Baku* | | | | |
| Ishimbai-Ufa | 1936 | 166 | 12 | — |
| Tuimaza-Ufa | 1940 | 150 | 12 | — |
| Stavropol-Syzran | 1940 | 94 | 12 | — |

Sources: Assembled from TsUNKhU, 1934, p. 92, and 1936a, p. 126, plus an unpublished paper of James H. Blackman.

Table 20 lists most of the lines in operation in 1940 in the USSR. On the eve of the First Five Year Plan, a crude oil line from Grosny in the North Caucasus to the Black Sea port of Tuapse came into operation. In 1930, a second line between Baku and Batumi was completed. In 1932, a petroleum products pipeline from the North Caucasus up to Trudovaya in the Donbas industrial area came into operation. In order to supply petroleum products to the growing industry of the Urals and Western Siberia, a crude oil line from Guryev, at the northern end of the Caspian Sea, up to Orsk in the southern Urals was completed in 1936. The crude oil was refined at Orsk and thereafter distributed throughout eastern territory. Toward the end of the 1930's, with the rapid growth of crude petroleum extraction in the so-called "Second Baku" oil fields, several short lines from fields to a refinery at Ufa or to railheads were placed in operation. Since 1945, there has presumably been considerable construction of short gathering lines in the Second Baku area and elsewhere, but details are not available. In addition, a natural gas line was built from Saratov on the Volga to Moscow, and construction of others has brought the total for gas pipelines to about 3000 kilometers in 1955.[8]

The basic fact about Soviet pipeline transportation of crude oil is that to date it has remained relatively small. As the detailed record in Table 51 shows, pipelines carried about 1 billion ton-kilometers of traffic annually at the beginning of the five-year plan period. By 1940 a level of almost 4 billion ton-kilometers had been reached. This was raised by 1950 to about 5 billion, and by 1955 to almost 14 billion ton-kilometers. A fourteenfold growth in 27 years is impressive, of course, but relative to the traffic carried by other means of transportation, especially railroad tank cars, pipeline petroleum traffic still remains a very junior partner.

Rough calculations for the six-year period 1935–1940 indicate that the railroads handled about 49 per cent of petroleum freight traffic measured in ton-kilometers, and about 41 per cent of petroleum tons originated. River barges were responsible for about 16 per cent of the total ton-kilometers, and 13 per cent of tons originated. Tankers on the Caspian Sea and elsewhere accounted for some 30 per cent of petroleum ton-kilometers, and 33 per cent of tons originated. Consequently the balance handled by pipelines came to about 6.5 per cent of ton-kilometers and 13 per cent of tons originated. Railroads carried petroleum an average distance of 1173 kilometers; river traffic moved an average distance of 1200 kilometers; maritime traffic had an average haul of 860 kilometers, and pipeline traffic moved only 500 kilometers on the average.

The relative role of pipelines does not seem to be increasing. Expansion of crude oil output in the Second Baku fields, and maldistribution of refinery capacity with respect to this new locational situation, have increased rather than decreased the burden on railroads. However, the Sixth Five Year Plan calls for even more marked growth in pipeline traffic than has been demanded under earlier (unfulfilled) plans, and pipelines may now be entering a long-delayed period of impressive absolute growth.

In a unified transportation system, the various carriers would be appropriately linked together so that two or more carriers would jointly handle a shipment whenever it was economically feasible. Considerable attention has been given to such joint shipments by Soviet transportation authorities, especially in recent years, but their volume is still very small. Generalizations are difficult in the absence of detailed data, yet Soviet discussions make it clear that serious difficulties stand in the way of expanded joint shipments of freight. This can be illustrated in three different connections.

Consider first the case of petroleum. Joint maritime-inland waterway shipments from Baku north to a roadstead below Astrakhan, at the mouth of the Volga, and then up the Volga River, have long been the backbone of Russian petroleum traffic. Nevertheless the railroads have come to share significantly in this traffic, taking consignments at middle Volga River ports for distribution to Moscow and elsewhere. Similarly, joint pipeline maritime-rail shipments from Baku via Batumi and Odessa to the Leningrad region have been traditional. Yet there are complaints that such routes are on occasion bypassed in favor of all-rail tank car shipments from Baku straight up to central and northwestern European Russia.

Timber presents another case of joint shipment conditions that appear very unsatisfactory to railroad authorities. Traditionally, a huge volume of timber has come down the Volga River, perhaps starting at points farther north along the Kama River, consigned to the black-earth region, the eastern Ukraine or to the Caucasus. It would be transferred to railroad cars at Volga River ports, Makhach Kala, or Baku. However, a railroad writer complained in 1950 that in the preceding year only 15 per cent of the timber consigned to Caucasian destinations, and 0.5 per cent of the timber for the Donbas, moved in this way.[9] He said affairs had reached a point where timber floated down the upper Kama is lifted to the banks at Molotov and thence railed all the way to the Donbas or the Caucasus. Such practices are not thought by Soviet writers to be consistent with operation of a unified transportation system.

Another form of joint shipment widely developed in the West involves use of trucks to complete rail shipments arriving at major rail centers. In addition, though this is not strictly a question of joint shipments, trucks in the West have largely supplanted the railroads for short freight movements around major industrial centers. Railroad officials in the USSR have complained bitterly for many years that such short-haul traffic still falls too heavily on the railroads.[10] Scattered references from 1935 through 1952 indicate that some 12 per cent of railroad tons originated moves for distances less than thirty miles, and about a quarter of originated rail tonnage moves for distances up to sixty miles. Soviet railroad writers contend that in a rationally unified transportation system this short-haul traffic would be carried by trucks. For a variety of understandable reasons, however, it has proved difficult so far to reduce the railroads' share of short movements.

Why is it that joint use of the major carriers has been so difficult to develop in the Soviet economy? Perusal of Soviet transportation literature suggests that there are at least four compelling reasons. Three of them serve to explain the reluctance of shippers themselves to make use of joint shipments. The fourth concerns the real cost of joint transportation operations.

One important factor militating against joint use of railroad and river or sea carriers has been the element of speed. Transportation Commissar Rudzutak explained as long ago as 1927 that the so-called "goods shortage" put a premium on rapid deliveries and thus hindered the river carriers in competition with railroads.[11] Precisely the same reasoning was used by Koldomasov in 1949. He pointed out that when everything was being mobilized for rapid postwar reconstruction and expansion of the economy, speed of shipment was a decisive influence on the division of traffic, especially between railroad and river carriers.[12] A related point, of course, concerns the seasonal availability of transportation; water carriers are not continuously prepared to offer service. Shippers apparently feel that water carriers are less reliable than the railroads. In an article imbued with heart-felt indignation, G. Smirnov, a railroad traffic agent in the Volga Valley, complained of his clients' "hydrophobia."[13] When urged by him to make more use of river shipments, shippers in his territory had cited several reasons for preferring the railroads: shortage of the proper crating material, consignments too heavy for river handling, potential damage to metal parts from river moisture, and interrupted access to river landings during the spring thaw.

A third factor influencing shippers in their choice among carriers is the level of freight rates. In recent years considerable effort has been made to increase the attractiveness of internal waterway and coastal maritime movement during the open navigating season, through concessions of special low freight rates. However, the difference in rates is sometimes not large enough to be effective. For example, the cost of shipping a ton of timber from Tavda in the Urals to Stalino in the Donbas by rail entirely was 82 rubles in 1951. By rail-water shipment, using the Kama-Volga route from Molotov to Stalingrad, it was 56 rubles. Similarly, all-rail shipment of a ton of timber from Kotlas in northern European Russia south to Tbilisi in the Caucasus cost 126 rubles; by rail-water shipment, using the Volga from Gorky to Astrakhan, it cost 105 rubles.[14] Sometimes, as Smirnov pointed out in his hydrophobia article, rail-water shipment is more expensive than all-rail movement. He stated, for example, that shipping a 20-ton car of flour from Ekaterinovka, west of Saratov, down to Stalingrad cost 460 rubles by rail, but that if the Volga were used from Saratov south, the cost of combined shipment was 666 rubles. Attempts are now made to eliminate such anomalies, as they appear to railroad officials, but shippers are evidently hard to convince.

A factor of fundamental importance here is the real cost of transshipment operations. Mass movement of freight, both by railroads and by water carriers, is very cheap indeed; the terminal costs of loading and unloading are large by comparison, as is well known in all transportation analysis. Labor costs of loading and unloading are high, and even mechanization leaves the cost substantial. Where rivers are frozen during part of the year, as in most of the USSR, storage facilities and stockpiling costs raise the real cost of joint rail-water shipments still further. These costs, reflected in transshipment charges, raise a genuine barrier to the growth of joint shipments, and one which is evidently respected by Soviet officials.

Soviet railroads were experimenting in the late 1930's with the use of large containers for handling less than carload lot shipments and merchandise freight, and this program of *kontainerizatsia,* greatly expanded since 1948, may provide a partial answer to the high costs of transshipment. A similar program has been well developed in the United Kingdom. However, in spite of strenuous campaigning in connection with the ill-fated Malenkov consumer goods program, Soviet kontainerizatsia still covers only part of small-scale shipments, which in turn are a minute fraction of all shipments. The day may come when Soviet carriers will make use of trailers on flat cars or of trailer ships, both now coming into use in the United States. Until then, transshipment will remain, for most commodities, expensive and difficult.

Wherever two or more carriers are available for handling freight traffic, it seems clear that a certain amount of competition between them is inherent in the situation. Broad ideological slogans relating to ownership of the means of production may not really be relevant. Certainly unification of a complex, multicarrier transportation system cannot be expected to follow automatically from nationalization or from the operation of a planned economy. Examination of this one detailed aspect of Soviet transportation tends to support a conclusion — one which has seemed applicable elsewhere in the economy — that the resource allocation problems of a modern industrial economy cut across ideological boundaries. There is no evidence that the Soviet transportation system is any more "unified" than the American transportation system. In a purely technical sense, the reverse appears more accurate. In each economy, difficult technical problems are confronted, and political slogans do not aid appreciably in solving them.

Assigning proper roles to each of the major carriers is very much a matter of debate throughout the world. Supporters of each major carrier can make it appear extremely attractive. In addition to writers indentified with transportation, geographers frequently discuss broad transportation matters, and offer judgments on the relative merits of various carriers. My impression is that geographers frequently underestimate the importance of transshipment costs and overvalue the contribution of inland waterways. The Soviet government appears to share these misconceptions, if that is what they are.

The evidence of the present chapter certainly suggests that most Soviet publicity concerning water transportation and her unified transportation system tends to be misleading. Much the same can be said for Soviet truck and pipeline transportation. Over the period analyzed in the present study, these minor carriers have contributed very little toward solution of the USSR's transportation problems.

The geography and technological history of each economy is different, and consequently its transportation system is unlikely to duplicate that of other economies. The present dominance of railroads in the USSR has no precise counterpart among other major industrial powers, and yet this does not mean that the proportions among the major carriers in the USSR are incorrect and therefore likely to change. It is nevertheless interesting to speculate about possible development in the future. All carriers will expand, but which will grow most rapidly?

The outlook for river and sea transportation, on present evidence, in spite of Soviet publicity, does not appear promising. On the other hand, while it is true that enormous investment will be required, the USSR appears well launched on a large-scale, gradual program for developing automobile transportation. It is not clear why pipeline transportation has been so little developed until recently; higher-priority uses for scarce steel supplies may have been a factor, and the oil industry (responsible for pipelines) may have lacked cost-reducing initiative. In any case, transfer of the center of petroleum production from the Caspian Sea region to mid-continental fields now appears to be stimulating the growth of pipelines.

Taken altogether, then, it seems probable that the percentage share of total ton-kilometers handled by trucks and pipelines will increase in the coming years. If the water carriers' share does not fall, the increase will be at the expense of the railroads. This, oddly enough, will be considered a boon by railroad officials. It should be emphasized, nonetheless, that structural changes of this kind take place slowly, and that there is no early prospect of any marked diminution in the railroads' role.

# 9 THE GEOGRAPHY OF COMMODITY TRANSPORTATION

Most of this study is concerned with general questions of economic policy and with historical analysis of transportation development. It is focused on freight transportation, and its quantitative heart is, of course, the annual volume of freight traffic. Such an aggregate is heterogeneous in composition and reflects a complex web of geographic movements; it therefore presents something of a dilemma for the investigator. It is only too easy to be submerged in a mass of commodity and regional detail, and yet a review of the main trends in commodity composition and regional traffic flows must be part of an adequate treatment of the subject. The present chapter is an attempt to provide a brief survey of Soviet railroad freight traffic seen in these two aspects. While it will clearly not compel the close attention of the general reader (who may wish to pass directly to Chapter 10, on passenger transportation), it may prove useful for anyone interested in related aspects of Soviet economic development.

The prerevolutionary Russian economy was, as we have seen, concentrated in European Russia and oriented toward the West. Much of the railroad network was built to facilitate the export of wheat and other grains from central European Russia, first to Baltic Sea ports for northern European customers, and later to Black Sea ports for shipment to southern European markets. Among the major commodity groups, grains held first place in rail traffic until the last few years before 1913. Thus in the inherited pattern of interregional transportation, a fundamental element had been the flow of grains northwestward (for domestic consumption as well as export) and southwestward from central European Russia.

The rapid industrialization process that had been well under way in Russia since around 1885 had at its heart, from a freight traffic standpoint, the coal, iron ore, and iron and steel shipments originating in the eastern Ukraine. Even before the revolution, this region was shipping out large quantities of coal, steel products, grain, and other commodities, straining the capacity of lines leading outward, especially those leading north toward Moscow.

In northwestern European Russia, the capital of St. Petersburg and its environs were supplied with grain from the south and southeast. Industry here utilized coal imported from the Dombrovo field in Poland or from England. Freight traffic throughout the rest of the empire was scattered and much thinner than the flows involved in these major movements. Some grain moved west out of Western Siberia into European Russia, and some cotton moved northwest out of Central Asia toward the textile centers around Moscow. Crude oil and kerosene originating around Baku or on the northern slopes of the Caucasus Mountains moved north to central European Russia, as well as going for export to Black Sea ports. But in general, the outward grain flow, outward flow from the Ukraine, and incoming flow toward St. Petersburg dominated the situation.

It has already been indicated that fundamental changes in this inherited regional structure were both forced on the Bolsheviks and actively fostered by them. One way of characterizing the pattern that evolved between 1928 and 1940 is in terms of the letter "T." In European Russia the dominant flow of traffic is north-and-south; stretching out toward the east, the traffic runs primarily in an east-west direction. The resulting pattern is roughly like that of a "T," or can perhaps better be likened to a Russian "G," since there is no leftward or western arm. During the interwar period, this "T" or "G" pattern was strengthened in several ways.

As we pointed out earlier, it was necessary to supply industry around Leningrad (formerly St. Petersburg) with coal from the Donbas. There was also increased need for petroleum products, carried north by railroad tank cars from Odessa after shipment across the Black Sea. A very large northward traffic in coal and other commodities from the eastern Ukraine became an even more dominant feature of the interwar period than it had been before. It required construction of a heavy duty line, an account of which appeared in Chapter 3.

In the Ural economic region and Western Siberia, development of the so-called "second iron and steel base" generated a huge volume of freight traffic. This east-west movement in the region adjacent to European Russia, combined with substantial interregional movement between this area and European Russia, had the effect of strengthening the right arm of the "T." Especially toward the end of the 1930's, rapid development of industry and armament production in Eastern Siberia and the Soviet Far East gave rise to a considerably enhanced freight traffic at this farthest end of the USSR.

It was overbalanced in the eastward direction, since these regions were importing more, by volume, than they were exporting. There was, however, very little export abroad from this end of the country.

By contrast with the prerevolutionary situation, one notes a marked reduction in the flow of grain and other primary commodities toward Baltic and Black Sea ports. Industrial growth around Moscow and Leningrad intensified the net import balance of these regions and the northward flow of heavy freight to them. Industrial growth in the Ural region and Western Siberia stimulated a considerable two-way freight flow between this part of the USSR, Moscow and Leningrad, and the eastern Ukraine.

Again, other elements of the pattern were less important. The southward flow of building timber, pit props, finished lumber, pulpwood, and paper products from northern regions to centers of industry and population was, of course, greatly intensified by the forced industrialization drive. And the northward flow of petroleum from the Caucasus also increased appreciably. In this connection, however, there was a marked diminution in the relative role of water-borne freight traffic, especially on the Volga River, since there appears to have been a shift of traffic from river barges to rail tank cars.

We have seen that World War II brought about substantial changes in the regional structure of the Soviet economy. The so-called eastern regions have expanded both absolutely and relatively, while the western areas of European Russia occupied by the Nazis have lost ground, even though they have more than regained their prewar industrial levels.

Nevertheless, from a freight traffic point of view, Moscow and Leningrad are still voracious consumers of heavy freight. The eastern Ukraine is still a substantial exporter of primary and fabricated output. Industrial growth in the Ural region and the Kuzbas has not yet brought them up to equality with the old eastern Ukrainian industrial complex. The trend has been, however, for a significantly higher rate of growth in this second industrial base than in the south of European Russia, so that within another decade the junior base may assume the lead.

It appears that the Volga Valley, which tended to lag behind somewhat in growth during the thirties, has been the scene of especially rapid growth during and since the war. Consequently, where there used to be primarily through freight traffic crossing this region to or from Central Asia, Kazakhstan, and the southern Urals, it is now combined with significant local origination and termination of heavy freight traffic. The "T" or "G" of the interwar period now appears to be further modified by a diagonal connecting the Donbas with the "second iron and steel base," passing through the Volga Valley. Moreover, the concentrated shuttle of coal and iron ore between the two ends of the Ural-Kuznetsk Kombinat has been somewhat diffused at each end, and a larger north-south freight flow between this region and Central Asia has developed. Consequently the lateral (east-west) arm of the "T" is broadening and the angle between the two arms is being filled in.

Farther east, there appears to be less evidence than during the late 1930's of rapid industrial development. On the other hand, since 1949 an increasing volume of freight traffic to and from China has moved overland along the Trans-Siberian Railroad, and south through Manchuria or (since 1955) through the Mongolian People's Republic. The result will be a broadening in this farthest end of the "T's" arm, especially when the Alma Ata-Lanchow line across Singkiang comes into operation.

*Table 21. Regional pattern of rail freight tons originated and terminated, USSR, 1949*
*(percentages of USSR total)*

| Region | Tons originated | Tons terminated |
|---|---|---|
| Northwest | 6 | 7 |
| Baltic | 3 | 3 |
| North | 5 | 3 |
| Center | 8 | 15 |
| South | 28 | 24 |
| Caucasus | 3 | 3 |
| Southwest | 12 | 11 |
| Total "west" | 65 | 66 |
| Ural region | 12 | 12 |
| Kazakh SSR & Central Asia | 6 | 6 |
| West Siberia | 8 | 7 |
| East Siberia | 5 | 4 |
| Soviet Far East | 4 | 5 |
| Total "east" | 35 | 34 |

Source: Derived from absolute estimates in Table 55.

To sum up, Table 21 presents a rough percentage distribution of esti-mated Soviet rail tons originated and terminated in 1949. It will be seen that some 65 per cent of the country's freight traffic still was being generated by economic activity in European Russia, and that the east's share was about 35 per cent. Within European Russia, the eastern Ukraine still accounted for about 25 per cent of total freight traffic. Thus, while the Bolshevik regime has made substantial modifications in the regional pattern bequeathed to them, the recent structure is a recognizable descendant of its prerevolutionary forerunner.

In Soviet freight traffic records, the several hundred commodity classifications are grouped into major commodity groups on lines appreciably
different from those of other countries. For several decades there have been
eight major commodity groups on which attention has been concentrated.

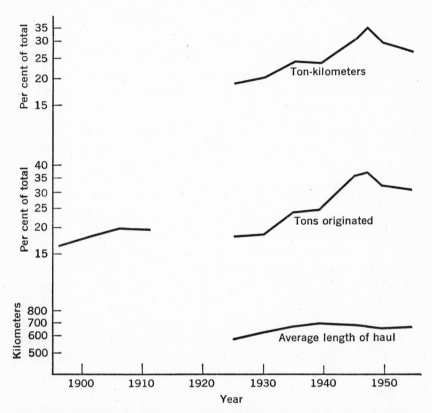

*Chart 20. Position of coal in railroad freight traffic, Russia and USSR, five-year
averages, 1894–1913 and 1923–1940, selected periods, 1945–1955. Source: absolute annual data in Tables 53 and 54.*

Without access to the detailed underlying records, one is perforce limited to
analysis of trends in these eight groups as compiled by Soviet record-keepers,
and one cannot recombine the constituent parts to make up groupings that
could be compared with those of, say, the United States. Even the analysis
of Soviet major commodity group traffic is limited by incomplete release
of data in recent years. Nevertheless, a review of broad traffic trends pro-

vides a skeletal insight into one aspect of the industrialization process, and in the section which follows, each group will be discussed briefly.

*Coal and Coke.* Chart 20 presents a summary record of coal movement on the railroads during the last six decades. One can see that, even before the turn of the century, coal accounted for about one sixth of total rail freight originated on the Russian railroad system. At that time first place was held by grain traffic, but in 1907, for the first time, coal surpassed grain in its share of total rail tons originated. Since then coal has been the most important single commodity carried, at least in terms of originated tonnage.

With economic restoration in the 1920's, coal's share of rail traffic rose close to its prerevolutionary level. Forced industrialization under the five-year plans pushed up coal's share to almost one quarter of total traffic in the middle and late 1930's. World War II saw still a further rise, to a peak around 37 per cent in the postwar year of 1947. Since then other traffic has grown more rapidly than coal traffic, and coal's share appears to be subsiding somewhat.

In the 1920's coal usually moved about 600 kilometers. Under the five-year plans, this average length of haul rose steadily to 701 in 1940. The drastic shift in coal sources brought about by the Nazi invasion led to a further lengthening; in 1942 it reached a peak of 886 kilometers. However, restoration and postwar advance has brought the average haul back to the neighborhood of 670 kilometers. It will be noted that while coal used to have an average haul above the average for all freight, in the late 1930's this relationship was reversed, and since then coal's average haul has been below that of all freight. Even with the slower growth in coal than in other freight tonnage, and a tendency for other hauls to rise more than coal's, coal accounts for some 30 per cent of the railroad's over-all work, measured in ton-kilometers.

This commodity group covers anthracite and bituminous coal, sub-bituminous coal, lignite, and coke. Coke appears to account usually for about 5 per cent of total tons originated for the commodity group. The average haul for coke has been significantly above that for coal, being in the neighborhood of 900 kilometers in the postwar period.

The geographic pattern of coal shipments that took shape during the 1920's and 1930's was briefly sketched in the preceding section. During and since World War II, the pattern has been somewhat modified. Donbas coal now moves to a lesser degree northwest toward Leningrad, and on a much more substantial scale northeast toward the various industrial centers along the Volga River.[1]

Discussing plans for the rebuilding of Leningrad in 1945, one author said that most of its coal would come from the newly developed Vorkuta coal field. Gas and shale oil were to come from the districts immediately southwest of the Leningrad region. It appears that, in addition, Leningrad

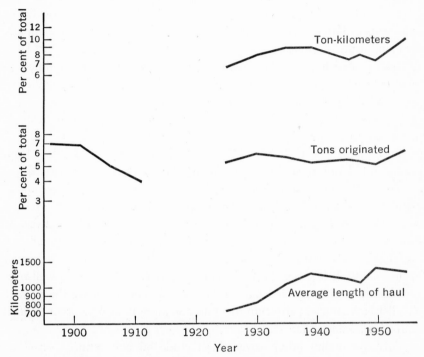

*Chart 21. Position of petroleum in railroad freight traffic, Russia and USSR, five-year averages, 1894–1913 and 1923–1940, selected periods, 1945–1955. Source: absolute annual data in Tables 53 and 54.*

in 1945 was once more receiving substantial coal from the coal fields of Poland.[2] Around Moscow, use of lignite from the sub-Moscow fields to the south has increased greatly. A geographer writing in 1947 pointed out that even though sub-Moscow lignite had only 43 per cent of the heating capacity of Donets Basin coal, nevertheless it was well worth using in Moscow. The average haul for sub-Moscow coal was then between 150 and 200 kilometers, while Donets coal came in from 1,000 to 1,200 kilometers away. Hence substitution of 100 tons of sub-Moscow lignite for 43 tons of Donets coal landed in Moscow would save the railroad about 30,000 ton-kilo-meters.[3]

The locational forces tending to raise the average distance over which coal is shipped do not appear to be abating, and the government conse-quently continues its strong campaign against them. For example, it was pointed out by L. M. Kaganovich, in his major address of May 1954 to railroad officials, that: "Coal accounts for 30 per cent of all carloadings. Shipments of Kuznets, Karaganda, and Ural coal are growing more rapidly than shipments of Donets coal, which requires the railroads to export large amounts of coal for long distances from Kuzbas and Karaganda almost to Moscow. Coal shipments for 2600 kilometers or more in 1953 were 7.1 per cent of total shipments, as against 5.9 per cent in 1952." [4]

*Petroleum and Petroleum Products.* Railroad tank car movement of petroleum was important on the Russian railroad system in the 1890's, as can be seen in Chart 21. Since pipeline traffic has not yet developed ap-preciably, railroad movement of crude and refined petroleum has remained an important element in railroad operations. During the 1930's, it accounted for more than 5 per cent of total railroad tons originated, and this level has been maintained since World War II. Under the impact of the five-year plans, the average distance for petroleum movement rose substantially, to over 1200 kilometers at the close of the 1930's. There was some reduction in the middle 1940's, but the distance recently has risen again to well over 1200 kilometers. Since this length of haul is substantially above the average for all freight traffic, petroleum accounts for more than 8 per cent of total railroad ton-kilometers.

This commodity group covers both crude oil and refined petroleum products. In the early 1930's, crude oil accounted for over half the total originated tonnage on the railroads, but this proportion fell below one half thereafter, and in 1947 crude oil accounted for about 43 per cent of rail tank car shipments. In 1947, the average haul for crude oil was about 600 kilometers; for heavy fuel oil it was about 950 kilometers, and for benzine it was over 1400 kilometers.[5]

Petroleum is shipped from the Caucasus, and from the so-called Second Baku region, to major Soviet industrial centers and to Machine-Tractor Stations in the agricultural regions of the USSR. Before the war, heavy movement north on the Caspian Sea and up the Volga River was associated with transshipment to rail tank cars at Stalingrad, Saratov, Gorky, and Yaroslavl for consignment to Moscow; also there was transshipment at Kuibyshev and Molotov for eastern consumers, and at Rybinsk for consignment to Leningrad. In 1939 only 13 per cent of the petroleum products reaching the Moscow district (*oblast*) arrived by all-water shipment. The 1939 percentage of all-water petroleum shipment to Leningrad oblast was only 9 per cent.[6]

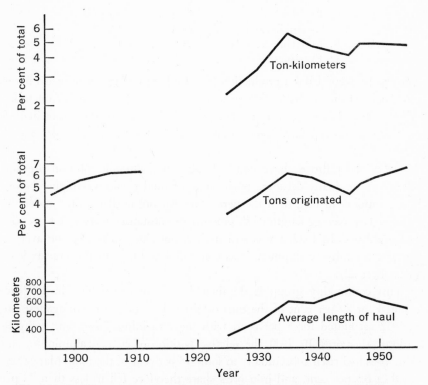

*Chart 22. Position of ores in railroad freight traffic, Russia and USSR, five-year averages, 1894–1913 and 1923–1940, selected periods, 1945–1955. Source: absolute annual data in Tables 53 and 54.*

The rapid growth of crude oil production in the region between the Volga and the Urals, combined with delay in the provision of local refining capacity, have laid a heavy burden on the railroads of the area and raised substantially the railroads' national share of petroleum traffic. Tank car loadings on the Ufa and Kuibyshev railroads in 1953 reached eight times their 1940 level, while in 1955 a railroad specialist wrote that "improper location of oil refineries leads to annual shipment of over five million tons of crude oil by rail from Bashkir and Tatar fields to the center and north Caucasus

. . . involving more than four billion extra ton-kilometers and forty-five hundred extra tank cars."[7] The percentage division of petroleum traffic among major carriers (measured in ton-kilometers) changed between 1940 and 1953 as follows:[8]

| Carrier | 1940 | 1953 |
|---|---|---|
| Railroads | 55.2 | 69.1 |
| Internal waterways | 18.3 | 12.3 |
| Maritime vessels | 20.8 | 11.8 |
| Pipelines | 5.7 | 6.8 |

The rise of Second Baku production has also led to a large southward barge movement of oil on the Volga; from 10 per cent of Volga petroleum traffic in 1940, these downstream shipments had already reached 40 per cent in 1948 and since then must have come to outweigh the traditional upstream movement.[9]

*Ores.* The railroads have handled substantial amounts of iron ore and other ores for many decades. Their share of total traffic was higher before the revolution, in fact, than the percentage for ore until recently under the Soviets. The average length of shipment rose substantially from the twenties to the thirties. In 1945 it was still higher, but since that time the average distance for rail ore shipments has come down almost to the prewar level (see Chart 22).

This commodity group is dominated by iron ore, which in 1932 accounted for 89 per cent of the tons originated on railroads. Manganese ore in 1932 accounted for 8 per cent, with the remaining 3 per cent going to various other ores. By 1940, the relative position of copper, aluminum, and other ores had risen substantially to some 18 per cent of the total. Manganese stood at 8.5 per cent, and iron ore's share therefore fell to less than 74 per cent. Points of origin and termination for this commodity group are determined by the location of ore deposits and refining facilities; detailed discussion does not seem appropriate here.

*Iron and Steel.* As a major element in an industrial economy, this commodity group has understandably assumed increasing importance during the Soviet period. Before the revolution it had come to account for over 3 per cent of total rail tons originated. During the Second Five Year Plan period, this percentage was exceeded and almost 5 per cent of rail traffic was accounted for by iron and steel. In the postwar period the fraction has risen to more than 6 per cent.

The average distance traveled by iron and steel shipments has steadily lengthened, from a level around 750 kilometers in the middle 1920's to 1000 kilometers at the close of the 1930's, and about 1060 kilometers in 1955 (see Chart 23). Evidently this is one price paid for the increased dispersion of industrial activity away from the eastern Ukraine and toward the east. The combined effect of larger relative originated tonnages and longer average hauls has been to raise the percentage of total rail ton-kilometers in this commodity group from around 4 to around 8 per cent.

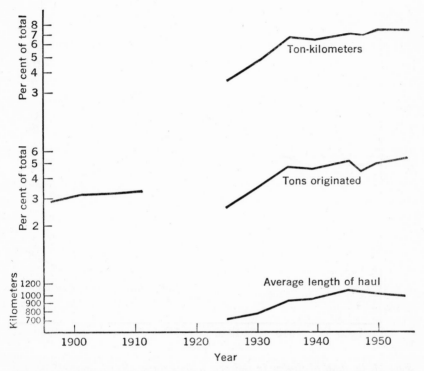

Chart 23. Position of iron and steel in railroad freight traffic, Russia and USSR, five-year averages, 1894–1913 and 1923–1940, selected periods, 1945–1955. Source: absolute annual data in Tables 53 and 54.

The detailed classifications included in this commodity group fall under the three categories of pig iron, ingot steel, and rolled steel products. In 1933, pig iron accounted for 40 per cent, ingots for 10 per cent, and rolled products for 50 per cent of the total tons originated in the group. By 1937 these percentages had shifted to 26, 17, and 57 respectively. In 1947, pig iron's share was 30 per cent, ingots had dropped to 5 per cent, and rolled products had risen to 65 per cent. These proportions make it appear that the railroads had achieved some success in inducing steel works to fabricate their output a little more before shipping it elsewhere.

The average distance for pig iron shipments in 1947 was about 950 kilometers; for ingots it was 966 kilometers. Shipment of rolled steel was for an average distance of 1234 kilometers, and the average haul for other

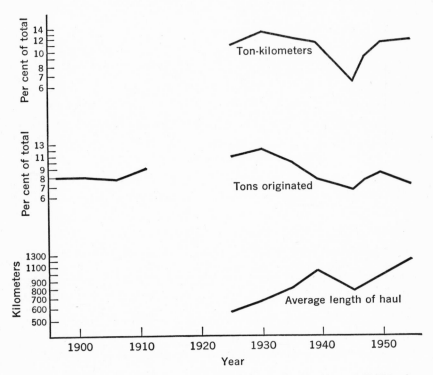

*Chart 24. Position of timber in railroad freight traffic, Russia and USSR, five-year averages, 1894–1913 and 1923–1940, selected periods, 1945–1955. Source: absolute annual data in Tables 53 and 54.*

rolled products in 1947 was 1414 kilometers. These are all considerably in excess of the average for all freight traffic.[10]

*Timber.* Railroad timber traffic in this traditionally wood-using country has always been large. Before the revolution it accounted for some 8 per cent of total originated rail tonnage. In the middle 1920's this percentage rose to 11 per cent, and, with the construction boom of the First Five Year Plan, it rose to 12 per cent. Thereafter it subsided to 10 per cent during the

Second Five Year Plan period, and to around 8 per cent at the close of the decade (see Chart 24).

One consequence of the Nazi invasion was a pronounced shift in the geography of timber freight traffic, reducing its average haul and altering its direction of movement. There was also a relative shrinkage in its position within total rail tons originated, though this has been largely restored since the war. Recently, there has been an alarming tendency for the average distance of timber shipments to rise.

During World War II, timber felling dropped sharply in outlying parts of the USSR.[11] The hard-pressed Russians turned to local forests, even cutting "water-protecting forests." There was also a substantial shift from coal to wood for municipal heating and even for firing railroad locomotives. All this brought the average distance for timber movement on the railroads from 1019 kilometers in 1940 to a low of 632 kilometers in 1942.

In recent years a different tendency has asserted itself. Timber supplies in the settled regions of European Russia are proving insufficient, and an increasing volume of imports is arriving from the Urals and farther east. In 1940, these imports from the east made up about 25 per cent of total timber shipments; in 1952 the expectation was that such long haul imports would amount to 35–40 per cent, and to even more in the future.[12]

The timber commodity group contains a considerable variety of sub-classifications, broadly grouped under the headings of "round logs" or undressed timber, sawn timber, and railroad ties. Undressed timber includes pit props and other mine timbers, round building timber, and other rough lumber. In 1937, sawn timber made up one third of total tons originated in the commodity group; this percentage in 1940 was 27.4 per cent. Wartime dislocations brought the proportion of sawn timber down to 17.8 per cent in 1945, and by 1953 it was still only 20.6 per cent. Railroad ties, which were 12.2 per cent of the total in 1937, and 12.1 per cent in 1940, dropped to about 11 per cent in the early postwar period, and 8.9 per cent in 1953. This meant that the balance of undressed timber, which was 55 per cent in 1937 and 61 per cent in 1940, reached 73 per cent in 1947, and 70.5 per cent in 1953.[13]

Undressed timber appears to move generally for shorter distances than all timber; sawn timber in 1947 moved for 957 kilometers and ties moved for 877 kilometers, as compared with an average for the entire commodity group of 831 kilometers. Pit props and mine timber moved an average distance of 1120 kilometers, with the balance of undressed lumber moving an average distance in 1947 of 580 kilometers.[14]

*Firewood.* Firewood is an interesting but minor component of Soviet railroad freight traffic. Before the revolution this commodity accounted for over 5 per cent of total rail tons originated, indicating the extent to which it was used for heating purposes all over Russia. During the turmoil between

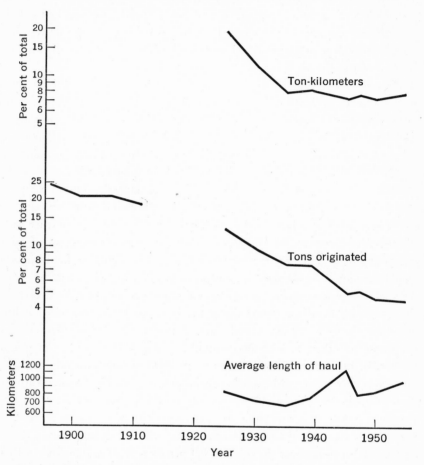

*Chart 25. Position of grain in railroad freight traffic, Russia and USSR, five-year averages, 1894–1913 and 1923–1940, selected periods, 1945–1955. Source: absolute annual data in Tables 53 and 54.*

1914 and 1923, it replaced coal in many uses, including the firing of loco-motives. During the five-year period 1923–1927, it still constituted almost 14 per cent of rail tons originated and 6 per cent of total ton-kilometers.

With the onset of the five-year plan period, firewood's share gradually declined, to less than 4 per cent at the close of the 1930's. By 1949 its share had fallen below 3 per cent. A pronounced postwar shrinkage in the average distance moved by firewood has brought its share of total rail ton-kilometers below 1 per cent. Presumably increasing urbanization and improving fuel technology will lead to gradual elimination of this category altogether.

*Grain.* As Chart 25 clearly shows, grain's role in railroad freight traffic has undergone a revolutionary transformation in recent decades. In the 1890's it accounted for almost one quarter of total rail tons originated. Since then its relative position has steadily decreased. During the early 1920's, it still accounted for one eighth of originated rail tonnage, but the forced industrialization drive brought grain's share down below 8 per cent in the middle and late 1930's. Currently it accounts for only about 5 per cent of rail tons originated.

The average length of grain shipments on the railroads was decreasing from the 1920's through the middle 1930's, but showed some tendency to rise on the eve of World War II. The war brought a substantial lengthening of average hauls for grain, to a level around 1150 kilometers in 1945. Even with the restoration of agriculture in occupied areas, the average length of haul for grain in 1949–1950 was still 830 kilometers, and by 1954–1955 it had risen again to around 970 kilometers. In the context of Soviet location policy, such a long and rising haul for grain and flour must be interpreted as showing the strength of forces generating interregional exchange, against which government efforts have so far proved ineffective.

Measured in ton-kilometers, railroad grain traffic has fallen relatively from a level accounting for almost 20 per cent of the railroad system's freight operations on the eve of forced industrialization. During 1947–1955, grain's share of total rail ton-kilometers ran between 5 and 6 per cent.

This commodity group includes both unprocessed wheat, rye, and other grains, and the milled products produced from them. In 1937, milled products made up one third of total rail tonnage in this commodity group. Since then, the proportion of unprocessed grain has risen, and in 1947 milled products made up only about one quarter of the total.[15]

Among the major commodity groups, this one fluctuates most markedly over the seasons. In late summer and early fall, a pronounced seasonal peak arises, with the peak month substantially above the monthly average. In 1940, it was 65 per cent above the annual average per month, and in 1946 the peak month was 206 per cent of the year's monthly average.

By contrast with certain mineral products, this group is also characterized by wide dispersion in points of origination. In 1940, grain originated at

4545 different railroad stations. From a railroad operating point of view, such widespread and fragmented shipments constitute a most bothersome problem. To the extent that the regime succeeds in dispersing population more evenly over Soviet territory, there will also be a tendency for consumption centers

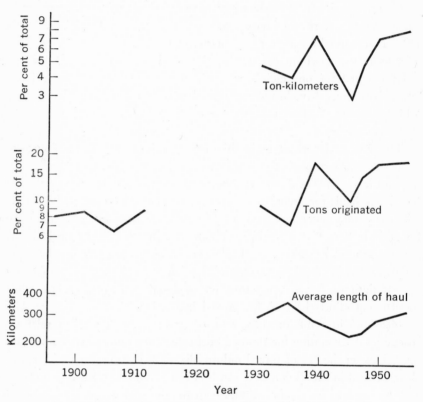

*Chart 26. Position of mineral building materials in railroad freight traffic, Russia and USSR, five-year averages, 1894–1913 and 1923–1940, selected periods, 1945–1955. Source: absolute annual data in Tables 53 and 54.*

to increase in number and spread out territorially. The slender evidence available to date does not reveal any marked progress in the government's drive to have each region develop its own grain supply, so that interregional grain movement can be reduced. In 1954, with a good crop in the first season of the "virgin lands" program, the average haul for grain rose from 949 to 997 kilometers. This program is not to supply the east, but European Russia.

*Mineral Building Materials.* Railroad traffic in mineral building materials has been substantial for many years. Before the revolution, it accounted for some 8 per cent of total rail tons originated. Since the average haul for items in this commodity group is generally short, the group accounted during the early and middle 1930's for less than 5 per cent of total ton-kilometers.

The record shown in Chart 26 is complicated by a change in coverage for this commodity group that extended its range substantially. Nevertheless, comparing the last prewar years with 1945 and 1949, it is clear that wartime dislocations markedly reduced the relative share of mineral building materials traffic in the wartime period. By 1949 this share had been essentially restored.

The change in coverage affecting this group reflects the construction drive. Until about 1933, the group covered only so-called "principal" mineral building materials; thereafter "other" mineral building materials were added to form a commodity group more than twice as large. Four items were traditionally considered to be "principal" building materials: building stone, bricks, cement, and lime plus limestone. Three categories were included in "other mineral building materials": gravel and sand, earth and clay, and a small miscellaneous category of new mineral building materials.[16] The position of limestone flux for blast furnaces was uncertain. Column 2 of the tabulation in note 16 shows that the relative position of sand, gravel, earth, and clay steadily increased during the 1930's to reach some 70 per cent by the end of the decade. If one examines the trend for principal mineral building materials alone, there is evidence of an absolute drop after 1937, presumably connected with a slackening in widespread construction of brick and stone buildings.

This commodity group has the shortest average length of haul of any among the major categories. It has sometimes been argued by geographers outside the USSR that a shortage of mineral materials on the steppes of Russia has been a serious impediment to industrial construction and road-building in that country. Short average hauls belie this supposition. In connection with stone ballasting for railroads, for example, a technical discussion in a railroad journal indicates that the average length of haul for ballast over several years was in the neighborhood of 150 kilometers.[17]

*"Other" Freight Traffic.* In Soviet freight traffic records of the kind released during the last twenty years, after these eight commodity groups are discussed, all other rail freight traffic is relegated to a residual category of "other" traffic. Even in prerevolutionary days, "other" traffic accounted for almost a quarter of total rail tons originated. During the Soviet period,

its proportion has been unclear because of the changing coverage in the mineral building materials commodity group; however, in the early and middle 1930's, about 30 per cent, rather than 24 per cent, of total rail tons originated was placed in the "other" category.

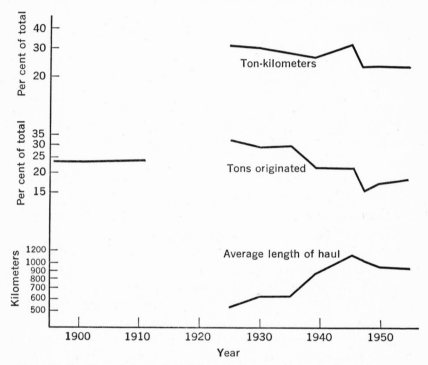

*Chart 27. Position of "other" freight in railroad freight traffic, Russian and USSR, five-year averages, 1894–1913 and 1923–1940, selected periods, 1945– 1955. Source: absolute annual data in Tables 53 and 54.*

With the transfer of sand and gravel, earth and clay, to the mineral-building materials commodity group, the share of "other" freight traffic in total tons originated dropped to 22 per cent on the eve of World War II. By 1949 this percentage had fallen to about 17 per cent. There has been a substantial lengthening in the average distance traveled by items in this residual category, and its share in total railroad operations is therefore higher, being in the postwar period roughly one quarter of total rail ton-kilometers (see Chart 27).

In Table 22, scattered data for 1937 and 1940 show some of the smaller freight traffic items included in this miscellaneous commodity group. It will be seen that over 50 million tons in the industrial subgroup remain unspecified. Similarly, in the agricultural subgroup, some 15 million tons fall in the "not elsewhere classified" category. Presumably these opaque aggregates cloak those rail movements about which the Soviet government felt it most necessary to be secretive. It will be noted that even for 1937

Table 22. Composition of "other freight" commodity group, 1937 and 1940
(millions of metric tons originated)

| Item | 1937 | | 1940 | |
|---|---|---|---|---|
| *Industrial:* | | | | |
| Peat | 9.5 | | — | |
| Mineral fertilizer | 5.0 | | — | |
| Machines | 3.9 | | 9.5 | |
| Chemicals | — | | 8.9 | |
| Sugar | 4.0 | | — | |
| Salt | 4.1 | | — | |
| Unspecified items | 53.9 | | 73.1 | |
| Subtotal | | 80.4 | | 91.5 |
| *Agricultural:* | | | | |
| Sugar beets | 8.9 | | 7.9 | |
| Cotton | 1.6 | | 1.8 | |
| Other technical crops | — | | 6.3 | |
| Potatoes | 2.8 | | — | |
| Livestock products | 1.5 | | — | |
| Fish products | 1.3 | | — | |
| Unspecified items | 15.4 | | 18.4 | |
| Subtotal | | 31.5 | | 34.4 |
| Total | | 111.9 | | 125.9 |

Sources: The 1937 items are from Vol'fson, 1941, p. 272, and the subtotals are derived from Galitskii, 1939, p. 15. The 1940 items are from Povorozhenko, 1947, p. 63, and Naporko, 1954, p. 180; the subtotals are derived from approximate data in Kaganovich, 1954b, p. 7.

and 1940 the residual remaining unaccounted for, while large in absolute terms, is a fairly small fraction of total rail traffic. Perhaps eventually this residual can be reduced still further.

A summary of the detailed material in the present chapter is scarcely possible. We have reviewed the geographic pattern of Soviet freight transportation, and surveyed the content of each major commodity group in railroad freight traffic, noting in each case any large-scale changes that have occurred during the last few decades. The available sources would permit a far more meticulous treatment of these topics than has been presented here, if it were required for special studies.[18] But perhaps in closing this discussion, one general observation would be appropriate.

Both the commodity composition of Soviet freight traffic and its regional distribution show a considerable degree of stability over the period from the 1880's to the 1950's. Coal has displaced grain as the leading commodity group, and traffic growth in the eastern regions has reduced the dominance of south and central European Russia, but the changes have been slow and evolutionary. The implications of this finding are several. It suggests that for this range of problems, at least, planning for the future may be more feasible, and predictions of the future may be more reliable, than might otherwise be supposed. And it also testifies to the strength of the basic locational determinants of transportation activity that were sketched in Chapter 1. Finally, the record may counsel a certain skepticism whenever one reads glowing Soviet accounts of plans for massive regional trans-formations in a short period of time. Even a revolutionary regime has found it necessary to make haste slowly in this field.

# 10 PASSENGER TRANSPORTATION

In transportation there is a noticeable contrast between the ordinary citizen's interest on the one hand, and the emphasis of those responsible for managing transportation activity on the other. The outsider is likely to think first and mainly of passenger transportation when he considers the major carriers. But for railroads, internal waterways, and maritime carriers, the physical and financial focus of attention is usually on freight traffic. Both passenger and freight transportation are of course important for the growth of an economy, but there is a sense in which the movement of persons is less fundamental than the movement of raw materials and finished commodities. The movement of commodities is for the most part an intermediate form of production, a service contributed in the value-adding process before the commodity passes to a final consumer. It is, therefore, a "producers' service." Passenger transportation, on the other hand, is frequently a "consumers' service." It is true that much urban passenger transportation carries workers to and from their jobs, and that intercity passenger movement may reflect business trips rather than personal travel. Nevertheless, most outlays on passenger travel come from household expenditures, while most freight bills are charged to enterprise accounts. The distinction is symbolized in Soviet economic methodology by the fact that freight services are considered "productive" and are included in aggregate national income, while passenger service is excluded as being "unproductive."

Soviet citizens, and foreigners traveling in the USSR, have thus naturally paid attention to prevailing conditions of passenger transportation service, while the Soviet government and the carriers themselves have regularly tended to concentrate on freight transportation. Had the regime been attempting primarily to raise the standard of living promptly, instead of driving to build heavy industry, more resources would presumably have been devoted to consumer goods in general, and to passenger service in particular. But even in a consumer-oriented economy such as our own, passenger services are typically peripheral in the operations of most railroads, water carriers, and trucking firms. Consequently there is an inherent psychological tendency, evidently independent of governmental forms, for the suppliers of transportation services to reflect the division of resources between their two types of operation, relegating passenger service to secondary status, while the general public tends to judge the carriers' performance almost entirely in terms of passenger transportation.

This chapter is designed to set forth briefly the main features of the record for Soviet passenger transportation. It will not go as far into the subject as might seem desirable for the sake of human interest, since the present study is concerned primarily with policies of resource management in a period of economic development. There is, moreover, another factor that confines an analysis of passenger transportation in the USSR even more narrowly than is justified by our terms of reference. Because the Soviet government has not been much interested in passenger transportation, Soviet books and journals seldom discuss it. It is therefore more difficult to piece together a satisfactory picture of passenger operations than it is to discern the main features of the freight traffic situation. Of necessity, the major emphasis here is on description, covering historical trends in the volume of passenger movement, and the conditions under which travelers and commuters move about. Of equal interest are certain simple comparisons among time series that are significantly related in a developing economy. Has the relative volume of passenger transportation kept pace with other indices of economic growth? The relationships examined seem significant, not only for an understanding of the record to date, but also in considering the prospects for Soviet passenger transportation in the future.

The broad category of passenger transportation can be usefully divided into two somewhat overlapping divisions: urban or metropolitan, and long-distance or intercity. The former is a function of urban growth, while the latter may reflect a number of diverse forces at work. The stormy years of the prewar forced industrialization drive in the USSR witnessed sharp changes in the volume of passenger transportation, and the changes differed appreciably in these two divisions. For the period as a whole, the rise in urban transportation was more marked than the rise in intercity passenger movement. At the same time, short-term changes within the period were more pronounced for intercity passenger traffic than they were for urban carriage.

As can be seen from the record in Chart 28, total intercity passenger traffic more than tripled between 1928 and 1940. The growth, however, was by no means uniform. During the period of the First Five Year Plan, with its large-scale movement from village to city, its opening up of new mining and manufacturing centers, and its resettlement of unco-operative

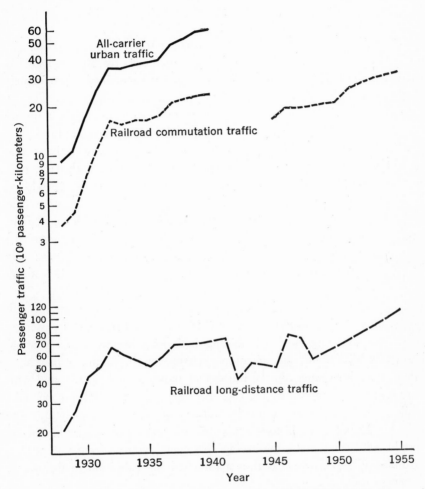

*Chart 28. Passenger traffic, urban and intercity, USSR, 1924–1955. Source: Tables 56 and 57.*

peasants, total passenger-kilometers in long-distance movement rose 3.1 times, from 23.1 to 72.6 billion. This great spurt, culminating in 1932, the year of crop failures and famine, was followed by a three-year decline in long-distance travel. It may be presumed to reflect in part a reduction in demand. The forces stimulating internal migration during the First Five Year Plan period relaxed after 1932. At the same time the ability of the carriers to provide adequate passenger service grew weaker. The railroads, accounting for over nine tenths of the total, were in the throes of a serious freight traffic crisis that evidently diverted both attention and resources from the passenger service.

The downward trend of intercity passenger traffic was reversed in 1936 and 1937, with total long-distance passenger-kilometers reaching and slightly exceeding the 1932 peak level. Thereafter the level remained approximately constant through 1939 and rose about 5 per cent in 1940.

When one views the prewar period as a whole, it appears that the industrialization drive called for a higher level of long-distance travel than had been associated with the previous pattern of economic activity, that this higher level was reached very quickly, and that from then on only very modest additions can be observed. No single variable can be selected to investigate causal relationships here, but perhaps total population is at least one major factor to be separated from the others. Rough calculations suggest that in 1926 the average citizen traveled about 150 kilometers per year, close to the 170 kilometers estimated for 1913. During the peak year of 1932, this figure rose to about 450 kilometers per year, and in 1939 it was still approximately 430 kilometers.

Scattered information makes it possible to discover, at least for the railroads, something about the manner in which the great increase of passenger traffic was accommodated. Combining both long-distance and commutation (suburban) traffic, one can compare changes in the volume of passenger-kilometers with changes in the number of passenger cars in use, and with the total mileage moved by the cars. Between 1928 and 1932, for example, while traffic rose 240 per cent, the number of passenger cars in use rose only by 22 per cent. Consequently the number of passenger-kilometers "produced" each year by the average passenger car rose from one million to three million. There was thus a threefold intensification in the use of passenger cars.[1]

This intensified use of passenger equipment was achieved partly through crowding each car more heavily with passengers, and partly through keeping each car more continuously in use. Again comparing 1928 and 1932, it seems that the extent of crowding rose by some 80 per cent, while the yearly distance run by a car increased some 50 per cent. The average "population" of a passenger car dropped off somewhat from 1932 to 1935, but even then it was 55 per cent above the level of 1928. After the 1932 peak, there was also some fall in the average yearly distance run by a passenger car; in 1935 it was 25 per cent above the 1928 level. Hence even at the trough of the post-1932 slump in passenger travel, the ratio of annual passenger-kilometers to cars in use was still more than 90 per cent above its preplan level.

These statistics give rough numerical expression to the human facts of turbulence and overcrowding so abundantly testified to in the accounts of Soviet writers and foreign visitors for this period. Passenger journeys on Soviet railroads in the early 1930's were, by all reports, a demanding experience. Not only were the trains crowded, but they ran slowly and there were frequent lengthy stops. As is shown in a comparison of prewar and postwar passenger train speeds (see Table 24), the scheduled terminal-to-terminal speeds for the fastest passenger trains on eight major routes in the USSR in 1934 varied between 20 and 36 miles per hour. By 1937 the speeds on these eight routes, including all stops, were scheduled between 22 and 38 miles per hour. These were the showcase trains. For the network as a whole, taking account of all passenger trains operated, the actual average speed including all stops was almost constant at 18 miles per hour in 1932, 1934, and 1935.[2]

In the 1928–1940 period, while passengers on the railroads were confronted with the conditions described, the railroads nevertheless raised substantially the average unit revenue collected per passenger-kilometer. The over-all average of course reflects changes in the composition of traffic according to class of accommodation and length of journey, as well as changes in the fares charged for a given distance and accommodation; no attempt is made here to surmount the index-number problem involved.[3] But the combined price and market-basket changes led to the following index trend, taking the realized unit passenger revenue in 1928 as 100: 1933, 230; 1938, 284; 1940, 351.[4] As between the two main divisions of passenger service, long-distance and commutation, the railroads' output shifted appreciably toward commutation service, which accounted for 25 per cent of total railroad passenger-kilometers in 1940, compared to 16 per cent in 1928. Since fares per mile are higher for short distances than for long, this change in composition would have tended to raise realized unit passenger revenue even if individual fares had remained constant. Hence the indicated index rise overstates the actual price change. By comparison with price changes for most consumer goods and services in the USSR over this period, the railroad passenger fare increase seems to have been a relatively modest one.

Turning now to the short-haul division of passenger transportation, we find a similar record of rapid growth over the 1928–1940 period, character-ized by much the same timing. There are, however, significant differences. The explosive growth of the First Five Year Plan period was a little later getting under way; on the other hand, it had not been preceded, as in the case of long-distance traffic, by a slight drop in 1927. From 1929 through 1932, urban passenger movement increased 3.1 times, while intercity move-ment was rising 2.4 times. In 1933 the volume of urban passenger transporta-tion on the railroads fell off somewhat, reflecting the railroads' difficulties, but the other urban carriers almost made up the deficiency, with the result that total urban passenger-kilometers remained approximately constant and did not suffer the absolute drop visible in intercity traffic. During 1934–1936, small gains were registered. Thus we can say that the transportation crisis discussed in Chapter 3 affected passenger movement mainly in its long-distance forms, with a much less pronounced impact on urban pas-senger transportation.

Toward the close of the decade, substantial increases were registered, and the rate of growth in urban movement was notably higher than in intercity movement. This was especially due to the expanding contribution of nonrailroad carriers. The railroads began the industrialization drive with about 40 per cent of the urban passenger traffic. As the population of cities rose rapidly, the railroads' share increased to over 48 per cent in 1932, and over 46 per cent in 1933–1934. Thereafter the other carriers began to pull ahead, lowering the railroads' share to 42 per cent by the end of the decade. The trend for urban passenger-kilometers is shown in Chart 28. It must be noted that the underlying data do not permit a fully satisfactory distinction between urban and intercity movement; the division employed in this analy-sis is only approximate. During these years autobus traffic is placed wholly in the urban category, and river traffic wholly in the intercity category, though a small amount of each actually lay in the other division. The rail component is composed of suburban, or commutation, traffic defined roughly as it is in Western practice. The data obtained thereby seem dependable enough to support the general analysis based on them.

This rapid growth in urban passenger transportation was one conse-quence of the expansion of Soviet cities attending the five-year plans. It would be interesting to compare it with a series for urban population, year-by-year, but the latter is not at present available. However, it is possible to compare urban passenger-kilometers with an annual series for the non-agricultural labor force, and the results are instructive.[5] A scatter diagram shows considerable evidence of systematic relationship, as might be expected;

and the fitting of a straight line by the least-squares method, with the labor force series taken as the independent variable, yields a relationship that "predicts" the observed values with an average percentage error of plus or minus 7.2 per cent. Clearly, the rise in urban passenger transportation was directly associated with the expansion of the labor force.

However, inspection of the scatter diagram also shows that the increment of passenger traffic associated with a given addition to the nonagricultural labor force increased during the prewar period of forced industrialization. A curve that was concave upward would describe this emerging relationship more precisely.

Certainly the most dramatic development in Soviet urban transportation before the war was the building of the Moscow subway. It seems to have been one of a handful of key symbols of modernization, employed to sustain and encourage the Soviet people during this stern era of transformation from a backward to an advanced economy. The emphasis in the subway was on beauty. Each station was conceived as representing one part of the country, or as a display of one form of building material. When the subway first opened, on May 15, 1935, it was 11.4 kilometers (7 miles) long, but by the end of 1938 it had been extended to a route distance of 26.5 kilometers (16.5 miles). The number of passenger cars in use rose from 74 in 1935 to 271 at the end of 1938. During 1940, the daily average number of passengers carried by the subway was about 1,024,000 riders.

In length and total capacity the Moscow subway was very small by comparison with the much older systems of such cities as London and New York. And the density of its traffic, while higher than implied by a well-known anecdote among Western observers, was not outstanding. In 1939, for example, 332,000,000 passengers were carried and 669,000 trains were dispatched, indicating an average of about 496 passengers per train. In the total public transportation of Moscow, excluding taxis and droshki, the subway system handled 11 per cent of the passengers in 1939, the balance being divided among streetcars (61 per cent), suburban railroad service (15 per cent), and buses (13 per cent). The data are somewhat inadequate, but it seems safe to conclude that the Moscow subway before the war had not become a major feature in the city's physical functioning, however great the éclat it provided psychologically.

The general trend of Soviet passenger traffic over the whole period from 1940 through 1955 is roughly similar to that of freight traffic and other production indicators. The Second World War brought a considerable setback, which has more than been made up, as can be seen from the record in Chart 28. It is worthwhile, however, to sketch a few major details of the record, and note the ways in which it differs from the general pattern of postwar Soviet development.

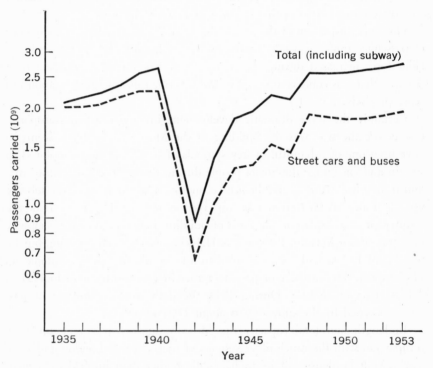

*Chart 29. Moscow annual passenger transportation, 1935–1953. Source: Table 41.*

First of all, the drop in intercity railroad passenger-kilometers after 1941 appears to be a result of incomplete enumeration. Soviet passenger statistics have for many years covered "paying passengers only," and this presumably meant that World War II troop movements do not appear in railroad passenger records.[6] If they could be estimated and added to the recorded long-distance total, it can be assumed that, at the very least, a considerable part of the 1942–1945 decline would be eliminated. As for railroad commutation traffic, no data have come to hand, but a genuine drop here would be expected on the basis of known destruction and evacuation of the major cities of European Russia. It probably showed some recovery in 1943 and 1944, but in 1945 was still substantially below the 1940 level.

Continuing the discussion of Moscow subway traffic, we find that in-

complete evidence for the war and postwar period gives a surprising perspective on the extent to which the capital was evacuated during the war,
and the slowness with which the capital has grown since the war. The
record of Moscow's passenger traffic is presented in Chart 29.

It will be seen that from 1935 through 1940, the service of these carriers
was steadily expanding, with the new subway's percentage share rising
rapidly from 2 to 14 per cent. Suburban railroad traffic, not covered by
the table, was rising more rapidly than was this aggregate, having been
depressed in 1935. To the extent, therefore, that the number of persons
carried per year by Moscow's public transportation agencies provides an
index to the size of the city's population, the evidence suggests that it increased by one third from 1935 to 1940.

When the Nazi invasion threatened Moscow in late 1941, the city was
harassed by German bombers, and the government moved temporarily to
Kuibyshev. The number of passengers carried by these agencies in 1941
dropped some 40 per cent from the 1940 level. In calendar 1942, it appears
that city passenger traffic was running at only one third the 1940 level.
Again, the crude deduction is that the change in the city's population must
have been of the same order of magnitude. Wartime shortages of fuel for
buses and electricity for street cars may explain why the subway's share
rose from 14 to 30 per cent of the city's traffic. There was recovery in 1943
and 1944, but even in 1945 the index for Moscow passenger traffic stood
at 74 per cent of its 1940 level.

The fragments on which the latter part of Chart 29 is based allow a
considerable margin of error around the estimates set down above. What
does seem incontrovertible is that from 1948 through 1952 the passenger
traffic of these carriers was at the 1940 level, and not significantly above
it. Has the same been true of the city's population? It has been government
policy ever since the Eighteenth Congress in 1939 to prevent any further
rise in the population of Moscow, and perhaps the policy has been successful.

The Soviet population estimates released in 1956 suggest that at the end
of 1955 Moscow's population was 17 per cent larger than in 1939. The index
for Moscow passenger traffic in 1953 was about 7 per cent above its 1939
level, indicating a relative falling behind in traffic growth. It is possible,
of course, that an important variable has been omitted here, one that would
eliminate this apparent tendency if it were adequately recognized. There
has certainly been some expansion since 1940 in the number of private
passenger automobiles and taxis used in the city. While nothing suggests
that this growth has been comparable to the postwar mushrooming of

passenger automobile traffic in United States metropolitan areas, inclusion of Moscow passenger-car traffic in the index above might bring it into line with national population trends. However, on any plausible assumption about the number of millions of passenger rides annually that might be added thereby, the traffic data tend to confirm that Moscow's population has not grown more rapidly than the national average, as it had been doing before the war.

Let us turn back now from urban traffic to long-distance passenger travel. A glance at Chart 28 will show that the slow rise from wartime levels of paying passenger movement was interrupted in 1946 and 1947 by a remarkable temporary boom. It had not been expected by the government. Reviewing prospects for the coming year, the Minister of Railroads in early 1946 stated that the number of passengers carried would be more than 10 per cent higher than it had been in 1945.[7] Presumably, the underlying plan figures anticipated roughly an equal rise in both suburban rail traffic and long-distance carriage. As events actually unfolded, suburban traffic rose something like 15 per cent, which was not drastically different from the plan, but the number of long-distance passengers more than doubled, and though the average length of trip dropped by a fourth in 1946, the volume of passenger-kilometers was fully 60 per cent above 1945! One can only speculate about the reasons for this great surge of passenger travel; presumably, persons evacuated eastward during the war were returning to their homes in unexpected numbers, and perhaps demobilized military personnel traveled as paying passengers to an unanticipated extent. In any case, the incident provides a striking example of the difficulty of "planning" a consumers' service for even so short a period as the ensuing year.

In 1947 the number of long-distance passengers rose still further, but the average trip grew shorter, so that long-distance passenger-kilometers fell off slightly, though remaining above the 1940 level. In 1948, however, the slender evidence available indicates that intercity passenger traffic fell off almost 30 per cent, to a level not far above 1945. Again it appears that planning officials were taken by surprise. The collegium of the railroad ministry reviewed the passenger situation in November 1948 and found the annual target (for both intercity and commutation traffic) being only 92 per cent fulfilled.[8] Evidently the year's target for combined traffic was set close to the 1947 figure. At least there does not seem to have been a large planned reduction indicating government restriction of travel. The fall appears rather to reflect a decline in demand, once the immediate postwar internal migration peak had passed.

Since 1948 there has been a steady rise in the volume of long-distance passenger traffic on the railroads, with the 1940 level being reached again in 1951 and moderate growth continuing thereafter. From a railroad operating point of view, the important change lies in the fact that freight ton-kilometers in 1953 had reached a level 91 per cent higher than in 1940, while passenger-kilometers in 1953 were only 20 per cent above their 1940 level. Since technically speaking there is more than a grain of truth in the notion that passenger trains merely get in the way of the important movement, namely that of freight trains, this relative displacement of passenger by freight operations is unquestionably a boon to hard-pressed operating officials.

Unfortunately, comprehensive data for passenger traffic carried in river and sea craft, by airlines, and in intercity bus travel are not easily available and have not been estimated for this study. However, it seems most probable from news stories, travelers' reports, and photographs that passenger travel by air and intercity bus has expanded very rapidly in recent years. There was so little before the war that the present volume cannot yet be very large, but the 20 per cent rise from 1940 to 1953 indicated by railroad data alone might appear as a 25 per cent rise if the other minor carriers were included for both years. Even so, it is clear that passenger travel ranks with food and other consumer goods in the rate of growth it has experienced in the USSR since World War II.

Reduced passenger traffic after 1940 was of course not intended by Soviet policy but imposed by the Nazi invasion, and the slow recovery thereafter reflects in large part the severity of the destruction wreaked by their retreating armies. The Soviet totals for destruction were compiled in connection with presentation of a reparations claim against the German economy, and at least in the case of railroad locomotives and freight cars, substantial evidence makes it clear that the totals are misleadingly large. A similar tendency toward exaggeration may have been present in connection with passenger facilities too, but even after a mentally supplied discount, the figures are shocking.

Before the invasion there were 3913 passenger stations on the Soviet railroad system; during the war some 2436 of them, or 62 per cent, were destroyed.[9] The number of passenger cars was reduced by 35 per cent.[10] The damage to roadway and track, bridges, water-supply facilities, and maintenance shops, which was reviewed in Chapter 5, affected passenger movement as well as freight traffic. There was clearly a Herculean job to be done in rebuilding the railroads. As we saw in Chapter 6, the key year for recovery of freight traffic was 1948, when it surpassed the 1940 level. This was also the year when the second main track was restored to operation on several major routes, and when the active stock of freight locomotives and freight cars rose very substantially. Yet in passenger operations, at least in long-distance traffic, it was a year of reduced traffic.

It appears that since not everything could be done at once, first priority was given to restoration of facilities for freight traffic, with secondary rank going to passenger facilities. This can been seen very clearly in connection with the restoration of passenger stations. Table 23 records the annual

*Table 23. Number of railroad passenger stations restored, USSR, by year, 1946–1954*

| Year | Number | Cumulative total | Plan target |
|------|--------|------------------|-------------|
| 1946 | — | 822 | — |
| 1947 | 28 | 850 | — |
| 1948 | 30 | 880 | — |
| 1949 | 106 | 986 | — |
| 1950 | 322 | 1308 | — |
| 1951 | 136 | 1444 | — |
| 1952 | 99 | 1543 | 140 |
| 1953 | 91 | 1634 | 130 |
| 1954 | 100[a] | 1734[a] | 140 |

[a] Estimated.

Sources: S. A. Andreev, in Levin, 1947, p. 143, refers to 2436 out of 3913 stations destroyed and then states that by Jan. 1, 1947, over 800 had already been restored, with a target for the Fourth Five Year Plan period of 1500 to be restored. An index of annual numbers for 1947–1951, plus the absolute number for 1951 and target for 1952, were given in *Gudok*, 2 Aug. 1952, p. 2. The actual 1952 number and 1953 target appear in *Gudok*, 2 Aug. 1953, p. 2. B. P. Beshchev gave the 1953 number and 1954 target in *Gudok*, 23 April 1954, p. 3, and the 1954 target appears in *Gudok*, 16 May 1954, p. 3.

number restored since the war. Roughly one third of the destroyed stations had been restored by the end of 1946, but little further progress was made in 1947–1948. With 1949, more intensive effort was devoted to passenger stations and some 560 were restored in the next three years. Since then the rate of restoration seems to have fallen off. If we assume 1954 plan fulfillment in proportion to that of 1952–1953, and add another hundred to the cumulative total through 1953, it appears that there were still 700 destroyed stations unaccounted for. It may be that many of these were not in fact "destroyed," but only lightly damaged, and that they have been returned to service without being included among those "restored."

Earlier in the chapter there was mention of passenger train speeds, and it may be well now to show how they were affected by the wartime destruction of railroad facilities. In Table 24, perspective is given through comparison of 1946 scheduled speeds with those of two prewar years, and with speeds established for 1949, after most of the damage had been repaired. For each of the four years, eight major routes have been selected, illustrating traveling conditions on the principal interregional lines. To give an American reader a further basis for comparison, Table 24 also presents illustrative data for the fastest scheduled trains on eight arbitrarily selected United States routes. In every case for both countries, these are average speeds

Table 24. Scheduled terminal-to-terminal passenger train speeds, selected routes in the USSR, 1934, 1937, 1946, 1949, and in the United States, 1953

| Terminals | Miles between terminals | Average miles per hour | | | |
|---|---|---|---|---|---|
| | | 1934 | 1937 | 1946 | 1949 |
| *USSR* | | | | | |
| Moscow–Minsk | 469 | 35.9 | 38.1 | 19.7 | 25.5 |
| Moscow–Kiev | 538 | 23.6 | 30.2 | 19.2 | 24.4 |
| Moscow–Rostov | 844 | 26.8 | 32.4 | 20.6 | 27.5 |
| Leningrad–Murmansk | 900 | 23.6 | 26.7 | 17.4 | 23.4 |
| Moscow–Sochi | 1234 | 24.9 | 30.5 | 19.1 | 26.5 |
| Moscow–Tashkent | 2090 | 21.0 | 21.8 | 18.9 | 21.2 |
| Moscow–Alma Ata | 2497 | 20.4 | 22.4 | 18.8 | 21.1 |
| Moscow–Vladivostok | 5800 | 26.2 | 27.3 | 22.0 | 26.5 |
| *United States* | | 1953 | | | |
| New York–Washington | 227 | 59.2 | | | |
| Washington–St. Louis | 882 | 45.2 | | | |
| Seattle–San Francisco | 904 | 44.1 | | | |
| New York–Chicago | 908 | 56.8 | | | |
| Chicago–New Orleans | 921 | 55.8 | | | |
| Boston–Miami | 1619 | 52.2 | | | |
| Chicago–Seattle | 2189 | 48.6 | | | |
| New York–Los Angeles | 3125 | 47.7 | | | |

Sources: The Soviet data for 1934 and 1937, converted from kilometers into miles, are drawn from a table presented in Khachaturov, 1939, p. 557. The 1946 data were computed through dividing the shortest scheduled elapsed time shown in MPS, 1946, by the route distance shown therein. The 1949 data were similarly computed from the 1949 edition of this same official time-table. The United States data were supplied by the Bureau of Railway Economics, Association of American Railroads, based on *The Official Guide of the Railways*, January 1953.

including all scheduled stops between terminals, and are not necessarily those maintained in practice. It should be noted, too, that these are the showcase trains, and that the ratio of total passenger train-miles to total passenger train-hours (that is, the actual average speed of all passenger trains operated) is substantially lower in each country.

Noting first the impact of the Nazi invasion on Soviet passenger train speeds, one sees that deteriorated track, roadway, and signaling facilities forced at least a one-third reduction on those of the selected routes (the first five in the table) that pass through formerly occupied territory. There was some fall also on the routes in unoccupied territory, presumably reflecting inadequate maintenance during the war. By 1949, these reduced speeds had been substantially improved, and trains were generally traveling at or above their 1934 speeds, though they had not yet regained their 1937 levels.

Before World War II, the main line west from Moscow to Poland via Minsk showed the highest of the eight listed speeds, but evidently it was badly damaged in the war, and its speeds since then remain substantially slower. The highest 1949 speed among these eight routes appears on the main line south from Moscow to Rostov-on-Don (near the eastern tip of the Sea of Azov), where an average of 27.5 miles per hour was scheduled. Actually there does appear to be at least one faster schedule in the 1949 timetable; the Red Arrow Express (Courier No. 1) between Leningrad and Moscow was scheduled to cover the 406 miles in exactly twelve hours, at an average speed, including five stops, of 33.8 miles per hour.[11] On the longest continuous railroad passenger journey in the world, from Moscow to Vladivostok on the Pacific Coast (5810 miles), a scheduled speed of about 27 miles per hour was maintained in both 1937 and 1949.[12]

On American railroads, where rail weight, track alignment, and roadbed conditions permit much higher speeds, the 1953 speeds on eight showcase routes range from 44 to 59 miles per hour, or roughly double the Soviet speeds. It should be noted that United States speeds have been slowly rising in recent years, from a system-wide average of 34 miles an hour in the early 1930's, and 36 miles an hour after the war, to a 1953 average of 39.1 miles per hour. As already indicated, there has not been a comparable rise in the USSR. The Soviet system-wide average in 1934 was about 18 miles per hour, and if the trend indicated in Table 24 for eight major routes is representative, the 1949 average was probably around 19 miles per hour.[13]

Large-scale investment would have been necessary to raise Soviet passenger-train speeds, not so much in locomotives and cars as in improved track and roadbed. There has been such improvement on key routes, but as shown in Chapter 6, it has facilitated vastly higher freight traffic density, while the evidence here indicates that passengers have benefited very little.

Before ending this brief discussion of passenger transportation, in which the railroads account for nine tenths of the long-distance movement, some notice should be given to the other carriers. River boats and coastal steamers carry passengers on the Volga, the Caspian and Black seas, and other water routes, but the volume of traffic involved is very small. Airlines in 1949 maintained some 179 scheduled domestic routes and often provided the principal means of reaching isolated communities in the east and north.

Probably the most rapidly growing passenger carrier in the postwar period has been the intercity bus. With very few all-weather paved roads available before the war, such service could scarcely exist. Since the late 1940's it has grown to unite many of the major cities in European Russia. The 1949 timetable lists 51 scheduled intercity services, and there may well be 200 or so by now.[14]

# PART III

## RAILROADS AS A SECTOR OF THE ECONOMY

# 11 RAILROAD COSTS AND REVENUES

In evaluating the performance of Soviet transportation, we cannot rely on output data alone. The record of physical performance is clearly an initial prerequisite for any analysis whatsoever. And with a few additional series in physical units, covering the chief inputs used, certain tests of operating effectiveness can be applied. But it will not be possible to say whether more or fewer resources should have been applied to transportation in the USSR during the 1928–1940 and postwar periods until a fairly comprehensive structure of ruble data for the whole economy has been worked out. Then the policy decisions made by the Bolshevik regime can be weighed in numerical terms; the costs and benefits associated with each alternative can be estimated, and an informed judgment of Soviet planned industrialization will become possible.

At present the task has only begun. We are still in the stage of piecing together continuous series for the most important magnitudes, with wholly inadequate subsidiary detail concerning their constituent parts. And at the same time it is proving necessary to build a framework of theory that can give meaning to the many unique features of Soviet economic institutions.[1] The Soviet price system has evolved since the 1920's into a complex barrier to welfare-economics analysis. When some prices are padded with enormous sales taxes and others are artificially understated by means of subsidies, and when the whole price structure is distorted through unequal degrees of price inflation, the task of reaching defensible conclusions regarding the effectiveness of Soviet economic activity, in a welfare-economics sense, becomes difficult indeed. But there is hope that in time our increasing knowledge will make such judgments possible.

In the present chapter a regrettably incomplete compilation of ruble data for railroad transportation will be reviewed. The data are too meager to support many firm conclusions. It is, however, necessary to begin with the fragments at hand, in the hope that gaps can later be filled. If the crude financial records for each major sector of the economy are made available, they can be expected to reinforce each other, permitting critical analysis, sector by sector, which could not be attained through study of any one sector in isolation.

It is probably unnecessary to begin with a caveat concerning the nature of these data. The physical series discussed throughout this study, while frequently subject to some doubt, are nevertheless considerably more reliable than Soviet financial statistics. One reason is that the data in tons and kilometers are far more abundant. The Soviet government has devoted single-minded attention to getting results in physical terms, and as a consequence most of its publications emphasize nonmonetary records. Budgetary matters have always constituted an exception, of course, along with banking operations. But in the published records of the People's Commissariat of Transportation, for example, something like a hundred pages of operating data will be found for every page of cost and revenue information. Increasing attention has been given to cost minimization, in ruble terms, and postwar manuals indicate clearly that elaborate financial records are now compiled for the railroads. As yet, however, detailed statistics based on these records have not appeared in the available literature.

Since the reliability of aggregate statistics turns very largely on the presence or absence of detailed information concerning their constituent elements, this paucity of financial information for railroads is serious. Continuous series for *total* operating revenues and costs can be assembled, but detailed breakdowns of costs and revenues are difficult to find. The case is different for traffic data, where regional breakdowns and commodity-group breakdowns greatly increase the confidence that can be placed in aggregate figures. Interpretation of the financial records presented in this chapter is relatively hazardous, precisely because supporting detail is so far lacking.

Though the evidence is slender, it seems likely that an additional difficulty arises from fairly substantial changes in the form and coverage of financial records during this period. The thorough and comprehensive operating records that had become well established by 1928 required only minor modification in the 1930's. Financially, on the other hand, a tradition of uniform, inclusive reports was lacking, and government concern for efficient use of resources seems to have induced a gradual expansion of record-keeping. During the course of the expansion, especially in connection with cost data, classifications and definitions have been changed from time to time. Consequently some of the trends disclosed in this chapter may reflect changes in reporting methods rather than changes in the underlying facts.

Finally, of course, there are the problems associated with monetary inflation. The ruble as a unit of account for the forced industrialization period leaves much to be desired. As will be shown below, the railroad sector shows a smaller degree of price inflation than many other sectors of

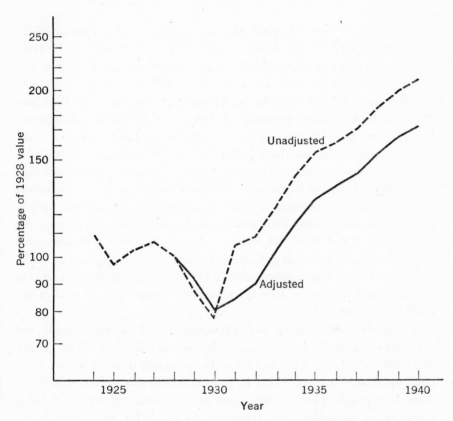

*Chart 30. Average unit operating costs, USSR railroads, 1924–1940. Source: Table 42.*

the economy, at least for the 1928–1940 period. However, wage rates, construction costs, and the prices charged for railroad transportation all rose appreciably during the 1930's, and this means that financial records require deflation for proper intertemporal comparisons. A few preliminary efforts in this direction will be made in the ensuing discussion, but they

will be recognized as first steps only. Where the underlying data are fragmentary, elaborate analysis is premature.

In Chart 30, we begin by recording two estimates for the average unit
cost of railroad operations annually from the late 1920's through 1940. The
output unit involved is a "cumulated ton-kilometer," obtained through
adding freight ton-kilometers and passenger-kilometers, using no (that is,
equal) weights.[2]

Both series of Chart 30 exhibit the same general trend: an initial fall in
unit operating costs, followed by a steady rise from 1930 onwards. By 1940,
the level of unit costs was between 73 per cent and 110 per cent above the
1928 level. The unadjusted series, however, exaggerates the rise in unit
costs between 1928 and 1940. At the beginning of the period, no allowance
was made in computing operating costs for capital repairs to rolling stock,
or for depreciation of fixed plant and equipment. Later, however, these
costs were recognized and included in the total. In order to preserve comparability, therefore, such costs must be either included or excluded throughout. Since the objective presence of these cost elements cannot be eliminated
through mere nonrecognition, it is clearly preferable to estimate and include
them for the early years. The result of doing so, of course, is to raise the
level of base-period costs and hence to show a smaller rise in costs over
the whole period. Although the amounts added to operating costs for 1926–
1930 are no more than approximations, the resulting adjusted series seems
clearly to provide a more accurate indication of cost trends than does the
unadjusted series.

It appears, then, that the unit operating cost of carrying freight and
passengers combined on Soviet railroads rose only by some 80 to 100 per
cent between 1928 and 1940. In view of the pronounced rise in money wage
rates, materials costs, and prices in general during this period, such a rise
seems surprisingly small. To the extent that our data will support detailed
investigation, it should prove rewarding to search for an explanation of
this limited rise. The basic cost data assembled in Table 68 make possible
the computations presented in Chart 31, which throw some light on the
question.

In general, the structure of railroad costs, when grouped under the three
broad headings of "labor," "depreciation," and "other," shows changes
consistent with what we know about the period. Using depreciation as a
measure of the direct costs associated with railroad fixed plant and equipment, its role in 1926–1930 (had it been charged at 4 per cent of fixed assets)
would have been a large one, amounting to some 20 per cent of total operat-

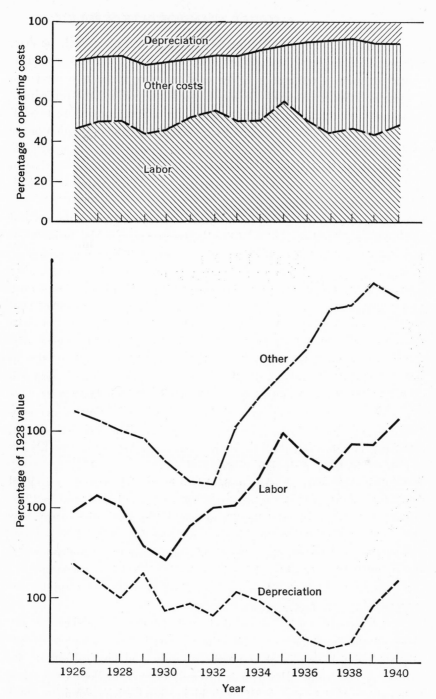

Chart 31. Relations among components of railroad operating cost, USSR, 1926–1940. Source: Table 43.

ing costs. As utilization of the railroads' fixed plant was intensified, the share of depreciation in operating costs fell steadily to 1938. The rise in 1939–1940 reflects government recognition of the need for more adequate depreciation charges; a 1939 decree raised the rate applied and codified the procedure.[3] Labor costs, on the other hand, accounted for a fluctuating share of total operating costs and ended the period with about the same proportion of the whole as they had in the late 1920's. It appears that in 1935, when Kaganovich's campaign against backlogs was in full swing, the share of labor in total costs rose some ten points as a result of additional hiring, though wage rates were also rising.

With labor's share showing no upward or downward trend, the reduced share estimated for depreciation of fixed assets was matched by an increased share for the residual of "other" operating expenses. This category includes the cost of coal and other fuel, of materials for current maintenance, and of repairs to rolling stock (excluded from recognized operating expenses until the middle 1930's). Its rise from 33 per cent to about 45 per cent of total operating costs reflects both an enlarged physical flow of current material inputs into the railroad production process and a substantial upward drift in their prices. Analysis of the unit cost indexes in Table 43 indicates that in 1935–1940 these fuel-materials-repairs costs were the ones primarily responsible for higher railroad operating costs as a whole. Unit labor costs were only some 40 to 60 per cent above their 1928 level, and estimated depreciation charges per unit of railroad output were at just about their hypothetical 1928 level. For the "other" category, however, unit cost was about 125 per cent above the level of the late 1920's.

At first, unit costs of current nonlabor inputs fell as output spurted forward, but with 1933 the gains since 1928 were eliminated, and in 1936–1937 the index rose substantially. There were widespread price increases in 1936, amounting to about 110 per cent over 1928 for coal and 70 per cent over 1928 for steel [4] — and the railroads of course were very large consumers of both. The railroads achieved notable gains in the efficiency of locomotive fuel consumption, but they were not sufficient to counteract the influence of higher prices on fuel expenses.

Special interest attaches to trends in unit labor cost, and here we are fortunately in a position to examine the separate influence of money wage rates, with which unit labor cost varies directly, and physical output per worker, on which unit labor cost is inversely dependent. Both were rising during this period in the USSR, with higher productivity dominant until

1932, and money wage increases dominant thereafter. The record is set forth in Chart 32.

The productivity of operating workers on Soviet railroads at the end of the 1930's was over 250 per cent of the 1928 level, and with no change in money wage rates, this would have meant a 65 per cent drop in labor cost per unit of traffic. Money wages, however, far from remaining constant,

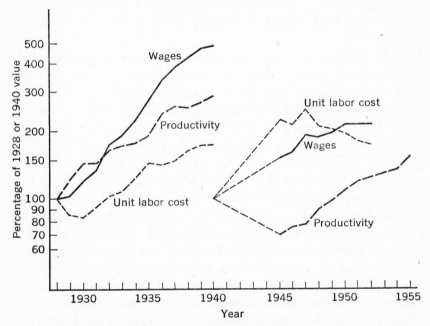

Chart 32. *Average operating wages, productivity, and unit labor costs, USSR railroads, 1928–1940 and 1945–1955. Source: Table 44.*

rose to almost five times their 1928 level. The combined effect, therefore, was to make average unit labor cost at the end of the period almost 75 per cent higher than it had been on the eve of the five-year plans.

The record discloses a number of factors contributing to the rise in labor productivity, though it would be difficult to ascribe weights to their relative contribution. First of all, we may note that in several respects the nature or quality of the service being produced was altered.[5] Between 1928 and 1932, the share of passenger-kilometers in cumulated ton-kilometers rose from 20 per cent to 32 per cent. This was the period of mass travel in connection with the growth of new production centers and the disorganization follow-ing upon "liquidation of the kulaks as a class." Evidently the "productivity" of labor in the passenger sector, measured in terms of passenger-kilometers per railroad passenger employee, rose in proportion as the trains grew more crowded. And this increased output of an appreciably deteriorated service, as noted above, accounted for an expanding share of total output. Between 1932 and 1935, the absolute volume of passenger traffic declined substantially, with the result that freight's share of accumulated ton-kilometers returned to its previous level, around 80 per cent, where it remained for the rest of the 1930's.[6]

In the freight sector, there were several changes in the nature of the service produced that reacted on railroad costs. The average length of haul for all commodities rose from 600 to 700 kilometers between 1928 and 1940. Since the costs associated with beginning and ending each trip were not increased by the lengthening of the intervening journey, the effect, in the absence of other factors, would have been to reduce railroad freight costs somewhat.[7] In another dimension, the average speed of freight train move-ment rose by 45 per cent, from a 1924–1928 average of 8.4 miles per hour (including stops), to a 1938–1940 average of 12.2 miles per hour. (For yearly figures and more detail, see Table 73.) Since in this range of speeds operat-ing costs probably do not rise proportionately with speed, the improvement must have tended to lower shipping costs. It was obtained through sub-stantial investments in better roadway and rolling stock, but the investment sums were not (in the main, at least) charged against current operating expenses. Still another development that tended to reduce freight shipment costs was the altered seasonal pattern of railroad traffic, as noted in Chapter 1. An appreciably larger fraction of each year's traffic came to be carried in the half year from May through October, when weather conditions favor transportation.

The product-mix in railroad freight transportation shifted under the impact of forced industrialization away from such commodity groups as grain and firewood, and even more toward the raw materials and fuels that had always had a prominent role in freight traffic. The relative growth of coal traffic, for example, at the expense of wheat shipments, meant that the rolling stock could be loaded more fully, the number of originating centers was reduced, and block marshaling of trains could be employed more widely. These changes in the nature of the service being provided all tended to lower the cost per ton-kilometer.

Higher productivity for labor, therefore, and in fact for all the inputs contributing to railroad output, resulted from changes in the nature of the output. But labor productivity was also improved through changes in the quantity and quality of the inputs themselves. It is a world-wide common-place that output per man-hour rises with the introduction of more, or more advanced, capital equipment. The discussion in Chapter 4 emphasized the importance of capital development programs in surmounting the freight traffic bottlenecks on key trunk lines. Hence, without attempting to isolate and measure their specific effect, we can confidently point to improved roadway, motive power, rolling stock, yard facilities, and so on as important factors tending to raise labor productivity. If we could assemble the under-lying data for an index of physical productivity per unit of capital input, and for a price index measuring the annual operating charge per unit of capital, we could then study their separate influences on the average current cost of capital equipment per unit of output. If we take depreciation charges as a rough measure of capital consumption costs, the crude data of Table 43 do suggest that during the 1928–1940 period greater physical productivity was periodically offset by higher "prices," that is, depreciation rates, charged for the services of capital plant and equipment.

Still another factor tending to raise the effectiveness with which inputs were used, and thus to restrain the rises in unit shipping costs, was the extensive training program for railroad workers. In this sector, as in most industrial sectors, the government's industrialization program included a sustained drive to raise the qualifications of workers at all levels of operation. This was not only a question of improving skills and introducing workers to more advanced equipment, but also a matter of tightening discipline and raising performance standards.[8]

Thus it appears that changes in the kind of service produced, in the quality and amount of other inputs used, and in the quality of labor itself all contribute to an explanation of the rise in labor productivity between 1928 and 1940. The fact that unit labor costs nevertheless rose reflects a rise in money wage rates that outstripped the productivity gains.

Before turning from railroad costs to the revenue side of their operations, we should give brief attention to trends in the cost of building new railroad capacity. A thorough review would have to be based on detailed records covering the many components of a railroad line, and providing information on such things as changes in the quality of construction and differences in the difficulty of terrain. Without access to such material, it is possible only to form a general impression of trends, subject to a wide margin of impre-cision. A beginning in this direction has already been made by Naum Jasny, and the present section will merely add a few more fragments of evidence to his discussion.[9] In summary, he finds the cost of building new railroad lines, in thousands of rubles per kilometer, to have risen roughly as follows:

| | |
|---|---|
| 1927 | 120 |
| 1928 | 125 |
| 1932 | 286 |
| 1939 | 800 |
| 1946 | 800 |

Jasny's figures for the early years are derived from the first two five-year plans, and thus represent averages covering a long list of building projects. They receive support from the indications of the cost of specific lines, given in the accompanying tabulation.[10]

| Termini | Date | Length (kilometers) | Cost (millions of rubles) | Cost per kilometer (rubles) |
|---|---|---|---|---|
| Semipalatinsk-Lugovaya (The Turk–Sib Railroad) | 1928–1930 | 1,441 | 203.5 | 141,000 |
| Proposed lines in the territory of the Ural–Kuznets Kombinat: | 1931–1937 | 20,851 | 2,817.8 | 135,000 |
| Ural–Bashkiriia | | 5,865 | 857.4 | 146,000 |
| West Siberia | | 5,182 | 804.4 | 155,000 |
| Kazakhstan and South Siberia | | 4,804 | 556.0 | 116,000 |
| Unspecified | | 5,000 | 600.0 | 120,000 |

In the middle 1930's, the major railroad project was the so-called Moscow-Donbas trunk line, which was put together mainly through renovating segments of several old grain-export lines, plus the construction of one additional link. The chairman of the government commission that accepted the line from the builders for permanent operation stated that the total cost of establishing the trunk line between Moscow and Valuiki (755 kilometers) was 434 million rubles.[11] This amounted to 57.5 million rubles per kilometer, which represents merely the cost of renovating an existing line.

An announcement of the building program for 1938 provides a certain amount of information on expected costs for five lines under construction at that time, indicated in the tabulation on the opposite page.[12] The average for these five projects is 341 thousand rubles per kilometer, clearly a striking increase over the 135 thousand used by Gibshman in 1931. It is possible that the costs noted in the 1938 dispatch refer only to the

| Termini | Length (kilometers) | Cost (millions of rubles) | Cost per kilometer (rubles) |
|---|---|---|---|
| Chelyabinsk–Sinarskaya | 157 | 86.0 | 548,000 |
| Gur'ev–Kandagach | 519 | 191.5 | 369,000 |
| Karaganda–Balkhash | 488 | 120+ | 246,000+ |
| Krasny Liman–Kupyansk | 73 | } 56.5 | } 325,000 |
| Kanash–Cheboksary | 101 | | |

amounts budgeted for that year's work, and thus that the full cost of these lines was appreciably higher. Even excluding this possibility, the indicated 1938 level is 2.53 times the 1931 level.

Jasny's 1939 figure of 800 thousand rubles per kilometer of new line is derived from a proposed 1940 project and from a 1940 article by another respected railroad engineer. The 1946 figures come from the postwar five-year plan and from postwar discussions by railroad writers. Two additional fragments reinforce the impression that figures around this level were indeed being used by railroad technicians and suggest, perhaps, that 700 rather than 800 would be a more accurate 1939 estimate. A. E. Gibshman, writing in *Tekhnika Zheleznykh Dorog*,[13] used 600–800 thousand rubles per kilometer as the cost "in prewar prices" of reconstructing through building new line. T. S. Khachaturov, in his latest book,[14] repeats his previously employed figure of 700 thousand rubles per kilometer, calling it the "cost at 1939 prices" of some 300,000 kilometers of railroad line that would have been required to carry 1939 freight traffic, if the railroad system had continued with the traffic density obtaining in 1913.

Jasny's cautious judgment in concluding his brief review is that the cost of building new railroad lines probably rose between 1928 and 1948 by more than 500 per cent, that is, from an index of 100 to more than 600. The scattered fragments adduced above are entirely consistent with this view. It may prove necessary when additional evidence is collected to raise his base period figures a little and lower those for the end of the 1930's. On the other hand, the postwar figures may have to be raised. In any case, it is clear that we do not yet have enough detailed evidence to assemble a continuous and reliable index.

Turning now to the revenue side of Soviet railroad operations, we may begin with a brief review of the general policies that have determined railroad receipts, as they evolved before and during the period of forced industrialization. The topic is inherently fascinating for any outside observer acquainted with the large body of economic literature dealing with freight rate theory and practice in Western economies. There is, more-

over, a considerable body of discussion of these matters in Soviet transportation and economic journals, especially during the middle and late 1920's. On
the other hand, the actual policies employed since 1917 began with the
simplest possible approach to these problems and only gradually came to
reflect the intricacies familiar to Western economists. That is to say, the
early decision-makers established bases for financing railroad operations that
seemed quite independent of the advanced discussion by contemporary
Soviet transportation specialists.

At the end of the 1930's, the impact of economic thought began to be
reflected in the actual structure of freight rates. Since that time, both the
literature and the rates themselves have become much more interesting
objects for analysis by an outside observer. Hence it seems appropriate to
divide the present discussion into two sections. The first will recount the
major developments in this field during the 1920's and early 1930's, em-
phasizing the obvious characteristics of the actual rate structures themselves.
The literature will be deliberately passed by. In the following section, both
theory and practice will be reviewed in somewhat more detail, with some
attention given to the theoretical implications of recent policy.

The history of railroad revenues since the Bolshevik revolution of 1917
begins with a chaotic situation in which the railroads, being swept into the
over-all government budget, obtained, in a sense, no normal revenues at
all. The hyperinflation of the War Communism period, together with the
excessive spread of centralized control, made such receipts as accrued to the
railroads' account either of only nominal value or of mainly intrabudgetary
significance. Thus the revenue aspects of railroad operations began, from a
long-run point of view, rather inauspiciously. It appears that all subsequent
developments can be seen as measures taken, step by step, to move from
this primitive and formless situation toward an articulated and rational set
of effective relative prices for transportation services.

On July 1, 1920, the first Soviet freight rate schedule was established for
the railroads.[15] It was extremely simple, all commodities being classed for
rate purposes into a mere seven groups. Four of these set up carload rates
for the twenty-six commodity groups deemed of greatest national importance,
and the remaining three set up less than carload rates for all other freight,
classed simply by weight. Between January 1 and August 15, 1921, all
government and co-operative organizations were relieved of the necessity of
paying either freight or passenger charges on railroad traffic, but a government decree of July 9, 1921 ended this brief attempt to reduce such transactions to internal bookkeeping. At the end of 1922, the rate structure was

revised, with twelve rate groups being established to apply to all commodities and nine special rate groups being set up for the most important commodity groups. The government used railroad freight rates as instruments of government policy, making them low for clients in the "socialist sector" and high for clients in the "capitalist sector" of the economy. In 1923 the rates for shipment of kerosene, salt, sugar, iron, and other consumer goods were lowered considerably during the government's attack on the "scissors crisis." At the end of 1922, special low freight rates, such as had existed in prerevolutionary days,[16] were re-established on coal, iron ore, and so on, moving from certain centers to certain favored destination points. These preferential rates were intended to provide indirect financial assistance to heavy industry, whose rapid recovery was a major concern of the government at this time.

Along with these elaborations of the rate structure itself, several small increases in the general level of rates were introduced to keep railroad operating revenues above operating expenses. Freight increases totaling 19 per cent and passenger increases amounting to 30 per cent were imposed in 1925 and 1926. On December 1, 1926, as one of several techniques for harassing the private sector of the economy and siphoning off funds to finance expansion of the state-operated sector, a series of supplementary freight charges, ranging from 50 to 100 per cent, was levied on all private freight shipments. The process of differentiating commodity groups more thoroughly continued; in 1926 the twelve general rate groups were subdivided into twenty-eight, and as of January 1, 1929 the number was extended to thirty-eight.

The decision to embark on an extensive program of capital development brought with it a government request, on November 30, 1927, that railroad freight rates should be reviewed to see how they could facilitate the program. On September 4, 1928 the government issued a directive stating that freight rate revisions should promote the development of new regions and new sources of raw materials, should induce industry and agriculture to locate their facilities more "expediently," and in general should assist the planned industrialization of the country. The thorough review evidently took a good deal of time. Another government directive, on February 26, 1930, laid down these additional (and contradictory) principles for the new rate system:

1. Individual freight rates should be "brought close to" the costs of shipping that particular commodity.

2. Those commodities selected for special treatment should be charged a rate covering 65 per cent of their shipping costs; all others should be

charged enough to cover their own costs, make up the deficiency on the first group, and yield revenue for the railroads' own capital development.

3. The structure of rates should be differentiated both by type of commodity and by length of haul.

During the course of the year, the new rate schedules were finally completed, to go into effect January 1, 1931. In response to the directives quoted above, the revisions carried a whole series of preferential rates, grafted on to the old structure.

The most widely discussed had existed at least since the decree of the Council of People's Commissars on September 4, 1928, which set a rate of 0.38 kopeks per ton-kilometer plus a 10 per cent handling charge, or total of 0.418 kopeks per ton-kilometer, on coking coal moving from the Kuznets Basin in Western Siberia to Magnitogorsk in the southern Urals.[17] On iron ore moving in the reverse direction, from Magnitogorsk to Kuznetsk, the same low rate applied. It was about one third the coal rate and one half the iron ore rate for the same distance in the general schedule. Preferential rates for coal from the sub-Moscow fields (58 per cent below the general rate) and from the Donets Basin in the eastern Ukraine (45 per cent below the general rate) were maintained to aid industrial consumers around Moscow, Leningrad, and other manufacturing centers.[18]

Pervading the whole structure of freight rates, the 65 per cent rule cited above offered a general subsidy to heavy industry in the form of an artificially low freight bill. The burden of offsetting these below-cost charges was placed on the "other freight" category, on fabricated commodities, on consumer goods, and on refined petroleum products. To some extent also it was placed on passenger travel. Such a distortion of the price structure for railroad freight service is quite understandable in terms of government objectives, and fits neatly into the well-known pattern of over-all government policy. The below-cost rates on coal, for example, fortified by additional concessions on key routes, supplemented the below-cost prices placed on the coal itself at pit heads. At the other end of the spectrum, the inflated freight charges levied on shipments of most consumer goods added their not inconsiderable toll to the turnover taxes (sales taxes) that were the major device for financial industrial development.

An impression that the structure of Soviet freight rates reflects only the stern, distorting pressure of a government intent on building up heavy industry would, however, be quite incorrect. Other factors can produce the same effects. Low rates for primary commodities and high rates for fabricated commodities arise in large part out of the fact that the railroads can handle bulk minerals, for example, more cheaply than they can handle fragile and space-using finished goods. There is also the matter of ability to pay — practically all rate-making systems give some consideration to a commodity's value as well as to its weight. The valuable, fabricated commodity can "afford" to pay a higher rate per ton-mile than the bulky, low-priced, raw material, in the sense that any given charge will be a far smaller percentage of its delivered price. Thus, for both these reasons, one would expect to find heavy industry in Russia paying freight rates on its inputs well below the rates on fabricated output and consumer goods, even under the most benign of administrations. What is at issue here is the question of *additional* differentials consciously driving primary-product rates below the railroads' operating costs. Without having at hand substantial statistical evidence showing the degree of cost-price discrepancy involved, it nevertheless seems clear that the injunction of the Council of People's Commissars was carried out.[19]

Another feature of the 1930 freight rate revisions that deserves emphasis is the marked reduction of ton-mile charges for long hauls. It gave effect to the government's desire to foster rapid development of the outlying frontier regions of the country. Not content with establishing progressively lower rates as the length of haul increased for each commodity group in the general rate schedules, the new system provided special low rates for certain freight moving to and from the Soviet Far East, Central Asia, and the Caucasus. It will be seen that this was a logical concomitant of the regional specialization, economies-of-scale phase of Soviet theory and practice.

Between 1931 and 1935, while the schedule of rail freight rates remained constant, the composition of traffic changed and the average length of haul rose. The relative tonnage of "sweeteners" (to use an American industrial term), that is, of commodities paying high freight rates, contracted, while the position of coal, ores, and similar bulk commodities expanded. With an increased length of haul, the average revenue per ton-mile yielded by the 1930 schedule tended to drop off. Consequently the two developments combined led to a fall in the average unit revenue from freight traffic. In early 1936, therefore, the government raised freight rates generally by about 20 per cent, effective April 1, but the structure of the schedule remained unaltered.[20]

As the 1930's drew to a close, the Soviet government arrived at a new, drastically modified policy for territorially organizing the economic activity of the USSR. It was a major theme at the Eighteenth Congress of the Communist Party, held March 10–21, 1939, and one of its immediate consequences was a new schedule of rail freight rates launched April 1. The most interesting characteristic of the new schedule was its explicit recognition of the role such prices play as market forces. Of course the relative-price impact of freight rates had not been completely unnoticed before, but the new approach heralded a profound difference in the degree of attention given to it. Whereas formerly the emphasis had been on special low rates to subsidize weak or high-cost enterprises, freight rates were now thought of as a means to penalize or discourage so-called "irrational, excessively long, and cross hauls." The former approach did not seek to encourage the use of one carrier rather than another, or one route rather than another, but to improve the financial showing of clients paying freight bills on necessary raw material supplies. Under the policy launched in 1939, on the other hand, the structure of freight rates was altered to present clients with freight-bill alternatives that, with much greater stress being laid on *khozraschet* (meaning in practice "cost-minimization" for each enterprise), would induce them to use transport services more sparingly.

Since the objective of the new location policy was to make regions more self-sufficient, the new schedule obviously needed to discourage long-distance shipments. Consequently, for all commodity groups the extent to which rates per ton-kilometer fell as length of haul increased was reduced. The rates for very long hauls were still well below the initial rates, but it became much more expensive than before for enterprises to import raw materials or other inputs from far-off sources of supply. The effect was, therefore, to lift the cost umbrella, if we may so term it, sheltering the nearby but low-grade source of supply. That is to say, where formerly a purchasing enterprise might have lower cost per unit of output from importing high-quality raw materials and paying a substantial freight charge, than from using poor local resources, the 1939 freight rates altered the relevant freight charges so that now it became more attractive to use the resources near at hand. Rates for all distances were raised, but the long-haul rates were raised to a greater extent than the medium-haul rates. Consequently the purchasing enterprise might now find it cheaper to substitute added tons of nearby resources for the now more expensive ton-kilometers previously involved with the long-haul imports.

The present study does not venture extensively into the field of Soviet railroad freight rates. If such an examination were undertaken, however, given the climate of economic objectives and policies, it would be more revealing to investigate the relations between distance and total freight bills than between distance and freight rates per ton-kilometer. This is because the basic question at issue in the setting of Soviet freight rates has been, not how to attract business, but how the territorial flow of inputs and outputs among regions should be organized. In particular, given the location of an enterprise, should its inputs come from far away or close at hand? To the extent that the answer depends on relative costs, it depends on an exami-

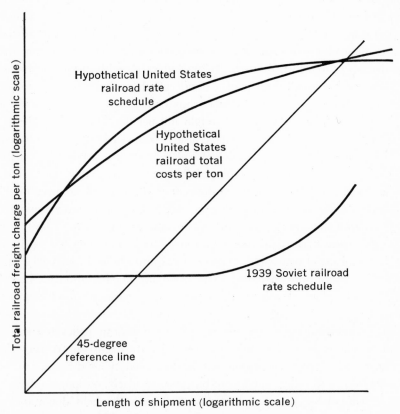

Chart 33. *Relations between freight bill and length of shipment, USSR and (hypothetical) United States railroads.*

nation of the size of relative freight bills facing the enterprise. The knowledge that freight rates per ton-kilometer are lower for long than for short distances is insufficient. For example, if a percentage increase in distance were always exactly matched by an equivalent percentage decrease in the ton-kilometer rate, the total freight bill would remain constant. Under these conditions the rate structure would be neutral with respect to influences on a firm's choice (regionally) among suppliers. Hypothetically, the rate structure could be such as to produce an absolutely smaller freight bill as distances increased, and in this case the firm would be encouraged to obtain its inputs from distant sources.

Actually, of course, cases in which the total freight bill facing an enterprise declines with longer-haul imports are quite unusual. They may result from preferential rates for certain points of origin or termination, or from comparisons along particular special routes. But in examining a general rate schedule of the Soviet type, freight bills will be found to vary directly rather than inversely with distance. The relevant structural question turns on the *extent* to which the total freight bill varies with distance. This may be illustrated through the use of a simple graph, such as the one shown in Chart 33, where the horizontal axis shows the length of a shipment, and the vertical axis records the total freight bill per ton.[21] The three curves of the graph illustrate the general shape of a 1939 Soviet freight rate, the hypothetical shape of a United States railroad freight rate, and the hypothetical shape of railroad costs per ton shipped. The scale on each axis is logarithmic rather than arithmetic. This transformation is useful in connection with distances as a means of bringing out clearly the important variations associated with short distances, while at the same time recording data for very long distances. It is useful in connection with observations on total freight bills as a means of conveying accurate visual impressions of *relative* changes at various levels. For convenience a 45° reference line has also been inserted, showing the slope signifying equiproportionate variation of distance and freight bill.

The basic difference between Soviet and American policy toward railroad freight rates is strikingly illustrated by these curves. At very short distances, where the competition of trucks is severe, United States rail rates are held down to reduce the loss of business. Similarly, on long hauls where inland waterways offer an alternative, rail rates are held down to keep traffic that might otherwise shift to water carriers. The result is a curve tending to be concave toward the $x$ axis.[22] Soviet railroads since 1939 have had essentially the opposite objectives in each case, and it is not surprising, therefore, to find that a typical 1939 Soviet rate curve is convex toward the $x$ axis.

In order to encourage clients to shift their demands toward trucks for very short hauls, and river carriers (wherever feasible) for long hauls, the Soviet railroad rate structure sets relatively high charges at each extreme of the distance scale. Hence while the addition to a freight bill for a given increment of distance is less than proportionate up to about 500 kilometers, thereafter the percentage increase in the freight bill exceeds a given percentage increase in the length of haul.

The hypothetical cost curve, showing for any given aggregate tonnage how the railroad's costs would vary with distance, assumes a given initial fixed cost together with a constant direct cost per distance unit. Using ordinary scales it would be a straight line. Its position with respect to the United States revenue curve assumes, following Hoover, that competitive forces push rail freight charges below cost for very short and very long hauls. In the absence of detailed cost-revenue data by distance for Soviet railroads, the Soviet curve is arbitrarily placed for easy visibility, and does not purport to assert any relationship with Soviet railroad costs.

With sufficient time, it would be possible to apply the technique illustrated here to several Soviet schedules and analyze the differences. In general, the 1939 schedules would probably curve upward much more sharply than the schedules introduced in 1931. Perhaps interesting contrasts among the schedules for different commodity groups would emerge. In all such comparisons, it would be possible to form at least visual impressions of the extent of variation in "regression" or "progression" at various points along the distance scale.[23] The pattern set in the 1939 and 1949 schedules apparently involves, starting from a distance zone that is "normal" for each commodity group, "progressive" rates per ton-kilometer for longer distance and "regressive" changes in rates applied to shorter distances.

The new freight rates established in 1939 reflected considerable attention to the competitive position of the railroads in relation to river and maritime carriers. However, in the extensive revisions introduced on January 1, 1949, the financial pressures have been made even more severe. Flat penalty rates are added to schedule rates during the navigation season for all those rail routes that parallel a functioning river route. Substantial reductions in rates are offered during navigation season on combined rail-water shipments where feasible. Similar provisions apply in situations where coastal maritime shipment is an alternative. This appears to be the principal structural modification made by the 1949 schedules, which seem to maintain more or less unchanged the relations established in 1939 between distance and freight bills. In the case of coal, at least, the rate pressure against short hauls seems to have been made stronger — evidently to encourage a shift of traffic toward trucks.

If attention is turned from the relative structure of freight rates to changes in their average level over time, a familiar price index problem presents itself. It is not difficult to obtain selected individual freight rates for a set of commodities for most of the years of the Soviet period. But the task of combining them into a single time series for the price of railroad freight transportation services is a formidable one. For one thing, each of the major commodity groups is in itself a composite of many specific products and rates. For another, there are the many exceptional or preferential rates, formally analogous to off-list prices in the industrial pricing field in the United States. Additional complications are introduced by the variation of freight rates with distance. Under these circumstances a substantial statistical computation would have to be made to produce an index of Soviet railroad freight rates, and the writer has not undertaken it.

However, the methodological rationale that would be appropriate seems clear. Relatively detailed information is at hand concerning originated tonnage and average length of haul for perhaps thirty of the most important commodities in the years through 1940. Almost complete price data are available in the schedules of 1926, 1931, 1939, 1949, and 1950. It should be possible to construct a set of weights for an appropriate year or years, say 1934 or 1937, taking into account both the average haul and the tonnage originated. The commodities for which traffic data were available could be made to stand for larger commodity groups, according to familiar procedures. In selecting the freight rate to be utilized, it would seem best to employ the average rate per ton-kilometer established for the distance zone within which each commodity's average length of haul fell during the weighting year. It would probably not be possible to take accurate account of the preferential rates applicable to situations like the Magnitogorsk-Kuznets shuttle, substantial though they have been. Comparisons between the observed revenue per ton-kilometer for a commodity group and the computed schedule rate for that group will disclose a gap, largely due to such preferential rates. The literature gives an impression, which could be tested through this kind of comparison, that the pervasiveness of specially reduced rates for specific points of origin and termination has gradually decreased since the period of the First Five Year Plan. To the extent that this is so, of course, the upward course of rail freight rates actually charged has been somewhat more marked than the trend of schedule rates alone would reveal.

Even without presenting the results of a computed price index for Soviet railroad freight transportation services, it is possible to review the trend in freight revenues, which on a ton-kilometer basis will at least indicate the aggregate result of changes in price together with changes in the composition of the service performed. For this and other purposes, we pass now to a review of railroad income.

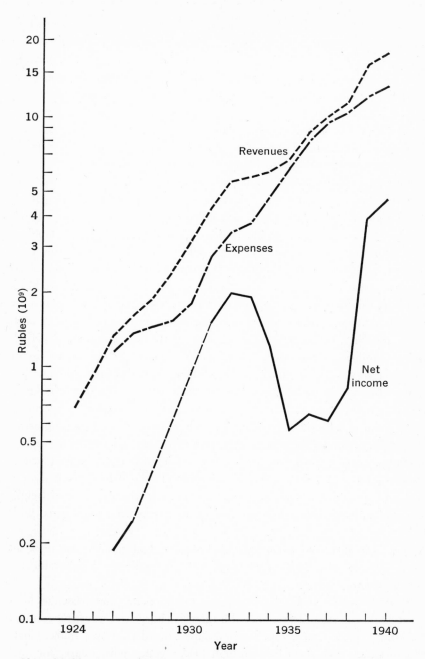

*Chart 34. Total operating revenues, expenses, and net income, USSR railroads, 1924–1940. Source: Tables 67 and 68.*

Since fundamentally Soviet railroad revenues have been designed to cover railroad expenses and growth, it is appropriate to begin with an over-all comparison between total operating revenues and total operating expenses in the years under review. Trends for the years 1926 through 1940 are shown in Chart 34, which also indicates the size of net operating income and the so-called "operating ratio." The latter, a financial measure widely applied in Western railroad financial analysis, shows the percentage relationship between expenses and revenues; the operating ratio and the profit ratio combined will add up to 100 per cent.

The opening years of the industrialization drive led to greatly improved financial results for the railroads. Revenues grew more rapidly than expenses, the margin of net income expanded, and the operating ratio dropped substantially. However by 1934 the traffic difficulties described in Chapter 3 had spread to create a financial crisis as well. A sharp rise in operating costs brought the operating ratio up over 90 per cent in 1935, where it remained for four years. The freight rate increases of 1939 were evidently introduced to correct this situation; they produced almost a fivefold rise in net income over 1938, and reduced the operating ratio thereafter to around 75 per cent.

Within the over-all changes in operating revenues during this period, several significant trends were at work. From 1929 to 1933 the great rise of passenger travel combined with a more than doubled average revenue per passenger-kilometer to shift the composition of total revenue markedly toward passenger traffic. Freight traffic, which contributed 68 per cent of total revenues in 1927–1929, contributed only 45 per cent in 1933. Thereafter the percentage of total revenue derived from freight operations rose again, reaching 70 per cent in 1940. The contribution of ancillary activities (such as baggage and mail carriage and terminal services) decreased relatively also, so that passenger traffic at the end of the period, even with the share of freight restored, contributed about 25 per cent of total revenues, as compared with 17 per cent in 1928–1929. The absolute amount of passenger revenue, reflecting both increased traffic and higher fares, had reached, by 1940, an index value of 1405 (with 1928 taken as 100), while the index value for freight revenue was 949.

Examination of realized revenue per ton-kilometer and passenger-kilometer makes it even clearer that the financial burden of covering railroad operating expenses was shifted substantially toward passenger traffic. Chart 35 shows the trends from 1924 through 1940, together with a curve for total operating revenue per "cumulated" ton-kilometer.

In the pre-plan base period, average passenger fares were somewhat below the average rate collected per ton-kilometer of freight, but this relationship was soon reversed. Drastic increases from 1929 through 1933 raised the passenger charge to almost twice the freight charge, though the latter had been raised in 1931. The gap thereafter was narrowed, especially with the increase of freight rates in 1939, but passenger fares remained about 50 per cent above the freight level. As indicated earlier in this chapter (see note 4), the estimated cost to the railroads of moving a passenger one kilometer has been somewhat higher than the cost of moving a ton of freight one

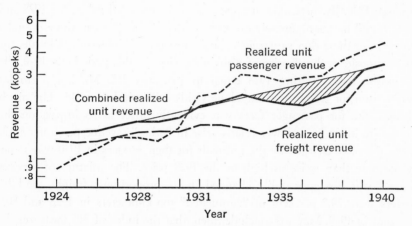

Chart 35. *Average revenue per ton-kilometer, passenger-kilometer, and "cumulated" ton-kilometer, USSR railroads, 1924–1940. Source: Table 69.*

kilometer, by perhaps 5 to 20 per cent. Comparison with the indicated relationship in charges, however, makes it clear that passenger traffic under the five-year plans yielded considerable net revenue to the railroads, who were thus enabled to apply it to freight-traffic deficits or capital development. In this respect the financial position of Soviet railroads stands in marked contrast with that of United States railroads, who typically suffer losses on their passenger traffic, covered by net income derived from freight operations.

Apart from the marked rise in the curve for total operating revenue per "cumulated" ton-kilometer, its most noteworthy characteristic is the five-year depression in its level between 1933 and 1938. It reflects the composite influence of contractions in freight, passenger, and "other" revenue per unit of traffic. The drop in unit freight revenue has already been explained as a consequence of shifts in the composition of traffic toward low-paying heavy freight. Shrinkage in the unit revenue from passenger traffic and other operations was evidently associated with similar changes, though the details are not clear from present evidence. In any case the record shows that the railroad system, confronted with a physical transportation crisis in the middle 1930's, was simultaneously confronted with serious financial problems as well. Not until 1939, three years after elimination of the physical traffic backlogs, was the system restored to satisfactory financial condition.

If the 1933–1938 sag in total unit revenue is ignored, a (logarithmic) straight line would provide a close fit for the observed values from 1924 through 1940. By inspection, it appears that the recorded values for 1928 and 1940 would lie approximately on such a fitted curve. We can therefore take the ratio of these two values as a rough measure of the terminal results for the composite realized price of railroad services in this period. By 1940, the composite index, setting 1928 equal to 100, was 215. Making a similar comparison for freight revenue alone yields a 1940 index of 214. The much sharper rise for passenger fares was evidently offset in its impact on the composite index by a slower relative rise in "other" revenue per traffic unit. Thus the price charged by the railroads for their services in 1940 was somewhat more than twice as high as the 1928 price. The mixture of services offered was not appreciably changed in its proportions: freight ton-kilometers were 79.2 per cent of "cumulated" ton-kilometers in 1928 and 80.9 per cent in 1940. May we conclude, then, that the index of 215 measures the pure price change, that changes in the nature of the service performed can safely be ignored?

Evaluation of changes in the quality of freight and passenger service on the Soviet railroads is rather difficult. As the preceding chapter has made clear, conditions of passenger travel between 1928 and 1940 were extremely poor by Western standards. They were especially bad in the early 1930's. But were they worse in 1940 than they had been in 1928, or was some small improvement visible? In the freight traffic sector, certain trends indicating a less valuable service are counteracted by others suggesting higher quality performance. Relatively more low-grade commodities were carried in 1940 than in 1928, and line-haul services increased at the expense of terminal services (another way of describing a longer average haul). These changes point toward a deteriorated product. But, on the other hand, the speed of freight movement increased between 1928 and 1940 by 44 per cent (see Table 73), a development that clearly constitutes an appreciable improvement. If the higher speeds in freight service outweigh the changes in commodity composition and average haul, and if the net improvement in freight service (80 per cent of total output) outweighs such deterioration in passenger service as may be assumed, the conclusion is perhaps warranted that, on balance, the quality of the services rendered by railroad transportation in 1940 was not significantly different from the 1928 level. It would follow, then, that the realized composite price index value of 215 for 1940 measures a pure price change for an equivalent set of services.[24]

Since freight traffic accounts for 70 per cent of all operating revenues and for 80 per cent of "cumulated" output, it may be helpful to examine somewhat more closely the sources, within total freight traffic, of the major contributions to revenue. Table 25 provides precentage breakdowns for three recent years on this point.

Table 25. *Composition of railroad freight revenue, USSR, by major commodity group, 1937, 1940, and 1950 (per cent)*

| Commodity Group | 1937 | 1940 | 1950 |
|---|---|---|---|
| Coal and coke | 14.8 | 13.5 | 20.8 |
| Petroleum | 9.7 | 11.3 | 8.7 |
| Ores | 2.9 | 2.7 | 2.9 |
| Iron and steel | 7.5 | 5.1 | 5.6 |
| Mineral building materials | 6.1 | 5.3 | 7.4 |
| Timber | 9.1 | 7.2 | 9.0 |
| Grain | 6.9 | 10.8 | 5.1 |
| Firewood | 1.5 | 1.2 | 1.2 |
| All other freight | 41.5 | 42.9 | 39.3 |

Sources: The 1937 data are computed through the use of realized unit revenue figures for each commodity group given in Vol'fson, 1941, p. 653, and ton-kilometer data from Table 53. The mineral building materials figure has been adjusted to cover "all" mineral building materials. The 1940 and 1950 percentages are given in Vinnichenko, 1952, p. 150.

With certain exceptions, the contribution of each major freight commodity group to railroad revenues exhibits considerable stability over time. Such changes as appear reflect either or both of two factors: a relative change in the ton-kilometers of freight carried, and a relative change in realized revenue per ton-kilometer. Traffic and output evidence in the case of coal, whose share rose from 14 per cent to 21 per cent between 1940 and 1950, makes it clear that most of the rise reflects a marked increase in coal traffic. The change in relative grain revenue, on the other hand, appears to be due, not to an absolute fall in the ton-kilometers of grain carried, but to a relaxation of the stiff composite freight rate established for this commodity group in the 1939 rate schedules.

The years for which details happen to be available fortunately are placed so as to bring out clearly the effect of the rate schedule changes in 1936 and 1939. The relative shifts become readily apparent in Table 26, where each rate is shown as a percentage of the average rate for all freight. For example, in the 1931 schedule, which still applied in 1935, the rate collected per ton on all ores averaged only 39 per cent of the over-all rate, whereas in the case of crude oil and refined petroleum products the composite freight rate per ton was 134 per cent of the over-all average. In 1937, per-ton revenue for both commodity groups was higher, reflecting the 1936 schedule increases, but the rise for ores was much sharper than the rise for petroleum. Consequently their relation to the over-all average was reduced to 54 per cent and 113 per cent respectively. By 1940 the position had changed again, slightly, with petroleum rising to 129 per cent and ore rising to 57 per cent of the rate for all freight.

*Table 26. Average realized unit revenue, by major commodity group, USSR railroads, 1935, 1937, and 1940*

| | 1935 | | 1937 | | 1940 | |
|---|---|---|---|---|---|---|
| Commodity group | Revenue (kop./ ton-km) | Group rate as percentage of rate for all freight | Revenue (kop./ ton-km) | Group rate as percentage of rate for all freight | Revenue (kop./ ton-km) | Group rate as percentage of rate for all freight |
| Coal and coke | 1.09 | 73 | 1.24 | 64 | 1.60 | 52 |
| Petroleum and products | 2.01 | 134 | 2.21 | 113 | 3.93 | 129 |
| Ores | 0.59 | 39 | 1.05 | 54 | 1.74 | 57 |
| Iron and steel | 1.63 | 109 | 1.96 | 101 | 2.47 | 81 |
| Mineral building materials | 1.11 | 74 | 1.45 | 74 | 2.37 | 78 |
| Timber | 1.08 | 72 | 1.44 | 74 | 2.09 | 69 |
| Grain | 1.41 | 94 | 1.78 | 91 | 4.18 | 137 |
| Firewood | — | — | 2.05 | 105 | 2.62 | 86 |
| Other freight | — | — | 3.14 | 161 | 4.70 | 154 |
| All freight | 1.50 | — | 1.95 | — | 3.50 | — |

Sources: The 1935 data are from a sample study for the month of June 1935, and do not cover all freight traffic. They are given in TsUNKhU, 1936a, p. 425. The 1937 data are from Vol'fson, 1941, p. 653. The 1940 data are computed through application of the percentages in Table 25 to the total freight revenue figure in Table 67, and through division by the ton-kilometer data in Table 53.

These comparisons reveal government policy at work. Railroad receipts per ton-kilometer of ore were relatively low; per ton-kilometer of crude and refined petroleum, they were relatively high. While it is true that shipping costs for the two commodity groups differ substantially, and in the same direction, it is evident that such relative freight rates favor heavy industry. However, the high oil rates were also meant to ration its use.

Evidence of another systematic policy emerges from the coal figures, which rise less rapidly than over-all rates, with the result that by 1940 the revenue collected by the railroads per ton-kilometer of coal was only half the average freight charge. At the same time the rates for crude and semifabricated iron and steel were raised less than proportionately, falling from a level 9 per cent above the over-all average to a point 19 per cent below it. Thus in a relative sense (though not absolutely, since the freight charges per ton were much higher in 1940 than in 1935) the iron and steel industry, the coal industry, and heavy industry generally received financial support from the railroad freight rate schedules.[25]

Government policy of another kind is revealed by the changes affecting grain and milled products. Here the 1931 and 1936 schedules yielded revenue per ton-kilometer 6 per cent and 9 per cent below the average for all freight. But in 1940 the realized rate was more than 2.3 times the 1937 rate, and was 37 per cent above the average revenue on total traffic. This was the most dramatic change for any major commodity group. It might be construed as a blow against the Soviet consumer. However, an alternative explanation would be that the 1939 schedules raised rail rates on grain (and on petroleum, too) largely to induce a transfer of traffic to river and coastal carriers, and that in 1940 the railroads' clients continued to ship by rail, paying, therefore, the penalty rates.

World War II produced substantial financial dislocations in the transportation sector, just as it affected other sectors of the Soviet economy. Detailed evidence, however, is so far either fragmentary or unclear. The major financial event for the railroads in the recovery years was a period of deficit operations from the fourth quarter of 1946 through 1948. Reconversion difficulties combined with unfavorable shifts in the composition of freight and passenger traffic to wipe out the slender margin of 1945 revenues over operating costs. Unit operating costs rose from 1945 through 1947, and though they were brought down appreciably in 1948, they still exceeded unit operating revenues. Consequently, a decree of the USSR Council of Ministers (No. 4207 of November 8, 1948) established a new schedule of railroad freight rates, to go into effect on January 1, 1949.[26] It was designed to yield an over-all average revenue per freight ton-kilometer of 5.75 kopeks, some 88 per cent above the realized unit freight revenue of 1940.[27]

The combined unit revenue for the railroads in 1949, taking account of passenger traffic too, was roughly 35–40 per cent higher than in 1948, and further success was achieved in reducing combined unit operating costs. Probably as a result of these developments, downward adjustments of many commodity rates were introduced as of January 1, 1950. A further reduction applicable to building materials was put into effect on July 1, 1950.[28] Evidently the 1949 increases went beyond the necessary level.

A rough measure of the extent to which World War II raised the aggregate sales price and internal cost level of the railroad sector of the Soviet economy is provided by the following tabulation (data from Tables 69 and 70).

| Year | Combined unit revenue (Kopeks) | (Index) | Combined unit cost (Kopeks) | (Index) |
|------|------|------|------|------|
| 1940 | 3.52 | 100 | 2.62 | 100 |
| 1950 (plan) | 4.54 | 129 | 3.62 | 138 |
| 1950 (actual) | 5.83 | 166 | 4.97 | 190 |

Additional evidence is required before the 1950 figures can be stated with precision, but it is probably safe to say that the composite charge for freight and passenger transportation on the railroads rose by about two thirds from 1940 to 1950, and that railroads costs rose by some 90 per cent. Moreover, there can be little doubt that the 1950 results for both revenue and costs were substantially higher than the targets for 1950 established in 1946. The postwar estimates above are considerably lower than the rates (around 7.5–8.0 kopeks) that have been estimated by Naum Jasny;[29] while various indirect considerations seem to support the lower figures, it must be admitted that neither set is based on convincing evidence.

Changes in the structure of railroad costs during the 1940's make it clear that higher labor costs were the principal factor underlying the indicated rise (see Table 68). Their proportion of total operating costs grew from 44 per cent in 1939 to 60 per cent in 1947, and this growth in turn was required by a combination of increased wages and lowered productivity. Substantial wage rate increases and bonus devices were put into effect on March 1, 1942, presumably to provide wartime incentives;[30] by 1945 the average wage for operating workers was 53 per cent above the 1940 level, and additional increases brought it to 193 per cent of the 1940 level in 1947. At the same time, deterioration of equipment and other dislocations had reduced the physical output per operating worker in 1945 to less than 70 per cent of the 1940 level, and by 1947 it had risen only to 78 per cent of the prewar figure (see Table 44). With money wages up, and labor productivity down, the combined effect was a 1945 index of labor cost per unit of output some 222 per cent of the 1940 base. Postwar wage adjustments preceded the rise in productivity, and by 1947 the labor cost index had risen to 248.

Since 1947, operating labor productivity has improved steadily, while the rise in money wage rates has been modest, so that labor costs per unit of output have been brought down substantially from their postwar peak. In 1950 the wage rate was more than double the 1940 rate, but productivity was only 10 per cent above prewar; unit labor cost was therefore roughly

93 per cent higher than in 1940. (Note that earlier the over-all unit cost for 1950 was estimated to be 90 per cent above 1940.) Wage increases in 1951–1955 have been modest, raising the wage index to 222 per cent of 1940, while productivity has advanced to a level 53 per cent above 1940, thus reducing unit labor costs to less than 50 per cent over their prewar level.

One of the other large components of railroad costs is fuel, primarily for stoking locomotives. World War II, especially with the temporary loss of Donbas coal output, led to a sharp deterioration in the railroads' coal supply, with the result that the amount of fuel consumed per thousand ton-miles of transportation service increased substantially. Sub-bituminous coal, lignite, and even firewood were substituted for regular bituminous locomotive fuel.[31] At the end of the war, the unit consumption index for locomotive fuel stood at 113 per cent of its 1940 level, and matters grew worse in the next two years.

With 1948 and 1949, fuel conditions improved rapidly, and the efficiency index reached the prewar level. The original 1950 target was more than achieved, and by 1952 the railroads were consuming only 83 per cent of the fuel per gross ton-mile required before the war.[32] In the absence of a price series, the influence of price changes on fuel expenses cannot be reviewed, but the record above suggests that gains in consumption efficiency have at least held down the rise of fuel expenses per unit of output.

# GROWTH RATES
12  FOR COMMODITY OUTPUT
AND FREIGHT TRAFFIC

In reviewing the background of Soviet transportation development, attention was drawn to a contest between, on the one hand, the government's objective of reducing the demand for transportation through locating
industry closer to sources of raw material and fuel, and on the other, various
forces jointly conspiring to maintain or even increase the need for transportation. We turned then to an account of the carriers' performance in
meeting the demands placed on them by forced Soviet industrialization, and
saw that the volume of freight traffic increased enormously. In preparation
for an evaluation of Soviet policy and prospects, it is now time to examine
in more detail the relation between growth in output and growth in freight
traffic — to see, that is, which side has been winning the contest. The reader
should be warned immediately that no clear verdict is available from the
fragmentary and complex evidence at hand. Nevertheless, the record of
trends in traffic-output relationships will prove at least to afford a general
impression of how matters stand.

An analysis of traffic-output relationships may be interesting also in
another way. If there are, as one would expect, stable relationships between
the physical volume of industrial production and the physical volume of
heavy freight traffic, knowledge of them would clearly be useful in planning
future development, and in analyzing prospects for growth. Mechanical
extrapolation of such relationships is a temptation to be avoided, of course,
but perhaps we can find a basis for provisional judgments, subject to revision with emerging evidence.

One way of summing up a vast composite of industrial activity is to add
together the tons of freight shipped by major carriers, or the ton-miles
(ton-kilometers) of transportation service performed by them. This miscellaneous physical aggregate will have the advantage of being in "real"
terms, free from distortions introduced by changing prices and value weights.

It has, however, no discernible rationale in a welfare-economics sense. The final products toward which the whole industrial process is directed do not have any major place in aggregate freight traffic (measured in tons or ton-kilometers). Nor does the value added at intermediate stages of production get measured through combining fragments of freight traffic incurred between stages. In a curious way it is almost as though summation of freight ton-kilometers is equivalent to concentrating on the weight *lost* in production (in Weberian terms) or on the values *not* added at each stage.

Although the relation between freight aggregates and output aggregates seems both oblique and obscure, value aggregates for Soviet industrial output present logically insoluble problems in continuity and comparability. Many writers have found it informative, therefore, in evaluating various Soviet or foreign estimates for the rate of industrial growth, to compare rates of growth in the value of production with rates of growth in freight traffic.[1] The material to be set forth below, while it would be quite inadequate for a thorough analysis of detailed relationships, is nevertheless revealing as regards over-all parallelism in growth trends for the two aggregates. It may thus prove useful in general appraisals of growth rates and growth relationships.

Even where analysis of relationships between large aggregates is both desirable and necessary, it will be more meaningful if internal relations among components of the large aggregates can also be examined. Consequently, in the present section, wherever sufficient detail can be assembled, comparisons between output and freight traffic for individual commodity groups will be made.[2]

There are, of course, serious coverage problems raised in attempting to compare similar categories. On neither side are the groups homogeneous or identically composed. For thoroughness one should, in principle, assemble output series for each of the components entering a freight-traffic commodity group. And on the traffic side, one should, at least for petroleum and timber, include the ton-kilometers performed by internal waterway, domestic maritime, and pipeline carriers. It has not been possible in the present study to carry through these refinements. There are also minor dating problems connected with records for some years. Until 1930, output series generally cover an economic year including three months of the preceding calendar year. The freight-traffic records used here, however, while covering economic years through 1927, are shifted to a straight calendar year

beginning with 1928. No serious distortion is introduced by such divergencies, given the larger uncertainties surrounding these aggregates.

As raw material for these comparisons, we need annual output series
for representative elements in as many commodity groups as possible, together with the freight-traffic records compiled in Appendix A of the present
study. Table 79 in Appendix E contains annual data for the years 1923

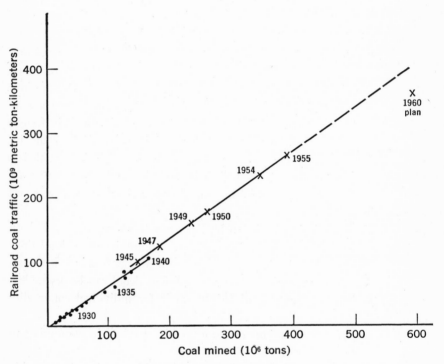

*Chart 36. Coal output and railroad coal traffic, USSR, by year, 1923–1940, selected
years, 1945–1955, and 1960 plan. Source: Tables 53 and 79.*

through 1940, and 1945 through 1955, covering physical output of coal, crude
petroleum, pig iron and rolled steel, and timber, as recorded in Soviet
sources. No doubt they suffer from various imperfections in detail, but as
crude indicators of output trends they are here considered fully acceptable.

Let us begin by examining relations between coal production and the
volume of coal traffic on the railroads. Chart 36 shows a scatter diagram

with coal production in tons on the $x$ axis, and railroad ton-kilometers of coal-and-coke traffic recorded on the $y$ axis. It is perfectly clear that a stable relationship has existed between the two over the period from 1923 through 1940, and again from 1945 through 1955. The relationship is so close in fact, in view of the tumultuous changes in Soviet industry since the early 1920's, that one gains considerable respect for the stability imbedded in Soviet industrial geography.

Closer inspection suggests that there may have been a slight change in the coal traffic-output relationship during 1928–1940. Up to 1935, increments in coal output were associated with somewhat lower increments in coal ton-kilometers than was true thereafter. The points for 1936–1940, that is, lie appreciably above a line carrying forward the previous trend.

Moreover, the six observations available for the 1945–1955 period indicate that the postwar relation between railroad coal traffic and national coal output is somewhat higher now than it was in the 1930's. Separate straight lines have been fitted to the eighteen prewar and six postwar years, and the postwar line has a slightly steeper slope as well as a slightly higher position. These lines have been fitted by the usual least-squares method, not because its rationale is applicable to time-series data, but because it provides a unique and repeatable measure of a relationship that could be just as well represented by several other lines in its vicinity. Both in the prewar and postwar periods, the fit is very close.[3] The largest absolute deviation between actual output and that indicated by the prewar line occurs in 1935, when the 61.0 billion ton-kilometers of actual coal traffic were 5.9 billion ton-kilometers short of the 66.9 billion indicated by the line. This is an error of 8.8 per cent. Making similar comparisons for each of the other years, and taking a simple arithmetic mean of the annual percentage deviations without regard for sign, one finds that in the first five years the average deviation was 15 per cent, when the absolute amounts were very small, but that the average for 1928–1940 was under 3 per cent. For the line fitted to the six selected years between 1945 and 1955, the average deviation of actual from "predicted" values is only 0.6 per cent.

What accounts for this close covariation between tons of coal mined and ton-kilometers of railroad coal traffic? The two series are clearly linked together technologically — almost all coal mined moves at least some distance by rail from pit head to consumer, and the railroads themselves consume 25–30 per cent of the coal produced. A rising trend in the average length of coal shipments has been counteracted in its effect by an increase in the efficiency of locomotive fuel consumption, so that the over-all parallelism has maintained great stability.

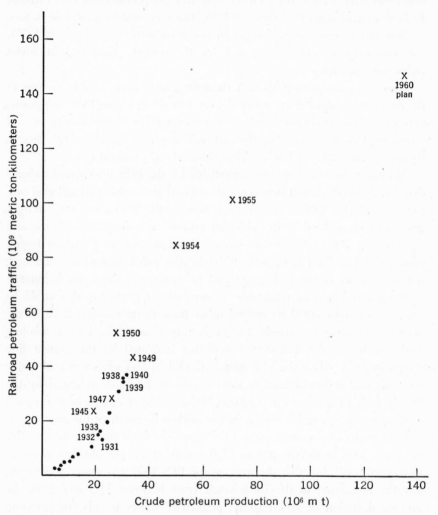

*Chart 37. Crude petroleum output and railroad petroleum traffic, USSR, by year, 1923–1940, selected years, 1945–1955, and 1960 plan. Source: Tables 53 and 79.*

It should be noted that the Sixth Five Year Plan calls for about 361 billion ton-kilometers of railroad coal movement to be associated with the 1960 target output of 593 million tons, while projection forward of the

1945–1955 relationship would imply a traffic level around 405 billion ton kilometers. The difference of 44 billion, representing roughly an 11 per cent reduction in coal traffic, presumably indicates the extent to which the government hopes that its traffic-minimizing program can be implemented in the case of coal (27 per cent of total rail ton-kilometers).

Turning now to the relation between the physical volume of crude petroleum extraction and railroad tank-car traffic, we have in Chart 37 a scatter diagram for the 1923–1940 period and six postwar years. The pattern disclosed is significantly different from that for coal. Up through 1931, there existed a stable relationship, which subsequently underwent substantial alternation. The rise of Soviet industry and mechanized agriculture brought with it a noticeable increase in the volume of freight traffic associated with crude petroleum production. While the relationship suggested by six postwar observations involves a noticeably lower ratio of petroleum traffic to crude oil output, it remains far higher than the pre-1932 ratio.

The 1960 railroad target for petroleum ton-kilometers is substantially below the level that would be required according to the recent relationship of this traffic to crude oil production, and at first sight it might appear that an unrealistic reduction is being demanded. However, this reduced railroad target is accompanied by a proposed sixfold expansion in the ton-kilometers carried by pipelines; what is anticipated is a shift of traffic from one carrier to another, but the traffic-output ratio is not altered in the Sixth Plan. Plotting the sum of rail and pipeline petroleum ton-kilometers against crude oil production for these same six postwar years, and fitting a least-squares line, discloses a close relationship; projected forward to 1960 it would call for combined traffic of about 230 billion ton-kilometers to accompany the 135 million tons of crude oil production. The Sixth Plan targets of 146 and 83 billion for rail and pipeline ton-kilometers, respectively, add to 229 billion. It would almost appear that the 1960 combined target was reached through the trend-projection method employed here!

Available data permit investigation of a third important commodity group — that of iron and steel. Here, since the freight traffic category is largely made up of rolled products and pig iron, with steel ingots playing a small role (see Chapter 9), an output series for pig iron has been added to an output series for rolled metal to yield a roughly comparable composite. Chart 38 discloses that in the 1928–1940 period the traffic-output ratio was stable but slowly increasing, that a curve concave upward would seem to provide the best fit. For this commodity group also it appears that

powerful forces were operating against the Soviet drive to reduce the ratio
of transportation to output.

The postwar observations perhaps show some progress toward a lower
traffic-output ratio. The high ratios of 1945 and 1947 are presumably to
be explained by the predominance of Ural and Kuzbas production in the
national total, at a time when the eastern Ukraine was producing very

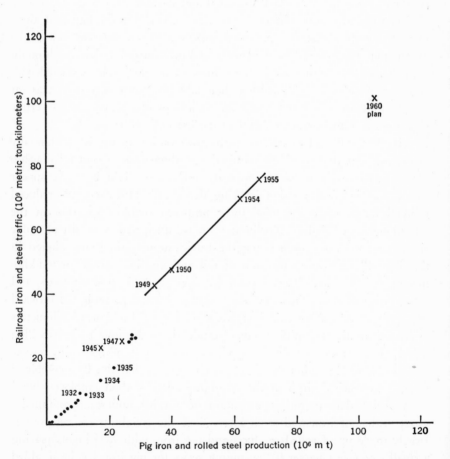

*Chart 38. Iron and steel production and railroad iron and steel traffic, USSR, by
year, 1923–1940, selected years, 1945–1955, and 1960 plan. Source: Tables 53
and 79.*

little. Even in 1949 and 1950, the traffic associated with iron and steel output was appreciably larger than what would have been involved under the

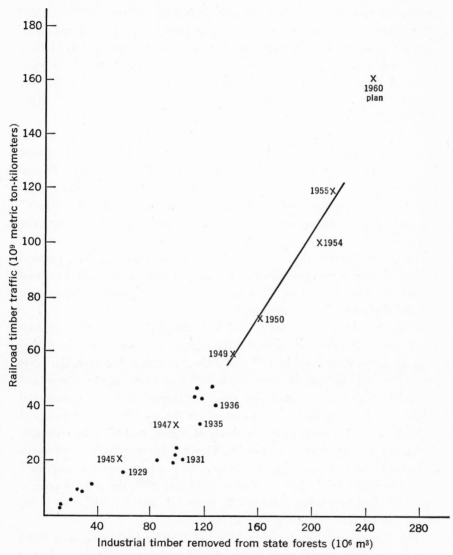

*Chart 39. Timber output and railroad timber traffic, USSR, by year, 1923–1940, selected years, 1945–1955, and 1960 plan. Source: Tables 53 and 79.*

prewar relationship. But by 1955, railroad traffic in iron and steel was approaching the relationship with iron and steel production that had characterized the late 1930's. A straight line fitted to the four 1949–1955 points indicates a new stable relationship (the deviations average about one third of one percent), which suggests that the 1960 combined pig iron and rolled steel target of 106 million tons would be associated with some 112 billion ton-kilometers of railroad iron and steel traffic. The Sixth Five Year Plan, however, calls for traffic of 100 billion, roughly 10 per cent below the postulated level. Again, the government's hope for a lower traffic-output ratio is evident.

Still another pattern comes to light with examination of relations between timber production and railroad timber traffic, as shown by Chart 39. Here one notes what is evidently a graphic indication of the railroads' faltering in the early 1930's. It was pointed out in Chapter 3 that the accumulated backlogs of unshipped freight which marked the "bottleneck" phase of railroad history bore heavily on the timber commodity group. The cluster of points lying substantially below an imaginary line running from the early 1920's through 1936 bears testimony to this fact. The physical volume of timber being removed from Soviet forests was greatly increased during the First Five Year Plan period, but no proportional increase in railroad timber traffic was registered.

With the attack on unshipped freight backlogs that came with Kaganovich's drive, the railroads brought the transport-output ratio for timber back to the previous level in 1935 and 1936. Thereafter, however, the years 1937–1940, and the postwar years 1945, 1947 and 1949, suggest a new and somewhat higher transport-output ratio for timber. Before the war, rail shipments of timber had come to move on the average over a thousand kilometers, as the European north, the Ural region, and West Siberia were drawn on to supply the old centers. During the war timber shipments grew much shorter, reflecting the emergency exploitation of scanty local sources in well-settled territory. But by 1954 and 1955, the prewar average length of haul was being substantially exceeded, and a further rise is expected during the Sixth Five Year Plan period.

The four observations between 1949 and 1955 lie fairly close to a fitted straight line, deviating from it by less than 5 per cent, and if the indicated relationship were to persist to 1960, the 264 million cubic meters of timber withdrawn from state forests would give rise to something like 155 billion ton-kilometers of rail timber traffic. The 1960 plan traffic target is not narrowly specified, but it appears to anticipate a slightly larger traffic volume, around 161 billion. Thus in this instance the evidence suggests government recognition of a stable or even rising traffic-output ratio.

Comparison of the volume of grain output with the volume of grain and milled-products freight traffic on the railroads shows that no significant relation between them exists. A straight line fitted to the widely scattered observations covering 1925–1955 would carry an average margin of error in the neighborhood of plus or minus 30 per cent. Much better results are obtained through comparing the physical volume of government grain procurement with rail freight traffic in grain and milled products. The relationship is not spectacularly close, but clearly a definite pattern existed in the 1928–1940 period.[4] Unfortunately, estimates for government grain procurement in 1945–1955 are not available, so possible changes in the transport-output relationship cannot be examined.

It is not difficult to understand why no close relationship should exist between harvests and railroad grain freight traffic. That portion of the crop which is set aside on the farm for seed and feed, and for work-day payments to local *kolkhozniki* (collective farm members), is presumably never put in railroad boxcars. Crop carry-over from one year to the next and government stockpiling both release railroad grain traffic from any necessary short-run relation with current harvests. Conversely, government procurement of grain for the urban population, armed forces, and export is much more likely to involve railroad shipments.

The four commodity groups compared above accounted in the 1923–1927 period for 41 per cent of total railroad ton-kilometers. Their share of total railroad ton-kilometers rose to 47 per cent during 1928–1932, and even further to 53 per cent and 51 per cent during the Second Five Year Plan period and the three years at the close of the decade. Recently, averaging together the four postwar years 1949, 1950, 1954, and 1955, it appears that these four groups have come to account for 58 per cent of total railroad ton-kilometers.

Unfortunately, however, the remaining 42 per cent of Soviet railroad freight traffic cannot be investigated with presently available materials. One large uncovered group is that for mineral building materials, which, it will be recalled, now consists to the extent of about 70 per cent of sand and gravel, earth and clay. It is possible to compile continuous output figures for production of cement, one of the four "principal" mineral building materials; however, even with its long hauls, it does not account for more than about 10 per cent of total ton-kilometers in this commodity group, and there is little reason to suppose that its production trends would accurately reflect production trends for the whole commodity group. The large residual commodity group of "other" freight is clearly too miscellane-

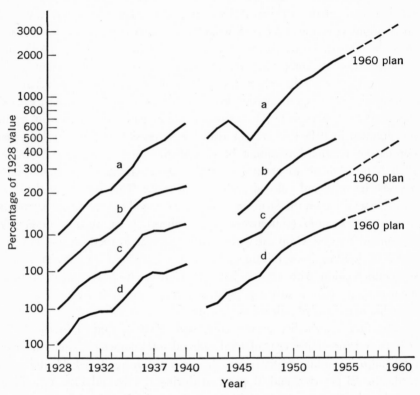

*Chart 40. Industrial output and freight traffic, USSR, 1928–1940, 1942–1955, and 1960 plan: a — official ruble series for gross output of all industry; b — Hodgman index of large-scale industrial production; c — aggregate freight traffic, carried by five carriers; d — railroad tons originated. Source: Table 45.*

ous for meaningful analysis. Along with a wide variety of fabricated commodities, this category includes a considerable number of agricultural products, which probably would vitiate use of a series like the Hodgman industrial output index as a production indicator for the group. It would be desirable to compare railroad freight traffic in ores with a production series for iron ore (accounting still for over three quarters of the railroad group), but the latter is not available on a continuous basis. Similarly, the minor commodity group of firewood should also be covered. A continuous prewar production series is available, but it has not yet been extended to the postwar period.

This section has shown that systematic relationships between production and railroad freight traffic exist for several major commodity groups covering primary raw materials and fuel for industry. Large gaps in the record, especially for recent years, have impaired the quality of conclusions to be drawn. Clearly a much more informed and painstaking analysis could be carried out in the transportation division of *Gosplan,* the Soviet Government Planning Committee. It would contribute notably toward clearer appreciation of Soviet transportation problems if such analyses were made and published.

The preceding examination of transport-output relationships for individual commodity groups, while it covers only half of total traffic, gives grounds for hope that significant relationships will be found between aggregate freight traffic and total industrial output. Such relationships have already been the subject of searching examination in the pioneer work of James H. Blackman, whose chapter in Abram Bergson's symposium on *Soviet Economic Growth* is a major contribution to our understanding.[5] Blackman has compared trends in aggregate freight traffic with a variety of series for over-all Soviet production. His work covers the period up through 1951, and in the present section an attempt will be made to carry it forward.

To that end, Chart 40 presents four annual indexes for 1928–1940 and 1942–1955. One curve shows the official Soviet series for gross industrial production of all industry, a series whose accuracy as a production indicator leaves a great deal to be desired, as pointed out in *Soviet Economic Growth* and elsewhere. A far preferable index of output trends has been computed by Donald R. Hodgman, in his *Soviet Industrial Production, 1928–1951,* and his series is also presented. Subject to minor reservations, it appears highly accurate for the 1928–1937 period, and while its coverage is sharply restricted thereafter, it is still a useful measure for later years.[6] Chart 40 also presents indexes for the ton-kilometers of freight traffic carried by five major carriers, and for railroad tons originated.

Examination of the curves discloses clear evidence of parallel movement among the four series, with significant differences. Both value series, during the prewar period and during the postwar period, tend to rise somewhat more rapidly than the traffic series. The slackened rate of growth in rail tons originated around 1932 and 1938 is less visible in the other three series. And the official Soviet output series shows marked discontinuities during World War II by comparison with the pattern of railroad freight traffic.

The degree of parallelism in the trends of these series can be brought out more clearly through the use of scatter diagrams. Using the Hodgman industrial production index as the most reliable indicator available for

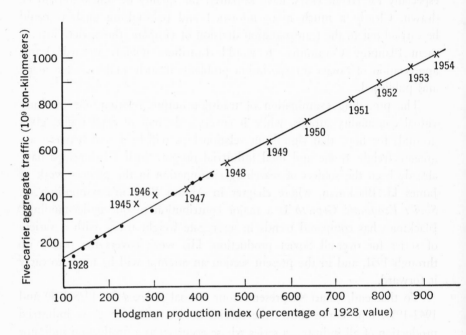

*Chart 41. Hodgman production index and five-carrier aggregate freight, USSR, 1928–1940 and 1945–1954. Source: Tables 45 and 52.*

over-all industrial output, and aggregate ton-kilometers of freight traffic carried by the five major carriers as an aggregate series for freight traffic, Chart 41 shows their relationship for 1928–1940 and 1945–1954. The co-variation is extremely regular. Straight lines have been separately fitted to two subperiods and inserted on the chart. It will be seen that except for 1945–1947, all twenty-three observations lie very close to the two straight lines.

Close correlation between large economic aggregates, causally connected through technology and geography, should occasion no surprise. These massive composites are but two facets of a single industrial process. Experiment shows that the close relationship indicated in this scatter diagram can be substantially reduced through comparison of annual percentage changes in the two series. From year to year, considerable divergencies have appeared. But such a test is, in a sense, misleading. Admittedly, the gross stability of the relation between these aggregates cloaks significant internal

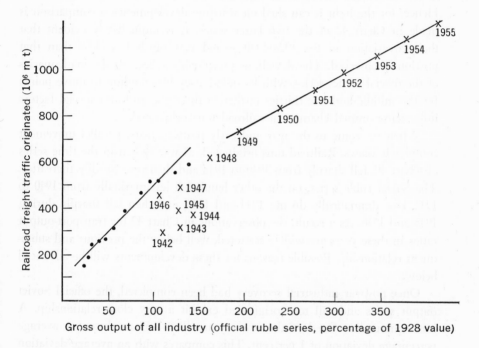

Chart 42. *Gross output of all industry and railroad tons originated, USSR, 1928–1940 and 1942–1955. Source: Tables 45 and 46.*

shifts in the composition of each over time. Nevertheless, offsetting movements appear to have eventuated in an over-all stability that has stubbornly persisted for over two decades. The record therefore suggests that we have here a useful instrument for projecting forward, into the near future at least, observed relationships in the past.

The least-squares line fitted to observations for 1928–1940 carries an average percentage deviation of actual from predicted values over this thirteen year period of 2.1 per cent. The record for postwar years, excluding 1945, 1946, and 1947 as special cases, is even better. Here a least-squares line fits the seven observations from 1948 through 1954 with an average percentage deviation of less than 0.5 per cent. The relationship between industrial production as measured by Hodgman and aggregate freight traffic is evidently a very close one indeed.

The two series just compared do not cover the years of World War II, as do the official Soviet series and the series for railroad tons originated. Hence, for the light it can shed on wartime developments, a comparison is made in Chart 42 of the two latter series. It is immediately evident that their covariation in the 1928–1940 period was much less close than that previously observed. The deviations presumably reflect all the inadequacies of the official Soviet series, with its inflationary bias tending to move points for the middle and late thirties farther to the right, and also special factors influencing annual changes in railroad tons originated.

When we come to the war and early postwar years, parallel movement completely ceases. Railroad tons originated, as was shown in the time series of Chart 40, fell sharply from 1940 to 1942 and then rose steadily thereafter. The Soviet ruble series, on the other hand, fell less markedly from 1940 to 1942, rose dramatically during 1943 and 1944, and then fell sharply during 1945 and 1946. As a result, the observations in Chart 42 for transport-output ratios in these years are widely scattered, well below the previous and subsequent relationship. Possible reasons for these developments will be advanced below.

Once postwar industrial recovery had been completed, the official Soviet output series and rail tons originated exhibit a very close relationship. A least-squares line fitted to the seven years 1949–1955 produces an average percentage deviation of 1 per cent. This compares with an average deviation of 6.1 per cent from the 1928–1940 fitted line. While the number of years covered is limited, it appears that still another stable relationship has been disclosed.

It will be seen that the postwar line is substantially below the 1928–1940 line, both in slope and position. This would seem to indicate either that Soviet industrial production is now associated with lower levels of rail tons originated than would have been true under prewar conditions, or that the official Soviet output index for the years 1949–1955 measures industrial output in a way quite different from that previously employed. The former conclusion is not consistent with what we have noted in the trends for several individual commodity groups (the change from ton-kilometers to tons originated has no systematic influence here), while the latter accords with what little is known about the introduction of new price weights for computing industrial output beginning with 1949 or 1950. It will be noted that the postwar fitted line seems to have approximately the same slope as a line connecting the five years 1936–1940, though it lies at a somewhat higher level. Perhaps this is an indication that, if rail tons originated provide a crude indicator for the physical volume of production, the growth trend indicated by the official Soviet production index for 1936–1940 contains no more upward bias than it contained in the growth trend suggested by the series in recent years. By contrast, the points for 1928–1935 can be interpreted as reflecting a different way of measuring output. Unfortunately, the pronounced upward bias in the production index for these years, which has been demonstrated by Hodgman and others, should appear in this scatter diagram as a *flatter,* rather than a steeper slope. Hence until further evidence is available, the significance of these 1928–1935 observations must remain obscure.

Coming forward now to the recent period, the stability of the 1949–1955 traffic-output relationship implies that projection forward to 1960 might be meaningful. The fitted 1949–1955 equation indicates that the Sixth Five Year Plan's goal of 1960 industrial output, with an index value of 3407 (1928 = 100), should, if the relationship persists, be associated with an index of 1190 for rail tons originated (1928 = 100). The rail tonnage actually called for in the plan has an index value of 1173, which suggests that no appreciable change in the traffic-output relationship, as measured by these two series, is envisaged by the government for the next five years.

There is some basis for arguing, however, that physical measures such as railroad tons originated may not always be an accurate reflection of aggregate values. This seems especially true in wartime periods. It was noted in the discussion of Chart 40 that the Soviet ruble series rose sharply from 1937 to 1940 and then, after a wartime peak in 1944, fell sharply through 1946. Railroad tons originated, on the other hand, rose slowly in 1937–1940 and exhibited no similar wartime peak. Does this mean that the Soviet series falsely reflects the facts?

American experience suggests that the answer is "no." If one adjusts the United States Department of Commerce series for the gross national product in 1947 dollars to a basis crudely comparable with the Soviet series, a similar 1944 peak is disclosed.[7] Our measure of total production includes the values generated in the production of services purchased by consumers, and also the values reflected in the compensation of general government employees. Neither of these is included in the Soviet series for gross output of all industry. Deducting them, therefore, from total United States gross

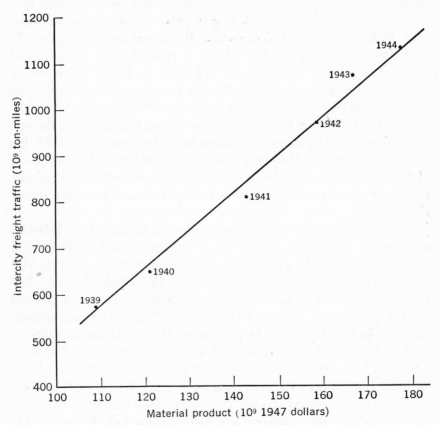

*Chart 43. United States gross private material product and total intercity ton-miles, by year, 1939–1944. Source: GNP data from United States Department of Commerce, 1954, p. 217 (see note 7, chapter 12); traffic data from ICC, 1954.*

national product, and setting the 1944 level equal to 100, it appears that in 1945 our gross private material product was 97 per cent of the 1944 level. The underlying data, it will be noted, are all computed in 1947 dollars, to minimize the distortions associated with changing price levels.

Evidently in both economies the 1944 wartime production peaks were followed by declines associated with the reconversion period. The United

States decline by 10 per cent from 1944 to 1946 was relatively modest; the Soviet fall to a 1946 level 26 points below the 1944 level was considerably sharper.

In the United States the decline was presumably a real one, in physical terms, though the valuation of military end-products may have played some slight role. In the USSR, on the other hand, high valuations placed on military end-products (even though their costs and prices are supposed to have fallen during the course of the war) probably accounts for the indicated 1944 production level, some 4 per cent higher than the 1940 level. In real terms, the physical output of the Soviet economy in 1944, especially in the consumer sector, was probably drastically lower than the 1940 level. One may ask, nevertheless, whether there is not some rational basis for a nation's putting a very high valuation on the output that is promoting its survival.

Still another comparison with American experience may serve to make the close association between freight traffic and industrial output in the USSR during the postwar period more credible. Chart 43 shows, for the six years 1939–1944, the relation between four-carrier intercity ton-miles of freight traffic in the United States and the American gross national product, less services and compensation of general government employees, measured in 1939 dollars. Obviously the two series moved together very closely. How is this to be explained?

The Soviet economy since 1928 has been directed by a stern and single-minded regime, whose objectives required maximum exploitation of every opportunity for growth. Twice during the 1930's, the upward trend was checked by what might be called an institutional or environmental bottleneck, but in neither case was the slackening due to withdrawal of pressure by the leadership. This pressure persisted after World War II, and has operated to exploit uniformly and smoothly the growth opportunities that were evidently still abundant in this relatively young industrial economy.

The United States between 1939 and 1944 went through a period with some of these same characteristics. Under wartime conditions, this country, too, was activated by stern and single-minded imperatives that gave rise to uniform upward movement. The potential for rapid growth lay in currently underutilized manpower and resources, and broadly speaking the supply side did not interpose prohibitive bottlenecks. Both freight traffic and industrial output rose together, in a systematically related way, similar to that observable in the USSR.

Comparison with United States experience during 1939–1946 thus appears to lend credibility to the asserted 1944 peak in Soviet wartime production and to the observed close relationship between output and freight traffic in a period of sustained expansion.

In concluding this review, it may be well to note that traffic-output relationships carry no direct implications for short-run Soviet growth prospects. The Sixth Five Year Plan, for example, specifies 1960 targets for gross industrial production and rail tons originated that are 65 per cent and 45 per cent, respectively, above their 1955 levels. These two targets are fully consistent with the 1949–1955 equation developed above, in the sense that they anticipate no noticeable change in the rail tonnage associated with a given value for the official production index. The traffic-output relationship, however, provides no check whatsoever on the plausibility of the output target. The official production index records an average growth rate of 14.6 per cent per year between 1949 and 1955, while the Sixth Five Year Plan calls for industrial growth at the rate of 10.5 per cent per year during 1956–1960. The reduced rate will clearly be easier to achieve than would a continuation of the 1949–1955 rate. But its feasibility depends on current factors such as prospects for additions to the labor force, and traffic-output relationships as such shed no light on these factors. Whether the availability of transportation capacity itself could be a limiting factor will be a question for consideration in the next chapter.

Our brief investigation thus reaches rather inconclusive results. The record of traffic and output for coal, oil, steel, and timber shows that the Soviet objective of reducing the volume of freight traffic associated with growing industrial production has not so far had much success. Additional output has led to additional freight traffic in a systematic way, and the forces tending to increase the traffic-output ratio seem to have been at least as strong as the government's drive to reduce it. When we turn to a comparison between aggregate freight traffic and two measures of aggregate industrial production, a similarly systematic relationship is disclosed. Both in 1928–1940 and 1949–1955, increments of industrial output have been associated with proportionate increases in freight traffic. An upward tendency in the ratio of traffic to output, however, would be counteracted by an upward bias in the production index, and vice versa, so that the apparent stability cannot be given any simple explanation. There is a tenuous indication that the post-1949 Soviet method of measuring aggregate industrial production leads to results somehow comparable with the results shown by the old index for 1936–1940, but the 1928–1935 traffic-output relations shown by the official index are at present uninterpretable. For the near future, on the other hand, it seems clear that the government is not pressing for any significant reduction in the traffic-output ratio during the current five-year plan period.

## 13 RAILROAD CAPITAL–OUTPUT RELATIONS

The process of industrialization seems always to involve more or less marked changes in the transportation sector of an economy, along with those centering in the industrial sector. As the narrative of earlier chapters has made clear, Soviet experience has been characterized by considerable expansion in the physical plant devoted to transportation, but even more so by dramatic increases in the intensity with which transportation facilities have been utilized. Soviet industrialization, that is to say, has been accompanied by very strenuous use of existing and augmented transportation capacity, without any growth in the transportation sector's *relative* share of total capital plant and equipment, while the output of transportation services has grown enormously.

That the possibility exists of using capital more intensively is obviously a matter of great interest for other countries wishing to industrialize. Capital equipment is expensive and scarce — if it can be made to perform more efficiently, given resources can be stretched to cover additional needs. In particular, to the extent that capital allocations to the transportation sector can be held down, additional resources are available to be plowed back into heavy industry and construction, whence capital plant and equipment originate. Hence it would be desirable to form some quantitative impression of what is possible in this sphere.

By the same token, it would be interesting to examine trends in the efficiency of transportation capital utilization because of their significance for Soviet economic growth prospects. It is clear that the USSR, having inherited a not inconsiderable transportation system, has exploited its position in order to concentrate on heavy industry. But this suggests the possibility that eventually, perhaps already, the inherited and augmented capacity will have reached its upper limit in intensity of use, so that further economic growth will require diversion of an increased fraction of investment into the transportation sector.[1]

The present chapter will assemble evidence bearing on these issues. It is confined to the railroads, since data on capital stock for the minor carriers are not readily available. Even for the railroads, statistics are fragmentary and their conceptual significance is unclear. The problem of measuring capital intensity, or of evaluating capital-output ratios, is a difficult one at best, and in the Soviet setting only very tentative findings can be expected.[2]

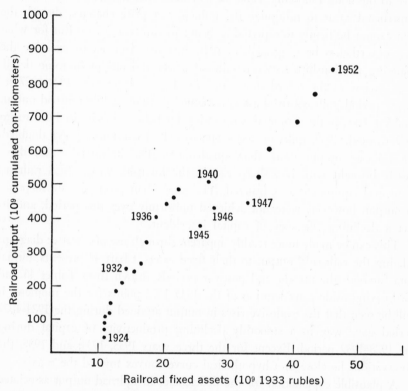

Chart 44. Railroad output and fixed assets, USSR, by year, 1924–1940 and 1945–1952. Source: Tables 46, 58, and 72.

To investigate the effectiveness with which Soviet railroad capital has been utilized, we need data for total railroad plant and equipment, on the one hand, and data for the output of the system, on the other. Neither is a simple magnitude. Quite apart from coverage problems, such as whether locomotive repair shops belong with the railroads or with industry, one faces difficult valuation problems, especially in making comparisons over a lengthy period of time. If a precise annual series could be built up from detailed records, increments in fixed assets could be brought into direct correspondence with data on annual investment. However, Soviet asset and investment records, at least those released to date, are full of obscurities, and it is not yet possible to handle the available data with full confidence.[3]

In Table 72, Appendix D, annual data for the years 1924–1940 and 1945–1952 are presented for railroad fixed assets, measured in rubles. Reference to the notes following Table 72 will show that the estimates have been constructed so as to minimize the influence of price changes, though the data cannot be firmly interpreted as being in constant prices. But for what may nevertheless be suggested, even by insecure data, let us examine the changing relationships between railroad assets and output in some detail.

A review of the record shows first of all that during the 1924–1927 recovery period, railroad fixed assets remained constant, while railroad output doubled. Clearly the system was operating far below capacity in 1924. From 1927 through 1939, railroad assets (measured in constant prices) doubled, but railroad output more than quadrupled. The industrialization drive clearly brought with it a sharp rise in the intensity with which railroad plant and equipment was utilized. The more than proportionate increases in output, however, were not achieved uniformly over this period, and in fact a declining efficiency of capital is evident.

This can be made more readily apparent through use of a scatter diagram relating the railroads' output to their fixed assets. Chart 44 presents annual data for both the prewar and postwar periods, drawn from Tables 46 and 72. Leaving aside consideration of the 1945–1952 points for the moment, it will be seen that the explosive rises in output attained during the 1924–1927 period gave way to a smoothly declining productivity of capital during the 1928–1939 period. Except for the three years 1933, 1934, and 1935, the observations lie close to a hypothetical curve convex toward the $x$ axis.

A plausible explanation for the deficiencies in railroad output associated with the asset levels of 1933–1935 would presumably center on the transportation crisis analyzed in Chapter 3. It will be recalled that growth in freight traffic fell off markedly, while there was simultaneously a considerable absolute decline in the volume of passenger traffic. Even though the railroads were receiving additions to their capital plant and equipment, operating difficulties prevented them from producing the large increments in transportation service that were required by the economy. After 1935, the reorganized NKPS under Kaganovich brought railroad capital productivity back up to the hypothetical long-run trend.

In terms of correlation analysis, it is worth inquiring whether other factors might not account for that portion of variation in railroad output which is not accounted for by variation in railroad fixed assets. For example, since labor input is a major element in the production of transportation services, annual changes in the railroad labor force should be examined for their relationship with railroad output. On the basis of labor-force data

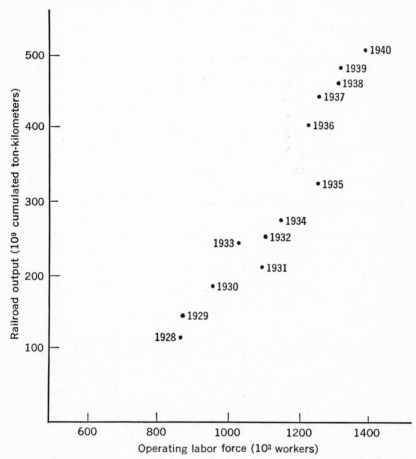

*Chart 45. Railroad output and labor force, USSR, 1928–1940. Source: Tables 58 and 66.*

in Table 66, Chart 45 presents a scatter diagram relating the railroad operating labor force to railroad output in physical terms. Clearly the relationship is less close than the relationship we saw for capital plant and railroad output. Moreover, it does not seem likely that changes in the labor force during 1933–1935 would account for the deficiencies in output. There was a fall in the average number of operating railroad workers from 1932 to 1933, but substantial increments in labor input were registered in 1934 and, a fortiori, in 1935. Consequently labor does not appear to be a factor that can reduce appreciably the unexplained variation in railroad output.

During the transportation crisis of the early 1930's, participants referred to steel shortages as a major problem, while supplies of coal for fuel were evidently not a serious restriction on railroad activities. Hence for a third possible explanatory factor, we may consider railroad consumption of iron and steel. Based on a rough series developed through combining Tables 34 and 78, a scatter diagram was constructed to investigate the relation between railroad steel consumption and railroad output. Year-to-year changes were quite erratic. The steel consumption figures cover steel for locomotives and freight cars, as well as steel for normal replacement, plus double-tracking and new construction. Without examining the record in detail, it is clear that steel consumption, like labor input, cannot noticeably reduce the unexplained variation in railroad output.

With data covering the railroads' output, and series for railroad assets, the railroad labor force, and railroad steel consumption, it would seem tempting to compute a railroad production function by means of multiple correlation. One might expect in this way to account systematically for most of the year-to-year changes in the output of the Soviet railroad system from 1928 through 1939. And if similar data could be assembled for years since World War II, a comparison could then be made to ascertain to what extent, if any, the Soviet railroad production function has changed. However, the scatter diagrams already presented suggest that such a computation would not be particularly fruitful, at least for the 1930's alone. The slump in railroad operations in 1933–1955 was not systematically related to any one of these three factors, but rather seems to have reflected malfunctioning of the system as a whole. As for allocating responsibility among the three factors, visual inspection makes it appear that capital plant and equipment is the most important factor in producing railroad transportation services, while the labor force is significantly but less closely correlated with output. Annual steel consumption by the railroads, on the other hand, is not very closely related to annual levels of output.

These comparisons suggest that further examination of relationships between changes in railroad capital plant and equipment on the one hand, and changes in railroad output on the other, should be meaningful. Let us begin by considering railroad output in a physical but intangible form. The break in trend from 1933 through 1935 suggests that two subperiods should be considered, first the 1928–1932 period and then the 1936–1939 period. In the opening years of forced industrialization, railroad assets rose from 11.5 to 14.2 billion rubles at 1933 prices, for an increment of 2.7 billion rubles. When tariff ton-kilometers of freight traffic are combined with passenger-kilometers as a measure of output, the 1932 level is found to be above the 1928 level by 135.1 billion ton-kilometers. Comparing these two increments, we find that in this first period, an increase of 100 billion cumulated ton-kilometers in output was associated with an increment of 2.0 billion rubles in assets. A similar calculation for the 1936–1939 period indicates that railroad assets rose by 3.3 billion rubles, while railroad output rose by 85.1 billion cumulated ton-kilometers. Hence in this period the additional assets associated with 100 billion cumulated ton-kilometers of output rose to 3.9 billion rubles, as compared with 2.0 billion earlier. There was almost a doubling in the amount of capital required to obtain a given increment in output.

Such a measurement, with output in physical terms, is less readily compared with others than a measurement using money valuation for railroad output. The value of transportation services is, as Harold Barger has shown, not easily determined.[4] Especially is this true when one draws raw data from the tangled web of Soviet economic records for the 1930's. Nevertheless, the following pages will seek to show that crude but instructive results may be obtained.

To begin with a simple example, suppose railroad output in the 1928–1939 period is valued according to a "typical" or mid-point price (unit revenue) for each of the two services. Examination of annual data in Table 69 will show that realized unit revenue was rising steadily in each service throughout the period, and that the 1934 levels were about halfway between 1928 and 1939 terminal values. Hence we might take 1934 combined unit revenue as a representative indicator for the gross value of railroad output. Resulting computations lead to an incremental capital-output ratio of 1.06 for 1928–1932 and 2.04 for 1936–1939.[5] On this basis, therefore, the previous finding (that twice as much capital was needed to obtain additional output in 1936–1939 as had been needed in 1928–1932) remains undisturbed.

Are these capital-output ratios unusually low? Rough impressions on this score can be obtained through comparisons with United States experience, though thoroughly detailed investigation of comparabilities in the underlying statistics would surely call into question the meaningfulness of such comparisons. In particular, grave doubts would arise concerning relations between asset valuation and the pricing of output in the two economies. Let us nevertheless make some experiments. Barger's record of United States railroad traffic development shows that from 1897 to 1907 there was a sustained period of rapid growth, perhaps in some respects not unlike the Soviet experience of the 1930's. It is possible to compute a capital-output ratio for this period along the lines employed above for Soviet railroads. The book value of road and equipment investment in American steam railroads on June 30, 1896 was 9,500 million dollars; by June 30, 1907 this total had risen to 13,030 million dollars.[6] For value weights measuring gross revenue from freight and passenger operations, like those involved in the Soviet computation, we turn to Barger's series for revenue per ton-mile and per passenger-mile. Taking 1902 values as representative mid-point values, and multiplying the physical volume of freight and passenger traffic in 1902 by these unit operating revenues, one obtains a figure of 0.89373 cents per "cumulated ton-mile." Thus valued, the increment in traffic from 1897 to 1907 comes to 1.421 million dollars. Hence the incremental capital-output ratio for this period on United States steam railroads was 2.48. Under conditions of rapid, steady growth, this capital-output ratio does not appear very much higher than the Soviet ratio for the late 1930's.

A second comparison with United States records will illustrate a serious complication associated with such measurements. Consider the period from 1938 through 1944, when again American railroads enjoyed a period of sustained and rapid growth in output. The book value of road and equipment investment on December 31, 1937 was 25,636 million dollars; by the end of 1944, this figure had risen to 26,632 million dollars. For a variety of reasons, the railroads' capital plant and equipment had risen only by 996 million dollars, or by less than 4 per cent. Output, on the other hand, rose dramatically. Using somewhat arbitrary revenue weights of 1.85 cents per passenger-mile and 0.96 cents per ton-mile as being crudely typical of this period, one obtains a figure of 1.012 cents per "cumulated ton-mile." Applying this to the increment in railroad traffic leads to a figure for output of 5,291 million dollars. The ratio, therefore, for this very unusual period, is 0.188 — that is, the incremental capital-output ratio for American railroads was only about 0.2.

Obviously, American railroads in the late 1930's were operating at only a small fraction of their capacity. But this was even more true of Soviet railroads on the eve of the plan period, as can be seen if 1924–1927 experience is examined. Applying the 1934 value weight of 1.88 kopeks per cumulated ton-kilometer to the 1924–1927 output increment, and using the asset series in 1933 prices, one finds an asset increase of 152 million rubles associated with an output increase of 1,026 million rubles, for an incremental capital-output ratio of 0.15. Neither the wartime experience of the United States nor the recovery period experience of the USSR can be taken to reflect capital-output ratios in the usual sense.

The lesson obviously is that capital-output ratios computed from actual output data rather than from capacity data, especially when computed over short periods of time, may be highly misleading. They will not necessarily show how much additional investment is required to obtain a specified increment in output. They may merely show how much additional capital was required, together with existing underutilized capital, to produce the observed increment in output.

From 1928 to 1932 in the USSR, while it was not possible to maintain the dramatic pace of the recovery period in this respect, there was clearly additional slack to be taken up, as was noted in the narrative of Chapter 3. However, this phenomenon, which is a confusing and misleading hindrance in historical capital-output analysis, should not on this account be thrust aside. From the point of view of an economy embarking on a purposive program of economic development, it holds great promise. Substantial gains in capital productivity may be realized through more intensive use of existing capital, before or along with the gains associated with absolute increments in the capital stock.

The comparisons so far made between capital and output have measured output in terms of the gross revenue derived from freight and passenger operations. It may be interesting to take a less gross measure of output, somewhat closer conceptually to value added by manufacture. If capital charges could be deducted from the capital increment measure, a true net capital coefficient would result. Soviet railroad asset records do not at present permit such computations to be made on the asset side. However, on the output side, one can at least deduct the cost of fuel and materials from railroad operating costs, thus giving a less gross measure of output. Returning to our Soviet data for the 1930's, we see that the 1934 structure of railroad costs and revenues, as shown in Tables 67 and 68, indicates that fuel and materials costs made up 15.8 per cent of combined freight and passenger revenues (wages had risen and coal prices were low in 1934). Deducting these reduces the value of the output increments by 15.8 per cent. This has the effect, naturally, of raising the computed incremental capital-output ratios for the two subperiods in the same proportion — that is, the 1928–1932 ratio becomes 1.23 and the 1936–1939 ratio becomes 2.39. If net output is taken to be measured by wages, estimated capital consumption, and retained income, then the adjustment goes still further. Along with fuel and materials expenses, one must exclude "other" expenses and current repairs to rolling stock; the result is to raise the computed incremental capital-output ratios to 1.40 for 1928–1932 and 2.69 for 1936–1939. It remains clear, after these adjustments, that capital effectiveness was notably lower at the end of the 1930's than it had been in the first burst of forced industrialization.

Still another aspect of the processes at work here can be brought out through examination of *average* capital-output ratios, that is, of trends in the relationship between the assets available in a year and the output they produced that year. Employing the average annual asset series "at 1933 prices" and converting the physical output series to value form through use of the 1.88 kopek conversion factor (representing average combined unit revenue in 1934) leads to the annual ratios given in the accompanying tabulation.

| Year | Asset-output ratio | Year | Asset-output ratio |
|---|---|---|---|
| 1924 | 11.97 | 1933 | 3.38 |
| 1925 | 8.82 | 1934 | 3.20 |
| 1926 | 6.37 | 1935 | 2.83 |
| 1927 | 5.75 | 1936 | 2.50 |
| 1928 | 5.20 | 1937 | 2.44 |
| 1929 | 4.37 | 1938 | 2.45 |
| 1930 | 3.59 | 1939 | 2.42 |
| 1931 | 3.30 | 1940 | 2.78 |
| 1932 | 2.99 | | |

Once again the trend toward intensive use of railroad plant and equipment is clearly evident. From 1924 to 1927, the ratio of assets to annual output was cut in half — or, put the other way, the average productivity of railroad plant in 1927 was twice what it had been in 1924. The downward trend continued unabated through 1932, only to be somewhat reversed in 1933 and 1934, under the impact of the transportation crisis. Thereafter the ratio improved slightly, and toward the close of the decade seemed stabilized at a level only one half that of 1928. From the government's point of view, this was clearly an achievement. The slight rise in the ratio in 1940 reflects the railroad plant and equipment incorporated along the western frontier, which was not very productive in its first year under Soviet control.

The relation between these average capital-output ratios and the incremental (that is, marginal) ratio previously discussed provides interesting material for speculation. When the average capital-output was falling rapidly, the marginal ratio was considerably below it; as the average ratio approached stability around 2.4, the marginal ratio rose to meet it. The formal properties of the relationship are such that if the average ratio had remained constant, the marginal ratio would have assumed the same value. We are here dealing, not with a production function in any short-run sense, but with something like an envelope curve enclosing the output functions of gradually expanding railroad plant. Reference to Chart 44 suggests (except for 1933–1935) a rather smooth curve.

If the underlying data were firm enough, and the forces at work were simple enough to justify an asserted "law," it might be argued that the Soviet railroad system was confronting an ironclad constraint associated with the technology of steam railroading. Continuing along the hypothetical curve, values would be soon reached beyond which the average ratio of assets to output would begin to rise, and the incremental ratio would increasingly exceed the average. The data, however, are not firm, and the engineering, geographic, and financial elements of the situation are not simple. Consequently we have here no more than speculation, especially since, as we shall see, new technology will invalidate old relationships.

Since growth in a capital stock arises from net investment, it would seem fruitful to examine relationships between investment increments and the growth of output, as a means of confirming or modifying the results obtained through study of asset changes. Using the series for annual (gross) investment in railroads assembled in Table 71, together with the previously-employed series for combined freight and passenger traffic output, a scatter diagram was constructed to bring out their covariation. In the 1928–1940 period, it was not particularly close. Logic would suggest that a given year's investment might only be reflected in additional output a year or two later, but lagged comparisons did not reveal any improvement in the relationship. Brief attempts to bring order into annual records for gross investment, depreciation allowances, and changes in railroad fixed assets make it immediately clear that the data are intricate and confused. In this respect the railroad figures appear to suffer from all the difficulties discussed by Kaplan and Campbell in their studies.[7] Portions of the sums allocated for railroad investment represent expenditures that do not increase fixed assets, for example, and the annual depreciation charges are by no means identical with book deductions from asset values. For these and other reasons, there seems little point at present in further examination of relationships between investment and railroad traffic growth in the USSR.

The postwar data on Soviet railroad assets so far available are fragmentary and indirect, but as crude estimates they have been entered on Chart 44. Apart from relative year-to-year changes, the principal uncertainty concerns their link with the prewar series. The fixed assets of the Soviet economy have been revalued at "1945 prices" and have probably been re-valued again since the 1949 price reforms.[8] The estimates offered here are interpreted, not as being in 1945 prices, but as linking up directly with the prewar series "in 1933 prices." It will be noted on Chart 44 that postwar points nevertheless lie below the trend indicated by prewar data. If these postwar estimates do in fact contain an upward revaluation component, then its removal would move postwar points on the graph to the left, bringing them closer to the prewar relationship, or even placing them above it. Until further evidence reduces these uncertainties, the available material should, of course, be interpreted with caution.

Annual relationships between railroad fixed assets and railroad output in physical terms show once again that in 1945–1947 reconversion and dis-organization hampered the effectiveness of the railroads' work. In 1948 and 1949, the recovery process generated rapid gains. The 1950–1952 record indi-cates a return to something like prewar relationships.

The postwar estimates permit computation of measures like those applied to the prewar period in the preceding section, though they can only be tentative in view of the fragility of the underlying evidence. Table 27 pre-

*Table 27. Postwar railroad assets and output, 1945–1952*

| Year | Assets at 1933 prices $(10^9 R)$ | Output at 1934 values $(10^9 R)$ | Ratio of assets to output |
|------|------|------|------|
| 1945 | 25.8 | 7.16 | 3.60 |
| 1946 | 27.8 | 8.12 | 3.42 |
| 1947 | 32.7 | 8.42 | 3.88 |
| 1948 | 34.5 | 9.85 | 3.50 |
| 1949 | 36.1 | 11.39 | 3.17 |
| 1950 | 40.2 | 13.07 | 3.08 |
| 1951 | 43.0 | 14.59 | 2.95 |
| 1952 | 46.0 | 15.94 | 2.89 |

Source: The asset estimates are from Table 72. The estimates for output at 1934 values reflect the 1.88 kopek composite unit revenue of 1934 (from column 3 of Table 69) applied to the output estimates in column 3 of Table 58.

sents annual figures for 1945–1952 covering railroad fixed assets "at 1933 prices," and railroad output of freight-plus-passenger service, valued at the composite unit revenue of 1934. The series are intended to be comparable to those of the prewar period, at least in their value basis.

Between 1947 and 1949, during the rapid recovery period, an increment of 3.4 billion rubles in railroad assets was associated with an increment of 2.97 billion rubles worth of output. The incremental capital-output ratio was therefore 1.14, not far different from the ratio characterizing the 1928–1932 period. Growth between 1949 and 1952, on the other hand, involved a 9.9 billion ruble addition to railroad assets and a 4.55 billion ruble increment in railroad output. The incremental capital-output ratio for this recent period therefore takes the value of 2.18, quite close to that of the 1936–1939 period in the USSR. The crude evidence seems to show, therefore, that Soviet railroads in the early 1950's faced approximately the same capital-output relationship they were confronting in the late 1930's.

In examining the third column of Table 27, it becomes evident that the *average* capital-output ratio has been declining throughout the postwar period, as it did before the war. Starting from a level of around 3.6 in 1945, it had fallen by 1952 to around 2.9. Again the level is not far different from that of the late 1930's. One notes also a gradual convergence between the average and marginal ratios. Smooth progression along the indicated trend would lead to a point at which the average ratio would rise, and the marginal ratio would increasingly exceed it.

If there were an envelope curve embodying technological limits on the Soviet railroad system, the implications would of course be extremely important. However, it is doubtful that any such deterministic force is at work. Soviet railroading to date has been overwhelmingly based on the steam locomotive, old-fashioned signaling, and poor-quality roadway. Recent developments and current plans make it clear that the Soviet government is initiating a gradual revolution in railroad motive power, following the American change to diesel-electric traction, and greatly expanding their use of electric traction. Similarly, important innovations in signaling, communications, and data-processing offer the prospect of radical improvements. While these developments will require a large absolute investment program, it seems likely that they will also open up possibilities for a new envelope curve (to return to the graphical concept), that is, that a given stock of railroad assets in the future can be associated with larger output than would have been possible using the old technology.

The postwar position of Soviet railroad fixed assets in the total assets of the economy does not seem to have undergone any marked change from the prewar situation until recently. In Chapter 3 it was shown that the railroads accounted in 1924 for some 17 per cent of the economy's fixed assets, and that in 1928 this share had fallen to 15 per cent (by one measurement). Another measurement for 1928 suggested a railroad share of 23 per cent, which by 1933 had fallen to around 16 per cent. In 1938 the railroads' share of the economy's fixed assets was "about one sixth," according to a 1945 railroad writer, and in mid-1940 a railroad writer used the figure of 15 per cent. Since the war, scattered remarks have continued along the same line. Khachaturov in his 1952 book said that "the transportation sector accounts for 20 per cent of the country's fixed capital, and railroads alone account for about 15 per cent." In a set of 1953 lectures, he stated that "the transportation sector's share of the economy's fixed assets exceeds 20 per cent, and more than two thirds of this amount is in the fixed assets of the railroads." Finally, the railroad newspaper in January 1955 reported railroad fixed assets as one sixth of the total for the economy.[9]

However, the 1956 statistical handbook presents indexes for the value of fixed assets in various sectors of the economy that indicate that the transportation and communications sector has been losing ground since 1950. If its share of total assets in 1950 was 22 per cent, then by 1954 it had dropped to about 20 per cent and by 1955 to about 19 per cent.[10] Within this sector, the railroads' proportion has probably also declined slightly, so that their 1955 fraction of the national total may be around 12 per cent. The valuation basis for these recent indexes has not been disclosed, and the lower railroad share may reflect exaggeration in other sectors. A decline is consistent, however, with recent trends in investment allocation, as will be shown below.

In the process of rapid economic growth, several policy questions revolve around the relative contributions of capital and labor. Which grows more rapidly, and which contributes most decisively to enlarged output? Our aggregate series provide only the grossest of clues, but they are perhaps worth examining briefly. As we have seen, the operating labor force on Soviet railroads has achieved substantial gains in productivity, just as railroad capital has been made to turn out more service than before. Neither input, that is, has expanded to anything like the degree that has characterized railroad output. But over the period from 1928 through 1952, railroad plant and equipment has grown a good deal more rapidly than has the operating railroad labor force. We find, for example, that by 1940 railroad fixed assets (including incorporations) were 2.33 times as large as the 1928 average, while the operating labor force was 1.7 times its 1928 size. Similarly, in the 1948–1952 period, railroad plant and equipment increased 33 per cent while the labor force rose 16 per cent. Railroad assets quadrupled from 1928 through 1952; the labor force doubled. It is clear, therefore, that the production of railroad ton-miles and passenger-miles in the USSR employs more capital relative to labor than it used to.

If one computes an assets-per-worker series as the quotient of railroad fixed assets (at "1933 prices") divided by the average annual operating labor force (from Table 66), one finds somewhat erratic year-to-year changes. Up through 1931 the labor force was increasing more rapidly than assets, and assets per worker dropped from around 13,500 rubles in 1928 to a little over 12,000. By 1939 they had risen to almost 17,000 rubles, and the 1939–1940 acquisitions brought the figure to around 18,400. In the postwar period railroad assets per worker rose from around 17,000 rubles in 1945 to 21,600 in 1948 and 24,800 by 1952. Though occasionally a labor increment outweighed an assets increment, the persistent trend has been clearly upward. In this sense, then, the Soviet railroad system has become more capital intensive, that is, the ratio of capital to labor has been increasing.

It is worth inquiring, however, whether the same trend is evident in connection with incremental ratios — have recent additions to the railroad labor force been associated with larger additions to railroad fixed assets than was true before the war? Trends for the industrial sector have been fruitfully examined by Gregory Grossman, who finds a striking tendency for Fifth Five Year Plan investment indicators to show high marginal capital intensity.[11] The evidence for Soviet railroads is somewhat less clear-cut, as indicated by the data in Table 28. During the 1928–1932 period a large

Table 28. Fixed asset and labor force increments, USSR railroads, selected periods, 1928–1952

| Period | Fixed assets (billions of rubles at 1933 prices) | Operating labor force (thousands) | Assets per worker | |
|---|---|---|---|---|
| | | | Rubles | Index (1928 = 100) |
| 1928–1932 | 2.70 | 242 | 11,160 | 100 |
| 1932–1936 | 4.57 | 111 | 41,170 | 369 |
| 1936–1939 | 3.26 | 99 | 32,930 | 295 |
| 1945–1948 | 8.70 | 88 | 98,860 | 886 |
| 1948–1952 | 11.50 | 261 | 44,060 | 395 |

Source: The increments are obtained through subtracting initial from terminal year figures for each period, from Table 72 for assets and Table 66 for the operating labor force. Asset per worker ratios are then obtained as quotients of column 1 over column 2, and not as changes in the annual figures.

number of workers were added to the railroad operating labor force; in the rest of the 1930's the increments were smaller. Capital additions, on the other hand, were most marked in the 1932–1936 period. The incremental capital-labor ratio for 1932–1936 was therefore 3.7 times the 1928–1932 ratio. For 1936–1939 the ratio was 3.0 times what it had been during the First Five Year Plan.

During the recovery period from 1945 through 1948, a most unusual combination of circumstances appears to have been at work. The railroad labor force did not contract much during the war and in 1945 was some 3 to 4 per cent above the 1940 level. The value of railroad fixed assets, however, reflected enemy damage in 1945 and prompt restoration thereafter. Consequently the incremental capital-labor ratio for 1945–1948 is 8.9 times as large as the 1928–1932 ratio. This sharp increase does not persist beyond the recovery period, however, at least as far as our slender evidence goes. For 1948–1952, the incremental ratio falls to a level 4.0 times the 1928–1932 level, not far from that of 1932–1936. Labor force growth between 1948 and 1952 was substantial, exceeding the early growth by some 8 per cent, and this served to offset in part the greatly increased absolute additions made to railroad fixed assets. On the whole, this sketchy record shows an upward drift in the ratio of capital increments to labor increments on Soviet railroads, but not a very marked one.

Just as the railroads' share of the economy's fixed assets appears to have declined recently, so does their share of total annual investment. In the Fourth Five Year Plan, the railroads were assigned 16 per cent of total investment; in the annual plan for 1947, however, they were allocated six out of fifty billion rubles, or a share of 12 per cent. In 1951, total investment rose 12 per cent over the preceding year, but investment in transportation rose only by 3 per cent, while investment in housing rose 20 per cent. The Fifth Five Year Plan, issued in 1952, called for twice as much investment in industry as during the Fourth Five Year Plan, for double the housing investment and 2.1 times the agricultural investment, but for an increase in the transportation sector of only 63 per cent. In 1953 Khachaturov told his audience that the transportation sector received about 15 per cent of total capital investment, and that three quarters of this went to the railroads, but he was evidently referring to previous practice. The 1956 report on Fifth Five Year Plan fulfillment stated that total government capital investment during the period had been 91 per cent larger than during the Fourth Five Year Plan period, and yet the reported rise for the transportation and communications sector was 48 per cent. Finally, in the spring of 1956 Khachaturov wrote that investment for all types of transportation in the USSR came to about 8 to 10 per cent of annual capital investment.[12]

Another change in Soviet transportation financing appears to have been inaugurated with the state budget for 1954. Unit revenue increases and cost reductions on the railroads since 1949 had made them very profitable, and the budget called for still further increases in railroad profitability during 1954. While ordinarily an enterprise's capital outlays are covered primarily through budget grants, with some assistance from retained income, the railroads were called on to finance all of their investment outlays out of retained income, and in addition to transmit some 2 billion rubles to the state budget. Moreover, the railroads were to receive only 30 per cent of the sector's capital allocation, instead of the customary 75 per cent. In 1955 the railroads covered their own investment outlays from retained income, and in addition contributed 6.4 billion rubles to the state budget. The recent policy appears to shift investment emphasis from the railroads to other carriers, and to use the railroads as a means for financing the growth of other parts of the economy.[13]

This review of the relation between railroad fixed capital and railroad output in the USSR has led to what may perhaps best be termed "provocative" conclusions. They seem very interesting, but their underlying statistical base is quite shaky. In a genuine sense, therefore, they should be considered preliminary observations. In general it is clear that railroad assets and railroad output are systematically related, and that the relation shows a declining trend in capital productivity from the 1920's to the 1950's. At the same time, both the marginal and the average capital-output ratios derived from Soviet records appear low in comparison with many that have been computed in the West. Attention to surrounding circumstances makes it clear that low incremental capital-output ratios based on historical records very likely reflect intensified use of a capital stock that was not being strained to capacity at the beginning of the period.

Prewar and postwar connections between average and marginal capital-output ratios for Soviet railroads are such as to raise the question of an "envelope curve" embodying technological limitations on the productivity of railroad capital, but progress in technology can clearly release new possibilities. Turning to relations between the supply of capital and the supply of labor, we find that the ratio of the capital stock to the operating railroad labor force has risen, but that the incremental capital-labor ratio has not risen very much.

Finally, a number of indirect observations suggest that the railroads since about 1953 have been receiving a smaller share of annual investment in the economy than they had previously received, and that their share of total fixed plant and equipment has fallen off somewhat. Obviously such a development reflects government recognition of the success achieved in steadily intensifying the use made of railroad fixed assets. Speculation about its implications will be reserved for our final chapter.

# 14 SOME THEORETICAL CONSIDERATIONS

When this study was undertaken, its main task seemed to consist of assembling a reasonably comprehensive record of Soviet transportation developments. The preceding chapters represent the fruit of that undertaking. But as the evidence took shape it became clear that its appraisal would raise difficult problems in the application of theoretical criteria. In this connection it would have been convenient to draw on a theory of transportation and location policy worked out by Soviet writers, but, as perhaps has been evident in earlier chapters, Soviet writers do not seem to have gone far enough to meet the purposes of this study. Or one might have expected to employ concepts drawn from Western location theory, as developed by such writers as Losch, Hoover, and Isard.[1] Western location theory, however, has generally concentrated on explaining historical developments or on defining partial equilibria in a market economy. The problems of Soviet transportation and location policy, on the other hand, have arisen in the search for suitable guidelines to govern future growth involving large, integrated expansion programs. In the absence of any conveniently available theoretical framework, it has thus been necessary to formulate a few theoretical standards for evaluating this specific body of material, and in the present chapter they will be set forth.

We should note at the outset that the dominant feature of all locational problems is the complexity of the factors bearing on them. This may imply that a theoretical framework for their evaluation must be so generalized as to provide impossibly vague standards for judgment. The difficulty can be met in part through the usual methods of partial analysis, taking certain factors as given and working out specific criteria for the others. But there remain several major issues in Soviet policy that require evaluation in more general terms, and here the present study reaches an impasse. Rigorous analysis would require both a more elaborate theory than has been worked out here and a much larger body of data than is yet available for the Soviet period. Tentative observations are nevertheless offered in this and the concluding chapter, but the reader should be conscious that they are anything but definitive.

Let us begin by considering the short-run question of specifying a proper cost-minimizing principle for transportation activities. Familiar notions of economic efficiency would lead us to say that freight carriers should constantly search out ways of concentrating their operations in space and time so as to minimize their own internal costs per unit of output (that is, per ton-kilometer). In general, this involves large traffic units permitting the carrier to enjoy economies of scale, and continuous use of transportation facilities in order to spread fixed costs over a large volume of traffic.

The carriers' clients, however, in collecting inputs and transforming them into various outputs, should also be attempting to minimize their own internal unit production costs, and as was suggested in the chapter on railroad operating practice, the two cost-minimizing objectives cannot help but conflict with each other in various respects. Many practices that lower unit costs for producers will raise unit costs for carriers, and vice versa. In such cases the obvious rule to apply would be that production and transportation should be so integrated as to minimize *combined* unit costs. This rule, however, is an intricate one.

Carriers produce ton-kilometers (or ton-miles) of transportation service, while enterprises produce tons (or other units) of output, so costs per ton-kilometer must be converted into costs per unit of output if *combined* unit costs are to be investigated. Even this simple transformation will involve complications. Moreover, the carrier's internal cost for a particular ton-kilometer is embedded in a heterogenous collection involving many commodity groups, many routes, and a variety of shipping conditions — the cost must therefore be estimated somewhat arbitrarily and be subject to alteration from a wide variety of influences. In addition, the freight charge collected by the carrier from the client need not be identical with the carrier's estimate of his internal costs for a shipment. An integrated review of production and transportation costs would as a result face formidable difficulties in attempting to select a scale of integrated production and transportation activities that would minimize *combined* unit costs.

The principle remains clear, however, and it has one practical consequence that can perhaps be useful, even if a full review of costs cannot be carried through. We can assume that the carrier and the producer will each tend to neglect the other's problems, and that any cost-reducing proposition advanced by one should be scrutinized for possible offsetting effects on the other. Errors in organizing economic activity can thereby be reduced.

A second short-run problem arises in specifying a proper relationship between transportation and other economic activities. Clearly distance is a barrier to be overcome in carrying out economic activity. The processes of production and consumption cannot, at least on any important scale, all take place at one single location. But when elements of economic activity are spatially diffused, some fraction of available resources must be devoted to overcoming the barrier, or friction, imposed by distance. The more resources are diverted into transportation, the less will be left for other uses.

On the other hand, the unification of geographically separated points by means of transportation facilities can be an immensely powerful instrument for increasing production. In the growth of output that has characterized Western economic history over the last few centuries, innovations facilitating low-cost transportation have played a primary role. One has only to think of maritime transportation for Great Britain, or railroad transportation for the American economy, to recognize the importance of this factor. Resources devoted to improving transportation facilities may yield immense dividends, increasing output by many times their initial cost. Thus transportation — and the resource diversity that gives rise to it — can be both a blessing and a curse. Resources used in transportation detract from total output, yet they may be the means of creating a larger output than before.

It follows, therefore, that some optimum volume of transportation capacity will characterize any given economy in any given stage of economic development. Inadequate transportation facilities will hinder production. Provision of excessive transportation capacity will waste resources. Somewhere in between there exists an optimum volume of transportation capacity and transportation services. The optimum will be one that maximizes current output, and not necessarily one that minimizes the volume of freight traffic. Excessive concentration on holding down the volume of freight traffic, in the interests of concentrating resources on the expansion of heavy industry, can lead, as we have seen, to backlogs of unshipped freight and a serious drag on industrial production. But even if such crises are avoided, an emphasis on minimizing freight ton-kilometers can lead to higher cost production, and therefore to a smaller total volume of production, than would be possible if additional freight traffic were permitted. An ideal short-run transportation policy will be one directed toward maximizing the economy's current output, providing all the transportation capacity that contributes effectively to this end.

Short-run criteria like the two rules just enunciated, however, require supplementation for application to a rapidly growing economy, and here we enter an even more complicated area. There is, for example, the problem of specifying a rule for the timing of transportation growth. The over-all policy objective presumably remains one of maximizing the economy's output; serious issues of defining the desired time-shape of the output stream immediately come to mind, but they will not be examined here. Given some time pattern for the over-all output objective, the long-run rule for providing transportation capacity can be restated in terms of avoiding the double errors of making it available either too early or too late. Additional transportation capacity, that is to say, should be brought into being just when it is needed.

Again, however, this simple long-run rule involves intricate complexities, which may be classified under the three headings of multiple objectives, joint costs, and locational interdependencies. The problem of multiple objectives regularly arises in economic analysis, though economists rightly or wrongly often concentrate attention on a single one, either ignoring the others or converting them into the same dimension. The single firm, for example, is usually considered to have the sole objective of maximizing the present discounted value of its anticipated future net earnings. Other influences on its behavior as an institution are ordinarily thought of as translatable into terms modifying its profit objective, or else as being insignificant. This approach has some relevance for a market economy, but not for an appraisal of Soviet policy.

The Soviet regime has had primarily political objectives: acquiring control of Russia, defending and consolidating it, obtaining voluntary or coerced consent from the Russian people, building effective military and economic national power. The leadership has found it increasingly necessary to recognize the purely economic rationale of allocating scarce resources so as to maximize the accomplishment of their objectives. But the point is that the objectives have been multiple. Consequently there have been multiple maxima, and they have not been easily translatable into a common dimension. Soviet economists have recognized this fact. The transportation economist T. S. Khachaturov, for example, in analyzing criteria for choosing investment projects, was careful to leave a wide loophole for the influence of "noneconomic" considerations in determining the final choice.[2] "National interests," as seen by the regime, might very well require the carrying out of an "uneconomic" project, or lead to rejection of a project with great earning power but low priority in the eyes of the leadership.

Over-all Soviet investment allocation decisions are broader than those made by a single firm responding to market forces, and partake of the atmosphere surrounding the concept of marginal social net productivity, as analyzed by A. C. Pigou. Social costs and benefits, indirect costs and benefits, very long run costs and benefits — all these can enter into the decision. Moreover, it is arguable that leading party policy-makers, acting on the doctrine that the party is the vanguard of the people in making choices, can introduce still a further degree of breadth into their decisions. In this setting, the quantitative calculations of engineer-economists require a larger set of reference points for fully rational decisions, including information on variables with quite mysterious contours. Ideally there should be functions expressing, in ruble terms, the impact of political, military, and doctrinal considerations, along with the usual cost and revenue functions, if policy alternatives are to be weighed with quantitative precision. Obviously we are a long way from this goal in Western public policy analysis, and with respect to the USSR we lack even more of the necessary information and understanding. Yet the presence of these noneconomic factors should be recognized, even if at present little more can be done.

A long-run transportation development policy necessarily involves also a plant location policy, and in this connection one encounters difficult joint-cost problems. Consider, for example, a large-scale program for expanding industrial capacity. It might be predicated on intensified use of existing transportation capacity, and locational cost comparisons might run largely in Weberian terms. But there will also be attractive alternatives requiring the building of a new rail line (or perhaps a canal, pipeline, or highway), and here joint cost problems arise. The new rail line is not likely to carry only a single commodity, and the feasibility of its construction will depend on the volume of other traffic to be expected under the program. If the cost of the rail line can be charged in large part against other traffic, the original production project requiring the line will be more attractive than otherwise. Along with internal joint-cost problems, rate-making policies must be considered, since freight rate charges will enter into selection of plant development locations even if freight charges are not used to allocate the initial cost of the new transportation capacity among its users.

The third group of problems in formulating criteria for long-run policy appears most clearly in connection with the locational decisions that determine the long-run need for transportation. Here partial analysis will be at its weakest. When a program for industrial growth is being translated into specific geographic terms, an obvious network of locational interdependencies clearly demands a general-equilibrium type of solution. The task is to find a pattern of plant location and transportation expansion that can be grafted onto the existing regional structure so as to maximize a stream of output from the whole interconnected set of enterprises. This is far more than a question of minimizing each new plant's freight bill. A new plant's demands for supplies will force readjustments in the geographic pattern of distribution of these supplies to some of its neighboring fellow producers. Distribution of the new plant's output, in turn, will alter previously established freight flows in this commodity, with resulting shifts for fellow producers and customers. Clearly an almost infinite variety of geographic patterns could be proposed for a given economy, and even the number worth serious investigation seems likely to be discouragingly large.

To sum up these general notions, we can say that an objective of increasing industrial production calls for (1) a transportation policy designed to provide additional transportation capacity on an adequate scale, but only as fast as, and in the locations where, it is needed; and (2) a location policy directed toward the elaboration of a geographic pattern of enterprises and transportation facilities that will promote efficient exchange of inputs and outputs among them. At the same time it has been obvious that these ideals involve a number of complex problems. Let us turn now to a consideration of practical means for solving the problems.

There is first the short-run problem of organizing the flow of freight traffic so as to maximize current production. In the USSR the guiding principle for a good many years has been that of minimizing the volume of freight traffic, and the procedure has centered around railroad review of clients' freight traffic plans. The principle has been blunted, however, in application. Railroad complaints have made it clear that a good deal of "unnecessary" transportation regularly takes place, and thoughtful railroad writers have acknowledged that the principle requires modification.[3] As a means of improving performance in this sphere, two suggestions appear relevant.

Recent developments in electronic computers and data-processing equipment make it possible for the first time to attack the problem with a reasonable expenditure of time and resources. Some of this equipment is already available in the USSR, and it clearly should be applied to short-run freight traffic problems.[4] If this is done, however, it should be accompanied by explicit recognition of cost-reducing possibilities open to clients through shipping arrangements that the railroads have all too often castigated as "irrational." It should be recognized, too, that an enterprise may be fully justified in obtaining inputs from more distant sources if its nearest supplier cannot provide delivery when it is necessary.

As a means for approaching the problem of multiple objectives, it has already been suggested that ruble functions be developed to provide rough indications of the valuation placed on various noneconomic benefits and costs associated with any projects under consideration. They could at least contribute to selection of the range of projects within which the most advantageous will lie, excluding those on either side that clearly do not meet the regime's joint criteria. It would no doubt continue to be necessary to make finer choices within this range on an intuitive or negotiated basis.

The extreme intricacy of a comprehensive theoretical solution for the joint cost and locational interdependencies problems raised above has been met in practice, both in market economies and in the USSR, through fragmentation of the problems and decentralization of the necessary decision-making. In Western practice, the adjustments that may or may not be made by suppliers, fellow producers, and customers of a new plant do not ordinarily concern the entrepreneur when he decides to build the new plant. They, like the freight carriers affected, are expected to adjust their own operations independently. With capital plant and equipment so relatively long-lived, it is clear that an entrepreneur who plunges ahead in an ill-considered and unco-ordinated decision on plant location may damage the interests of the over-all economy, since the adjustments of others merely minimize losses from a *fait accompli*. Our review of the Soviet record suggests, moreover, that ill-considered and unco-ordinated location decisions are not a monopoly of market economies.

Little is known concerning Soviet procedures for reaching locational decisions, but there is some evidence that certain institutional phenomena create difficulties. Unco-ordinated decisions may follow from the unavoidable subdividing of budget allocations for capital development. For each fiscal year, ministries receive allocations on capital account that, together with their own retained incomes, finance a loosely specified volume of new construction. Having been assigned strenuous production targets, the ministry will be under pressure to choose projects in terms of short-run expediency. Its location choices may cause difficulty for other ministries; for example, a new plant might require the railroad line serving it to build a second track, calling for a capital expenditure by the railroad ministry. But if capital outlays appear in the budget of some other ministry, they are a weaker barrier than if they must be charged against one's own ministerial capital allocation. It would not be easy to document the importance of this factor, but its existence is consistent with observed evidence.[5]

Another institutional limitation that is probably significant in the Soviet setting can perhaps be termed administrative sluggishness. It will be recalled that a shrill campaign has been waged over many years for "comprehensive" development of each region, with emphasis on development of subsidiary activities around major industrial centers. Now this is precisely the kind of economic growth that in earlier Western experience sprang up rapidly as individuals saw a need that could be met on attractive terms. Massive organizations were not called on to formulate and carry out diversified programs. Individual foresight and initiative provided the needed push. In the USSR, on the other hand, a large volume of exhortation is required to promote similar results, and the results have been observably slow in appearing. Centralized co-ordination appears in this case to operate more clumsily than has small-scale, decentralized enterprise elsewhere.

In reflecting on additional means for solving location and transportation problems, or for evaluating transportation and location policy, one is reminded of the legal phrase, "Further than this, deponent sayeth not." It would be possible to put some of these notions in the form of functional equations, probably with beneficial results in improved rigor and additional elaboration. It would also be possible to trace in much greater detail the interrelationships among factors that have been briefly outlined above. Both these tasks deserve attention in the future. For the present study, however, neither can be done with sufficient care, and it seems best therefore to stop at this point and turn to a general summing up of the material we have reviewed.

# A SUMMARY EVALUATION
## 15 OF SOVIET POLICY
## AND PROSPECTS

The time has now come to draw together the threads of this analysis and examine its implications. The record we have been reviewing is a complex one, in the sense that it has involved excursions into geography, technology, and ideology, as well as economics, but the material has been organized in a manner intended to facilitate an orderly review of national policy for this sector of the Soviet economy. The conclusions that appear to grow out of the evidence assembled in the preceding chapters can perhaps best be presented in three groups: first, a set of observations on the lessons implied for other countries seeking to industrialize rapidly; second, an appraisal of Soviet transportation and location policy in terms of its objectives and its execution; and third, a series of comments on the implications of this record for prospective Soviet economic growth.

Clearly, one lesson of Soviet experience is that inadequate attention to freight traffic capacity can lead to a bottleneck that will hinder the growth of the economy. A policy that concentrates too narrowly on heavy industry, neglecting the timely enlargement of transportation facilities and demanding impossible performance from the transportation personnel and equipment on hand, can lead to a serious crisis in the functioning of the economic system. In Chapter 3 an attempt was made to analyze the causes of the Soviet traffic crisis in the early 1930's, and to show that it could have been avoided.

The relevance of this lesson for other economies will depend, of course, not only on the structure of their own growth objectives, but also on the specific economic situation from which each country begins its industrialization drive. In seeking to explain the complex process through which Soviet industrial power was so rapidly enlarged during the 1928–1940 period, it seems important to note that the Soviet drive was launched from a not inconsiderable industrial base. The process of industrialization, as Professor Gerschenkron and others have shown, had been under way for at least fifty years. Much of the necessary foundation had already been laid. In particular, a transportation system had been established in European Russia, and it was by no means fully utilized. In the Urals and Western Siberia, railroad construction during the First World War, together with projects completed in the 1920's, provided a minimum network built ahead of traffic. The forced industrialization drive could therefore proceed through intensifying the utilization of existing capacity and through expanding it, without having to commit enormous resources to the task of laying down the primary network.

In pushing ahead on this basis, the government nevertheless permitted a serious transportation crisis to develop. It appears that the backlogs of unshipped freight, which hampered industrial growth for some three years, arose because of bad timing in the channeling of resources into expansion of carrying capacity. The margin of additional resources that would have been necessary to avert the crisis was not a large one. The government rested its hopes on prompt gains in operating efficiency, and at the time this may have appeared a well-calculated risk; with the benefit of hindsight, it appears to have gone too far.

Speculation about reasons for governmental policy mistakes runs onto very unsure ground, of course, and extensive analysis of many aspects of this complex period will be required before a satisfactory account can be given. One may expect, however, that the regime's absorption with the revolutionary upheavals arising out of collectivization of agriculture had a good deal to do with the matter. Stalin did not "turn his attention to transportation" until 1934. A second set of causal factors appears to have centered in the steel industry, where serious difficulties noticeably reduced steel availabilities in 1932 and 1933. To the extent that these were unavoidable, a measure of unavoidability may have attached to transportation difficulties as well. In any case, the record should suggest to other countries that formidable problems in these sectors of the economy may create crises in other sectors as well.

The transportation crisis was, however, rather promptly overcome, and Soviet experience in building a more effective transportation system provides significant material for analysis. Improvement can be traced to new equipment on the one hand, and increased labor productivity on the other; the two interacted in complex ways that are briefly touched on in Chapter 4. Some efficiency gains were achieved before much new equipment came into use, but then a limit was reached. Provision of substantial quantities of new plant and equipment then supported pronounced gains in output, plus notable further gains in efficiency, but once more a limit was reached. Again in the postwar period, after the recovery period was completed, a cycle of equipment improvement and efficiency gains was unfolded, and the process shows no sign of ending. The broad lesson is that more effective transportation performance involves the reciprocal interaction of both men and equipment, of both social and mechanical engineering. One would not expect precise numerical relationships to be transferable from one economy to another, but it may be helpful to recognize the character of this two-pronged drive to advance the limits of the transportation production process, and to note the points at which temporary limits have been reached.

A third and related lesson, pointed out in Chapter 13, concerns the possibility of using capital plant and equipment more intensively, or in technical terms, of lowering capital-output ratios. Discouraging implications for rapid economic growth have sometimes been drawn from the observation that capital-output ratios in the transportation sector appear to be relatively high; necessary improvements in this form of social capital are said to make a substantial levy on available capital resources. Soviet experience, however, and United States experience too, in certain periods, suggest that in fact transportation capital can be highly productive and therefore that relative optimism on this score is warranted.

As to locational matters, a fourth lesson of Soviet experience is that speed of industrial development and geographic dispersion of economic activity appear to be inversely related. If rapid growth of industry is a major objective, it is likely to foster the expansion of established industrial centers, and thus to conflict with an objective of building up an economy's underdeveloped regions. This is not to say, of course, that certain activities (mining in particular) will not develop rapidly in outlying areas, but Soviet experience and simple economic logic both demonstrate that industry can expand most cheaply and rapidly around existing concentrations of population and social capital. It follows that a balanced choice must be made, in formulating national economic development policy, between stimulating the growth of underdeveloped regions and rapidly enlarging the output of manufacturing industry.

As a corollary of this relationship, it can be observed that pronounced shifts in the regional distribution of economic activity require a good deal of time. The Soviet objective of spreading economic activity more evenly throughout the USSR has encountered a variety of objective difficulties that have impeded the grandiose schemes regularly promulgated by the regime. Without calling into question the objective itself, it is well to recognize the problems confronted in carrying it out, and to avoid undue expectations of rapid success. Perhaps other nations will progress more successfully in this respect, but, as Chapter 2 has shown, the experience of the USSR points up the difficulties involved.

For a sixth lesson arising out of the Soviet record, we may turn to the manner in which transportation and location policy principles have been enunciated. It should be evident from a review of the statements quoted in Chapter 2, seen in the light of the broad rules laid down in Chapter 14, that the party's general line in these matters has been far too sweeping. Perhaps simple prescriptions, set forth without qualifications, can be justified in terms of effective campaigning under strenuous conditions, but modest analysis readily demonstrates that such rules are exceedingly clumsy in application. At this point it appears that political technicians and economic technicians must resolve a conflict of procedure in administering national economic policy: rational and precise guidelines for organizing economic activity may not express the political force necessary to dislodge prevailing attitudes and dramatize the regime's objectives. If so, political *élan* will be obtained at the expense of economic rationality.

In this connection there is a related lesson to be learned from the nature of Soviet five-year plans. It has been shown in Chapter 6 that the Fourth and Fifth Five Year Plans (and this was also true of the three prewar plans) contained seriously inaccurate forecasts of the volume of transportation service to be required by the economy, and seriously misleading "plans" for the amount of new transportation capacity to be provided for meeting these needs. The list of specific investment projects to be completed during the next five years has proved to be merely an agenda from which actual construction projects have been drawn, and the record of actual construction has shown that very substantial delays in completion have regularly occurred. Here again there appears to be a conflict between political or psychological considerations and purely economic considerations in formulating five-year plans. Rational integration of prospective needs and resources for the various interdependent sectors of an economy would entail cautious and precise formulation of both output targets and construction programs. But such a plan would perhaps be insufficiently dramatic as a galvanizing force expressing the ambitious objectives of a determined regime. There may be a genuine case for overstating the objectives of a five-year plan in order to make it an active, goading instrument for rapid economic change. It would follow, of course, that administrators responsible for operating the economy would then have to piece together an informed and somewhat cynical set of expectations about the actual demands likely to confront them and the actual facilities likely to be made available for meeting these demands.

There is, finally, an eighth lesson to be drawn from the Soviet record, perhaps somewhat discouraging in its implications. Nationalization of transportation facilities, and centralized planning of transportation activities, have not so far proved to be successful means for organizing a smoothly functioning, unified transportation system. The material reviewed in Chapter 8, seen against the background set forth in Chapter 1, indicates that co-ordinated integration of multicarrier operations faces several practical difficulties that cannot be eliminated merely through political changes in ownership and control. There is clearly much progress to be made in this sphere, both in the USSR and in the United States, but there is no evidence to date that Soviet organizational techniques provide any keys to success.

Turning now to an appraisal of Soviet transportation and location policy, I would suggest three broad observations. All three are based on acceptance of over-all Soviet objectives as given, thus limiting the issue to questions of effectiveness in pursuing these objectives. It would clearly lie outside the scope of the present study to pass judgment on them, much as a Western observer may be tempted to do so.

First, there can be no doubt that the general policy of restricting the expansion of transportation facilities and the volume of freight traffic, in order to promote rapid growth of heavy industry, has been successful. Soviet heavy industry has grown very rapidly indeed, using in part the resources that might have gone into transportation expansion, and, after the initial mistake of permitting a freight traffic crisis in the early 1930's, the government has seen to it that transportation capacity has kept pace with the rest of the economy. However, it is entirely possible that more generous allocation of resources to expansion of transportation capacity, while reducing availabilities for industrial capital formation in the very short run, might nevertheless have facilitated absolutely larger additions to industrial capacity toward the end of the 1928–1940 period. While it is important to recognize the possibility, it has not been possible in the present study to investigate the issue.

The problem goes beyond a lack of historical data. In a few more years our time-series records will adequately crisscross the 1928–1940 period. But policy decisions at a point in time, and evaluations of them by later observers, involve marginal comparisons among alternative factor combinations and output assortments, given a background of technological possibilities and state preferences. The analysis can be dynamic in the sense that production functions describing Soviet technological possibilites in the 1930's should be reconstructed, not as static, old-fashioned ones, but as modernized, anticipatory, even hortatory ones. Nevertheless, as Norman Kaplan has pointed out,[1] tracing the path of actual developments over time does not yield much information about alternatives at any moment. (In technical terms, marginal rates of substitution along a particular isoquant on a production surface cannot be deduced from time-series records tracing a kind of scale line moving up along a [changing] surface.) For evaluating alternatives, one needs cross-section or structural data relating to a given year, and until such a framework has been reconstructed, one cannot adequately compare observed policy with alternatives to see if an optimum course was pursued.

A second broad finding concerns the effectiveness of Soviet transportation and location policy in enabling the USSR to emerge successfully from World War II. Given Soviet objectives, it appears on balance that Soviet policies found a rational middle ground between the conflicting forces at work. In 1947 a Soviet writer pointed out that the iron and steel devoted in World War II to the construction of Soviet tanks would have been sufficient for 60,000 kilometers of railroad line.[2] This is one instance of the larger fact that the resources not used in the 1930's to expand transportation capacity were used for heavy industry and armaments; the outcome of World War II gives crude approval to this policy from a Soviet point of view. Moreover, even without undertaking a careful military analysis, it can be argued that the strategic policy of retreating in depth proved pragmatically to have been a risk worth taking. For the railroads, it meant a conscious policy of failing to build up lateral lines near the Soviet western frontier, coupled with emergency construction in 1942 of a long lateral line near the edge of unoccupied territory. In the broad sphere of location policy, it meant expansion of industrial capacity during the 1930's in western territory later occupied by the Nazis, though safer production sites farther to the east could have been chosen instead. Again, the policy involved a calculated risk. Had industrial capacity in western and southern European Russia not been expanded, the increments obtainable farther east would undoubtedly have involved higher real costs, and come forward less promptly.

There are, of course, many other imponderables. Had Western Europe and the United States found effective ways to solve the problems arising out of the First World War, the Nazis might never have come to power and attacked the USSR. If there had been less implacable hostility on the Bolsheviks' part toward the West, the USSR might have had a far happier experience. An appropriate transportation and location policy would of course have been different under such conditions. Given, however, the actual framework and sequence of events, Soviet transportation and location policies appear to have been well designed to meet their environment.

The third judgment that seems warranted in evaluating the Soviet record concerns the way in which official policy has been employed. It was noted above that the party's general line has often substituted exhortation for precision. Furthermore, it can be said that official doctrine has at times been used to restrict rational thought. In this field, Soviet writers have occasionally encountered criticism for following reason outside the bounds of official slogans. A somewhat extreme postwar example relates to a thoughtful technical paper in a 1948 book. When it was reviewed, in *Planovoe Khoziaistvo* (Planned Economy) in 1949, the reviewer harshly criticized the paper, saying in effect that party policy should overrule objective evidence.[3] Discussion of location and transportation issues has often run in ritualistic terms that must have interfered with straight thinking about difficult problems.[4] A broader scope for objective technical analysis will unquestionably improve the solution of many present and future Soviet transportation problems.

Reflection on the implications of Soviet transportation experience for prospective Soviet economic growth leads to a single broad conclusion: that the transportation sector will not prove to be a retarding influence on industrial expansion in the next decade or so. The conclusion rests on a series of subconclusions concerning (a), the traffic-output ratio, (b) the eastward movement, (c) the capital-output ratio, and (d) the share of transportation investment in total Soviet capital formation. Each will be summarized below.

But before considering the role of transportation in fostering or hindering Soviet economic growth, one should perhaps defend the initial assumption that rapid Soviet economic growth will in fact continue. The basic premise must evidently be that the Soviet regime will continue to press forward vigorously in this direction. Given such a driving force, one must next consider the sources of industrial growth. Quantitatively, these sources in the USSR still appear very large. The Russian land mass contains huge absolute amounts of the raw materials and fuels on which industrial activity depends. The Soviet population of over 200 million people is very large, and while stringencies are currently evident, substantial additions to the nonagricultural labor force can be expected in the coming years. As for capital, the stern mechanism of the Soviet fiscal and allocation system brings forth each year a large volume of resources for capital formation. Quantitatively, then, the wherewithal for industrial growth appears impressive.

But qualitative aspects of the situation also require examination. Soviet natural resources, while abundant, are not always so rich as Soviet publicity implies. In many instances, recourse is already being had to deposits of progressively lower grades. In addition to technical deficiencies that raise the cost or reduce the productivity of such resources, there is the factor of distance. Many abundant resource deposits are thousands of kilometers from existing industrial centers, and their use, which is already generating large increments of freight traffic, will, in the future, add to the real cost of obtaining increments of industrial output.

On the other hand, qualitative improvement in the nonagricultural labor force appears to hold considerable promise for Soviet industrial growth. As Walter Galenson has shown,[5] labor productivity in Soviet industry is typically less than half as high as corresponding labor productivity in the United States. Thus while the quality of the Soviet resource base seems likely to deteriorate, the quality of its labor force appears certain to improve.

In connection with capital inputs, there may also be substantial potentialities for growth. On the one hand, Soviet industry, like Soviet railroads, makes very intensive use of its capital equipment, thereby perhaps already pressing on the upper limit of what can be expected. On the other hand, current technology appears to involve items of equipment whose productivity is very much higher than that characteristic of capital equipment some decades ago. In technical terms, the capital-output ratio may be lower now in many lines than was true in the past. For a concrete example in the railroad field, consider modern earth-moving equipment. Certainly 100,000 rubles invested now in a diesel-powered earth-mover or carryall will accomplish many times the work performed by an equivalently priced steam shovel of the early 1930's. The contrast with men using wheelbarrows is even more dramatic. Consequently, current railroad construction projects can take advantage of enormously more efficient technology than was available when the Turk-Sib Railway or the Moscow-Donbas trunk line was built, and photographs in the railroad newspaper make it clear that such modern equipment is already in use. Similar potentialities appear available in other sectors of the economy.

If it seems likely that there will continue to be substantial Soviet industrial growth in the next few years, what does this imply for the transportation sector? First, what can be anticipated for the relation between industrial output and the volume of freight traffic? The evidence of Chapter 12 suggests that the ratio of traffic to output, as measured there, is not likely to decline. It is more likely, in fact, to drift upward. If a relaxation of Soviet policy permitted more generous freight service to be made available, industrial production might well be facilitated, thus offsetting any upward trend in the traffic-output ratio. But beyond this possibility, there is some evidence of an unintended upward drift reflecting geographic forces at work. As noted in Chapter 1, wide locational dispersion of economic resources characterizes the Soviet land mass, and this dispersion, or maldistribution of inputs with respect to each other, is permanently embedded in the Russian environment. It may be exacting an increasing toll from the expanding economy.

In this connection one must weigh the prospects for the Soviet eastward movement. The Soviet economy, as shown in Chapter 2, is still marked by substantial "unevenness," in spite of ostensible government intentions. There is much to explain and even recommend this unevenness, as we have seen. What will be the consequences for transportation if it continues? Substantial growth around existing industrial centers will evidently be associated with an increasing volume of long-haul freight traffic bringing in the fuel and raw materials required at the centers and not locally available. Already European Russia's demands for coal and timber are raising transportation problems. This reaching out from established centers toward the east and north will, if it continues and grows, clearly tend to raise the traffic-output ratio.

Suppose, on the other hand, that Soviet policy leads toward creation of genuinely self-sufficient regional economies. The purpose would be, from a transportation point of view at least, to hold down increases in the numerator of the traffic-output ratio. It can be argued, however, that such a policy would simultaneously tend to hold down increases in the denominator of the ratio as well.

The weakly developed regions of the USSR vary among themselves greatly in their characteristics, but they share a common disability: unfavorable conditions for economic activity. Agriculture can be pursued, for example, only at relatively high real costs outside the so-called wedge territory. In the east and north, serious engineering difficulties raise the real cost of building dwellings, factories, railroads, highways, and industrial service installations. The problem of offsetting low winter temperatures is more serious in the east and north than in most of central and southern European Russia. In Central Asia and Kazakhstan, deficient water supplies create cost-raising problems.

This is not to suggest, by any means, that substantial increments of output cannot be obtained in the outlying regions of the USSR. What does seem clear, nevertheless, is that a given quantum of inputs applied here will produce a smaller total output than has been obtained at established centers. Or, putting it the other way around, the real costs associated with production of any given volume of output will be higher in these newer regions than in settled territory. If so, then the increments of production to be expected from a regional self-sufficiency policy will tend to be checked. Consequently, although the traffic-output ratio may not rise, the expansion of both numerator and denominator will be inhibited.

Parenthetically, the probable scope of the Soviet eastward movement in the near future deserves comment. Recent trends and current plans suggest that substantial growth will be concentrated in the regions adjacent to European Russia, and that the far-distant eastern regions bordering on the Pacific Ocean will not be greatly affected. In the Volga Valley, the Ural region, Kazakhstan, Central Asia, and Western Siberia, extending as far east as an industrial enclave around Irkutsk near Lake Baikal, notable development appears to be in prospect. But at the same time it will remain true that perhaps 40 per cent of Soviet territory will be relatively unproductive wilderness, except for isolated mining and military installations.

The argument up to this point has run in terms of an upward drift in the volume of transportation service to be associated with increments of Soviet industrial output, and this would imply that an increased flow of capital plant and equipment into transportation capacity will be necessary to meet the need. Here, however, one confronts another crucial ratio, that between assets and traffic, and the best present prediction appears to be that this ratio can be expected to fall. A downward trend in the volume of transportation assets required to turn out a given amount of transportation service would clearly tend to offset an upward trend in the traffic-output ratio. The crude evidence of Chapter 13 indicates, it will be remembered, that just such a downward tendency has characterized Soviet experience. Moreover there is reason to believe that the various technological innovations now on the horizon for Soviet railroads (such as electric and diesel-electric locomotives, improved signaling and communications, and electronic data-processing) will make continued reductions possible.

We have seen that while the average assets-to-traffic ratio (this is merely another name for the railroad capital-output ratio) has tended downward in both the 1928–1940 and 1945–1955 periods in the USSR, the incremental ratio at the end of each period has been higher than it was at the beginning. A rising incremental ratio would of course spell increasing marginal needs for transportation plant and equipment to keep pace with growing traffic. It may be misleading, however, to compare incremental ratios from 1928–1932 and 1945–1948 with the ratios existing in more normal periods; inability to maintain the extremely low ratios of these two periods need not rule out the possibility of stable, low ratios sustained for some time at a moderate level. In short, the slender evidence so far available seems consistent with a situation in which the average capital-output ratio for Soviet railroads will continue to decline slowly, while the marginal capital-output ratio continues to rise slowly.

The final relationship to be considered is that of transportation investment to total Soviet investment in the near future. It has been argued above that additional industrial production will call for additional freight transportation service on a rising scale, but that such service can probably be provided through less than proportionate increases in the transportation capital stock. It follows that the transportation sector will not have to make percentage demands on the national pool of investment resources that exceed its past percentage demands. The absolute sums, of course, will certainly be larger, but that is not the question. If transportation capital is proving increasingly effective, and the need for transportation is not expanding uncontrollably, then the transportation sector can make do with perhaps even a smaller share of total new investment than has been necessary in the past. Fragmentary evidence for recent years points in this direction, as we have seen. And for a final clue, one can point to the fact that the present Sixth Five Year Plan appears to allocate for transportation investment in the 1956–1960 period, not the 12 per cent of total investment which used to go to the railroads alone, but something in the neighborhood of 7 per cent for the whole transportation sector.[6] The evidence of the present study provides a basis for understanding this astonishing recent development; only the future can test conclusively its wisdom.

# BIBLIOGRAPHY

Where titles have been cited in the notes by other than the author's last name and the year of publication, the entry below begins with the special form employed. In the case of complex author entries, Library of Congress procedure is followed. Unless otherwise noted, all titles published in Moscow.

## 1. BOOKS AND PAMPHLETS

AAR, 1956. Association of American Railroads, Bureau of Railway Economics. *Railroad Transportation, A Statistical Record, 1921–1955*. Washington, D.C., 1956. 35 pages.

Armstrong, Terence. *The Northern Sea Route*. Cambridge, England: Cambridge University Press, 1952. 162 pages.

Avgustyniuk, Aleksandr Ivanovich, and V. Vakhman. *Transport sovetskoi derzhavy* (Transportation of the Soviet Realm). 1950. 102 pages.

Bakulin, S. N., and D. D. Mishustin. *Vneshniaia torgovlia SSSR za 20 let, 1918–1937 gg.; statisticheskii spravochnik* (USSR Foreign Trade During 20 Years, 1918–1937: Statistical Handbook). 1939. 264 pages.

Bal'zak, S. S., V. F. Vasiutin, and IA. G. Feigin, editors. *Ekonomicheskaia Geografiia SSSR, Chast I*. 1940. English translation: Chauncy D. Harris, editor. *Economic Geography of the USSR*. New York: Macmillan, 1949. 620 pages.

Baranskii, Nikolai Nikolaevich. *Ekonomicheskaia geografiia SSSR: uchebnik dlia 8 klassa srednei shkoly* (Economic Geography of the USSR: Textbook for the Eighth Grade of the Middle School), 8th ed. 1947. 394 pages.

Bardin, I. P., and N. P. Bannyi. *Chernaia metallurgiia v novoi piatiletke* (Ferrous Metallurgy in the New Five-Year Plan). 1947. 174 pages.

Barger, Harold. *The Transportation Industries, 1889–1946: A Study of Output, Employment and Productivity*. New York: National Bureau of Economic Research, 1951. 288 pages.

Beck, F., and W. Godin. *Russian Purge and the Extraction of Confession*. New York: The Viking Press, 1951. 277 pages.

Beckmann, Martin, C. B. McGuire, and Christopher B. Winsten. *Studies in the Economics of Transportation*. New Haven: Yale University Press, 1956. 232 pages.

Beliunov, S. A., and others. *Planirovanie na zheleznodorozhnom transporte* (Planning in Railroad Transportation). 1948. 324 pages.

Bergson, Abram. *The Structure of Soviet Wages*. Cambridge: Harvard University Press, 1946. 255 pages.

Bergson, 1953a. Abram Bergson, editor. *Soviet Economic Growth: Conditions and Perspectives*. Evanston, Illinois: Row, Peterson and Company, 1953. 376 pages.

Bergson, 1953b. Abram Bergson. *Soviet National Income and Product in 1937*. New York: Columbia University Press, 1953. 156 pages.

Bergson, Abram, and Hans Heymann, Jr. *Soviet National Income and Product, 1940–1948*. New York: Columbia University Press, 1954. 249 pages.

Bernatskii, Lev Nikolaevich. *Sverkhmagistral'* (Supertrunkline). 1925. 254 pages.

Bernstein-Kogan, Sergei Vladimirovich. *Osnovnye problemy transporta SSSR i perspektivy ego razvitiia: sbornik* (Basic Problems of Transportation in the USSR and Prospects for its Development: A Symposium). 1929. 121 pages.

—— *Ocherki geografii transporta* (Notes on Transportation Geography). 1930. 348 pages.

Beshchev, Boris Pavlovich. *Itogi raboty zheleznykh dorog za 1953 god i mery dal'neishego pod'ema raboty zheleznodorozhnogo transporta* (Results of the Railroads' Work During 1953 and Measures for a Further Rise in the Work of Railroad Transportation). 1954. 48 pages.

Blackman, James Horton. "Transportation Appendices" (mimeographed appendices to Chapter IV in Abram Bergson, ed., *Soviet Economic Growth*). September 1953. 88 pages.

BSE, 1932. *Bol'shaia sovetskaia entsiklopediia* (Large Soviet Encyclopedia), vol. 24. 1932. 800 columns.

BSE, 1947a. *Bol'shaia Sovetskaia entsiklopediia, dopolnitel'nyi tom: soiuz sovetskikh sotsialisticheskikh respublik* (Large Soviet Encyclopedia, Supplementary Volume: Union of Soviet Socialist Republics). 1947. 2026 columns.

BSE, 1947b. *Bol'shaia sovetskaia entsiklopediia* (Large Soviet Encyclopedia), vol. 55. 1947. 986 columns.

Bukharin, Nikolai Ivanovich, *defendant*. *Report of Court Proceedings in the Case of the Anti-Soviet "Bloc of Rights and Trotskyites"* . . . Moscow: People's Commissariat of Justice of the USSR, 1938. 799 pages.

Chernomordik, David Iosifovich. *Ekonomicheskaia Politika SSSR* (Economic Policy of the USSR). 1936. 382 pages.

Chudov, A. S. *Planovaia kal'kulatsiia sebestoimosti zheleznodorozhnykh perevozok* (Planned Calculation of the Cost of Railroad Shipments). 1947. 113 pages.

Clark, M. Gardner. *The Economics of Soviet Steel*. Cambridge: Harvard University Press, 1956. 400 pages.

Danilov, S. K., editor. *Ekonomika transporta* (Economics of Transportation). 1956. 612 pages. (Library of Congress author entry is Gibshman, A. E.)

DeWitt, Nicolas. *Soviet Professional Manpower: Its Education, Training and Supply*. Washington, D. C.: National Science Foundation, 1955. 400 pages.

Ezhov, A. I. *Moskovskii metropoliten* (The Moscow Subway). 1953. 31 pages.

Galitskii, A. E. *Planirovanie perevozok* (The Planning of Shipments). 1939. 90 pages.

General'nyi Shtab Vooruzhennykh Sil SSSR. *Stratigicheskaia Karta evropy* (Strategic Map of Europe). 1946. Scale, 1:2,500,000. Available in the Library of Congress Map Division.

Gerschenkron, Alexander. *A Dollar Index of Soviet Machinery Output, 1927–28 to 1937*. Santa Monica, California: The RAND Corporation, 1951. 357 pages.

Gibshman, A. E. *Transport v probleme uralo-kuznetskogo kombinata* (Transportation in the Problem of the Ural-Kuznetsk Combine). 1931. 59 pages.

Gibshman, A. E., and others. *Osnovy proktirovaniia zheleznykh dorog* (Principles of Surveying for Railroads). 1954. 459 pages.

Gokhman, O. V. *Puti soobshcheniia Finlandii* (Means of Communication of Finland). 1944. 62 pages.

Gorinov, 1948a. A. V. Gorinov. *Proektirovanie zheleznykh dorog* (Surveying for Railroads), 3rd ed., supplemented and revised, 3 vols. 1948. 575, 548, and 438 pages.

Gorinov, 1948b. A. V. Gorinov and N. P. Divnogorskii. *Razvitie tekhniki zheleznodorozhnogo transporta* (The Development of Railroad Technology). 1948. 97 pages.

Gosplan, 1930. Gosudarstvennaia planovaia komissiia Soiuza SSR. *Piatiletnii plan narodno-khoziaistvennogo stroitel'stva SSSR* (Five-Year Plan of National-Economic Construction of the USSR), 3rd ed., 3 vols. 1930. 1747 pages.

Gosplan, 1934. —— *Vtoroi piatiletnii plan razvitiia narodnogo khoziaistva SSSR, 1933–1937 gg.* (Second Five Year Plan of Development of the National Economy of the USSR, 1933–1937), 2 vols. 1934. 1262 pages.

Gosplan, 1935. —— *Narodno-khoziaistvennyi plan na 1935 god* (National-Economic Plan for 1935). 1935. 927 pages.

Gosplan, 1936. —— *Narodno-khoziaistvennyi plan na 1936 god* (National-Economic Plan for 1936), 2nd ed., 2 vols. 1936. 1170 pages.

Gosplan, 1937. —— *Narodno-khoziaistvennyi plan Soiuza SSR na 1937 god* (National-Economic Plan of the USSR for 1937). 1937. 177 pages.

Gosplan, 1939a. —— *Itogi vypolneniia vtorogo piatiletnogo plana razvitiia narodnogo khoziaistva Soiuza SSR* (Results of Fulfillment of the Second Five Year Plan of Development of the National Economy of the USSR). 1939. 157 pages.

Gosplan, 1939b. —— *Tretii piatiletnii plan razvitiia narodnogo khoziaistva Soiuza SSR, 1938–1942 gg., proekt* (Third Five Year Plan of Development of the National Economy of the USSR, 1938–1942, Draft). 1939. 232 pages.

*Gosudarstvennyi plan razvitiia narodnogo khoziaistva SSSR na 1941 god* (Government Plan of Development of the National Economy of the USSR for 1941). Baltimore: Universal Press, 1951. 746 pages.

Grigor'ev, A. N. *Khoziaistvennyi raschet otdeleniia zheleznoi dorogi* (Economic Accounting for a Railroad Division). 1955. 129 pages.

Gurevich, S., and S. Partigul. *Novyi pod'em narodnogo khoziaistva SSSR v poslevoennoi piatiletke* (The New Upswing of the National Economy of the USSR in the Postwar Five Year plan). 1949. 157 pages.

*History of the Communist Party of the Soviet Union (Bolsheviks), Short Course.* Moscow: Foreign Languages Publishing House, 1945 printing. 363 pages.

Hodgman, Donald, R. *Soviet Industrial Production, 1928–1951.* Cambridge: Harvard University Press, 1954. 241 pages.

Hoeffding, Oleg. *Soviet National Income and Product in 1938.* New York: Columbia University Press, 1954. 156 pages.

Hoover, Edgar M. *The Location of Economic Activity.* New York: McGraw-Hill, 1948. 310 pages.

IAkobi, Alexsandr Moritsevich. *Zheleznye dorogi SSSR v tsifrakh: statisticheskii sbornik* (Railroads of the USSR in Figures: A Statistical Handbook). 1935. 186 pages.

ICC. United States Interstate Commerce Commission. *Annual Report on the Statistics of Railways in the United States.* Washington, D.C.: Government Printing Office. Issued annually.

ICC. —— Bureau of Transport Economics and Statistics. "Intercity Ton-Miles, 1939–1952, With Adjustments of Motor-Vehicle Ton-Miles" (Statement No. 544, by Paul L. Ambelang). March 1954. 8 pages.

Ioffe, IA. A. *SSSR i kapitalisticheskie strany: statisticheskii sbornik* (The USSR and Capitalist Countries: A Statistical Handbook). 1939. 319 pages.

Isard, Walter. *Location and Space Economy.* New York: John Wiley and Sons, 1956. 350 pages.

Ivliev, I. V., and A. G. Kuz'min. *Finansirovanie kapital'nogo stroitel'stva zheleznykh dorog* (Financing Capital Construction of Railroads). 1946. 227 pages.

Izosimov, A. V. *Osnovnye sredstva zheleznykh dorog SSSR* (Fixed Assets of the Railroads of the USSR). 1952. 91 pages.

Jasny, Naum. *The Socialized Agriculture of the USSR.* Stanford: Stanford University Press, 1949. 837 pages.

—— *Soviet Prices of Producers' Goods.* Stanford: Stanford University Press, 1952. 180 pages.

Kaganovich, 1954a. Lazar Moiseevich Kaganovich. *Ob uluchshenii raboty i dal'neishem pod'eme vodnogo transporta* (On Improving the Work and [Obtaining] A Further Rise in Water Transportation). 1954. 99 pages.

Kaganovich, 1954b. —— *Uluchshit' rabotu i organizovat' novyi pod"em zheleznodorozhnogo transporta* (To Improve the Work and Organize A New Rise in Railroad Transportation). 1954. 103 pages.

Kattsen, I. *Metro Moskvy* (The Moscow Subway). 1947. 174 pages.

Khachaturov, Tigran Sergeevich. *Razmeshchenie transporta v kapitalisticheskikh stranakh i v SSSR* (Distribution of Transportation in Capitalist Countries and in the USSR). 1939. 716 pages.

—— *Zheleznodorozhnyi transport v velikoi otechestvennoi voine* (Railroad Transportation in the Great Patriotic War). 1943. 47 pages.

—— *Osnovy ekonomiki zheleznodorozhnogo transporta* (Economic Principles of Railroad Transportation). 1946. 374 pages.

—— *Zheleznodorozhnyi transport SSSR* (Railroad Transportation of the USSR). 1952. 262 pages.

—— *Transport i sviaz' v SSSR* (Transportation and Communications in the USSR). 1953. 48 pages.

Khanukov, Evgenii Davidovich, and V. I. Chernyshev, editors. *Voprosy ekonomiki zheleznodorozhnogo transporta: sbornik statei* (Economic Problems of Railroad Transportation: A Collection of Articles). 1948. 376 pages.

Kochetov, Ivan Vasil'evich, editor. *Zheleznodorozhnaia statistika* (Railroad Statistics). 1939. 363 pages.

Kochetov, I. V., *Statistika zheleznodorozhnogo transporta* (Statistics of Railroad Transportation). 1941. 598 pages.

—— *Zheleznodorozhnaia statistika* (Railroad Statistics). 1st ed., 1948, 309 pages. 2nd ed., 1953, 303 pages.

Kochnev, F. P. *Organizatsiia passazhirskikh perevozok na zheleznodorozhnom transporte* (Organization of Passenger Movement in Railroad Transportation). 1950. 331 pages.

Koldomasov, IU. I. *Osnovy planirovaniia perevozok na zheleznodorozhnom transporte* (Principles of Planning Shipments in Railroad Transportation). 1949. 299 pages.

Kolosovskii, Nikolai Nikolaevich. *Problema Sibirskoi sverkhmagistrali* (The Problem of a Siberian Supertrunkline). 1929. 193 pages.

—— *Velikaia Sibirskaia sverkhmagistral'* (The Great Siberian Supertrunkline). 1930. 63 pages.

Kommunisticheskaia partiia Sovetskogo soiuza. 17. S"ezd, Moscow, 1934. *XVII s"ezd Vsesoiuznoi kommunisticheskoi partii (b), 26 IAnvaria — 10 Fevralia 1934 g., Stenograficheskii otchet* (Seventeenth Congress of the All-Union Communist Party (B), January 26 — February 10, 1934, Stenographic Transcript). 1934. 716 pages.

—— Eighteenth Congress, Moscow, 1939. *XVIII s"ezd, 10–21 Marta 1939 g., Stenograficheskii otchet* (Eighteenth Congress, March 10–21, 1939, Stenographic Transcript). 1939. 742 pages. English translation: *The Land of Socialism Today and Tomorrow.* Moscow: Foreign Languages Publishing House, 1939. 488 pages.

—— *Kommunisticheskaia partiia Sovetskogo Soiuza v rezoliutsiiakh i resheniiakh s"ezdov, konferentsii i plenumov TsK* (Communist Party of the Soviet Union in

Resolutions and Decisions of Congresses, Conferences, and Central Committee Plenums), 7th ed., 2 vols. 1953. 2156 pages.

Kovalev, 1946a. Ivan Vladimirovich Kovalev. *Zheleznodorozhnyi transport v novoi stalinskoi piatiletke* (Railroad Transportation in the New Stalinist Five-Year Plan). 1946. 122 pages.

Kovalev, 1946b. ——— *Zheleznodorozhnyi transport v novoi piatiletke* (Railroad Transportation in the New Five Year Plan). 1946. 24 pages.

——— *Sovetskii zheleznodorozhnyi transport, 1917–1947 gg.* (Soviet Railroad Transportation, 1917–1947). 1947. 109 pages.

*Land of Socialism Today and Tomorrow, The.* Moscow: Foreign Languages Publishing House, 1939. 488 pages.

Lenin, Vladimir Il'ich. *Sochineniia* (Collected Works), 4th ed., 35 vols. 1941–1950.

Levin, B. I., editor. *Osnovnye voprosy piatiletnogo plana vosstanovleniia i razvitiia zheleznodorozhnogo transporta na 1946–50 gg.* (Basic Problems of the Five-Year Plan of Restoration and Development of Railroad Transportation in 1946–1950). 1947. 396 pages.

Lorimer, Frank. *The Population of the Soviet Union: History and Prospects.* Geneva: League of Nations, 1946. 289 pages.

Losch, August. *The Economics of Location* (translated from the second revised German edition of *Die raumliche Ordnung der Wirtschaft*). New Haven: Yale University Press, 1954. 520 pages.

Malenkov, Georgi Mikhailovich. *O zadachakh partiinykh organizatsii v oblasti promyshlennosti i transporta* (On the Tasks of Party Organizations in the Field of Industry and Transportation). 1941. 45 pages.

——— *Report to the Nineteenth Party Congress on the Work of the Central Committee of the CPSU (B).* Moscow: Foreign Languages Publishing House, 1952. 147 pages.

Migal', S. P. *Zarabotnaia plata na zheleznodorozhnom transporte, po osnovnoi deiatel'nosti* (Wages in Railroad Transportation, for the Basic Occupation). 1951. 87 pages.

Modzolevskii, I. V., and others. *Obshchii kurs zheleznykh dorog* (General Course on Railroads). 1951. 398 pages.

MPS, 1916. Russia. Ministerstvo putei soobshcheniia, Otdel statistiki i kartografii. *Statisticheskii sbornik ministerstva putei soobshcheniia* (Statistical Handbook of the Ministry of Means of Communication). Petrograd, 1916 and earlier years.

MPS, 1946. Russia (1923 — USSR) Ministerstvo putei soobshcheniia. *Ofitsial'nyi ukazetel' zheleznodorozhnykh, vodnykh i drugikh passazhirskikh soobshchenii na leto 1946 g.* (Official Timetable for Railroad, Water, and Other Passenger Transportation in the Summer of 1946). 1946. 456 pages.

MPS, 1947. ——— *Ofitsial'nyi ukazetel' passazhirskikh soobshcheniia, leto 1947 goda* (Official Timetable for Passenger Transportation, Summer 1947). 1947. 557 pages.

MPS, 1949a. ——— *Ofitsial'nyi ukazatel' passazhirskikh soobshchenii, po dannym na 21/IV 1949 goda* (Official Timetable for Passenger Transportation, as of April 21, 1949). 1949. 592 pages.

MPS, 1949b. Russia (1923 — USSR) Ministerstvo putei soobshcheniia, politicheskoe upravlenie. *Za vysokuiu rentabel'nost' predpriiatii zheleznodorozhnogo transporta: sbornik statei* (For High Profitability of Enterprises of Railroad Transportation: A Collection of Articles). 1949. 217 pages.

Naporko, A. G. *Ocherki razvitiia zheleznodorozhnogo transporta SSSR* (Notes on the Development of Railroad Transportation of the USSR). 1954. 285 pages.

Narodnyi komissariat vodnogo transporta, otdel statistiki. *Rechnoi transport v 1935 g.* (River Transportation in 1935). 1936. 465 pages.

NKPS *Materialy.* Russia (1923 — USSR) Narodnyi komissariat putei soobshcheniia, tsentral'nyi otdel statisticheskogo ucheta i uchetnosti. *Materialy po statistike zheleznodorozhnogo transporta* (Materials on the Statistics of Railroad Transportation), 141 vols. 1921–1935.

NKPS, 1944a. Russia (1923 — USSR) Narodnyi komissariat putei soobshcheniia, tsentral'nyi planogo-ekonomicheskii otdel. *Planirovanie ekspluatatsionnykh raskhodov zheleznykh dorog* (Planning Railroad Operating Expenses). 1944. 190 pages.

NKPS, 1944b. *Sbornik zakonodatel'nykh materialov dlia rabotnikov zheleznodorozhnogo transporta* (Collection of Legal Materials for Railroad Transportation Workers). 1944. 364 pages.

Notkin, Aleksandr Il'ich. *Ocherki teorii sotsialisticheskogo vosproizvodstva* (Notes on the Theory of Socialist Reproduction). 1948. 291 pages.

Novikov, Sergei Semenovich. *Sovetskie zheleznodorozhniki v velikoi otechestvennoi voine* (Soviet Railroadmen in the Great Patriotic War). 1945. 34 pages.

Obraztsov, Vladimir Nikolaevich. *Zheleznodorozhnyi transport v dni velikoi otechestvennoi voiny* (Railroad Transportation in the Days of the Great Patriotic War). 1943. 62 pages.

Obraztsov, 1948a. ——— *Istoriia razvitiia transporta Moskvy* (History of the Development of Moscow's Transportation). 1948. 31 pages.

Obraztsov, 1948b. ——— *Perspektivy elektrifikatsii zheleznodorozhnogo transporta v SSSR* (Prospects for Railroad Electrification in the USSR). 1948. 22 pages.

Obraztsov, 1948c. ——— *Vodnyi, vozdushnyi, avtodorozhnyi, gorodskoi, i promyshlennyi transport* (Water, Air, Automotive, City, and Industrial Transportation). 1948. 490 pages.

*O gosudarstvennom plane vosstanovleniia i razvitiia narodnogo khoziaistva SSSR na 1947 god* (On the Government Plan of Restoration and Development of the National Economy of the USSR in 1947). 1947. 30 pages. (Library of Congress entry under Russia (1923 — USSR) Laws, statutes, etc.).

*O piatiletnem plane vosstanovleniia i razvitiia narodnogo khoziaistva SSSR na 1946–1950 gg.* (On the Five-Year Plan of Restoration and Development of the National Economy of the USSR in 1946–1950). No date (probably 1946). 183 pages.

Ordzhonikidze, Grigorii Konstantinovich. *Industrial Development in 1931 and the Tasks for 1932, Report to the 17th Party Conference.* Moscow, 1932. 84 pages.

Pares, Bernard. *A History of Russia,* 4th ed., revised. New York: Alfred A. Knopf, 1944. 575 pages.

*Pennsylvania Railroad, 1947 Freight Traffic Density* (copyright 1949 by H. H. Copeland and Son, New York).

Potapov, V. P., and A. T. Deribas. *Kommercheskaia ekspluatatsiia zheleznykh dorog SSSR* (Commercial Operation of the Railroads of the USSR). 1950. 409 pages.

Povorozhenko, V. V. *Pogruzka i vygruzka na promezhutochnykh stantsiiakh bez ottsepki vagonov; organizatsiia i raschety* (Loading and Unloading At Intermediate Stations Without Uncoupling of Cars: Organization and Accounting). 1946. 83 pages.

——— *Organizatsiia gruzovoi raboty na zheleznodorozhnom transporte; perevozka gruzov* (Organization of Freight Work in Railroad Transportation: Freight Shipment). 1947. 517 pages.

——— *Organizatsiia gruzovykh perevozok i kommercheskoi raboty na zheleznodorozhnom transporte SSSR* (Organization of Freight Shipments and Commercial Work in Railroad Transportation of the USSR). 1951. 383 pages.

Prokopovich, Sergei Nikolaevich. *Narodnoe khoziaistvo SSSR* (The National Economy of the USSR). 2 vols. New York: Izdatel'stvo imeni Chekhova, 1952. 753 pages.

"Report on Railways of U.S.S.R.," vol. 1 (typewritten carbon copy on deposit in record group 219, National Archives, Washington, D.C.). 1930. 166 pages.

Rudzutak, IAn Ernestovich. *Transport v khoziaistve SSSR; doklad na III sessii TsIK SSSR, 17–18 Fevralia 1927 goda* (Transportation in the Economy of the USSR; Report at the Third Session of the Central Executive Committee of the USSR, February 17–18, 1927). 1927. 79 pages.

Rum, L. L., editor. *Kaspiisko-Aralskaia zheleznaia doroga v ekonomicheskom otnoshenii* (The Caspian — Aral [Sea] Railroad in Its Economic Aspects). St. Petersburg, 1914. 447 pages.

Russia. Departament zheleznodorozhnykh del' ministerstva finansov. *Svodnaia statistika perevozok po russkim zheleznym dorogam* (Summary Statistics of Shipments on Russian Railroads). St. Petersburg, various years.

Saharov, George M. "Survey of Russian Railways, Pre-War and Post-War" (mimeographed report). United States Interstate Commerce Commission, Bureau of Statistics, Statement No. 3910, File 6–A–12. March 1939. 137 pages.

Schwartz, Harry. *Russia's Soviet Economy.* New York: Prentice-Hall, 1950. 592 pages.

Scott, John. *Behind the Urals: An American Worker in Russia's City of Steel.* Boston: Houghton Mifflin, 1942. 279 pages.

Shashkov, Z. A. *Rechnoi transport v novoi stalinskoi piatiletke* (River Transportation in the New Stalinist Five-Year Plan). 1947. 141 pages.

Shishkin, S. N. *Khalkhin-Gol.* 1954. 60 pages.

Shul'kin, L. R. *Potreblenie chernykh metallov v SSSR; statisticheskii sbornik* (Consumption of Iron and Steel in the USSR: Statistical Handbook). 1940. 339 pages.

Shvetsov, V. N. *Statistika truda na zheleznodorozhnom transporte* (Labor Statistics in Railroad Transportation). 1956. 171 pages.

Simmons, Ernest J., editor. *Continuity and Change in Russian and Soviet Thought.* Cambridge: Harvard University Press, 1955. 563 pages.

SNK, 1929. Sovet narodnykh komissarov. *God raboty pravitel'stva, materialy k otchetu za 1927/28 g.* (A Year of Work of the Government, Materials for a Record of 1927–1928). 1929. 510 pages.

*Spravochnik po tarifam zheleznodorozhnogo transporta* (Guide to Railroad Freight Rates). 1949. 235 pages.

Stalin, Iosif Vissarionovich. *Problems of Leninism,* 11th ed. Moscow: Foreign Languages Publishing House, 1947. 642 pages.

—— *Sochineniia* (Collected Works), 13 vols. 1946–1953.

Stychinskii, S. P. *Perevozki khlebnykh gruzov na zheleznykh dorogakh* (Shipments of Grain Freights on the Railroads). 1952. 192 pages.

Suiazov, I. G. *Zheleznodorozhnye perevozki v mezhdunarodnykh soobshcheniiakh* (Railroad Shipments in International Communication). 1949. 174 pages.

Suslov, Sergei Petrovich. *Fizicheskaia geografiia SSSR; Zapadnaia Sibir', Vostochnaia Sibir', Dal'nii Vostok, Srednaia Aziia* (Physical Geography of the USSR: Western Siberia, Eastern Siberia, Far East, Central Asia). 1947. 543 pages.

Tsaregorodtsev, V. E., editor. *Sbornik lektsii o peredovykh metodakh raboty na zheleznodorozhnom transporte* (Collection of Lectures on Advanced Methods of Work in Railroad Transportation). 1948. 260 pages.

Tsentral'noe statisticheskoe upravlenie. *Itogi desiatiletiia sovetskoi vlasti v tsifrakh: 1917–1927* (Results of a Decade of Soviet Power in Figures: 1917–1927). 503 pages.

—— *Statisticheskii spravochnik SSSR za 1928* (Statistical Handbook of the USSR for 1928). 1929. 958 pages.

Tsentral'noe statisticheskoe upravlenie. *Slovar'-spravochnik po sotsialno-ekonomicheskoi statistike* (Dictionary-Handbook on Social-Economic Statistics). 1944. 269 pages.

TsSU, 1956. Tsentral'noe statisticheskoe upravlenie pri sovete ministrov SSSR. *Narodnoe khoziaistvo SSSR; statisticheskii sbornik* (National Economy of the USSR: Statistical Handbook). 1956. 262 pages.

TsUNKhU, 1932. Tsentral'noe upravlenie narodnogo-khoziaistvennogo ucheta. *Narodnoe khoziaistvo SSSR* (National Economy of the USSR). 1932. 670 pages.

TsUNKhU, 1934. Tsentral'noe upravlenie narodnogo-khoziaistvennogo ucheta Gosplana SSR. *Sotsialisticheskoe stroitel'stvo SSSR* (Socialist Construction in the USSR). 1934. 624 pages.

TsUNKhU, 1935. ——— *Sotsialisticheskoe stroitel'stvo SSSR* (Socialist Construction in the USSR). 1935. 752 pages.

TsUNKhU, 1936a. ——— *Sotsialisticheskoe stroitel'stvo SSSR* (Socialist Construction in the USSR). 1936. 772 pages.

TsUNKhU, 1936b. Central administration of economic and social statistics of the state planning commission of the USSR. *Socialist Construction in the USSR, Statistical Abstract.* Moscow: Soiuzorguchet, 1936. 538 pages.

TsUNKhU, 1936c. ——— *SSSR strana sotsializma: statisticheskii sbornik* (The USSR, Country of Socialism: Statistical Handbook). 1936. 210 pages.

TsUNKhU, 1936d. ——— *Transport i sviaz' SSSR v tsifrakh* (Transportation and Communication of the USSR in Figures). 1936. 63 pages.

TsUNKhU, 1936e. ——— *Trud v SSSR* (Labor in the USSR). 1936. 387 pages.

TsUNKhU, 1939. ——— *Sotsialisticheskoe stroitel'stvo SSSR, 1933–1938 gg.* (Socialist Construction in the USSR, 1933–1938). 1939. 200 pages.

Turetskii, SH. IA. *Vnutripromyshlennoe nakoplenie v SSSR* (Intra-Industrial Accumulation in the USSR). 1948. 397 pages.

Tverskoi, K. N. *Za bol'shevistkie tempy sotsialisticheskoi rekonstruktsii transporta* (For Bolshevik Tempos in the Socialist Reconstruction of Transportation). 1931. 128 pages.

——— *The Unified Transport System of the USSR.* London: V. Gollancz, Ltd., 1935. 176 pages.

Umbliia, V. E. *Osnovy organizatsii, normirovaniia i planirovaniia truda na zheleznodorozhnom transporte* (Principles of the Organization, Norm-Setting, and Planning of Labor in Railroad Transportation). 1st ed., 1947, 218 pages. 2nd ed., 1949, 260 pages.

United States Department of Commerce, Bureau of the Census. *Historical Statistics of the United States, 1789–1945.* Washington, D.C.: Government Printing Office, 1949. 363 pages.

——— Office of Business Economics. *National Income, 1954 Edition.* Washington, D.C.: Government Printing Office, 1954. 249 pages.

Universities-National Bureau Committee for Economic Research. *Capital Formation and Economic Growth.* Princeton: Princeton University Press, 1955. 677 pages.

Vedenisov, Boris Nikolaevich, and others. *Kratkii tekhnicheskii zheleznodorozhnyi slovar'* (Short Technical Railroad Dictionary), 2nd ed. 1946. 606 pages.

Verkhovnyi sovet. *Zasedaniia verkhovnogo soveta SSSR, vtoraia sessiia, stenograficheskii otchet* (Sessions of the USSR Supreme Soviet, Second Session, Stenographic Transcript). 1949.

Vinnichenko, N. G. *Finansirovanie zheleznykh dorog, po osnovnoi deiatel'nosti* (Financing of Railroads, for Their Basic Activity). 1st ed., 1948, 315 pages. 2nd ed., 1952, 332 pages.

VNII, 1946. Moscow. Vsesoiuznyi nauchno-issledovatel'skii institut zheleznodorozhnogo transporta. *Rezervy zheleznodorozhnogo transporta* (Reserves in Railroad Transportation). 1946. 163 pages.

Vol'fson, Lev IAkovlevich, S. K. Danilov, and N. S. Shil'nikov. *Zheleznodorozhnyi transport na rubezhe dvukh piatiletok* (Railroad Transportation on the Border [between] Two Five-Year Plans). 1934. 126 pages.

Vol'fson, L. IA., A. Korneev, and N. S. Shil'nikov. *Razvitie zheleznykh dorog SSSR* (Development of the Railroads of the USSR). 1939. 175 pages.

Vol'fson, L. IA., V. I. Ledovskoi, and N. S. Shil'nikov. *Ekonomika transporta* (Economics of Transportation). 1941. 684 pages.

Voznesenskii, Nikolai Alekseevich. *Piatiletnii plan vosstanovleniia i razvitiia narodnogo khoziaistva SSSR na 1946–1950 gg. Doklad . . . 15–18 Marta 1946 g.* (Five-Year Plan of Restoration and Development of the National Economy of the USSR. Report . . . March 15–18, 1946). 1946. 47 pages.

—— *The Growing Prosperity of the Soviet Union.* New York: Workers Library Publishers, 1941. 48 pages.

—— *Voennaia ekonomika SSSR v period otechestvennoi voiny* (War Economy of the USSR in the Period of the Patriotic War). 1947. 191 pages. A paper-bound English translation sponsored by the American Council of Learned Societies was published by the Public Affairs Press (Washington, D.C.), in 1948, and a similar translation was issued that year by the Foreign Languages Publishing House in Moscow, under the title *War Economy of the USSR in the Period of the Patriotic War.*

Vsesoiuznaia konferentsiia po razmeshcheniiu proizvoditel'nykh sil SSSR. *Trudy* (Transactions), at least 16 vols. 1932–1933.

*Vsesoiuznyi den' zheleznodorozhnogo transporta* (All-Union Railroadmen's Day). 1944. 80 pages.

Wellington, Arthur Mellen. *The Economic Theory of the Location of Railways,* 6th ed., corrected. New York: John Wiley and Sons, 1911. 950 pages.

Zagliadimov, D. P. *Organizatsiia dvizheniia na zheleznodorozhnom transporte* (Organization of Movement in Railroad Transportation). 1947. 595 pages.

Zagorskii, Konstantin IAkovlevich. *Ekonomika transporta* (Economics of Transportation). 1930. 368 pages.

*Zakon o piatiletnem plane vosstanovleniia i razvitiia narodnogo khoziaistva SSSR na 1946–1950 gg.* (Law on the Five-Year Plan of Restoration and Development of the National Economy of the USSR in 1946–1950). 1946. 93 pages.

Zelenovskii, A. See his article in *O piatiletnem plane.*

## 2. ARTICLES

Where only isolated data in a journal article have been cited in the text, the article is not listed here. The selected articles below are of more general interest, and the Russian titles have been translated. The journals in which they appear are as follows (with abbreviations given if they were used in the text).

*Bol'shevik.*
*Plan.*
*Planovoe Khoziaistvo* (Planned Economy), *Plan. Khoz.*
*Problemy Ekonomiki* (Problems of Economics), *Prob. Ekon.*
*Sotsialisticheskii Transport* (Socialist Transportation), *Sots. Trans.*
*Tekhnika Zheleznykh Dorog* (Railroad Engineering), *Tekhnika Zhel. Dorog.*
*Transport i Khoziaistvo* (Transportation and the Economy).

*Voprosy Ekonomiki* (Questions of Economics), *Vop. Ekon.*
*Voprosy Geografii* (Questions of Geography).
*Zheleznodorozhnyi Transport* (Railroad Transportation), *Zhel. Trans.*

In addition to the railroad newspaper *Gudok* (The Whistle), the following newspapers have been occasionally cited: *Izvestiia, Moskovskii Bol'shevik, Pravda,* and
*Trud.*

Ames, Edward. "A Century of Russian Railroad Construction: 1837–1936," *American
    Slavic and East European Review,* vol. 6, nos. 18–19 (December 1947), pp. 57–74.
Bernstein-Kogan, S. V. "Shifts in the Geography of Railroad and Water Transporta-
    tion over Thirty Years," *Voprosy Geografii,* 1947, sbornik no. 6, pp. 79–100.
Borisov, N. "Means of Further Improvement in the Work of the Traffic Service," *Sots.
    Trans.,* 1939, no. 6, pp. 24–32.
Breus, N., and A. Shleifman. "Railroad Rolling Stock and Its Utilization," *Plan. Khoz.,*
    1935, no. 8, pp. 72–92.
Chertkova, L. L., "Transportation in the Sixth Five-Year Plan," *Vop. Ekon.,* 1956, no.
    7, pp. 14–31.
Dubrovin, N. "The Principal Reserves for Raising the Profitability of Shipments,"
    *Zhel. Trans.,* 1946, no. 11/12, pp. 19–28.
Galitskii, A. "Inter-regional Shipments in the USSR," *Plan. Khoz.,* 1938, no. 7, pp.
    10–28.
——— "Railroad Freight Traffic in the Third Five-Year Plan," *Plan. Khoz.,* 1939, no.
    6, pp. 107–23.
——— "Transportation and the Location of Economic Activity," *Bol'shevik,* 1941, no.
    5, pp. 12–23.
——— "The Postwar Five-Year Plan for Railroad Transportation," *Plan. Khoz.,* 1946,
    no. 2, pp. 113–22.
Gaposhkin, F. "The Battle Against Gigantomania — A Great National-Economic Task,"
    *Plan. Khoz.,* 1939, no. 4, pp. 122–28.
Gibshman, A. E. "New Railroad Construction During Thirty Years," *Teknika Zhel.
    Dorog,* 1947, no. 10, pp. 13–16.
Grossman, Gregory. "Scarce Capital and Soviet Doctrine," *Quarterly Journal of Eco-
    nomics,* vol. 67, no. 3 (August 1953), pp. 311–43.
Hunter, Holland. "The Planning of Investments in the Soviet Union," *Review of
    Economics and Statistics,* vol. 31, no. 1 (February 1949), pp. 54–62.
——— "Soviet Railroads Since 1940," *Bulletins on Soviet Economic Development,*
    series I, no. 4 (September 1950), pp. 10–20 and 33–34.
——— "Transport — Russia's Achilles' Heel?," *Automotive Industries,* vol. 105, no. 6
    (September 15, 1951), pp. 39–43 ff.
——— "How the Russians Run Railroads," *Railway Age,* vol. 137, no. 9 (August 30,
    1954), pp. 24–26.
——— "Soviet Industrial Growth — The Early Plan Period," *Journal of Economic
    History,* vol. 15, no. 4 (September 1955), pp. 281–87.
——— "Soviet Railroads in World War II," *National Defense Transportation Journal,*
    vol. 11, no. 5 (1955), pp. 52–58.
Ivliev, I. "Restoration of the Prewar Profitability of Transportation — A Great Task,"
    *Zhel. Trans.,* 1948, no. 8, pp. 10–18.
Jasny, Naum. "Soviet Grain Crops and Their Distribution," *International Affairs*
    (London), vol. 28, no. 4 (October 1952), pp. 452–59.
Kazarin, I. "The Second Stakhanovite Year in Railroad Transportation," *Plan,* 1937,
    no. 3, pp. 39–45.

Khachaturov, T. S. "On the Principles for Construction of Railroad Freight Rates," *Transport i Khoziaistvo,* 1929, no. 2, pp. 54–66.

────── "Transportation and the Location of Economic Activity," *Prob. Ekon.,* 1939, no. 6, pp. 111–34.

────── "The Basic Economic Task of the USSR and Means for Development of Railroad Transportation," *Plan. Khoz.,* 1940, no. 10, pp. 30–43.

────── "On Restoration and Certain Prospects for the Development of Transportation," *Zhel. Trans.,* 1943, no. 9/10, pp. 15–25.

────── "The Organization and Development of Transport in the USSR," *International Affairs* (London), vol. 21, no. 2 (April 1945), pp. 220–35.

Kuchurin, S. "The New Freight Rates and Their Role in the Rationalization of Shipments," *Sots. Trans.,* 1939, no. 6, pp. 18–23.

Levin, B. I. "Basic Trends of the Five-Year Plan of Restoration and Development of Transportation," *Zhel. Trans.,* 1946, no. 2/3, pp. 8–19.

Nekrasov, N. "On the Location of the Motor Fuel Industry in the USSR," *Plan. Khoz.,* 1938, no. 1, pp. 35–59.

Obraztsov, V. "Railroad Transportation — The Main Means of Communication Between Front and Rear," *Plan. Khoz.,* 1944, no. 1, pp. 59–65.

Obraztsov, V., and Sergei Vladimirovich Zemblinov. "Problems of Railroad Transportation in the Third Five-Year Plan," *Plan. Khoz.,* 1937, no. 5/6, pp. 55–63.

Onufriev, T. "Construction of the Stalinsk-Magnitogorsk Trunkline," *Zhel. Trans.,* 1946, no. 2/3, pp. 90–98.

Piotrowski, A. "La Situation des Chemins de Fer de L'URSS en cas de Guerre," *Revue Economique Internationale,* vol. 4, no. 1 (October 1939), pp. 55–76.

Whitworth, Charles E. "The Russian Railways," *Annals of the American Academy of Political and Social Science,* vol. 230 (November 1943), pp. 150–58.

# NOTES

## INTRODUCTION

1. See Gerschenkron, 1951, pp. 1–24; Bergson, 1953b, pp. 4–9; DeWitt, 1955, pp. xxvi–xxviii and 259–61.

2. See his introduction to Hodgman, 1954, p. xi.

## CHAPTER 1. THE SOVIET GEOGRAPHIC SETTING IN HISTORICAL PERSPECTIVE

1. For general discussion, see Jasny, 1949, esp. chap. 7, and Balzak and others, 1949, chap. 6.

2. See Lorimer, 1946, esp. plate 14, facing p. 146.

3. Rapidly worsening iron ore supplies are a major Soviet problem, not confined to the Kerch deposits. Chap. 9 of Clark, 1956, provides an original and significant analysis of the evidence.

4. The rail distance between Dolgintsevo, center of iron ore loading, and Debaltsevo, center of coal shipments, by way of Verkhovtsevo, Dnepropetrovsk, Chaplino, and Yasinovataya, is 568 kilometers (354 miles). See MPS, 1947, pp. 260, 269, 342, and 352. Between the same two points, the distance by the southern route through Zaporozh'e is 604 kilometers (376 miles).

5. The 1911–1913 figures are from Ames, in *American Slavic and East European Review*, 1947, table on p. 58. The article provides excellent background for the present study. The 1914–1917 figures are from the notes to Table 59, Appendix B.

6. Rudzutak, 1927, pp. 32–33. Rudzutak became People's Commissar of Means of Communication on February 2, 1924, following Dzerzhinskii, who had been in charge since April 14, 1921. Rudzutak was a medium-rank "old Bolshevik," with the following official biography: Born 1887 in former Kurlandia on a farm. Worked in Riga and joined party there around 1907. Made member of VSNKh presidium in 1917, chairman of Glavvoda in 1918, chairman of TsK soiuza zheleznodorozhnikov in 1920. Elected to Central Committee of the Party in 1920, and to the Politburo in 1926. (This information is from an article by S. Chernov commemorating Rudzutsk's fifth anniversary as Narkom PS, in *Transport i Khoziaistvo,* 1929, 1, pp. 3–5.) He was purged in 1937 and is one of those mentioned in Khrushchev's speech of February 1956.

7. See Suslov, 1947, p. 141. He devotes pp. 140–163 to detailed discussion of permafrost.

8. For a thorough study, based on Soviet sources, see Armstrong, 1952.

9. See Balzak and others, 1949, pp. 12–13.

CHAPTER 2. SOVIET LOCATIONAL OBJECTIVES AND PROBLEMS

1. See V. I. Lenin, "Imperialism, the Highest Stage of Capitalism" (1917) for a general exposition. In Lenin's *Sochineniia,* 4th ed. (1948 printing), vol. 22, pp. 173–290; see esp. pp. 247–52.

2. In the absence of readily available ethnic data for earlier years, these are 1926 proportions obtained from Lorimer, 1946, p. 55.

3. General Marxist ideological notions are said to have fostered an autarkic policy also.

4. For a thoughtful review of these issues in the early period, see Alexander Erlich's paper in Simmons, ed., 1955, pp. 81–99.

5. Tverskoi, trans., 1935, pp. 167–68.

6. Obraztsov and Zemblinov, in *Plan. Khoz.,* 1937, no. 5/6, pp. 55–63. Obraztsov was a prominent engineering professor and politically acceptable spokesman for the railroads.

7. Kommunisticheskaia partiia Sovetskogo soiuza, *XVIII S"ezd, 10–21 Marta 1939 g., Stenograficheskii Otchet,* pp. 282–315. In the English translation (*The Land of Socialism Today and Tomorrow*) see especially pp. 124–25, 130–31, 134–36, 163–64.

8. *XVIII S"ezd,* pp. 240–69. For the specific passage in English see *Land of Socialism Today and Tomorrow,* pp. 338–41.

9. For the English text, see *ibid.,* pp. 429, 433–34, and 440.

10. Among the more informative are Khachaturov, in *Prob. Ekon.,* 1939, no. 6, pp. 111–34; Bal'zak, 1940; and Vol'fson, 1941.

11. Galitskii, in *Bol'shevik,* 1941, no. 5, pp. 15–16.

12. See Scott, 1942, pp. 69 and 273; also the Party Resolution on the Third Five Year Plan, in *Land of Socialism,* pp. 436–37.

13. See Gaposhkin, in *Plan. Khoz.,* 1939, no. 4, pp. 122–38.

14. Rudzutak, 1927, p. 22.

15. Speech at the Seventeenth Party Conference, reprinted in Ordzhonikidze, 1932, p. 84.

16. Galitskii, 1941, p. 21, estimated the combined "waste" at 40 per cent; the percentages in the text are presented by Khachaturov, 1946, p. 335.

17. See Galitskii, in *Plan. Khoz.,* 1946, no. 2, pp. 119–20.

18. See Vol'fson, 1941, p. 280.

19. Khachaturov, in *International Affairs,* 1945, p. 221. This is the text of a talk given in English before the Royal Institute of International Affairs at Chatham House on January 4, 1945, and is an informative introduction to the subject.

20. The comparisons in these two paragraphs are based on absolute data drawn from Soviet sources for a more detailed study by the author, of which only selected results are summarized here.

21. See *Gudok,* 18 Nov. 1955, p. 2, and MPS, 1949a, p. 489.

22. The Ural economic region usually consisted of the following administrative units: Molotov (formerly Perm) oblast, Udmurt ASSR, Sverdlovsk oblast, Bashkir ASSR, Chelyabinsk oblast, and Chkalov oblast. See for example, Baranskii, 1947, p. 76.

23. 1947, p. 74.

24. Malenkov, 1952, pp. 57–58.

25. This can be deduced from the statement of S. Tokarev in *Plan. Khoz.,* 1956, no. 2, p. 77, that 1955 industrial output was 85 per cent over 1950 for the USSR as a whole, including a 77 per cent rise in the east and an 88 per cent rise in European Russia.

26. *Pravda,* 30 Aug. 1955, p. 2.

CHAPTER 3. INDUSTRIALIZATION AND TRANSPORTATION

1. See Alexander Gerschenkron's comments in Bergson, 1953a, p. 26.

2. See Gerschenkron, "The Rate of Industrial Growth in Russia Since 1885," *Journal of Economic History*, 7:148–50 and 168–69 (Supplement 1947). See also Theodore H. Von Laue, "The Industrialization of Russia in the Writings of Sergei Witte," *American Slavic and East European Review*, 10:177–90 (October 1951), and "The High Cost and the Gamble of the Witte System," *Journal of Economic History*, 13:425–48 (Fall 1953).

3. See the definitive study by Abram Bergson, *The Structure of Soviet Wages* (Cambridge, 1946).

4. From his speech "The Tasks of Business Executives," here cited from *Problems of Leninism*, p. 358.

5. *History of the CPSU*, pp. 305 and 303.

6. See Gosplan, 1930, vol. 3, pp. 9–21.

7. Cited by Tverskoi, 1931, p. 65. K. N. Tverskoi was born in 1902, graduated in 1930 from the Economic Institute of Red Professors, and in 1932 became a professor there. About 1934 he was the head of the Transport Section of Gosplan, and wrote a book published in London, in English, as *The Unified Transport System of the USSR* (1935). In 1946 he was the assistant director of the Central Planning-Economic Section of the Ministry of Transportation.

This 1931 pamphlet is a strong attack on existing policy and many leaders in transportation. There may be significance in its having been published by the press for maritime transport literature rather than by the regular railroad publishing house.

The S. A. Bessonov referred to by Tverskoi may be the Sergei Alekseevich Bessonov who was a defendant in the 1938 purge trials. If so, he moved from transport work to government purchasing work in Berlin from 1931 to 1937 (see Bukharin, 1938, pp. 38–65, 715–18).

Tverskoi quoted Bessonov here from *Ekonomicheskaia Zhizn'*, 1 May 1930, and may have misrepresented his opponent's meaning. The original source was not available, however, at the time this material was consulted.

8. Kafman, in *Gudok*, no. 145 (1930), cited in Tverskoi, 1931, p. 72.

9. From his preface to Kolosovskii, 1929, p. v.

10. These and the preceding distances are taken from MPS, 1949a, pp. 84–85, 138–40, 419–22, 499, 511, and 515. The cutoff to Novosibirsk and the Kurgan-Sverdlovsk line were not built when the Ural-Kuznetsk Kombinat began, and are hence excluded: the route mileage is computed via Yurga and Tyumen. The second line into the Kuznetsk Basin cut the rail distance to the west by 28 miles, but the Omsk-Sverdlovsk line through Kurgan is no shorter than the line through Tyumen; in fact, it is 3 miles longer. See *ibid.*, pp. 419–20 and 474.

11. Gosplan, 1930, vol. 3, p. 180.

12. Gibshman, 1931, p. 7.

13. Kolosovskii, 1930, p. 52.

14. See SNK, 1929, p. 367. The September 1929 figure is from the following year's volume in this series, p. 322.

15. Tverskoi, 1931, pp. 37–38.

16. Vol'fson, 1941, p. 146.

17. Tverskoi, 1931, pp. 39–40.

18. Vol'fson, 1941, p. 146.

19. *Ibid.*, pp. 201–02.

20. *Ibid.,* pp. 150, 202.

21. The four are reviewed in an editorial in *Zhel. Trans.,* 1947, no. 11, p. 6. The first two are published in full in NKPS, 1944b, pp. 36–50.

22. For an itemized list, see Vol'fson, 1934, pp. 99–100.

23. Rudzutak, 1927, pp. 22 and 31–32.

24. *Kommunisticheskaia partiia Sov. Soiuza v rezoliutsiiakh,* 7th ed., vol. 2, 1953, pp. 258–59.

25. Stalin, *Sochineniia,* vol. 12, p. 337. In the next paragraph Stalin castigates the river carriers severely for not even having regained the prewar level of traffic.

26. Tverskoi, 1931, p. 37.

27. Kommunisticheskaia partiia Sovetskogo soiuza, 1934, p. 27.

28. Voroshilov's remark is on p. 227, *ibid.* For the other speeches, see pp. 202–09 and 587–93 (Andreev), 281–85 (Rudzutak), 545–46 (Kaganovich), 362–64 (Molotov), 383–85 (Kuibyshev), 457–59 (Piatakov), 41–43 (Amosov, Head of the Northern railroad), and 61–64 (Zimin, NKPS Political Admin.).

29. Annual data for operating revenues and expenditures are compiled in Tables 67 and 68. They are taken directly from Soviet railroad records. In every case the values involved are smaller than those shown in the government budget. The explanation on the revenue side is probably nonoperating revenue collected, and on the expenditure side is assumed to be nonoperating, that is, capital, outlays covered from the budget.

30. TsUNKhU, 1934, pp. 20–21.

31. Shul'kin, 1940, p. 9.

32. B. I. Shlifshtein, in Vsesoiuznaia konferentsiia, vol. 4 (*Uralo-Kuznetskii Kombinat*), p. 313.

33. See Clark, 1956, pp. 315–20.

34. Guttsait and Spivak, in *Plan. Khoz.,* 1937, no. 3, pp. 65–86.

35. Bardin, 1947, p. 32.

36. The term "nonfarm" is slightly misleading, in that Soviet records include some agricultural workers, such as tractor drivers, in the nonfarm labor force. During these years they average about 12 per cent of the total.

37. See TsUNKhU, 1934, pp. 316–17, and 1936a, pp. 512–13.


## CHAPTER 4. SURMOUNTING THE TRANSPORTATION CRISIS

1. Cited in Chernomordik, 1936, p. 301.

2. Engineering characteristics of 16 locomotive classes are set forth in Gorinov, 1948a, vol. 1, p. 83. The comparison above is between an FD locomotive, first built in 1931, and the "U" modification of E class locomotives (respectively, 33,450 and 26,100 kilograms of tractive effort).

3. "Chronicle of the Battle and of Victories," *Gudok,* 30 July 1938, p. 2.

4. See Voroshilov's speech in Kommunisticheskaia partiia Sovetskogo soiuza, 1934, p. 226.

5. *Gudok,* 30 July 1938, p. 2. See also Vol'fson, 1941, pp. 154–57, and Breus and Shleifman, in *Plan. Khoz.,* 1935, no. 8, pp. 72–92.

6. Excerpts appear in *Pravda,* 2 Aug. 1935, and are reprinted in NKPS, 1944b, pp. 19–23.

7. The 1956 Railroadmen's Day editorial in *Gudok* rephrased the notions as fol-

lows: "It is a great honor to work on the railroads, the main nerve of the country's economic life, 'one of the principal bases of our whole economy,' as V. I. Lenin said. But railroadmen also have a great responsibility to see that the railroads at all times function with the precision of a timepiece" (*Gudok,* 22 July 1956, p. 1).

8. See Vedenisov, 1946, pp. 234–35; Vol'fson, 1941, p. 158; Avgustyniuk, 1950, pp. 51–52.

9. A story in *Gudok,* 24 May 1938, p. 1, lists five railroad Stakhanovites who had already been raised to high-level positions; four were the heads of railroads, and the fifth was deputy chief of the NKPS locomotive administration.

10. See the remarks of L. Bel'skii, deputy head of NKPS, in *Gudok,* 30 July 1938, p. 2, and those of the head of NKPS political sections, S. Bagaev, in *Gudok,* 20 July 1938, p. 2.

11. *Gudok* in late April and early May carried a number of reports on the meetings.

12. Beck and Godin, 1951, pp. 70–71 and 26–27. See also pp. 109–11.

13. See Table 65. In 1937, 50 per cent of the freight car stock still was equipped with hand couplings, and 83 per cent had hand brakes.

14. See Table 76, where annual figures for each element of freight car turnaround time are tabulated.

15. This would be an interesting question for analysis by an ex-Soviet *émigré* with a railroading background.

16. "Report on Railways of U.S.S.R.," 1930. The conclusions are summarized on pp. 1–2. This manuscript contains no indication of the membership of the group who wrote the report. However, it may be inferred that this was the so-called "Budd Mission" from the fact that at the end of October 1930, Mr. Budd gave an address entitled "Some Observations on the Railways of the USSR" at a Washington meeting of railroad officials. See Ralph Budd, "Some Observations on the Railways of the USSR by President of the Great Northern Railway," Association of Practitioners before the ICC, *Report* of first annual meeting, Washington, D.C., October 30–31, 1930, pp. 232–48. Available in the library of the Bureau of Railway Economics, Association of American Railroads, Washington, D.C.

17. Khachaturov, 1939, p. 471.

18. For a review of previous surveys and presentation of a recommended low-gradient route, see Bernatskii, 1925.

19. The termini were Uzlovaya and Venev. See NKPS *Materialy,* vol. 85, p. 165 and vol. 115, p. 222.

20. Stated by V. Antonov in a history of the Turk-Sib line, in *Zhel. Trans.,* 1947, no. 11, pp. 61 and 64.

21. See Shermergorn, in *Plan. Khoz.,* 1934, no. 11, pp. 84–96.

22. See the story in *Gudok,* 18 April 1938, p. 3.

23. See story in *Gudok,* 20 Aug. 1939, p. 2; also Vedenisov, 1946, p. 273; Khachaturov, 1939, pp. 598–601; Tverskoi, 1935, pp. 125–126; Balzak, 1949, pp. 454 and 461 (the transportation chapter was written by Khachaturov).

24. See Khachaturov in *International Affairs,* 1945, p. 224.

25. Vol'fson, 1941, p. 512.

26. See *Gudok,* 30 Oct. 1940, p. 4. A premature reference was given by Tverskoi, 1935, p. 127. For a map showing the route double-tracked, see General'nyi Shtab Vooruzhennykh Sil USSR, 1946.

27. See *Gudok,* 23 Aug. 1939, p. 3; 29 Sept. 1939, p. 2; 8 June 1940, p. 2.

28. Calculations based on data in Kochetov, 1949, pp. 45–46.

CHAPTER 5. SOVIET RAILROADS IN WORLD WAR II

1. See, for example, Pares, 1944, pp. 340 and 423–26.

2. See Khachaturov, 1939, pp. 470–71.

3. Piotrowski in *Revue Economique Internationale,* 1939, pp. 55–76.

4. *Ibid.,* p. 75. His prediction was not far off: the annual average for 1940 was 97,852 and for the first six months of 1941, 106,598, but these include traffic in the territory acquired along the western frontier. Higher levels could be sustained, of course, for shorter periods of time; in July 1940, for example, average daily carloadings reached 108,000 (*Gudok,* 4 Aug. 1940, p. 2).

5. *Gudok,* 30 July 1938, p. 4.

6. *Gudok,* 15 Oct. 1938, p. 2.

7. *Pravda,* 4 Aug. 1940, p. 1.

8. Stalin's statement of 2 Sept. 1945 on the end of the war with Japan, cited from *Tekhnika Zhel. Dorog,* 1945, no. 9, p. 1. On the 1939 engagement, see Shishkin, 1954.

9. *Moskovskii Bol'shevik.* 4 Aug. 1940, p. 1.

10. *Plan. Khoz.,* 1944, no. 1, p. 61.

11. A summary of the speech appeared in *Pravda* on May 24, and in *Gudok* and *Izvestiia* on May 25, 1954. For a condensed translation, see *Current Digest of the Soviet Press,* vol. 6, no. 24, pp. 26–31 (July 28, 1954). A more complete text appeared as a 101-page pamphlet, cited in the bibliography under Kaganovich, 1954b. My article appeared in *Automotive Industries,* Sept. 15, 1951, pp. 39–43ff. A preliminary version of the present chapter appeared in the *National Defense Transportation Journal,* vol. 11, no. 5, pp. 52–58 (September–October 1955).

12. For a somewhat more detailed discussion, see my "Soviet Railroads Since 1940," *Bulletins on Soviet Economic Development,* series 1, no. 4 (September 1950), p. 19.

13. "The operating length of the railroad network decreased at the beginning of 1943 by 40 per cent compared with 1941. The locomotive stock decreased over the same period by 15 per cent, and the number of freight cars by 20 per cent, in spite of the fact that a considerable part of the rolling stock on occupied railroads was evacuated to the eastern regions of the USSR" (Voznesenskii, 1947, p. 100).

14. *Gudok,* 13 Sept. 1942, p. 1.

15. N. Khrulev, in *Gudok,* 25 Sept. 1942, p. 2, reprinted from *Pravda,* 23 Sept. 1942. Khrulev is listed as People's Commissar of Transportation, though Kaganovich is supposed to have held the portfolio. Perhaps Kaganovich's supervision was only nominal.

16. *Pravda,* 1 Aug. 1943, p. 1.

17. I. V. Kovalev, in *Plan. Khoz.,* 1945, no. 5, p. 5.

18. IU. I. Koldomasov states the haul for military supplies during World War II, but does not specify any year or years. See Koldomasov, 1949, p. 63.

19. We are told that: "In the first six months of the war, more than 1,200,000 cars were used just to ship evacuated freight and people to the depths of the country" (*Gudok,* 11 July 1945, p. 2); "From June 1941 through December 1941 . . . around 1,500,000 cars . . ." (*Gudok,* 31 May 1946, p. 2): "From June 1941 through February 1942, more than 1,500,000 cars . . ." (*Zhel. Trans.,* 1947, no. 11, p. 9).

From June 22 through December 31 was 192 days, so the implied average daily carloadings are in the range of 6,260 to 7,820. Average *total* daily carloadings in the first half of 1941 were at a level of 107,000 and for the year 1942 were around 43,000. In between, they may have been in the 70,000–80,000 range.

The average net load per car during the first half of 1941 was around 17 tons (see

Table 46). Assuming the same factor for evacuation freight, the figure for cars converts into 23–26 million tons originated. The average length of haul for the first half of 1941 was 693 kilometers, and for all of 1941 was 732 kilometers. A simple average, which understates the rise, yields 771 kilometers for the second half. Multiplying tons originated by this factor gives 17–20 billion metric ton–kilometers, and the conversion factor of 0.68494 reduces this to its short ton–mile equivalent.

For the estimate of military traffic, see the notes to Table 39.

20. "In 1943–1945 alone, 360 kilometers of second track and 432 kilometers of track at junctions and stations were laid in the Urals and on the lines joining the Urals with Siberia" (Bernstein-Kogan, in *Voprosy Geografii,* Sbornik No. 6, 1947, p. 89). See also Voznesenskii, 1947, pp. 102–03.

21. L. P. Belousov, "The Reconstruction of Roadway Destroyed by the German Wreckers" (in Russian), *Tekhnika Zhel. Dorog,* 1944, no. 10/11, p. 28. See also *Tekhnika Zhel. Dorog,* 1943, no. 7/8, pp. 1–2; *Zhel. Trans.,* 1945, no. 1, pp. 41–52; and *The Railway Gazette* (London), vol. 82, no. 7 (February 16, 1945), pp. 166–67, which reproduces photographs of a German track-wrecking machine captured in the Ukraine, and of wrecked railroad line in Poland.

22. Khachaturov, in *Zhel. Trans.,* 1943, no. 9/10, p. 22.

23. These assorted observations on the amount of destruction and reconstruction are compiled from the following sources: *Gudok,* 22 June 1945, and 13 July 1945; *Zhel. Trans.,* 1946, no. 7, pp. 92–93, and 1947, no. 11, p. 21; Voznesenskii, 1947, pp. 101–102; *Gudok,* 25 July 1943, p. 3; *Vsesoiuznyi Den',* 1944, p. 73; *Tekhnika Zhel. Dorog,* 1944, no. 7, p. 9, and 1945, no. 7/8, p. 2; Turetskii, 1948, p. 152; Kovalev, 1946a, p. 121 and p. 59; Zagliadimov, 1947, p. 466.

24. Whitworth, in *Annals of the American Academy of Political and Social Science,* November 1943, pp. 156–57.

25. See *Pravda,* 13 Sept. 1945.

26. "In the first half of this year, freight car workers converted 7405 'trophy' cars from the west European to our native gauge" (*Vsesoiuznyi Den',* 1944, p. 71).

27. Schwartz, 1950, pp. 512–13.

28. The Soviet press carried a report by the USSR Foreign Trade Commissariat on allied aid during the period June 22, 1941–April 30, 1944, in considerable detail, giving amounts "dispatched" and "landed" from the United States, Great Britain, and Canada, in thousands of tons. Out of 10,100,000 tons dispatched, 8,796,000 were recorded as landed, indicating an average loss of 13 per cent (see *Gudok,* 11 June 1944, p. 1). Shipments from June 1944 through the middle of 1945 must have shown a much smaller percentage of loss, hence the 13 per cent figure should be reduced appreciably when discussing the entire war period.

29. The cases cited in this paragraph were reported on page 4 of *Gudok* for July 29, August 12, August 14, and September 9, 1942. The editorial appeared on September 18.

30. *Pravda,* 16 April 1943.

31. Novikov, 1945, p. 11.

32. See items in *Gudok,* 1 Dec. 1938, p. 1; 5 Dec. 1938, p. 3; 4 Nov. 1938, p. 1; 28 Sept. 1939, p. 1.

33. Obraztsov, 1943, p. 14.

34. B. F. Zhigachev, "Living Block Signaling on Railroad Sections Near the Front" (in Russian), *Tekhnika Zhel. Dorog,* 1942, no. 5/6, pp. 36–39.

### CHAPTER 6. POSTWAR RECOVERY AND EXPANSION

1. See Table 45.

2. G. M. Malenkov's statement at the Nineteenth Congress that "the war retarded our industrial development for eight or nine years" suggests an official view that the recovery period extended through 1949.

3. This tabulation is based on the Fourth, Fifth, and Sixth Five Year Plans, in conjunction with Tables 46, 56, 59, 60, and 63.

4. Kovalev, 1946b, p. 11.

5. Construction plans are discussed by Onufriev, in *Zhel. Trans.,* 1946, no. 2/3, p. 90–98, and by Levin, 1947, pp. 291–95. Route lengths for portions already built are given in MPS, 1947.

6. See Rum, 1914; Gosplan, 1930, vol. 1, p. 454, and vol. 2, pp. 328, 331, 350–56; Zagorskii, 1930, p. 273; Obraztsov and Zemblinov, in *Plan. Khoz.,* 1937, no. 5/6, p. 62.

7. See G. Khodzhaev, "The Chardzhou-Kungrad Railroad" (in Russian), *Zhel. Trans.,* 1947, no. 7, pp. 17–21, and "An 'Affair' of Rails" (in Russian), *Gudok,* 5 Jan. 1949, p. 2; Verkhovnyi Sovet, 1949, p. 54; *Gudok,* 11 Nov. 1949, p. 1.

8. See "Report on Railways of U.S.S.R." vol. 1, 1930, pp. 3–4 and 87–88.

9. Grossman, in *Quarterly Journal of Economics,* 1953, pp. 311–43.

10. Obraztsov, 1948b, pp. 15–16.

11. V. Terekhov in *Gudok,* 5 March 1955, p. 3.

12. Kaganovich, 1954b, p. 70.

13. *Gudok,* 21 Feb. 1956, p. 3.

14. See the remarks of Deputy Minister Robel' in *Gudok,* 2 Nov. 1955, p. 2.

15. The 1955 outputs appear in TsSU, 1956, p. 56. The 1960 target for electric locomotives appears in *Pravda,* 20 Jan. 1956, p. 3, and the 1960 diesel-electric target is given in *Gudok,* 12 Feb. 1956, p. 2. The intervening years are arbitrarily interpolated.

### CHAPTER 7. SOVIET RAILROAD OPERATIONS

1. I was told in the USSR that this passage exaggerates the railroads' position.

2. See *Railway Age,* 28 Nov. 1955, pp. 30–31.

3. Khachaturov, in *International Affairs,* 1945, pp. 223–28.

4. A. P. Mikheev, in Tsaregorodtsev, ed., 1948, p. 54.

5. At the end of 1929, steam locomotives made up 98.9 per cent of total locomotives in service; at the end of 1930, 98.7 per cent. See ICC, *Annual,* 1940, p. 16.

6. See Table 65.

7. "Report on Railways of U.S.S.R.," vol. 1, 1930, pp. 1–2. This report appears to have been written by members of the so-called "Budd Mission"; see Chap. 4, note 16.

8. The Soviet figure is converted from one in kilograms per meter in *Zhel. Trans.,* 1956, no. 2, p. 9. The United States figure is from AAR, 1956, p. 9.

9. The Soviet data employed in this chapter are drawn from the relevant tables of the appendices. The United States figures come from two sources: annual volumes of the Interstate Commerce Commission, *Statistics of Railways,* and annual pamphlets of the Association of American Railroads, *Statistics of Railways of Class I.* The 1921–1955 record is conveniently summarized in AAR, 1956.

10. The Krasnyi Liman-Osnova figure appears in Vedenisov, 1946, p. 455. The Novosibirsk-Chulymskaya figure was given in Kovalev, 1947, p. 65.

11. The 1947 figure is from *Pennsylvania Railroad,* and refers to the Columbia–

Shocks Mills section of the Philadelphia Division, some 85 miles west of Philadelphia, where 1947 density was found to be 62,540,000 short ton–miles per road mile. At this point east-bound traffic from Chicago and St. Louis comes together, and passes over a common route until it divides into northward or southward flows along the seaboard. The section is 7 miles long, and carries no passenger movement.

In 1944, average freight traffic density on the Pennsylvania Railroad system was 18 per cent above the 1947 level (*ibid.*), and on this particular section it must have been at least 18 per cent greater, since the Marietta Army Supply Depot is located at its western end, and in 1944 large quantities of materiel were being shipped east to the Atlantic seaboard.

T. S. Khachaturov noted the relation between maximum densities on USSR and United States railroads in the following 1946 passage: "In the United States there are sections of four-track trunk lines with a load factor for freight traffic of up to 50 million [metric] ton-kilometers [55 million short ton–kilometers] per kilometer of road; this figure could be even higher in case of necessity" (Khachaturov, 1946, p. 339).

12. It was reported in *Gudok,* 18 Jan. 1956, p. 1, that on parts of the Trans-Siberian trunk line, density was approaching 77 million (short) ton-miles per mile, and a 1955 average of 53.7 million was reported for the whole Omsk-Novosibirsk section (392 miles) in *Zhel. Trans.,* 1956, no. 8, p. 37.

## CHAPTER 8. INTERCARRIER RELATIONS IN FREIGHT TRANSPORTATION

1. Traffic on the Baltic–White Sea Waterway is reported in *Gudok,* 2 Aug. 1938, p. 4, and in BSE, 1947a, column 1945.

2. For more thorough analysis, yielding somewhat different results, see George Y. Nowak's Appendix T-B in the forthcoming National Bureau of Economic Research study of Soviet economic growth.

3. For relevant data, see TsUNKhU, 1936b, pp. 320–21, and Koldomasov, 1949, p. 44.

4. See Kaganovich, 1954a, p. 77.

5. See Koldomasov, 1949, p. 44.

6. For detailed discussion of United States practice, see ICC, Statement No. 544, 1954.

7. Reported annual percentage increases in the freight traffic carried by trucks under the new ministry's jurisdiction are, of course, misleading to the extent that they relate to traffic previously carried by trucks belonging to other ministries; the 1954 increases of 66 per cent in ton-kilometers and 75 per cent in tons originated appear to involve this difficulty.

8. See the article on gas by A. Polezhaev in *Bulletin of the Institute for the Study of the History and Culture of the USSR* (Munich), vol. 2, no. 8 (August 1955), pp. 33–40, esp. p. 38.

9. See the article by I. Aksenov, in *Gudok,* 6 Oct. 1950, p. 3.

10. G. S. Raikher seems to have specialized in this topic. See his articles (in Russian), "The Battle Against Irrational Short-Haul Shipments," *Sots. Trans.,* 1940, no. 3, pp. 8–11; "Freeing the Railroads from Short-Haul Shipments," *Zhel. Trans.,* 1945, no. 10/11, pp. 70–73; and his chapter in Levin, 1947.

11. See Rudzutak, 1927, pp. 47–50.

12. See Koldomasov, 1949, p. 25. A table of comparative shipping times on the Volga and neighboring rail lines appears on page 26.

13. See the article by G. Smirnov, Head of the Shipment Planning Section on the Ryazan-Ural Railroad, in *Gudok*, 4 June 1952, p. 2.

14. I. Solov'ev in *Gudok*, 6 Sept. 1951, p. 3.

## CHAPTER 9. THE GEOGRAPHY OF COMMODITY TRANSPORTATION

1. See N. Sharapov, in *Gudok*, 6 July 1951, p. 1.

2. See L. Volodarskii, in *Plan. Khoz.*, 1945, no. 5, pp. 61–72.

3. See A. E. Probst, in *Voprosy Geografii*, 1947, no. 6, p. 68.

4. See Kaganovich, 1954b, p. 22.

5. See Koldomasov, 1949, p. 192.

6. See Khanukov, 1948, p. 129.

7. See A. Galitskii, in *Plan. Khoz.*, 1954, no. 6, p. 49, and G. Raikher in *Gudok*, 22 Oct. 1955, p. 4.

8. See B. V. Krich, in *Zhel. Trans.*, 1955, no. 10, p. 54.

9. See V. P. Moronov, in *Rechnoi Transport*, 1952, no. 6, p. 16.

10. For an informative discussion of the current situation and future prospects for railroad iron and steel shipments, see an article by the engineer I. Pomerantsev, in *Gudok*, 24 Sept. 1953, p. 3.

11. For this and the following discussion see Koldomasov, 1949, pp. 199ff.

12. See B. Shiskov, in *Gudok*, 17 Sept. 1952, p. 3, and N. Sharapov, in *Gudok*, 6 July 1951, p. 1.

13. For the recent percentages, see the informative article by M. Epshtein, Deputy Head of the Transport Section of Glavlesosbyt, in *Gudok*, 15 June 1954, p. 2.

14. See Koldomasov, 1949, p. 198.

15. *Ibid.*, p. 217.

16. Annual rail tons originated figures for 1932–1937, covering "principal" mineral building materials, and for 1938–1940, covering "all" mineral building materials, appear in Table 53. Using data for the larger coverage during 1932–1937 from IAkobi, 1935, p. 126, and Vol'fson, 1939, p. 149, together with an estimate for the restricted coverage in 1940 derived from Naporko, 1954, p. 180, and interpolated estimates for 1938–1939, one obtains the following breakdown, in thousands of metric tons:

| Year | "Principal" MBM | "Other" MBM | Total | Percentage of "principal" |
|---|---|---|---|---|
| 1932 | 24,678 | 20,468 | 45,146 | 54.7 |
| 1933 | 18,582 | 14,234 | 32,816 | 56.6 |
| 1934 | 20,713 | 23,739 | 44,452 | 46.6 |
| 1935 | 29,402 | 31,844 | 61,246 | 48.0 |
| 1936 | 35,400 | 56,480 | 91,880 | 38.5 |
| 1937 | 41,500 | 60,878 | 102,378 | 40.5 |
| 1938 | 38,000 | 55,500 | 93,500 | 40.6 |
| 1939 | 35,000 | 71,100 | 106,100 | 33.0 |
| 1940 | 32,000 | 79,700 | 111,700 | 28.6 |

17. See S. N. Popov, in *Tekhnika Zhel. Dorog*, 1944, no. 9, p. 14.

18. For a recent review, by commodity group, including simple flow diagrams, see Danilov, 1956, chapter 7.

## CHAPTER 10. PASSENGER TRANSPORTATION

1. The comparisons here and in the following paragraph are based on the following underlying series, drawn from TsUNKhU, 1936b, pp. 307–308:

|  | 1913 | 1928 | 1932 | 1935 |
|---|---|---|---|---|
| Billions of passenger-kilometers | 25.2 | 24.5 | 83.7 | 67.9 |
| Thousands of passenger cars in use | — | 22.9 | 28.0 | 32.3 |
| Billions of axle-kilometers for passenger cars | 5.60 | 4.24 | 7.94 | 7.57 |
| Million passenger-kilometers per car | — | 1.07 | 2.99 | 2.07 |
| Passengers per axle | 4.50 | 5.78 | 10.6 | 8.98 |

2. See *ibid.*, p. 309.

3. The Moscow-Leningrad railroad fare is reported for selected years by Janet G. Chapman, in the *Review of Economics and Statistics,* 36:154 (May 1954).

4. Derived from computed absolute data in Table 69, col. 2.

5. The series covers workers and employees in the Soviet economy, as compiled and adjusted by Warren Eason (see Bergson, 1953a, p. 110). It includes a small number of persons at Machine-Tractor Stations, and is thus not strictly "nonagricultural."

6. Descriptions of wartime Soviet railroading frequently mention large troop movements, and, with the number of intercity railroad passengers in 1942–1945 down to roughly 40 per cent of the 1940 level, there does not appear to be room for them in the recorded total. Soviet railroad statistics make provision for a kind of "40-and-8" movement; when freight cars carry people instead of freight, the load is recorded as four tons for a two-axle car or eight tons for a four-axle car (see *Gudok,* 29 June 1952, p. 3). Hence wartime troop movements probably were recorded as one item in the residual category of "other freight."

7. I. V. Kovalev, in *Gudok,* 6 Feb. 1946, p. 2.

8. See report in *Gudok,* 21 Nov. 1948, p. 3.

9. G. Ter-Minasov, in *Zhel. Trans.,* 1945, no. 5/6, p. 44.

10. Zagliadimov, 1947, p. 466.

11. See MPS, 1949a, pp. 138–43.

12. When the Moscow-Pekin Express was put into service in early 1954, it was scheduled to take "somewhat more than 8 days." Taking this to be 8½ days, and dividing by 9028 kilometers (Moscow-Otpor, 6704 kilometers and Man'chzhuriia-Pekin, 2324 kilometers), it appears that the average speed was to be 27.5 miles per hour. See *Gudok,* 29 Dec. 1953, p. 4; 16 Jan. 1954, p. 1; 2 Feb. 1954, p. 2; and 10 Feb. 1954, p. 1.

13. Since 1953 there has been improvement; a 1955 average of 34.2 kilometers per hour (21.3 miles per hour) is given by Khachaturov in *Vop. Ekon.,* 1956, no. 3, p. 85.

14. For 1949, see MPS, 1949a, pp. 578–84 and 546–60.


## CHAPTER 11. RAILROAD COSTS AND REVENUES

1. Bergson, 1953a, provides a convenient reference to recent work in this field. Considerable results have already been achieved: see Bergson, 1953b; Bergson and Heymann, 1954; and Hoeffding, 1954.

2. For more detailed discussion, see the notes to Tables 42, 58, and 68.

3. On railroad treatment of depreciation, see V. Vasil'ev, in *Transport i Khoziaistvo,* 1929, no. 6/7, p. 110, and Kochetov, 1941, pp. 315–16. For the 1939 railroad depreciation regulation, see *Finansovoe i Khoziaistvennoe Zakonodatel'stvo,* vol. 15

(1939), no. 15/16, p. 26. For a review of general Soviet depreciation policy, see Robert W. Campbell, "Accounting for Depreciation in the Soviet Economy," *Quarterly Journal of Economics,* 70:481–506 (November 1956).

4. See Abram Bergson, Roman Bernaut, and Lynn Turgeon, "Prices of Basic Industrial Products in the USSR, 1928–1950," *Journal of Political Economy,* 64:303–28 (August 1956), esp. pages 323 and 326.

5. For stimulating discussion of this and other points, see Jasny, 1952, chap. 3, "Railway Costs and Rates," pp. 31–42.

6. The influence on total unit costs of changes in the ratio between freight and passenger traffic is not entirely clear, since segregation of joint costs to ascertain unit costs per ton-kilometer and passenger-kilometer is somewhat arbitrary. For the three years 1925/26–1927/28, S. I. Zhilov (NKPS *Materialy,* vol. 93, 1929, pp. 10–30) made a careful computation indicating the following costs:

|  | 1925/26 | 1926/27 | 1927/28 |
|---|---|---|---|
| Kopeks per passenger-kilometer | 1.360 | 1.575 | 1.526 |
| Kopeks per ton-kilometer | 1.293 | 1.327 | 1.273 |
| Percentage excess of passenger cost over freight cost | 5.2 | 18.7 | 19.9 |

The evidence for recent years is fragmentary and conflicting. Chudov, 1947, p. 16, states: "According to 1945 accounts, the cost of one passenger-kilometer is only 7 per cent above [sic] the cost of one ton-kilometer. However, the difference is greater on individual roads." One year later, in a chapter probably prepared by Chudov, it was reported that: "According to the accounts for 1946, the cost of one passenger-kilometer was only 7 per cent lower [sic] than the cost of one ton-kilometer" (p. 291 in Beliunov, 1948). As Jasny notes (1952, p. 32, n. 3), illustrative data for a single road in a 1948 book show "a cost per passenger-kilometer almost 25 per cent higher than per ton-kilometer."

7. According to D. Chernomordik, writing in *Vop. Ekon.,* 1948, no. 9, p. 30 (cited by Jasny, 1952, p. 33), the average cost per ton-kilometer for a 1000-kilometer haul is 89.5 per cent of the average cost for a 500-kilometer haul. Evidently a rise in the average haul of all freight from 600 to 700 kilometers would be associated with a drop of about 2.1 per cent. Jasny suggests a drop of about 6 per cent, due partly to a typographical error in the source from which he obtained a 1928 average haul figure (498 instead of 598).

8. The report of the American railroad officials in the summer of 1930 laid considerable stress on "safety, orderliness, cleanliness, and better care of material supplies" as elements in an improvement program (see "Report on Railways of U.S.S.R.," vol. 1, 1930, pp. 2ff). Stricter punctuality has been a major theme in Soviet railroad literature for many years. The existence of a campaign to raise skills and improve discipline does not, of course, constitute clear evidence of realized gains. Indirectly, the growth of traffic carried per operating worker implies that workers performed more effectively. However, as argued above, much of the gain can be imputed to changes in output, and in other factors of production. Analysis of railroad labor's record on this score by an *émigré* railroad technician with personal experience in the field would be most useful.

9. Jasny, 1952, pp. 119–21.

10. The Turk-Sib figure is from Tverskoi, 1935, p. 162. Whether it is the original planned cost or the final recorded cost is not clear. The Ural-Kuznets Kombinat proposals are from Gibshman, 1931, p. 49.

11. *Gudok,* 20 Aug. 1939, p. 2.

12. *Gudok,* 14 May 1938, p. 1.

13. 1947, no. 10, p. 13.

14. Khachaturov, 1952, p. 140.

15. This summary is based on Vol'fson, 1941, pp. 616–24, and Povorozhenko, 1947, pp. 446–51.

16. See Saharov, 1939, pp. 67–75.

17. For an incisive analysis of this feature of the Ural-Kuznetsk Kombinat, see Clark, 1956, chapter 12.

18. These preferential coal rates are puzzling. Evidently only coal receivers at nonmajor centers and coal shippers at minor fields failed to obtain special rates. But this meant penalizing, relatively, just those consuming and producing localities ostensibly being favored under over-all governmental policy.

19. Data cited below for the postwar period suggest that the discrepancies were both large and chronic.

20. For a complete list of the new rates, see *Finansovyi i Khoziaistvennyi Biulletin',* 1939, no. 23/24 (30 Aug. 1939), pp. 21–27.

21. The reader familiar with current methods of demonstrating cost-price relationships in economic textbooks will recognize the formal similarity of approach here with the use of total cost and revenue curves. By the same token, the approach is identical with that of a break-even chart as used in business analysis.

22. The transformation from ordinary to log-log scales tends to make curves with a positive slope less than one "turn downward," and thus to increase the concavity of this curve. Compare the sketch, with ordinary scales, in Hoover, 1948, p. 21.

23. Leaving aside the small-scale distance zones established in the freight books for the convenience of clerks, rail freight rates are constructed in exactly the way that the United States personal income tax is levied. For example, the 1949 rate on coal in the distance zone from 151 to 500 kilometers was 4.10 rubles (the charge for 150 kilometers) plus 3.11 kopeks for each additional kilometer. Hence the terms "progressive" and "regressive" can be meaningfully applied.

24. Compare Jasny's conclusion (Jasny, 1952, pp. 39–40): "In 1940 the actual unit charge was about double that in 1926–27, but it would have been two-and-half times higher if the composition of the transported goods and the average haul remained unchanged."

25. Incidentally, the changes in relationship between the average revenue collected per ton-kilometer of coal and of iron ore are significant for the steel industry. They make ore more expensive and coal less so, relatively. Given the location of Soviet steel plants, this means that cost disadvantages are imposed on plants near coal but far from ore. An opposite trend would have been more rational. See Clark, 1956, chapters 8 and 9, and Walter Isard, "Some Locational Factors in the Iron and Steel Industry," *Journal of Political Economy,* 56:203–17 (June 1948).

26. For the rates themselves, see *Spravochnik po tarifam,* 1949. The decree is cited by Koldomasov, 1949, p. 156.

27. For the intended unit freight revenues for all railroad traffic and twelve commodity groups, see Koldomasov, 1949, p. 28. For the 1940 figure, see Table 69.

28. See Potapov, 1950, p. 349.

29. See Jasny, 1952, pp. 36–38.

30. The decree appears in *Pravda,* 17 March 1942. There was evidently a wage increase in 1941 also ("After the increase of railroad workers' wages in 1941 . . . ,"— Khachaturov, 1946, p. 54), and it does not seem to have been anticipated in the 1941

annual plan. The 1940 average was 356 rubles per month for operating workers, and the 1941 plan figure was 357.

31. In 1940, 85 per cent of the railroads' fuel was bituminous coal; petroleum accounted for 8 per cent, lignite for 6 per cent, and firewood for 1 per cent. In 1943 these proportions shifted to 64, 7, 17, and 12 per cent respectively (see Tsaregorodtsev, 1948, p. 126). A 1943 account of wartime railroad operations stated that "on roads running through forested regions, locomotives have been switched over entirely to wood firing" (Obraztsov, 1943, p. 12).

32. In Soviet records, locomotive fuel is converted into "coal equivalent" units of 7,000 calories per metric ton, and consumption is measured in kilograms of fuel per 10,000 gross ton–kilometers of freight and passenger movement. Trends in this measure since 1939 have been as follows:

| Year | Fuel consumption | Index (1940 = 100) | Year | Fuel consumption | Index (1940 = 100) |
|------|------|------|------|------|------|
| 1939 | 249 | — | 1949 | 232 | 94 |
| 1940 | 248 | 100 | 1950 (plan) | 242 | 98 |
| 1945 | 281 | 113 | 1950 (actual) | 221 | 89 |
| 1946 | 286 | 115 | 1951 | 212 | 85 |
| 1947 | 291 | 117 | 1952 | 207 | 83 |
| 1948 | 257 | 104 | | | |

Sources: *1939* — T. S. Khachaturov in *Plan. Khoz.*, 1940, no. 10, p. 40. *1940* — Notkin, 1948, p. 147. *1945* — Levin, 1947, p. 177. *1946, 1947, 1948* — I. Ivliev in MPS, 1949b, p. 26. *1949* — *Gudok*, 9 April, 1950, p. 3. *1950 plan* — Levin, 1947, p. 177. *1950 actual* — *Gudok*, 4 Feb. 1951, p. 3. *1951* — *Gudok*, 16 Sept. 1952, p. 3. *1952* — *Gudok*, 27 May 1953, p. 2.

## CHAPTER 12. GROWTH RATES FOR COMMODITY OUTPUT AND FREIGHT TRAFFIC

1. See Alexander Gerschenkron, "The Soviet Indices of Industrial Production," *The Review of Economic Statistics,* 29:221 (November 1947); and Hodgman, 1954, pp. 95–96.

2. An excellent review of this field was made by N. G. Bochkarev, in his paper, "On the Question of Relations Between the Volume of Production and the Volume of Shipments in the USSR" (in Russian), pp. 352–376, in Khanukov, 1948. However, the statistical methods applied here, to fuller records, appear more informative than the simple device he used.

3. The equations for the least-squares straight line indicating the regression of railroad coal traffic on coal production, and for the other lines to be presented in this chapter, are as follows, with traffic taken as the dependent variable $y$, and output as the independent variable $x$:

coal, 1923–1940: $y = -4.8 + 0.654\ x$;

coal, 1945–1955: $y = -2 + 0.686\ x$;

petroleum, 1945–1955 (regression of rail plus pipeline traffic on crude oil output): $y = -10.9 + 1.78\ x$;

iron and steel, 1949–1955: $y = 8.2 + 0.986\ x$;

timber, 1949–1955: $y = -66 + 0.839\ x$;

five-carrier ton-kilometers on Hodgman index of industrial production, 1928–1940: $y = 11 + 0.94\ x$;

five-carrier on Hodgman, 1948–1954: $y = 55 + 0.84\ x$;

rail tons originated on official index of industrial production, 1928–1940: $y = 70 + 0.52\ x$;

rail tons on official index, 1949–1955: $y = 212 + 0.287\ x$.

4. The grain harvest series employed in the first test was that compiled by Jasny, 1949, pp. 792–93, and in *International Affairs,* 1952, pp. 452–459. Jasny's estimates for barn crops net of various losses are clearly preferable to the official Soviet harvest data for comparison with freight traffic data, since grain which does not reach the barn does not enter into railroad transportation. The 1928–1940 government procurement series came from his 1949 book, p. 794.

5. Bergson, 1953a, chap. 4.

6. See my review in the *Journal of Economic History,* 1955, pp. 281–87.

7. The underlying United States data (in billions of 1947 dollars) are listed below (see United States Department of Commerce, 1954, p. 217). Line 1 shows gross national product; line 2 personal consumption expenditure on services; and line 3, total compensation of general government employees. Line 4 shows what may be called "gross private material product": gross national product less services and government payrolls. Line 5 shows an index for this measure, with its 1944 level taken as 100.

|    | 1940  | 1941  | 1942  | 1943  | 1944  | 1945  | 1946  | 1947  | 1948  |
|----|-------|-------|-------|-------|-------|-------|-------|-------|-------|
| 1. | 176.6 | 198.2 | 223.6 | 248.9 | 268.2 | 263.1 | 233.8 | 232.2 | 243.9 |
| 2. | 37.4  | 38.9  | 40.1  | 42.0  | 43.7  | 45.6  | 49.8  | 51.3  | 53.5  |
| 3. | 13.0  | 16.5  | 24.8  | 39.9  | 46.2  | 45.1  | 22.6  | 16.7  | 16.6  |
| 4. | 121.2 | 142.8 | 158.7 | 167.0 | 178.3 | 172.4 | 161.4 | 164.2 | 173.8 |
| 5. | 68    | 80    | 89    | 94    | 100   | 97    | 90    | 92    | 97    |

## CHAPTER 13. RAILROAD CAPITAL—OUTPUT RELATIONS

1. For brief but thoughtful discussion, see Gregory Grossman's comments in Bergson, 1953a, p. 17.

2. For a broad analysis of Soviet incremental capital output ratios, see the article by Alexander Eckstein and Peter Gutmann, "Capital and Output in the Soviet Union, 1928–1937," *Review of Economics and Statistics,* 38:436–44 (November 1956).

3. Most of our present understanding is due to the impressive work of Norman Kaplan; see his chapter in Bergson, 1953a, pp. 37–87, and his underlying RAND papers RM–735, P–277, and P–277 revised.

4. Barger, 1951, esp. pp. 163–82 and 191–213.

5. With combined unit revenue of 1.88 kopeks per cumulated ton-kilometer, the gross value increments are 2539 million rubles for 1928–1932 and 1600 million for 1936–1939.

6. See United States Department of Commerce, 1949, p. 204.

7. For Kaplan, see note 3 above; for Campbell, see the reference given in note 3, chap. 11.

8. Four over-all prewar figures, in 1945 prices, were given in Voznesenskii, 1947, p. 12. Railroad figures for 1923 and 1939, of a size suggesting the application of postwar price levels, appear in Kochetov, 1948, p. 196.

9. The first remark is from Khachaturov's 1952 book, p. 62, and the second from his 1953 pamphlet, p. 5. The *Gudok* quotation appeared in the 18 Jan. 1955 issue, p. 2.

10. See TsSU, 1956, p. 32. Converting the indexes from a 1940 to a 1950 base, one finds that by 1955 "all" assets had increased by 53 per cent and "productive" assets by 63 per cent, including rises of 72 per cent for industry, 85 per cent for agriculture, and 33 per cent for the transportation and communications sector.

11. See his paper in the Universities–National Bureau volume, 1955, pp. 171–288, with comments by Norman Kaplan, Abram Bergson, and Alexander Erlich.

12. For the 1947 annual plan, see *O gosudarstvennom plane,* 1947, pp. 14–15. The

1951 results were reported in *Gudok*, 23 May 1952, p. 2, and the Fifth Five Year Plan intentions appear in *Rechnoi Transport*, 1952, no. 6, p. 1. For Khachaturov's remarks, see Khachaturov, 1953, p. 5, and *Gudok*, 7 March 1956, p. 2.

13. See the "Law on the Government Budget of the USSR for 1954"; Kaganovich's speech to the Supreme Soviet, in *Gudok*, 28 April 1954, pp. 2–3; B. P. Beshchev's speech to the Twentieth Congress, in *Gudok*, 24 Feb. 1956, p. 4.

## CHAPTER 14. SOME THEORETICAL CONSIDERATIONS

1. The most authoritative analyses in English are Hoover, 1948, Losch, 1954, and Isard, 1956. For a rewarding analysis of railroad-building policy, see the classic work of Wellington, 1911.

2. See a summary of his 1946 analysis in my article in *Review of Economics and Statistics*, 1949, pp. 54–62.

3. For an amusing and critical description of importunate shippers, see F. Bogatyrev's letter in *Gudok*, 2 July 1952, p. 3. For sensible discussion of an exception to the traffic-minimizing principle, see Koldomasov, 1949, pp. 112–13. The discussion was criticized, however, in a review by A. Mots, in *Plan. Khoz.*, 1950, no. 2, p. 95.

4. Dispatches referring to Soviet electronic computers appear in the *New York Times* in 1955: 27 Nov., Section 1, p. 37; 30 Nov., p. 10; 11 Dec., pp. 1 and 24; 12 Dec., p. 4. For the kind of methodology which would be appropriate, see Beckmann, 1956.

5. A different form of the argument is given by Clark, 1956, pp. 216–28.

## CHAPTER 15. A SUMMARY EVALUATION OF SOVIET
## POLICY AND PROSPECTS

1. See Universities–National Bureau, 1955, pp. 207–14 and 225–28.

2. A. M. Firsovich, in *Gudok*, 14 Sept. 1947, p. 2.

3. The paper was by N. G. Bochkarev, pp. 352–76, in Khanukov, 1948. The review was by P. Krylov, in *Plan. Khoz.*, 1949, no. 4, pp. 83–91.

4. The reader can easily satisfy himself on this point by glancing at Balzak, 1949, especially pp. 145–66.

5. See Galenson, 1955, pp. 240–47.

6. Bulganin's speech on the Sixth Five Year Plan (*Pravda*, 22 Feb. 1956, p. 5) gave a plan investment total and minimum subtotals for industry, agriculture, and social investment. The subtotals account for 920 out of 990 billion rubles, leaving a maximum of some 7 per cent for the transportation and communications sector (which he referred to separately, without stating a figure). Perhaps some transportation investment appears in the broad categories, but the reduced share seems indisputable. Moreover, statements comparing Sixth Plan targets with 1951–1955 results indicate that transportation only obtained some 7 per cent of over-all investment grants during the Fifth Plan period.

# APPENDICES

Table 29.  Seasonal index of average daily carloadings, USSR
railroads, 1921–1938, by month and quarter (average
for the year = 100)

| Period | Unadjusted series[a] | Adjusted series[b] |
|---|---|---|
| Month | | |
| January | 92 | 90 |
| February | 93 | 92 |
| March | 97 | 95 |
| April | 98 | 100 |
| May | 100 | 104 |
| June | 103 | 106 |
| July | 101 | 105 |
| August | 100 | 104 |
| September | 107 | 104 |
| October | 109 | 105 |
| November | 104 | 101 |
| December | 96 | 94 |
| Quarter | | |
| First | 94.0 | 92.4 |
| Second | 100.3 | 103.3 |
| Third | 102.7 | 104.3 |
| Fourth | 103.0 | 100.0 |

[a]Calculated on the basis of all 18 years.

[b]Adjusted to give effect to the pattern that became typical in the 1930's.

Sources: Calculated by the link-relatives method applied to data from NKPS
*Materialy*, vol. 53, p. 11 and vol. 104, p. 11; from TsUNKhU, 1936b, p. 340; and
from Kochetov, 1941, p. 61.

313

Table 30. Distribution (per cent) of total road operated, USSR railroads, by ruling gradient, 1913, 1933, 1940

| Ruling gradient (per cent) | 1913 | | 1933 | | 1940 | |
|---|---|---|---|---|---|---|
| | In class | Cumulated | In class | Cumulated | In class | Cumulated |
| Less than 0.01 | 32.7 | 32.7 | 32.2 | 32.2 | 26.7 | 26.7 |
| 0.01–0.40 | | | 25.2 | 57.4 | 33.0 | 59.7 |
| 41–.50 | 40.8 | 73.5 | 5.2 | 62.6 | 13.8 | 73.5 |
| .51–.60 | | | 9.5 | 72.1 | | |
| .61–.80 | 22.4 | 95.9 | 17.1 | 89.2 | 13.0 | 86.5 |
| .81–1.00 | | | 7.4 | 96.6 | 9.4 | 95.9 |
| 1.01–1.20 | 2.7 | 98.6 | 1.5 | 98.1 | 3.3 | 99.2 |
| 1.21–1.50 | | | 1.3 | 99.4 | | |
| Over 1.50 | 1.4 | 100.0 | 0.6 | 100.0 | 0.8 | 100.0 |

Sources: The 1913 percentages are from Bernstein-Kogan, 1930, p. 275. Figures from January 1, 1934, covering both the absolute number of kilometers in each class and its percentage share, are given by IAkobi, 1935, p. 112. The 1940 percentages appear in Gorinov, 1948a, vol. 1, p. 382.

Table 31.  Gross industrial output, USSR, by territory, 1940–1944
(billions of rubles at "1926–27 prices"[a])

| Territory | 1940 | 1942 | 1943 | 1944 |
|---|---|---|---|---|
| Occupied west | 45.7 | — | 2.7 | 8.3 |
| Middle band | 70.1 | 50.8 | 54.8 | 61.1 |
| East | 22.7 | 52.2 | 63.5 | 67.6 |
| Total USSR | 138.5 | 103.0 | 121.0 | 137.0 |

[a]The "1926–27 prices" officially used to compute industrial output impart a systematic upward bias; for discussion, see Hodgman, 1954, chap. 1.

Sources: Voznesenskii, 1947, gives the 1940 occupied west output as 33 per cent of the USSR on p. 157, and gives its 1943 and 1944 output on p. 61. He gives 1942 and 1943 figures for the Ural region, West Siberia, and Kazakhstan plus Central Asia on pp. 49–52. The estimates for "east" above consist of totals for these three regions, plus crude estimates for East Siberia and the Soviet Far East. The 1940 output for this latter territory is estimated at 5.0 billion rubles. For 1942 and 1943 the observed percentage increases in West Siberia were applied to this base figure on the assumption of proportionate increases in the two territories. Voznesenskii's 1944 figure for the "eastern regions" is 106.5 per cent of his 1943 figure; this factor was applied to the above 1943 estimate for "east" to obtain a 1944 estimate.

The 1940 USSR total is given by Voznesenskii on p. 12. The 1942 and 1943 estimates were derived from Voznesenskii's remarks by Professor Gerschenkron in the *American Economic Review*, 38:650 (September 1948). The 1944 USSR total is 361 billion less the 1942 and 1943 totals; Voznesenskii stated in introducing the Fourth Five Year Plan that this was the total gross output of large-scale industry in 1942–1944.

Given these estimates, the amounts recorded for "middle band" territory result in each case as residuals. Some small error results from failure to observe the distinction between "large-scale" and "all" industry.

Table 32. Railroad traffic and facilities indexes, USSR, by year, 1928–1940 and 1948–1955

| Year | Freight traffic Annual percentage increase | Freight traffic Index | Passenger traffic Annual percentage increase | Passenger traffic Index | Road operated, index | Freight locomotives, index | Freight cars, index |
|---|---|---|---|---|---|---|---|
| | | 1928 = 100 | | 1928 = 100 | 1928 = 100 | 1928 = 100 | 1928 = 100 |
| 1928 | 14.4 | 100.0 | 10.7 | 100.0 | 100.0 | 100.0 | 100.0 |
| 1929 | 21.0 | 121.0 | 30.7 | 130.7 | 100.2 | 104.8 | 115.2 |
| 1930 | 18.6 | 143.4 | 61.8 | 211.5 | 100.2 | 109.4 | 126.8 |
| 1931 | 13.6 | 162.9 | 19.4 | 252.5 | 104.4 | 115.4 | 138.5 |
| 1932 | 11.3 | 181.3 | 35.5 | 342.1 | 106.0 | 122.2 | 140.8 |
| 1933 | 0.1 | 181.5 | −10.3 | 307.0 | 106.8 | 125.5 | 143.6 |
| | | 1932 = 100 | | 1932 = 100 | 1932 = 100 | 1932 = 100 | 1932 = 100 |
| 1933 | 0.1 | 100.1 | −10.3 | 89.7 | 100.6 | 102.6 | 102.0 |
| 1934 | 21.4 | 121.5 | − 5.0 | 85.3 | 102.1 | 117.8 | 102.0 |
| 1935 | 25.4 | 152.5 | − 4.9 | 81.1 | 102.8 | 122.3 | 109.2 |
| 1936 | 25.3 | 191.0 | 13.6 | 92.2 | 103.8 | 110.9 | 121.7 |
| 1937 | 9.7 | 209.6 | 17.8 | 108.6 | 104.1 | 112.2 | 130.4 |
| 1938 | 4.4 | 218.9 | 0.8 | 109.4 | 104.1 | 112.0 | 137.7 |
| 1939 | 5.8 | 231.6 | 2.3 | 111.9 | 108.4 | 117.3 | 140.8 |
| 1940 | 5.9 | 245.2 | 4.5 | 117.0 | 117.1 | 120.6 | 150.0 |
| | | 1948 = 100 | | 1948 = 100 | 1948 = 100 | 1948 = 100 | 1948 = 100 |
| 1948 | 27.2 | 100.0 | −20.9 | 100.0 | 100.0 | 100.0 | 100.0 |
| 1949 | 17.3 | 117.3 | 8.1 | 108.1 | 100.6 | 102.8 | 109.2 |
| 1950 | 15.1 | 135.0 | 7.7 | 116.5 | 101.2 | 105.7 | 112.2 |
| 1951 | 12.5 | 151.8 | 12.4 | 131.0 | 101.9 | 113.5 | 117.0 |
| 1952 | 9.5 | 166.2 | 9.4 | 143.4 | 102.6 | 117.1 | 120.4 |
| 1953 | 7.6 | 178.8 | 9.8 | 157.4 | 103.6 | 118.5 | 124.2 |
| 1954 | 7.4 | 192.0 | 9.9 | 171.7 | 104.3 | 114.5 | 132.3 |
| 1955 | 13.3 | 217.5 | 9.5 | 188.0 | 104.7 | 109.3 | 133.5 |

Source: Derived from absolute data in Tables 46, 56, 59, 61, and 63. Coverage details are discussed in the notes to each table.

Table 33.  Government budget revenue and expenditure in railroad sector,
1924–1932 (millions of rubles at current prices)

| Year | Government revenues | Government expenditures | Balance to the railroads |
|---|---|---|---|
| 1924[a] | 694.6 | 739.8 | 45.2 |
| 1925[a] | 989.9 | 929.0 | −60.6 |
| 1926[a] | 1415.8 | 1340.6 | −75.2 |
| 1927[a] | 1701.0 | 1763.3 | 62.3 |
| 1928[a] | 1923.4 | 1984.6 | 61.2 |
| 1929[a] | 2305.3 | 2217.3 | −88.0 |
| 1930 | 3049.4 | 2717.7 | −331.7 |
| Special quarter[b] | 925.9 | 903.4 | −22.5 |
| 1931 | 4445.9 | 4274.9 | −171.0 |
| 1932 | 5378.5 | 5580.5 | 202.0 |

[a]Fiscal year including 3 months of the preceding calendar year.
[b]The fourth quarter of 1930.  In 1931 calendar-year accounting was adopted.
Source: TsUNKhU, 1934, pp. 440–42.

Table 34. Consumption of rolled steel, USSR railroads and total USSR, by year, 1931–1938

| Year | Direct railroad consumption | | Railroad equipment consumption | | Total railroad consumption | | Total USSR consumption | | Railroads' percentage share | Percentage reduction in nonrailroad consumption if railroad consumption— | |
|---|---|---|---|---|---|---|---|---|---|---|---|
| | Metric tons (10³) | Index (1931 = 100) | Metric tons (10³) | Index (1931 = 100) | Metric tons (10³) | Index (1931 = 100) | Metric tons (10³) | Index (1931 = 100) | | Increased 10% | Increased 20% |
| 1931 | 574.8 | 100.0 | 349.5 | 100.0 | 924.3 | 100.0 | 5216.8 | 100.0 | 17.7 | 2.2 | 4.3 |
| 1932 | 533.7 | 92.8 | 461.7 | 132.1 | 995.4 | 107.7 | 4500.2 | 86.3 | 22.1 | 2.8 | 5.7 |
| 1933 | 513.0 | 89.2 | 371.3 | 106.2 | 884.3 | 95.7 | 4288.8 | 82.2 | 20.6 | 2.6 | 5.2 |
| 1934 | 902.7 | 157.0 | 511.6 | 146.4 | 1414.3 | 153.0 | 5718.7 | 109.6 | 24.7 | 3.3 | 6.6 |
| 1935 | 1140.1 | 198.3 | 1121.6 | 320.9 | 2261.7 | 244.7 | 7648.8 | 146.6 | 29.6 | 4.2 | 8.4 |
| 1936 | 1501.6 | 261.2 | 1236.1 | 353.7 | 2737.7 | 296.2 | 9779.1 | 187.5 | 28.0 | 3.9 | 7.8 |
| 1937 | 1491.2 | 259.4 | 956.2 | 273.6 | 2447.4 | 264.8 | 9800.7 | 187.9 | 25.0 | 3.3 | 6.7 |
| 1938 | 1254.8 | 218.3 | 731.8 | 209.4 | 1986.6 | 214.9 | 9516.6 | 182.4 | 20.9 | 2.6 | 5.3 |

Source: Compiled from tables in Shul'kin, 1940, pp. 20–28. The figures for railroad equipment cover locomotives, freight cars, and passenger cars. Equipment for street railways and mine transport is included. But steel going into automobiles, trucks, shipbuilding, and aircraft is excluded.

Table 35.  Total iron and steel consumption, USSR railroads and total USSR,
by year, 1932–1938

| Year | Railroad consumption ($10^3$m t) | | | Total USSR consumption ($10^3$m t) | Percentage consumed by railroads |
|------|--------|-----------|-------|--------|--------|
|      | Direct | Equipment | Total |        |        |
| 1932 | 717.8   | 718.1   | 1,435.9 | 7,598.6  | 18.9 |
| 1933 | 707.5   | 654.0   | 1,361.5 | 7,862.3  | 17.3 |
| 1934 | 1,195.5 | 895.8   | 2,091.3 | 10,970.5 | 19.1 |
| 1935 | 1,506.1 | 1,586.4 | 3,092.5 | 13,764.2 | 22.5 |
| 1936 | 1,842.4 | 1,643.0 | 3,485.4 | 16,531.7 | 21.1 |
| 1937 | 1,891.3 | 1,273.4 | 3,164.7 | 17,398.2 | 18.2 |
| 1938 | 1,544.0 | 965.7   | 2,509.7 | 17,044.3 | 14.8 |

Source: Compiled from tables in Shul'kin, 1940, pp. 20–28. The USSR total is
net of the pig iron consumed by the iron and steel industry itself, since this is a
feedback that reappears in the amounts consumed in more fabricated form.

Table 36. Railroad labor force, USSR, by year, 1925–1935

| Year | Railroad labor force | | | Total USSR nonfarm labor force | | | Railroad as percentage of total USSR | Percentage reduction in nonrailroad labor force if railroad labor force— | |
|---|---|---|---|---|---|---|---|---|---|
| | No. of persons (10³) | Index (1928 = 100) | Annual percentage increase | No. of persons (10³) | Index (1928 = 100) | Annual percentage increase | | Increased 10% | Increased 20% |
| 1925[a] | 806.4 | 83.0 | — | 8,532.0 | 73.6 | — | 9.5 | 1.0 | 2.1 |
| 1926[a] | 962.0 | 99.1 | 19.3 | 10,173.4 | 87.7 | 19.2 | 9.5 | 1.0 | 2.1 |
| 1927[a] | 1,006.4 | 103.6 | 4.6 | 10,943.7 | 94.4 | 7.6 | 9.2 | 1.0 | 2.0 |
| 1928 | 971.0 | 100.0 | -3.5 | 11,599.0 | 100.0 | 6.0 | 8.4 | 0.9 | 1.8 |
| 1929 | 984.0 | 101.3 | 1.3 | 12,167.9 | 104.9 | 4.9 | 8.1 | .9 | 1.8 |
| 1930 | 1,084.0 | 111.6 | 10.2 | 14,530.9 | 125.3 | 19.4 | 7.5 | .8 | 1.6 |
| 1931 | 1,320.0 | 136.0 | 21.8 | 18,989.5 | 163.7 | 30.7 | 7.0 | .7 | 1.5 |
| 1932 | 1,526.5 | 157.2 | 15.6 | 22,942.8 | 197.8 | 20.8 | 6.7 | .7 | 1.4 |
| 1933 | 1,473.7 | 151.8 | -3.5 | 22,325.3 | 192.5 | -2.7 | 6.6 | .7 | 1.4 |
| 1934 | 1,603.2 | 165.1 | 8.8 | 23,681.2 | 204.2 | 6.1 | 6.8 | .7 | 1.5 |
| 1935 | 1,788.6 | 184.2 | 11.6 | 24,769.9 | 213.6 | 4.6 | 7.2 | .8 | 1.6 |

[a]The figures for 1925–1927 cover a 12-month period including 3 months of the preceding calendar year.

Sources: The 1925–1932 data are from TsUNKhU, 1934, pp. 306–07; for 1928–1935 from TsUNKhU, 1936a, pp. 508–09.

Table 37. Railroad coal consumption, USSR, by year, 1923–1935

| Year | Railroad consumption | | | Total USSR production | | | | Per cent reduction in nonrailroad consumption if railroad consumption — | |
|---|---|---|---|---|---|---|---|---|---|
| | Metric tons (10³) | Annual percentage increase | Index (1928 = 100) | Metric tons (10³) | Annual percentage increase | Index (1928 = 100) | Percentage of total production consumed by railroads | Increased 10% | Increased 20% |
| 1923[a] | 3,381 | — | 34.2 | 12,700 | — | 35.8 | 26.6 | — | — |
| 1924[a] | 4,709 | 39.3 | 47.7 | 16,328 | 28.6 | 46.0 | 28.8 | — | — |
| 1925[a] | 4,810 | 2.1 | 48.7 | 16,520 | 1.2 | 46.5 | 29.1 | — | — |
| 1926[a] | 7,207 | 49.8 | 72.9 | 25,770 | 56.0 | 72.6 | 28.0 | — | — |
| 1927[a] | 8,904 | 23.5 | 90.1 | 32,275 | 25.2 | 90.9 | 27.6 | — | — |
| 1928[a] | 9,880 | 11.0 | 100.0 | 35,510 | 10.0 | 100.0 | 27.8 | — | — |
| 1929[a] | 10,686 | 8.2 | 108.2 | 40,067 | 12.8 | 112.8 | 26.7 | 3.6 | 7.3 |
| 1930[b] | 13,479 | 26.1 | 136.4 | 47,780 | 19.3 | 134.6 | 28.2[b] | 3.9 | 7.9 |
| 1931 | 15,201 | 12.8 | 153.9 | 56,752 | 18.8 | 159.8 | 26.8 | 3.7 | 7.3 |
| 1932 | 16,789 | 10.4 | 169.9 | 64,664 | 13.9 | 182.1 | 26.0 | 3.5 | 7.0 |
| 1933 | 18,168 | 8.2 | 183.9 | 76,205 | 17.8 | 214.6 | 23.8 | 3.1 | 6.3 |
| 1934 | 20,898 | 15.0 | 211.5 | 93,940 | 23.3 | 264.5 | 22.2 | 2.9 | 5.7 |
| 1935 | 23,816 | 14.0 | 241.1 | 108,900 | 15.9 | 306.7 | 21.9 | 2.8 | 5.6 |

[a]The years 1923–1929 cover a 12-month period including 3 months of the preceding calendar year. This applies to both series.
[b]For 1930, the railroad consumption figure has been shifted forward to a calendar-year basis, while the total production figure remains on a fiscal-year basis. Consequently the rise in the railroads' percentage share is largely spurious.

Sources: Railroad consumption data for 1923–1932 are from IAkobi, 1935, pp. 72–73. Railroad consumption figures for 1933–1935 are from TsUNKhU, 1936a, p. 436; the same source gives total production figures for 1923–1934 on pp. 100–01. The 1935 production figure is from Ioffe, 1939, p. 150.

Table 38. Indexes of railroad operating averages, USSR, by year, 1923–1940

| Year | Gross ton-kilometers per freight train-hour | | Locomotive-kilometers per locomotive day | | Freight car turnaround time[a] | |
|------|------------------|------------|------------------|------------|------------------|------------|
| | Annual percentage increase | Index (1928 = 100) | Annual percentage increase | Index (1928 = 100) | Annual percentage increase | Index (1928 = 100) |
| 1923[b] | — | — | — | 77.8 | — | 61.8 |
| 1924[b] | — | — | 7.1 | 83.3 | 6.9 | 66.0 |
| 1925[b] | — | 86.7 | 5.1 | 87.6 | 19.4 | 78.8 |
| 1926[b] | 1.1 | 87.7 | 1.2 | 88.7 | 7.2 | 84.5 |
| 1927[b] | 7.7 | 94.4 | 7.3 | 95.2 | 10.6 | 93.5 |
| 1928 | 5.9 | 100.0 | 5.0 | 100.0 | 7.0 | 100.0 |
| 1929 | -1.4 | 98.6 | 10.2 | 110.2 | 3.6 | 103.6 |
| 1930 | 0.6 | 99.2 | 1.2 | 111.5 | 9.1 | 113.1 |
| 1931 | 11.6 | 110.8 | 4.2 | 116.1 | -2.5 | 110.2 |
| 1932 | 8.2 | 119.9 | 3.1 | 119.7 | 2.5 | 112.9 |
| 1933 | -4.0 | 115.1 | -0.7 | 118.9 | -2.3 | 110.3 |
| 1934 | 9.8 | 126.4 | 3.1 | 122.5 | 9.4 | 120.7 |
| 1935 | 11.6 | 141.1 | 12.2 | 137.5 | 13.8 | 137.3 |
| 1936 | 30.6 | 184.3 | 22.8 | 168.9 | 13.3 | 155.5 |
| 1937 | 10.1 | 203.0 | 5.7 | 178.6 | -2.7 | 151.3 |
| 1938 | 3.1 | 209.2 | 2.1 | 182.4 | -7.2 | 140.4 |
| 1939 | 3.8 | 217.1 | 0.2 | 182.7 | 3.7 | 145.7 |
| 1940 | 5.4 | 228.7 | 1.6 | 185.5 | -1.6 | 143.3 |

[a]The annual percentage increase, and the index based on 1928, are computed as reciprocals in order to make them comparable with the other 2 series. They may be thought of as relating to the average number of trips per year made by a freight car.

[b]The data for 1923–1927 relate to a 12-month period including 3 months of the preceding calendar year.

Source: Derived from absolute data in Tables 73–75. Details of definition and coverage are discussed in the notes to each table.

Table 39.  Military traffic, USSR railroads, 1940–1945, average
daily carloadings

| Year | Military traffic | | Nonmilitary traffic | | Total traffic | |
|---|---|---|---|---|---|---|
| | Cars (2-axle units) | Index (1940 = 100) | Cars (2-axle units) | Index (1940 = 100) | Cars (2-axle units) | Index (1940 = 100) |
| 1940 | 2,600 | 100 | 95,252 | 100 | 97,852 | 100 |
| 1941 (2nd half) | 7,100 | 273 | 67,900 | 69 | 75,000 | 77 |
| 1942 | 12,100 | 465 | 30,570 | 32 | 42,670 | 44 |
| 1943 | 13,500 | 519 | 32,080 | 34 | 45,580 | 47 |
| 1944 | 16,900 | 650 | 38,610 | 41 | 55,510 | 57 |
| 1945 (to May) | 17,100 | 658 | — | — | — | — |

Sources: The total traffic series is taken from Table 46.  The military traffic
series is only approximate, and therefore the estimates for "nonmilitary traffic,"
obtained as residuals, are also subject to a considerable margin of error.

For total military traffic, we have the statement: "During 47 months of war
with Germany, more than 19 million cars of military freight were shipped"
(*Gudok*, 31 May 1946, p. 2).  For allocating this total to time periods, we have
the statements: "Taking average daily carloadings of military freight in 1942 as
100, they were 111.8 in 1943 and 139.5 in 1944" (N. Vasil'ev in *Zhel. Trans.*,
1947, no. 11, p. 35); and "Military freight increased in 1944 by 150–200 per cent
compared to 1941–1942" (*Gudok*, 20 July 1945, p. 2).  These indexes can be
plotted on semilog paper and, with the assumption added that carloadings during
January–May 1945 continued at the rate for the second half of 1944, crude
estimates of the level at the midpoint of each six month period can be read off.
Distributing the total according to those indexes, and dividing by the number of
days involved, converts the absolute subtotals into average daily carloadings.

The total distributed in this way was 19 million cars, though the statement
reports "more than" 19 million.  Thus the series for military carloadings above
may be slightly low, as appears to be born out in juggling the fragments.  The
underestimate may be appreciable for the second half of 1941.  The 1940 figure
for military traffic is an unfounded estimate based on "reasonable" relationships
with total carloadings and 1941 military traffic, and is used merely to obtain a
rough base for the two indexes.

Table 40. Per cent composition and average hauls, USSR rail freight traffic, by commodity group, selected periods, 1894–1955

| Commodity group | 1894–1898 | 1899–1903 | 1904–1908 | 1909–1913 | 1923–1927 | 1928–1932 | 1933–1937 | 1938–1940 | 1945 | 1947 | 1949–1950 | 1954–1955 |
|---|---|---|---|---|---|---|---|---|---|---|---|---|
| **Percentage of total ton-kilometers** | | | | | | | | | | | | |
| Coal and coke | — | — | — | — | 19.2 | 20.3 | 24.3 | 23.9 | 31.4 | 35.5 | 30.2 | 27.4 |
| Petroleum and products | — | — | — | — | 6.7 | 8.0 | 8.9 | 9.0 | 7.6 | 8.0 | 8.4 | 10.2 |
| Ores | — | — | — | — | 2.3 | 3.3 | 5.5 | 4.6 | 4.0 | 4.7 | 4.7 | 4.6 |
| Iron and steel | — | — | — | — | 3.7 | 5.0 | 7.1 | 6.8 | 7.6 | 7.4 | 8.0 | 8.0 |
| Mineral building materials | — | — | — | — | — | 4.9 | 4.1 | 7.6 | 3.0 | 5.0 | 7.4 | 8.2 |
| Timber | — | — | — | — | 11.3 | 13.5 | 12.3 | 11.7 | 6.6 | 9.4 | 11.7 | 12.0 |
| Grain | — | — | — | — | 19.6 | 12.0 | 8.1 | 8.3 | 7.4 | 5.8 | 5.4 | 5.9 |
| Firewood | — | — | — | — | 5.6 | 2.7 | 1.6 | 1.4 | .9 | 1.1 | .8 | .5 |
| Other | — | — | — | — | 31.6 | 30.3 | 28.1 | 26.7 | 31.5 | 23.1 | 23.4 | 23.1 |
| **Percentage of total tons originated** | | | | | | | | | | | | |
| Coal and coke | 16.4 | 18.2 | 20.0 | 19.8 | 18.2 | 19.0 | 24.0 | 24.3 | 36.0 | 37.3 | 32.3 | 30.7 |
| Petroleum and products | 7.0 | 6.7 | 5.0 | 4.0 | 5.2 | 5.9 | 5.6 | 5.2 | 5.4 | 5.3 | 5.1 | 6.2 |
| Ores | 4.5 | 5.6 | 6.2 | 6.3 | 3.4 | 4.5 | 6.1 | 5.7 | 4.5 | 5.2 | 5.7 | 6.6 |
| Iron and steel | 2.9 | 3.2 | 3.3 | 3.4 | 2.7 | 3.6 | 4.9 | 4.8 | 5.4 | 4.7 | 5.2 | 5.7 |
| Mineral building materials | 8.0 | 8.7 | 6.7 | 9.0 | — | 9.8 | 7.4 | 18.7 | 10.6 | 15.3 | 18.6 | 19.0 |
| Timber | 8.0 | 8.0 | 7.8 | 9.1 | 11.0 | 12.1 | 10.0 | 7.9 | 6.7 | 7.8 | 8.6 | 7.4 |
| Grain | 24.7 | 20.8 | 20.9 | 18.7 | 13.0 | 9.8 | 7.8 | 7.8 | 5.1 | 5.2 | 4.7 | 4.6 |
| Firewood | 5.3 | 5.6 | 6.5 | 5.9 | 13.9 | 6.2 | 4.3 | 3.8 | 4.4 | 3.8 | 2.6 | 1.4 |
| Other freight | 23.2 | 23.2 | 23.6 | 23.8 | 32.6 | 29.1 | 29.9 | 21.8 | 21.9 | 15.4 | 17.2 | 18.4 |
| **Average length of haul (kilometers)** | | | | | | | | | | | | |
| Coal and coke | — | — | — | — | 586 | 634 | 673 | 699 | 693 | 679 | 668 | 679 |
| Petroleum and products | — | — | — | — | 712 | 812 | 1,061 | 1,225 | 1,115 | 1,074 | 1,314 | 1,262 |
| Ores | — | — | — | — | 362 | 443 | 597 | 576 | 702 | 647 | 592 | 535 |
| Iron and steel | — | — | — | — | 747 | 823 | 975 | 1,000 | 1,124 | 1,120 | 1,102 | 1,066 |
| Mineral building materials | — | — | — | — | — | 302 | 373 | 286 | 228 | 235 | 287 | 330 |
| Timber | — | — | — | — | 567 | 670 | 816 | 1,042 | 780 | 866 | 971 | 1,233 |
| Grain | — | — | — | — | 837 | 732 | 683 | 755 | 1,153 | 798 | 827 | 973 |
| Firewood | — | — | — | — | 221 | 258 | 253 | 258 | 157 | 201 | 234 | 302 |
| Other | — | — | — | — | 537 | 619 | 622 | 868 | 1,140 | 1,071 | 977 | 958 |
| Total | — | — | — | — | 553 | 597 | 664 | 708 | 794 | 715 | 717 | 762 |

Table 41.  Moscow passenger transportation, by year, 1935–1953

| Year | Subway | | Number of passengers on street cars and buses (10⁶) | Total[a] | |
|------|--------------------------------|-------------------|-----------------------|----------------------------|----------------------|
|      | Number of passengers (10⁶) | Percentage share | | Number of passengers (10⁶) | Index (1940 = 100) |
| 1935 | 41 | 2.0 | 1997 | 2038 | 77 |
| 1936 | 111 | 5.2 | 2022 | 2133 | 81 |
| 1937 | 155 | 7.1 | 2045 | 2200 | 83 |
| 1938 | 213 | 9.0 | 2150 | 2363 | 90 |
| 1939 | 332 | 12.9 | 2238 | 2570 | 97 |
| 1940 | 377 | 14.3 | 2263 | 2640 | 100 |
| 1941 | 260 | 17 | 1270 | 1530 | 58 |
| 1942 | 200 | 23 | 670 | 870 | 33 |
| 1943 | 390 | 28 | 1000 | 1390 | 53 |
| 1944 | 559 | 30 | 1301 | 1860 | 70 |
| 1945 | 617 | 31.7 | 1333 | 1950 | 74 |
| 1946 | 668 | 30.4 | 1528 | 2196 | 83 |
| 1947 | 670 | 31.5 | 1460 | 2130 | 81 |
| 1948 | 673 | 26 | 1917 | 2590 | 98 |
| 1949 | 700 | 27 | 1890 | 2590 | 98 |
| 1950 | 725 | 28 | 1865 | 2590 | 98 |
| 1951 | 750 | 28.5 | 1880 | 2630 | 100 |
| 1952 | 775 | 29 | 1905 | 2680 | 102 |
| 1953 | 800 | 29 | 1940 | 2760 | 105 |

[a]Excluding railroad commutation traffic.

Sources: 1935, 1939, 1945, and 1946 data for subway and other carriers appear in Obraztsov, 1948c, p. 314.  Similar data for 1936–1938 appear in TsUNKhU, 1939, p. 137, and for 1940 in Obraztsov, 1948a, p. 22.  The 1941–1946 subway data are from Kattsen, 1947, pp. 53–56.  The subway's percentage share in 1944 appears in *Gudok*, 10 Sept. 1947, p. 4; its 1948 traffic and share in *Gudok*, 30 Dec. 1949, p. 3; its 1950 share in *Gudok*, 14 May 1950, p. 2; its rough 1952 share in Ezhov, 1953, p. 14; and its 1953 traffic (2.2 million per day) in *Gudok*, 8 Aug. 1953, p. 4.  The absolute data above for 1941–1944 and 1947–1953 are interpolated accordingly.

Table 42.  Railroad unit cost and revenue indexes, USSR,
by year, 1924–1940 (1928 = 100)

| Year | Cost indexes | | Revenue indexes | |
|------|------|------|------|------|
|      | (A)  | (B)  | (C)  | (D)  |
| 1924 | 108.6 | — | 82.2 | 85.9 |
| 1925 | 96.9 | — | 85.2 | 87.8 |
| 1926 | 103.0 | — | 89.0 | 90.6 |
| 1927 | 107.2 | — | 95.0 | 95.9 |
| 1928 | 100.0 | 100.0 | 100.0 | 100.0 |
| 1929 | 86.7 | 91.1 | 100.0 | 101.2 |
| 1930 | 78.2 | 79.5 | 105.2 | 105.4 |
| 1931 | 104.5 | 84.2 | 128.6 | 122.8 |
| 1932 | 109.0 | 89.8 | 133.8 | 132.4 |
| 1933 | 124.2 | 102.5 | 143.1 | 143.8 |
| 1934 | 140.9 | 114.9 | 133.6 | 134.2 |
| 1935 | 155.0 | 127.6 | 127.3 | 127.9 |
| 1936 | 162.3 | 134.7 | 144.1 | 133.3 |
| 1937 | 171.3 | 141.5 | 154.6 | 138.8 |
| 1938 | 186.0 | 153.5 | 169.8 | 152.5 |
| 1939 | 199.8 | 164.5 | 224.3 | 201.6 |
| 1940 | 210.0 | 172.6 | 238.8 | 214.9 |

Column headings:
   (A) Total operating cost per "cumulated ton-kilometer" (combining passenger-kilometers with *tariff* ton-kilometers).
   (B) Unit cost obtained through dividing total operating costs (including imputed depreciation, 1928–1930) by the sum of passenger-kilometers and *operating* ton-kilometers.
   (C) Combined  freight and passenger revenue divided by "cumulated ton-kilometers."
   (D) Sum of freight, passenger, and other revenue divided by "cumulated ton-kilometers."
   Source: Derived from absolute data in Table 69, columns 5, 7, 3, and 4.

Table 43. Relations among components of railroad operating cost, USSR,
by year, 1926–1940

| Year | Percentage composition | | | Indexes per cumulated[a] ton-kilometer (1928 = 100) | | |
|------|-------|--------------|-------|-------|--------------|-------|
|      | Labor | Depreciation | Other | Labor | Depreciation | Other |
| 1926 | 45.7 | 20.1 | 34.2 | 98.0  | 121.4 | 110.5 |
| 1927 | 49.6 | 17.9 | 32.5 | 107.6 | 109.8 | 106.7 |
| 1928 | 49.6 | 17.6 | 32.8 | 100.0 | 100.0 | 100.0 |
| 1929 | 43.6 | 22.2 | 34.2 | 80.7  | 115.8 | 95.8  |
| 1930 | 45.5 | 20.2 | 34.3 | 74.1  | 92.9  | 84.3  |
| 1931 | 51.9 | 19.8 | 28.3 | 90.1  | 97.0  | 74.2  |
| 1932 | 55.3 | 17.8 | 26.9 | 100.1 | 91.0  | 73.6  |
| 1933 | 49.6 | 17.7 | 32.7 | 102.3 | 103.0 | 102.0 |
| 1934 | 50.7 | 15.0 | 34.3 | 118.7 | 99.2  | 121.2 |
| 1935 | 59.9 | 12.4 | 27.7 | 154.4 | 89.8  | 107.7 |
| 1936 | 50.5 | 10.3 | 39.2 | 136.3 | 78.6  | 159.5 |
| 1937 | 43.9 | 9.5  | 46.6 | 125.1 | 75.9  | 200.6 |
| 1938 | 46.7 | 8.9  | 44.4 | 144.3 | 77.8  | 207.5 |
| 1939 | 43.6 | 10.3 | 46.1 | 144.7 | 95.9  | 231.9 |
| 1940 | 47.8 | 11.2 | 41.0 | 166.8 | 110.5 | 215.9 |

[a]"Cumulated" ton-kilometer is defined in the notes to Table 58.

Sources: Computed from data in Tables 68 and 58 (column 3). For 1926–1930, depreciation adjustment included. For 1936, 1938, and 1940, labor cost estimated on basis of wage and labor-force data; depreciation estimated as interpolated percentage of average assets from Table 72.

Table 44.  Average operating wages, productivity, and unit labor costs
USSR railroads, by year, 1928–1940 and 1945–1955

| Year | Average monthly wage | | Productivity Index | Index of unit labor cost |
|------|--------|--------|-----------|-----------|
|      | Rubles | Index  |           |           |
|      |        | 1928 = 100 | 1928 = 100 | 1928 = 100 |
| 1928 | 74.2 | 100.0 | 100.0 | 100.0 |
| 1929 | 78   | 105.4 | 122.8 | 85.8  |
| 1930 | 89   | 120.3 | 144.7 | 83.1  |
| 1931 | 100  | 135.1 | 146.0 | 92.5  |
| 1932 | 129  | 174.3 | 167.0 | 104.4 |
| 1933 | 141  | 190.5 | 174.1 | 109.4 |
| 1934 | 165  | 223.0 | 178.4 | 125.0 |
| 1935 | 202  | 273.0 | 190.6 | 143.2 |
| 1936 | 250  | 337.8 | 237.6 | 142.2 |
| 1937 | 284  | 383.8 | 258.9 | 148.2 |
| 1938 | 311  | 420.3 | 256.2 | 164.1 |
| 1939 | 343  | 463.5 | 268.2 | 172.8 |
| 1940 | 356  | 481.1 | 277.4 | 173.4 |
|      |      | 1940 = 100 | 1940 = 100 | 1940 = 100 |
| 1945 | 544  | 152.8 | 68.8  | 222.1 |
| 1946 | 573  | 161.0 | 75.4  | 213.5 |
| 1947 | 686  | 192.6 | 77.6  | 248.2 |
| 1948 | 673  | 189.0 | 90.0  | 210.0 |
| 1949 | 710  | 199.4 | 99.2  | 201.0 |
| 1950 | 752  | 211.4 | 109.5 | 193.1 |
| 1951 | 768  | 215.8 | 119.5 | 180.6 |
| 1952 | 769  | 216.0 | 123.6 | 174.8 |
| 1953 | 772  | 217.1 | 131.0 | 165.7 |
| 1954 | 781  | 219.4 | 136.1 | 161.2 |
| 1955 | 788  | 221.5 | 152.7 | 145.1 |

Sources: 1928–1935 annual wages for *all* railroad labor appear in TsUNKhU,
1936a, pp. 512–13. Average monthly wages for operating workers alone appear in
*Plan*, 1937, no. 3, p. 40, for 1932 and 1933, and in Vol'fson, 1941, p. 553, for
1934–1937.  Operating wages averaged 3.6 per cent over wages for all railroad
labor in 1932–1935, and this factor was applied to obtain the 1928–1931 estimates above.  Data for 1938–1940 are given in Migal', 1951, p. 68.  The 1940
and 1945 monthly wage figures are from Umbliia, 1947, pp. 176–77; Migal', 1951,
p. 86 gives figures for 1946 and 1949.  Percentage relationships with 1940 are
given for 1947 by I. Ivliev in *Zhel. Trans.*, 1948, no. 8, p. 12; for 1948 in
Umbliia, 1949, p. 197, and, for 1952 in *Gudok*, 9 July 1953, p. 3.  The wage
estimates for 1950–51 and 1953–55 are derived from 1950–1955 indexes given in
A. A. Chertkova's 1956 pamphlet, *Proizvoditel'nost' truda na zhel. transporte
SSSR*, p. 47.
  The productivity index is derived from Table 66, using column 4, for 1928–
1940 and column 2 for 1945–1955 figures (the respective 1940 figures are 397.2
and 368.0 thousand cumulated ton-kilometers).  The index of unit labor cost is
the ratio of the wage index the productivity index.

Table 45. Two industrial production indexes and two freight traffic
indexes, USSR, by year, 1928-1940 and 1942-1955, plus 1960 plan
(1928 = 100)

| Year | Hodgman index | Five-carrier ton-kilometers | Official index | Rail tons originated |
|------|------|------|------|------|
| 1928 | 100 | 100 | 100 | 100 |
| 1929 | 120 | 120 | 120 | 120 |
| 1930 | 139 | 145 | 146 | 153 |
| 1931 | 164 | 167 | 176 | 165 |
| 1932 | 172 | 183 | 202 | 171 |
| 1933 | 192 | 189 | 213 | 172 |
| 1934 | 229 | 226 | 254 | 203 |
| 1935 | 295 | 280 | 312 | 249 |
| 1936 | 344 | 342 | 401 | 309 |
| 1937 | 371 | 366 | 446 | 331 |
| 1938 | 388 | 377 | 498 | 330 |
| 1939 | 407 | 393 | 578 | 354 |
| 1940 | 430 | 409 | 646 | 379 |
| 1942 | — | — | 507 | 186 |
| 1943 | — | — | 597 | 200 |
| 1944 | — | — | 672 | 237 |
| 1945 | 263 | 309 | 593 | 253 |
| 1946 | 304 | 332 | 495 | 288 |
| 1947 | 375 | 357 | 603 | 314 |
| 1948 | 464 | 447 | 761 | 397 |
| 1949 | 560 | 523 | 912 | 471 |
| 1950 | 646 | 598 | 1119 | 534 |
| 1951 | 742 | 671 | 1304 | 582 |
| 1952 | 804 | 737 | 1454 | 639 |
| 1953 | 877 | 793 | 1626 | 684 |
| 1954 | 959 | 859 | 1841 | 724 |
| 1955 | — | 976 | 2065 | 811 |
| 1960 (plan) | — | 1516 | 3407 | 1173 |

Sources: The Hodgman index for the output of large-scale industry is from
Hodgman, 1954, pp. 89, 134, plus a 1954 estimate of Abram Bergson in *Foreign
Affairs*, 34:219 (January 1956). The 1938 and 1939 estimates were inserted by
the present writer on the assumption of approximately uniform growth, somewhat
faster in 1940 than in 1938-1939.

The official index for the output of all industry is taken from TsSU, 1956,
pp. 46 and 50, except for 1942-1944. The 1944 index figure is from G. M.
Malenkov's report to the Nineteenth Congress (Malenkov, 1952, p. 53). He gave
a 1943 index figure interpreted here as covering large-scale industry only, on
p. 11 of the same report. Voznesenskii, 1947, p. 46, stated that 1943 output
(again interpreted as being large-scale only) was 17 per cent over 1942. In his
March 1946 report (Voznesenskii, 1946, p. 7), he stated that large-scale industrial output in 1942-1944 totaled 361 billion rubles, and this permitted estimation of 1944 as a residual. With these figures for large-scale industrial output,
converted into "1926-27 rubles," and in the perspective of similar figures for
surrounding years covering both series, plausible additions were made to the
1942 and 1943 figures to obtain estimates for all industry, which were then
chained into the index.

The index for five-carrier ton-kilometers is derived from the final column of
Table 52, and that for rail tons originated is derived from column 3, Table 46.

## APPENDIX B. Freight and Passenger Traffic

This appendix groups together the principal freight and passenger traffic series for the five major carriers of the USSR. The thoroughness of treatment varies considerably, reflecting the importance of the carrier and the availability of data. Since the railroads dominate the scene so conclusively, primary attention is given to them. The figures presented for the other carriers are sufficient to give an accurate indication of their role, but could be substantially extended by anyone wishing to make a specialized study.

For the years since 1945, many references will be made to the reports of the Central Statistical Administration under the USSR Council of Ministers. These have appeared in *Pravda, Izvestiia,* and other major newspapers, and for the sake of brevity a full citation will not be given; instead the annual report for 1954 (for example), which appeared on January 21, 1955, will be referred to as the "1954 CSA report." The full list of references is as follows:

| *CSA Report for—* | *Published on—* |
|---|---|
| 1946 | January 21, 1947 |
| 1948 | January 20, 1948 |
| 1949 | January 18, 1950 |
| 1950 | January 26, 1951 |
| Fourth Five Year Plan results | April 17, 1951 |
| 1951 | January 29, 1952 |
| 1952 | January 23, 1953 |
| 1953 | January 31, 1954 |
| 1954 | January 21, 1955 |
| 1955 | January 30, 1956 |
| Fifth Five Year Plan results | April 25, 1956 |

In addition, draft versions of the Fourth Five Year Plan will be found in *Pravda,* on March 15, 1946; of the Fifth Five Year Plan, on October 12, 1952; and of the Sixth Five Year Plan, on January 15, 1956.

Table 46.  Railroad freight traffic,[a] USSR, by year, 1913–1955, plus 1960 plan

| Year | Metric ton-kilometers[b] ($10^6$) | Average length of haul (km) | Metric tons originated ($10^3$) | Average net load per car (m t) | Average daily[c] carloadings (2-axle units) |
|------|------|------|------|------|------|
| 1913[d] | 65,696 | 496 | 132,400 | 13.24 | 27,400 |
| 1914 | 62,900 | 512 | 122,900 | — | — |
| 1915 | 75,600 | 600 | 126,100 | — | — |
| 1916 | 91,200 | 620 | 147,400 | — | — |
| 1917 | 63,032 | 547 | 115,244 | — | — |
| 1918 | 14,157 | 381 | 37,202 | — | — |
| 1919 | 17,514 | 574 | 30,515 | — | — |
| 1920 | 14,354 | 357 | 40,259 | — | — |
| 1921 | 15,715 | 415 | 37,910 | — | — |
| 1922[e] | 16,065 | 402 | 39,926 | 11.47 | 9,590 |
| 1923[e] | 23,523 | 405 | 58,043 | 13.55 | 11,741 |
| 1924[e] | 33,747 | 500 | 67,489 | 13.68 | 13,517 |
| 1925[e] | 47,438 | 568 | 83,454 | 13.14 | 17,398 |
| 1926[e] | 68,904 | 590 | 116,750 | 13.32 | 24,007 |
| 1927[e] | 81,650 | 601 | 135,934 | 13.36 | 27,868 |
| 1928 | 93,389 | 598 | 156,237 | 13.24 | 32,333 |
| 1929 | 112,950 | 602 | 187,626 | 13.32 | 38,601 |
| 1930 | 133,918 | 561 | 238,732 | 14.11 | 46,335 |
| 1931 | 152,129 | 589 | 258,283 | 14.34 | 49,354 |
| 1932 | 169,270 | 632 | 267,906 | 14.28 | 51,415 |
| 1933 | 169,485 | 632 | 268,075 | 14.34 | 51,224 |
| 1934 | 205,746 | 649 | 317,075 | 15.59 | 55,717 |
| 1935 | 258,066 | 664 | 388,533 | 15.63 | 68,098 |
| 1936 | 323,381 | 669 | 483,179 | 15.36 | 86,160 |
| 1937 | 354,839 | 686 | 517,349 | 15.78 | 89,833 |
| 1938 | 370,500 | 718 | 516,300 | 16.07 | 88,046 |
| 1939 | 392,000 | 708 | 553,600 | 16.24 | 93,374 |
| 1940[f] | 409,000 | 705 | 580,000 | 16.70 | 95,150 |
| 1940[g] | 415,000 | 700 | 592,600 | 16.59 | 97,852 |
| 1941[h] | 460,000 | 693 | 664,000 | 17.01 | 106,958 |
| 1942 | 228,000 | 786 | 290,000 | 18.60 | 42,670 |
| 1943 | 256,000 | 817 | 313,000 | 18.80 | 45,580 |
| 1944 | 297,000 | 801 | 371,000 | 18.30 | 55,510 |
| 1945 | 314,000 | 794 | 395,300 | 17.48 | 61,950 |
| 1946 | 335,100 | 744 | 450,600 | 17.74 | 69,580 |
| 1947 | 350,900 | 715 | 491,100 | 17.64 | 76,260 |
| 1948 | 446,300 | 720 | 619,800 | 18.66 | 90,980 |
| 1949 | 523,500 | 712 | 735,100 | 19.00 | 105,990 |
| 1950 | 602,300 | 722 | 834,300 | 19.32 | 118,300 |
| 1951 | 677,500 | 745 | 909,400 | 19.50 | 127,800 |
| 1952 | 741,800 | 744 | 997,600 | 19.75 | 138,400 |
| 1953 | 798,100 | 747 | 1,068,400 | 19.80 | 147,800 |
| 1954 | 856,800 | 757 | 1,131,400 | 19.82 | 156,400 |
| 1955 | 970,900 | 766 | 1,267,000 | 20.49 | 169,400 |
| 1960 (plan) | 1,374,000 | 750 | 1,832,000 | 22.66 | 221,500 |

[a]All revenue and nonrevenue freight carried in commercial trains, including freight on narrow-gauge lines, but excluding nonrevenue freight carried in work trains.

[b]To convert to short ton–miles, multiply by 0.68494.

cFor the early years, the average daily carloadings series covered freight cars and tank cars in commercial trains, excluding traffic on narrow-gauge lines. The latter is probably now included. Reporting methods were changed in January 1934 in such a way as to reduce the series thereafter by 1–1½ per cent compared to what would have been reported previously (see note in IAkobi, 1935, pp. 114–15).

dAdjusted to exclude traffic carried in the regions later ceded by the new government.

eFor a 12-month period including 3 months of the previous calendar year.

fExcluding traffic in the regions acquired during 1940.

gIncluding traffic for all of 1940 in the regions acquired during 1939, and for approximately July-December 1940 in the regions acquired during 1940.

hFirst half-year only, at annual rates.

## Notes to Table 46

Columns 1, 3, and 5 of Table 46 represent basic data, while columns 2 and 4 are derived from them. Total ton-kilometers divided by total tons originated equals the average length of haul. Total tons originated divided by (365 times average daily carloadings) equals average static net load per car.

The ton-kilometers recorded here are "tariff" ton-kilometers, based on distances for which shippers are charged. A somewhat larger series for "operating" ton-kilometers, 1928–1955, showing actual distances moved as recorded in trip reports, can be derived using column 1 of Table 58.

Sources for Table 46 are as follows:

*1913.* All three figures appear in many sources. Here taken from IAkobi, 1935, pp. 20–21.

*1914–1916.* Soviet railroad statisticians faced the problem of adjusting the records of the Ministry of Means of Communication to exclude operations in the western parts of the Russian empire which were ceded by the new government. This was done very thoroughly for 1913. The records for 1914–1916 probably showed some decline in comprehensiveness and accuracy due to the pressure of war, and in any case were not later subjected to thorough published reworking by the new People's Commissariat of Means of Communication. The figures above for tons originated appear in BSE, 1932, vol. 24, p. 763. They are repeated and extended to estimates of average length of haul and total ton-kilometers in Khachaturov, 1943, p. 6.

*1917–1921.* The government agency responsible for collecting and processing railroad statistics was the People's Commissariat of Means of Communication (hereafter referred to as the NKPS, its Russian initials). It resumed publication quite promptly of the detailed records which had been regularly released by its predecessor, the Ministry of Means of Communication. The early volumes of its *Materialy po statistike zheleznodorozhnogo transporta* were chiefly concerned, however, with the state of railroad motive power and rolling stock, and only scanty freight traffic data for 1917–1920 were published in them. The above figures are taken from TsUNKhU, 1934, p. 258. The figures for calendar 1921 are supported by NKPS *Materialy* ... figures for the economic year, October 1, 1920–September 30, 1921: 14,405 million ton-kilometers, 366 kilometers average length of haul, and 39,372 thousand tons originated (vol. 36, p. 2).

*1922–1933.* The ton-kilometer and tons originated data are conveniently grouped in IAkobi, 1935, pp. 20–21. His 1922–1924 figures coincide with those in the NKPS series, vol. 36, p. 2; his 1925–1927 data agree with those in vol. 115, p. 4.

Notes to Table 46 (*Continued*)

The 1928–1934 figures are supported by enumerations of constituent commodities and regions appearing in many sources.

The average daily carloadings series is here taken from NKPS, *Materialy...*, vol 53, p. 11, for 1922–1925, and vol. 104, p. 11, for 1924–1927. The 1928–1933 figures are here taken from TsUNKhU, 1936b, p. 340.

*1934–1937.* The ton-kilometer and tons originated figures are given by G. Raikher, in *Prob. Ekon.*, 1940, no. 2, p. 89. The average daily carloadings series comes from Kochetov, 1941, p. 61.

*1938–1939.* The ton-kilometer figures are taken from Gorinov, 1948a, vol. 1, p. 30. The tons originated figure for 1938 is from TsUNKhU, 1939, p. 105, and for 1939 from *Gudok*, 4 Aug. '40, p. 2. The average daily carloadings figures are from Kochetov, 1941, p. 60.

*1940.* The smaller of the two ton-kilometer figures was reported by N. A. Voznesenskii in his keynote address of February 18, 1941 (Voznesenskii, 1941, p. 7). The larger began to appear in 1946, and is here taken from an article by I. V. Kochetov in *Zhel. Trans.*, 1946, no. 5/6, p. 65, together with a tons-originated figure of 592.6 million and the associated length-of-haul figure of 700 kilometers. However, IU. I. Koldomasov, a careful writer, presented a 1940 length-of-haul figure of 705 kilometers in a table in *Zhel. Trans.*, 1946, no. 10, p. 39, and it has been repeated elsewhere. It is here assumed that the longer average haul is associated with the smaller volume of traffic, that is, it relates to a total originated tonnage of 580 million. The difference of 12.6 million tons and 6 billion ton-kilometers, with an average length of haul of 476 kilometers, can plausibly be ascribed to six-month's operations in the Baltic republics, the net area ceded by Finland, Bessarabia, and Northern Bukovina. The larger 1940 carloadings figure is taken from Kochetov, 1948, p. 56; the smaller is obtained through applying the frequently cited net load of 16.7 tons to the reduced estimate for tons originated.

*1941, first half year.* Voznesenskii, 1947, p. 15, states that rail freight traffic (*gruzooborot*) reached 90 per cent of the level planned for 1942. This term usually applies to ton-kilometers rather than tons originated. An average length-of-haul figure of 693 kilometers for the first half of 1941 is given by N. G. Bochkarev in Khanukov, 1948, p. 354. These two together yield the tons originated figure. The carloadings figure is from an editorial in *Zhel. Trans.*, 1947, no. 11, p. 8.

*1942–1944.* The ton-kilometer estimates are derived from the statement by N. A. Voznesenskii in his March 15, 1946 speech that the average annual level of rail freight traffic (*gruzooborot*) in 1942–1944 was 3.4 times the corresponding level in Russia during 1915–1917. Multiplying the 1915–1917 estimates above by 3.4 yields a 1942–1944 total of 781 billion ton-kilometers. This was divided among the three years on the basis of two statements: (1) "In the third year of the war, operating ton-kilometers increased 13 per cent over 1942" (*Zhel. Trans.*, 1944, no. 10/11, p. 18), and "Tariff ton-kilometers in 1944 were 116.0 percent of 1943" (Naporko, 1954, p. 200). As explained in the notes to Table 58, "operating" ton-kilometers exceed "tariff" ton-kilometers slightly, and the gap was increasing at this time. Applying a ratio of 104.9/105.2 converts the 1943/1942 rise to an estimated 12.7 per cent for tariff ton-kilometers.

The average daily carloadings series is derived from the following statements: "ADC of all freight increaesed in 1943 by 6.8 per cent over 1942, and in 1944 by 21.8 per cent over 1943" (*Zhel. Trans.*, 1947, no. 11, p. 9) and "ADC in 1945

## Notes to Table 46 (*Continued*)

increased by 11.6 per cent over 1944" (I. V. Kovalev, head of the NKPS, *Gudok* 6 Feb. '46, p. 2). For 1945, see below. The 1942 estimate is consistent with Voznesenskii's remark (1947, p. 102), that ADC in that year was "1/2.3 of its 1940 level," that is, was 42,540 cars per day.

The 1942 average length of haul is given as 86 kilometers over 1940 in Naporko, 1954, p. 192, and this leads to 1942 estimates for tons originated and load per car. The 1944 average load per car was given in *Zhel. Trans.*, 1946, no. 1, p. 68, and in conjuction with the carloadings estimate permitted computation of 1944 tons originated and average haul. Naporko on p. 200 gives 1944 tons originated as 118.3 per cent of 1943; applied to the 1944 estimate, this implies a 1943 figure which in turn leads to estimated 1943 average haul and average load.

Voznesenskii's remark (1947, p. 103) that in 1943 Soviet railroads "shipped" 2.8 times as much freight as the railroads of tsarist Russia had done in 1915, on a network of almost equal length, implies roughly 350 million tons originated in 1943, as compared with the 313 shown above. Such a figure would involve implausibly erratic trends in both average haul and net load per car. If he is interpreted as referring to ton-kilometers, and as meaning 1916 instead of 1915 (the usual Soviet comparison is between 1942–1944 and 1915–1917), then the implied 1943 figure of 255 billion is fully consistent with the 256 shown above.

*1945–1955*. The 1945 ton-kilometer figure was given by Gorinov, 1948a, vol. 1, p. 30, and the 1945 average haul by Povorozhenko, 1951, p. 46, among others. Division produces a tons originated estimate. The 1950, 1954, and 1955 figures for these three measures appear in TsSU, 1956, p. 177. Danilov, 1956, p. 179, gives annual percentage increases in ton-kilometers and tons originated, 1946–1954, and the estimates above are compromises obtained by chaining percentage increases forward and backward from the absolute data. The average hauls result by division. Average daily carloadings in 1945 and 1946 are determinable from the following statements: (1) "ADC at the end of the five-year plan must be 86 per cent above 1945" (Beliunov, 1948, p. 10); (2) "ADC in 1946 increased by 7630 cars over 1945" (Zagliadimov, 1947, p. 21); and (3) "The five-year plan anticipates a growth of 65 per cent in ADC" (*Gudok*, 8 Oct. '48, p. 1). The 1947 estimate is 23 per cent over 1945 (*Gudok*, 14 July '48 p. 3); the 1948 estimate is 19.3 per cent over 1947 (*Gudok*, 21 Jan. '49, p. 2); and the 1949 estimate is 16 per cent over 1948 (*Gudok*, 18 Jan. '50, p. 2). The 1950–1955 estimates are derived from indexes based on 1913, 1940, and 1950 in TsSU, 1956, pp. 28–30. Estimated net loads per car are quotients of tons originated over (365 times average daily carloadings). Comparison of the results with alternative absolute figures and estimates derived from previously reported relationships shows that Soviet records change slightly as revised data replace early reports, and that small uncertainties due to rounding remain. In general, however, the figures above appear to be within plus-or-minus 1 per cent of the underlying Soviet absolute data.

*1960 plan*. The ton-kilometer figure is in the Sixth Five Year Plan. The planned average haul was given by Deputy Minister S. I. Bagaev (*Gudok*, 5 April '56, p. 2) as 21 kilometers below 1955, and until appearance of the TsSU handbook the 1955 average haul was reported as 771 kilometers (for example, CSA report on fifth Five Year Plan fulfillment, *Gudok*, 25 April '56, p. 3). Division leads to the tons originated estimate. The rough estimate for carloadings is derived from the statement that 57 per cent of the growth in carloadings during the Sixth Five Year Plan is to result from reduction in average freight car turn-around time, and the estimated 1960 target for net load per car results by division.

Table 47.  Freight traffic on internal waterways, USSR, by year, 1928–1940 and 1945–1955, plus 1960 plan

| Year | Ton-kilometers ($10^6$) | Annual percentage increase | Average length of haul (km) | Metric tons originated ($10^3$) | Annual percentage increase |
|---|---|---|---|---|---|
| 1928 | 15,902 | — | 868 | 18,333 | — |
| 1929 | 18,429 | 15.9 | 794 | 23,204 | 26.6 |
| 1930 | 22,855 | 24.0 | 625 | 36,595 | 57.7 |
| 1931 | 27,011 | 18.2 | 603 | 44,761 | 22.3 |
| 1932 | 25,106 | −7.1 | 534 | 47,043 | 5.1 |
| 1933 | 25,829 | 2.9 | 578 | 44,717 | −4.9 |
| 1934 | 28,987 | 12.2 | 544 | 53,294 | 19.2 |
| 1935 | 33,932 | 17.1 | 524 | 64,708 | 21.4 |
| 1936 | 31,150 | −8.2 | 446 | 69,912 | 8.0 |
| 1937 | 33,050 | 6.1 | 494 | 66,900 | — |
| 1938 | 32,030 | −3.1 | 481 | 66,580 | −0.5 |
| 1939 | 34,550 | 7.9 | 476 | 72,650 | 9.1 |
| 1940 | 35,900 | 3.9 | 492 | 72,900 | 0.3 |
| 1945 | 18,200 | — | 505 | 36,100 | — |
| 1946 | 20,900 | 14.8 | 537 | 38,900 | 7.8 |
| 1947 | 26,700 | 27.8 | 529 | 50,500 | 29.8 |
| 1948 | 34,200 | 28.1 | 525 | 65,200 | 29.1 |
| 1949 | 39,800 | 16.4 | 504 | 78,900 | 21.0 |
| 1950 | 45,900 | 15.3 | 502 | 91,500 | 16.0 |
| 1951 | 51,600 | 12.4 | 499 | 103,400 | 13.0 |
| 1952 | 57,800 | 12.0 | 504 | 114,700 | 10.9 |
| 1953 | 58,800 | 1.7 | 509 | 115,500 | 0.7 |
| 1954 | 62,400 | 6.1 | 487 | 128,200 | 11.0 |
| 1955 | 67,400 | 8.0 | 485 | 139,100 | 8.5 |
| 1960 (plan) | 121,000 | — | 584 | 207,000 | — |

Notes to Table 47

The data for freight transportation on Soviet internal waterways (rivers and canals), given in Table 47, are complicated by serious coverage problems. For example, until the early 1930's it was usual to include in total traffic some estimate of the volume of timber floated loose or in rafts without being towed. Since then this traffic has been excluded from the records. That the difference is substantial can be seen from the accompanying tabulation, in millions of ton-kilometers.

| Year | Total river traffic | Traffic moved with power | Percentage moved with power |
|---|---|---|---|
| 1929 | 28,172 | 18,429 | 65.4 |
| 1930 | 33,376 | 22,855 | 68.5 |
| 1931 | 38,756 | 27,011 | 69.7 |
| 1932 | 36,127 | 25,106 | 69.5 |

Notes to Table 47 (*Continued*)

Column 1 is from TsUNKhU, 1934, p. 279; column 2 is taken from Table 47.

Even if attention is confined to traffic moved with power, slight differences in coverage for the later years remain. They seem to depend mainly on inclusion or exclusion of traffic administered by organizations outside the People's Commissariat of Water Transport (divided in 1939 into River Fleet and Maritime Fleet Commissariats, and now renamed Ministries). Their effect is to increase the difficulty of assembling a reliable series of figures with constant coverage, and Table 47 probably contains several figures wide of the facts by perhaps 5 per cent. However, it has not seemed worthwhile to spend the additional time which would be necessary to isolate and explain such relatively small differences in coverage are as involved. A similar compilation (unpublished) was made some years ago by James H. Blackman, and where references to Soviet sources below include the notation "(via JHB)," they indicate observations generously made available to me by him.

The sources for Table 47 are as follows:

*1928.* TsUNKhU, 1936a, p. 443.

*1929–1935.* Narodnyi Kommissariat Vodnogo Transporta, Otdel Statistiki, *Rechnoi Transport v 1935 g.*, 1936, p. 6. These data cover NKVT traffic only. They seem preferable to figures in the *Sots. Stroit.* volumes and elsewhere which coincide in some cases and deviate up or down in others.

*1936.* The tons originated figure is from a statistical supplement in *Plan. Khoz.*, 1937, no. 8, p. 197. A rounded figure of 31.1 billion ton-kilometers is given as part of a 1929–1938 series (coinciding with the NKVT figures through 1935), by N. I. Plotnikov in *Vodnyi Transport*, 1940, no. 9, p. 3. It has been raised to conform with the average haul given for this year as part of a 1935–1939 series by A. Galitskii in *Plan. Khoz.*, 1941, no. 1, p. 45.

*1937.* Plotnikov gives 33.0 and 66.9 for 1937. The former is raised slightly to conform with the average haul. This is consistent with the 33.1 figure given by Vol'fson, 1941, p. 203.

*1938.* Plotnikov gives 32.0 and 66.6. The former is raised slightly and the latter lowered, to fit the length of haul figure. This is consistent with a statement in *Vodnyi Transport*, 1940, no. 1/2 p. 1, giving a preliminary figure for 1939 ton-kilometers of 35,066 million, "9.5 per cent more than 1938."

*1939.* *Vodnyi Transport*, 1940, no. 3, p. 1, gives 35.0 and 72.6. Voznesenskii in his Eighteenth Conference speech used a figure of 34.6, and this figure is repeated by Galitskii in the article cited above, together with a length of haul of 474 kilometers. The latter, in turn, is given by Khachaturov, 1946, p. 239. The two tonnage figures have been adjusted to come as close as possible to the stated average haul.

*1940.* Z. A. Shashkov, head of the River Fleet since 1939, gives data on pages 18–19 of his 1947 book which indicate figures of around 35.8 and 72.8, with a stated average length of haul of 491 kilometers, and these three figures are given in Gorinov, 1948b, p. 6. A length of haul figure of 492 appears on p. 42 of A. Zelenovskii's article in the pamphlet, *O Piatiletnem Plane ... 1946–1950 gg.* (no author or date). The figures have been adjusted to conform as closely as possible to each other. Kochetov, 1948, p. 20, gives larger figures of 35.9 and 73.7 with a stated average haul of 488 kilometers; the haul is given also by Beliunov, 1948, p. 71. The tons originated figure might include traffic on territory acquired in 1940, though it does not appear to have been added to

Notes to Table 47 (*Continued*)

ton-kilometers. The 1956 statistical handbook gives 35.9 and 72.9 as total 1940 river traffic, including 35.8 and 72.3 carried by the River Fleet Commissariat itself.

*1945–1955.* Postwar observations by Minister Shashkov, or in the journal *Rechnoi Transport,* seem to refer to ministry traffic only, while the Central Statistical Administration in its annual reports and 1956 handbook adds a small amount of short-haul traffic by other organizations. The 1945 and 1946 estimates above probably cover ministry traffic only, but the 1947–1955 series is derived from CSA data and appears to have the larger coverage. For benchmarks we have absolute 1950, 1954, and 1955 data from TsSU, 1956, p. 181. The 1945 ton-kilometer figure is derived from Shashkov, 1947, p. 19, and the tons originated figure is from *Trud,* 6 March '46 (via JHB). Ton-kilometers in 1946 were given as 58.2 per cent of 1940 in *Rechnoi Transport,* 1947, no. 5, p. 1 (via JHB), and Shashkov, 1947, p. 138, gave 1946 tons originated as 2,760,000 over 1945.

The crude estimates for 1947, 1948, and 1949 are derived by working back from 1950 tons originated by applying CSA-reported annual percentage increases during 1948–1950, and then multiplying by interpolated average haul estimates to obtain ton-kilometer figures. The estimates for 1951–1953 are derived through applying CSA annual percentage increases where available, plus an interpolated average haul for 1952 and a *Rechnoi Transport* statement (1953, no. 2, p. 3) that 1952 traffic (*gruzooborot*) was 26 per cent above 1950.

*1960 plan.* The Sixth Five Year Plan calls for river ton-kilometers "about 80 per cent above 1955," and the ministry's length-of-haul target is a rise from 515 kilometers in 1955 to 620 kilometers in 1960 (*Rechnoi Transport,* 1956, no. 4, p. 5). Assuming a proportionate increase in the planned haul for all river traffic leads to the tons originated estimate shown above.

Table 48. Maritime freight traffic, USSR, by year, 1928–1940
and 1945–1955, plus 1960 plan

| Year | Ton-kilometers ($10^6$) | Annual percentage increase | Average length of haul (km) | Metric tons originated ($10^3$) | Annual percentage increase |
|---|---|---|---|---|---|
| 1928 | 9,100 | — | 1,152 | 7,900 | — |
| 1929 | 10,400 | 14.3 | 1,143 | 9,100 | 15.2 |
| 1930 | 13,200 | 26.9 | 1,065 | 12,400 | 36.3 |
| 1931 | 16,000 | 21.2 | 1,067 | 15,000 | 21.0 |
| 1932 | 20,100 | 25.6 | 1,331 | 15,100 | 0.7 |
| 1933 | 24,400 | 21.4 | 1,506 | 16,200 | 7.3 |
| 1934 | 27,600 | 13.1 | 1,221 | 22,600 | 39.5 |
| 1935 | 34,100 | 23.6 | 1,307 | 26,100 | 15.5 |
| 1936 | 41,100 | 20.5 | 1,343 | 30,600 | 17.2 |
| 1937 | 36,400 | −11.4 | 1,238 | 29,400 | −3.9 |
| 1938 | 33,900 | −6.9 | 1,119 | 30,300 | 3.1 |
| 1940 | 23,800 | — | 763 | 31,200 | — |
| 1945 | 28,700 | — | 1,635 | 17,600 | — |
| 1946 | 28,400 | −1.0 | 1,428 | 19,900 | 13.1 |
| 1947 | 32,700 | 15.1 | 1,351 | 24,200 | 21.6 |
| 1948 | 34,800 | 6.4 | 1,293 | 26,900 | 11.2 |
| 1949 | 38,200 | 9.8 | 1,235 | 30,900 | 14.9 |
| 1950 | 39,700 | 3.9 | 1,178 | 33,700 | 9.1 |
| 1951 | 40,400 | 1.8 | 1,110 | 36,400 | 8.0 |
| 1952 | 44,000 | 8.9 | 1,058 | 41,600 | 14.3 |
| 1953 | 48,000 | 9.1 | 1,048 | 45,800 | 10.1 |
| 1954 | 56,600 | 17.9 | 1,167 | 48,500 | 5.9 |
| 1955 | 68,900 | 21.7 | 1,283 | 53,700 | 10.7 |
| 1960 (plan) | 144,000 | — | 1,752 | 82,200 | — |

## Notes to Table 48

Table 48 covers all maritime freight traffic, both "domestic" (tonnage originating and terminating at Soviet ports) and "overseas" (originating or terminating at non-Soviet ports). The sources for Table 48 are as follows:

*1928.* Compiled from Soviet sources by J. H. Blackman and taken from an unpublished paper of his.

*1929–1938.* Series given by N. I. Plotnikov in *Vodnyi Transport*, 1940, no. 9, p. 3.

*1940.* TsSU, 1956, p. 181.

*1945.* According to Povorozhenko, 1947, p. 66, maritime traffic made up 7.9 per cent of a ton-kilometer total in which the railroads accounted for 86.4 per cent. Average haul from A. Zelenovskii, 1946, p. 42. Tons originated obtained by division.

*1946.* Povorozhenko, 1951, p. 42, gives 7.2 per cent as maritime traffic's share of a total in which railroad traffic made up 84.9 per cent. Average haul from Koldomasov, 1949, p. 24. Tons originated obtained by division.

*1947–1955.* Absolute data for 1950, 1954, and 1955 appear in TsSU, 1956, p. 181. Annual percentage increases in ton-kilometers during 1947, 1952, 1953, and 1954, were reported in CSA annual reports; similarly, 1948–1951 and 1953–1954 annual rises in tons originated are stated in these reports. These percentages were chained onto the benchmark data to obtain the estimates above,

Notes to Table 48 (*Continued*)

except that for 1948 and 1949 average hauls had to be interpolated between the 1947 and 1950 figures to permit estimation of ton-kilometers for 1948 and 1949.

*1960 plan.* The ton-kilometer target is given as almost 2.1 times 1955 and 6 times 1940 by V. Bakaev, Minister of the Sea Fleet, in *Morskoi Transport*, 1956, no. 3, p. 3; he also states the tons originated target as 53 per cent over 1955. The average haul results by division; its increase over 1955 is consistent with his prediction that intersea traffic (grand cabotage) will triple and that foreign trips will increase 70 per cent.

Coverage problems in compiling a record of Soviet maritime freight traffic are more serious than those for freight traffic on internal waterways. There are three classes of traffic and several organizations involved, so that we are frequently in great doubt about the precise meaning of a statistical fragment. If the relative positions of the traffic categories and the carrying organizations had shown general stability, one could with some confidence extend available fragments to fill the gaps in the evidence. Unfortunately, however, there have been abrupt and substantial changes during the 1928–1950 period, a fact which requires us to minimize the extrapolation or transfer of relationships among the variables.

Table 48 owes much to the pioneer research of J. H. Blackman, whose work in compiling a time series for aggregate freight traffic led him to collect maritime traffic data. The desirable coverage for his study, as for the present one, is one which takes account of all freight traffic carried between points in the USSR, that is, all "domestic" traffic, but which excludes all traffic originating or terminating abroad. It should include any domestic traffic carried in foreign ships and exclude any freight carried between non-Soviet ports in Soviet ships, if what we are interested in is the contribution of maritime carriers to the transportation activities of the Soviet economy. There is no evidence that Soviet ships carried any appreciable amount of traffic between foreign ports in the period 1928–1950. On the other hand, a considerable volume of freight traffic has been carried by non-Soviet ships between Soviet ports in some of the years here under review.

Data for the years through 1935 are available in considerable detail from the records of the People's Commissariat of Water Transportation. However, their records fail to include a small volume of traffic carried by ships under other Soviet organizations, and their information with respect to the operations of non-Soviet vessels seems quite incomplete. After the mid-1930's detailed information grows thinner, and especially in the postwar period the references become vague indeed. Juxtaposition of fragments makes it seem highly probable that the series about which most Soviet comments have come to be made is not the "domestic" traffic series, but the "all traffic" series. In other words, the figures stated or implied in recent years appear to include freight originating or terminating abroad along with purely internal traffic.

Table 48 covers "all traffic," even though it would be preferable to exclude shipments originating or terminating abroad. It probably does not cover the freight carried in non-Soviet ships, though ideally their operations between Soviet ports should be included. The reasons for compiling and presenting the series in this form are as follows: it offers the least danger of changes in comparability over the period, since it appears to be the one about which the most direct information is given; and isolation of the domestic component in the gross total requires more information than has yet been made available on the extent of changes in the relative position of the three traffic classes. The volume of "overseas" traffic depends on the scale of Soviet foreign trade, and this obviously has shown wide variation over the last two decades.

Table 49. Domestic and foreign maritime freight traffic, USSR, by year, 1928–1940 and 1945–1951 (millions of metric ton–kilometers)

| Year | Domestic traffic | | | Foreign traffic | Total |
|------|---------|----------|----------|---------|-------|
|      | Intrasea | Intersea | Combined | | |
| 1928 | —      | —      | 5,000  | 4,100  | 9,100  |
| 1929 | 4,500  | 1,400  | 5,900  | 4,500  | 10,400 |
| 1930 | —      | —      | 8,300  | 4,900  | 13,200 |
| 1931 | —      | —      | 10,200 | 5,800  | 16,000 |
| 1932 | 8,400  | 5,400  | 13,800 | 6,300  | 20,100 |
| 1933 | 9,450  | 6,650  | 16,100 | 8,300  | 24,400 |
| 1934 | 13,400 | 2,500  | 15,900 | 11,700 | 27,600 |
| 1935 | 13,600 | 1,500  | 15,100 | 19,000 | 34,100 |
| 1936 | 15,200 | 1,500  | 16,700 | 24,400 | 41,100 |
| 1937 | 16,000 | 1,500  | 17,500 | 19,400 | 36,400 |
| 1938 | 17,540 | 3,100  | 20,640 | 13,260 | 33,900 |
| 1939 | 18,350 | 4,150  | 22,500 | 6,000  | 28,500 |
| 1940 | 20,190 | 1,380  | 21,570 | 1,550  | 23,120 |
| 1945 | —      | —      | 13,000 | 15,700 | 28,700 |
| 1946 | —      | —      | 17,000 | 11,600 | 28,600 |
| 1947 | —      | —      | 19,000 | 13,900 | 32,900 |
| 1948 | —      | —      | 21,000 | 13,500 | 34,500 |
| 1949 | —      | —      | 25,000 | 12,300 | 37,300 |
| 1950 | —      | —      | 27,000 | 11,100 | 38,100 |
| 1951 | —      | —      | 29,000 | 11,300 | 40,300 |

Notes to Table 49

The difference between "all" maritime traffic and "domestic" traffic as estimated by Blackman is shown in Table 49. Sources for this table are as follows:

The "total" figures are transcribed from Table 48. The "combined domestic" series is taken from p. 6 of Blackman's "Transportation Appendices," the separately reproduced, September 1953 appendix to Chapter IV of Bergson, ed., *Soviet Economic Growth, 1953*. The estimates for "foreign" traffic are residuals obtained by subtraction.

The division of domestic traffic between "intrasea" (petty cabotage) and "intersea" (grand cabotage) movements is estimated for 1929 and 1932–1935 through converting the ton-miles data in TsUNKhU, 1936a, p. 480, to ton-kilometers and expanding them by about 15 per cent to correspond to Blackman's fuller coverage. The estimated division for 1936–1940 is carried through as follows:

Vol'fson, 1941, p. 211, gives 1937 intrasea as 16.0; Khachaturov, *Osnovy*, 1946, p. 300, gives it as 17. It is here assumed that Khachaturov was in fact

Notes to Table 49 (*Continued*)

giving combined traffic, and his figure is rounded up to make room for intersea traffic. His 1939 figure of 23 is similarly interpreted but rounded down.

The 1940 combined and total figures are adjusted to fit rounded data given by Kochetov, 1948, p. 20, and Gorinov, 1948b, p. 6, together with Koldomasov's remark (1949, p. 44) that intrasea was 93 per cent of 1940 total ton-miles. However, following Blackman, the smaller figure is taken to cover combined traffic rather than intrasea alone.

For intrasea traffic, a statement in *Morskoi Flot*, 1955, no. 2, p. 1, that the 1954 level was 2.7 times the prewar level, was used to get from 54.5 for 1954 to 20.19 for 1940. The remark will not fit the larger 1940 figures.

A. Galitskii, in *Plan. Khoz.*, 1941, no. 4, p. 30, stated that intrasea shipments in 1940 were 10 per cent larger than in 1939, and this was applied to the 1940 ton-kilometers estimate. G. M. Malenkov, in his Feb. 15, 1941 report(Malenkov, 1941, p. 5) stated that 1940 intrasea traffic was 15.1 per cent above 1938; this also was applied to the 1940 ton-kilometers estimate.

The 1939 intersea traffic figure is obtained by subtraction, and the 1938 figure is interpolated between 1937 and 1939. The 1938 combined traffic is then obtained by addition. The 1939 total traffic is interpolated between 1938 and 1940, yielding 1939 foreign traffic by subtraction.

Table 50.  Automotive freight traffic, USSR, by year, 1928–1940
and 1945–1955, plus 1960 plan

| Year | Ton-kilometers ($10^6$) | Annual percentage increase | Average length of haul (km) | Metric tons originated ($10^3$) | Annual percentage increase |
|---|---|---|---|---|---|
| 1928 | 147 | — | — | — | — |
| 1929 | 380 | 157.0 | — | — | — |
| 1930 | 610 | 61.1 | — | — | — |
| 1931 | 840 | 37.9 | — | — | — |
| 1932 | 1,070 | 27.5 | 9.5 | 113 | — |
| 1933 | 1,800 | 68.1 | 9.8 | 183 | 62.0 |
| 1934 | 3,500 | 94.5 | 0.0 | 350 | 91.3 |
| 1935 | 5,500 | 57.2 | 12.5 | 440 | 25.7 |
| 1936 | 8,400 | 52.7 | 10.5 | 800 | 81.8 |
| 1937 | 8,700 | 3.6 | 10.9 | 800 | 0 |
| 1938 | 8,770 | 1.0 | — | — | — |
| 1939 | 8,840 | 0.8 | — | — | — |
| 1940 | 8,920 | 0.9 | 10.4 | 858 | — |
| 1945 | 4,400 | — | 13.4 | 328 | — |
| 1946 | 7,500 | 70 | 12.0 | 625 | 91 |
| 1947 | 10,800 | 44 | — | — | — |
| 1948 | 13,300 | 23 | — | — | — |
| 1949 | 17,000 | 28 | — | — | — |
| 1950 | 20,100 | 18 | 10.8 | 1,859 | — |
| 1951 | 24,100 | 20 | — | — | — |
| 1952 | 27,700 | 15 | — | — | — |
| 1953 | 31,400 | 13 | — | — | — |
| 1954 | 37,500 | 19 | 11.3 | 3,306 | — |
| 1955 | 42,500 | 13 | 11.4 | 3,730 | 13 |
| 1960 (plan) | 85,000 | — | — | — | — |

### Notes to Table 50

The sources for Table 50 are as follows:

*1928–1939.* Compiled from Soviet sources by J. H. Blackman and presented in rounded form in his 1953 appendix, p. 6.

*1940.* Gorinov, 1948b, p. 6.

*1945.* Povorozhenko, 1947, p. 66, gives this as 1.2 per cent of a total in which the railroads accounted for 86.4 per cent.  The average haul is from Zelenovskii, 1946, p. 42, and the tons originated figure results by division.

*1946.* Koldomasov, 1949, p. 24, gives this as 1.9 per cent of a total in which the railroads account for 84.9 per cent, and gives the average haul on the same page.  Tons originated result by division.

*1947–1955.* TsSU, 1956, p. 183, gives absolute data for 1950, 1954, and 1955, to which annual percentage increases reported for 1948–1953 in CSA reports have been chained on.  The 1950 ton-kilometer target is stated in the Sixth Five Year Plan as "twice 1955."  A distinction should be noted between the truck traffic handled by the USSR Ministry of Auto Transport and Paved Roads, which became a Union-Republic Ministry in September 1953, and the traffic carried by the trucks of various other organizations.  The former is perhaps roughly comparable to "for hire" or "common carrier" traffic in the United States, and has only recently attained any prominence.  The average length of haul makes it clear that there is as yet no appreciable volume of intercity traffic comparable to what is recorded in the United States.  Division

Notes to Table 50 (*Continued*)

of truck traffic between common carrier and "other" in recent years is shown in the accompanying tabulation, in billions of metric ton-kilometers.

| Year | Common-carrier | Other | Total |
|------|---------------|-------|-------|
| 1940 | 0.3 | 8.6 | 8.9 |
| 1950 | 0.9 | 19.2 | 20.1 |
| 1951 | 1.0 | 23.1 | 24.1 |
| 1952 | 1.1 | 26.6 | 27.7 |
| 1953 | 2.5 | 28.9 | 31.4 |
| 1954 | 4.2 | 33.3 | 37.5 |
| 1955 | 9.3 | 33.2 | 42.5 |
| 1960 (plan) | 40.0 | 45.0 | 85.0 |

The common-carrier data are from TsSU for 1940, 1950, and 1954–1955, plus other clues for 1951–1953 and the Sixth Five Year Plan for 1960.

Table 51.  Pipeline traffic, USSR, by year, 1928–1940 and 1945–1955, plus 1960 plan (millions of metric ton-kilometers)

| Year | Traffic | Year | Traffic |
|------|---------|------|---------|
| 1928 | 680 | 1945 | 3,200 |
| 1929 | 1,130 | 1946 | 3,600 |
| 1930 | 2,230 | 1947 | 3,900 |
| 1931 | 2,620 | 1948 | 4,200 |
| 1932 | 2,860 | 1949 | 4,600 |
| 1933 | 3,380 | 1950 | 5,000 |
| 1934 | 3,500 | 1951 | 6,100 |
| 1935 | 2,540 | 1952 | 7,300 |
| 1936 | 3,550 | 1953 | 8,700 |
| 1937 | 3,650 | 1954 | 10,300 |
| 1938 | 3,750 | 1955 | 14,000 |
| 1939 | 3,750 | 1960 (plan) | 83,000 |
| 1940 | 3,850 | | |

Notes to Table 51

Sources for Table 51 are as follows:

*1928–1934.* Estimated from Soviet sources by J. H. Blackman; in rounded form the series appears in his 1953 appendix, p. 6.

*1935–1936.* Derived through applying average hauls of 516 and 500 kilometers to the tons originated figures of 4.8 and 6.9 million, respectively, given by N. Nekrasov, *Plan. Khoz.*, 1938, no. 1, p. 53.

*1937–1940, 1945–1955.* TsSU, 1956, pp. 173 and 176 gives indexes for pipeline ton-kilometers which, when applied to the 1960 target of 83 billion stated in the Sixth Five Year Plan, yield the estimates above for 1940, 1950, 1954, and 1955. The 1946 estimate is derived as 0.9 per cent of a total in which railroad traffic was 84.9 per cent (Povorozhenko, 1951, p. 42). Estimates for 1937–1939, 1945, 1947–1949, and 1951–1953 are inserted in proportion to changes in crude oil production, as given in TsSU, 1956, p. 69.

Table 52. Freight traffic carried by five major carriers, USSR,
1928-1940 and 1945-1955, plus 1960 plan (millions of metric ton-kilometers)

| Year | Railroad | River | Sea | Auto | Pipeline | Total |
|------|----------|-------|-----|------|----------|-------|
| 1928 | 93,380 | 15,902 | 9,100 | 147 | 680 | 119,209 |
| 1929 | 112,950 | 18,429 | 10,400 | 380 | 1,130 | 143,289 |
| 1930 | 133,918 | 22,855 | 13,200 | 610 | 2,230 | 172,813 |
| 1931 | 152,129 | 27,011 | 16,000 | 840 | 2,620 | 198,600 |
| 1932 | 169,270 | 25,106 | 20,100 | 1,070 | 2,860 | 218,406 |
| Total | 661,647 | 109,303 | 68,800 | 3,047 | 9,520 | 852,317 |
| Percentage | 77.6 | 12.8 | 8.1 | 0.4 | 1.1 | — |
| 1933 | 169,485 | 25,829 | 24,400 | 1,800 | 3,380 | 224,894 |
| 1934 | 205,746 | 28,987 | 27,600 | 3,500 | 3,500 | 269,333 |
| 1935 | 258,066 | 33,932 | 34,100 | 5,500 | 2,540 | 334,138 |
| 1936 | 323,381 | 31,150 | 41,100 | 8,400 | 3,550 | 407,581 |
| 1937 | 354,839 | 33,050 | 36,400 | 8,700 | 3,650 | 436,639 |
| Total | 1,311,517 | 152,948 | 163,600 | 27,900 | 16,620 | 1,672,585 |
| Percentage | 78.4 | 9.1 | 9.8 | 1.6 | 0.9 | — |
| 1938 | 370,500 | 32,030 | 33,900 | 8,770 | 3,750 | 448,950 |
| 1939 | 392,000 | 34,550 | 29,800 | 8,840 | 3,750 | 468,940 |
| 1940 | 415,000 | 35,900 | 23,800 | 8,920 | 3,850 | 487,470 |
| Total | 1,177,500 | 102,480 | 87,500 | 26,530 | 11,350 | 1,405,360 |
| Percentage | 83.8 | 7.3 | 6.2 | 1.9 | 0.8 | — |
| 1945 | 314,000 | 18,200 | 28,700 | 4,400 | 3,200 | 368,500 |
| 1946 | 335,100 | 20,900 | 28,400 | 7,500 | 3,600 | 395,500 |
| 1947 | 350,900 | 26,700 | 32,700 | 10,800 | 3,900 | 425,000 |
| 1948 | 446,300 | 34,200 | 34,800 | 13,300 | 4,200 | 532,800 |
| 1949 | 523,500 | 39,800 | 38,200 | 17,000 | 4,600 | 623,100 |
| Total | 1,969,800 | 139,800 | 162,800 | 53,000 | 19,500 | 2,344,900 |
| Percentage | 84.0 | 6.0 | 7.0 | 2.2 | 0.8 | — |
| 1950 | 602,300 | 45,900 | 39,700 | 20,100 | 5,000 | 713,000 |
| 1951 | 677,500 | 51,600 | 40,400 | 24,100 | 6,100 | 799,700 |
| 1952 | 741,800 | 57,800 | 44,000 | 27,700 | 7,300 | 878,600 |
| 1953 | 798,100 | 58,800 | 48,000 | 31,400 | 8,700 | 945,000 |
| 1954 | 856,800 | 62,400 | 56,600 | 37,500 | 0,300 | 1,023,600 |
| Total | 3,676,500 | 276,500 | 228,700 | 140,800 | 7,400 | 4,359,900 |
| Percentage | 84.3 | 6.3 | 5.3 | 3.2 | 0.9 | — |
| 1955 | 970,900 | 67,400 | 68,900 | 42,500 | 14,000 | 1,163,700 |
| Percentage | 83.4 | 5,8 | 5.9 | 3.7 | 1.2 | — |
| 1960 (plan) | 1,374,000 | 121,000 | 144,000 | 85,000 | 83,000 | 1,807,000 |
| Percentage | 76.0 | 6.7 | 8.0 | 4.7 | 4.6 | — |

Table 52 is recapitulated from Tables 46-51. The 1939 sea figure is interpolated to fill out the row.

Table 53.  Railroad freight traffic, USSR, by major commodity group,
1913, 1923–1940, selected years, 1945–1960 plan

| Commodity group | 1913 | 1923 | 1924 | 1925 | 1926 | 1927 |
|---|---|---|---|---|---|---|
| *Millions of metric ton-kilometers* | | | | | | |
| Coal and coke | 12,800 | 3,230 | 6,445 | 8,035 | 13,545 | 17,837 |
| Petroleum | 3,100 | 2,054 | 2,216 | 3,258 | 4,481 | 5,023 |
| Ores | 2,500 | 226 | 404 | 995 | 1,820 | 2,316 |
| Iron and steel | — | 228 | 528 | 2,036 | 3,002 | 3,681 |
| Mineral building materials | — | — | — | — | — | — |
| Timber | 5,100 | 2,476 | 3,374 | 5,133 | 8,414 | 9,365 |
| Grain | 10,000 | 5,488 | 7,909 | 9,366 | 12,066 | 15,279 |
| Firewood | 1,700 | 2,527 | 2,620 | 2,195 | 3,076 | 3,754 |
| Other freight | — | — | — | — | — | — |
| Total | 65,696 | 23,523 | 33,747 | 47,438 | 68,904 | 81,650 |
| *Thousands of metric tons originated* | | | | | | |
| Coal and coke | 26,339 | 8,004 | 12,258 | 14,552 | 21,957 | 27,029 |
| Petroleum | 5,799 | 3,336 | 3,463 | 5,012 | 5,621 | 6,490 |
| Ores | 8,927 | 815 | 1,506 | 2,935 | 4,753 | 5,887 |
| Iron and steel | 4,567 | 479 | 822 | 2,696 | 3,968 | 4,718 |
| Mineral building materials | — | — | — | — | — | — |
| Timber | 12,170 | 5,822 | 7,190 | 9,742 | 12,930 | 15,077 |
| Grain | 18,264 | 8,914 | 10,721 | 10,597 | 14,181 | 15,479 |
| Firewood | 8,583 | 14,846 | 12,446 | 9,553 | 12,303 | 14,987 |
| Other freight | — | — | — | — | — | — |
| Total | 132,400 | 58,043 | 67,487 | 83,454 | 116,750 | 135,934 |
| *Average length of haul (kilometers)* | | | | | | |
| Coal and coke | 485 | 403 | 526 | 552 | 617 | 660 |
| Petroleum | 601 | 617 | 640 | 650 | 797 | 774 |
| Ores | 278 | 278 | 269 | 339 | 383 | 393 |
| Iron and steel | — | 469 | 642 | 755 | 756 | 780 |
| Mineral building materials | — | — | — | — | — | — |
| Timber | 415 | 425 | 469 | 527 | 651 | 621 |
| Grain | 547 | 615 | 738 | 884 | 851 | 987 |
| Firewood | 197 | 170 | 210 | 230 | 250 | 250 |
| Other freight | — | — | — | — | — | — |
| All freight | 496 | 407 | 500 | 568 | 590 | 601 |

| Commodity group | 1928 | 1929 | 1930 | 1931 | 1932 |
|---|---|---|---|---|---|
| *Millions of metric ton-kilometers* | | | | | |
| Coal and coke | 18,676 | 21,538 | 25,393 | 30,951 | 37,512 |
| Petroleum | 6,348 | 7,779 | 10,445 | 13,003 | 15,143 |
| Ores | 2,782 | 3,472 | 3,909 | 5,019 | 6,713 |
| Iron and steel | 4,479 | 5,327 | 6,675 | 6,779 | 9,792 |
| Mineral building materials | 3,753 | 4,603 | 7,011 | 8,700 | 8,685 |
| Timber | 11,673 | 15,384 | 20,335 | 20,128 | 22,075 |
| Grain | 14,738 | 16,173 | 14,615 | 16,247 | 17,684 |
| Firewood | 3,436 | 3,576 | 3,826 | 3,328 | 3,514 |
| Other freight | 27,504 | 35,098 | 41,709 | 47,947 | 48,152 |
| Total | 93,389 | 112,950 | 133,918 | 152,129 | 169,270 |
| *Thousands of metric tons originated* | | | | | |
| Coal and coke | 30,358 | 35,125 | 41,380 | 47,837 | 56,691 |
| Petroleum | 8,719 | 10,216 | 13,197 | 15,761 | 17,004 |

Table 53  (*Continued*)

| Commodity group | 1928 | 1929 | 1930 | 1931 | 1932 |
|---|---|---|---|---|---|
| *Thousands of metric tons originated (Continued)* | | | | | |
| Ores | 7,018 | 8,969 | 9,869 | 10,887 | 12,725 |
| Iron and steel | 5,692 | 6,876 | 8,258 | 8,614 | 10,710 |
| Mineral building materials | 13,728 | 17,382 | 25,693 | 27,019 | 24,678 |
| Timber | 17,392 | 22,246 | 30,922 | 30,683 | 32,394 |
| Grain | 15,523 | 19,178 | 24,326 | 25,708 | 23,767 |
| Firewood | 12,748 | 12,978 | 15,126 | 13,750 | 13,880 |
| Other freight | 45,059 | 54,656 | 69,961 | 78,024 | 76,057 |
| Total | 156,237 | 187,626 | 238,732 | 258,283 | 267,906 |
| *Average length of haul (kilometers)* | | | | | |
| Coal and coke | 615 | 613 | 614 | 647 | 662 |
| Petroleum | 728 | 761 | 792 | 825 | 891 |
| Ores | 397 | 387 | 396 | 461 | 528 |
| Iron and steel | 786 | 775 | 808 | 787 | 914 |
| Mineral buildings materials | 273 | 265 | 273 | 322 | 352 |
| Timber | 671 | 692 | 658 | 656 | 681 |
| Grain | 949 | 843 | 601 | 632 | 744 |
| Firewood | 269 | 276 | 253 | 242 | 253 |
| Other freight | 610 | 642 | 596 | 615 | 633 |
| All freight | 598 | 612 | 561 | 589 | 632 |

| Commodity group | 1933 | 1934 | 1935 | 1936 | 1937 |
|---|---|---|---|---|---|
| *Millions of metric ton–kilometers* | | | | | |
| Coal and coke | 44,501 | 53,870 | 60,979 | 76,715 | 82,650 |
| Petroleum | 15,856 | 19,419 | 22,823 | 28,200 | 30,370 |
| Ores | 8,474 | 10,782 | 15,996 | 17,880 | 19,290 |
| Iron and steel | 9,700 | 13,542 | 18,743 | 25,200 | 26,320 |
| Mineral building materials | 6,042 | 7,910 | 11,202 | 13,450 | 15,770 |
| Timber | 19,705 | 24,099 | 33,842 | 40,100 | 43,670 |
| Grain | 17,744 | 17,481 | 20,634 | 23,100 | 26,800 |
| Firewood | 3,319 | 3,772 | 4,659 | 4,670 | 5,040 |
| Other freight | 44,144 | 54,901 | 69,188 | 94,066 | 104,929 |
| Total | 169,485 | 205,746 | 258,066 | 323,381 | 354,839 |
| *Thousands of metric tons originated* ' | | | | | |
| Coal and coke | 66,556 | 81,881 | 94,679 | 113,990 | 116,571 |
| Petroleum | 16,539 | 20,338 | 22,385 | 26,000 | 24,730 |
| Ores | 15,611 | 20,007 | 25,972 | 29,170 | 30,481 |
| Iron and steel | 11,023 | 14,020 | 19,118 | 25,500 | 26,215 |
| Mineral building materials | 18,582 | 20,713 | 29,402 | 35,400 | 41,500 |
| Timber | 28,632 | 32,431 | 42,196 | 47,800 | 46,859 |
| Grain | 26,673 | 25,718 | 30,024 | 33,550 | 38,900 |
| Firewood | 14,048 | 15,403 | 18,251 | 17,900 | 19,328 |
| Other freight | 70,411 | 86,564 | 106,507 | 153,869 | 172,765 |
| Total | 268,075 | 317,075 | 388,533 | 483,179 | 517,349 |
| *Average length of haul (kilometers)* | | | | | |
| Coal and coke | 669 | 658 | 644 | 673 | 709 |
| Petroleum | 959 | 955 | 1,020 | 1,086 | 1,228 |
| Ores | 543 | 539 | 616 | 613 | 633 |
| Iron and steel | 880 | 963 | 980 | 989 | 1,004 |

Table 53 (*Continued*)

| Commodity group | 1933 | 1934 | 1935 | 1936 | 1937 |
|---|---|---|---|---|---|
| *Average length of haul (kilometers) (Continued)* | | | | | |
| Mineral building materials | 325 | 382 | 381 | 380 | 380 |
| Timber | 743 | 802 | 839 | 932 | 1,078 |
| Grain | 665 | 680 | 687 | 688 | 689 |
| Firewood | 236 | 245 | 255 | 261 | 261 |
| Other freight | 627 | 634 | 650 | 611 | 607 |
| All freight | 632 | 649 | 664 | 668 | 686 |

| Commodity group | 1938 | 1939 | 1940 | 1945 | 1947 | 1949 |
|---|---|---|---|---|---|---|
| *Millions of metric ton-kilometers* | | | | | | |
| Coal and coke | 84,300 | 90,200 | 106,800 | 98,700 | 124,500 | 161,300 |
| Petroleum | 35,800 | 34,100 | 36,900 | 23,800 | 28,000 | 43,100 |
| Ores | 17,400 | 17,600 | 19,700 | 12,500 | 16,500 | 24,800 |
| Iron and steel | 26,300 | 27,000 | 26,200 | 23,900 | 25,900 | 42,300 |
| Mineral building materials | 29,300 | 31,000 | 28,200 | 9,600 | 17,600 | 37,200 |
| Timber | 46,700 | 47,400 | 43,600 | 20,700 | 33,300 | 59,500 |
| Grain | 30,900 | 33,700 | 32,800 | 23,300 | 20,300 | 29,800 |
| Firewood | 5,400 | 5,100 | 5,800 | 2,700 | 3,700 | 4,900 |
| Other freight | 93,800 | 105,900 | 115,400 | 98,800 | 81,100 | 120,600 |
| Total | 370,500 | 392,000 | 415,000 | 314,000 | 350,900 | 523,500 |
| *Thousands of metric tons originated* | | | | | | |
| Coal and coke | 120,800 | 128,800 | 152,500 | 142,300 | 183,300 | 241,800 |
| Petroleum | 28,400 | 29,000 | 29,500 | 21,300 | 26,100 | 36,800 |
| Ores | 28,900 | 30,700 | 35,200 | 17,800 | 25,500 | 40,400 |
| Iron and steel | 25,800 | 26,600 | 27,100 | 21,300 | 23,100 | 38,200 |
| Mineral building materials | 93,500 | 106,100 | 111,700 | 41,900 | 75,000 | 135,300 |
| Timber | 43,400 | 46,000 | 42,800 | 26,500 | 38,400 | 63,200 |
| Grain | 40,300 | 44,100 | 44,600 | 20,200 | 25,500 | 34,600 |
| Firewood | 20,300 | 19,900 | 23,100 | 17,400 | 18,500 | 21,300 |
| Other freight | 115,100 | 122,400 | 126,100 | 86,600 | 75,700 | 123,500 |
| Total | 516,300 | 553,600 | 592,600 | 395,300 | 491,100 | 735,100 |
| *Average length of haul (kilometers)* | | | | | | |
| Coal and coke | 698 | 700 | 701 | 693 | 679 | 667 |
| Petroleum | 1,260 | 1,178 | 1,234 | 1,115 | 1,074 | 1,172 |
| Ores | 602 | 574 | 612 | 702 | 647 | 614 |
| Iron and steel | 1,019 | 1,016 | 966 | 1,124 | 1,120 | 1,107 |
| Mineral building materials | 320 | 292 | 253 | 228 | 235 | 275 |
| Timber | 1,078 | 1,031 | 1,019 | 780 | 866 | 941 |
| Grain | 768 | 764 | 736 | 1,153 | 798 | 863 |
| Firewood | 266 | 256 | 252 | 157 | 201 | 229 |
| Other freight | 815 | 867 | 917 | 1,140 | 1,071 | 977 |
| All freight | 718 | 708 | 700 | 794 | 715 | 712 |

| Commodity group | 1950 | 1954 | 1955 | 1960 (plan) |
|---|---|---|---|---|
| *Millions of metric ton-kilometers* | | | | |
| Coal and coke | 178,200 | 234,700 | 266,700 | 361,000 |
| Petroleum | 52,000 | 84,500 | 101,600 | 147,000 |
| Ores | 27,800 | 40,500 | 40,500 | 67,000 |
| Iron and steel | 47,500 | 69,700 | 69,700 | 100,000 |
| Mineral building materials | 46,700 | 68,400 | 82,100 | 119,000 |

Table 53  (*Continued*)

| Commodity group | 1950 | 1954 | 1955 | 1960 (plan) |
|---|---|---|---|---|
| *Millions of metric ton–kilometers (Continued)* | | | | |
| Timber | 72,200 | 100,100 | 119,900 | 161,000 |
| Grain | 30,900 | 53,100 | 55,100 | 79,000 |
| Firewood | 4,500 | 4,600 | 5,200 | — |
| Other freight | 142,500 | 201,200 | 220,200 | 340,000[a] |
| Total | 602,300 | 856,800 | 970,900 | 1,374,000 |
| *Thousands of metric tons originated* | | | | |
| Coal and coke | 266,100 | 349,300 | 389,000 | 570,000 |
| Petroleum | 43,200 | 69,900 | 77,600 | 135,000 |
| Ores | 48,400 | 75,300 | 83,400 | 136,000 |
| Iron and steel | 43,300 | 64,600 | 71,800 | 97,000 |
| Mineral building materials | 157,500 | 209,800 | 245,600 | 350,000 |
| Timber | 72,400 | 84,300 | 94,100 | 124,000 |
| Grain | 38,800 | 53,200 | 58,000 | 78,000 |
| Firewood | 18,900 | 16,000 | 16,400 | — |
| Other freight | 145,700 | 209,000 | 231,100 | 342,000[a] |
| Total | 834,300 | 1,131,400 | 1,267,000 | 1,832,000 |
| *Average length of haul (kilometers)* | | | | |
| Coal and coke | 670 | 672 | 686 | 633 |
| Petroleum | 1,205 | 1,210 | 1,309 | 1,085 |
| Ores | 574 | 538 | 532 | 490 |
| Iron and steel | 1,095 | 1,078 | 1,055 | 1,035 |
| Mineral building materials | 296 | 326 | 334 | 340 |
| Timber | 998 | 1,187 | 1,274 | 1,300 |
| Grain | 798 | 997 | 950 | 1,010 |
| Firewood | 241 | 290 | 314 | — |
| Other freight | 978 | 963 | 953 | 994[a] |
| All freight | 722 | 757 | 766 | 750 |

[a]Includes firewood.

## Notes to Table 53

The content of each commodity group shown in Table 53 is discussed in Chapter 10. The sources of Table 53 are as follows:

*1913.* The tons originated data are from IAkobi, 1935, pp. 22–25. The ton-kilometers estimates were made by Vol'fson, and are scattered through pages 219–267 of *Ekonomika Transporta* (1941), together with the related average length of haul figures.

*1923–1934.* IAkobi, 1935, pp. 26–27.

*1935.* TsUNKhU, 1936a, pp. 420–22.

*1936.* Vol'fson, 1939, p. 149, gives 1935–1936–1937 tons originated for the eight major groups to the nearest hundred thousand tons; slightly different figures appear in Gosplan, 1937, pp. 122–23, repeated in the journal, *Plan*, 1937, no. 3, p. 41. For all but firewood, percentage increase over 1935 are given by S. Semenov in *Sots. Trans.*, 1937, no. 1, p. 8, and these were used to check on the last significant digit.

Average length of haul figures for coal and coke, and for firewood, in 1935, 1936, and 1937 are given in Kochetov, 1939, p. 23. The figures for mineral build-

Notes to Table 53 (*Continued*)

ing materials ("principal" only) and for grain have been assumed at their 1935 value. The other four average hauls are given by A. Galitskii in *Plan, Khoz.*, 1938, no. 7, pp. 18–24. The ton-kilometer estimates above are the product of tons originated times average haul.

*1937.* Tons originated figures to the nearest thousand tons are given for all but mineral building materials and grain by A. Galitskii in *Plan Khoz.*, 1939, no. 6, p. 108. Vol'fson gives these two, rounded off, plus length of haul and ton-kilometer data for all groups in tables scattered between pages 219 and 267 of *Ekonomika Transporta* (1941). The figure assumed to cover "principal" mineral building materials only is from Khachaturov, 1939, p. 547, and the average length of haul is assumed.

*1938.* A percentage distribution of tons originated was published by a British writer in 1943 (cf. Whitworth, in *Annals of the American Academy of Political and Social Science*, 230:154, Nov. 1943). No primary source was cited, but Mr. Whitworth was described by the editor of the volume as having visited Russia, and it may be that the data were seen by him there. The first six average haul figures are given by S. Kuchurin in *Sots. Trans.*, 1939, no. 6, p. 19, and the last two by A. Golovanov in *Gudok*, 11 Dec. '40, p. 3. Tons originated of firewood were given as 20.3 million in *Gudok*, 16 July '39, p. 2. The ton-kilometer estimates above are the product of tons originated times average haul.

*1939.* A percentage distribution of ton-kilometers for each of the eight groups is given by N. Peskov in *Sots. Trans.*, 1940, no. 6, p. 8. The mineral building materials and firewood average hauls are from Koldomasov, 1949, p. 15. The tons originated estimates result by division. Whitworth, p. 154, gives somewhat different figures for coal, petroleum, ores, and iron and steel, evidently drawn from Kochetov, 1941, p. 495, but it is here felt more reliable to accept the fuller set of data assembled from the writers cited.

*1940.* Absolute data appear in TsSU, 1956, pp. 178–80. There appears to have been a recent small change in the coverage of the ore commodity group, and the ore figures above are derived from Kochetov, 1953, pp. 29 and 31, since they appear more comparable with 1939 and earlier years than the TsSU data.

*1945. Kochetov*, 1953, pp. 29 and 31, gives percentage shares in tons originated, and average hauls, for each commodity group. Applying the percentages to the annual total shown in Table 46 produces absolute tons originated estimates, and multiplication by average hauls leads to ton-kilometer estimates. The latter add up to the Table 46 annual total, thereby providing a check on the individual estimates.

*1947.* Koldomasov, 1949, pp. 184–230, gives average haul data for all but mineral building materials and "other," and percentage-of-total data for all but mineral building materials, firewood, grain, and "other," covering both ton-kilometers and tons originated. The grain tons originated estimate is derived from an annual index given by Stychinskii, 1952, p. 13. Mineral building materials, firewood, and "other" estimates have been inserted at internally consistent levels which are plausible in relation to 1945 and 1949 traffic data.

*1949.* The procedure outlined for 1945 was repeated here, based on the same source.

*1950, 1954, 1955,* All data appear in TsSU, 1956, pp. 178–80.

*1960 Plan.* These are rough estimates derived from G. S. Raikher's discussion in *Zhel. Trans.*, 1956, no. 4, pp. 35–40.

Table 54. Railroad freight traffic, Russia, by major commodity group, 1894–1913 (millions of poods originated: 1 pood = 16.38 kilograms)

| Commodity group | 1894 | 1895 | 1896 | 1897 | 1898 | 1899 | 1900 |
|---|---|---|---|---|---|---|---|
| Coal and coke | 392 | 399 | 445 | 511 | 565 | 664 | 730 |
| Petroleum | 159 | 180 | 197 | 225 | 220 | 243 | 271 |
| Ores | 92 | 104 | 114 | 160 | 168 | 239 | 248 |
| Iron and steel | 63 | 64 | 76 | 95 | 112 | 128 | 133 |
| Mineral building materials | 151 | 183 | 209 | 262 | 324 | 387 | 374 |
| Timber | 180 | 203 | 219 | 239 | 277 | 310 | 324 |
| Grain | 732 | 710 | 701 | 620 | 710 | 692 | 780 |
| Firewood | 140 | 142 | 142 | 154 | 164 | 192 | 225 |
| Other freight | 581 | 609 | 644 | 688 | 737 | 843 | 873 |
| Total | 2490 | 2594 | 2747 | 2954 | 3277 | 3698 | 3958 |

| | 1901 | 1902 | 1903 | 1904 | 1905 | 1906 | 1907 |
|---|---|---|---|---|---|---|---|
| Coal and coke | 744 | 742 | 823 | 834 | 782 | 971 | 1114 |
| Petroleum | 278 | 272 | 311 | 326 | 229 | 210 | 205 |
| Ores | 202 | 203 | 244 | 295 | 231 | 314 | 353 |
| Iron and steel | 123 | 122 | 147 | 158 | 144 | 159 | 173 |
| Mineral building materials | 335 | 318 | 363 | 348 | 285 | 294 | 334 |
| Timber | 314 | 313 | 373 | 356 | 323 | 370 | 414 |
| Grain | 809 | 955 | 1011 | 989 | 967 | 1079 | 1030 |
| Firewood | 236 | 244 | 240 | 251 | 240 | 297 | 359 |
| Other freight | 950 | 1004 | 1047 | 1013 | 1015 | 1222 | 1218 |
| Total | 3991 | 4173 | 4559 | 4570 | 4216 | 4916 | 5200 |

| | 1908 | 1909 | 1910 | 1911 | 1912 | 1913 |
|---|---|---|---|---|---|---|
| Coal and coke | 1129 | 1100 | 1089 | 1297 | 1464 | 1709 |
| Petroleum | 226 | 240 | 269 | 299 | 278 | 269 |
| Ores | 300 | 308 | 348 | 407 | 498 | 560 |
| Iron and steel | 173 | 172 | 199 | 238 | 264 | 291 |
| Mineral building materials | 355 | 495 | 494 | 637 | 644 | 751 |
| Timber | 432 | 490 | 560 | 627 | 647 | 731 |
| Grain | 982 | 1252 | 1270 | 1282 | 1200 | 1297 |
| Firewood | 411 | 376 | 346 | 396 | 430 | 438 |
| Other freight | 1240 | 1288 | 1484 | 1627 | 1687 | 1938 |
| Total | 5248 | 5721 | 6059 | 6810 | 7112 | 7984 |

## Notes to Table 54

The data in Tabel 54 appear in various issues of the *Svodnaia statisika perevozok po russkim zheleznykh dorog,* published by the Department Zhelezno-dorozhnyi Del'Ministerstva Finansov (see under Russia. Department). They are here taken from pp. 3–6 of the 1901 volume and pp. 7–11 of the 1911, 1912, and 1913 volumes. The coverage of the series appears to be constant over the period, in contrast with many of the figures contained in contemporary statistical handbooks, especially those made up for international expositions.

Table 55. Railroad freight traffic, USSR, by region, 1928, 1934, 1940, 1949

| Region | 1928 Metric tons originated (10³) | 1928 Percentage of total | 1934 Metric tons originated (10³) | 1934 Percentage of total | 1940 Metric tons originated (10³) | 1940 Percentage of total | 1949 Metric tons originated (10³) | 1949 Percentage of total |
|---|---|---|---|---|---|---|---|---|
| Northwest | 17,868 | 11.4 | 32,583 | 10.3 | 43,800 | 7.4 | 44,000 | 6.0 |
| Baltic | — | — | — | — | 14,500 | 2.5 | 19,000 | 2.6 |
| North | 7,274 | 4.7 | 16,370 | 5.2 | 32,100 | 5.4 | 33,000 | 4.5 |
| Center | 22,904 | 14.7 | 39,407 | 12.4 | 60,400 | 10.2 | 62,000 | 8.4 |
| South | 52,829 | 33.8 | 113,268 | 35.7 | 201,300 | 34.0 | 208,000 | 28.2 |
| Caucasus | 4,892 | 3.1 | 8,197 | 2.6 | 14,300 | 2.4 | 19,000 | 2.6 |
| Southeast | 22,965 | 14.7 | 37,423 | 11.8 | 63,400 | 10.7 | 92,000 | 12.5 |
| Subtotal "West" | 128,732 | 82.4 | 247,248 | 78.0 | 429,800 | 72.5 | 477,000 | 64.7 |
| Urals | 10,483 | 6.7 | 25,421 | 8.0 | 56,500 | 9.5 | 87,000 | 11.8 |
| Kazakhstan | 1,366 | 0.9 | 4,206 | 1.3 | 27,800 | 4.7 | 45,000 | 6.1 |
| Central Asia | 3,028 | 1.9 | 6,381 | 2.0 | | | | |
| W. Siberia | 5,451 | 3.5 | 18,215 | 5.7 | 38,300 | 6.5 | 61,000 | 8.3 |
| E. Siberia | 2,403 | 1.5 | 7,282 | 2.3 | 21,100 | 3.6 | 35,000 | 4.7 |
| Far East | 2,780 | 1.8 | 8,085 | 2.5 | 19,100 | 3.2 | 32,000 | 4.3 |
| Subtotal "East" | 25,511 | 16.3 | 69,590 | 21.9 | 162,800 | 27.5 | 260,000 | 35.3 |
| Total USSR | 156,237[a] | | 317,075[a] | | 592,600 | | 737,000 | |

| Region | 1928 Metric tons terminated (10³) | 1928 Percentage of total | 1934 Metric tons terminated (10³) | 1934 Percentage of total | 1940 Metric tons terminated (10³) | 1940 Percentage of total | 1949 Metric tons terminated (10³) | 1949 Percentage of total |
|---|---|---|---|---|---|---|---|---|
| Northwest | 19,855 | 12.7 | 40,821 | 12.9 | 52,700 | 8.9 | 53,000 | 7.2 |
| Baltic | — | — | — | — | 18,500 | 3.1 | 23,000 | 3.1 |
| North | 6,093 | 3.9 | 11,529 | 3.6 | 21,400 | 3.6 | 22,000 | 3.0 |
| Center | 35,255 | 22.6 | 58,658 | 18.5 | 109,000 | 18.4 | 108,000 | 14.7 |
| South | 45,702 | 29.2 | 94,160 | 29.7 | 168,600 | 28.5 | 183,000 | 24.7 |

Table 55 (*Continued*)

| Region | 1928 | | 1934 | | 1940 | | 1949 | |
|---|---|---|---|---|---|---|---|---|
| | Metric tons terminated (10³) | Percentage of total | Metric tons terminated (10³) | Percentage of total | Metric tons terminated (10³) | Percentage of total | Metric tons terminated (10³) | Percentage of total |
| Caucasus | 5,547 | 3.6 | 8,946 | 2.8 | 15,000 | 2.5 | 19,000 | 2.6 |
| Southeast | 18,354 | 11.7 | 28,523 | 9.0 | 53,900 | 9.1 | 78,000 | 10.6 |
| Subtotal "West" | *130,806* | *83.7* | *242,637* | *76.5* | *439,100* | *74.1* | *486,000* | *65.9* |
| Urals | 9,794 | 6.3 | 26,588 | 8.5 | 55,200 | 9.3 | 87,000 | 11.8 |
| Kazakhstan | 1,536 | 1.0 | 4,904 | 1.5 | 26,100 | 4.4} | 42,000 | 5.7 |
| Central Asia | 3,568 | 2.3 | 6,953 | 2.2 | | — | | |
| W. Siberia | 3,628 | 2.3 | 13,437 | 4.2 | 32,600 | 5.5 | 55,000 | 7.5 |
| E. Siberia | 1,903 | 1.2 | 7,476 | 2.4 | 18,000 | 3.0 | 31,000 | 4.2 |
| Far East | 4,276 | 2.7 | 9,628 | 3.0 | 21,600 | 3.7 | 36,000 | 4.9 |
| Subtotal "East" | *24,705* | *15.8* | *68,986* | *21.8* | *153,500* | *25.9* | *251,000* | *34.1* |
| Total USSR | 156,237[a] | | 317,075[a] | | 592,600 | | 737,000 | |

[a] In 1928, 1,994,000 tons originated and 726,000 tons terminated were not distributed by region. In 1934, 237,000 tons originated and 5,452,000 tons terminated were not distributed by region. Hence the constituent figures will not add to the two annual totals.

## Notes to Table 55

The regions in Table 55 are defined as follows:

*Northwest.* In 1928 and 1934, Leningrad, Western, and Kalinin oblasts, plus the Belorussian SSR. In 1940 and 1949, Leningrad, Smolensk, V. Luki, Kalinin, Novgorod, and Pskov oblasts, plus the Belorussian SSR.

*Baltic.* In 1940 and 1949, the Estonian, Latvian, and Lithuanian SSR's.

*North.* In 1928 and 1934, Northern, Vyatka, and Gorky krais, plus the Tatar and Karelian ASSR's. In 1940 and 1949, Vologda, Arkhangel, Kriov, and Gorky oblasts, plus the Karelo-Finnish SSR and the Komi, Tatar, Chuvash, Mari, and Udmurt ASSR's.

*Center.* In 1928 and 1934, Moscow, Ivanovo, Kursk, and Voronezh oblasts. In 1940 and 1949, Yaroslavl, Kostroma, Ivanovo, Vladimir, Moscow, Kaluga, Tula, Ryazan, Tambov, Bryansk, Orel, Kursk, and Voronezh oblasts.

*South.* The Ukrainian SSR plus Crimea.

*Caucasus.* The Georgian, Armenian, and Azerbaidzhan SSR's plus Abkhaz ASSR.

*Southeast.* In 1928 and 1934, Kuibyshev, Saratov, Stalingrad, Azov-Black Sea, and N. Caucasus krais, plus Dagestan ASSR. In 1940 and 1949, Penza, Ulyanovsk, Kuibyshev, Saratov, Stalingrad, Rostov, Astrakhan, and Grozny oblasts; Krasnodar and Stavropol krais; and Dagestan, N. Osetin, and Mordva ASSR's. In 1928 the territory of what became Orenburg oblast was probably included with Kuibyshev oblast, though in 1934 and later it has been grouped with the "Ural" subregion.

*Urals.* In 1928, Ural oblast plus Bashkir ASSR. In 1934, Sverdlovsk, Chelyabinsk, and Orenburg oblasts, plus Bashkir ASSR. In 1940 and 1949, Chelyabinsk, Kurgan, Sverdlovsk, Molotov, and Chkalov oblasts, plus Baskhir ASSR.

*Kazakhstan.* In 1928 and 1934, the Kazakh ASSR. In 1940 and 1949, the Kazakh SSR.

*Central Asia.* In 1928, Uzbek and Turkmen SSR's, plus Kirgiz ASSR. In 1934, Uzbek, Turkmen, and Tadzhik SSR's, plus Kirgiz ASSR. In 1940 and 1949, the Uzbek, Turkmen, Tadzhik, and Kirgiz SSR's.

*West Siberia.* In 1928, West Siberian krai. In 1934, Omsk oblast and West Siberian krai. In 1940 and 1949, Kemerovo, Novosibirsk, Omsk, Tomsk, and Tyumen oblasts, plus Altai krai.

*East Siberia.* In 1928, East Siberian krai, plus Yakut and Buryat-Mongol ASSR's. In 1934, Krasnoyarsk and East Siberian krais, plus Yakut and Buryat-Mongol ASSR's. In 1940 and 1949, Krasnoyarsk krai, Irkutsk and Chita oblasts, and Yakut and Buryat-Mongol ASSR's. For 1949, add Tuva A. O.

*Far East.* In 1928 and 1934, the Far Eastern krai. In 1940 and 1949, Primorskii and Khabarovsk krais.

Sources for Table 55 are as follows:

*1928.* 1929 data for 26 regions, together with precise percentage increases over 1928, appears in TsUNKhU, 1934, pp. 263-64. The derived 1928 figures have been consolidated as nearly as possible into the groupings taken by the 1940 data.

*1934.* Data for 35 regions appear in TsUNKhU, 1936a, p. 487. They are more finely classified than a similar tabulation in TsUNKhU, 1936c, pp. 8-9, and have been used here to form groupings as much as possible like the 1940 breakdown.

## Notes to Table 55 (*Continued*)

*1940.* These are estimates, based on the accompanying tabulation, which is given by S. V. Bernstein-Kogan in *Voprosy Geografii*, Sbornik no. 6 (1947) pp. 87–88. These data, applied to twice the 1940 total of 592.6 million tons originated, can be converted into absolute figures. But the content of the

| "Groups of regions" | Percentage distribution of the sum of tons originated and tons terminated | Percentage excess of tons originated over tons terminated |
|---|---|---|
| Northwest and north | 8.15% | −17.0 |
| West | 2.78 | −21.5 |
| Center | 18.80 | −29.0 |
| South | 31.20 | 19.5 |
| Southeast | 9.90 | 17.5 |
| Urals and West Siberia | 15.40 | |
| East Siberia and Far East | 6.75 | |
| Central Asia and Kazakhstan | 4.55 | 6.5 |
| Transcaucasus | 2.47 | −5.0 |

"groups of regions" is undefined, and only becomes clear when the data are compared closely with figures compiled for 1937.

The 1937 information can be extracted from a distribution of the sum of tons originated and terminated in each of nine regions, defined as to their political boundaries, given by Vol'fson, 1941, p. 207, plus 1937 figures for tons originated in eleven regions (not all of which coincide with the former), given by A. Galitskii in *Plan. Khoz.*, 1939, no. 6, p. 109, together with a few miscellaneous fragments for particular regions. It is necessary to separate several combined regions, which can be done by projecting trends evident through inspection of data for 1933–1935. Assuming continuity in the basis on which the records were compiled, inspection of the 1937 and 1940 data side by side makes the exact definition of the vague 1940 groupings considerably clearer. It appears that Bernstein-Kogan condensed his data in the following manner:

His "center" is a combination of the regions previously known as "center" and "north." There was almost no change in the figures here between 1937 and 1940, so his 1940 figures were divided on the basis of the ratios existing in 1937.

His "southeast" combines the regions previously known as "Volga Valley" and "North Caucasus." Changes here between 1937 and 1940 were substantial, so a 1940 division was not attempted.

His "northwest and north" is equivalent to the 1937 grouping, "west and northwest," that is, the former "north" region appears, not here, but consolidated with the "center." The small figures he gives indirectly for "west" appear to relate to the Baltic SSR's, since the order of magnitude of tons originated in this region is the same as the estimate derived for this territory in Table 46.

The 1937 information for the Urals, Siberia, and the Far East permits separation of his two territories into four, assuming no pronounced change in the relative roles of these regions between 1937 and 1940. However, a similar separation of Central Asia from Kazakhstan was not attempted, in the absence of information about trends in the two regions.

*1949.* The estimated 1949 tons originated total for the entire USSR was divided among regions by projecting forward the 1940 pattern, and then adjusting it for known or probable trends in each region. There had been a substantial

Notes to Table 55  (*Continued*)

shift of traffic, relative but not absolute, between 1937 and 1940, as traffic in the northwest, north, and center grew much less rapidly than traffic in Asiatic Russia. In view of the drastic changes brought on by World War II, and the government's continued efforts to relocate toward the east, we would expect to find this trend accentuated between 1940 and 1949. Several pieces of evidence make it possible to approximate the probable magnitude of the shift.

Average daily carloadings on the six railroads grouped in the Urals *okrug*, whose territory corresponds roughly to the Ural region above, plus most of West Siberia and Kazakhstan, had grown by 1948 to 129.4 per cent of their 1940 level (*Gudok*, 28 Jan. '49, p. 1). If their 1949 increase in ADC equaled the nationwide average (15.9 per cent, the 1949 level was 50 per cent over 1940. Now tons originated vary directly with carloadings except as the net load per car changes, and the latter rose 15.5 per cent between 1940 and 1949 for the railroad system as a whole. However, the net load per car in this territory has regularly been well above the network-wide average, and probably rose less than 15 per cent over this period. If it rose, say, 10 per cent, then 1949 tons originated were about 165 per cent of 1940. On the Sverdlovsk railroad alone, however, the volume of shipments in 1949 was reported as about 52 per cent over the prewar level (*Gudok*, 9 Dec. '49, p. 3).

If developments during this period conformed to the pattern observable for the 1920's and 1930's, the percentage gains in relatively well-established areas were somewhat lower than percentage gains in the newest areas. Arbitrarily, therefore, a cautiously estimated over-all increase of 60 per cent was divided among the five regions of Asiatic Russia as follows:

| | |
|---|---|
| Urals | 54 per cent |
| Kazakhstan and Central Asia | 62 |
| West Siberia | 59 |
| East Siberia | 66 |
| Far East | 68 |

To the extent that freight traffic in some regions increased more rapidly than the national average, other regions must have experienced growth at rates below the national average. The occupied parts of European Russia suggest themselves immediately as regions where perhaps even the 1940 level of traffic had not been regained by 1949. This general observation is borne out by a comparison of two statements, the first made in December, 1939, and the second in mid-1948:

"The railroads of the south, and in the first place the North Donets, South Donets, Stalin, Southern, Odessa, and Southwestern roads ... load 70 per cent of all coke shipped by the railroads, 54 per cent of the ores, 50 per cent of the coal and metal, and 37 per cent of the grain" (*Gudok*, 25 Dec. '39, p. 3).

"In 1948 the railroads of the Donets *okrug* (N. Donets, S. Donets, Stalin, Southern, Southeastern, and Stalingrad roads), are loading 34.2 per cent of the network's coal, 46.3 per cent of the ores, 33.1 per cent of the iron and steel, and 20.8 per cent of the grain" (*Zhel. Trans.*, 1948, no. 8, p. 39).

The railroads involved are not identical, and the years compared are not 1940 and 1949, but it is clear that the relative position of the territory labeled "south" in Table 55 had contracted. If we assume that the 1948 carloading

## Notes to Table 55 *(Continued)*

plans for the Donets okrug indicate its share of 1949 tons originated, and assume moreover that these four commodity groups make up the same proportion of the region's total ton originated as they bear to the national total (clearly not the case), then, using the 1947 ratios of these commodity groups to total tons originated for the USSR (1940 ratio for grain), we can estimate this okrug's approximate share of total tons originated in 1949. It comes to around 240 million. The roads involved, however, operate partly in the territory labeled "southeast" in Table 55, while some of the roads operating in the "south" are not included. On balance, a figure around 210 million tons for "south" is indicated. We can add the information that carloadings on the Stalin railroad in 1949 were 2.3 times their 1946 level (*Gudok*, 11 April '51, p. 3), suggesting recovery from the low levels of the immediate postwar period, and that total traffic (*gruzooborot*) on the S. Donets railroad in 1950 was "higher than before the war" (*Izvestiia*, 13 June '51, p. 2). Also, we have the statement that in the fourth quarter of 1950, carloadings on railroads of the Donets okrug were higher than the total 1913 carloadings in tsarist Russia (*Gudok*, 13 Dec. '50, p. 3) which permits a rough calculation suggesting that this okrug accounted for about 25 per cent of the network's carloadings.

For the territory labeled "center" in Table 55, we have two fragments: "Railroads of the central okrug already last year considerably exceeded the prewar level of carloadings" (*Gudok*, 5 April '50, p. 2), and "carloading on the Moscow–Donbas railroad have increased considerably over the 1940 level" (*Gudok*, 20 Dec. '50, p. 3).

Using these rather indirect clues to the volume of tons originated in the south and center, plus a variety of general evidence, such as that the southeast expanded rapidly during the war, while on the other hand Caucasian petroleum production suffered seriously, the 1949 values which would have resulted from continuation of the 1940 pattern were adjusted to reflect changes of a plausible magnitude. The tons terminated figures were carried forward similarly, with the balance between them indicated for 1940 by Bernstein-Kogan's percentages being moderately abated to allow for some success in the government's regional self-sufficiency program. The resulting set of estimates is provisional, and can certainly be made more accurate as additional data become available.

Table 56. Railroad passenger traffic, USSR, total, long-distance,
and commutation, by year, 1913, 1922–1955

| Year | Passenger-kilometers (millions) | Average trip (kilometers) | Number of passengers (thousands) |
|---|---|---|---|
| | *Total traffic* | | |
| 1913[a] | 25,215 | 136 | 184,800 |
| 1922[b] | — | — | 76,641 |
| 1923[b] | 13,931 | 114 | 121,786 |
| 1924[b] | 15,434 | 100 | 154,376 |
| 1925[b] | 19,040 | 90 | 211,825 |
| 1926[b] | 23,366 | 89 | 262,686 |
| 1927[b] | 22,110 | 87 | 254,200 |
| 1928 | 24,484 | 84 | 291,118 |
| 1929 | 32,004 | 88 | 365,239 |
| 1930 | 51,777 | 93 | 557,704 |
| 1931 | 61,813 | 85 | 723,681 |
| 1932 | 83,748 | 87 | 967,053 |
| 1933 | 75,154 | 81 | 927,028 |
| 1934 | 71,421 | 76 | 945,206 |
| 1935 | 67,936 | 74 | 919,121 |
| 1936 | 77,200 | 78 | 991,600 |
| 1937 | 90,942 | 80 | 1,142,700 |
| 1938 | 91,661 | 78 | 1,177,800 |
| 1939 | 93,726 | 74 | 1,267,100 |
| 1940 | 97,972 | 73 | 1,343,500 |
| 1941 | — | — | — |
| 1942 | — | — | — |
| 1943 | — | — | — |
| 1944 | — | — | — |
| 1945 | 66,200 | 79 | 843,000 |
| 1946 | 97,800 | 89 | 1,095,000 |
| 1947 | 95,100 | 83 | 1,144,000 |
| 1948 | 75,200 | 71 | 1,055,000 |
| 1949 | 81,300 | 75 | 1,080,100 |
| 1950 | 87,600 | 75 | 1,163,800 |
| 1951 | 98,500 | 75 | 1,315,300 |
| 1952 | 107,800 | 75 | 1,442,400 |
| 1953 | 118,400 | 78 | 1,508,200 |
| 1954 | 129,100 | 82 | 1,573,600 |
| 1955 | 141,400 | 86 | 1,641,400 |

| Year | Passenger-kilometers (millions) | Average trip (kilometers) | Number of passengers (thousands) |
|---|---|---|---|
| | *Long-distance traffic* | | |
| 1913[a] | 23,674 | 189 | 125,500 |
| 1922[b] | — | — | — |
| 1923[b] | — | — | — |
| 1924[b] | 13,354 | 180 | 74,256 |
| 1925[b] | 16,357 | 155 | 105,477 |
| 1926[b] | 20,158 | 153 | 131,863 |
| 1927[b] | 18,866 | 154 | 122,414 |
| 1928 | 20,645 | 154 | 134,091 |
| 1929 | 27,397 | 158 | 173,396 |
| 1930 | 44,314 | 184 | 240,492 |
| 1931 | 50,209 | 204 | 245,901 |

Table 56  (*Continued*)

| Year | Passenger-kilometers (millions) | Average trip (kilometers) | Number of passengers (thousands) |
|------|------|------|------|
| | *Long-distance traffic (Continued)* | | |
| 1932 | 66,996 | 221 | 303,073 |
| 1933 | 59,136 | 199 | 297,619 |
| 1934 | 54,559 | 211 | 258,320 |
| 1935 | 51,136 | 224 | 228,110 |
| 1936 | 59,300 | 238 | 249,000 |
| 1937 | 69,500 | 254 | 273,400 |
| 1938 | 69,400 | 255 | 272,600 |
| 1939 | 69,500 | 243 | 286,150 |
| 1940 | 73,200 | 215 | 340,400 |
| 1941 | 74,700 | 300 | 249,000 |
| 1942 | 42,800 | 333 | 129,000 |
| 1943 | 52,500 | 367 | 143,000 |
| 1944 | 50,800 | 400 | 127,000 |
| 1945 | 49,300 | 448 | 110,000 |
| 1946 | 78,400 | 314 | 250,000 |
| 1947 | 75,200 | 256 | 294,000 |
| 1948 | 55,300 | 307 | 180,000 |
| 1949 | 61,000 | 339 | 180,000 |
| 1950 | 66,400 | 318 | 209,100 |
| 1951 | 73,400 | 343 | 213,900 |
| 1952 | 80,400 | 368 | 218,800 |
| 1953 | 89,300 | 393 | 227,200 |
| 1954 | 98,500 | 418 | 235,600 |
| 1955 | 109,500 | 452 | 242,400 |

| Year | Passenger-kilometers (millions) | Average trip (kilometers) | Number of passengers (thousands) |
|------|------|------|------|
| | *Commutation traffic* | | |
| 1913[a] | 1,541 | 26.0 | 59,300 |
| 1922[b] | — | — | — |
| 1923[b] | — | — | — |
| 1924[b] | 2,080 | 26.0 | 80,120 |
| 1925[b] | 2,683 | 25.2 | 106,348 |
| 1926[b] | 3,208 | 24.5 | 130,821 |
| 1927[b] | 3,244 | 24.6 | 131,786 |
| 1928 | 3,839 | 24.4 | 157,027 |
| 1929 | 4,607 | 24.0 | 191,843 |
| 1930 | 7,463 | 23.5 | 317,212 |
| 1931 | 11,604 | 24.3 | 477,780 |
| 1932 | 16,752 | 25.2 | 663,980 |
| 1933 | 16,018 | 25.4 | 629,409 |
| 1934 | 16,862 | 24.5 | 686,886 |
| 1935 | 16,800 | 24.3 | 691,011 |
| 1936 | 17,900 | 24.1 | 742,600 |
| 1937 | 21,400 | 24.6 | 869,300 |
| 1938 | 22,300 | 24.6 | 905,200 |
| 1939 | 24,200 | 24.65 | 981,100 |
| 1940 | 24,800 | 24.7 | 1,003,100 |
| 1941 | — | — | — |
| 1942 | — | — | — |

Table 56 (*Continued*)

| | Commutation traffic (*Continued*) | | |
|---|---|---|---|
| 1943 | — | — | — |
| 1944 | — | — | — |
| 1945 | 16,900 | 23.0 | 733,000 |
| 1946 | 19,400 | 22.9 | 845,000 |
| 1947 | 19,400 | 22.8 | 850,000 |
| 1948 | 19,900 | 22.7 | 875,000 |
| 1949 | 20,300 | 22.6 | 900,000 |
| 1950 | 21,200 | 22.2 | 954,700 |
| 1951 | 25,100 | 22.8 | 1,101,400 |
| 1952 | 27,400 | 22.4 | 1,223,600 |
| 1953 | 29,100 | 22.7 | 1,281,000 |
| 1954 | 30,600 | 22.9 | 1,338,000 |
| 1955 | 31,900 | 22.8 | 1,399,000 |

[a]Adjusted to exclude passenger travel in the areas later ceded by the new government.

[b]For 12 months including 3 months of the preceding calendar year.

### Notes to Table 56

In Soviet railroad statistics, passenger traffic is recorded primarily on the basis of ticket reports, and hence covers paying passengers only. Three types of movement are distinguished: suburban, local, and through. Suburban movement is movement on commutation tickets, or within commutation zones designated by government order for roughly 100 kilometers around major cities. The precise definition is somewhat unclear. See Vedenisov, 1946, p. 383; TsSU, 1944, p. 139; Kochetov, 1941, pp. 75–84; Kochetov, 1948, pp. 71–81; and Kochetov, 1953, pp. 66–69, esp. p. 68. Local movement differs from through movement in being confined to a single railroad administration, but the two are here combined into a single category of "long-distance traffic," equivalent to the United States category of "noncommutation" or "other" passenger traffic.

The sources for Table 56 are as follows:

*1913 and 1922–1933.* The data for all three parts of the table are from IAkobi, 1935, pp. 36–37.

*1934–1935.* All three series are given in TsUNKhU, 1936a, p. 427.

*1936.* The figures are drawn from a table in Vol'fson, 1941, p. 365.

*1937–1940.* The total traffic figures are from Beliunov, 1948, p. 77, and the number-of-passenger breakdown between suburban and long-distance traffic is from Zagliadimov, 1947, p. 496. See also Beliunov, 1948, p. 77, and Gorinov, 1948a, vol. I, p. 250. The passenger-kilometer breakdown for 1937 and 1938 is from Vol'fson, 1941, p. 365; the 1940 breakdown is from Zagliadimov, 1947, p. 469. On the basis of average-trip figures for 1937, 1938, and 1940, a 1939 average trip for suburban traffic was estimated. Multiplication then produced a 1939 suburban passenger-kilometers estimate. Subtraction of this figure from the total traffic figure led to a 1939 estimate for long-distance passenger-kilometers, which then permitted computation of the implied average long-distance trip.

*1941–1944.* Kochnev, 1950, p. 33, presents a graph showing the monthly number of passengers carried in long-distance movement for each year from 1933 through 1943. Reading off the monthly levels, to three significant digits, and adding them by year produces yearly totals essentially identical with those already obtained through 1940. The 1941–1943 figures above are such sums, subject to a compiling error of perhaps ± 2 million. The 1944 estimated number

## Notes to Table 56 (*Continued*)

of passengers is a rough average between 1943 and 1945. Given the observed long-distance average trip up through 1940 and in 1945, an arbitrary series of average trips was inserted for 1941–1944, leading to long-distance passenger-kilometer estimates by multiplication. That they cannot be very accurate is suggested by the statement that "[total] passenger-kilometers in 1944 were 45.5 per cent higher than in 1943" Naporko, 1954, p. 200).

*1945–1947.* For 1945, the total number of passengers was given in *Gudok*, 2 June '46, p. 1, and total passenger-kilometers were implied by S. A. Andreev's statement (Levin, 1947, p. 138) that the 1950 target of 98 billion would be 48 per cent above 1945. For 1946, the total passenger-kilometer figure was given in *Gudok*, 25 April 47, p. 1, and the number of passengers was given as 250,000 more than in 1945 in *Gudok*, 1 Jan. '47, p. 2. For 1947, A. Svistunov, in *Zhel. Trans.*, 1948, no. 10, p. 24, stated that "in 1947 sea, river, and air transport together produced 5.1 billion passenger-kilometers, while the railroads produced 95.1 billions."

The 1945–1947 number-of-passenger figures for long-distance movement are given by S. N. Prokopovich, in his *Narodnoe Khoziaistvo SSSR* (New York, 1952), vol. II, p. 162, presumably from a Soviet source. Subtracting them from the 1945 and 1946 totals leads to estimated numbers of suburban passengers. Released data for 1950–1952 indicate that the average trip in suburban movement is shorter than before the war; the 1945–1949 average suburban trips above are interpolated to reflect a downward trend, and suburban passenger-kilometers in 1945–1946 then result by multiplication. For 1947, the reported fall in total passenger-kilometers, combined with the rise in number of long-distance passengers, shows that there must have been a sharp fall in long-distance average trip. The assumed number of suburban passengers leads to the set of estimates above for 1947; they are not very firm.

*1948–1955.* Absolute 1949 and 1951 total figures are given by Kochetov, 1953, p. 68, and 1951 breakdowns between long-distance and suburban traffic appear on p. 70. Absolute 1950 and 1954 data for all three categories are given by Danilov, 1956, p. 248. Total traffic data for 1955 appear in TsSU, 1956, p. 177. The figures in Table 56 for 1948, 1952, and 1953, and the 1949 and 1955 breakdowns, are estimates. For 1948 total passenger-kilometers, the statement in *Gudok*, 23 Oct. '49, p. 2, that traffic had grown 9 per cent over the preceding year, was applied to the 1949 figures. The 1947–1949 suburban number-of-passengers, and 1948–1949 long-distance number-of-passengers, are interpolated at plausible levels. The 1952 data are derived from indexes given by Gibshman, 1954, p. 93, for 1953, but shifted to 1952 on grounds of plausibility. The 1953 estimates are arithmetic means between 1952 and 1954, and are subject to considerable doubt. The 1955 breakdown is derived by projecting forward the growth trend in number of suburban passengers and their recent average trip.

Table 57.  Total passenger traffic, USSR, by carrier, 1928–1940
(millions of passenger-kilometers)

| Year | Railroad | River | Sea | Auto | Other urban | Air | Total |
|---|---|---|---|---|---|---|---|
| 1928 | 24,484 | 2,150 | 300 | 380 | 5,220 | 3 | 32,537 |
| 1929 | 32,004 | 2,460 | 400 | 480 | 5,920 | 4 | 41,268 |
| 1930 | 51,777 | 4,050 | 600 | 630 | 9,070 | 6 | 66,133 |
| 1931 | 61,813 | 4,060 | 700 | 770 | 13,130 | 9 | 80,482 |
| 1932 | 83,748 | 4,570 | 1,000 | 1,040 | 16,860 | 13 | 107,231 |
| Total | 253,826 | 17,290 | 3,000 | 3,300 | 50,200 | 35 | 327,651 |
| Percentage | 77.5 | 5.3 | 0.9 | 1.0 | 15.3 | 0.0 | — |
| 1933 | 75,154 | 3,720 | 900 | 1,290 | 17,210 | 19 | 98,293 |
| 1934 | 71,421 | 3,500 | 800 | 720 | 18,380 | 32 | 94,853 |
| 1935 | 67,936 | 2.900 | 900 | 1,010 | 19,390 | 40 | 92,176 |
| 1936 | 77,200 | 2,710 | 800 | 1,300 | 20,300 | 75 | 102,385 |
| 1937 | 90,942 | 3,100 | 800 | 2,940 | 23,860 | 94 | 121,736 |
| Total | 382,653 | 15,930 | 4,200 | 7,260 | 99,140 | 260 | 509,443 |
| Percentage | 75.1 | 3.1 | 0.8 | 1.4 | 19.5 | 0.1 | — |
| 1938 | 91,661 | 3,200 | 800 | 3,200 | 26,100 | 136 | 125,097 |
| 1939 | 93,726 | 3,300 | 800 | 3,840 | 28,960 | 184 | 130,810 |
| 1940 | 97,972 | 3,430 | 800 | 3,810 | 29,990 | 181 | 136,183 |
| Total | 283,359 | 9,930 | 2,400 | 10,850 | 85,050 | 501 | 392,090 |
| Percentage | 72.3 | 2.5 | 0.6 | 2.8 | 21.7 | 0.1 | — |

Sources: The railroad data are transcribed from Table 56.  Figures for the
other carriers have been compiled from Soviet sources by J. H. Blackman, and
are here adapted from an unpublished paper of his.

Table 58.  Combined output, USSR railroads, by year, 1928–1955
(billions of ton-kilometers)

| Year | (1) | (2) | (3)[a] | (4)<br>(3) plus (1) | (5)<br>(3) plus<br>(1) and (2) |
|---|---|---|---|---|---|
| 1928 | 3.7[b] | 2.0 | 117.9 | 121.6 | 123.6 |
| 1929 | 5.6[b] | 2.3[b] | 145.0 | 150.6 | 152.9 |
| 1930 | 8.7 | 2.6 | 185.7 | 194.4 | 197.0 |
| 1931 | 11.9 | 3.0[b] | 213.9 | 225.8 | 228.8 |
| 1932 | 7.9 | 3.4 | 253.0 | 260.9 | 264.3 |
| 1933 | 7.3 | 2.7 | 244.7 | 252.9 | 254.7 |
| 1934 | 11.7 | 4.4 | 277.1 | 288.8 | 293.2 |
| 1935 | 10.7 | 4.1 | 326.0 | 336.7 | 340.8 |
| 1936 | 9.6 | 3.4 | 400.6 | 410.2 | 413.6 |
| 1937 | 13.0 | 4.6 | 445.7 | 458.7 | 463.3 |
| 1938 | 13.9 | 4.1[b] | 462.2 | 476.1 | 480.2 |
| 1939 | 15.6[b] | 3.6[b] | 485.7 | 501.3 | 504.9 |
| 1940 | 17.5 | 3.1 | 513.0 | 530.5 | 533.6 |
| 1941 | — | — | — | — | — |
| 1942 | 11 | — | — | — | — |
| 1943 | 13 | — | — | — | — |
| 1944 | 24 | — | — | — | — |
| 1945 | 33.6 | — | 380.2 | 413.8 | — |
| 1946 | 30.2 | — | 432.9 | 463.1 | — |
| 1947 | 24.6 | — | 446.0 | 470.6 | — |
| 1948 | 17.9 | — | 521.5 | 539.4 | — |
| 1949 | 15.7 | — | 604.8 | 620.5 | — |
| 1950 | 12.6 | — | 689.9 | 702.5 | — |
| 1951 | 20.3 | — | 776.0 | 796.3 | — |
| 1952 | 29.7 | — | 849.6 | 879.3 | — |
| 1953 | 45.9 | — | 916.5 | 962.4 | — |
| 1954 | 54.2 | — | 985.9 | 1040.1 | — |
| 1955 | 65.1 | — | 1112.3 | 1177.4 | — |

Footnotes to Table 58

[a]"Cumulated" ton-kilometers.
[b]Estimated.
Column headings:
    (1) Excess of "operating ton-kilometers" over "tariff ton-kilometers."
    (2) Nonrevenue freight carried in noncommercial ("work") trains.
    (3) Sum of total passenger-kilometers and total tariff ton-kilometers.

## Notes to Table 58

*Column (1).* While in several years the amounts involved in the two adjustments here considered are outweighed by larger uncertainties, the tabulation at least will serve to reduce the avoidable imprecision associated with the combined output series. Since 1930, Soviet railroads have reported "operating ton-kilometers" of freight traffic as well as "tariff ton-kilometers," the former being derived from engineers' trip reports and the latter from waybills. The principal factor generating an excess of operating over tariff ton-kilometers is circuity, that is, movement of traffic over a route longer than that for which the client is charged. In United States records, the "short line" distances which would correspond with Soviet "tariff" distances are not ordinarily computed; Soviet "operating" ton-kilometers therefore should be used in comparisons with United States performance data.

*Column (2).* Soviet freight traffic statistics include with revenue freight the shipments made by the railroads for their own (or other railroad administrations') accounts if these shipments move in "commercial" trains. The small amounts shown in column (2) relate to nonrevenue freight carried in noncommercial trains. (See Kochetov, 1948, p. 34.)

*Columns (3)–(5).* Column (3) shows the sum of total passenger-kilometers from Table 56 and total tariff ton-kilometers from Table 46, giving equal weights to passengers and tons; these are the "cumulated" (*privedennye*) ton-kilometers frequently employed in Soviet operating measurements. Column (4) presents the sum of passenger-kilometers and *operating* ton-kilometers, while column (5) also includes work train ton-kilometers. There will be occasion in connection with labor productivity and operating cost computations to make use of all three coverages.

Sources for Table 58 are as follows:

The figures in column (1) for the excess of operating over tariff ton-kilometers are based on absolute data for the former: IAkobi, 1935, p. 21, gives 1930–1934 figures; Tverskoi, in *Prob. Ekon.*, 1937, no. 5/6, p. 97, gives 1932–1936 figures; Kochetov, 1948, p. 82, gives 1932, 1937 and 1940 figures; and *Gudok*, 9 March '39, p. 3, gives 1933 and 1938 figures. The estimates for 1928, 1929, and 1939 have been inserted as plausible percentages of tariff ton-kilometers in those years. Percentage excesses of 5.2 and 7.99 in 1943 and 1944 are given by Beliunov, 1948, p. 61; a percentage of 4.9, midway between 1940 and 1943, was assumed for 1942, and the percentages were then applied to estimated wartime tariff ton-kilometers from Table 46.

The "cumulated" figure of 413.8 billion for 1945 is taken from Umbliia, 1947, p. 45 (where it appears in a table headed 1946, though comparison of the table with other data on p. 16 and p. 22 makes it clear that the heading should be 1945), and is supported by I. Ivliev's statement (*Zhel. Trans.*, 1947, no. 1, p. 23) that the 1950 target of 648 billion would be 56.3 per cent above 1945. Strenuous efforts were made during the Fourth Five Year Plan period to reduce the excess of

## Notes to Table 58  (*Continued*)

operating over tariff ton-kilometers—in the first quarter of 1948 it was 5.6 per cent as compared with 1945's 10.6 per cent (B. Levin, in *Zhel, Trans.*, 1948, no. 8, p. 20). For 1950 it was evidently reduced to 2.1 per cent; G. Nedopekin and A. Nikolskii, in *Gudok*, 1 July '51, p. 3, stated that while the average trip of a freight car in 1950 exceeded the average freight length of haul by 9.8 per cent, it exceeded the average *operating* length of haul by only 7.6 per cent, and applied to the 1950 data of Table 46, this suggests a 1950 operating ton-kilometer figure of 614.9 billion.

By 1953 and 1954 the percentage excess appears to have increased again. The reported traffic densities in 1953 of 7.1 million ton-kilometers per kilometer of road operated (A. Galitskii, in *Plan, Khoz.*, 1954, no. 6, p. 56) and in 1954 of 7.6 million (G. Raikher, in *Gudok*, 22 Oct. '55, p. 3) are higher than those computed from data in Tables 46 and 59; if they are interpreted as reflecting use of operating ton-kilometers, they imply percentages excesses of 6.4 per cent in 1953 and 6.9 per cent in 1954. With these observations as benchmarks, the estimates above were inserted for 1946–1949 and 1951–1952 by assuming percentage excesses of 9, 7, 4, 3, 3, and 4 respectively. A 1952 level of 4 per cent is consistent with A. Smetenin's remark (*Gudok*, 5 April '53, p. 3) that on the Orenburg RR in 1952 it was 7.2 per cent; on the S. Ural RR, 5.3 per cent; on the Sverdlovsk, Yaroslavl, Kishinev, and Vinnitskaya, 3.5 per cent; and on the N. Donets, Ordzhonikidze, and Kazan RR's 2.5 per cent. 1955 and 1960 plan densities of 8.6 and 11.6 million are given by G. S. Raikher, *Zhel. Trans.*, 1956, no. 4, p. 40.

The work train traffic data for 1928, 1930, 1932, 1937, and 1940 are given by Kochetov, 1948, p. 239, and for 1933–1935 can be computed from the "cumulated" output series given by I. Kazarin in *Plan*, 1937, no. 3, p. 40. His preliminary 1936 figure is raised on the basis of labor force and output-per-worker data in Vol'fson, 1941, p. 553. The 1929, 1931, and 1938–1939 estimates are inserted as crude means between neighboring years.

Table 59. Total road operated, USSR railroads, by year, 1917–1955,
plus 1960 plan (kilometers)

| Year | (1) Annual average | (2) Rise of (1) during year | (3) At end of year | (4) Rise of (3) during year | (5) Added for permanent operation | (6) Other changes (net) |
|---|---|---|---|---|---|---|
| 1917 | 63,252 | — | — | — | 995 | — |
| 1918 | 26,790 | −36,462 | — | — | 1,089 | −11,690 |
| 1919 | 31,494 | 4,704 | — | — | 73 | — |
| 1920 | 56,819 | 25,325 | — | — | 200 | — |
| 1921[a] | 67,531 | 10,712 | — | — | 203 | — |
| 1922[a] | 69,430 | 1,899 | — | — | 120 | — |
| 1923[a] | 69,640 | 210 | 69,494 | — | 251 | — |
| 1924[a] | 73,858 | 4,218 | 73,987 | 4,493 | 1,578 | 2,915 |
| 1925[a] | 74,399 | 541 | 74,429 | 442 | 292 | 150 |
| 1926[a] | 74,594 | 195 | 74,744 | 315 | 1,321 | −1,006 |
| 1927[a] | 75,753 | 1,159 | 75,893 | 1,149 | 1,218 | −69 |
| 1928[a] | 76,887 | 1,134 | 76,923 | 1,030 | 418 | 612 |
| 1929 | 77,010 | 123 | 76,938 | 15 | 483 | −468 |
| 1930 | 77,073 | 63 | 77,861 | 923 | 1,058 | −135 |
| 1931 | 80,248 | 3,175 | 80,958 | 3,097 | 2,645 | 452 |
| 1932 | 81,564 | 1,316 | 81,815 | 857 | 815 | 42 |
| 1933 | 82,080 | 516 | 82,614 | 799 | 848 | −49 |
| 1934 | 83,247 | 1,167 | 83,493 | 879 | 837 | 42 |
| 1935 | 83,818 | 571 | 84,367 | 874 | 517 | 357 |
| 1936 | 84,649 | 831 | 84,931 | 564 | 622 | −58 |
| 1937 | 84,910 | 261 | 84,889 | −42 | 278 | −320 |
| 1938 | 84,919 | 9 | 84,950 | 61 | 380 | −319 |
| 1939 | 88,400 | 3,481 | 91,850 | 6,900 | 1,367 | 5,533 |
| 1940 | 95,526 | 7,126 | 106,102 | 14,252 | 2,865 | 11,387 |
| 1941 | 90,000 | −5,526 | 74,000 | −32,102 | 2,125 | −34,227 |
| 1942 | 68,900 | −21,100 | 62,900 | −11,900 | 2,830 | −14,730 |
| 1943 | 72,300 | 3,400 | 81,646 | 18,746 | 1.075 | 17,671 |
| 1944 | 93,800 | 21,500 | 106,000 | 24,354 | 1,960 | 22,394 |
| 1945 | 108,900 | 15,100 | 112,868 | 6,868 | 150 | 6,718 |
| 1946 | 113,489 | 4,780 | 114,110 | 1,242 | 405 | 837 |
| 1947 | 114,456 | 967 | 114,802 | 692 | — | — |
| 1948 | 115,148 | 692 | 115,493 | 691 | — | — |
| 1949 | 115,839 | 691 | 116,184 | 691 | — | — |
| 1950 | 116,530 | 691 | 116,875 | 691 | — | — |
| 1951 | 117,318 | 788 | 117,761 | 886 | — | — |
| 1952 | 118,162 | 844 | 118,563 | 802 | — | — |
| 1953 | 119,253 | 1,091 | 119,943 | 1,380 | — | — |
| 1954 | 120,124 | 871 | 120,304 | 361 | — | — |
| 1955 | 120,506 | 382 | 120,707 | 403 | — | — |
| 1960 (plan) | 126,500 | — | 127,200 | — | — | — |

[a]12-month period including 3 months of the preceding calender year.

365

## Notes to Table 59

Columns 1, 3, and 5 represent basic data; columns 2, 4, and 6 are derived from them. In particular, the final column shows for each year the number of kilometers of road operated which were added to (or subtracted from) the total at the end of the preceding year, through adjustments other than the entry of newly completed construction into permanent operation. Thus, for each year, column 6 equals column 4 minus column 5.

Those familiar with railroad statistics in other countries will recognize that many minor changes give rise to such adjustments. From time to time, here and there on a large railroad network, a few kilometers of road will be retired or reclassified; maintenance of way operations may extend to altering roadway location and hence to a change in the distance between termini. In the USSR, there have been many instances of transfer from an individual enterprise to the NKPS of portions of road. Previously considered the property of the enterprise, they became "common carrier" lines, administered by the NKPS. Conversely, there may be instances of transfer from the NKPS to some other organization of short portions of road for operating purposes. It follows that changes in total road operated from one year to the next will not be identical with the amount of new line placed in operation, though in normal times this may be the largest single component in the aggregate.

The figures in column 5 show the amount of new line which each year was accepted by the NKPS for "permanent" or "regular" operation, as distinct from "temporary" operation. The difference is both technical and administrative. Since a complete railroad line is an elaborate engineering plant which includes, in addition to the roadbed, track, and superstructure, such indispensible facilities as bridges, water-supply equipment, locomotive-servicing installations, stations and terminals, signaling equipment, line switching facilities, yard switching trackage, locomotive and train crew accommodations, storage space, and maintenance facilities, it is obvious that merely because a train has run from point A to point B, one cannot necessarily say that a new line is "completed." The first stage is the opening of a line for "working movement," that is, for work equipment moving to the scene of construction. After that the new line will go into "temporary" operation, during which it will begin to carry revenue freight and passengers, while ancillary facilities are finished. Finally, a commission of NKPS and other government officials will conduct a thorough inspection, and when any remaining inadequacies are eliminated to its satisfaction, the line will be accepted for permanent operation and will be added to the total operated by the NKPS (now the MPS).

These details are pointed out here because year-to-year changes in total road operated cannot be accurately compiled unless the distinction between temporary and permanent operation is explicitly recognized. Outside observers frequently notice the opening of working movement at a construction project and seem to identify it with final completion of the line, though in fact the latter may not come for several more years. When line in temporary operation is added unknowingly to total road operated, the result is to exaggerate the length of available roadway at that moment, and to confuse the record of year-by-year additions to the network, since such line will be entered too early.

The sources for Table 59 are as follows:

*1917–1933.* The foundation for accurate data on the total length of railroad roadway inherited by the Soviet government, to which subsequent additions have

Notes to Table 59 (*Continued*)

been made, is Vol. 42 of the NKPS *Materialy po Statistike Zheleznodorozhnogo Transporta*, published in 1926. It presents the results of an exhaustive inventory, as of September 30, 1924, of all railroad line in the USSR, carried to the nearest hundredth of a kilometer. One of the tabulations shows the date each section of line was placed in permanent operation, and from it one can arrive at the precise total inherited by the new regime, after making two adjustments. In early 1918 the government ceded a considerable territory along its western frontier, and this territory contained 11,689.96 kilometers of roadway. The enumerators in 1924 were not able to date certain short spurs with a total length of 1,590 kilometers. Hence the gross total enumerated on September 30, 1924, of 84,564.38 kilometers must be reduced by the former and increased by the latter. It has been thought more accurate here to allocate the undated spurs uniformly over the whole period of Russian railroad construction than to imply that they were all built in 1924. This requires raising the figures for each year by 1.0188, the ratio of 86,154.38 to 84,564.38.

Leaving aside the record for 1838–1912, not directly germane to the present study, the figures for the years immediately preceding the change of regime were as follows:

|      | Total road built at end of year | Added for permanent operation during year |
|------|-------------------|-------------------|
| 1913 | 71,475.08 | — |
| 1914 | 74,395.04 | 2,919.96 |
| 1915 | 77,373.82 | 2,978.78 |
| 1916 | 81,646.02 | 4,272.20 |
| 1917 | 82,641.00 | 994.98 |

Thus the Soviet government inherited 83,641 kilometers of roadway, and after ceding 11,690 kilometers had left a total of 70,951 kilometers (44,087 miles). However, during 1917 the average length of road operated was somewhat smaller, being 63,252, just as in 1913 in USSR territory average road operated was 58,549 kilometers out of a total at the end of 1913 of 59,785 kilometers.

Because 11,166 kilometers of line were added to the network between the end of 1913 and the end of 1917, while 11,690 kilometers were then lost in territorial adjustments, there is the possibility of misleading comparisons between the railroad systems before and after the Revolution. These misleading comparisons have indeed been made, both by outside observers and by Soviet writers. For example Vladimir Nikolaevich Obraztsov, dean of Soviet railroad writers, wrote in *Pravda* (17 April '38, p. 4) that "the Soviet government inherited from Tsarist Russia 58,549 kilometers of road (without the Chinese Eastern)." Here the 1913 annual average operated is used, excluding line in ceded territory and ignoring new construction during the first World War. Less inaccurate is Bernstein-Kogan's statement (*Voprosy Geografii*, Sbornik No. 6, 1947, p. 83); "We recall that in 1913, on the territory of Russia there were 58.5 thousand kilometers of railroad. Up to 1917, this figure rose to 68.2 thousand kilometers." He had previously given the figures of 70.2 and 58.5 for 1913, so there is only left a slight underenumeration of new construction. In the current literature one finds more accurate statements, such as that by the woman reporter, Marietta Shaginian, "We received from old Russia 70,000 kilometers of railroad" (*Gudok*, 5 Nov. '47, p. 3), or the recent statement by Deputy Minister of the MPS, V.

## Notes to Table 59 (*Continued*)

Kurochkin: "Before the Revolution the railroad network of Russia consisted of 25 state and 13 private railroads, with a total length of about 70,000 kilometers." It is to be hoped that the tabulation above will eliminate any misunderstanding remaining among students of the Soviet period.

The data for the annual average length of road operated from 1917 through 1933, and for the end-of-year figures from 1923 through 1933, are taken from IAkobi, 1935, pp. 6–7. They are identical with figures for 1921–1932 in various volumes of the NKPS *Materialy*, and are repeated for some or all of these years in such statistical handbooks as TsUNKhU, 1934, pp. 248–49, or TsUNKhU, 1932, p. 194. Through 1924 they are adjusted upward to include a proportionate share of the 1,590 kilometers of undated spurs mentioned above. They thus exceed slightly the data of Vol'fson, 1941, pp. 506–507, where each year's principal new lines are itemized. For 1925–1933, the unadjusted Vol'fson figures (*ibid.*, pp. 507–511), are used.

*1934–1935.* Both the annual average and the end-of-year figures for line operated in 1934 and 1935 come from TsUNKhU, 1936a, pp. 440–41; the figures for new line are from Vol'fson, 1941, p. 511.

*1936–1937.* For 1936 and 1937, it is necessary to select from several variant figures. Ioffe, 1939, p. 293, gives a series for annual average road operated with 85,080 and 85,280 kilometers for these two years, and a preliminary end-of-the-year estimate for 1936 of 85,200 kilometers appears in *Plan. Khoz.*, 1937, no. 3, p. 239. These however, appear to be generous estimates, probably including some new line only in temporary operation. A detailed figure of 84,889 kilometers in operation at the end of 1937 is given in a thorough review of Soviet railroad construction by A. E. Gibshman, in *Tekhnika Zhel. Dorog*, 1947, no. 10, p. 14, and acceptance of the above figures in conjunction with this one would indicate an appreciable fall in road operated during 1937. A more plausible estimate of the annual average can be derived from the datum that in 1937 the density of freight traffic in thousands of ton-kilometers per kilometer of road operated was 4,179. Dividing 354,839 million ton-kilometers by 4,179 yields a figure of 84,910 kilometers of road operated. The 4,179 is given by Vol'fson, 1941, p. 204, and repeated by V. N. Obraztsov in *Plan. Khoz.*, 1944, no. 1, p. 61. A similar figure results from the indication in Gorinov, 1948a, vol. I, p. 251, that in 1937 the density of passenger traffic in thousands of passenger-kilometers per kilometer of road operated was 1,071. Division of 90,942 million passenger-kilometers by 1,071 yields 84,913 kilometers of road operated. On the other hand, a passenger density figure of 1,069 is given for 1937 by Vol'fson, 1941, p. 365, as part of a series for 1934–1938 which appears to be using somewhat different coverages.

At any rate, accepting the 1937 end-of-the-year figure from Gibshman, and a 1937 annual average of 84,710 kilometers, one can then approximate an end-of-year figure for 1936 by assuming that the annual average is a simple arithmetic mean between them, that is, that the changes proceeded steadily throughout the year. This 1936 figure, in turn, permits calculation of an arithmetic mean for the 1936 annual average of road operated. As shown below in connection with new line placed in operation, there was some shrinkage of line operated in any case, and this calculating procedure minimizes the erratic fluctuations involved.

The Vol'fson figure for 1936 line placed in operation is 900 kilometers, but their itemization of lines clearly includes several lines prematurely. It appears

Notes to Table 59  (*Continued*)

from the information that the length of line placed in permanent operation during the period of the Second Five Year Plan was 3,102 kilometers (Bernstein–Kogan, p. 85), that the figure of 900 kilometers covers both 1936 and 1937. Gorinov, 1948a, vol. 1, opp. p. 21, provides a map showing all new line placed in permanent operation between 1917 and 1946 in the USSR, with a date placed beside each piece of construction. Compiling a list from the map, and sorting it by year, one finds a total of 622 kilometers for 1936, and none for 1937. It is here assumed that, nevertheless, 278 (900–622) kilometers came into operation in 1937. According to A. E. Gibshman's tabulation, new line during 1933–1937 totaled 3,380 kilometers, but this is not here accepted. It will be seen that developments during 1936–1938 included appreciable negative adjustments (net), and use of larger construction figures would simply bring with it larger residual negative adjustments.

*1938.* The 1938 end-of-year figure is from N. Borisov, in *Sots. Trans.*, 1939, no. 6, p. 25, and the annual average is the arithmetic mean between the 1937 and 1938 year-end figures. The estimate for new line is compiled from Gorinov's map.

*1939–1940.* Figures for these years are complicated by the problem of determining just when the roughly 16,000 kilometers of additional roadway acquired along the western frontier were placed in operation. Poland was invaded on September 18, 1939, and the railroads in the regions added to the Belorussian and Ukrainian SSR's were being reorganized during October and November. *Gudok* of Dec. 11, 1939, reported the NKPS order establishing four new railroad administrations for this territory. Khachaturov reported in *Sots. Trans.*, 1939, no. 11, p. 8, that "the railroads of western Belorussia and western Ukraine come to 6.7 thousand kilometers," but not all of this may have been operated immediately.

The war with Finland began on December 4, 1939, and in the spring of 1940 there was an exchange of territory such that "about 900 kilometers of railroad line" passed to the USSR (Gokhman, 1944, p. 23). Bessarabia and northern Bukhovina were acquired late in the spring, and the NKPS organized the Kishinev railroad in July (*Gudok*, 25 July '40, p. 4). In early August 1940, the three Baltic republics were taken over and the 7,050 kilometers of railroad thus acquired were being reorganized under NKPS administration at the end of that month (*Gudok*, 28 Aug. '40, p. 4).

Vol'fson, 1941, p. 164, gives a figure of 86,300 kilometers for 1939 before the incorporations, and Gorinov 1948a, p. 30, gives a 1939 figure of 88,400, which is here taken to be the annual average. Together with the 1938 year-end figure, it yields a 1939 year-end estimate of 91,850. The figure of new line placed in permanent operation is the sum of the lines read off Gorinov's map.

The 1940 year-end figure appears in several sources and evidently includes all acquisitions and completed line as of December 31, 1940. It is here taken from Gibshman, 1947 article, p. 14. The 1940 annual average is an arithmetic mean between the 1939 and 1940 year-end figures, and the 1940 new line estimate is compiled from Gorinov's map.

*1941–1945.* These wartime data are rough estimates, based on fragmentary remarks concerning the total length of railroad line occupied by the Nazis and

Notes to Table 59  (*Continued*)

the extent of reconstruction during various periods of the war, as follows: "Road operated at the beginning of 1943 had been reduced by 40 per cent compared to the beginning of 1941" (Voznesenskii, 1947, p. 100); "During 1943, the railroad network increased by 18,746 kilometers over 1942, or by 29.8 per cent" (Naporko, 1954, p. 199); "In 1943–1944, 43,000 kilometers of line were repaired and put into operation in the devastated areas" (Turetskii, 1948, p. 152). The end-of-year figure for 1945 is dated Jan. 1, 1946 in Zagliadimov, 1947, p. 7. The annual averages are computed as arithmetic means between year-end estimates. The data for new line are compiled from Gorinov's map.

*1946–1955.* The 1946 and 1950–1955 end-of-year figures are from Shvetsov, 1956, p. 52, and estimates for 1947–1949 are inserted on the assumption of even growth. The large increase during 1953 reflects entry into permanent operation of three sizeable projects: Mointy–Chu, 438 kilometers; Akmolinsk–Pavlodar, also 438 kilometers; and Kulunda–Barnaul, 342 kilometers. A more precise allocation for 1947–1949 could be derived from the map opp. p. 610 in Danilov, 1956, but has not been carried through here. The estimated annual averages are arithmetic means between year-end figures.

Table 60.  Length of second and other tracks, electrified line, and
narrow-gauge line, USSR railroads, by year, 1921–1955,[a] plus 1960 plan
(kilometers)

| Year | Second tracks | Yard tracks | Total trackage | Electrified line | Narrow-gauge line |
|---|---|---|---|---|---|
| 1921[b] | — | — | — | — | 1,938 |
| 1922[b] | — | — | — | — | 1,672 |
| 1923[b] | 14,319 | — | — | — | 1,534 |
| 1924[b] | 14,637 | 11,393 | 100,017 | — | 1,312 |
| 1925[b] | 14,781 | — | — | — | 1,258 |
| 1926[b] | — | — | — | — | 1,129 |
| 1927[b] | — | — | — | — | 1,097 |
| 1928 | 15,609[b] | 30,549 | 123,081 | — | 1,004 |
| 1929 | 16,017[b] | — | — | 18 | 1,005 |
| 1930 | 16,383 | — | — | 55 | 1,005 |
| 1931 | 17,481 | — | — | 64 | 996 |
| 1932 | 18,993 | 36,757 | 137,565 | 153 | 1,003 |
| 1933 | 19,483 | 37,431 | 139,528 | 350 | 1,004 |
| 1934 | 20,907 | 38,828 | 143,228 | 379 | 1,003 |
| 1935 | 22,810 | 39,187 | 146,364 | 907 | 1,097 |
| 1936 | — | — | — | 1,352 | — |
| 1937 | 24,500 | 40,611 | 150,000 | 1,632 | — |
| 1938 | 24,861 | — | — | 1,680 | — |
| 1939 | — | — | — | 1,714 | — |
| 1940 | 28,700 | 48,849 | 183,651 | 1,870 | — |
| 1941 | — | — | — | — | — |
| 1942 | 14,640 | — | — | — | — |
| 1943 | 16,680 | — | — | — | — |
| 1944 | — | — | — | — | — |
| 1945 | 20,800 | 47,504 | 181,172 | 2,038 | — |
| 1946 | 22,200 | — | — | 2,154 | 4,260 |
| 1947 | — | — | — | — | — |
| 1948 | — | — | — | — | — |
| 1949 | — | — | — | — | — |
| 1950 | 24,800 | 51,900 | 193,600 | 3,085 | — |
| 1951 | — | — | — | 3,490 | — |
| 1952 | — | — | — | 3,690 | — |
| 1953 | 27,600 | — | — | 4,260 | — |
| 1954 | 28,500 | — | — | 4,860 | — |
| 1955 | 29,500 | 55,700 | 205,900 | 5,352 | — |
| 1960 (plan) | 36,100 | 59,300 | 222,600 | 13,500 | — |

[a]At end of year.
[b]As of September 30 rather than December 31.

## Notes to Table 60

Sources for Table 60 are as follows:

*Second tracks*. These figures include a small amount of third or fourth main track (222 kilometers at the end of 1934). The 1923–1933 data are from IAkobi, 1935, pp. 6–7, except for the 1924 figure, which is from NKPS *Materialy*, vol. 36, p. 36. The 1928 and 1929 figures relate to Sept. 30. The 1934–1935 figures are from TsUNKhU, 1936a, p. 440. The 1937 estimate is based on the statement in Vol'fson, 1941, p. 512, that during the Second Five Year Plan, 5.5 thousand kilometers of second tracks were laid. N. Borisov gave the 1938 figure in *Sots. Trans.*, 1939, no. 6, p. 25. Kaganovich's statement at the Eighteenth Congress that more than 8000 kilometers of second track were laid during 1933–1938 evidently includes some 2000 kilometers of unfinished line.

For 1940, one must choose between the frequent statement that during 1928–1940, 9,100 kilometers of second tracks were built (cited from Zagliadimov, 1947, p. 13), and the alternative statement which substitutes the figure of 13,100 kilometers in the same sentence (Gorinov, 1948b, p. 63). Both the Third Five Year Plan and progress reports in *Gudok* during 1938–1940 make it clear that several thousand kilometers of double-tracking were under way. The larger figure may be presumed to reflect completion of these projects by the end of 1940, plus the 1,700 kilometers incorporated on the territory added to the Ukraine and Belorussia (Khachaturov, in *Sots. Trans.*, 1939, no. 11, p. 7). and whatever second track there was in the Baltic countries, Bessarabia, and northern Bukhovina. The largest single double-tracking project of the 1930's was the Trans-Siberian from Chelyabinsk to Vladivostok; completion of the Karymskaia-Khabarovsk portion was announced at the Eighteenth Congress, and Khachaturov reported in BSE, 1947a, col. 1803, that the whole distance (7,150 kilometers) had been double-tracked before the war. Since the 1949 timetable distance between Chelyabinsk and Vladivostok was 7,416 kilometers (MPS, 1949a, pp. 442–48), it appears that 266 kilometers of single-track line remain, or that this amount had already been double-tracked long before.

The 1942 and 1943 estimates are derived from the statement (Naporko, 1954, p. 199), that the "unfolded length" of main track increased in 1943 by 20,783 kilometers or by 26.8 per cent, along with his statement that the network increased by 18,746 kilometers or by 29.8 per cent. While it was claimed that around 20,000 kilometers of second track were occupied by the Nazis (Khachaturov, 1946, p. 257), and 17,513 kilometers were damaged or destroyed (*Gudok*, 13 July '45, p. 2), the length out of operation at the end of 1942 seems to have been more like 15,000 kilometers (28,700 minus 14,640 plus allowance for additional construction in unoccupied territory). Reconstruction during the war was put at 7,846 kilometers (*Zhel. Trans.*, 1946, no. 7, p. 92) and the Fourth Five Year Plan called for restoration of an additional 6,788 kilometers (*Gudok*, 27 March '46, p. 2).

The 1945 figure is the 1950 target of 33,600 (Gorinov, 1948b, p. 64) less the planned additions of the Fourth Five Year Plan, and can also be derived as 19 per cent of the first main track route mileage (*Zhel. Trans.*, 1946, no. 4, p. 56). "In 1946...1,400 kilometers of second track were restored and newly laid "Minister I. V. Kovalev, *Gudok*, 1 Jan. '47, p. 1). The estimate assigned to the end of 1954 is derived from Deputy Minister Robel's statement (*Gudok*, 2 Nov. '55, p. 2) that the length of double track line had increased during two postwar five-year plans by 37 per cent. Since double-tracking of the 806-kilo-

Notes to Table 60 (*Continued*)

meter Akmolinsk–Kartaly line was finally completed on Nov. 24, 1955 (*Gudok*, 25 Nov. '55, p. 1), a year-end figure for 1955 was put at 1,000 kilometers higher than 1954. Rough figures for 1950 and the 1960 plan then result from the draft Sixth Five Year Plan target of building 6,600 kilometers of second track, or 40 per cent more than during the Fifth Five Year Plan period.

*Yard tracks.* This category appears to correspond to "yard switching tracks" in United States usage, and perhaps also includes "way switching tracks." For 1925, 1928, 1932–1935, and 1937, obtained as total trackage less first and second tracks. The 1940 estimate reflects the statement (Naporko, 1954, p. 170) that 1940 was 18,300 kilometers over 1928. The 1945 figure is from Zagliadimov, 1947, p. 24. For 1955, the estimate is based on Deputy Minister Robel's statement (*Gudok*, 2 Nov. '55, p. 2) that the ratio of yard track to road operated had risen during two postwar five-year plans from 42 per cent to 46 per cent. A crude estimate for 1950 is inserted as 44 per cent of road operated at that time. The 1960 target is stated as 49 per cent of road operated.

*Total Trackage.* The 1924 figure is from NKPS, *Materialy*, no. 42, p. 109. The 1928 and 1932–1935 figures are from TsUNKhU, 1936a, p. 400. Vol'fson, 1941, p. 493, gives the slightly rounded 1937 figure. For the remaining years, the total is the sum of first, second, and yard tracks.

*Electrified line.* 1928–1934—These data for the end of each year are from IAkobi, 1935, p. 10.

1935—TsUNKhU, 1936a, p. 440.

1936—K. Tverskoi, in *Prob. Ekon.*, 1937, no. 5/6, p. 104.

1937—Vol'fson, 1941, p. 484, give this total with a list of the constituent lines, divided into suburban and long-distance lines.

1938—N. Borisov, in *Sots. Trans.*, 1939, no. 6, p. 25.

1939—It was reported in *Gudok*, 4 Aug. '39, p. 4, that total electrified line at that time came to 1,690 kilometers, plus another 24-kilometer line just put into operation and another still (Olen'ya–Murmansk, 113 kilometers) said to be going into operation but only put into "temporary" operation on October 14 (*Gudok*, 15 Oct. '39, p. 4), and therefore deferred to 1940 for the present table.

1940—*Gudok*, 27 July 1940, p. 3, reported the figure of 1870 kilometers, which has been repeated since the war (for example, Kovalev in *Zhel. Trans.*, 1947, no. 8, p. 4) as a total electrified "during the Stalin Five Year Plans." A figure of 1887 kilometers is given in Obraztso, 1948b, p. 10, as the total up to the middle of 1941.

1945—This figure results from subtracting the 5325 kilometers scheduled for construction in the Fourth Five Year Plan from the planned figure of 7363 kilometers at the end of 1950 (both given in I. V. Kovalev, 1946a, pp. 37–38).

1946—Kovalev, *Gudok*, 1 Jan. '47, p. 1, reported an annual increase of 116 kilometers.

1950–1955—These estimates are derived from the following sources: (1) annual index numbers based on 1937 for 1950–1954, in *Gudok*, 28 June '55, p. 3; (2) Khrushchev's statement (*Gudok*, 15 Feb '56, p. 5), that 2267 kilometers were electrified during the Fifth Five Year Plan; and (3) annual construction increments for 1953–1955 reported by I. S. Sal'nikov, Deputy Head of the MPS Electrification Administration, in *Zhel. Trans.*, 1956, no. 3, p. 14. The Sixth Five Year Plan construction target first appeared as 8500 kilometers, but quickly became 8100.

Notes to Table 60 (*Continued*)

*Narrow-gauge line.* 1921–1933—IAkobi, 1935, pp. 6–7.
1934–1935—TsUNKhU, 1936b, p. 302.

1946—V. Losev, in *Zhel. Trans.*, 1947, no. 1, p. 73. The rise since 1935 is due in large part to acquisition of narrow-gauge line in the Baltic republics and western Ukraine, including over 700 kilometers in the Latvian SSR (Vedenisov, 1946, p. 241), 693 kilometers in the Estonian SSR (BSE, 1947a, col. 1936), 526 kilometers in the Lithuanian SSR (BSE, 1947a, col. 1877), and 190 kilometers in Trans-Carpathian oblast (BSE, 1947b, col. 831). As part of the "new lands" program in Kazakhstan, a 1954 plan for hurried construction of 1,850 kilometers of narrow-gauge line in western Siberia and Kazakhstan is currently in progress.

Table 61. Number of locomotives, USSR, by year, 1924–1940, 1945–1955

| | (1) | (2) | (3) | (4) | (5) | (6) | (7) | (8) |
|---|---|---|---|---|---|---|---|---|
| | | "Under railroad orders" | | | | | (6) as percentage— | |
| Year | Total | Freight | Passenger | Combined[a] | "Working fleet"[a] | Road freight service | of (2) | of (5) |
| 1924[b] | — | — | — | 19,900 | 6,100 | 2,080 | — | 34.2 |
| 1925[b] | — | — | — | 20,100 | 6,700 | 2,830 | — | 42.2 |
| 1926[b] | — | — | — | 19,000 | 8,700 | 3,830 | — | 44.0 |
| 1927[b] | — | — | — | 18,400 | 9,000 | 4,080 | — | 45.3 |
| 1928 | — | 12,500 | 2,600 | 15,100 | 9,300 | 4,360 | — | 46.9 |
| 1929 | — | — | — | 15,300 | 11,100 | 4,570 | — | 41.1 |
| 1930 | — | — | — | 15,700 | 12,000 | 4,770 | — | 39.7 |
| 1931 | 19,200 | — | — | 17,200 | 12,500 | 5,030 | — | 40.2 |
| 1932 | 20,100 | 14,900 | 3,000 | 17,900 | 12,400 | 5,330 | 35.8 | 43.0 |
| 1933 | 21,000 | 15,400 | 3,200 | 18,700 | 12,700 | 5,470 | 35.5 | 43.1 |
| 1934 | 22,100 | 16,000 | 3,400 | 19,400 | 13,800 | 6,280 | 39.3 | 45.5 |
| 1935 | 23,000 | — | — | 20,300 | 14,200 | 6,520 | — | 45.9 |
| 1936 | 23,600 | — | — | — | — | 5,910 | — | — |
| 1937 | — | — | — | — | — | 5,980 | — | — |
| 1938 | — | — | — | — | — | 5,970 | — | — |
| 1939 | — | — | — | — | — | 6,250 | — | — |
| 1940 | — | — | — | — | — | 6,430 | — | — |
| 1945 | — | — | — | — | — | 6,070 | — | — |
| 1946 | — | — | — | — | — | 6,870 | — | — |
| 1947 | — | — | — | — | — | 6,910 | — | — |
| 1948 | — | — | — | — | — | 7,770 | — | — |
| 1949 | — | — | — | — | — | 7,990 | — | — |
| 1950 | — | — | — | — | — | 8,210 | — | — |
| 1951 | — | — | — | — | — | 8,820 | — | — |
| 1952 | — | — | — | — | — | 9,100 | — | — |
| 1953 | — | — | — | — | — | 9,210 | — | — |
| 1954 | — | — | — | — | — | 8,900 | — | — |
| 1955 | — | — | — | — | — | 8,490 | — | — |

[a]Freight and passenger locomotives combined.
[b]12-month period including 3 months of the preceding calendar year.

## Notes to Table 61

The sources for the columns are as follows:

(1) The 1932 and 1937 figures come from Vol'fson, 1941, p. 469. The 1935 and 1936 figures come from Gosplan, 1937, pp. 120-21. They apparently cover locomotives held by organizations other than the railroads, in addition to those "under railroad orders." That such locomotives exist is indicated by data in the 1941 annual plan (*Gosudarstvennyi plan,* 1941, pp. 452-53), which shows that repairs were to be made on 8000 NKPS steam locomotives, and in addition on 1300 steam locomotives belonging to such commissariats as iron and steel, coal, and the NKVD administration for corrective labor camps (*GULAG*).

(2)—(4) The combined series (4) for 1924-1934 is given by IAkobi, 1935, p. 44, and a 1935 figure given is in TsUNKhU, 1936a, p. 430, where the division between freight (2) and passenger (3) locomotives for 1928 and 1932-1934 is also given.

(5) The series for 1924-1934 is from IAkobi, 1935, p. 44, who gives data for the last three years permitting the exclusion of locomotives undergoing boiler washes (since they had not been included previously). A 1935 figure including such locomotives appears on p. 417, of TsUNKhU, 1936a, and it has been reduced here by about the same proportion as applied in 1934.

(6) This is a synthetic series, compiled by combining traffic data with locomotive performance data. Briefly, total ton-kilometers of freight traffic, divided by the average net weight per train, yielded total train-kilometers, which is in general the same as total "principal" locomotive-kilometers. For each year, putting this on a daily basis, and dividing by the average daily run per operating freight locomotive (average locomotive-miles per locomotive-day), indicates the average number of freight locomotives at work in road freight service. For details see Table 74.

Kochetov, 1948, p. 90, gives a 1940 breakdown in percentages of the location of all locomotives under railroad orders as follows:

| | | |
|---|---:|---:|
| In the working fleet | | 55.5 |
|     Freight service | 30.1 | |
|     Passenger service | 8.4 | |
|     Switching | 14.0 | |
|     Other auxiliary work | 3.0 | |
| Bad-order | | 21.7 |
| Stored by individual railroads | | 18.1 |
| In process of transfer | | 4.7 |

In addition to the serviceable locomotives stored by the individual railroads, Kochetov states that the NKPS in 1940 maintained a separate reserve stock of locomotives. The indicated ratio of locomotives in road freight service to the total stock is surprisingly low, but at least his data tend to support the order of magnitude of the synthetic series compiled above for locomotives in road freight service. Locomotives "in process of transfer" are those reported on daily field reports as, for example, having been dispatched to another depot but not yet relocated.

Table 62.  Number of locomotives produced, USSR, by year,
1925–1940, 1950–1955

| Year | Steam locomotives | | | Electric locomotives |
|------|--------|-----------|----------|-----------|
| | Freight | Passenger | Combined | |
| 1925[a] | 46 | 55 | 101 | — |
| 1926[a] | 72 | 142 | 214 | — |
| 1927[a] | 182 | 182 | 364 | — |
| 1928[a] | 308 | 150 | 458 | — |
| 1929[a] | 408 | 140 | 548 | — |
| 1930[a] | 587 | — | 587 | — |
| Special quarter[b] | 178 | — | 178 | — |
| 1931 | 812 | — | 812 | — |
| 1932 | 681 | 148 | 829 | 1 |
| 1933 | 725 | 182 | 907 | 17 |
| 1934 | 844 | 222 | 1,066 | 19 |
| 1935 | 1,146 | 372 | 1,518 | 34 |
| 1936 | — | — | 1,194 | — |
| 1937 | — | — | 1,214 | 32 |
| 1938 and 1939 | — | — | 2,085 | — |
| 1940 | — | — | 914 | — |
| 1936–1940 | 4,116 | 1,291 | 5,407 | — |
| 1929–1940 | 9,497 | 2,355 | 11,852 | — |
| 1950 | — | — | 985 | 102 |
| 1951 | — | — | — | 113 |
| 1952 | — | — | 255 | 110 |
| 1953 | — | — | 671 | 148 |
| 1954 | — | — | 758 | 158 |
| 1955 | — | — | 654 | 194 |

[a]12 months including 3 months of preceding calendar year.
[b]Last three months of calendar 1930.

### Notes to Table 62

Sources for this table are as follows:

*1925–1934.* IAkobi, 1935, pp. 86–87. The totals are broken down by producing plant, and exclude imports. The latter are apparently included in the slightly larger totals given in TsUNKhU, 1936a p. 163.

*1935.* TsUNKhU, 1936a, p. 163.

*1936–1937.* Ioffe, 1939, p. 165.

*1929–1940.* These totals are given by Minister I. V. Kovalev, 1946, p. 6, as having been received by the railroads during the years of the five-year plans. The preceding totals for 1938–1939 and for 1936–1940 result by subtraction, using the 1940 combined figure from TsSU, 1946, p. 56, which also presents the 1937 and 1940 figures for electric locomotives.

*1950–1955.* The 1950, 1954, and 1955 data are from TsSU, 1956, p. 56. Estimates for intervening years result from applying annual per cent rises given in CSA reports.

Table 63.  Railroad rolling stock, USSR, by year, 1924–1940, 1945–1955, plus 1960 plan

| Year | Freight cars (10³ 2-axle units) | | | (3) as percentage— | | Passenger cars (10³ 2-axle units) | | Total cars under RR orders (10³ 2-axle units) |
|---|---|---|---|---|---|---|---|---|
| | (1) Under railroad orders | (2) Working fleet | (3) Road service | of (1) | of (2) | Under railroad orders | Working fleet | |
| 1924[a] | 423.5 | 234.9 | 216.3 | 51.1 | 92.1 | — | 8.0 | — |
| 1925[a] | 433.5 | 250.3 | 233.2 | 53.8 | 93.2 | — | 10.3 | 456.7 |
| 1926[a] | 436.4 | 319.3 | 300.0 | 68.7 | 94.0 | 20.3 | 12.3 | 471.6 |
| 1927[a] | 450.3 | 334.8 | 314.9 | 69.9 | 94.1 | 21.3 | 14.4 | 494.9 |
| 1928 | 472.0 | 363.0 | 341.4 | 72.3 | 94.0 | 22.9 | 14.6 | 518.9 |
| 1929 | 494.5 | 414.1 | 393.3 | 79.5 | 95.0 | 24.4 | 16.1 | 532.2 |
| 1930 | 507.2 | 457.5 | 433.0 | 85.4 | 94.6 | 25.0 | 18.2 | 556.0 |
| 1931 | 529.4 | 494.1 | 472.8 | 89.3 | 95.7 | 26.6 | 19.6 | 573.8 |
| 1932 | 545.8 | 496.5 | 480.7 | 88.1 | 96.8 | 28.0 | 21.8 | 585.1 |
| 1933 | 555.4 | 502.6 | 490.2 | 88.3 | 97.5 | 29.7 | 23.0 | 595.9 |
| 1934 | 565.2 | 506.7 | 490.3 | 86.7 | 96.8 | 30.7 | 23.5 | 636.9 |
| 1935 | 604.6 | 536.6 | 525.0 | 86.8 | 97.8 | 32.3 | — | — |
| 1936 | — | — | 585.0 | — | — | — | — | — |
| 1937 | — | — | 627.0 | — | — | — | — | — |
| 1938 | 757.4 | 679.0 | 662.1 | 87.4 | 97.5 | — | — | — |
| 1939 | — | — | 677.0 | — | — | — | — | — |
| 1940 | — | — | 721.2 | — | — | — | — | — |
| 1945 | — | — | 676.5 | — | — | — | — | — |
| 1946 | — | — | 700.7 | — | — | — | — | — |
| 1947 | — | — | 732.9 | — | — | — | — | — |
| 1948 | — | — | 789.7 | — | — | — | — | — |
| 1949 | — | — | 862.8 | — | — | — | — | — |
| 1950 | — | — | 886.1 | — | — | — | — | — |
| 1951 | — | — | 924.0 | — | — | — | — | — |
| 1952 | — | — | 950.8 | — | — | — | — | — |
| 1953 | — | — | 981.4 | — | — | — | — | — |
| 1954 | — | — | 1044.8 | — | — | — | — | — |
| 1955 | — | — | 1055.4 | — | — | — | — | — |
| 1960 (plan) | — | — | 1174.0 | — | — | — | — | — |

[a]12 months including 3 months of the preceding calendar year.

Notes to Table 63

Sources for this table are as follows:

The data in columns (1) and (2) for 1924–1934 are from IAkobi, 1935, p. 44, and include freight cars carrying work train freight as well as those in commercial trains. The 1935 figures are from TsUNKhU, 1936a, pp. 416 and 430. *Gudok*, 9 March '39, p. 3, states that between 1934 and 1938 the number of freight cars increased 34 per cent in 2-axle units, and this percentage is applied to both columns to yield 1938 estimates.

Column (3), showing the average number of freight cars in road service each year, is a synthetic series, compiled through combining data on average daily carloadings with data on the average turnaround time of freight cars. In general, the number of cars loaded each day times the number of days it takes a car to complete a trip equals the total number of cars in road service at that moment. For details, see Table 75.

The passenger car series for 1924–1934 come from IAkobi, 1935, p. 44; and the 1935 figure is from TsUNKhU, 1936a, p. 430.

Table 64.  Freight car stock, USSR railroads, by type, 1928, 1932, 1937, 1940

| Type of car | 1928 | | | 1932 | | | 1937 | | | 1940 | | |
|---|---|---|---|---|---|---|---|---|---|---|---|---|
| | 2-axle cars | 4-axle cars | 2-axle units[a] | 2-axle cars | 4-axle cars | 2-axle units[a] | 2-axle cars | 4-axle cars | 2-axle units[a] | 2-axle cars | 4-axle cars | 2-axle units[a] |
| Box cars | 313,300 | 12,400 | 337,900 | 312,900 | 20,300 | 353,600 | 268,300 | 45,600 | 359,400 | 254,500 | 53,600 | 361,600 |
| Gondola and hopper cars | 6,100 | 8,500 | 23,200 | 9,400 | 7,600 | 24,600 | 8,700 | 33,000 | 74,700 | 7,300 | 59,200 | 125,700 |
| Flat cars | 74,800 | 700 | 76,100 | 92,800 | 700 | 94,100 | 158,300 | 8,500 | 175,300 | 151,500 | 22,000 | 195,500 |
| Tank cars | 27,200 | 2,500 | 32,200 | 28,800 | 8,100 | 45,000 | 29,300 | 19,900 | 69,200 | 25,200 | 23,400 | 72,000 |
| Refrigerated cars | 6,800 | 200 | 7,200 | 9,600 | 4,500 | 18,700 | 8,800 | 8,300 | 25,400 | 8,400 | 10,000 | 28,500 |
| Other cars[b] | 9,300 | 1,200 | 11,800 | 10,500 | 800 | 12,000 | 14,100 | 2,800 | 19,700 | 13,000 | 6,200 | 25,400 |
| Total | 437,500 | 25,500 | 488,400 | 464,000 | 42,000 | 548,000 | 487,500 | 118,100 | 723,700 | 459,900 | 174,400 | 808,700 |

a Figures in 2-axle units may not agree with data derived as the 2-axle component plus twice the 4-axle component, due to rounding errors.

b This category includes special-type cars plus cars of the five listed types leased to other organizations, administered by other organizations, or being scrapped.

## Notes to Table 64

These estimates are derived from two percentage tables given by Kochetov, 1948, p. 220. One shows the number of physical units of each of the five types, and of total cars "on hand," as percentages of their number in 1928, and the other shows the percentage of each type having four axles in 1928, 1932, 1937, and 1940, together with the four-axle percentage for the whole freight car stock.

Since the Soviet freight car stock contains both European-type two-axle cars and the four-axle, two-truck type familiar on United States railroads, Soviet railroad statisticians have adopted the convention of multiplying the physical number of four-axle cars by two and combining the result with the physical number of two-axle cars to yield the number of "two-axle *units*."

The practice introduces a number of confusing elements into the analysis of freight train performance, and explains why, for example, no attempt is made in the present study to compile a series for the average number of cars per freight train. Figures on the number of axles per train, even if divided by the average number of axles per car, convey misleading impressions. Moreover, as will be seen from an inspection of trends in the number of cars of a given type, this statistical device serves to mask several cases of actual decline in the number of cars on hand, where presumably the addition of new cars was insufficient to offset attrition of the existing stock.

The absolute 1928 figures used as a base for Kochetov's percentages are taken from the NKPS *Materialy* ... , vol. 104, p. 39. Kochetov does not state whether his percentages apply to an annual average or to the end of each year, but a comparison of the totals implied by his data with the series in Table 64 indicates that he was comparing end-of-year figures. However, the 1928 statistics in vol. 104 were published for the economic year, and show an average for September rather than a January 1, 1929 census. IAkobi, 1935, p. 44, gives data for both "1927/28" and "1928," and the ratio between his respective figures for the total freight car stock under railroad orders was applied to the NKPS data to raise each figure by 1.01768.

There is additional uncertainty concerning the coverage of Kochetov's percentages, since the "total on hand" is slightly larger than the total "under railroad orders." For all these reasons, the computed absolute data have been rounded off, and are not as accurate as series derived less circuitously.

Table 65. Rolling stock characteristics, USSR railroads, by year,
1928–1940, 1945–1955[a] (per cent)

| Year | Cars equipped with automatic brakes | Cars equipped with automatic couplings | Cars equipped with four axles |
|------|------|------|------|
| 1928 | 8.06 | — | 5.5 |
| 1929 | — | — | — |
| 1930 | 5.6 | — | 6.9 |
| 1931 | — | — | — |
| 1932 | 10.6 | 0.1 | 8.3 |
| 1933 | 17.0 | — | 9.0 |
| 1934 | 26.0 | 0.5 | 10.5 |
| 1935 | 32.6 | — | 12.1 |
| 1936 | — | — | 15.6 |
| 1937 | 49.7 | 17.2 | 19.6 |
| 1938 | 60.1 | 23.8 | 22.7 |
| 1939 | 68.4 | 31.2 | 24.9 |
| 1940 | 72.7 | 38.0 | 27.5 |
| 1945 | 71.1 | 41.5 | — |
| 1946 | — | — | 28.0 |
| 1947 | — | — | — |
| 1948 | — | — | — |
| 1949 | — | — | — |
| 1950 | 76.0 | 52.5 | 36.4 |
| 1951 | — | — | — |
| 1952 | — | — | — |
| 1953 | 81.4 | 66.5 | 50.0 |
| 1954 | 85.0 | — | 53.4 |
| 1955 | 87.0 | 77.0 | — |

[a]At end of year.

## Notes to Table 65

The 1928, 1930, and 1932–1935 data come from TsUNKhU, 1936a, p. XLI, and from page 22 of TsUNKhU, 1936b (for 1930 figures). The 1932 percentage for automatic couplings is from Kochetov, 1948, p. 220, and the 1934 percentage is from Naporko, 1954, p. 228.

The 1936–1939 percentages of 4-axle cars are taken from Povorozhenko, 1948, p. 24. His 1940 figures, which appear frequently, seem rounded. The 1937–1939 data for brakes and couplings are given by Zagliadimov, 1947, p. 29.

The 1940 percentages for brakes and couplings are given by Kovalev, 1946, pp. 43–44, and the 1940 percentage for 4-axle cars appears on p. 220 of Kochetov, 1948.

The 1945 percentage of automatic brakes is derived from the statement (B. Podshivalov, in *Gudok*, 6 June '51, p. 2), that outfitting of freight cars with automatic brakes increased during the (postwar) Five Year Plan by 6.9 per cent (though this procedure is not accurate). The 1945 couplings percentage is derived (through deliberate misinterpretation), from Kovalev's statement (1946a, p. 43), that "the number of freight cars equipped with automatic couplings will increase by 33.5 per cent and reach 75 per cent." The 1946 4-axle percentage is from *Gudok*, 20 Apr '55, p. 3.

The 1950 percentages for automatic brakes and couplings were given by B. Podshivalov in *Gudok*, 6 June '51, p. 2. The percentage of 4-axle cars is derived

Notes to Table 65 (*Continued*)

from his 76 per cent over-all figure plus the information that "in the postwar Five Year Plan, 97 per cent of the four-axle and 64 per cent of the two-axle freight cars have been equipped already with automatic brakes (Modzolevskii, 1951, p. 153). All three 1953 percentages were given by Minister B. P. Beshchev in his speech in *Gudok*, 5 May '54, p. 3. The 1954 couplings percentage was reported by Deputy Minister Robel' in *Gudok*, 2 Nov '55, p. 2, and the 1954 4-axle percentage appeared in *Gudok*, 20 April '55, p. 3. The brakes and couplings percentages for 1955 are given in the CSA report on the Fifth Five Year Plan.

Table 66.  Operating labor force and labor productivity,
USSR railroads, by year, 1928–1940, 1945–1955

| Year | Average operating labor force (thousands) (1) | Productivity (thousands of "cumulated" ton-kilometers per operating worker-and-employee) | | |
|------|------|------|------|------|
| | | (2) | (3) | (4) |
| 1928 | 863 | 136.6 | — | 143.2 |
| 1929 | 868 | 167.0 | — | 175.8 |
| 1930 | 951 | 195.3 | 204.4 | 207.2 |
| 1931 | 1094 | — | 206.4 | 209.1 |
| 1932 | 1105 | — | 236.1 | 239.2 |
| 1933 | 1022 | — | — | 249.3 |
| 1934 | 1148 | — | — | 255.5 |
| 1935 | 1249 | — | — | 273.0 |
| 1936 | 1216 | — | — | 340.2 |
| 1937 | 1250 | — | — | 370.7 |
| 1938 | 1309 | — | — | 366.9 |
| 1939 | 1315 | — | — | 384.0 |
| 1940 (a) | 1325 | 382.6 | 395.1 | 397.2 |
| 1940 (b) | 1394 | 368.0 | 380.6 | 382.8 |
| 1945 | 1502 | 253.2 | 275.4 | — |
| 1946 | 1560 | 277.5 | — | — |
| 1947 | 1562 | 285.6 | — | — |
| 1948 | 1575 | 331.2 | — | — |
| 1949 | 1657 | 365.1 | — | — |
| 1950 | 1712 | 403.0 | — | — |
| 1951 | 1765 | 439.7 | — | — |
| 1952 | 1867 | 455.0 | — | — |
| 1953 | 1901 | 482.0 | — | — |
| 1954 | 1968 | 501.0 | — | — |
| 1955 | 1980 | 561.8 | — | — |

Notes to Table 66

The railroad labor force is a diverse one, raising many problems of inclusion and exclusion. For a thorough analysis, see A. David Redding's "Employment and Labor Productivity in USSR Railroads, 1928–1950," RAND P-327 of 15 Sept. 52, and its published version in *Soviet Studies*, 5:32–43 (July 1953). While it has been possible to carry certain minutiae farther here than could be done by Redding in 1952, great reliance is placed on his pioneer work.

Notes to Table 66 (*Continued*)

The annual averages in column (1) cover only those workers and employees "connected with railroad operations," roughly half the total employed in the railroad sector, and exclude those working in locomotive and car building and repair plants, construction of new lines, and certain other minor activities. When not given directly in Soviet sources, they can be estimated as quotients of railroad output divided by an output-per-worker series compiled from numerous Soviet remarks. In this connection, columns (2), (3), and (4) correspond to the output coverages shown in Table 58; (2) is the sum of passenger-kilometers and tariff ton-kilometers, (3) is the sum of passenger-kilometers and operating ton-kilometers, and (4) also adds work-train traffic.

Slight changes in coverage have produced a considerable diversity of Soviet railroad operating labor productivity figures, but most can be successfully reconciled. The following changes have occurred: the excess of operating over tariff ton-kilometers was included in output from 1930 to 1949; work-train freight was included from 1932 to 1947; for 1932–1935, TsUNKhU Gosplana compiled a railroad operating labor force series somewhat smaller than the NKPS series; and records for 1940 both include and exclude the workers and output added to the Soviet railroad system through acquisitions along the western frontier.

The sources for Table 66 are as follows:

The 1928–1932 labor force figures are from TsUNKhU, 1936e, p. 278. The 1934–1937 figures are from Vol'fson, 1941, p. 553, and the 1933, 1938, and 1939 figures are derived from Kochetov, 1941, p. 260. Use of the smaller TsUNKhU labor force coverage for 1932–1935 leads to the following data (headings keyed to Table 66):

|      | (1)  | (2)   | (3)   | (4)   |
|------|------|-------|-------|-------|
| 1932 | 1016 | 249.0 | 256.8 | 260.1 |
| 1933 | 992  | 246.7 | 254.0 | 256.8 |
| 1934 | 1111 | 249.4 | 259.9 | 263.9 |
| 1935 | 1209 | 269.6 | 278.5 | 281.9 |

These figures plus the productivity figures computed in Table 66 will reproduce almost all reported Soviet productivity data for these years and assign them to their proper coverage. Compare, for example, those given by I. Kazarin in *Plan*, 1937, no. 3, p. 40. It is assumed here that if the reduction from 1935 to 1936 in labor force, as shown by Vol'fson, could have been explained as a change from NKPS to TsUNKhU coverage, Vol'fson would have noted the change. The 1928 and 1929 productivities in column (4) are computed on the basis of output estimates in Table 58.

For 1940, the (a) line reflects estimates for USSR territory as of January 1940, while the (b) estimates are interpreted as including operations on the territory acquired during the year. Umbliia, 1947, p. 16, gives 1940 productivity as 397.2, with a footnote adding that inclusion of Baltic and Kishinev railroads makes the figure 364.0. Naporko, 1954, p. 184, gives 1940 productivity as 382.6, and states that 1940 output, with 1935 productivity, would have required another 600,000 operating workers. TsSU, 1956, p. 180, gives the 1940 operating labor force as 1,394,000, and in conjunction with a 1940 figure of 513,000,000,000 for cumulated output, it yields 368,000 as the productivity per worker. Experimentation shows that 1940 cumulated output must have been approximately as follows (in billions of ton-kilometers):

Notes to Table 66  (*Continued*)

|  | (2) | (3) | (4) |
|---|---|---|---|
| Territory as of January 1940 | 506.9 | 523.5 | 526.3 |
| Increment on new territory | 6.1 | 7.0 | 7.3 |
| Territory as of December 1940 | 513.0 | 530.5 | 533.6 |

An addition of 69,000 operating workers is broadly consistent with the figure of 115,000 in *Gudok*, 6 Aug. '40, p. 1, for the number added to Soviet railroads by the acquisitions, if the 115,000 covered nonoperating workers too.

The 1945–1955 labor force series is derived through chaining on to absolute 1950, 1954, and 1955 data from TsSU, 1956, p. 180, together with railroad output figures from Table 58 (using tariff ton-kilometers), the indexes for output per worker given by Naporko, 1954, p. 246, for 1945–1950, and by TsSU, 1956, p. 34, for 1950–1955. Since 1949, the excess of operating over tariff ton-kilometers has been excluded from Soviet labor productivity computations, and previous 1945–1948 data revised. The 1945 figure of 275.4, given by Umbliia, 1947, p. 45, clearly has column (3) coverage. However, his 1940 figure of 364.0, which was the base for percentage reference during the Fourth Five Year Plan, has uncertain coverage; he may have taken column (2) in January 1940 territory and divided by 1,394,000 workers, without remarking on the reduced coverage involved. A check on the productivity and output series for 1950–1955 is provided by absolute labor force data in Shvetsov, 1956, p. 52, which confirm the estimates in Table 66, except that his 1950 figure is 1,713.1 thousand (and his 1946 figure is 1,518.0).

# APPENDIX D. Railroad Finances

Table 67. Railroad operating revenues, USSR, by year, 1924–1940,
1945, 1950 (millions of rubles)

| Year | Freight revenues | Passenger revenues | Combined revenues | Other revenues[a] | Total operating revenue |
|---|---|---|---|---|---|
| 1924[b] | 432,021 | 137,422 | 569,443 | 122,381 | 691,824 |
| 1925[b] | 599,762 | 198,484 | 798,246 | 157,515 | 955,761 |
| 1926[b] | 880,980 | 275,873 | 1,156,853 | 212,688 | 1,369,541 |
| 1927[b] | 1,091,166 | 296,845 | 1,388,011 | 241,917 | 1,629,928 |
| 1928 | 1,333,772 | 327,351 | 1,661,123 | 269,651 | 1,930,774 |
| 1929 | 1,643,540 | 417,652 | 2,061,192 | 342,070 | 2,403,262 |
| 1930 | 1,959,388 | 793,741 | 2,753,129 | 453,051 | 3,206,180 |
| 1931 | 2,440,224 | 1,435,959 | 3,876,183 | 426,785 | 4,302,968 |
| 1932 | 2,723,227 | 2,049,319 | 4,772,546 | 715,959 | 5,488,505 |
| 1932 | 2,616,703 | 2,315,275 | 4,931,978 | 831,850 | 5,763,828 |
| 1934 | 3,044,100 | 2,175,700 | 5,219,800 | 871,900 | 6,091,700 |
| 1935 | 3,883,000 | 1,964,600 | 5,847,600 | 982,800 | 6,830,400 |
| 1936 | 5,846,200 | 2,291,400 | 8,137,600 | 612,200 | 8,749,800 |
| 1937 | 6,915,200 | 2,797,900 | 9,713,100 | 425,100 | 10,138,200 |
| 1938 | 7,595,400 | 3,465,000 | 11,060,400 | 484,100 | 11,544,500 |
| 1939 | 11,375,500 | 3,978,600 | 15,354,100 | 687,000 | 16,041,100 |
| 1940 | 12,660,000 | 4,600,000 | 17,260,000 | 796,000 | 18,056,000 |
| 1945 | 9,900,000 | 7,800,000 | 17,700,000 | 1,040,000 | 18,740,000 |
| 1950 | 30,400,000 | 8,300,000 | 38,700,000 | 2,260,000 | 40,960,000 |

[a]"Other revenues" cover receipts from carriage of baggage and mail, loading and unloading, storage, weighing and refrigeration fees, fines collected from shippers or receivers, miscellaneous receipts from rental of railroad equipment, real estate, and so on, and from other sources unrelated to the volume of traffic.
[b]12 months including 3 months of the preceding calendar year.

## Notes to Table 67

Sources for Table 67 are as follows:
*1924-1927.* NKPS *Materialy*, vol. 104, p. 4.
*1928-1930.* NKPS *Materialy*, vol. 128, pp. 28–29.
*1931-1933.* IAkobi, 1935, pp. 64–65.
*1934-1935.* TsUNKhU, 1936a, pp. 437–38.
*1936.* Kochetov 1939, p. 268.
*1937.* Vol'fson, 1941, p. 653.
*1938.* The total revenue figure is given by Vol'fson, 1941, p. 650, and by Vinnichenko, 1948, p. 46. The division into components is based on the statement by A. Svistunov in *Zhel. Trans.*, 1948, no. 10, p. 24, that in 1938 revenue from passenger transport made up 30 per cent of total operating revenue, and on the assumption that the ratio of "other" to total operating revenue in 1938 was the same as the 1937 ratio. This yields a residual figure for freight revenue which produces an estimated unit revenue of 2.050 kopeks per ton-kilometer. Since Vol'fson, 1941, p. 624, states that the 1938 average unit revenue for freight was 2.0 kopeks per ton-kilometer, the division appears reasonably accurate.

Notes to Table 67 (*Continued*)

*1939.* Kochetov, 1941, p. 295.

*1940.* The total appears in Vinnichenko, 1948, p. 46, and a percentage breakdown permitting its distribution into elements is given in the second edition of his book, 1952, p. 148.

*1945.* The estimate for total operating revenue is explained in the notes to Table 70. It has been divided on the basis of the statement that "in 1945 the revenue ... from freight, passengers, and baggage made up 96 per cent of total railroad revenues" (Kochetov, 1948, p. 230), using the 1940 ratio of baggage revenue to total revenue to transfer baggage receipts to "other" revenue; plus the information that the average unit revenue for 9 months of 1945 was 3.16 kopeks per ton-kilometer (N. Dubrovin, *Zhel. Trans.*, 1946, no. 11/12, p. 24). This rate seems clearly to cover freight alone, and is extended to the whole year. It leads to a residual for passenger revenues which implies a very high unit revenue per passenger-kilometer (11.78 kopeks). This, however, may reflect an abnormally low proportion of commutation traffic and abnormally high proportion of long-distance traffic, along with some wartime rate increases.

*1950.* The estimate for total operating revenue is explained in the notes to Table 70. The division comes from a percentage breakdown supplied by Vinnichenko, 1952, p. 148.

Table 68. Railroad operating expenses, USSR, by year, 1926–1940,
1945–1947, 1950 (millions of rubles)

| Year | Wages | Fuel | Materials | Other expenses | Sub-total | Depre-ciation | Rolling stock repair | Total |
|---|---|---|---|---|---|---|---|---|
| 1926[a] | 678 | 149 | 213 | 144 | 1,184 | — | — | — |
| 1927[a] | 837 | 182 | 266 | 101 | 1,386 | — | — | — |
| 1928[a] | 884 | 209 | 295 | 81 | 1,469 | — | — | — |
| 1929[a] | 877 | 232 | 252 | 95 | 1,456 | — | 110 | 1,566 |
| 1930[a] | 1,032 | 270 | 221 | 148 | 1,671 | — | 137 | 1,808 |
| Special quarter[b] | 297 | 90 | 46 | 21 | 454 | — | 37 | 491 |
| 1931 | 1,447 | — | — | — | 2,235 | 551 | — | 2,786 |
| 1932 | 1,899 | — | — | — | 2,823 | 613 | — | 3,436 |
| 1933 | 1,876 | 508 | 221 | 509 | 3,114 | 671 | — | 3,785 |
| 1934 | 2,468 | 537 | 288 | 624 | 3,917 | — | — | 4,867 |
| 1935 | 3,774 | 575 | — | — | 5,516 | 780 | — | 6,296 |
| 1936 | — | — | — | — | — | — | — | 8,099 |
| 1937 | 4,183 | 1,482 | 801 | 1,545 | 8,011 | 900 | 608 | 9,519 |
| 1938 | — | — | — | — | — | — | — | 10,711 |
| 1939 | 5,269 | 2,064 | 934 | 1,836 | 10,103 | 1,240 | 750 | 12,093 |
| 1940 | — | — | — | — | — | — | — | 13,419 |
| "War year"[c] | 6,960 | 1,800 | — | 1,690[d] | 10,450 | 1,150 | 650 | 12,250 |
| 1945 | 10,610 | 2,610 | 940 | 1,610 | 15,770 | 1,880 | 770 | 18,420 |
| 1946 | 13,870 | 2,800 | — | 3,890[d] | 20,560 | 2,680 | 1,100 | 24,340 |
| 1947 | 17,090 | 3,070 | — | 4,320[d] | 24,480 | 2,700 | 1,220 | 28,400 |
| 1950 | 15,800 | 6,900 | — | 5,400[d] | 28,100 | 5,100 | 1,700 | 34,900 |

[a]12 months including three months of the preceding calendar year.
[b]"Special quarter" is the Soviet designation for October-December 1930.
[c]Probably calendar 1943. These figures are approximate.
[d]Includes materials.

### Notes to Table 68

The sources for this table are as follows:

*1926.* NKPS *Materialy,* no. 85, p. 159.

*1927.* NKPS *Materialy,* vol. 104, p. 160.   This breakdown appears preferable to the one given in vol. 85, p. 159, since it distributes 49 million rubles the latter had left in "other expenses."

*1928—Special quarter, 1930.* NKPS *Materialy,* vol. 128, pp. 17–19.   In this case also, revised figures for 1928 have been preferred over those given in no. 104.

*1931-1932.* NKPS *Materialy,* vol. 136, p. 12.

*1933.* IAkobi, 1935, p. 178, itemizes expenses making up the subtotal.   The total given by Kochetov and Vinnichenko (see below) was then used to obtain amortization expense by subtraction.

*1934.* TsUNKhU, 1936a, p. 439.   The difference between the itemized subtotal and the gross total for operating expenses in 1934 is 950 million rubles. It will be seen that this is larger than the amortization allowance made in the preceding and following years, and hence it probably is a combination of amortization expense with something else, perhaps rolling-stock repairs.

Notes to Table 68  (*Continued*)

*1935.*  Kochetov, 1939, p. 286.

*1937.*  Vol'fson, 1941, gives a percentage breakdown on p. 655 and the absolute total on p. 654, together with figures for amortization and rolling-stock repairs (both annual and medium).  Their figure for "other expenses" has been raised to include an undistributed item of 86.4 million rubles for "other expenses of the center."

*1939.*  Kochetov, 1941, p. 316, gives figures for all but rolling-stock repairs, which he consolidates into "other expenses."  Khachaturov, 1946, p. 54, gives a percentage breakdown consistent with Kochetov's absolute data, and states a separate percentage for rolling-stock repairs.

*1926–1940.*  Totals for railroad operating expenses in every year of this period appear in the summary tabulations provided by Vinnichenko, 1948, pp. 37–46. Apart from minute discrepancies in 1929–30 and 1935, his figures agree with those accompanying the breakdowns cited in the table.  Totals conforming to those above for 1933–1936 are also given by Kochetov in his 1939 volume, p. 286.

*"War year."*  These approximate figures are based on the statement that "railroad expenses exceed 12 billion rubles a year" (p. 3), and a percentage breakdown of operating expenses in a "war year" (pp. 67–68), appearing in NKPS, 1944.  They most likely relate to calendar 1943.

*1945.*  The estimate for total operating expenses is explained in the notes to Table 70.  The individual figures are based on a percentage breakdown given in Khachaturov, 1946, p. 54.

*1946.*  The total is an estimate explained in the notes to Table 70, and the breakdown is based on a percentage distribution given in Umbliia, 1947, p. 7.

*1947.*  The estimated total is explained in the notes to Table 70, and a percentage breakdown of 1947 operating expenses given in Beliunov, 1948, pp. 148–149, is the basis for the individual figures.

*1950.*  A percentage breakdown provided in Naporko, 1954, p. 239, was applied to estimated total expenses from Table 70.

Table 69. Unit operating revenues and expenses, USSR railroads,
by year, 1924–1940 (kopeks)

| Year | (1) | (2) | (3) | (4) | (5) | (6) | (7) |
|------|-----|-----|-----|-----|-----|-----|-----|
| 1924[a] | 1,280 | 0.890 | 1.158 | 1.407 | 1.353 | 0.054 | — |
| 1925[a] | 1.264 | 1.043 | 1.201 | 1.438 | 1.207 | 0.231 | — |
| 1926[a] | 1.279 | 1.181 | 1.254 | 1.484 | 1.284 | 0.200 | — |
| 1927[a] | 1.336 | 1.343 | 1.338 | 1.571 | 1.336 | 0.235 | — |
| 1928[a] | 1.428 | 1.337 | 1.409 | 1.638 | 1.246 | — | 1.466 |
| 1929[a] | 1.455 | 1.305 | 1.422 | 1.658 | 1.080 | — | 1.336 |
| 1930[a] | 1.463 | 1.533 | 1.483 | 1.727 | 0.974 | — | 1.166 |
| 1931 | 1.604 | 2.323 | 1.812 | 2.011 | 1.302 | 0.709 | 1.234 |
| 1932 | 1.609 | 2.447 | 1.886 | 2.169 | 1.358 | 0.811 | 1.317 |
| 1933 | 1.544 | 3.081 | 2.016 | 2.356 | 1.547 | 0.809 | 1.502 |
| 1934 | 1.480 | 3.046 | 1.883 | 2.198 | 1.756 | 0.442 | 1.685 |
| 1935 | 1.505 | 2.892 | 1.794 | 2.095 | 1.931 | 0.164 | 1.870 |
| 1936 | 1.808 | 2.968 | 2.031 | 2.184 | 2.022 | 0.162 | 1.979 |
| 1937 | 1.949 | 3.077 | 2.179 | 2.274 | 2.135 | 0.139 | 2.076 |
| 1938 | 2.050 | 3.780 | 2.393 | 2.498 | 2.318 | 0.180 | 2.249 |
| 1939 | 2.902 | 4.245 | 3.161 | 3.303 | 2.490 | 0.813 | 2.410 |
| 1940 | 3.051 | 4.695 | 3.365 | 3.520 | 2.616 | 0.904 | 2.529 |

[a]The data for 1924–1927 are all for a 12-month period including 3 months of the preceding calendar year. The revenue data for 1928, 1929, and 1930 remain on an economic-year basis; hence comparisons can be seriously misleading.

Column headings:

(1) Unit freight revenue per tariff ton-kilometer.

(2) Unit passenger revenue per passenger-kilometer.

(3) Combined unit revenue per "cumulated" ton-kilometer.

(4) Total operating revenue per "cumulated" ton-kilometer.

(5) Unit cost per "cumulated" ton-kilometer, using tariff ton-kilometers.

(6) Net income per "cumulated" ton-kilometer, that is, column (4) minus column (5).

(7) Unit cost per "cumulated" ton-kilometer, using operating ton-kilometers.

## Notes to Table 69

All figures in the first six columns are computed from the financial data in Tables 67 and 68, divided by the sum of passenger-kilometers from Table 56 and tariff ton-kilometers from Table 46. Column (7) shows the unit cost of railroad operations, including the ton-kilometers of freight movement performed by commercial trains but not charged to clients, that is, movement in excess of the tariff distances between points of origination and termination. For the years 1928–1930, column (7) also reflects inclusion in costs of the computed depreciation charge discussed in chapter 11. The 1934–1939 figures are from Vol'fson, 1941, pp. 639–50, and the 1940 figure is from Koldomasov, 1949, pp. 50–51.

Table 70. Postwar USSR railroad revenues and expenses, by year,
1945–1950

| Year | Total operating revenue ($10^6$R) | Total operating expense ($10^6$R) | Net income ($10^6$R) | Profit or loss (per cent) |
|---|---|---|---|---|
| 1945 | 18,740 | 18,420 | 320 | 1.7 |
| 1946 | 20,800 | 24,600 | −3,800 | −15.4 |
| 1947 | 21,200 | 29,200 | −8,000 | −27.4 |
| 1948 | 23,770 | 30,420 | −6,650 | −21.9 |
| 1949 | 40,290 | 32,890 | 7,400 | 22.5 |
| 1950 (plan) | 29,400 | 23,450 | 5,950 | 25.4 |
| 1950 (actual) | 40,960 | 34,900 | 6,060 | 17.4 |

| Year | Railroad output[a] | Unit revenue (kopeks) | Unit cost (kopeks) | Unit margin (kopeks) |
|---|---|---|---|---|
| 1945 | 413.8 | 4.53 | 4.45 | 0.08 |
| 1946 | 463.1 | 4.49 | 5.32 | −0.83 |
| 1947 | 470.6 | 4.50 | 6.20 | −1.70 |
| 1948 | 539.4 | 4.41 | 5.64 | −1.23 |
| 1949 | 620.5 | 6.49 | 5.30 | 1.19 |
| 1950 (plan) | 648.0 | 4.54 | 3.62 | 0.92 |
| 1950 (actual) | 702.5 | 5.83 | 4.97 | 0.86 |

[a]Billions of "cumulated" ton-kilometers, combining passenger-kilometers with
*operating* ton-kilometers.

Notes to Table 70

The estimates in Table 70 are derived from indirect evidence with varying
degrees of precision, and the recent appearance of additional information makes
it clear that many of the figures require substantial revision. Interpretation of
available fragments is complicated by at least two factors: cost comparisons
sometimes refer to unit freight costs alone rather than to combined unit costs,
and cost computations since 1949 have employed tariff rather than operating ton-
kilometers as a divisor. I. Ivliev, in *Vop. Ekon.*, 1956, no. 10, pp. 38–39, states
that the 1947 and 1948 deficits were 1.9 billion and 0.88 billion rubles respectively, while the 1949 and 1950 profits were 8.6 and 6.3 billion rubles. Other
fragments cast doubt on certain unit cost data in Table 70 also, but it has not
yet proved possible to reconcile the evidence and produce a consistent set of
estimates.

The basis for the table will be clear if, instead of reviewing sources year by
year, we retrace the sequence of steps involved in its construction. I. Ivliev, in
*Zhel. Trans.*, 1947, no. 1, pp. 22–30, stated that "railroad revenues in 1950 will
be 162 per cent of 1940" (p. 25), and that "the planned rate of profit for 1950 is
to be 25.4 per cent" (p. 24). Given 1940 revenue, this led to absolute revenue,
expense, and net income figures for the 1950 plan. Kovalev, 1946a, p. 87,
stated that the planned 1950 revenue would be 56.9 per cent over 1945, and
added that 1950 net income would be around 6 billion rubles; Ivliev remarked
that the 1950 rate of profitability would be more than 18 times above 1945. This
led to absolute 1945 figures for total revenue, expense, and net income. It was
stated in *Gudok*, 23 July '47, p. 3, that 1946 railroad revenues were 11 per cent

Notes to Table 70 (*Continued*)

over 1945. K. Tverskoi reported in *Gudok*, 14 Jan. '49, p. 2, that "since the fourth quarter of 1946, the railroads have been working under subsidy" (at a loss), and a *Gudok* editorial of 12 Apr. '50 stated that the railroads in 1949 "crossed over to join the profitable sectors of the economy."

For 1950, it was reported by Vinnichenko, 1952, p. 35, that the "profitability of shipments was 17.4 per cent, exceeding the planned level of profitability by 2.2 per cent." Since the *rate* of profitability planned for 1950 was 25.4 per cent, this was taken to mean that absolute 1950 net income was 2.2 per cent above the 1950 target. The profitability rate is given as 17.3 per cent on p. 215, and (apparently rounded) as 25 per cent on p. 199. Given planned absolute 1950 net income, this led to realized absolute 1950 net income, revenue, and expense estimates.

Dividing total 1950 operating expenses by total "cumulated" ton-kilometers, using operating ton-kilometers, produced a realized 1950 unit cost. It has frequently been stated that the cost of shipment in 1950 "fell 2.2 per cent more than was intended by the five-year plan" (Vinnichenko, 1952, p. 35), yet realized 1950 unit costs, instead of being "more than 18 per cent below 1945" (Ivliev, *Zhel. Trans.*, 1947, no. 1, p. 26), as intended by the five-year plan, were apparently about 8 per cent *above* 1945. The statement could be considered "true," however, if it were interpreted to mean that 1950 unit costs were over 20 per cent below the postwar peak (1947 unit costs), thus conviently avoiding any mention of the rise between 1945 and 1947. One must also accept the coincidental appearance of the figure 2.2 per cent in two distinct connections.

If this assumption is followed, it leads to a 1947 unit cost estimate. Cost of shipment in 1948 was stated as 9.1 per cent below 1947 (Speech of B. P. Beshchev, new Minister of Transportation, before the USSR Supreme Soviet, reported in *Gudok*, 13 March '49, p. 2). The 1945 unit cost figure was obtained by division, and this left 1946 and 1949 to be filled in. If the two values are interpolated as arithmetic means between the preceding and following years, the series is complete, and can be used to complete a series for total operating expenses.

The 1949 percentage of profitability was given by Vinnichenko, 1952, p. 215, and this led to estimated absolute net income and total operating revenue for 1949. Unit revenue for 1947 was assumed at the 1946 level; this led to 1947 total revenue. 1948 operating income was given as 12.1 per cent more than in 1947 (I. Ivliev's article in MPS, 1949b, p. 23). The 1948 and 1949 unit revenues were obtained by division.

Several figures for unit cost in 1945, 1946, 1947, and the 1950 plan have appeared in the literature, and are ably discussed by Naum Jasny in chapter 3 of his *Soviet Prices of Producers' Goods* (Stanford, 1952). As he points out there, some of the figures relate, or may relate, only to the freight component of "cumulated" ton-kilometers; this probably explains some of the discrepancies between the unit figures estimated above and the implications of other Soviet data. There is also uncertainty regarding the coverage of the traffic data used to obtain unit figures, and until these ambiguities are resolved, the record must remain substantially uncertain.

Table 71. Annual investment in railroads and the whole economy, USSR,
by year, 1925–1940, and plan goals

| Year | Investment (10⁹ rubles) | | Percentage invested in railroads |
| | In railroads | In the whole economy | |
|---|---|---|---|
| 1925[a] | 0.220 | 1.220 | 18.03 |
| 1926[a] | 0.430 | 2.138 | 20.11 |
| 1927[a] | 0.715 | 3.664 | 19.51 |
| 1928 | 0.731 | 4.088 | 17.88 |
| Total | 2.096 | 11.110 | *18.87* |
| 1929 | 0.873 | 5.885 | 14.83 |
| 1930 | 1.112 | 9.786 | 11.36 |
| 1931 | 1.910 | 15.681 | 12.18 |
| 1932 | 2.569 | 20.086 | 12.79 |
| Total | 6.464 | 51.438 | *12.57* |
| 1st FYP period[b] | 6.398 | 50.502 | *12.67* |
| 1933 | 2.107 | 19.707 | 10.69 |
| 1934 | 2.928 | 25.528 | 11.47 |
| 1935 | 4.038 | 27.693 | 14.58 |
| 1936 | 4.428 | 31.750 | 13.95 |
| 1937 | 3.576 | 32.813 | 10.90 |
| Total[c] | 17.077 | 137.491 | *12.42* |
| 1938 | 4.650 | 35.700 | 13.03 |
| 1939 | 4.950 | 34.300 | 14.43 |
| 1940 | 5.000 | 38.000 | 13.16 |
| Total | 14.600 | 108.000 | *13.52* |
| *Plan goals* | | | |
| First FYP | 8.899 | 78.354 | 11.36 |
| Second FYP | 15.765 | 120.083 | 13.13 |
| 1935 plan | 3.357 | 21.190 | 16.79 |
| 1936 plan | 4.762 | 32.365 | 14.71 |
| 1937 plan | 5.553 | 32.600 | 17.03 |
| 1938 plan | 5.000 | 38.500 | 12.99 |
| Third FYP | 24.245 | 188.300 | 12.88 |
| 1941 plan | 6.500 | 48.140 | 13.50 |
| Fourth FYP | 40.100 | 250.300 | 16.02 |

[a]1925 and 1926 cover a 12-month period including 3 months of the preceding calendar year. The 1927 figures cover a 15-month period, from Oct. 1, 1926 through Dec. 31, 1927.

[b]These figures cover the last 3 months of calendar 1928, in addition to calendar 1929–1932. It is apparent that they are slightly less inclusive than the annual data.

[c]These figures are the total for the Second Five Year Plan period.

## Notes to Table 71

This table owes a great deal to the thorough research of Norman Kaplan, whose studies of Soviet investment have required the classification of voluminous and refractory ruble data. See his chapter in Bergson, ed., *Soviet Economic Growth*, and his RAND Memoranda RM-735 and P-277 Revised. Figures for annual investments in the railroads differ somewhat, and for investments in the whole economy differ substantially, depending on whether several relatively minor forms of investment, such as capital repairs, projects financed internally, and small equipment outlays, are included or excluded. In order to trace government policy over time with respect to the railroads' share of total investment, it is necessary, if possible, to maintain the same degree of inclusiveness or exclusiveness for the annual investment figures. This is especially true of the series for total investment in the whole economy. The data above are, in general, *inclusive*, which has the effect of showing a lower percentage of total investment being channeled into railroad development than would be shown by a series excluding these various adjustments. With constant coverage, however, the year-to-year trend would probably appear much the same.

Sources for Table 71 are as follows:

*1925–1928.* TsUNKhU, 1934, p. 300. The total represents addition of each column, and the percentage is then taken, independently of the annual ratios.

*1929–1932.* TsUNKhU, 1936a, p. 384. Again, the four-year total is based on these figures.

*First Five Year Plan period.* Gosplan, 1934, vol. 1, p. 442.

*1933–1937.* Annual data for the first four years were directly available from various sources, but figures for 1937 have had to be estimated as residuals. This requires careful treatment of the early years, in order to maintain a coverage comparable to that of the summary compilation for the Second Five Year Plan period. The 1933 and 1934 figures are from TsUNKhU, 1936a, pp. 386–87, and include investment outlays "for special purposes." The 1935 figures are from TsUNKhU, *SSSR Strana Sotsializma; Statisticheskii Sbornik,* 1936c, p. 8 (via NK). They are higher than the figures in Gosplan, 1937, pp. 142–43, and are used here to reduce the 1937 residuals. Data for 1936 are here taken from the journal *Plan,* 1937, no. 4, p. 9; they appear also in the 1937 plan cited above. The 1937 figures were obtained by subtracting from the 1933–1937 totals cited below the four annual figures appearing in the table. Their accuracy and comparability hinge on constancy of coverage for the years concerned, and it is by no means certain that this has been achieved. Totals for the Second Five Year Plan period are found in Gosplan, 1939a, p. 71.

*1938–1940.* Summary data for the periods 1933–1937 and 1934–1938 can be used, in conjunction with 1933 data, to obtain 1938 figures as residuals (the 1934–1938 data appear in TsUNKhU, 1939, p. 113). The figures are 4,657 million rubles for the railroads and 37,364 million rubles for the whole economy. Rough data for 1940 and for the period 1938–1940 were given by N. Voznesenskii in his February 18, 1941, speech (available in English as *Economic Results of the USSR in 1940 and the Plan of National Economic Development for 1941,* Moscow, 1941, or as *The Growing Prosperity of the Soviet Union,* New York, 1941). They make it possible, in turn, to obtain figures for 1939 as residuals. Annual estimates for investment in the whole economy have been carefully worked out by Norman Kaplan, and his 1938 estimate seems preferable to the residual given above.

Notes to Table 71 (*Continued*)

For railroads alone, Voznesenskii stated that "in 1941, the railways will be assigned 6,500 million rubles by the state for capital investment, which exceeds the assignments made in 1940 by nearly 55 per cent" (*Economic Results*, p. 25). If we assume that actual 1940 investment equaled the budgetary assignment, and that the amount assigned (presumably to the NKPS) equaled the investment in "railways" (though neither assumption is fully tenable), then the statement implies railroad investment of 4,200 million rubles in 1940. We also have the statements that "during three years of the Third Five Year Plan period, investment in railroads totaled 12.3 billion rubles" (Kovalev, 1947, p. 34), or the same sentence with the figure "12.2 billion" (Ivliev, 1946, p. 18). Experimentation makes it appear that both statements exclude "noncentralized investment," and in the following illustrative tabulation (in millions of rubles) both have been increased, for the inclusive series, by the ratios applying to over-all investment:

|  | Inclusive | | | Exclusive | | |
|---|---|---|---|---|---|---|
|  | Railroads | Whole economy | Percentage in railroads | Railroads | Whole economy | Percentage in railroads |
| 1938 | 4,650 | 35,700 | 13.03 | 4,100 | 29,200 | 14.04 |
| 1939 | 4,950 | 34,300 | 14.43 | 3,950 | 29,300 | 13.48 |
| 1940 | 5,000 | 38,000 | 13.16 | 4,200 | 32,000 | 13.13 |
| Total | 14,600 | 108,000 | *13.52* | 12,250 | 90,500 | *13.54* |

Table 72. Railroad fixed assets, USSR, by year, 1923–1940, 1945–1952
(millions of rubles)

| Year | Assets at current prices | | | Assets at 1933 prices | | |
|---|---|---|---|---|---|---|
| | Annual average | Beginning of year | Annual increment | Annual average | Beginning of year | Annual increment |
| 1924 | 7,467 | 7,495 | −56 | 11,071 | 11,112 | −83 |
| 1925 | 7,427 | 7,439 | −25 | 11,011 | 11,029 | −37 |
| 1926 | 7,455 | 7,414 | 82 | 11,053 | 10,992 | 122 |
| 1927 | 7,569 | 7,496 | 147 | 11,223 | 11,114 | 218 |
| 1928 | 7,824 | 7,643 | 362 | 11,529 | 11,332 | 394 |
| 1929 | 11,179 | 11,129 | 100 | 11,920 | 11,726 | 388 |
| 1930 | 11,475 | 11,229 | 491 | 12,548 | 12,114 | 868 |
| 1931 | — | 11,720 | — | 13,275 | 12,982 | 586 |
| 1932 | — | — | — | 14,233 | 13,568 | 1,330 |
| 1933 | 14,828 | 14,844 | −32 | 15,563 | 14,898 | 1,330 |
| 1934 | — | 14,812 | — | 16,646 | 16,228 | 836 |
| 1935 | — | — | — | 17,371 | 17,064 | 614 |
| 1936 | — | — | — | 18,802 | 17,678 | 2,247 |
| 1937 | — | — | — | 20,425 | 19,925 | 1,000 |
| 1938 | — | — | — | 21,275 | 20,925 | 700 |
| 1939 | — | — | — | 22,063 | 21,625 | 875 |
| 1940 | — | — | — | 26,850 | 22,500 | 8,700 |
| 1941 | — | — | — | — | 31,200 | — |
| 1945 | — | — | — | 25,800 | — | — |
| 1946 | — | — | — | 27,800 | — | — |
| 1947 | — | — | — | 32,700 | — | — |
| 1948 | — | — | — | 34,500 | — | — |
| 1949 | — | — | — | 36,100 | — | — |
| 1950 | — | — | — | 40,200 | — | — |
| 1951 | — | — | — | 43,000 | — | — |
| 1952 | — | — | — | 46,000 | — | — |

## Notes to Table 72

Perplexing coverage and valuation problems make it extremely difficult to compile a continuous and comparable series for railroad fixed assets. These estimates are therefore subject to considerable uncertainty, as will become clear in the following notes.

The 1924–1934 fixed asset data "at current prices" come from four sources. The 1924–1929 figures for the beginning of each year (October 1 of the preceding calendar year) are given by Bernstein–Kogan, 1929, p. 23, together with annual data for investment, and for estimated depreciation not covered out of operating expenses. They probably involve a 1924 inventory using 1913 records to which a price revaluation factor was applied, together with subsequent additions valued at current prices. The 1929–1931 figures are from the NKPS *Materialy*, vol. 128, pp. 18–19 (for Oct. 1, 1928, Oct. 1, 1929, and Jan. 1, 1931), and are probably at 1930 prices. The Oct. 1, 1928 figure is 1.3901 times Bernstein-Kogan's figure for the same data of 8005.6 million rubles. The Jan. 1, 1933 figure is from an editorial in the Gosplan journal, *Plan*, 1937, no. 4, p. 11. The Jan. 1, 1934 figure is from TsUNKhU, 1936a, p. 442, where a footnote explains that a 1929–1932 inventory was taken, starting from 1913 prices multiplied by

Notes to Table 72 (*Continued*)

1.65, and supplemented by additions valued at current prices. Where possible, annual averages computed as arithmetic means of successive beginning-of-year figures have been inserted, together with annual increments.

The series "at 1933 prices" reflects an attempt to minimize the influence of revaluations, but its components are by no means secure. TsUNKhU, 1934, pp. 20–21, presented annual averages for 1928–1933, "at 1933 prices"; Kochetov, 1939, p. 265, repeated them, with 50 million rubles added for 1933, and his figures appear above. Midpoints between annual averages are placed in the beginning-of-year column for 1929–1933, and extended to obtain estimates for 1928 and 1934. The ratio of 11,332 to 7,643 was then used to transform Bernstein-Kogan's 1924–1927 data to a series "at 1933 prices," and the annual averages were computed as means between Oct. 1 figures.

The Jan. 1, 1933 and 1934 figures of 14.8 billion rubles do not seem consistent with a 1933 annual average of 15.6 billion "at 1933 prices"; the former must have been at some lower price level. Hence a Jan. 1, 1934 estimate "at 1933 prices" was inserted by adding to the 1933 average one half the difference between the 1932 and 1933 averages. The Jan. 1, 1935 figure from TsUNKhU, 1936a, p. 442, appears to fit smoothly into the series. Kochetov, 1939, p. 266, gives itemized data for Jan. 1, 1936 and 1937; in his 1941 book he repeats the 1934 and 1937 data on p. 338, and the 1935 and 1937 data on p. 176. Annual averages are then computed as means between successive January 1 figures. In Soviet records, annual averages are obtained by noting the exact *month* when additions come into service (see example in Vinnichenko, 1948, p. 63), while the present approach assumes they come into service uniformly throughout the year; but the resulting error is probably not large.

For post-1937 values, we have a statement by B. Levin, head of the Technical-Expert Section of the NKPS, in *Gudok*, 7 Nov. '40, p. 3, that railroad assets increased 32 per cent from 1934 to 1940, and a statement in Ivliev, 1946, p. 18, that railroad fixed assets on Jan 1, 1941, were 31.2 billion rubles, having risen by more than 74 per cent over the period from 1937 through 1940 inclusive. The 32 per cent rise, applied to a Jan. 1, 1934 figure of 14,812 million rubles, leads to a 1940 figure of 19,552, lower than the 1937 figure; applied to the Jan. 1, 1935 figure it produces an estimate, presumably for Jan. 1, 1940, of 22,524 million rubles. This is used above, though it may well be too low, since application of the Jan. 1, 1940, percentage breakdown of railroad total assets given in Kochetov, 1953, p. 187, indicates an absolute fall from 1937 to 1940 in ruble values for rolling stock and structures. Ivliev's figure presumably reflects the assets brought in with 1939–1940 territorial acquisitions and also may reflect revaluations arising out of a capital inventory taken in 1940 (see Kochetov, 1941, p. 326).

The 1938 and 1939 January 1 figures are inserted on the basis of (a) some probable delayed carryover into 1937 of 1935–36 investment programs, and (b) the rising 1937–1940 trend for completion of new railroad line. Annual averages are then calculated as arithmetic means of the January 1 figures, and the annual increments are differences between succeeding January 1 figures. Kochetov, 1948, p. 196, states that railroad fixed assets rose from 30.5 billion rubles in 1923 to 60.9 billion in 1939. The 1923 figure is four times the contemporary estimate; clearly a radical upward revaluation has been made. There was probably a stocktaking as of January 1, 1946, using 1945 prices like those

Notes to Table 72 (*Continued*)

referred to in Voznesenskii, 1947, p. 12, with conversion factors used for upward revaluation of data for earlier years.

The 1945–1952 estimates rest on two fragile pieces of evidence. In Izosimov, 1952, it is stated that "railroad fixed assets grew more than 1.5 times during the first postwar five-year plan, shown in the accompanying graph" (p. 22). The graph on p. 23 contains figures written over each of the years, 1946 through 1950, in terms of an index with 1945 equal to 100, but the vertical scale is headed "expenses" (*raskhody*) in percentages of 1945! Are the indexes for fixed assets or for annual capital outlays? Here the former is assumed, following his text. The other fragment is Kaganovich's statement, at the March 1954 meeting with water transport officials (Kaganovich, 1954a, p. 16), that railroad assets increased 4 times from 1928 to 1952, while fixed assets in water transport increased 6 times. Applying a factor of 4.0 to the 1928 annual average yields a 1952 figure (in "1933 prices") of 46.0 billion rubles. Then, arbitrarily assuming a 7 per cent increase in railroad fixed assets during 1951, and during 1950, one obtains a 1950 estimate of 40.2 billion. With it and Izosimov's indexes, the 1945–1949 estimates were obtained.

Clearly these estimates are subject to a very wide margin of error. They imply that 1945 fixed assets were only a billion rubles below the 1940 level; this would be plausible if wartime construction and acquisitions came close to offsetting the damage sustained during the war. And they do not appear to leave room for any very substantial upward revaluation associated with the 1949 price changes. Taken in conjunction with postwar investment data indicating that between 1945 and 1951, inclusive, some 34.2 billion rubles worth of fixed assets was added to the railroads' plant and equipment, the implication is that roughly 14 billion rubles worth of retirement was recorded. The asset estimates may therefore reflect a correct order of magnitude.

Indexes for the value of fixed assets by sector, with the basis of valuation unstated, appear for 1928, 1940, and 1950 in TsSU, 1956, p. 32, but they do not provide a close check on the estimates above, since they relate to the more inclusive sector of "transportation and communications." Railroads accounted for 73 per cent of the sector's fixed assets in 1928, according to TsUNKhU, 1934 data, and 68 per cent in 1933; their share has probably continued to decline gradually. Kaganovich told water transportation officials that their (river and sea carriers) assets had grown six fold from 1928 through 1952, while rail assets grew four fold. This would imply for rail and water together a 1952 index of 454, with 1928 as 100. The TsSU indexes are 434 for 1950 and 542 for 1954. Communications assets probably grew still more rapidly, so the four fold relationship for rail assets (used to anchor the postwar series above) appears to fit into the TsSU series fairly well.

Table 73. Freight train performance, USSR railroads, by year, 1923-1940 and 1945-1955

| Year | Total freight train-kilometers (10³) | Average weight[a] | | Average speed (km/hr) | | Gross ton-kilometers per freight train-hour |
|------|------|------|------|------|------|------|
| | | Gross | Net | Ex-cluding stops | In-cluding stops | |
| 1923[b] | 81,379 | — | 272 | 18.3 | 12.5 | — |
| 1924[b] | 101,734 | — | 320 | 20.4 | 13.3 | — |
| 1925[b] | 124,237 | 740 | 371 | 20.6 | 13.5 | 9,990 |
| 1926[b] | 170,604 | 765 | 395 | 20.9 | 13.2 | 10,100 |
| 1927[b] | 194,898 | 818 | 411 | 20.9 | 13.3 | 10,880 |
| 1928 | 218,813 | 817 | 420 | 21.1 | 14.1 | 11,520 |
| 1929 | 252,471 | 854 | 443 | 21.1 | 13.3 | 11,360 |
| 1930 | 266,861 | 937 | 523 | 21.8 | 12.2 | 11,430 |
| 1931 | 293,033 | 967 | 549 | 22.3 | 13.2 | 12,760 |
| 1932 | 320,322 | 966 | 543 | 23.0 | 14.3 | 13,810 |
| 1933 | 326,365 | 959 | 533 | 22.3 | 13.8 | 13,260 |
| 1934 | 386,219 | 994 | 555 | 23.5 | 14.7 | 14,560 |
| 1935 | 449,987 | 1,035 | 590 | 24.4 | 15.7 | 16,250 |
| 1936 | 500,700 | 1,160 | 661 | 29.8 | 18.3 | 21,230 |
| 1937 | 536,300 | 1,199 | 677 | 31.4 | 19.5 | 23,380 |
| 1938 | 542,200 | 1,262 | 703 | 31.9 | 19.1 | 24,100 |
| 1939 | 573,300 | 1,296 | 711 | 32.7 | 19.3 | 25,010 |
| 1940 | 595,700 | 1,298 | 726 | 33.0 | 20.3 | 26,350 |
| 1945 | 489,600 | 1,247 | 710 | 29.1 | 17.2 | 21,450 |
| 1946 | 526,400 | 1,219 | 694 | — | 16.0[c] | 19,500 |
| 1947 | 529,600 | 1,239 | 709 | — | 16.5[c] | 20,400 |
| 1948 | 601,300 | 1,340 | 772 | — | 17.3 | 23,180 |
| 1949 | 669,000 | 1,390 | 806 | — | 18.3 | 25,440 |
| 1950 | 738,200 | 1,427 | 833 | 33.8 | 20.1 | 28,680 |
| 1951 | 803,900 | 1,472[c] | 868[c] | 34.3 | 21.6 | 31,800 |
| 1952 | 840,400 | 1,517 | 918 | 34.8 | 23.1 | 35,040 |
| 1953 | 863,000 | 1,577 | 978 | 34.9 | 23.4 | 36,900 |
| 1954 | 866,000 | 1,657 | 1,052 | 35.2 | 22.9 | 37,950 |
| 1955 | 906,400 | 1,758 | 1,143 | 37.1 | 24.7 | 43,420 |

[a]Excluding weight of locomotive and tender, and computed through dividing freight ton-kilometers (gross or net) by principal locomotive-kilometers, so as to reflect both loaded and empty movement.

[b]12 months including 3 months of the preceding calendar year.

[c]Interpolated.

### Notes to Table 73

*Total freight train-kilometers.* This series covers (at least through 1934) operations on wide gauge track only, excluding a small amount of work on narrow-gauge track. The latter may now be included. The data for 1923-1934 are taken from IAkobi, 1935, p. 48, and the 1935 figure is from TsUNKhU, 1936a, p. 430.

### Notes to Table 73 *(Continued)*

The rest of this series has had to be approximated through combining two other series, in the absence of direct published information. The average net weight of a freight train (including empty hauls) results from dividing net ton-kilometers of freight carried by total (loaded plus empty) freight train-kilometers. Consequently, if a series for net ton-kilometers per year is divided by a series for average net train weight, the result should approximate freight train-kilometers. Unfortunately, even for the years when all three series are available, the relationship does not quite hold, no doubt because of slight differences in compilation and coverage which are inadequately explained in Soviet statistical handbooks. However, the discrepancies are not serious. The traffic series employed in this connection by Soviet railroad statisticians is "operating" ton-kilometers, which measures the actual distance traveled by each ton originated, a slightly larger total than the "tariff" ton-kilometers for which shippers are charged. Thus for the present computation the data of column (1) in Table 58 were added to ton-kilometers as recorded in Table 46, and the sum was divided by estimated net train weights to obtain the train-kilometer estimates for Table 73.

*Average weight.* Figures for both gross and net weights from 1923 through 1934 are given by IAkobi, 1935, p. 56. Average gross freight train weights for the years 1935–1940 appear in Khanukov, 1948, p. 294. Net train weights for 1935–1937 are given in Ioffe, 1939, p. 305; for 1939 in Khachaturov, 1952, p. 132; for 1940 by B. E. Peisakhzon in *Tekhnika Zhel. Dorog*, 1946, no. 8/9, p. 5. The figure for 1938 is estimated through interpolating a figure such that the ratio of net to gross train weight is halfway between the 1937 and 1939 ratios.

Postwar discussion is seldom explicit, but statistical links and occasional direct references make it clear that the remarks refer to gross rather than net train weight. 1945 was given as 94.8 per cent of 1941 by Tverskoi in *Zhel. Trans.*, 1946, no. 11/12, p. 17, while gross weight in the first half of 1941 was 1315 tons (*Tekhnika Zhel. Dorog*, 1947, no. 12, p. 5). Tverskoi gave 1946 as 28 tons less than 1945 in *Zhel. Trans., 1947*, no. 10, p. 23. The 1947 figure was indicated by Ivliev's statement (*Zhel. Trans.*, 1948, no. 8, p. 12) that it was 4.6 per cent lower (than in 1940). B. P. Beshchev, in *Trud*, 1 May '49, p. 3, indicated that 1948 was 42 tons over 1940, and the implied 1340-ton figure is confirmed by its relationships with 1954–1955–1960, as shown in this table. The 1949 estimate is a crude mean between the *Gudok* editorial statements that the standard for the new summer schedule would be 27 tons over 1949 and 119 tons over 1940 (14 May '50, p. 1)

Train weight in 1950 was reported as 10 per cent over 1940 in the CSA report of 17 April '51, and as more than 14 per cent over 1945 by B. Podshivalov in *Gudok*, 6 June '51, p. 2. The 1951 estimate above is an arithmetic mean between 1950 and 1952. The 1952 level was given as 13.2 per cent over 1948 in a *Gudok* editorial, 15 Dec. '53, p. 1. For 1953, we have the statement (*Gudok*, 15 May '55, p. 3) that gross weight in 1954 was 5.1 per cent higher, combined with the statement that 1954 was 16.1 per cent over 1950 (*Gudok*, editorial, 26 April '55, p. 1 and repeated as "gross" by M. Lin'kov in *Gudok*, 30 Sept. '55, p. 2). Moreover Grigor'ev, 1955, p. 12, gives 1954 as 23.7 per cent over 1948. The draft Sixth Five Year Plan called for a 1960 gross train weight of 2200 tons, 25 per cent over 1955, and 1955 was given as 6 per cent over 1954 in the 1955 CSA report.

Notes to Table 73 (*Continued*)

Net train weight above is estimated in relation to gross train weight. For 1945–1946, there is Minister Kovalev's statement that some 14,000 freight trains, carrying 10 million tons of freight, were being dispatched daily (*Zhel. Trans.*, 1946, no. 7, p. 8—10/14 implies a net weight of 715 tons per train), and Tverskoi's computation that an extra 27,000 trains were made up to handle 19 million tons of freight representing underloading of cars (*Zhel. Trans.*, 1946, no. 11/12, pp. 14–15—19/27 implies a net weight of 704 tons per train). The indicated ratio of net to gross train weight is around 57 per cent. In 1954 Kaganovich said the net weight of a train was "roughly two thirds" of its gross weight (Kaganovich, 1954b, p. 68), and V. Zvonkov, Corresponding Member of the USSR Academy of Sciences, said in *Gudok*, 20 Aug. '55, p. 4, that the tare weight of freight cars averaged 55 per cent of the actual weight of freight being carried. The ratio of 100 to 155 is 64.5 per cent. A *Gudok* editorial of 8 Feb. '56 stated that freight ton-kilometers (apparently gross) rose during the Fifth Five Year Plan by 51.9 per cent, and this leads to an indicated 1950 ratio of 58.4 per cent for net to gross train weight. These ratios, and the prewar Soviet ratios around 55–57 per cent, are higher than the United States ratio (around 45 per cent), presumably reflecting the sparseness of light-loading commodities in the composition of Soviet freight traffic. The surprising rise in the ratio between 1950 and 1954 may reflect the growing proportion of 4-axle cars in the freight car fleet.

With these 1945, 1950, and 1955 benchmarks, ratios for the intervening years were assumed as follows:

| 1945 | 56.9 | 1951 | 59.0 |
|------|------|------|------|
| 1946 | 56.9 | 1952 | 60.5 |
| 1947 | 57.2 | 1953 | 62.0 |
| 1948 | 57.6 | 1954 | 63.5 |
| 1949 | 58.0 | 1955 | 65.0 |
| 1950 | 58.4 |      |      |

*Average train speeds.* The series for the average speed of freight trains, excluding stops, is termed in Russian "technical" speed, while the series for average freight train speed, including stops, is termed either "commercial" or "section" speed (see Vedenisov, 1946, p. 468). The former excludes the time a train is halted at any point en route (see *ibid.*, p. 412).

The data for 1923–1933 are taken from IAkobi, 1935, p. 56. Figures for both series from 1934 through 1937 are given in Khanukov, 1948, p. 300, and for the first series are continued through 1940 on p. 294. The 1938 figure for average speed including stops is given as 138.4 per cent of its 1933 level in *Gudok*, 9 March '39, p. 1, or as 12.8 kilometers less than 1938 "technical" speed of 31.9 kilometers per hour in *Gudok*, 16 May '39, p. 2. Both 1939 figures are given in Khachaturov, 1952, p. 132, and both 1940 figures in Khanukov, 1948, p. 300.

The 1945 figure for speed including stops appears in Levin, 1947, p. 105. A 1949 estimate is based on the statement in *Gudok*, 11 Dec. '49, p. 3, that "at the present time 'commercial' speed is 1.9 kilometers per hour below the prewar level," and a 1948 figure then follows from the statement that "commercial" speed in 1949 increased by 1 kilometer per hour over 1948 (*Gudok*, 24 May '50, p. 1). The 1946 and 1947 estimates are inserted as crude interpolations to obtain estimates for the last column in Table 73. The 1945 estimate for average "technical" speed is based on turnaround time data explained in the notes to

## Notes to Table 73 (*Continued*)

Table 76. The 1950 estimates for both measures of speed are based on the statements of B. Podshivalov, in *Gudok*, 6 June '51, that "during the five years ... of the postwar five-year plan ... the technical speed of freight trains increased by 16 per cent" (p. 2), and "commercial speed in 1950 was 17 per cent above 1945" (p. 3).

1951-1953 train speeds were estimated on the basis of A. Galitskii's statement in *Plan. Khoz.*, 1954, no. 6, p. 54, that 1953 commercial speed was 16 per cent over 1940, 1953 technical speed was 1.9 kilometers per hour above 1940 and 0.1 kilometers per hour above 1952, and that the gap between commercial and technical speeds in 1953 was 11.5 kilometers per hour. 1951 technical speed is placed halfway between 1950 and 1952; commercial speed for 1951 and 1952 is placed to reflect plausible closing of the gap between the two speeds. 1954 speeds are computed on the basis of M. Trubikhin's statement (*Gudok*, 2 April '55, p. 2) that, during four years of the Fifth Five Year Plan, commercial speed rose 14 per cent and technical speed a little more than 4 per cent, reducing the gap between them by 1.4 kilometers. 1955 technical speed is reported as 3.3 kilometers per hour over 1950, and 1.9 kilometers per hour over 1954, in *Zhel. Trans.*, 1956, no. 1, p. 25. The rise in commercial speed during 1955 is given as 1.8 kilometers per hour in *Gudok*, 11 Jan. '56, p. 3.

*Gross ton-kilometers per freight train-hour.* This series, while not compiled by Soviet railroad statisticians, is widely used by American railroad analysts as a central measure of operating efficiency. It would normally be computed as the quotient of total gross ton-kilometers (or ton-miles) divided by total freight train-hours. The former is equivalent to total freight train-kilometers times average gross weight per freight train. The divisor is equivalent to total freight-train kilometers divided by the average speed of a freight train in kilometers per hour. It will be seen that in such a computation the train-kilometers cancel out, and in effect the measure results from multiplying average gross train weight by average train speed. This column in Table 73 has therefore been computed as the product of the second column times the fifth column.

Table 74. Locomotive performance, USSR railroads, by year, 1921–1940, 1945–1955, plus 1960 plan

| Year | All locomotives (millions of annual locomotive-kilometers) | | | | Locomotives in freight service | |
| | Road principal | Road other | Switching | Total | Kilometers per loco.-day | Turnaround time (hr)[a] |
|---|---|---|---|---|---|---|
| 1921[b] | 123.8 | 16.3 | 58.2 | 198.3 | — | — |
| 1922[b] | 123.0 | 15.1 | 63.9 | 202.0 | — | — |
| 1923[b] | 148.8 | 17.5 | 63.1 | 229.4 | 107.0 | — |
| 1924[b] | 173.9 | 21.4 | 63.2 | 258.5 | 114.6 | — |
| 1925[b] | 214.4 | 24.0 | 62.5 | 300.9 | 120.5 | — |
| 1926[b] | 286.7 | 32.8 | 84.1 | 403.6 | 122.0 | — |
| 1927[b] | 315.3 | 38.4 | 86.2 | 439.9 | 130.9 | — |
| 1928 | 339.4 | 43.8 | 102.3 | 485.5 | 137.5 | — |
| 1929 | 374.4 | 51.9 | 111.5 | 537.8 | 151.5 | — |
| 1930 | 426.5 | 65.7 | 129.7 | 621.9 | 153.3 | — |
| 1931 | 475.6 | 81.0 | 148.0 | 704.6 | 159.7 | — |
| 1932 | 545.5 | 94.9 | 164.1 | 804.5 | 164.6 | 32.1 |
| 1933 | 557.8 | 92.3 | 169.9 | 820.0 | 163.5 | 33.8 |
| 1934 | 634.9 | — | — | 921.8 | 168.5 | 32.4 |
| 1935 | 666.4 | — | — | 989.7 | 189.1 | 28.4 |
| 1936 | — | — | — | — | 232.3 | 22.4 |
| 1937 | — | — | — | — | 245.6 | 20.9 |
| 1938 | — | — | — | — | 250.8 | — |
| 1939 | — | — | — | — | 251.2 | — |
| 1940 | — | — | — | — | 255.1 | 20.3 |
| 1945 | — | — | — | — | 220.9 | 23.8 |
| 1946 | — | — | — | — | 210.0[c] | 23.2 |
| 1947 | — | — | — | — | 210.0[c] | — |
| 1948 | — | — | — | — | 212.0 | — |
| 1949 | — | — | — | — | 229.5 | — |
| 1950 | — | — | — | — | 246.3 | — |
| 1951 | — | — | — | — | 249.7[c] | — |
| 1952 | — | — | — | — | 253.1[c] | — |
| 1953 | — | — | — | — | 256.6 | — |
| 1954 | — | — | — | — | 266.7 | — |
| 1955 | — | — | — | — | 292.3 | — |
| 1960 (plan) | — | — | — | — | 406.0 | — |

[a]Average number of hours per complete locomotive trip.
[b]12 months including 3 months of the preceding calendar year.
[c]Interpolated.

## Notes to Table 74

Sources for the table are as follows:

*All locomotives.* The data for 1921–1932 are taken, rounded off to the nearest hundred thousand, from TsUNKhU, 1934, pp. 250–51. IAkobi, 1935, p. 47, gives a more detailed breakdown for 1923–1933. Neither source separates locomotive-miles in freight service from locomotive-miles in passenger service except for principal locomotive miles; hence it is not possible to present a breakdown of principal, helper, and light locomotive miles in each service, as is done in ICC

## Notes to Table 74 (*Continued*)

records. The series for "Road, other" locomotive-kilometers shows the sum of helper and light locomotive-kilometers. The series for "Switching" locomotive-kilometers includes, along with yard (and line?) switching, an allowance for time spent standing idle under steam. The latter made up about 6 per cent of total locomotive-kilometers in the early 1930's. Figures for 1934 and 1935 are taken from TsUNKhU, 1936a, p. 430.

*Daily kilometers per locomotive.* This is the series known in American practice as "locomotive-miles per locomotive-day." It is computed as the quotient of locomotive-kilometers in road operations (both principal and other), divided by total locomotive-days for the "working fleet" (see Kochetov, 1948, p. 138), and almost always seems to relate only to locomotives in freight service. It will be seen that, since the numerator here combines "other" road locomotive-kilometers with principal locomotive-kilometers, use of this series to approximate the number of locomotives in road freight service will systematically understate their number, by possibly 15 per cent. However, year-to-year trends should not be much affected, since the ratio of auxiliary to principal locomotive-kilometers is very stable.

The data for 1923–1933 are taken from IAkobi, 1935, p. 56; and for 1934–1935 from TsUNKhU, 1936a, p. 431. The 1936 figure is from Vol'fson, 1941, p. 409. A revised figure for 1937 is given by Povorozhenko and Peisakhzon in *Tekhnika Zhel. Dorog.* 1947, no. 12, p. 5. The 1938 figure was mentioned indirectly by Kaganovich in his speech at the Eighteenth Congress, which appears in *Gudok*, 18 March '39, p. 3, with the phrase "87.3 kilometers above 1933." The 1939 figure appears in Khachaturov, 1952, p. 132, and the 1940 figure is given in TsSU, 1956, p. 177.

B. Podshivalov gives a 1945 figure of 220.9 kilometers and a 1950 target of 270 kilometers in *Zhel. Trans.*, 1946, no. 8/9, p. 10. The 1946 and 1947 values in parentheses are crude estimates reflecting disorganized operations, inserted for use in estimating number of locomotives.

Estimates from 1948 on reflect the growing importance of electric and diesel-electric locomotives in freight operations, where their daily mileage considerably exceeds that of steam locomotives. Steam daily mileages for 1950, 1954, and 1955 appear in TsSU, 1956, p. 177. P. G. Muratov, head of the MPS Locomotive Administration, gives 1955 electric and diesel daily mileages in *Zhel. Trans.*, 1956, no. 3, p. 30, together with percentage increases over 1950. Targets for each appear in the Sixth Five Year Plan. Weighting each by its share in total gross freight ton-kilometers leads to the average mileages shown in Table 74. The weights applied are as follows:

|          | 1950  | 1955  | 1960 |
|----------|-------|-------|------|
| Steam    | 94.2% | 85.5% | 55%  |
| Electric | 3.6   | 9.0   | 30   |
| Diesel   | 2.2   | 5.5   | 15   |

Danilov, 1956, p. 327, gives the 1950 figures; the 1955 estimates carry forward his 1954 proportion between electric and diesel for application to their 1955 combined share of 14.5 per cent (*Zhel. Trans.*, 1956, no. 2, p. 39, and *Pravda*, 22 Feb. '56, p. 5). The 1960 figures for electric and diesel are assumed on the basis of existing shares and government plans. For alternative figures, see L. Chertkova's article in *Vop. Ekon.*, 1956, no. 7, p. 27.

## Notes to Table 74 (*Continued*)

The 1950 average daily mileage is used to obtain 1949 and 1948 estimates through the statements that 1950 was 8.2 per cent over 1949 (*Gudok*, 13 July '51, p. 3), and that 1949 was 18 kilometers above 1948 (*Gudok*, 23 Apr. '50 p. 3). 1953 is given as 4.2 per cent above 1950 in *Gudok*, 2 Nov. '54, p. 3, and 1954 is estimated through weighting the steam mileage. 1951 and 1952 are interpolated on the assumption of even growth.

*Turnaround time.* This series is computed as the quotient of total locomotive-hours recorded for the "working fleet" (excluding time spent in pusher service), divided by the number of locomotives dispatched with trains per day (see Kochetov, 1948, p. 138). The data for 1932–1937 are from Vol'fson, 1941, p. 409, and for 1940 from Gorinov, 1948b, p. 19.

The 1945 estimate is derived from E. Ashkenazi's statement, in *Zhel. Trans.*, 1946, no. 7, p. 59, that "turnaround time for locomotives in 1945 was 18 per cent over the 1940 level, which was equivalent to a daily waste of 1150 locomotives." N. Chelnokov, in *Zhel. Trans.*, 1947, no. 5, p. 43, stated the 1945 figure as 24 hours. Incidentally, the relationship stated by Ashkenazi, when applied to the values of 23.8 hours and 20.3 hours for 1945 and 1940 respectively, permits calculation of the average number of freight locomotives in use. Converting the turnaround time figures into fractions of a day, we have: 0.846 (N plus 1150) equals 0.992 N, and this yields an estimate of 5860 locomotives, not far from the number estimated through a quite different approach in Table 61 (6070 locomotives).

The 1946 estimate derives from G. Sokolov's statement, in *Gudok*, 27 April '47, p. 3, that it speeded up by 2.5 per cent. It appears that in 1949 locomotive turnaround time improved by 2 hours (*Gudok*, 23 April '50, p. 3), and in 1950 by 1.7 hours (*Gudok*, 20 June '51, p. 3), but the intervening years have not yet been located.

Table 75. Freight car performance, USSR railroads, by year, 1923–1955,
plus 1960 plan

| Year | Average freight car trip | | | | Turnaround time (days) | Kilometers per day |
|------|--------------|-------------|--------------|--------------------|----|----|
|      | Loaded (km) | Empty (km) | Total (km) | Percentage empty | | |
| 1923[a] | 522.3 | 298.5 | 820.8 | 30.1 | 17.1 | 48.0 |
| 1924[a] | 582.2 | 318.6 | 900.8 | 32.5 | 16.0 | 56.3 |
| 1925[a] | 634.0 | 263.8 | 897.8 | 29.9 | 13.4 | 67.0 |
| 1926[a] | 650.3 | 261.0 | 911.3 | 28.9 | 12.5 | 72.9 |
| 1927[a] | 646.6 | 261.9 | 908.5 | 29.1 | 11.3 | 80.4 |
| 1928 | 636.6 | 255.8 | 892.4 | 28.7 | 10.56 | 84.6 |
| 1929 | 641.5 | 248.0 | 889.5 | 27.9 | 10.19 | 87.3 |
| 1930 | 611.3 | 224.5 | 835.8 | 26.9 | 9.34 | 89.5 |
| 1931 | 643.5 | 227.8 | 871.3 | 26.1 | 9.58 | 90.9 |
| 1932 | 664.3 | 245.3 | 909.6 | 27.1 | 9.35 | 97.3 |
| 1933 | 673.0 | 260.7 | 933.7 | 27.9 | 9.57 | 97.6 |
| 1934 | 731.6 | 297.2 | 1028.8 | 28.9 | 8.75 | 117.5 |
| 1935 | 719.0 | 268.0 | 987.0 | 27.2 | 7.69 | 128.4 |
| 1936 | 697 | 256 | 953 | 26.9 | 6.79 | 140.3 |
| 1937 | 721 | 255 | 976 | 26.1 | 6.98 | 139.8 |
| 1938 | 749 | 292 | 1041 | 28.0 | 7.52 | 138.4 |
| 1939 | 757 | 296 | 1053 | 28.1 | 7.25 | 145.2 |
| 1940[b] | 732 | 295 | 1027 | 28.7 | 7.37 | 139.9 |
| 1941 | 746 | — | — | — | 6.92 | — |
| 1942 | — | 385 | — | — | 13.8 | — |
| 1943 | — | 439 | — | — | 12.6 | — |
| 1944 | — | 398 | — | — | 11.4 | — |
| 1945 | 961 | 335 | 1316 | 27.0 | 10.92 | 120.5 |
| 1946 | — | — | — | — | 10.07 | — |
| 1947 | 768 | — | — | — | 9.61 | — |
| 1948 | 784 | 306 | 1090 | 28.1 | 8.68 | 125.6 |
| 1949 | — | — | — | — | 8.14 | — |
| 1950 | 793 | 303 | 1096 | 27.6 | 7.49 | 146.3 |
| 1951 | — | — | — | — | 7.23 | — |
| 1952 | — | — | — | — | 6.87 | — |
| 1953 | 821 | 314 | 1135 | 27.7 | 6.64 | 170.9 |
| 1954 | 837 | 321 | 1158 | 27.7 | 6.68 | 173.3 |
| 1955 | — | — | 1186 | — | 6.23 | 190.3 |
| 1960 (plan) | — | — | — | — | 5.30 | — |

[a]12 months including 3 months of the preceding calendar year.
[b]First half of the year only.

Notes to Table 75

Sources for this table are as follows:
*1923–1933.* These figures are given by IAkobi, 1935, p. 55, and by TsUNKhU, 1934, pp. 254–57, except for the lengths of empty and total trip in 1923–1927. However, since the total trip is equal to average kilometers per day times the number of days required for a complete trip (turnaround time), values for the total trip have been computed and inserted. The length of empty trips then results by subtraction. For the first two years, the derived percentage of empty-car movement differs somewhat from the figures these two sources record, but for 1925, 1926, and 1927 the correspondence is very close.

Notes to Table 75 (*Continued*)

*1934–1935.* All values are given in TsUNKhU, 1936a, p. 432.

*1936–1940.* Vol'fson, 1941, p. 409 gives 1936 and 1937 figures for the last three columns which permit computation of values for the first three columns.

Turnaround time for 1938 is given in TsUNKhU, 1939, p. 105; the 1939 value is given in Khachaturov, 1952, p. 132; and the 1940 value is given in Zagliadimov, 1947, p. 384.

Car-kilometers per car-day in 1938 are stated as 141.8 per cent of 1933 in *Gudok*, 9 March '39, p. 1; for 1939, are given in Khachaturov, 1952, p. 132, and for 1940, are given in Khanukov, 1948, p. 304.

The percentage of empty movement in 1939 is given by A. Malukhin in *Gudok*, 2 July '40, p. 3, and 1938 is stated to have been 1.3 per cent less. The 1939 figures are confirmed all around by the fact that the computed average loaded trip corresponds exactly to the figure of 757 kilometers given by Khanukov, 1948, p. 308.

Zagliadimov, 1947, p. 384, give absolute figures for the average total and empty trip in 1940; their figure of 300 kilometers for the latter is apparently rounded, since the writer cited below, who gave the wartime empty-trip figures, used 295 kilometers for 1940. The percentage of empty-car movement is obtained by division.

*1941–1945.* The average loaded trip in the first half of 1941 is given by Povorozhenko and Peisakhzon in *Tekhnika Zhel. Dorog*, 1947, no. 12, p. 4, and the turnaround time is given on the next page. The 1942–1945 figures for the average empty trip of a freight car come from an article by R. Robel, in *Zhel. Trans.*, 1946, no. 7, p. 30. Voznesenskii presents the 1942 and 1943 turnaround figures in his 1947 book, p. 104.

The 1945 length-of-trip data come from Zagliadimov, 1947, pp. 384 and 374, and the percentage of empty-car movement is then arrived at by division. 1945 turnaround time likewise comes from this source, and the kilometers-per-day figure is then computed as the quotient of total trip divided by number of days per trip.

*1946–1955.* The loaded car trips for 1947, 1948, and 1950 are derived from G. Nedopekin's statement (*Gudok*, 1 July '51, p. 3), that they were 7.4 per cent, 8.9 per cent, and 9.8 per cent above average length of haul. The 1948 percentage of empty movement is an arithmetic mean between the monthly extremes of 35.6 per cent to 42.3 per cent in 1948 (percentage empty to loaded) reported in *Gudok*, 9 March '49, p. 3, and it permits computation of empty trip, total trip, and car-kilometers per day (given turnaround time). Car-kilometers per day in 1950 were stated as 4.6 per cent over 1940 in the CSA report of 17 April '51, and taken with turnaround time, they yield estimated total trip. Empty trip and percentage empty follow by subtraction.

1946 turnaround time was given as 0.85 days less than 1945 by Zagliadimov, 1947, p. 21. Tverskoi gave 1947 as 2.65 days above the 1950 target (6.96 days) in *Gudok*, 14 Jan. '49, p. 2, and it was also reported as 32 hours less than 1945 in *Zhel. Trans.*, 1948, no. 2, p. 4. The 1948 figure was less than 1947 by 0.92 days (*Gudok*, 30 Nov. '49, p. 1). 1950 is given in TsSU, 1956, p. 177, and the 1949 estimate reflects the 8 per cent improvement reported in the 1950 CSA report.

Beshchev, 1954, p. 10, gives 1953 turnaround as 17.5 hours less than 1940 and 5.5 hours less than 1952. An estimate for 1951 is indicated by the informa-

## Notes to Table 75 (*Continued*)

tion that the 1952 annual plan called for a 5.5 hour reduction (Ivliev in *Gudok*, 10 April '52, p. 3), and that it was overfulfilled by 0.7 hours (*Gudok*, 2 Aug. '53, p. 2). The 1954 and 1955 turnaround figures appear in TsSU, 1956, p. 177.

The 1953 percentage of empty movement is given by B. Shishkov in *Gudok*, 7 April '54, p. 3. The 1953 total trip is derived as the product of technical speed times time in motion, the latter from Table 76. Loaded and empty trips result by application of the percentage, and daily car-kilometers result as the quotient of total trip over turnaround time. Daily car-kilometers for 1954 are given by Danilov, 1956, p. 282; 1954 total trip results as a product. The 1954 movement empty percentage is stated by A. Galitskii in *Plan. Khoz.*, 1954, no. 6, p. 55, and it leads to figures for loaded and empty trip. Daily car-kilometers in 1955 are given as 36 per cent over 1940 by Khachaturov in *Vop. Ekon.*, 1956, no. 3, p. 89, and 1955 total trip results by multiplication.

*1960 plan.* Stated in the Sixth Five Year Plan.

Table 76.  Breakdown of freight-car turnaround time, USSR railroads,
by year, 1932–1940, 1945–1955 (hours)

| Year | Loading and unloading | At technical stations[a] | At way stations | In motion | Total |
|---|---|---|---|---|---|
| 1932 | 52.1 | 106.2 | 24.0 | 41.7 | 218.0 |
| 1933 | 52.7 | 109.1 | 25.8 | 41.8 | 229.4 |
| 1934 | 46.0 | 92.2 | 26.7 | 45.8 | 210.7 |
| 1935 | 38.8 | 82.5 | 22.8 | 40.5 | 184.6 |
| 1936 | 33.5 | 76.9 | 19.7 | 31.7 | 162.8 |
| 1937 | 32.6 | 85.2 | 18.7 | 31.0 | 167.5 |
| 1938 | 34.8 | 91.2 | 21.9 | 32.6 | 180.5 |
| 1939 | 32.0 | 84.7 | 21.8 | 35.5 | 174.0 |
| 1940 | 37.1 | 86.7 | 19.5 | 33.6 | 176.9 |
| 1945 | 50.5 | 134.8 | 31.2 | 45.3 | 261.8 |
| 1950 (plan) | 32.0 | 87.0 | 18.0 | 30.0 | 167.0 |
| 1950 (actual) | 51.7 | 73.6 | 22.1 | 32.4 | 179.8 |
| 1953 | 48.3 | 62.6 | 16.0 | 32.5 | 159.4 |
| 1954 | 47.3 | 62.3 | 17.8 | 32.9 | 160.3 |
| 1955 | 43.9 | 57.6 | 16.0 | 32.0 | 149.5 |

[a]The term "technical" station appears to mean classification and division
points where trains lose their identity in the records, whereas way stations are
all points at which a train stops between origin and destination. In other words,
the last two categories listed above show, in combination, the time spent "in
trains."

## Notes to Table 76

Sources for this table are as follows:

*1932.* Using the 1932 total from Table 75, and the 1940 data explained below,
the 1932 breakdown was taken from M. Breev, in *Zhel. Trans.*, 1945, no. 1, p. 11,
who tabulated the number of hours of improvement under each heading.

*1933–1935.* All data given by TsUNKhU, 1936a, p. 433.

*1936–1938.* These figures appear in an article by N. Borisov, in *Sots. Trans.*,
1939, no. 6, p. 25.

*1939.* Povorozhenko, 1946, p. 7, gives a percentage division of 1939 turnaround time which, when applied to the total from Table 75, yields the above
absolute figures.

*1940.* The absolute total given in TsSU, 1956, p. 177, is distributed according
to the percentage breakdown given in Voznesenskii, 1941, p. 30.

*1945 and 1950 plan.* Zagliadimov, 1947, p. 384, gives absolute figures for the
total and its components. However, it is evident that the classification "in
trains" covers both time in motion and time at way stations, and that their
"other" classification must be a sub-category of time at "technical" stations.
This is clear both from their version of the 1940 breakdown, and from computations based on the information in Kochetov, 1948, p. 139, that the time a car
spends "in motion" is calculated as the quotient of total trip over technical
speed of train movement, while the time spent at intermediate stations is obtained
as the quotient of total trip divided by commercial speed, minus time in motion.
The time spent in motion in 1945 is given by V. V. Povorozhenko on p. 11 of
VNII, 1946, and when divided into 1945 total trip, it yields the estimate for
technical speed used in Table 75.

## Notes to Table 76 (*Continued*)

*1950 actual.* Hours at way stations and in motion are derived as quotients of total trip over technical-minus-commercial speed, and over technical speed, respectively. Time at technical stations is estimated as 6.4 hours per station times 11.5 stations, based on data in Zagliadimov, 1947, p. 384, and *Gudok*, 6 June '51, p. 3. Loading and unloading time results as a residual.

*1953–1955.* A percentage breakdown for 1953 is given in Kaganovich, 1954b, p. 31, and for 1954 by Khachaturov in *Vop. Ekon.*, 1956, no. 3, p. 95. Approximate 1955 percentages are given by A. Chertkova in *Gudok*, 5 June '56, p. 4, but the figures above are derived from total trip and train speed data, plus a percent for technical stations from Deputy Minister N. A. Gundobin, in *Zhel. Trans.*, 1956, no. 5, p. 10.

Table 77. Total fixed assets, USSR, by economic sector, 1924 and 1928

| Economic sector | Assets (10⁶ rubles) | | Percentage increase |
|---|---|---|---|
| | 1924[a] | 1928[a] | |
| Agriculture | 23,020 | 27,533 | 19.6 |
| Industry | 6,647 | 8,818 | 32.7 |
| Electric power plants | 235 | 683 | 190.6 |
| Railroads | 9,556 | 9,992 | 4.6 |
| Other transportation | 1,229 | 1,462 | 19.0 |
| Communications | 212 | 291 | 37.3 |
| Trade and storage | 404 | 688 | 70.3 |
| Administrative and social-cultural | 1,374 | 1,905 | 38.6 |
| "Communal economy" | 2,246 | 2,469 | 9.9 |
| City housing | 2 | 404 | — |
| Total USSR | 55,144 | 64,699 | 17.3 |

[a] October 1.
Source: Tverskoi, 1931, p. 48.

Table 78. Rails supplied to USSR railroads, by year, 1923-1936

| Year | Industry records | | Railroad records | | | Fulfillment (per cent) |
|---|---|---|---|---|---|---|
| | Rails supplied ($10^3$m t) | Index (1928 = 100) | Rails supplied ($10^3$m t) | Index (1928 = 100) | Planned supply ($10^3$m t) | |
| 1923[a] | — | — | 45.5 | 16.4 | — | — |
| 1924[a] | — | — | 59.1 | 21.3 | — | — |
| 1925[a] | — | — | 109.0 | 39.2 | — | — |
| 1926[a] | — | — | 189.7 | 68.2 | — | — |
| 1927[a] | — | — | 224.6 | 80.8 | — | — |
| 1928[a] | 352.2 | 100.0 | 278.0 | 100.0 | — | — |
| 1929[a] | 335.0 | 95.1 | 249.7 | 89.8 | 300 | 83.2 |
| 1930[a] | 397.7 | 112.9 | 307.5 | 110.6 | 390 | 78.8 |
| 1931 | 454.0 | 128.9 | 345.4 | 124.2 | 597 | 57.9 |
| 1932 | 427.0 | 121.2 | 284.6 | 102.4 | 550 | 51.7 |
| 1933 | 516.9 | 146.8 | 317.2 | 114.1 | 530 | 59.8 |
| 1934 | 786.8 | 223.4 | 529.9 | 190.6 | 550 | 96.4 |
| 1935 | — | — | 628.3 | 226.0 | 700 | 89.4 |
| 1936 | — | — | 838.2 | 301.5 | 1126 | 74.4 |

[a] 12 months including 3 months of preceding calendar year.
Sources: Industry records—these figures appear in the section on the iron and steel industry in TsUNKhU, 1936a, p. 135; railroad records—the data for 1923-1928 are from IAkobi, 1935, p. 89. The 1929-1936 data are from Kochetov, 1939, p. 232. His figures for 1931-1934 are larger than IAkobi's (considerably so in 1931) and are here accepted as conforming better in trend to the industry data; planned supply—these figures, together with the percentage of fulfillment, are given by Kochetov, 1939, p. 232.

Table 79.  Output of coal, petroleum, pig iron and rolled steel,
and timber, USSR, 1923–1940 and 1945–1955

| Year | Coal ($10^6$ m t) | Petroleum ($10^6$ m t) | Pig iron and rolled steel ($10^6$ m t) | Timber ($10^6$ m$^3$) |
|------|------|------|------|------|
| 1923 | 12.7 | 5.2 | 0.8 | 13.1 |
| 1924 | 16.3 | 6.0 | 1.4 | 13.4 |
| 1925 | 16.4 | 7.0 | 2.7 | 21.4 |
| 1926 | 25.7 | 8.3 | 4.5 | 28.1 |
| 1927 | 32.3 | 10.2 | 5.7 | 26.2 |
| 1928 | 35.5 | 11.6 | 6.7 | 36.0 |
| 1929 | 40.1 | 13.7 | 7.9 | 60.0 |
| 1930 | 47.8 | 18.5 | 9.6 | 96.7 |
| 1931 | 56.8 | 22.4 | 9.2 | 104.1 |
| 1932 | 64.4 | 21.4 | 10.6 | 99.4 |
| 1933 | 76.3 | 21.5 | 12.2 | 98.0 |
| 1934 | 94.2 | 24.2 | 17.4 | 99.7 |
| 1935 | 109.6 | 25.2 | 21.9 | 117.0 |
| 1936 | 126.8 | 27.4 | 26.9 | 128.1 |
| 1937 | 128.0 | 28.5 | 27.5 | 114.2 |
| 1938 | 133.3 | 30.2 | 28.0 | 114.7 |
| 1939 | 146.2 | 30.3 | 27.2 | 126.1 |
| 1940 | 165.9 | 31.1 | 28.0 | 117.9 |
| 1945 | 149.3 | 19.4 | 17.3 | 61.6 |
| 1946 | 164.1 | 21.7 | 19.5 | 80.3 |
| 1947 | 183.2 | 26.0 | 22.3 | 99.0 |
| 1948 | 208.2 | 29.2 | 27.9 | 132.4 |
| 1949 | 235.5 | 33.4 | 34.4 | 151.3 |
| 1950 | 261.1 | 37.9 | 40.1 | 161.0 |
| 1951 | 281.9 | 42.3 | 45.9 | 184.5 |
| 1952 | 300.9 | 47.3 | 51.9 | 184.6 |
| 1953 | 320.4 | 52.8 | 56.8 | 179.9 |
| 1954 | 347.1 | 59.3 | 62.1 | 205.8 |
| 1955 | 391.0 | 70.8 | 68.6 | 214.0 |
| 1960 (plan) | 593.0 | 135.0 | 105.7 | 264.0 |

Sources: The 1923–1927 coal and petroleum data are from TsUNKhU, 1934,
pp. 79 and 88; the iron and steel figures are derived from series presented in
Clark, 1956, p. 10, and the timber data are from an unpublished report by Mirko
Lamer (on file at the Russian Research Center, Harvard University).  All figures
for 1928–1940, 1945–1955, and 1960 plan are transcribed from TsSU, 1956, pp.
60–78.

# INDEX

Administrative sluggishness criticized, 271

Agricultural "wedge," 5

Andreev, A. A.: criticized at 17th Congress, 53; speech at 17th Congress, 55

Assets per worker, railroad, 260–61

Automatic brakes: annual data, 382–83

Automatic couplings: annual data, 382–83

Backlogs of unshipped freight, 51–53, 59–60

Barger, Harold: on transportation prices, 253

Bakulin, A. V.: Commissar of Transportation 1937–38, 80

Bessonov, S. A.: on output and traffic growth, 45; as purge victim, 296n

Blackman, James Horton: source of pipeline data, 155; on traffic–output relationships, 239

Bochkarev, N. G.: on traffic–output relationships, 307n

Budd mission report: selective application of, 83; on electrification, 123–24; identified, 298n

Capital–output ratios: lower with modern equipment, 279. *See also* Railroad capital-output ratios

Chapman, Janet G.: on rail passenger fares, 304n

Chardzhou–Kungrad line: construction of, 119–20

Clark, M. Gardner: on definitions of deposits, 7, 8; on ore supplies, 294n; on conflicting interests, 306n

Climatic influences: permafrost, 12–13; freezing of rivers and seas, 13–14; seasonal traffic pattern, 14–16; railroad seasonal index, 313

Coal fields: Donbas, 6–7; Sub-Moscow, 7; Asiatic Russia, 7–8; distribution of reserves, 7–8

Coal traffic, 165–68

Collectivization: relation to transportation crisis, 43, 273

Comprehensive regional development: defined, 29; stimulated by private initiative, 271

Concentration and differentiation: policy defined, 83–86

Container shipments, 159

Cost-minimizing: conflicting interests in, 128, 265

Crosshauls: defined and discussed, 31

Cumulated ton-kilometers (cumulated output): defined, 202, 363; annual data, 362

Donbas: early growth, 8–9

Donbas–Krivoi Rog shuttles: distances, 294n

Eastward movement: relation to location policy, 22–23; inhibited by emphasis on rapid growth, 24–25; trends during 1928–1940, 32; opposite trend, 37–38; prospects, 280–81

East-west boundary: discussed, 34; and Volga Valley region, 37–38

Economic policy: passive or purposive, xxi

Economies of scale: and evenness of location, 23–24; in freight transportation, 46

Electrification of railroads: issues in, 122–26; annual data, 371

Electronic computers: recommended for traffic planning, 269; availability in USSR, 309n

Firewood traffic, 173–75

Freight car-miles per car-day: in United States and USSR, 138; annual data, 406

Freight cars: number on line, 49–50, 75, 77, 115–16; evacuated during 1941–42, 93–94; wartime losses exaggerated, 105; two-axle and four-axle, 121–22; availability in United States and USSR, 130; annual data, 378; by type, 380; per cent four-axle, 382

Freight car trip, average: loaded and empty, 406

Freight car turnaround time: trends in, 79–80, 95–96; in United States and USSR, 129; index, 322; annual data, 406; components, 409

Freight rates, railroad. *See* Railroad freight rates

Freight traffic: as a "producers' service," 181

Freight traffic density: frequency distributions of, 86–87; during 1942–1945, 96–98; over-